The Seven Veils of Our Lady of Guadalupe

The Seven Veils of Our Lady of Guadalupe

The "New Evangelization" in Light of the Apparition of Our Lady of Guadalupe

Miguel Guadalupe

Queenship
PUBLISHING COMPANY
P.O. Box 220 • Goleta, CA 93116
(800) 647-9882 • (805) 692-0043 • Fax: (805) 967-5843

Library of Congress Number # 97-065316

Published by:
    Queenship Publishing
    P.O. Box 220
    Goleta, CA 93116
    (800) 647-9882 • (805) 692-0043 • Fax: (805) 967-5843

Printed in the United States of America

ISBN: 1-882972-79-1

Contents

Preliminary Note ix

Preface to the Seven Books xxvii

Book One – The Dimensions of the Holy Rosary 1
    The Rosary in the Image of Our Lady of Guadalupe 1
    The First Meditation: The Rosary as Symbol of
    Covenant of God with Man 5
    Second Meditation: The Interior House of the Rosary 9
    The Third Meditation on the Rosary 77
    The Fourth Meditation: The Rosary and the Holy Angels 90
    The Fifth Meditation: Interpretation of the
    Individual Prayers of the Rosary 95
    Conclusion 101
    Scholion (Example for Unfolding a Mystery) 106

Book Two – The Extension of the Cross Over the World 111
    The First Four Crusades. 113
    Brief Chronology of the Birth of Mexico
    and the Apparitions of Our Lady 121
    The "Fifth Crusade" and the Mission of Our Lady
    in the "New Evangelization" 125
    Mexico at the Threshold of Modern Times 127
    The Help of St. Michael and of the Angels
    for this Mission of Mexico in and for the Virgin 131
    The New Evangelization as "Reform of the Church" . . . 140
    I. To the Church at Ephesus 144

II.   To the Church at Smyrna 148

III.   To the Church at Pergamum 151

IV.   To the Church at Thyatira 153

V.   To the Church at Sardis 156

VI.   To the Church at Philadelphia 159

VII. To the Church at Laodicea 162

The Four Living Creatures 168

A Broader Perspective on the History of America 174

Book Three – The Message of Our Lady of
Guadalupe and St. Michael the Archangel 185

The Message of the Image According to
the Spanish Background 185

The Aztec View 186

A Combined Perspective 204

The Message of the Cross in the Revelation
of Our Lady of Guadalupe 207

The Sign of the Cross in the Apparition of
the Virgin of Ocotlán 211

The Relationship Between the Apparition of Our Lady
on the Hill of Tepeyac (1531) and the Apparition
of St. Michael in San Bernabé, Capula (1631) 220

The Prophecy of Daniel in Relation to St. Michael 223

The Prophecies of the "Two Witnesses" 233

Book Four – The Movement of Ransom in the
Sign of the Lamb of God 237

A Eucharistic Vision of the Image
of Our Lady of Guadalupe 237

The Mystery of the Lamb of God 237

The Triple Sign for the Eucharistic 240

Presence of Our Lord in the Image
of Our Lady of Guadalupe 240

The Movement of Ransom in the Nine Large
Flowers on the Gown of Our Lady of Guadalupe 247

The Movement of Ransom in the Stars in the
Mantle of Our Lady of Guadalupe 264

Book Five – The Way of the Cross of Blessed Juan Diego . . 307
    Foreword 307
    First Station 309
    Second Station 312
    Third Station 315
    Fourth Station 320
    Fifth Station 322
    Sixth Station 324
    Seventh Station 326
    Eighth Station 329
    Ninth Station 331
    Tenth Station 335
    Eleventh Station 339
    Twelfth Station 340
    Thirteenth Station 344
    Fourteenth Station 347
    Our mission in the common priesthood 349
    The Holy Rosary 350

Book Six – Proclaiming the Good News 361
    Foreword 361
    Part One – Introduction: Word and Light 362
    The "Apocalyptic Mass" 366
    Interpretation of the Apocalypse as Apocalyptic Mass . 369
    Part Two – The Beauty of Revelation in Mary 398

Book Seven – The Seven-Fold Candelabra 433
    Introduction 433
    Three Orders of "Seven" 434
    The Seven Steps of Trinitarian Interpretation 437
    The Movement of the Spiral in the
       Seven-Fold Candelabra 442
    The Seven-fold Candelabra of Book One 443
    The Seven-Fold Candelabra of Book Two 451
    The Seven-Fold Candelabra of Book Three 459
    The Seven-Fold Candelabra of Book Four 466
    The Seven-Fold Candelabra of Book Five 472
    The Seven-Fold Candelabra of Book Six 481
    Seven-Fold Candelabra of Book Seven 489

Appendix I - The Nican Mopohua. 497
    Plans of the Wisdom of God 497
    The Nican Mopohua 499
    Epilogue. 516
    "Call" in the Name of Holy God 517
    Beauty and Order. 518
    A Structural Analysis of the Nican Mopohua 518
    Resumé. 529

Appendix II – Analysis of the Structure of the First Apparition
   as Recorded in the Nican Mopohua (Prologue to Verse 39) 529
    General Review of the First Encounter
       According to its Seven Main Parts 542
    Similitude of the Nican Mopohua with
    the Gospel of St. John 546

Appendix III – One Way of Praying the Seven Veils 549

Preliminary Note

The Authenticity of the Image

The Seven Veils of Our Lady of Guadalupe helps us to enter deeper into the contemplation of the Guadalupan apparition in its three-fold dimensions of word, image and implied correlations.

It is necessary to rid ourselves of any serious doubts concerning the authenticity of the image from the beginning. The greater number of attacks with respect to the image of Guadalupe are best presented in J. Benitez's "exposé": *Disconcerting Discoveries.* Surely, it is not the first time such "discoveries" have been alleged, but here, it is crucial that we respond lest they might be misunderstood or disturbing to the faith of some. There is nothing more dangerous than a half or a poorly understood truth, one that is easily twisted so as to confuse the innocent. It is not our aim to prove or disprove his thesis regarding these "discoveries," but to simply put things into the right perspective.

The grace of technology, if utilized well for the greater glory of God, has the capacity of bringing us closer to reality. But we must begin here by saying that the term "reality" is an "enigmatic" concept, especially if it is restricted to material reality. By use of a Christian discernment, technology can help us arrive at a more realistic and detailed understanding of the reality of things, but we must always keep in mind that material reality is a reflection of a deeper and invisible Spiritual reality. What holds true for the word of God, that the subordinate sciences of archeology, philology, history, etc., help us to understand the word of God in a deeper way, is also true for the deeper study of the image of Our Lady of Guadalupe. It is extremely important that investigation is never done out of personal curiosity, like that of reporters who fish for sensational news, but for the "greater honor and glory of God" and for the salvation of souls.

The unfortunate thing about these "disconcerting discoveries" is their negative undertone with respect to matters of faith. Necessarily, the Image of Our Lady of Guadalupe is a matter of faith! Numerous popes as well as pontifical action confirm this. The Virgin of Guadalupe is not only the Queen of Mexico and Latin America, but has been pontifically proclaimed "Empress of the Americas and the Philippine Islands."[1] Although we do not encounter a negative tendency with Benitez, we must take into account that he is a journalist and "lives" on "sensationalism and innovation." His profession aspires to "raising questions," not necessarily limited to the facts, but always insinuating doubt in relation to matters of faith. What "disconcerts" a critical reader is the "security with which he speaks of 'a retouched image,' a false moon and an angel that falls in pieces." This is a typical "reporting style," rapidly classifying "the discoveries," although in the end, on the backcover of the book, he humbly concludes: *"that the reader make his own conclusions on that which, in my opinion constitutes one of the most astonishing enigmas of the Twentieth Century."* We find the same attitudes in the video "Los Enigmas

---

[1]   1667 — Papal bull by Pope Clement IX declaring December 9 as the Feast of Our Lady of Guadalupe.

April 24, 1754 — the Sacred Congregation grants a Mass and Office Proper to Our Lady of Guadalupe

May 25, 1754 — Papal bull by Pope Benedict XIV proclaiming the Virgin of Guadalupe as Patroness of Mexico

October 12, 1895 — First papal coronation by Pope Leo XIII (up until 1975 Our Lady of Guadalupe has had 160 Solemn Coronations, nineteen of them having been pontifical. Remember also that it is this same pope who gives the exorcism prayer of St. Michael to the church.)

August 24, 1910 — Pope Pius X declares the Virgin of Guadalupe as the Patroness of Latin America,

December 10-12, 1933 — Pius XI gives a pontifical crowning of the Virgin of Guadalupe and five hundred bishops implore the extension of the Mass and Office Proper for the whole world,

May 31, 1966 — The Virgin of Guadalupe receives a golden rose from His Holiness Pope Paul VI

de Guadalupe."[2] Behind its title is the hidden insinuation: *"One day, this enigma will be clarified!"* The optimism in the "unlimited progress of science" shines forth; one day, science will substitute faith!

There are strict laws governing the painting of icons, not only in relation to their "geometric structure," but also in relation to the painter (normally a person consecrated to God), because sacred icons represent the dogmas of the faith. They are like an official catechism which does not permit any personal liberties in the interpretation of the truths of the faith. In the case of the image of the Virgin of Guadalupe, we certainly have to deal with the most perfect icon ever created. It does not permit the slightest change, because this would consequently produce a change in the truth it announces. Although we are not yet capable of reading it in the light of the Holy Spirit, as an "image not made by human hands," it is really the most perfect and profound summary of our Christian faith.

Even with the Franciscans in the very beginning, there have been attacks against the image. At the onset of His public ministry, Our Lord Jesus Christ also encountered the same opposition. We must simply accept that things cannot be otherwise. Wherever the light of God breaks through the darkness of this world it becomes a challenge of combat to the fallen angels and their followers. Aware of the living presence of Our Lady in the image, the church in Mexico has supported and officially permitted "inquiries" since 1661. It was then that the first "process" of confirming the authenticity of the "miracle" of the image of Guadalupe was done. Mr. Benitez himself confesses that the Mexican Chancery very benignly permitted him to consult the report of Smith and Callahan,[3] a work which these two scientists had humbly deposited into the hands of the Bishop of Mexico without any benefit to themselves (quite a noble and selfless act for scientists!). The transcendence of their discoveries made them cede their personal and professional gain in the "hiding" or the "selling" of their findings.

---

[2]   Jaime Morrison, Video Visa Al5311
[3]   cf. *Applied Infrared Photography*, 1977

We will consider three distinctive data in the image of Our Lady of Guadalupe which will help better discernment of the authenticity of the image:

- The dimension of the Incarnation
- The diverse "strata" of the image
- The character of "dialogue" in the image

The Dimensions of the Incarnation in the Image of the Virgin of Guadalupe

The Incarnation as the fundamental criteria of Christian discernment. This is the fundamental difference between our and other religions, i.e., that God has made Himself known through the Incarnation of His Son Jesus Christ through Mary! In the image Our Lady is not hovering in the air. She revealed herself through her servant Juan Diego, the boy present at her feet. It is he and his uncle Bernardino, only witness of her apparitions, that brought her down to the soil of Mexico. It is through them that she wanted to make known the true God.

But remember: the absolute truth of God, for us Christians, is revealed in a "contingent manner," adapting itself to our manner of being, of thinking, and of speaking. More than four hundred years ago Pascal very clearly expressed that it is a sign of the loss of faith, that more and more we have to deal with a "god of philosophers" and not with the God of Abraham, Isaac and Jacob! The knowledge of God, to which this image gives us a glimpse, is a living knowledge, so necessarily it is a "Sign of Contradiction" which requires the answer of our faith!

Because the image is put in the hands of man, necessarily it will arouse controversy. Attacks always have been, only now they are supported with the nimbus of science. Referring to the "Aztec and Spanish elements" on and around the image of the "young Jewess," professors Callahan and Smith's infra-red studies allude that the areas which were "touched up" in the past may have been "added a century later." The simplest way to refute this doubt are the four painted copies of the image in the 16th century. Two of them date to the year 1540. The first has been studied by the historian Estrada and is found in the city of Guatemala. The second is found in the city of Puebla. Both of these copy images contain the same elements as does the original[4] and thus testify to the authenticity of the original. The fourth is a copy of the image commissioned by Montufar, former Bishop of Mexico, and sent by him to King Philip II of Spain in 1570. It was present in the Admiral's cabin in the victory of the Battle of Lepanto, 1571; it also contains the so called "disconcerting features" and thus renders Callahan's theory void. Don Valeriano in his epilogue of the Nican Mopohua, 1543–45, also gives a detailed description of the image in all its details, those also discussed by "modern science."

The image being always under the control of the ecclesiastical authority could not be touched by foreign hands. The faithful served as guards. Even with the remote chance that "retouching" might have been permitted, it would act as another proof of its having been incarnated by the people to whom it was given. Almost all painted copies of the image of the Virgin or of the saints manifest this "adaptation" to time, place or to man's way of life! Even today, within the church, we continue to adorn the image of the Virgin according to the liturgical season of the year. With a fervent faith we conclude then that these religious customs act as a testimony of the Incarnation within the salvation history of the church.

Lucifer fell because he would not submit to the plan of the Incarnation of the Son of God. From the beginning of the history of the church there has existed a battle against images with respect to religious cult. The first to revolt were the "iconoclasts." They were followed by Protestantism in all its forms backing their argument with Ex 20:4 and Lev 26:1. The deepest reason for images is that Our Lord Jesus Christ Himself is *the image of the invisible God*.[5] There are three images of Our Lady, believed to be carved by St. Joseph and painted by St. Luke: one in Guadalupe, Spain, the other in Nazaré, Portugal, the third in Czestochowa, Poland.

---

[4] Both copies have the rays of the sun, the moon, the golden flower brocade, the stars and the angel.

[5] Col 1:15

Which is the true one? This question never was decided. The church has never made a definitive decision with respect to these legends. Is the Virgin less present in a copy? Certainly, heaven must laugh over our disputes, and yet even in these "unreconcilable differences" there are significances, which only the eternal wisdom of God is capable of revealing to us in heaven!

One surety exists: man needs images: this holds true not only for the Aztecs with their official proclamations by pictures, it holds true in special way for modern man: images are more complex than words, easier understood. Heaven meets us more than half way. Not only do they represent something of the invisible reality of the reign of God, but they serve as "crystals," helping to concentrate our faith, guiding us in the light of the Holy Spirit. All of the previously mentioned images are really focuses of crystallization of utter religious importance. Without finding the statue of Our Lady of Guadalupe, there would not have been a conquest of the New World. Without Our Lady of Nazaré the navigators to the New World would not have had "the Star of the Sea" to guide them, and without Our Lady of Czestochowa, Poland would not be the Catholic nation that it has become.

One can not imagine that the church, after the death of Fray Juan de Zumarraga (sixteen years after the apparitions), conceded in allowing the alleged Native Indian, Marco, to "approximate" the "young Jewess" to the "liking" of the Mexican people. This is pure conjecture at best and fanciful at that. There would be so many criteria to meet, most of which could not have been achieved with the technology available in the 16th century, needless to say that of skill or artistic style and form. In 1531, painting in Spain was barely at the inception stage. The great Renaissance art movement did not enter Spain but two generations following. The image is even further removed from the Mexican art tradition of the Mayas, Toltecs, Aztec or Olmecs. They were wonderful sculptors and jewelers, and artists in featherwork and weaving, but in painting their work was yet crude and hieroglyphic. Moreover, lacking the necessary technology, early representations were relatively crude.

When Professor Fritz Hahn took fibers from the tilma to Nobel Prize winner Richard Kuhn, then director of the Wilhelm Institution's Chemistry Department, the latter stated that "There is no coloring of any kind in the fibers. The materials used to produce what resembled colors were unknown to science, being neither animal, vegetable, nor mineral dyes. The use of synthetic coloring was ruled out since that was developed three centuries after the creation of the image. Professor Francisco Champs Ribera, in 1954 and in 1966, did an exhaustive study of the picture. He concluded that he had found "no brush strokes." At any rate, if later research would show any thing else, the modifications were so marvelously adapted to the "original," that no one had discovered them until now!

We need the Spirit's Gift of Wisdom in order to better understand that an important "interior" criteria of authenticity for a work of art is the overall harmony of its integral parts. There should not exist "dissonance or shocking contrasts," in whatever type or consideration that they may appear, i.e., diverse styles, or the use of unusual or obsolete colors.

Even Benitez concedes, *"that the additions and the retouches, taken as a whole, are fascinating in their effect. As if accomplished by use of magical art, the decorations accentuate the beauty of the original and elegantly portray the Virgin Mary. It is as if God and man had worked together in the creation of a master work."*[6] These "details," from the spiritual point of view, give the image its "incarnative nature," its "Sitz im Leben." If there truly be "retouches," we hold that they were merely painted overlays and that they in no way challenge the authenticity nor the message of the image.

It is the will of God that this "young Jewess" (Mary seems to have been thirteen years of age in the moment of Annunciation) be made "incarnate" amongst this people as if she were one of them, which in fact is what has happened! This image necessarily encompasses the entirety of her life, on earth as well as in heaven: from the "young maiden" to the "woman clothed with the sun" and this conclusion can only be reached through the Spirit's Gift of Wisdom.

Certainly, one of the hidden tendencies of "demystification" of the image of Guadalupe is to make us forget about the apocalyptic dimension of Tepeyac. The way of life of the Aztecs was pro-

---

[6] cf. *El Misterio de la Virgen de Guadalupe*, pg. 102

foundly shaken by the violent entry of the Spaniards into their country. The entire world will be shaken when before the eyes of mankind she indeed be recognized as the "woman clothed with the sun"! Already in this very image, she is the Spirit's Gift of Counsel that God gives humanity today, a humanity which is at the brink of auto-destruction. If the "retouches" in the image could truly be verified, then they would be a "sign," just as is the abundant "Guadalupan" literature, that for more than 460 years, this image has continued to challenge all Americans, proponents and opponents alike!

The image of Our Lady of Guadalupe exacts a response, in the same way that the word and the commandments of God do. The triune God asks of us a triple response:

- The Father to the commandments,
- The Son to His words,
- and the Holy Spirit offers us Mary His Spouse to love, to emulate, to imitate! He challenges us to allow Him to form us in Her image, which is in fact, that of her Son, and to allow her to form us as she helped to form the human Jesus, and so allow the Spirit of God to transform us into that image of Jesus which the Father seeks in each one of us. For only in, through and with Mary will we enter heaven. This is the Spirit's Gift of the Science of the cross we have to learn by giving our response of faith.

The security safe which protects the image today is in direct contrast to the "neglectfulness" with which the image was cared for during the first two hundred years following its miraculous appearance. How many more millions would have touched, revered it or have been converted? God certainly is more capable of protecting it than any of today's most advanced or sophisticated security systems. Indeed, the Virgin of Guadalupe is the "honor of our race" and deserves the protection of her children, but being behind a bomb-proof glass places her far from personal contact and makes her "prisoner of love."

She asked for a "sacred house" where she could "reveal Him, give birth to Him in making Him known." She wants with all her personal love, compassionate gaze, help and salvation to give us

God. She did not ask for a glass vault to be protected from the people! She said that "Truly I am your compassionate Mother, yours and of all the people who live as one in this land and of all the other people of different lineages who love me, those who cry to me, those who seek me, and those who confide in me, because there I will listen to their weeping, to their sorrows, in order to remedy, to cure all their various afflictions, their necessities, their sufferings."[7] If her present glass vault residence is modern man's response to her maternity, then it is we who have become somewhat indifferent to a loving Mother's tender plea.

The image has remained under the guardianship and protection of the church, throughout the ups and downs of time. The so called "retouches," if that is what they are, remain under its responsibility. In everything, from the discoveries of her eyes to the investigations with the infra-red rays, there is a confirmation that there is a "nucleus of enigmas" that cannot be humanly explained; "the image is of divine origin!" As the details of the "retouches," as Benitez confirms, harmoniously integrate themselves into the overall outcome of the image, they also form part of the message of the Virgin. All of the investigations on the image of the Virgin of Guadalupe, above all, the fact that the image meets all the criteria of the "golden rectangle"[8] clearly demonstrate that there does not exist an icon, painted by God Himself, more sacred than this.

In this sense, the image is a point of union, not only between North and South America, but also between Asia and Europe, between the western and eastern churches. In the spiritual battle of these end times, the fallen angel attacks even that which is most sacred. We recall the words of Our Lord in His apocalyptic sermon: *"Therefore, when you see the abomination of desolation, which was spoken of by Daniel the Prophet, standing in the holy place ..."*[9] announcing the great tribulation of the end times. The enemy has many hidden means of entrance, including the "Holy of

---

[7] Nican Mopohua, vs. 26-32

[8] There exists in the image perfect symmetry, both from top to bottom and from east to west. The presence of the "golden rectangle" will be treated further in this book.

[9] cf. Mt 24:15

Holies,"[10] and we must remain vigilant, asking for the Gift of Fortitude so as to be able to resist these attacks which try to rob us of the most precious treasure of our faith.[11] The Virgin of Guadalupe is a sign of union in the very light of the Most Holy Trinity. Only if we resist all of these insidious attacks with fortitude will we, with Mary, be able to one day enter heaven![12]

God's Presence abides in an image like that of Guadalupe, even after the event, not only by His creative act, but sustaining it in the "current of life." In particular through the radiation which emanates from her. This is why she has touched the hearts of millions and the sphere of her influence extends far beyond the American continent. Let us remember with great gratitude that because of Mary's influence and protection, the disintegration of the faith and the corruption of morality, so much fomented in this country by a Free Mason government, which have swept Europe and the rest of the world since World War II, have been less felt in Mexico, with exception of the capital. She has helped Mexico to go on in the fear of God. Yet we have no idea what their apocalyptic influence will be on the world tomorrow, even though today the image of Our Lady is encountered as if locked up in a "temple of the New Age," as her enemies so proudly call it. The missionary image leaving the Basilica on December 12, 1992, on her pilgrimage through Latin America, and year earlier to the United States of America to end abortion, are a clear sign that she is starting her mission in our times: preparing for the second coming of her Son.

The Truth of God is consummated in us only if it is incarnated. Only if it is assimilated does it take on flesh from our flesh. This is only possible in the measure that Mary accepts our blemished heart within her Immaculate Heart. This is the message she gave in one of her apparitions in Germany following the second World War: *"exchange your heart with My own and offer it thus to*

---

[10] St. Margaret Mary told of seeing the devil even in the chapel.

[11] cf. Mt 10:22

[12] A prime example is the current stance of the abortionists, who now admit that they are "killing something". "Because before the abortion, it was alive and after the abortion it is no longer alive." These clinics now call themselves "houses of healing" and even have a workbook to help the mother deal with her guilt, even requiring her to write a letter to her unborn child.

the Father!" Basically, this is the same proposition that St. Louis Marie Grignon de Montfort brings to our awareness in his treatise, *True Devotion to Mary*, three hundred years ago. This can not be a one time pious act, but has to be a deep conversion, a daily even hourly act. Only in this manner will we arrive at the transformation of our heart into the heart of Mary and so will we be able to enter through her to the Most Sacred Heart of Our Lord Jesus Christ. Only by means of her, who meditated and pondered the word and deeds of her Son in her Immaculate Heart, will we truly become pious, only then the mysteries of Our Lord Jesus Christ will become flesh in us.

It is in meditation that we enter more profoundly into the plans of the mercy of God for these our times which exceed all human understanding, and only by meditation will we arrive at loving Our Lord more. St. Ignatius recommends the same in the final meditation of his spiritual exercises. True piety is the imitation of Mary, in her unconditional surrender to the will of God. This will transform the Gift of Piety into heavenly beatitude.

The Diverse "Strata" of the Image

The infra-red rays reveal something of the technique of the great painters. Their process of painting involved many different layers. They initiated with the placement of the "golden rectangle" on their canvas, followed with different drafts, and slowly came to a final product of their most primitive intuition. This idea of different strata or layers can also be seen by analogy in the image of Our Lady of Guadalupe. Miguel Cabrera, the famous Mexican painter, verifies that four different procedures were used in the image of Our Lady of Guadalupe which normally never come together: oil, tempera, watercolors, and etching.[13] He also insists that human brushstrokes are not to be found!

In analogy to these four different techniques of painting, and coming back to the idea of different layers, we could speak also of different "layers" in the image of Guadalupe. The "first layer" would

---

[13] *Maravilla Americana*, Miguel Cabrera, 1756, facsimile, 1977, ed. Jus, pg. 13

be the "young Jewess," discovered by the infra-red rays, and found at the foundation of the actual image. This discovery coincides with the tender words of Juan Diego, directed to the Virgin on the Tuesday morning encounter, while in search for a priest for his dying uncle Juan Bernardino: "My young child, my daughter, the smallest."[14] It is not only a manner of speaking. She really is the "daughter" who wills to grow in his heart and through him in all the hearts that will be opened to her message.

A secret parallelism with the announcement of the birth of the Lord in Bethlehem to the shepherds is apparent. It is no coincidence that the Holy Virgin, in her first encounter with him, speaks in the same way to him: "Listen, my son, the youngest, little John…" (vs.23) and "my son, the smallest…" (vs.26) and at the end of the first encounter: "Have you heard, my son, the youngest…?" (vs. 37) Remember also that in the Greek of the New Testament, the term "pais" signifies "child," but it also signifies "servant." This second connotation is also applied to the angels, as God's most faithful servants, only surpassed by the servant of God, Mary! This coincides with the "the child" at the feet of Our Lady being "an adult child" having passed through the fire of God's purification.

The plans of the mercy of God can only be executed by those who are pure and abnegated servants of God, just as the Virgin and the seer are. There is a profound affinity between their souls, both want to serve God with the entirety of their beings! Only through the purity and humility of Mary, so apparent in Juan Diego, will the people of the "New World" attain their freedom from the bondage of Satan and its service to the demons. We dare say that it is Mary, in the person of Juan Diego, who is victorious in the battle, for she is "unequal in her power against the demons!" The seer recognizes himself and his mission in Mary. Once again, the cognitive verdict of the pre-Socrates philosophers, proves its profound truth: "simile simili cognoscitur" — "knowledge only through similarity." Juan Diego was only capable of knowing the "child Mary" because he himself was a "pure child," pure in his

---

[14] Nican Mopohua, vs. 110

heart! This is the spiritual base of the image: It is necessary that we be reborn of the Immaculate Heart of Mary, washed by the blood of Christ.

The "second stratum or layer" in the image corresponds to the corredemptive mission of Mary, which not only began at the foot of the cross, but at the very moment of the Annunciation, when after having meditated the words of the Angel, she gave her crystalline "yes" to God. This "stratum" is reflected in the image, above all in the battle of light and darkness of her rose colored gown.

The "third layer" represents the mission of Mary as Mother of the church and of the universe, which began at the foot of the cross and extended itself through to the end of her earthly life in Ephesus, where she lived with St. John. It was also during this time that St. John was prepared for his apocalyptic mission. This last mission, with and for the church, finally extended over the whole church and the universe. It is symbolically present in her blue mantle containing forty-six stars; the horizontal addition of forty-six is ten and signifies the omnipotence of God!.

The "fourth layer" is her heavenly glorification, made visible to us in her mission as "the woman clothed with the sun," the stars about her head, and the moon beneath her feet. This final mission of the Virgin in the history of salvation is indicated by whatever is gold in the image: Cabrera distinguishes two forms of gold, admiring how it adheres to the weave of the tilma. How can God's glory ever come together with the dust of this earth? One form of the gold certainly represents the eternity of God. The other, the reflection of His eternal essence on us frail human vessels.

Recognizing exactly "four painting styles" and "four strata" in the life of the Virgin represented in the image, we can, in light of the four Gospels be confirmed that this sacred image, "not made by human hands" is another "gospel," a "gospel of light." Her message, identical to that of the Apocalypse, announces the "Final Victory of the cross of the Lord" and thus can truly be called "the Fifth or the Last Gospel"! Only "through the four directions of the wind" can we, in a "synopsis," intuit the truths of God. Many images in the Middle Ages were frequently represented as such; the life of the Lord, of Mary or of a Saint, in a single image, was represented in its totality.

In what way did the hand of God, or any other inspired one, paint these strata? We may never exactly know. In any case, the technical curiosity of our day has awakened us from a "pietistic" comprehension: from pious devotees of the Virgin, we must become confessors, and if necessary martyrs! We are not only to contemplate the image of Our Lady of Guadalupe from time to time or in pious moments. As the "child Mary" entered into the heart of Juan Diego, so also must the image of Mary enter into our hearts, transforming us according to her own image, which is none other than that of her Beloved Son. Whoever truly loves something tends to resemble the "beloved object": this is the final reason that the Virgin remains with us in her image: In contemplating it, our life should become more temperate and concentrated on the only valid goal necessary in the life of man: God!

The question, "How was this image made?" is of little importance to him who truly loves the Virgin. Love seeks out the beloved. Love does not investigate the "beloved" as an object so as to conquer, for many times this only serves as a means of demonstrating our intelligence and superiority. He who loves Our Lady of Guadalupe does not love an object, but a living person with a history, with unique way of adapting herself to us and our weaknesses, and all through love. If it is true that retouching was done to her face during the time of persecution, 1926-29, while hidden in a private home as Benitez affirms, then we can conclude that she suffered it for the love of God and for us. Does she not suffer disfiguration by all the insidious spiritual retouches that have political or pseudo-religious aims, presenting her as "mother of revolution and liberation" — Miguel Hidalgo, as symbol of the "eternal feminine" — on behalf of the esoterics, or as "mother of all gods" — metaphysical workshops of Guadalajara, claiming that she has left her "Christian disguise," by leaving the old sanctuary "entering the temple of the New Age," the new basilica of Guadalupe!

God in His infinite patience, magnanimity, and mercy toward us poor sinners permits these "sacrileges" just as He permitted the martyrdom of His Son in His most cruel passion. He, who with bleeding heart, experiences the passion of the Lord in His church today, will understand well that the passion of the Lord in His

Mystical Body, the church, is entering its final phase: the way to Golgotha! We will always find the Mother with the Son, even when all the apostles left and so many priests deny Him, she remains faithful under the cross and next to her St. John, representing the purity of the priesthood in the Spirit of Mary!

In the New Basilica, as if in a "babylonic captivity," she shares the captivity of her Son in the church of today, with its lack of faith and horrendous sacrileges committed both openly and secretly! Like the Lord, she remains firm in the midst of her enemies. Her merciful glance is capable of converting even her most outrageous enemies if they find the grace of repentance. The image truly is Her presence in our midst, partaking in all of our miseries, afflictions and desperations in a world that is so evil and is constantly falling more into the tight hold of the devil. Her presence is the living testimony of heaven that God has not abandoned us. But at the same time she ever more urgently calls us to take refuge beneath her protective mantle, the only secure place in this anarchic world, the only warm place in this world which is progressively being transformed into a freezer. It is in her, in the midst of the confusion, attacking even the Christian doctrine, that we yet find the pure truth of God which is His infinite love for us poor sinners!

The Character of Dialogue in the Image

Lastly, the image of Our Lady is the image of God Himself in His only begotten Son, through Whom all things were made. The more an image approximates the image of God, the greater the work of art. In this sense, there isn't any doubt that the image of the Virgin of Guadalupe is the world's greatest masterpiece. It certainly isn't by coincidence that by the very same hand of God we receive another image, of no lesser value: that of His Son, in the Holy Shroud of Turin. It would be lengthy to account its adventurous history, but it has many parallels with that of the Virgin! It has been investigated in our times in the same "scientific way" as the image of Guadalupe, and there are sufficient proofs that reveal it to truly be the authentic image of Christ. These two images, are the presence of the two witnesses of which the Apocalypse speaks.[15] They are the final call for conversion preceding the judgment over the church and the world.

The image is God's invitation to reestablish dialogue with man, a dialogue which was lost in paradise. It was first renewed in God's dialogue with Mary by the mediation of the Angel St. Gabriel. God then extends this grace to "all men of good will," like the poor and humble pastors of Bethlehem. It can continue only in the purity of the hearts of Jesus and Mary. We will only enter into this dialogue in: silence, listening, obedience, poverty, sincerity, and fidelity. Mary is the first human creature who gave the just response to God, a continual "fiat" until the moment of her death. She continues her response in heaven in representation of all of us in the church, the Mystical Body of her Son.

The dialogue between the Mother of God and the seer, Juan Diego, is the most lucid example of the dialogue with God in the spirit of a child. It reflects the crystalline character of the dialogue of the Lord with Nicodemus as accounted in the Gospel of St. John and with the Samaritan woman.[16] Truly it is the dialogue of the "child Mary" with the "child Juan Diego," in which all the surrounding nature of Tepeyac participates. That this dialogue has come to us in the Nican Mopohua is another miracle of the grace of God. It is a grace that God has reserved for these times, because only now is it available to everyone.[17] Just as the Virgin shines forth in the apparitions, so here also, in the grace of God, does the promise of the consummation of all things. The dialogue between God and man through Mary, in this "paradise of Tepeyac," is restored. If we become children at heart, then we also can take part in this promise of the Virgin clothed with the light.

We must grasp the folds in Mary's mantle tightly so as to ascend with her in her "Assumption" from the dust of this earth. Like Juan Diego, if we are humble of heart, then we also will be called to help in the construction of the reign of Mary. This reign must precede the second coming of Our Lord Jesus Christ when He comes as judge of the living and the dead. With the apparition of the Vir-

---

[15] cf. Rv 11:3-14

[16] cf. Jn 3-4

[17] cf. Book III

gin in Mexico the foundation of the reign of Mary has been set. The last phase of the battle against the enemy has begun, and it will principally unfold in the "New World."

The attack against the image has its parallel in the demystification of the word of God. This only underlines its strategic importance in the spiritual battle that has come to its climax in our days. In preparation for the apocalyptic battle, together with the holy angels, Our Lady is calling her children to form her "white army." We recall that the first martyrs of the New World were the three children of Tlaxcala, beatified in 1990 by our Holy Father, together with the seer of Tepeyac, Juan Diego. They give testimony to that which the Immaculate Heart of Mary asks of us: martyrdom, be it the white martyrdom of Juan Diego or the red one of the three children from Tlaxcala.

According to a legend, it is in the very place where the mercy of God initiated His work, the center of Mexico, being reflected in the Virgin's dress just beneath her praying hands, where the ultimate and final battle will unfold. It is here where the cry of St. Michael was first heard: "Who is like unto God!" in the apparition of St. Michael the Archangel in San Bernabé.[18] This is like the "third tone" in the "harmony" of the these apparitions. Mary will conquer the serpent, and St. Michael will liberate the people of God from their bondage!

---

[18]   cf. Book II

Preface to the Seven Books

How to Use These Books

Before entering the "workshop" of these books:

- ask your good Guardian Angel to help you,
- take time to contemplate the image of Our Lady of Guadalupe,
- read and reread the beautiful dialogue of the Virgin and her seer in the Nican Mopohua.[19]

First and foremost, in, with and through Mary, this book is one of prayer, meditation and contemplation and wants to help us to come closer to God and give the answer of love God is expecting from us.

Only in Mary are we able to give the right response to God.

- Our prayer is first of all answering the call of God's unique love for us. It is not necessarily a response by words, but finds its simplest and deepest expression in adoration.

- Meditation is pondering the word given to us by God. It is a word that includes all created things, because everything can become a "message of God" to and for us. We must only penetrate deeper so as to uncover that deeper interior mes-

---

[19] The Nican Mopohua is found in Book III

sage, because God's message is not on the surface of things, but in the depths of them.

- Contemplation is a step further. It is looking at things as an image of the invisible God, because everything was created in view of the Son, it is Him we should look out for in all things, because He alone is the perfect image of the invisible Father.[20]

A Book of Seven

It is beneficial to the reader to understand from the onset that this book corresponds with the holy number "7," the number which is to be understood as the "symbol" of the action of the Holy Spirit through Christ in this world. In as much as our meditations are open to His action can and will He guide and transform us into new creatures in Christ. This is why mere reading does not suffice. It is prayer that we need and this book is meant to be prayed from the beginning unto the end. This task of prayer will require the entirety of our forces: intellectual, spiritual and physical, so as to deeply understand the many correlations which will open up before our interior eyes.[21] The image of Our Lady of Guadalupe is a "Gospel," not by the word, but by the light. It is quite transparent to the structure and order of the Gospel of St. John (the same we will also see with the structure and order of the holy rosary), this is why we chose this order as the pattern for this book of prayer which should help us to understand deeper about the "Last Gospel of Light." The structure of the Gospel of St. John is that of the seven Sacraments, and this in an apocalyptical light.

---

[20] cf. Col 1:15

[21] Fátima in Lucia's … When the children were praying with the angel the prayer of adoration and reparation, they were really praying with all their physical and spiritual forces; this is why also after praying they felt without forces anymore. Francisco confessed that he was hardly able to walk. Remember also the Lord's prayer in the garden of Gethsemane. His effort to reach the Father was so great that it made His blood go out of the veins.

The first sign occurs in the second chapter when the Lord, at the marriage feast at Cana, revealed His glory so that the disciples believed in Him.[22] As the sign is performed at a marriage, marriage is seen as a Sacrament and becomes transparent for a deeper reality which is the covenant of God with man by His Son Jesus Christ. St. Paul, in the fifth chapter of his letter to the Ephesians, confirms this transparence of matrimony to the covenant of God.[23] As it is the first "sign," it englobes all further signs, and therefore also all the other Sacraments. The deeper sense of matrimony as covenant of God with mankind covers all the further steps of the Gospel of St. John. This is why the Priesthood, the last "sign" (Jn 21:), is the last step in consummating the Covenant of God with man. Man must be transformed according to the image of the Son sacrificied on the cross; this is why we are all called to participate in the eternal priesthood of Christ.

When man fell out of God by his first sin, more and more he lost the understanding that life is sacrifice. In the sense of "unless a grain of wheat falls into the ground and dies it remains a single grain …"[24] the life and mission of Jesus Christ is the exemplification of this truth; St. John, in his sermon on the Good Shepherd, explains that only the Son of God has the power for this sacrifice: "I have the power to lay down My life and to take it up again, and this mission I receive from My Father."[25] Only in Him and through Him, poor sinners that we are, are we allowed (it is a grace!) to share in His sacrifice and so lay down our life for our brothers as He did.

Our Lord Himself is the "great sign," He alone is the sacrament of salvation, and only through, with and in Him man can also become "sign" in the "sign." This is why Mary also, who was the first

---

[22] cf. Jn 2:12

[23] cf. Eph 5:32: "Great is this mystery I related to the relation of Christ and His church."

[24] cf. Jn 12:24

[25] cf. Jn 10:18

allowed to enter into His steps is "the great sign" (Rv 12:1)[26] only in partaking in the greater sign of her Son. She is, poetically expressed, "the morning star" that announces the "rising of the sun." St. John, the Beloved Apostle of Our Lord, through Mary is the next to share in this grace and together with him all those who extend their arms to embrace the cross.[27] When, at the end of times, she appears as this "great sign" before the eyes of the whole world, we know that the time has come to consummate the history of salvation. This happens in 1531 with the apparition of Our Lady on Tepeyac, when at the same time in Europe by the Reformation, "modern times" begin.

In this "great sign" mysteriously the presence of Christ the King as the great sign is veiled under the symbol of the four-petalled flower in the center of her person.[28] When we consider the second and glorious coming of Our Lord Jesus Christ as something conspicuous, we fail to consider the words of the angels at the ascension, as well as the image the Father has given us in the image of Our Lady of Guadalupe. The Virgin is "Teotokos," the God bearer. She comes robed in the splendor and glory of heaven.

---

[26] This can also be seen symbolically in the image of Guadalupe: under her hands, in the white ermine hand-cuffs, we discover the small "omega" (last letter of the Greek alphabet). It is necessarily the small omega, because the omega is reserved for her Son alone.

[27] This is why the messenger of Our Lady of Guadalupe, depicted in the boy at her feet, necessarily has to appear "crucified". He is, in the "great sign", sign for the way we have to take up our cross in these last times: in and through the mediation of Mary. This is the holy will of God the Father, to pass on His cross to us in these last times through Mary. (cf. Lucia's vision in Tuy where this truth is being shown in a wonderful image.)

[28] Christ, disappearing on the day of His ascension before His disciples, is "veiled by a cloud before their eyes". When they still continued looking up to heaven while He was going away, two men with white vestments came and said "Men of Galilee, why are you looking up to heaven? This Jesus Who has been taken away from you will return in the same way as He left." Acts 1:9-11

This testimony of the Acts is literally fulfilled when we look closer to the image of Our Lady of Guadalupe. She is coming precisely veiled in a cloud and her entire figure, together with her vestments, is another set of six veils, about which we have to speak more in detail at the beginning of Book Four: there are seven veils around the mysterious presence of the Lord in the four petalled flower.

But she herself is veiled in a cloud bearing the Lion of Judah in her womb. The "great sign" in another perspective is no other than that of the cross. But this time, it is not the cross as we meet it on the hill of Golgotha, but one transformed by the permanent meditation of Mary into "the four-petalled flower," which is another sign for the Lamb of God. This is also the title Our Lord receives already in the first chapter of St. John by St. John the Baptist pointing to Him.[29]

Resuming, there is a trinitarian significance of the concept of "sign" as we find it with St. John which will also be the key to our deeper interpretation of the image of Our Lady of Guadalupe:

1. It is transparent to the "great sign" which becomes visible in the "great sign" of Our Lady in the heavens of these last times. The Sacraments of the church are only unfolding the sacrament which is Our Lord Himself.
2. It represents the sign of the cross as the sign of salvation by which everything will be recapitulated in God.
3. The image given to this sign in the Apocalypse, prepared already in the Gospel of St. John, is that of the Lamb of God. It is a "rounded sign," because it has passed through the heart of Mary in continual meditation. This will be the end of history when the church as the Mystical Body of Christ will have taken into its heart the cross in the same way as did Our Lady when she stood with St. John three hours beneath the cross.[30]

---

[29] cf. Jn 1:36

[30] cf. lectures on the "Seven Days of Creation" with St. John, an interpretation of the Gospel of St. John according to its Spiritual structure (not yet published).

   For a better understanding of the concept of "sign" refer to the following citations:
   - Jn 2:11: the "sign" at the marriage of Cana, the principle sign for the covenant of God with man
   - Jn 2:18: it is always a "sign" of contradiction (purification at the temple)
   - Jn 2:23: it is the "sign" which will awaken the faith in the heart of those who look up to Jesus
   - Jn 3:2: it is the "sign" which cannot be overseen and so makes Nicodemus ponder more profoundly about the necessity to be born again
   - Jn 4:54: it the "sign" which will restitute to man his integrity (healing of the servant of the royal

St. John's Gospel in Relation to the Seven Sacraments

7. This is the aim of the covenant: that we become a royal priesthood (Holy Orders) (cf. Jn 21)[31]

6. We have to die to the old man and become new men in Christ (extreme unction) (cf. Jn 11)[32]

5. Our part in confirmation is to be confessors (cf. Jn 9)

---

30 cont.

- Jn 6:2: it is an extra-ordinary "sign" as can be seen in the multiplication of the bread. But its deeper significance should be penetrated. (cf. 6:14,26)
- Jn 7:33: The simple people are closer in understanding the "sign" than the sophisticated Pharisees.
- Jn 9:16: More and more the "sign" is revealing its separating power as already indicated in the second citation (healing of the blind man)
- Jn 10:41: St. John could only point out to the "sign".
- Jn 11:47: It is because of the "many signs" Jesus did that the Pharisees decide that there is no other way than "to do away with Him".
- Jn 12:18: The "sign of Jesus" is becoming more and more glorious: He is even attracting the Greeks, representing the pagans, who came to the Feast of Pasach (cf. also 12:37).
- Jn 20:30: This last citation, like a clasp on a chain, returns to the first: Jesus is the great sign, so whatever signs in the understanding of St. John will be performed, they must be referred to this one and unique "sign" Who is the Son of God.

[31] The movement of descent and ascension in reality is a perfect circle in resemblance to the "circle of light" which is the triune God: the Father sends the Son to the earth, the Son returns to the Father having fulfilled His Holy will. In this ring of salvation we have to enter wherever and whenever God will call us. Entering makes us "sons in the Son". Something of this ring of beatitude, which is the life of God, we can see in the halo of the saints. They best exemplify that sanctity is the full participation in the sacrifice of Christ on Golgotha. That St. John begins his Gospel with the Sacrament of matrimony clearly points out that natural life is orientated from the beginning to supernatural life.

[32] The passion of Our Lord, announced already at the end of Chapter 11 (11:55–57), extends, in another seven steps, to the end of the Gospel. The entire life of Christ is seen in the symbolism of His descent (end of Chapter 11) and His ascension again to the Father. The same symbolism we find depicted in the image of Our Lady in what we will later call: "the movement of ransom", starting from her eyes, going down to the lowest point of her gown and lifting up again into the light on the left side of her gown.

4. The Eucharist will help us to grow deeper in this covenant (cf. Jn 6)
3. By way of penance we profit from its graces (cf. Jn 5:1-18)
2. By way of baptism we enter into this covenant (cf. Jn 3:1 - 4:54)[33]
1. Matrimony is a sign for this covenant of God with man (cf. Jn 2:1-11)

Another Sequence of the Books

Book One: Another symbol of the covenant of God, as we will later see, is the holy rosary. The more we meditate on its structure, the more we will see that it is quite similar to that of the image of Our Lady of Guadalupe representing the structure of the reign of God. As such it will become for us the key for a deeper interpretation of the message and the image of Our Lady of Guadalupe.

Book Two: The next step is to better know the historical background: the Spaniards conquering Mexico opened the door for the baptism of this great continent of America.[34]

Book Three: It is not the Spaniards, first of all, who bring the good news to the New World, but Our Lady appearing on the hill of Tepeyac in 1531. By this apparition she gives quite a different orientation to the evangelization of this country and Latin America.

---

[33] As the vocation of the first apostles (cf. Jn 1:35-51), present at the marriage of Cana, and the purification of the temple (cf. Jn 2:13-22) form part of the first "sign" performed at the wedding feast at Cana, so also the "sign" of baptism is exposed in a triple way: in relation to the Father, baptism is shown as "rebirth" (cf. the dialogue with Nicodemus, Jn 3:1-21); in relation to the Son, baptism is shown as conversion to the "fountain of divine life" (cf. the dialogue with the Samaritan woman, Jn 4:1-41); and in relation to the Holy Spirit, baptism is shown as "call to the pagans" and "promise of a new family in Christ" (cf. the healing of the son of the royal dignitary, Jn 4:46-54).

[34] Here, we especially recommend for Spanish readers the beautiful book of Jose Luis Guerrero: "Flor y Canto del Nacimiento de Mexico," to which we will first of all refer.

She takes up all the light scattered in their pagan religion and concentrates it on the person of Our Lord Jesus Christ as the sacrificial victim Who will take away all our sins.

Book Four: Only by meditating can we find out about the trinitarian perspective of her message hidden under the symbols of the flowers and the stars. This beautiful order, reflecting the fourth day of creation is nothing else but the flourishment of the one four petalled flower which is a symbol for her Son she wants to bring to the New World.

Book Five: To bring her message to the bishop, she has chosen the purest crystal amoung the Aztecs: Juan Diego, who will reflect all the light she brings down from the Father. But wherever light enters into this world of sin, it has to break the walls of darkness and so the mission of Juan Diego really is a way of the cross.

Book Six: Only after these five first steps are we able to intuit the deeper significance of the message and image of Our Lady of Guadalupe. It is really an apocalyptic message in the light of chapter 12 of the Apocalypse. In order to better understand that the "woman clothed with the sun" is suffering "birth pangs," we have to relate her message and image to the Apocalypse as "apocalyptic Mass." The passion of Our Lord is seen in the light of glory — looking to its fruit: the new Jerusalem and its splendor, already prophesied in the Beatitudes of St. Mathew.

Book Seven: This book is a book of multiple relations. It is like the "workshop" for the *Seven Veils of Our Lady of Guadalupe*. It will help one to deeply meditate the beauty of this apocalyptic Message which will finally bring about the transfiguration of the whole creation into the new Jerusalem. The deeper this beauty penetrates, the more we will already partake in it now.

The Beauty of the Revelations of God as an Order of Signs

This book on Our Lady of Guadalupe is a genuine attempt at discovering the marvelous order of the reign of God already present among us, only hidden from our vision because we are yet too blind to see it. It is for this reason that we must first ask the help of our holy angel, because he is the closest representative of this holy order of the things of God. He will teach us to be silent, listening and obedient as Mary was, and by way of him we will learn to be poor, sincere and faithful, because only in stretching out for these qualities of Mary and asking for them in all humility are we given this first glimpse into this "reign of beauty."

It is our holy companion who will help us to look at things and persons in the ingenuous way of a child: in admiration - a word so applicable in understanding the crystalline relation of Juan Diego to Our Lady. Admiration is the starting point of Greek philosophy. The grasping for things in an egotistical effort of self-indulgence is that which dissembles the modern man from genuinely seeing things in a child-like perspective. Before any attempts to better understand the why's or before any analysis of details, our first approximation to the image of Our Lady of Guadalupe should be to admire its perfection.

As anarchy and disorder are taking over more and more, we should more intensively look out for the order of the reign of God. The more man loses his orientation in the exterior world, the more he has to orientate himself with the eternal order of the things of God. This is not only a spiritual order, because otherwise we would fall in the error of the Gnostics. It is an order, already incarnated in this world through Christ and the mysteries of His life and His continued presence in the church, first of all by the Sacraments.

According to the terms of this world, it is neither an invisible order, nor a visible one, but an order of the signs which are always to be found on the limit between the visible and the invisible world. This order is closest to us in the seven Sacraments of the church, as we have seen them in the Gospel of St. John. By way of the Sacraments and their incarnation in our life, it will also become an order in our human life and in the creation that surrounds us.

So as to better understand more of this order of signs we necessarily have to go to the limit between the visible and the invisible worlds and this means on our side that again and again we have to die to the old Adam and the old Eve in us in order to look over to the other side where Christ is seated at the right hand of the Father. In this perspective the crisis the church is undergoing can be interpreted as a challenge of God's apocalyptic love to come closer to His open heart and to experience the power of His cry on the cross, "I thirst!"

This fourth last word of Our Lord from the cross: "I thirst!" is like the interweaving connective thread which will help us to find our way through these meditations. It is the cry of God's love to bring us back to the Father: angel, man and the whole of creation. It is a cry of the "harvest;" with the holy angels being sent out as the harvesters.[35] Lastly, this cry is not only audible, but also visible in the merciful eyes of Our Lady of Guadalupe in her God-made image. It is our good Guardian Angel who will help us to enter deeper into this "country of the beauty of God" which is the image of Our Lady of Guadalupe.

Classical philosophy speaks to us of three "transcendental" properties of all existence: "unum, verum, bonum" — "oneness, veracity, and excellence." The word "transcendental" connotes that these qualities are transparent for the ultimate cause of all existence: God. For this reason also, the revelations of God must reflect these three qualities, moreover having their relation to the three divine persons: The first to the Father, the second to the Son, and the third to the Holy Spirit, but there is also a relation to the four greater attributes of God: Oneness to the holiness of God, veracity to the wisdom of God, and excellence to the justice of God. The fourth transcendental, beauty, corresponds to the omnipotence of God.

In the history of salvation we can follow four steps of revelation in concordance with the four transcendentals. The first phase of the knowledge of God in the Holy Spirit is that of the unity of

---

[35] cf. Mt 13:39

God, expressed in monotheism. The second is that of true God —
by means of Jesus Christ and His death on the cross. The third is
that of just God, which is made manifest by the mission of the
church in this world": *"He that believes and is baptized shall be
saved, but he who does not believe shall be condemned"*(Mk
16:16). The fourth coincides with the last phase of salvation history: the Apocalypse, in whose final chapters the new Jerusalem
descends as the consummated revelation of the mystery of the most
Holy Trinity!

Within this pattern we can also see the history of Mexico, as
Guerrero explains it: already in the Aztec religion existed an understanding of One God, Ometéotl, although it was yet dimmed by
the "many other gods," one more expression of the impossibility
of man in understanding the "true God" in His essence. Guerrero
interprets these "gods" as a deficient human manner of approaching the unfathomable concept of God; this for two reasons: we are
creatures, and moreover, we are sinners! The dual or opposing concept of God (male and female) allowed entry of the Christian view
of the opposition between the Father and the Son, most apparent in
the death of the Son on the cross (cf. Mk 15:34-35), an opposition
that is only resolved in the Holy Spirit through the Resurrection.

The concept of true God above all shines forth in the experience of the Mexican people throughout the Spanish conquest,
which practically eliminated their culture. Only by their holocaust
is the true God revealed. Christ sacrificed can only be known by
sacrifice.

The just God is apparent in the revelation of the Virgin of
Guadalupe correcting the violent manner of the Spaniards preparing the way for the Gospel.[36] This direct intervention of God by
way of Our Lady in Mexico is really unique in the whole history of
salvation and caused Pope Benedict XIV to exclaim: *"taliter non*

---

[36] Being horrified by the practice of human sacrifices, the Spaniards thought that
the best way to put an end to it was to kill the pagan priests which they did
shortly after having arrived.

fecit nullae nationi!" (Psalm 147)[37] The beauty of this intervention we can admire already now in the image of Our Lady. It will be the omnipotent God Who in the reign of Mary will bring the history of salvation to its consummation.

The image of Our Lady of Guadalupe really is like a "Fifth Gospel" synthesizing the four-fold revelation of the synoptic Gospels and that of St. John. It preannounces the unity of faith in the One God of three persons at the end of time, as Christ prays for in His high priest prayer: *"that all may be one..."* (Jn 17:21). The Virgin words to Juan Diego *"I am the Mother of all those in these lands that desire to be one!"*[38] are addressed to all men of goodwill.

The message of Guadalupe is a message of light of the omnipotent God Who will fulfill in and by Mary whatever He has promised to those who belive in Him.[39]

Close to Our Lady, we meet St. Michael, who already helped in the first separation of darkness and light. Even though the image and the circumstances of the apparition of Our Lady of Guadalupe are clearly apocalyptic,[40] man must be repeatedly reminded of this. This is part of the mission of St. Michael in his apparition in San Bernabé-Capula one hundred years later in 1631 about one hundred kilometers east of Tepeyac.[41] St. Michael is subordinate to Our Lady: as chief of the heavenly hosts, he has to

---

[37] Already here, we should transcend the local limits of the apparitions of Our Lady in Mexico. The same way she helped those poor pagans to get out of the darkness of the most abominable idolatry, so she will finally help all mankind to be freed from the clutches of Satan, prince of this world. She really is the help of Christians.

[38] cf. Nican Mopohua vs. 30

[39] This interpretation is part of the name Guadalupe as it is understood by the Spanish. The message of Our Lady as the "woman clothed with the sun" is a message of light piercing the growing darkness of this world. This light is different from the light of the Incarnation. In this apocalyptic light the final separation of light and darkness will be completed.

[40] Recall the first meeting with Our Lady in a nature completely transformed similar to the material structure of the new Jerusalem. (cf. Rv 21)

[41] For further information on the apparition of St. Michael in San Bernabé-Capula, 1631, refer to Book Two.

bring about the victory of the light of God through Mary.[42] In the image of Our Lady of Guadalupe, the angels, so to speak, are "in" Our Lady. Their presence, according to their spiritual-invisible nature, is indicated by signs, as for example: the golden rays around Our Lady.[43] God wants our complete attention to be concentrated on Our Lady as bearer and witness of the "mystery of God." As the angels in the history of salvation necessarily drew back before the light of Christ and limited their visible presence to the "key points" of the life of Christ,[44] so the angels will also "withdraw" visibly in awe before the awesomeness of God Who will reveal Himself through and by Mary.

The more we are nearing the end of time, the angels must be seen in their essence as being light of the light of God. This is why we should not look out for new visible appearances of angels, but learn to meet them in our conscience. Already in the Gospel of St. John, in the narration of the Resurrection, the angels appear directly only to those who still lack faith in the reality of God-Spirit, like Mary Magdalene. St. John recognizes their presence by way of the order in the arrangement of the shroud and the head wrapping in the tomb.[45] Holy order is always the clearest sign of the presence of the angels. The image of Our Lady of Guadalupe is a

---

[42] Unfortunately, man all too soon forgets the importance of these heavenly admonitions; not only did the apparitions of Our Lady become more and more a symbol of Mexico's national pride, insidiously disfigured by the enemy, but also the world-wide importance of the apparition of St. Michael was gradually lost. Today it has become merely a "devotion" of the simple people in the locality immediately surrounding the sanctuary.

This "babylonic captivity" is a clear sign for those who can still see that the battle is being waged ever more fiercely. The sanctuary of Our Lady in Mexico has become a "temple of the New Age" with some almost hidden relics of our Christian faith. The feast of St. Michael commemorated in the months of September and October is now primarily an occasion for the worldly pleasures of the pilgrims who still go there.

[43] cf. Heb. 1:7; "He makes the angels as Spirits and servants to fire tongues."

[44] Meditate the five mysteries of the fifteen decades of the Rosary which deal with the angels. (The Annunciation, the nativity, the agony in the garden, the Resurrection, and the Ascension)

[45] cf. Jn 20:7

Gospel of light to be contemplated in the three different forms of revelation that come to us as: image, word and light.

The universe, created in view of the Son of God is threefold because it should be a reflection of the triune God: so there are the three worlds, the angelic, the material creation and that of man.[46] This is also explained in the beginning of the Letter to the Hebrews: *"God, who at sundry times and in diverse manners spoke in times past to the fathers by the prophets, last of all in these days He has spoken to us by His Son ... "*[47] All revelation, not only that of the word, culminates in the revelation of the Son of God; already, creation is a revelation of God: *"For since the creation of the world His invisible attributes are clearly seen. His everlasting power and His divinity have become visible, recognized through the things He has made."*[48]

Part of the revelation of God through the cosmos are the stars of heaven. They remind us that we are nothing in comparison to the immensity of the world of the stars, the bounds of which increase daily as revealed through the discoveries of modern science. It is so great that man would feel annihilated in the face of it. This is in fact the reaction of the majority of men who do not have the support of faith. Necessarily, they feel lost in the immensity of this universe and are unable to discover what man's mission should be there in. How good God is in letting us see in the stars on the mantle of the Virgin, representing the constellations seen in the heavens on December 12, 1531,[49] that this marvelous world is uniquely oriented to His Son, speaking to us of Him all the while! Even the stars are prophets especially if we see them in relation to the hierarchical order of the holy angels. They are part of the "Gospel of light" which is the image of the Virgin of Guadalupe. Because all creation is *"... the brightness of His glory and the image of His substance...."*[50]

---

[46] cf. Col 1:15

[47] Heb 1:1-3

[48] cf. Rom 1:20

[49] cf. Book Four: "The movement of ransom in the Sign of the Lamb of God."

[50] Heb 1:3

Book One

The Dimensions
of the Holy Rosary

The Rosary in the Image
of Our Lady of Guadalupe

In *The Last Gospel of God*,[1] the author calls our attention to a chain of pearls which seems to have all the qualities of the rosary, including a cross with a Corpus Christi on it. The manner in which we behold the image of Our Lady of Guadalupe is not so much a "searching for material details" as it is an interpretation of the Spiritual value of symbols in their analogy.

The "analogy of all being," *analogia entis*, signifies the transparency of the material world to a higher Spiritual world, of which it is only a reflection. Material details become "pure signs" the more we ascend in the light of God. Little by little, the material

---

[1] James D. Halloway is among the first to probe deeper into the symbolic character of the image of Our Lady of Guadalupe in an effort to reveal something of its deeper "Spiritual message."

world has to be left behind. The "outward face" becomes thinner and thinner without losing its last relation to the material thing. It is for this reason that certain things, at higher "levels," have a variety of meanings, but an analogy to the material thing always remains. A beautiful example is St. John's description of the triune God in the first chapter of the Apocalypse. His "vision" is on the level of symbols: the exterior signs are but an indication of a higher Spiritual reality. God, Whom we cannot imagine, is beyond the signs; the signs are only frail landmarks. This is why we should see the rosary not in relation to special material details of the image, but in view of the message the Virgin Mother of God was sent to bring. The rosary in the image of Guadalupe is not a particular chain, Our Lady herself is a living rosary!

As a sign of her mission, she sent Juan Diego to the bishop with his tilma full of roses. As the original text of the apparition states, it was at the exact moment that the seer opened his tilma that the roses fell before the feet of the bishop and that her image appeared on the tilma.[2] This implies that it was not there before. Mary is the "rose" of God's grace, who brought God's love into the darkness of this continent.

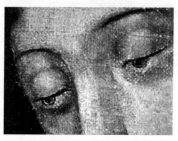

God's bounty for us poor sinners is again brought to image for us by way of the eyes of the Virgin of Guadalupe. As a loving mother, she bows down to us, her children, and offers us the "covenant of God." She is the bridge from heaven to earth. She is the "gate of heaven," the *Porta Coeli*, and she offers us the rosary as a type of rope ladder. The rosary is like an umbilical cord or life line binding us to our Mother and by means of which we may climb up into the light of God's promise.

Within the image of Our Lady of Guadalupe something like fishing instruments can be seen: a beam of light, a hook and a net. Is not the rosary itself "a fishing instrument" of Our Lady? By way of the mysteries of Christ she will attract, capture, and save

---

[2]   cf. Nican Mopohua, vs. 181-183

souls from the stormy seas of this world. The individual roses brought by Juan Diego to the bishop as the "sign" can be seen as symbols of the mysteries of Christ's life, passion and Resurrection; not only the fifteen traditional mysteries, but also the myriads of mysteries, apparent or hidden, of His life found in the Gospels. In the image of Our Lady all these mysteries are synthesized in the nine large golden flowers.

The nine small golden flowers act as a type of vine-trellis on which the nine larger ones climb. In them, we can also see "reigns of grace"[3] to be conquered by our praying and living the mysteries. That there are nine in number again reminds us of the new man in Christ who must be born in us.[4] By her personal meditation and contemplation, Mary has opened a deeper comprehension of the

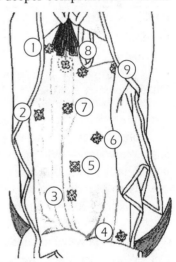

mysteries of the life of her Son. Little by little, our life should become more like hers, a "blossoming rosebush" for the greater glory of God in Jesus Christ and the salvation of souls.

The formal structure of the rosary is reflected in the four columns visible in the image. They can be seen as symbols of the columns of the house in our souls and in the church in which the triune God can dwell. Our Lady, is at the door to take us in.

---

[3] Symbolically, Mary can be seen as the "country" God's love has conquered by the Precious blood of His Son. As poor sinners we are allowed to enter this "country" by the attraction of her loving glance. And just as everything in the reign of God is order and beauty, so also can we imagine that this "country" is divided in different "provinces" or "reigns of grace" corresponding to the special merits, virtues and graces of Mary.

[4] cf. *A Little Catechism on the Holy Rosary in Relation to the Image of Our Lady of Guadalupe,* m.g., May 8, 1994, Fátima: II. 2.b. The 3 x 3 circles as "a way of birth"

Resuming the first trinitarian relationship between the image of Our Lady of Guadalupe and the rosary:

- The Virgin herself is the living rosary, moving the mysteries of Christ in her heart.
- The rosary is a fishing instrument for the salvation of souls.
- The pearls of the rosary are the individual mysteries, which together form the house of God, the house of salvation.

Over and over again, as manifested in the holy rosary, so also do we find a trinitarian rhythm in the image of Our Lady of Guadalupe, revealing the presence of the triune God.[5]

Another important element of construction, in the image as well as in the rosary, is the cross. Our Lady does not carry a cross, but she herself *is* the cross: she is crucified, in and with her Son. Other elements of construction are the numeric relations: with five, seven, nine, twelve.

There are four promises which hold true for the image of Guadalupe and the rosary:

- With Mary's help, by the mysteries of the life, death and Resurrection of her Son, we will find our way to the door of heaven,
- With Mary's help the battle between darkness and light will finally end in the victory of the light;
- With Mary's help we will participate in this victory even in this life, in the measure that by her mediation the mysteries of the life, death and Resurrection of her Son, Our Lord Jesus Christ, become incarnate in us and
- With Mary's help we will participate, already here on earth, in the order of the reign of God.

We present five meditations on the rosary:

The first meditation will focus on the covenant of God the Father with mankind. The rosary is considered as a symbol of this

---

[5] By a "trinitarian rhythm" we want to signify that, in the image as well as in the rosary, there is a harmonious repetition of elements in relation to the three persons of the most holy Trinity.

covenant. It is likened to an umbilical cord uniting us more intimately with God through Our heavenly Mother.

The second meditation is "the interior house of the rosary." It will present the rosary, structured in likeness of the cross, as our Spiritual house here on this earth. As such, it will become our shelter in these apocalyptical times, when the church will increasingly lose its secular property and become a church "in tents" (as the Israelites on their way out of Egypt), on pilgrimage in its ascent to Golgotha.

The third meditation presents the "movements" in the rosary. The rosary is not only an empty house, but it is filled with the life of Christ. We only have to enter these movements in order to participate in the "trinitarian rhythm" of God's life in Christ, in which we are called to participate for all eternity.

The fourth meditation is an unfolding of the formal beauty of the individual prayers of the rosary. Everything in God is beauty and harmony, not only in the image of Our Lady of Guadalupe, but also in this "picture of life" which is the rosary.

The fifth meditation is an invitation to share the rosary with our good Guardian Angel, with St. Gabriel and all the other angels. It is thus that it becomes an apocalyptic prayer: the invincible power of the cross against the powers of hell.

The First Meditation: The Rosary as Symbol of Covenant of God with Man

Expression of the Bounty of God with Men

At no other time in the history of the created world is the overflowing bounty of God's love more apparent than in the passion of the only begotten Son. God's goodness descends upon us by way of the cross. We get a better idea of this considering the life of Padre Pio of Pietrelcina. For fifty years his life made visible the bloody sacrifice of Christ on Golgotha. In this way he exemplifies the true mission of the priest. Not only is the priest called to represent the holy sacrifice of Christ in its liturgical dimensions, but he is also invited to participate in the same sacrifice with his entire life. The more the Lord can realize His passion in us, the more His graces can flow on the barren soil of this earth. The rosary is meant to remind us that our lives should be integrated into the life, suffering and Resurrection of Our Lord, and as such it becomes for us an inseparable link to the mystery of the holy Mass.

This is also the deeper meaning of our praying the Liturgical Hours of the Divine Office throughout the day to continue our participation in the holy Mass. The rosary is another psalter with the same mission, especially if we tend for the "perpetual rosary."[6] By way of Our Lady and the praying of her rosary, the many who are unable to assist at daily Mass can partake in and be united with the continual flow of graces coming down from Golgotha.[7] From the very beginning, the Spiritual power of the holy rosary was evident. St. Dominic used it as heaven's weapon in overcoming the existing schism in southern France. Meditating the sacred mysteries of the rosary helped the schismatics to come back to Christ.

The rosary is really a prayer of "autumn and harvest," a bringing of the "crop of life" into the heart of Mary. Autumn is the time when the light begins to fail and darkness increases. The fullness of summer growth has come to an end and the last ears of corn are gathered. But before the darkness of winter fully takes over, nature bursts open with the most beautiful colors, as if desperately trying to enter into the deeper transparency of light. As the colors of nature symbolize its beauty and diversity, so also do all the different mysteries of Christ's life, death and Resurrection. All the sacred

---

[6] Here we understand the "perpetual rosary" first of all as continuing in, with and through Mary to ponder the life of the Son of God in our heart as she did — trying to carry the Lord in the holy Eucharist, like St. Therese of Lisieux: "from one communion to the next." St. Anthony M. Claret was also graced with the permanence of the Eucharistic presence. This presence of Our Lord is not only a Spiritual one, as understood by the monks of first Christian era, but it is a sacramental presence. The Lord wants to live in us, body and soul, for the sanctification and the salvation of souls.

[7] In this last century, Christian missionaries were again permitted to enter China. Although all priests had been expelled in the XVI Century, it was found that many Christian communities had preserved the faith during the clerical and sacramental absence of the Lord by the mere recitation of the holy rosary.

mysteries of Our Lord are synthesized in the "sheaf" of the Most Holy Bread, Our Lord in the holy Eucharist. The holy Virgin then, can be likened to the "barn of the harvest," the tabernacle, in which God has brought in and conserved the crop of the Redemption wrought by His Son.

Praying the mysteries of the rosary with our heart, as Our Lady of Fátima recommends, enables our contemplation to become Spiritual bread for the life of the world. The bread which synthesizes the harvest of this world is heavy. As the bringing in of the crop is not a casual pastime, so neither can we say is the praying of the rosary. As a prayer of "harvest," it is hard work! All the sufferings of the world must be integrated into the mysteries of Our Lord. By way of Mary and Our Lord Jesus Christ they must be brought before the throne of God. The rosary is a prayer of harvest in which we try to bring in our little participation in the mysteries of Christ's life. Our hands will never be empty, because we can always unite our little efforts with the effort of Our Lord Jesus Christ on the cross and with that of Our Lady at the foot of the cross. There is nothing in our life which would fall outside of the myriads of mysteries of the life and passion of Our Lord Jesus Christ. By way of the mysteries of the life, passion and Resurrection of Our Lord, God the Father wants to bind together the threefold creation (material, angel and man) in Christ His Son.[8]

We can distinguish three covenants of God with man which make up for the treason of angel and man. The first covenant of God, by way of Moses through the laws of the Ten Commandments, constituted Israel as a nation set apart, peculiarly belonging to God. This first covenant is the foundation for the two that follow. The second covenant, by our Lord Jesus Christ through His death on Golgotha, completely fulfills the law of God over man and angel. The "third covenant" is the consummation of the second by way of the Holy Spirit in the Mystical Body of Christ in the

---

[8]　The three parts of creation are symbolized in the rosary in the following way: the wooden pearls represent the material creation, the words we speak represent the life of man who is related to the word and our meditation links us with the holy angels, the instruments of the Holy Spirit.

church, bringing her to perfection at the end of times. As the people of Israel fell away from the first covenant, with only a remnant entering into the new covenant with Christ, so also now in these end times will there only be a remnant who will fulfill the third covenant with God.

These three covenants can be related to the three rosaries:

- The Joyful Mysteries, with the Old Testament being its fulfillment
- The Sorrowful Mysteries correspond with the new covenant of God by way of the death of His Son Jesus Christ on the cross and
- The Glorious Mysteries correspond with the promise of the Apocalypse that all things will be made new: *"There will be a new heaven and a new earth."*[9]

The third covenant will not only be a restoration of man's dignity, but a rearrangement of the order of the angels: God will redistribute the empty places of the fallen angels. In the end the number of men and angels united in the eternal praise of God will be equal.[10]

The Principle of Meditation: Repetition

Only by a repetitive praying of the rosary can we enter more deeply into the mysteries of creation, Redemption and consummation. Repetition is not, and never should be, automatic or sterile. Neither should it be associated with or confused with the false circle: the serpent biting its tail.[11] It is an organic process, and is best un-

---

[9]   Rv 21:1,5

[10]   This could be deduced from the measure of the walls of the new Jerusalem: there is an identical measure of man with that of the angels. (cf. Rv 21.16) Remember that the measure of man is in the Incarnated Son of God. Only in Him and through Him can man and angel come together: be one as He is one with the Father and the Holy Spirit. The wall of the holy city is 144 cubits high — recall the 144 rays on the image of Our Lady of Guadalupe — she is the most perfect reflection of the "measure of her Son."

derstood in the symbol of the spiral; ever open to new upward growth. This mysterious yet organic action is witnessed in plants, trees, seashells, even in the spiral nebulas of far-off solar systems. All life ultimately tends toward God, not in a linear, but in a vertical upward spiral movement. The three liturgical seasons of the church have a part in this spiral movement; they are to lead us into a deeper participation of the mysteries of Christ and His Holy Spirit in the church.

We accept every cross that God places on our shoulders more easily, remembering that the tears and prayers of the maternal heart of Our Lady have polished smooth all the hard and cutting edges of the cross. Our repetitive praying with Mary will transform our suffering and trials into pearls of grace for the greater glory of God. Our meditation must be ongoing and life-long, because the aim of contemplative prayer is to incarnate the life of Christ in our lives. At the end of our life, by way of Mary and our angel, we should be able to hand over the rosary of our life, completely integrated in the rosary of the life of Our Lord Jesus Christ, so as to be a *"pleasing sacrifice, holy and acceptable"* to the Father.[12]

Second Meditation: The Interior House of the Rosary

Only by a true meditation of the mysteries of the holy rosary[13] will we discover it to be a "house" in which we may take shelter and dwell on our earthly pilgrimage.

The principle of construction of the rosary is the central mystery around which the remaining four revolve.[14] These four surrounding mysteries can be compared to the four columns of a house.

---

[11] We will speak more about the "circle" in the second meditation on the "interior house of the rosary."

[12] cf. I Pt 2:5

[13] In all of her apparitions, Our Lady consistently recommends a deeper praying and meditation of the holy rosary.

[14] cf. The Four Mysteries Surrounding the Central Mystery, pp. 79 ff.

Joyful		Sorrowful		Glorious	
Vis.		Scour		Ascend.	
Finding	Annun.	Cruc.	Agony	Coron.	Resur.
Pres.		C. Cross		Assum.	

The essence of a "Spiritual house" is that it should be a place of "rest," one where we can contemplate God. In the folly of God, this house is built upon the cross; the same cross below which the heart and soul of Mary were transpierced. By the sorrowful heart of Mary, the "sword" of the cross has been transformed into the key to the mysteries of Christ. The Virgin's contemplation of the cross of Her Son has transformed it into a house of treasures. "House" should not be understood in a material way. It is here first of all symbol of home and shelter in an organic sense, as something which is growing under the grace of God. As God is a living God, so also the house in which He wills to abide should be a living house. This is why, ultimately, the house of God is Mary.

The Order of the Reign of God: As an Order of Organic Growth

We must learn to pray the rosary in accordance with the First Commandment of God: *"Hear, oh Israel, you shall love the Lord your God with all your heart, with all your soul and with all your strength."*[15] Praying in this manner will help us to make it a prayer of life and get away from any automatism and monotony which kill the spirit. St. Paul reminds us that we are unable to pray as we ought. This is why we must implore the Holy Spirit to intercede for us and teach us how to pray.[16] Man's original sin caused him to fall from his created dignity. If it were not for the mercy and help of God, man would be incapable of finding his way back to intimacy with God. God Himself takes up man again to His heart in and through the merits of the cross of His Son. The cross is the

---

[15] Dt 6:4-5 and Mk 12:29-30
[16] cf. Rom 8:26

richest of all the symbols of salvation. It can be seen as a ladder which we ascend, and in this perspective, the rosary can be likened to a rope tied to the cross helping us to ascend to the heart of Jesus, and through Him to the Father!

As an organic and symbolic structure, the cross can be compared to a tree, with its four main constituents: the roots, the stem and the branches, the leaves (sometimes flowers) and finally the fruit. These constituents again are symbols for the four stages of Spiritual "growth." We find them also in the Gospels as the four periods of Christ's life: His infancy, His first apostolate in Galilee, His way to Jerusalem and His passion and Resurrection in the Holy City of Jerusalem. We find them again in the four "encounters" of Juan Diego with Our Lady of Guadalupe.[17] This is another sign that God reveals Himself through the cross of His Son also in a formal way. In the end, in a veiled manner, these four stages converge into one, as the four different gospels become "one" in the "fifth gospel" of the image of Our Lady of Guadalupe.[18] The same is true for the mysteries of Christ's life. They are synthesized into the one mystery of the cross. It is thus that the cross becomes the axle of all the mysteries of the rosary, the Joyful and Glorious Mysteries as well as the Sorrowful.

Because each of us must give a personal response to God, the cross is necessarily the one foundation of the house which God wills to construct in us with the help of the angels. Thus will the cross be the key that opens the gates of heaven for us! As our response is always to the triune God, every step of "construction" must necessarily be threefold, i.e., orientated to the three divine persons. Thus we arrive at the holy number 4 (stages) x 3 (each stage in a threefold

---

[17] 1st encounter — December 9, 1531, dawn; 2nd encounter — December 9, afternoon; 3rd encounter — December 10, afternoon; 4th encounter — December 12, dawn; See Nican Mopohua vs. 3, 47-48, 68/88 and 99/106.

[18] cf. The manuscripts of lectures on the interpretation of the "synoptic gospels" and the "writings of St. John," Anapolis, Brazil. The four apparitions of Our Lady of Guadalupe also converge in the "fifth apparition" to Juan Bernardino, where the Virgin reveals her name and heals the uncle of Juan Diego. (cf. also Nican Mopohua vs. 120, 121 and 203) It is a promise that in the end she will heal mankind from the deepest wound: that of original sin.

manner) = 12: symbol of the new Jerusalem with its 12 gates open for mankind to enter into the house of the Father.

The Four Steps of the Construction of the House of God within Us

Symbols in the Spiritual realm can be seen under different perspectives, which according to a purely logical interpretation might even seem contradictory. In our case, how can the four steps of growth be symbolized in the growth of a tree and at the same time be seen in the form of a quadrangle; or put even more clearly, what relation is there between the organic spiral growth of a living organism and the constructive form of a quadrangle? This question already preoccupied Pythagorean philosophers. Symbolically, how finally will our life become round, having so many edges?

Because man fell away from God through original sin, he fell out of the order of God and so needs to be reformed and educated at the very root of his being.[19] This is why everyday we should remember that we have to start with Our Lord in the Holy Bread, best received in humility. In the description of the holy city,[20] we find the way man must proceed so as to reach his goal. This description should not only be seen in a static, but also in a dynamic way. It represents the way we are to take so as to arrive at God.[21]

---

[19] This image of "root" can be explained by another symbol: the seed. Within the seed, dynamically there is already the whole structure of any organism. If within the seed something is in disorder, then the whole growth will be is disorder or may not come about. This is why, in order to restore humanity, God the Father put the "new seed" of His Beloved Son in the soil of our earth. Only in Him, dying and resurrecting with Him will we become new men. So the root of all being is the life of Our Lord Jesus Christ, as He Himself emphasized speaking about Himself as the Bread of Life. The sermon about the "Bread of Life" unfolds this mystery left to mankind in the Holy Eucharist. (cf. Jn 6) So, ultimately, the "root" of all new growth is this tiny little bread of the Holy Eucharist.

[20] Rv 21:11-27

[21] Remember that the new Jerusalem will be built upon the foundation of the holy cross; so we are to simply proceed on the way of the cross of Our Lord Jesus Christ with its twelve stations, three to each direction of the wind as are the twelve gates of the new Jerusalem.

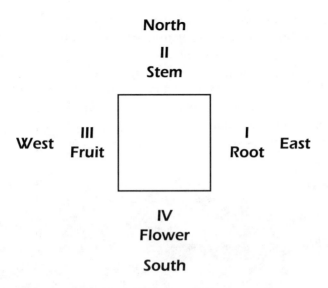

- We start in the East I, because it is the region of the rising of the sun (the sun being the noblest symbol of God). Only when we are first orientated to God do we have the right starting place.
- We proceed North II. The direction signifies darkness and battle. We are yet unsure if we will really reach the goal; only the light of God in our hearts can orient us securely amidst the trials and tribulations of this life. We must be on guard so as not to fall prey to the dark abyss of sin.[22]
- This is why, in all the darkness around and in us, we must turn our gaze to the South III, region of light, so as to continue on our pilgrimage; this is where the cross on Golgotha is pointing to. The light of God which first penetrated our hearts in the East must make us "children of light."
- Only thus we can enter into the West IV, the region of the setting of the sun (the symbolic region of the final combat of light against darkness!).

---

[22] cf. Rv 2:24

The great counter-sign of the last times against Our Lady is the Antichrist and his reign of disorder, rearing its head up against God. The celestial hierarchy, invisibly representing the order of the reign of God, will come to our help. The church will withstand the impact of the devil only if it reflects the order of the holy angels. This holds true also for everyone of us individually. Only by a life of union with our heavenly companion will we be able to find our way to God and become instruments of God for the renewal of the church.

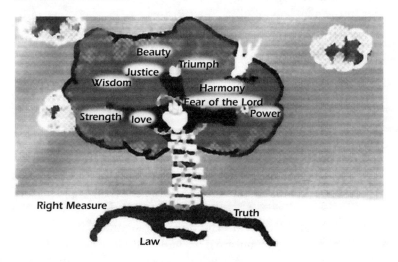

In the root of all life we find three entities:[23]

Only in the cross can man once again learn how to give the right response to God. The science man has to learn in the "school of his life" is first of all the science of the cross the fathers of the church call "staurologia." Unfortunately, this sacred science is no longer taught in the seminaries and is even less lived. There is a great pursuit in the sciences, religious as well as natural, but no school or degree of higher learning can teach or qualify what the simple uneducated learns by way of suffering. The wisdom of man is vanity to God. Man must return to the wisdom of God in the folly of the cross.

---

[23] Three always points out to the triune God and four to the house of God. But we already mentioned that "house" and "inhabitant," in this case, are one.

Right Measure

Because of sin most men live in "disequilibrium," even in basic things; we have lost the living of the virtue of right measure: in our eating, sleeping, work habits and scheduling of time. Our life is stress. We want to "make it" by our own forces. The atomic explosion in the material world is simply a symbol of the atomic explosion occurring in mankind. Psychology considers man as a bundle of reactions and sentiments. These modern tendencies throw man "out of orbit," causing him to lose his right order of things before God.

Man has lost his created purpose, his sense of order, his priorities, his center. He can no longer find himself in God. When by his own means he tries to return to order, he opts for violent means, always resulting in more violence: wars and battles and ultimately in the destruction of the world. We have to find a new starting point: only in Christ can we start a new life!

Right measure is best explained with the parable of the tiny mustard seed that only by falling into the ground and dying will sprout and bring forth fruit. It is the smallest of all the seeds, but grown into a tree the birds of heaven come and nest in it.[24] As from a tiny little seed, so also must the life of God grow in us — in right measure! It is God Who will plant His seed into our hearts and it is He Who will care for its growth. Our part is only humble collaboration.

Law

According to the apocalyptic sermon of the Lord,[25] the outstanding "sign of the times" is disorder and anarchy. It is not difficult to note the prevalence of anarchy and lawlessness, so much so that love is stifled and almost killed. The world is becoming colder and colder. Even our Catholic churches are suffering what the Protestants and the sects call "reformation." The sorrowful reality is that we are on the verge of becoming another assembly of people, looking to God in a confused and purely horizontal level.

---

[24] cf. Mt 13:31-32, Mk 4:30-32

The first and foremost law of God, the cross of Our Lord Jesus Christ, has been lost. Our Christian social principles have been exchanged for humanistic values, making secular humanism the rule of the day. We have to find our way back to the law of God, governing not only the entire universe, but ordered to the governing of our individual and personal lives. Why don't we remember that at our side there is a representative of the order of the reign of God who is completely integrated in the will of God: our Guardian Angel. He is ever willing to help us find our way out of the anarchy of this world!

He will help us to recognize that the law of God is not only universal, but adapted to our very own existential and personal condition. We must stand on this law as on firm ground. Anarchy has infiltrated even in the church in such a subtle way that many times we don't even note it. The church continues to teach faithful observance of the laws, but man continues to act as a spoilt child, preferring his own whims over any type of established form.

With anarchy as the "rule of the day," an open entry for the Antichrist, head of all lawlessness, has been paved. We have confused arbitrariness with liberty. There is a lack of responsibility towards any authority constituted by God, a perfect reflection of the "liberty" of the Freemasons, who are the "constructors" of anarchy.[26] As less and less we find the law of God in our environment, we must discover it more and more in our hearts. Remember the word of the prophets: *"At the end of time I will write my law in your hearts."*[27] It is the law of conversion to the living God.

---

[25] Mt 24

[26] Be on guard against the seductive teachings of the esoteric cults! They also mention the "laws," trying to hide the anarchy behind. Naturally, the fallen angels, as Spiritual creatures, know much better than we about the laws of this created world, but they employ all their intelligence to use them for their negative plans.

A simple, but striking example is, when in the New Age movement, they tell us to avail ourselves of the "cosmic energy" in order to "overcome" ourselves (to become "supermen"); unfortunately this energy is that of the fallen angels who have retained their natural power.

[27] Jer 31:33 and Ez 37:14.

Truth

God's house in us should be constructed on both objective and subjective truth, on the eternal truth that comes to us from God and the unique truth of our personal vocation in the love of God that we must discover and live. These two fundamental truths have been set aside by the modern man. He has developed his "own goals" and falsely called them "truths." He has become "emancipated" in the school of the Freemasons and liberally constructs his own world of skyscrapers, state of the art computers, jets, space-shuttles and missiles. He has lost identity as to what he should be.[28] St. Paul discourses the end times: Because man will no longer crave the law and the truth of God, God will send him a Spirit of lies, and he will take along all those who look for their own truth, which is a lie before God.[29]

This chastisement is already upon us. Anyone who establishes his own life, on whatever ideology or "ism," builds his house on sand. In the end he will fall! Only in the light of the Holy Spirit and following the teaching of the church can we find our way back to truth. Our own conversion is the first step toward truth. The truth of God is the truth of reality. According to the teachings of the church the "realism" of St. Thomas is the fundament for a sane theology. We must come closer to reality as it is, not as we want it to be. As soon as we do not accept reality, as soon as we establish our own conditions of living, we fall into lie, and are prey to the one who is a liar and a murderer from the beginning; one lie gives birth to another, ad infinitum. The modern Babylon, the "city of man," looks very glamorous and enticing. Many a man is attracted and seduced by it. Only God's sober light can give us the right discernment by way of our Guardian Angel. We must begin to find truth in the little things of daily life.

---

[28] "Being of a certain gender shouldn't be an obstacle to ambition or psychological well-being. Enough money can alter your sex." This type of confusion, prevalent in our own day, causes human identity to be determined as a "convertible commodity."

[29] cf. II Thes 2:1-12.

We have tailored and customed our lives to purely human conventions, creating them to be expressions of "polite lies," beautiful images of the world's falsehood. Our life must undergo a reeducation starting at the root. More and more, our angel wants to bring us along the narrow path of truth. Our reformation and transformation into the image of Christ must begin at the root.

Human development studies tells us that while a child is yet in its mother's womb, it suffers all the conditions of the mother's life: her sentiments, her ideas and her lifestyle. Many times this prenatal influence on the child is so overwhelmingly predominant that the entire future of the child is defined within the womb.[30]

In the stem — "structure of all life" — we find three other entities:

The renovation of human life begins in the root, and therefore must grow out of measure, law and truth. They are the foundation for the structure of the house of God. Only in love can this house be a place where one feels at home and makes others feel at home. Fear of God reminds us that God should always be first. He is our aim and should be our point of reference in everything. Being that there is no other measure outside of God, the house must reflect something of His greatness. It must be a house of Justice where everyone can grow and develop according to the measure God has put into his heart.

Love

Over and over again, we will come to realize that the love of God is a sober and a wise love. His is the love of a father who sees further than the desires of His children. He does not instantaneously fulfill all wishes, but at times educates with severity and chastise-

---

[30] Silent retreats as well as the healing of memories show that these life studies are realities of deep Spiritual significance. The more deeply we enter into adoration and contemplation the more our buried memories and the roots of our sins will become unearthed. In the light of grace we might even come to intuit something of the conditions in which we were conceived. We must willingly entrust all our wounds and sins to the blood of Christ so as to be brought back into the right order of God. This is always best done in a deep confession.

ment. Left on our own we would indeed be lost. All the virtues necessary to build the house of God in our souls include, penetrate and compensate the other. They are one as in Christ, in Our Lady and in the saints. Each virtue presupposes and is dependent on the previous and becomes fundamental for the following. This inter-relationship is most apparent with the three virtues in this second step: there can be no love without the fear of God and no true fear without justice.

Fear of God

The fear of God is always linked to wisdom and therefore points to one of the entities of "flower."[31] We are only capable of growing in God if the interior light of the fear of God orientates our steps in the midst of the darkness of this world. Man must always remember that he is creature, that life is an entrusted gift enabling him to serve God and his neighbor. Fear of the Lord will enable us to be a "son in the Son," with the favor of the Father resting upon us. The apocalyptic events unsealing before our eyes will force us to learn what true fear of God is. Sometimes a "shaking up" is necessary for our waking up to the reality that "God is greater!" and then we fall down in adoration before Him. If we do not bow down in awe before God, we will be compelled to do so in fear of Him. The rosary teaches us to enter deeply into the mysteries of the life, passion and Resurrection of Christ, and it brings us to a living and life-giving "fear of the Lord." The fear of God is a fundamental element of our interior house and of all true religious life.

Justice

Even with the best efforts at establishing a "better" social order, there will always be abuses. Society as well as the individual of goodwill may aim for a true balance, but man is frail and his philanthropic efforts are easily converted into injustice. Adam's

---

[31] cf. Prov 9:10 and Sirach 1:9.

disobedience broke man's sense of right measure, and his broken-ness gives way to the "isms" in the political, economic and religious realms, but they all remain human efforts at "escaping" his prison of sin. The simplest definition of justice is: right measure with respect to God and fellow man.

The importance of justice in our lives is well understood by the evil one and this reason alone prompts his continual presentations of "simple solutions." Liberation theology is a perfect example of making a mere human perspective of justice an absolute principle. The justice of God is far greater than any human view or necessity. Here, by way of our angel, we still have to learn more.

In the "flower" of all growth we find another three entities. The following three virtues, amidst a world of violence and disharmony, appear like precious flowers growing in the desert. They, shining with the grace of God, are like the Castillian roses the Virgin asked Juan Diego to pick atop Tepeyac. These virtues seem to be the privilege of the saints; having grown in love, fear and the justice of God, they have become like mighty oak trees, immovable to the weathering of the storms of the times.

Wisdom

Today's predominant drive for secular knowledge is one of the major threats that is robbing the children of the world of the special graces of childhood. They are pushed at ever earlier ages to learn more, such that they become "little adults" before their time. Today we find the virtue of wisdom almost exclusively with the simple, many of whom are illiterate or with very little secular learning. Wisdom is a "science" acquired first of all in life and many times through sacrifice and suffering.

Beauty

"Beauty" is not a "virtue" in the common sense of the word, but it is like the fragrance of all the virtues of Our Lady. Because of our productive and functional mentality, beauty has also been lost in our churches and our families, because it is not considered practical nor useful in a technical sense. Beauty "shines by itself." It is a reflection of the greater beauty of God which we can only adore and admire.

Beauty is a sign of God's tender love for His children. At the beginning of the modern times, He "painted" the image of His most beautiful creature, so that in our world of "functional order" we would not forget; there is an inviolate "beauty" accessible to all those who reach out for her.

The image of Our Lady of Guadalupe not only draws our attention to Mary as a beautiful woman (as western art tries to depict), but as the icons of the eastern church portray, she most perfectly reflects the beauty of heaven and earth. She is the most perfect mirror of the "beauty of God."

We should not forget to look up to this living image in the praying of our rosary. We cannot always have it with us in a material way, but we can carry it in our hearts. More and more it should impregnate our soul, making it more beautiful in the eyes of God.

Harmony

In the image of Our Lady of Guadalupe, we see harmony as the reflection of heaven on earth. Beyond our limited and human conception, it is the promise of a greater and more beautiful life. The "equilibrium of all virtues" is a qualifying factor in the beatification process of any "holy person," quite contrary to the world's ideal of fomenting one "virtue" to the exclusion of the others.

In the "Fruit" of all creation we find another three virtues which will bring creation to its consummation: The words of St. Paul, *"...for when I am weak, it is then that I am strong"*[32] help us to understand these last three "virtues." They presuppose that man has surrendered himself completely to God; no longer is he "lord of his life." He is "bound" by someone Who will lead him where he does not want to go.[33] The "strength, "power" and the "triumph

---

[32] II Cor 12:10
[33] cf. Jn 21:18

of God" will be revealed when we have become nothing before Him. Only then can He use us as His instruments, as He likes and for whatever plan or intention that delights His holy will.

At this point, the house of God in our soul is growing into a "house of glory," touching the new Jerusalem coming down from heaven. It is easy to discover that the "house of God," in its root, construction, flower and fruit is related to the four elements discovered by the philosophers before Plato: fire, water, air and earth, and to the four directions of the wind: east, south, north and west.

The Spiritual reflections of these elements are: adoration, contemplation, reparation and mission. In the analogy of being we ascend from the natural elements to the more Spiritual concepts governing our lives. In whatever form the cross is a challenge to conform to the life of Christ. Only if we are cruciform will we be able to pass through that "one" gate of the twelve which is our destination in the new Jerusalem.

The Origin of the Rosary, Circle and Spiral

We have to learn more about the importance of the humble signs, otherwise it is difficult to understand "rectangle" as a symbol for a "house," a shelter for those who otherwise could not grow, develop or even survive. Another universal symbol is the circle. The rosary relates to both: to the rectangle as symbol of "house" and to the circle as symbol of life, coming from God in the person of Jesus Christ. The following meditation will help in the discernment of the circle as well as its deeper significance.

The first question we ask is: What is the root of this prayer, where does it come from? In a man-made world we are more prone to manipulate the things of God in the same manner as we do with the things of the world. Even with the rosary we have to remember it is not our prayer, but it is God-given. This is why we have to pray it, always lifting our soul up to Him, otherwise we fall into the rut of mechanical prayer, with little if any attention to what is being prayed. God is merciful and rich in compassion. He accepts even our miserable efforts especially when our intention to reach His heart is sincere. Our Guardian Angel, as the Guardian Angel of Portugal did with the shepherd children, will do everything to teach us the right way of praying.

Prayer is not just a technique to be learned in an automatic way. More and more it must become a conscious prayer. We must learn to pray the rosary with our angel so as to be more aware of what we pray. Praying the perpetual rosary is a way of allowing the mysteries of Christ's life to begin to penetrate deeper into our lives. Waking up during the night is an opportunity to pray at least one "Hail Mary" so as to remain in the current of the rosary.

"Current" is another interpretation of the circle. We experience something of this current in our own body: in the circulation of blood pumped by the heart. As a symbol of life, the circle penetrates the material, human and Spiritual worlds. It is a basic structure in the material creation, recognized in the construction of atoms, in the cross-section of rocks and trees, the beautiful unfolding of flowers, and the faraway formation of new solar systems. The symbol of circle is also part of the biological make-up of man. Without awareness, every cell within the human body undergoes a total renovation and reconstruction every seven years. Also in Spiritual life there are cycles in relation to our growth towards God.

As a universal law, the circle can never be a static reality, not even in heaven, for in eternity the greater love of God has no end. This reflection leads us to the spiral and its circular movement around a center(s). The circle is a perfect symbol for oneness and wholeness when understood in light of the spiral, for only then do we begin to recognize it as a living and vibrating reality equipped with the potential of leading us deeper into the living God, the origin and destiny of all life.

The geometrical properties of a circle are not hard to envision, for as a plane figure it has a limited circumference whose points are all found equidistant from its center. On the other hand, a globe is a sphere with similar properties. Like the circle, it has a single center, and is limited in all directions by a surface whose points are all equidistant from its center. The spiral (with a single center) is like the circle in that it is a curve revolving about a certain central point of reference, but it differs from the circle in that it does not close. The kind of spiral considered is determined by its proper geometric laws. Unlike the circle, the radius of the spiral is "living." It is not static. It can augment or decrease in measure depending on its type. The augmentation or decreasing in measure is what gives the spiral a shape like that witnessed in nature, i.e. the shell of a snail or the formation of a galactic nebula.[34] The cone is a solid body with an augmenting radius and change in the slant of the slope of the radius from the axis. Another type of spiral is that of the helix. It is a spiral that has the form of the solid body cylinder.

---

[34] See Book Six: "The Beauty of Revelation"; the Golden Rectangle and Fibonacci's Law which correlates "perfect dimension" in the world of nature with the golden proportion: a/b = a+b/a, pp. 27 ff.

Geometrical dimensions of the circle and the spiral

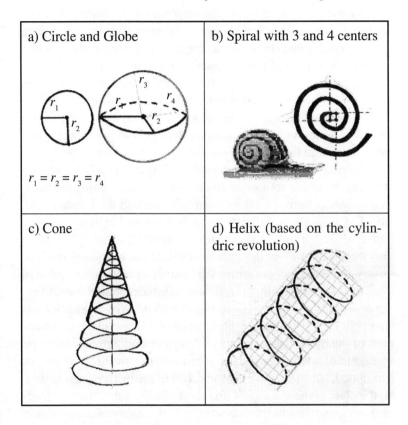

a) Circle and Globe	b) Spiral with 3 and 4 centers
$r_1 = r_2 = r_3 = r_4$	
c) Cone	d) Helix (based on the cylindric revolution)

In our Spiritual growth and union with God, we must always maintain the one dimensional perspective of God as the center and focal point of all our Spiritual life, aware though that God is not one dimensional, stagnant or limited to time or space. It is for this reason that the living, moving momentum of the spiral serves as a symbol of life over and above the singular dimension of the circle, for it respects the essential aspect of revolving about God, but not in a monotonous way. We must be alive in and for God. Like the spiral, we must gyrate about and move ever closer toward Him upon Whom the entirety of our existence rests.

The Circle and the Spiral as Symbol of Life

As we observe innocent children on a playground, we note that even without supervision or interference, they naturally seem to form circles and rings. Adults are no different in their childlike enjoyment on a whirling carrousel. Life is movement, moreover it is circular movement. Although most men seem ignorant of the fact, life has a center about which it revolves. We have become like Israel dancing about a molten golden calf while Moses intercedes atop Mt. Sinai. As poor sinners, we dance about our sinful habits and make them the center of our lives.

Praying "in a circle" is man's innate need to join in the hidden mystery of life, to come ever closer to its center. For this reason, it is a common form shared with our Moslem and the Hindu brothers. The rosary's circular structure is what makes it a *universal* prayer. It is not only a prayer for Catholic Christians. The mere fact that "catholic" means universal would automatically lend the rosary as the perfect prayer for the "universal church."

The circle is so much a religious symbol among the world religions, that it can be considered an archetype. Why is it a religious symbol? We have already pointed out that it is part of the construction of creation. Spiritual "cycles" are not only applicable to the religious minded. Aging causes us to reflect on life and on our childhood, sometimes even to the extent of instinctively going back to the places where we grew up. There are certain obligatory trials that we must pass in the course of life. If we do not pass them in the first run, we will be periodically visited by them in different ways. The "final exams" will be at the end of our life. It will be an overall consensus of all the other proofs.

The circle is a universal law of all life: the material, the human, and the Spiritual. The Seraphim adore God in a horizontal circle singing *"Sanctus, sanctus, sanctus…,"* day and night.[35] The Cherubim carry the word of God up and down in a vertical circle.[36]

---

[35] cf. Isaiah 6:2
[36] cf. Jn 1:51

We must accept and consciously participate in this law of the cycle as a reality of our life, for it is the normal way to perfection in both a positive and negative sense. To choose against this innate law would be a choice of auto-destruction.

The civilization of the modern world seems to have lost consciousness of this law. We focus on the stars with an incessant longing to conquer the solar system and a continual soliciting for the "self-made man/millionaire" literally knocks on the door of every household. But this vain search for a linear perfection only confirms man's fear of self and of any type of encounter with God. Far removed from man's conscience is the reality that his imprisonment is his own inescapable circle of sin.

Man runs in continual circles of illusion, but his ultimate illusion will be the temptation to think himself greater than or equal to God. This stance of Lucifer cast him out of reality, to fall out of God. The "hell prepared for the devil and his angels," which the three shepherd children of Fátima saw in the July apparition of 1917, is not a mere static reality, it is a dynamic one. Only at the end of time, when the devil has fallen to the deepest distance from God, will hell come to its completion. In a certain sense, the same is true of heaven. Only at the end of time when all the saints will have entered into their glory will it be complete, but even then, in the greater love of God, there is no static end.[37] Our success should never be measured with or by an exterior measure. Apparent success should always bring us back to the root and source. Only within the humble interior of the circle can reconstruction begin. With this small introduction we can already begin to intuit something of the profound relationship between the circle and spiral, a relationship in God to be found congruent.

---

[37] The blessed in heaven, living with and in the blessed Trinity, share in God's life of love by virtue of sanctifying grace. This participation and union in the love of God, limited by our human nature, will be the delight of the saints. Since God is life, we must then impute that heaven is not static, but is imminent life!

Christian Discernment of the Circle

A "Living" Circle

As Christians, we need a Christian discernment of this universal symbol of the "circle" in order not to fall into a pagan way of praying. Are we dealing with a circle or is it rather not a *spiral*? The true symbol for growth in all life forms, material, human and Spiritual, is the spiral.

The church's liturgical calendar is a guide for our entering more deeply into the life of Christ. The first liturgical season is Advent and is followed by Christmastide. After celebrating the Baptism of the Lord we return to ordinary time until the Lenten season begins, preparing us for Paschal and Eastertide. The Easter season is followed by Pentecost, and then again we enter ordinary time. These three liturgical seasons are repeated every year.

Our danger is in remaining on the same level, exteriorly entering the liturgical cycle, but without any penetration. A stagnant circling does not allow any growth or any fruit bearing. It is a form of lukewarmness that the Lord warns about in the letter to the church of Laodicea.[38] As Christians, we should know how to benefit from the living movement towards the living God in Christ. Man's unwillingness to enter more deeply into the mysteries of God is the real reason why his response to God in horizontal dimensions becomes his easy response to the first and great commandment. By norm, man doesn't want to change. He modifies his exterior environment, substituting God for personal ego, and then wonders why his Spirituality doesn't flourish. He has built his own prison: a God-forgotten egocentric world.

First and foremost, by life and example, it is the priest who must lead the flock deeper into the mysteries of the life of Christ. Religious feasts must be reconquered from their secular associations, for they were never established as mere occasions to be celebrated. They have become a sad consequence of our sinful condition as Christians in the church throughout the world. Like our

---

[38] See Rv 3:15-16; *"How I wish you were one or the other — hot or cold! But because you are lukewarm, neither hot nor cold, I will spew you out of my mouth!"*

monotonous and unfruitful praying of the rosary, our liturgical prayer also lacks a living interior participation. Fixed on our own egos we become open prey to the enemy, the "prince" of the "dead circle." Today's secular feasts, with a certain humanistic and philanthropic coloring, are symptoms of the "changing poles": Mother's and Father's Day, Day of the Child, of peace etc. Thanksgiving is known as "turkey day," the birth of the Son of God has been exchanged for Santa, elves, lots of presents, Christmas trees, eggnog and mistletoe, whereas the Resurrection of Christ is marketed with the Easter bunny, baskets, lots of candy and Easter break. Very inconspicuously, the secular "feasts" have filled the Spiritual void of man's soul. The majority are blinded to this reality simply because they are cut off from the living God. The more persistently we live in sin the more we enter the "dead circle": the serpent biting its tail.

Sin is the most irrational act in which man can participate. It blinds him to good, cuts him off from and causes him to fall even further from God. As it is a denial of the one reality it becomes the vicious circle that enslaves anyone who bows to its service. But the more our lives are conformed with grace the clearer our vision becomes with respect to this reality. The Roman Stoic philosophers referred this innate sinful state of man to the law of *"stoicheia,"* the "law of the elements." Their doctrine held that only through periodic catastrophes could man escape this circle.[39] This same Stoic philosophy has been modernized by the "New Agers" as a ploy in the proclamation and initiation of their "movement."

The Way Out of the Vicious Circle of Sin

Without faith there is no true exit from this vicious circle. Sooner or later, whether on the individual or collective level, the reality of a final catastrophe has to be faced. Existentialism encourages man to a heroic stoicism, but the ordinary man is hardly capable of facing death "heroically." Fidelity to these "isms" and philosophies by those who promote them is quite doubtful, when they really have to face their own death. Praying the rosary with a

---

[39] When the natural law is abused, nature itself strikes back as the only means of purifying and renewing life again.

living faith, as expression of a Christian life in and with Mary, is a practical way out of this vicious circle of a life condemned to death. Original sin makes all of us heirs of this vicious circle, but we are incapable of breaking its chains by ourselves. Our Redemption can only be found in the power of the cross and the Resurrection of Jesus Christ, the Son of God. Our proneness to the weakness of our human condition as well as the ease by which we can easily fall into mechanical prayer, should make us conscious that we need a constant and loving contrition, for only then can Our Lord lift us up from the dust of sin and renew us in a living faith.

Only by grace can our prayer ascend to God as in a spiral and so join the prayer of our holy angel who is ever at our side, hanging at the face of God. It is the angel who will best guide us into the depths of the different mysteries of the life of Christ and lead us into a deeper contemplation of a particular mystery, which has an existential importance for us at this moment. It is virtually impossible to meditate all fifteen mysteries of the rosary at once. It is better to concentrate on the one related to our life and find out in meditation how we can emulate the life of Christ in this mystery.

As the mysteries of the rosary represent the descent of the light of God into the darkness of this world and its victorious return to God, we should pray them looking up to the image of Our Lady of Guadalupe, for in her image this "movement" is depicted if we follow Our Lady's loving glance. It penetrates the darkness on the right side of her mantle and gown and ascends again into the light on her left side. In this way, in and by her we can more easily unite with the light of God and so arrive in the glorious light: He has overcome! It is thus that our prayer will have part in the spiral "movement of ransom," a movement of love initiating in the heart of the triune God and then descending by the Incarnation of the Son and the mediation of Mary. Our rosary will partake in both the divine and human center of the "spiral of ransom" and become a Christian rosary, one that enables the mysteries of Christ's life to incarnate in us.[40]

---

[40] See Book Four: *The Movement of Ransom in the Sign of the Lamb of God,* and *A Little Catechism on the Holy Rosary in Relation to the image of Our Lady of Quadalupe,* III. and IV.

The Three "Currents" of Life, word and Love in the Rosary

Life is movement and as God is life in abundance we necessarily will find in Him the origin of all movement. But as God's life rests in Himself it should be symbolized by a circular movement. As God is light, the most convenient symbol for this circular movement is "the circle of light," which necessarily is a threefold light, representing the three persons of the most holy Trinity. When God called creation into existence He let it have part in this light, created light from the uncreated light of God, and so it also has part in the three currents coming from the triune God: the current of life correlated primarily to the Father, because He is the origin of all life; the current of the word and force related to the Son; and the current of love related to the Holy Spirit. In their essence they are one, but they can be attributed, as dogma says, to the three different persons of the most holy Trinity.

The life of God comes to us in the person of Jesus Christ: "I am the Way and the Truth and the life…"[41] By the blood of Christ shed for us poor sinners on the cross, the Son will lift us up to the Father, and graft us back to the source of all life. With the Resurrection of Christ we, in the Holy Spirit, are connected to this "circulation of blood," made accessible to us by way of the Sacraments. Christ Himself wants to live His life in us. Each liturgical year is another invitation to the faithful to share in the Sacramental presence of the Son of God in His Mystical Body, the church.

---

[41] Jn 14:6

Within the "rosary of the liturgical year" we meet the other two currents (word and love) which are inseparably united with the current of life of the Father. The current of the word, will help us understand about the divine life in us and teach us how we have to collaborate with grace in order to bring forth fruit. The current of love in the Holy Spirit will unite us more intimately with the love of God in the Holy Spirit and by way of this love, with our brother in Christ who participates in the same liturgy. These three currents are also symbolically present in the ellipse of "ransom" ascending to God.[42] One day the spiral of our life will definitively enter into the circle of the life of God. By way of the Incarnation of Christ the spiral is now part of the life of God: we have become "sons in the Son" for all eternity.

The Circle With God as Center (Life of Order and Harmony)

The help of the holy angels is to guide us into the depths. We shouldn't only receive the Lord in Holy Communion, but we should keep Him in our hearts from one Communion to the next. Each Communion should bring us closer to the heart of our merciful Lord. As long as the mercy of God allows us to pilgrim through the vale of tears, we must endeavor all the more to enter deeper into the spiral of ransom. We must never forget that our angel has already passed his trial and has already been accepted into the beatific vision. His entire life revolves about God. As Guardian Angel, sent to be companion of one of us, he lives a "perpetual rosary" trying to serve His Lord in the mystery of His Incarnation in our life. It is in Christ and the mysteries of salvation that man and angel are called to share in order to become one in and through Him.

---

[42] The "movement of ransom," "spiral of ransom" and "ellipse of ransom" are interchangeable terms for the movement found in the image of Our Lady of Guadalupe. Creation (Joyful Mysteries), Redemption (Sorrowful) and Consummation (Glorious) are another inseparable trinitarian "unit." This is clearly demonstrated already in the second narration of creation, including the fall of man and the promise of Redemption.(Gen 2:4 - 3:24)

Also, Book IV: "The Movement of Ransom in the Sign of the Lamb of God" is an unfolding of this "movement."

This is why our life, like Our Lady's, should become a perpetual rosary; we begin with the mysteries of the Incarnation in the morning, we accompany Our Lord on His way of the cross during the day and we seek the promise of His Resurrection in the darkness of nightfall. Our Lady, in every detail of her life, is the perfect example and our best assistance in this way of love. She lived her magnificat by simply revolving about God. As seat of wisdom, she teaches us that our lives can only come to order and peace when they revolve about God.

There are circumstances or times when our attention is so entirely absorbed in a work that a conscious attention to our "praying always" is prevented, but this is the moment to call upon the angel to take over our part. He will continue fervently adoring God in our heart so that we do not fall out of the circle of love revolving about God. Of course, this requires that we slow down, that we become more conscious of our actions, our words and our thoughts, not only keeping in mind the dangers before us, but our promises before God.

Three Enemies to Fight:

The Ego

We must fight against three great enemies every moment of our lives. Primarily the battle is against our personal ego. We create a false circle when we put our ego in the center, such that everything we do revolves about us. There are those who speak about a thousand never-ending things, and their "never-ending story" usually revolves about their own ego which is a vicious circle they cannot escape. The only way out of this prison is by self-denial/sacrifice. God offers us many opportunities for sacrifice everyday. We have to learn to accept them. As we begin to walk with our angel we will become more sensitive to his voice and even eagerly look for sacrifices.[43] This humble and sacrificial walk will lift us up from the vicious circle of our life into the spiral of salvation, enabling us to fight the next enemy, the world.

---

[43] Remember the angel's advice to the three shepherd children: "offer continual sacrifices to God," cf. Memorias de Lucia, 2nd Ecition, p.56

The World

Today's world, surrounding us on all sides, is such a vicious circle that it is almost impossible to escape. It is easier to note with others than with ourselves, because a unique vicious circle seems to enwrap its victim as does a spider its prey. This is true for every individual, but also for any country. America, for example, is completely dominated by technology and commerce, by what is called "modern life." Everything, eating, sleeping, speaking, working, has become a horrible circle of enslavement. The particular captivity suffered by each country is determined by the devil in his attack against the realization of the country's unique mission according to the plan of God. The circle of the "world" can only be broken by the grace of the cross as sword.

Young people, in comparison with older people, are more sensitive to the pressure of the world and suffer the bonds of this captivity more painfully. This is one of the reasons why they desperately try to break through by use of violence. What they don't realize is that the more they struggle the tighter they tie the bonds. They race around in cars and on motorcycles at dangerously high speeds, break any laws, violate all forms of morality in forbidden pleasures, seek escape in the world of drugs, etc. They opt for the mask of "enthusiastic suicide," not realizing its author is the master of lies.

These poor children are only crying out to live, but the chosen means for attaining their end leads them to death. Behind their repugnance to any form of "prison" is something quite genuine and we should really try to guide them better. But we are unable to lead them to the freedom of the children of God, because we ourselves are bound by and held prisoners of our own vicious "pious" circle. Astutely, and with all the assistance of technology, the devil does everything in his power to hide the exit door of this captivity: *sacrifice!* The children of "this age" have everything at their fingertips. If they want candy, it's theirs; if they want to watch television, they can watch it; if they want to report or sue their parents for child abuse they are afforded all measures. They've never really been offered the opportunity to learn self-denial or any form of abnegation. Their world is one of licentiousness, and anything outside of self-gratification isn't acceptable to them. Secular humanism and the lie of progress fills young minds with the false ambition of touching the stars at the expense of their eternal souls.

If our young people are not brought back to the mystery of the cross, they will be lost, and the sacrifice of Christ will be forfeited. Only grace can release them from their prison and "standard of easy living." If we could bring them to pray the rosary their lives would slowly enter into the rhythm of God's love. Today's youth are victims of the contagion and rush of a Godless world and it is ours to practice Christian charity and patience with them. We must first of all pray and then be an example of a "living rosary." One day they will catch on and follow.

The Devil

Our third great enemy is the devil. He is a master at disproportionalizing our ego. We are absolutely nothing to him other than a "pawn" to be played in his eternal rejection of God. He may keep his temporal promises to those who succumb to him, but we must recognize his ploy of leading us deeper into his vicious circle for the sole purpose of isolating us from God. If we have escaped this "Egyptian captivity," it is owing to our good Guardian Angel and his constant effort at protecting us from the demonic wiles. The angelic world is of other dimensions in comparison to our short lived life; it is a comparison of light years to "one day."[44] Our angel sees clearer and farther than we and gently wills to bring us back to a living prayer, but our inflated ego must first be humbled. We must rid ourselves of the idea that we know and can accomplish everything by ourselves. We need prayer more urgently than ever to find out about this invisible world and live in it. By praying we will experience the power of prayer and so be convinced to pray always. Our good angel companion will assist us so that we will persevere to the end.[45]

---

[44] Ps 89:4 - Remember that all the angels were created in the beginning of the world. They are among the first "citizens" of the cosmos and therefore as modern astronomy confirms the immense dimension of time and space, so must we accept the greatness of dimensions and age of these first creations of God.

[45] cf. Mt 10:22

The Cross as Key to the Rosary

The Challenge of the Rosary to Take up the Cross

In order to pray the rosary, we must begin with both the physical as well as the symbolic embracing of the cross. Although it may appear to be an insignificant element to the prayer circle, it is exactly that which is lacking in the rosaries of the Hindus and Moslems. Their prayer beads are mere loops facilitating the repetition of their mantras. The cross is the key to the sacred circle containing the mysteries of salvation. It will help us to partake more deeply in the mysteries as it will finally open to us the door of heaven. With St. Paul we must proclaim: *"May I never boast of anything, but the cross of our Lord Jesus Christ! Through it, the world has been crucified to me and I to the world."*[46]

In the image of Guadalupe, the entire figure of the Virgin is cruciform. She is crucified with her Son. The only exterior sign of the cross, the little cross on the brooch at her neck, not only reminds us of the sails of the Spanish galleons which bore the sign of the cross to the New World, but of our inability to approximate the celestial gate without the precious "key of the holy cross"; here it becomes symbol of the "narrow door."[47] If we rely on our obligatory prayers, prayed in routine, we forget that there is no deception of the just God. "Christian" cannot be worn as a brandmark, oblivious to the privilege or implied responsibility. If our lifestyles do not reflect the creed we profess, then we are responsible for many of

---

[46] Gal 6:14

[47] cf. "A Little Catechism on the Holy Rosary in Relation to the image of Our Lady of Guadalupe," III. A.1.

our misled brothers and sisters who sincerely seek the light of God. We must be "crystalline" souls: the same interiorly before God as exteriorly before our brothers.

If we are incapable or even unwilling to accept the small crosses of the sacrifices in our daily living, then we are not worthy of the privilege of praying the rosary. When the mysteries of the rosary are contemplated, the Lord is present, and as in the Sacraments we must respect Him. The mysteries are more than the exterior sacramental of blessed beads. If we do not discern them as such then they will rise up in judgment against us.[48] The rosary and its sacred mysteries revolve about the axis of the holy cross.[49] The entirety of our lives, the deeper tones of our joyful and glorious experiences as much as the sorrowful, must relate to the cross. The more we surrender to the cross in all our life the more we will become cruciform as is Our Lady.

The Mystery of Opposition

False opposition is based on the *"non serviam"* = "I will not serve" of the fallen angel at the beginning of time. It is an opposition that is climaxing in our own day. True opposition, on the other hand, is a mystery fundamental in God Himself. It is a divine opposition, between Father and the Son, perfectly reflected in the *"Adsum"* of the Son to the Father's will, in His submission to "death on the cross."[50]

---

[48] Recall Our Lord admonishing the "present generation" (cf. Mt 12:42) for not recognizing the "greater than Solomon" in their midst. Recall also the admonition of St. Paul: "to discern this bread."(1 Cor 11)

[49] There is a fourfold opposition found in the rosary:
- an opposition within a single mystery,
- an opposition between the two mysteries of the exterior circles (1st and 5th, 2nd and 4th)(cf. "A Little Catechism on the Holy Rosary in Relation to the Image of Our Lady of Guadalupe")
- an opposition between the two exterior circles (1/5 with 2/4)
- an opposition between the Joyful and the Glorious Mysteries.

[50] cf. Phil 2:8

There is a threefold opposition, in relation to the three persons of the most Holy Trinity:

- Nature teaches us that true opposition is the fountain of fertility: the opposition between day and night, hot and cold, man and woman, young and old.
- In Redemption: The expiatory death of Christ, as the innocent lamb, on the cross.
- In our personal appropriation of the Redemption with the help of the Holy Spirit.

The opposition we find in the cross reveals the deeper Mystery of Opposition in the most Holy Trinity,[51] it is the reason for the eternal fertility of God. For all eternity, God the Father engenders the Son by the Holy Spirit.[52]

---

[51] This Mystery of Opposition in God is something we can only deduce from its reflection in creation, in salvation and by the experience in our own life. Again we are challenged to remember that the most important science we have to learn is that of the cross. Only thus will we come to recognize that the cross is not something exteriorly imposed on us, something we hang up on our walls as a symbol of piety or protection; it is really the deepest mystery of God Himself, in which we are called to share by way of the cross of the Son. Only by way of the cross in the Holy Spirit can we realize the idea which God the Father had on us for all eternity. It is through Mary that we come to understand that like a vine winds up on its support, so too must we grow suspended on the cross. This is beautifully seen in the image of Guadalupe in the flowers on her robe. See further in book IV.

[52] Here again we have a trinitarian Mystery: the eternal birth of the Son can be seen in a triple way:
- it is a birth in God Himself for all eternity,
- it is His birth in humility by Mary in Bethlehem,
- it is His birth by way of the Holy Spirit in the soul of the faithful.

    Over and over again we are to contemplate these "three births" in the mysteries of the rosary.

The more we understand that this Mystery of Opposition[53] pervades all being, the easier we will accept it in our personal way of the cross on this earth. Even the "crosses" that are consequences of our sins can be transformed into the true cross of Christ. Together with His sacred cross He has taken all our sins upon Himself. We only need *"a humbled and contrite heart...."*[54] When prayed in view of the cross, the rosary helps us to discern the oppositions of our own lives. True opposition is the motor of life. Considering the first two Joyful Mysteries, we see that hardly conceiving the Son of God, the Virgin sets off,[55] not only to assist Elizabeth, but to fulfill a prophecy.[56] Her conformability to the will of God is that

---

[53] To better understand this Mystery of Opposition of God, we should try to remember:
- The distance of the creature to the Creator. Only the Son could franchise this immense distance. We are able to evaluate better by what we have to come to know by the natural sciences: the greatness of the cosmos;
- The even greater abyss between the Holy God and us poor sinners which could only be franchised because the Son of God as the Innocent Lamb took on Himself the sins of the whole world. He became for us "sin" and suffered the just chastisement of the Father (man in no way by himself can make up for the offense done to the Holy God by our sins!);
- The incomprehensible condescendence of God with each of us. salvation is not only for the whole of mankind; Jesus Christ died for each of us personally, as if there existed no other soul to redeem but us.

    Beginning with the Reformation this most important truth has been more and more obliterated; even in faith we are more involved with ideologies (theologies) than the living God, "the God of Abraham, Jacob ... of Our Lord Jesus Christ!" (Pascal).

[54] cf. Psalm 51:17: This "humbled and contrite heart" includes a threefold condition:
- that we are poor sinners before the Father (we should see us in the mirror of the "prodigal son"); this we can do only in the grace of faith.
- we must look up in firm hope to the Son on the cross — only His Precious blood can wash us from our sins;
- only in the power of the Holy Spirit we can be transformed in to a "new man in Christ!"

[55] The Immaculata, not only conceives the Son of the Eternal Father for herself, but on behalf of all mankind.

[56] *"...while yet in his mother's womb, he will be filled with the Holy Spirit."* (Lk 1:15) and *"At the sound of your greeting the child in my womb leapt for joy."* (Lk 2:40)

which reflects true "opposition," a union of the two great commandments: love of God and neighbor.

We again encounter this opposition between the second and the fourth Joyful Mystery. In conformity to the will of God, Our Lady not only obediently carries her newly conceived Son to Elizabeth and His precursor, but also presents Him to His Father in the temple. Another opposition is between the first and the last Joyful Mystery. Our Lady must experience the loss of her Son in Jerusalem, so in finding Him, anew she will conceive Him again in her heart. This intuited threefold opposition of the Joyful Mysteries tends towards the central Mystery, the birth of Christ in the soul of man.

The Cross as Symbol of Holy Order (a Glorious Perspective)[57]

Already in the four elements and the four directions of the wind, the cross is recognized as the principle of all order in the created universe. By the will of the Father, the lifting up of Christ on the cross is a sign that in and through Him, for Whom all things were made,[58] all order violated by the rebellious angels at the beginning of time and through original sin will be restored. In this renewal of all things, the greater glory of the cross will become apparent before the eyes of the whole world. Only in the cross will the house

---

[57] All opposition finally is solved in the Holy Spirit:
- He is the "bond" between the Father and the Son;
- He helps the Son consummate the Redemption;
- He will help the church and every single Christian soul to realize the fullness of salvation.

This threefold mystery is seen in the "three births" of Our Lord in the three central mysteries of the Rosary:
- a Joyful Mystery in His birth in Bethlehem,
- a sorrowful mystery in His crowning with thorns, where He is first acknowledged as "king,"
- a glorious mystery in the descent of the Holy Spirit upon the apostles on Pentecost.

[58] cf. Col 1:16

of God become a reflection of the reign of God and the most Holy Trinity and so come to its consummation. This again is best seen in the image of Our Lady of Guadalupe — Mary is the "house of gold," the primitive image of the church as it should be according to the idea of God! The application of the "golden rectangle"[59] to the image of Our Lady of Guadalupe, reveals its unspeakable beauty and harmony which again is no other than the order of the cross, principle of all construction.

This same beauty and order underlies the construction of the holy rosary. Praying the rosary while looking up to the image of Our Lady of Guadalupe allows us to penetrate into the beauty of God we admire in Mary. The more we are in Mary the more she will help us to assimilate the "order of the cross" in an organic way. In an more administrative way of looking on the mysteries of faith we easily forget, that faith is the challenge to become a new man in Christ, it can not be "done" in a day and not by man alone![50] In this way the cross will grow into that tree where the birds of heaven will come to abide, and this "tree" started as a tiny mustard grain!

---

[59] Many of the world's great artists have employed the golden rectangle in the initial drafting of their work. By means of it, they aimed at attaining a certain harmony with respect to the overall work as well as with every single detail. In relation to the image of Our Lady of Guadalupe, the correspondence to the laws of the "golden proportion" testify on behalf of its perfection and best prove that nothing has been added by human hand. (For more information on the golden rectangle see Book Six: "The Beauty of Revelation")

[60] This is why meditating the mysteries of salvation is like "homeopathic medicine" which the body has to assimilate slowly. More and more, technical and chemical facilities have destroyed man's understanding for "organic growth," even in agriculture. Man knows better, he wants to be faster and more effective than God. Here again the luciferic Spirit behind the illusion of "progress" is revealed!

The Symbolic Importance of Numbers[61]

Modern civilization has reduced the value of numbers to mere economic and scientific terms and so deprived them of their symbolical character as signs for the order of creation and the reign of God. On the other hand, fallen out of the order of the cross, they serve esoteric speculations and magical practices. Already the pagan Pythagorean philosophers knew something of the Spiritual significance of numbers, because they have so much to do with "wisdom."[62] The symbolic importance of numbers in the Judeo-Christian world is apparent to any attentive reader of the Bible; and this not only in an material, but also in a formal perspective.[63] Numbers, one of the five books of the Pentateuch, gives a direct pur-

---

[61] In relation to numbers we must beware of two "heresies" very common today:
- an exclusively materialistic interpretation: as means of domination in economics, politics, administration etc.;
- a "Spiritualistic and gnostic" interpretation which by way of numbers is trying to find out the "secrets" of the invisible world; again with the goal to dominate and therefore as much in danger as the first one to become an instrument of the fallen angels.

[62] We should always soberly remember that the fallen angels retained their natural knowledge and power. Consequently, we can suppose that they have a great knowledge about things and laws of nature which we do not even think of. As the eastern world (Cain went to the east!) up to our days was almost impermeable for the Christian truth, it is quite natural that knowledge of the "other side" is much more common with them as in the formerly Christian West. Having lost our Christian discernment in our days, the doors are wide open to this "eastern wisdom"! It has become a substitute for the lost faith in Jesus Christ. In this perspective we should also see the ever more intensive penetration of this "wisdom" into Christian doctrine, morals and ascetics.

[63] Here again we need Christian discernment. God's wisdom and providence are most apparent in the guidance of his elected people, and this also in respect to the numbers. The number "1" in relation to the "One True God"; "3," alluding to the Most Holy Trinity, "4" to the directions of the wind, as symbol of protection (already in paradise, the four rivers!) and ultimately to the cross, "5" to the wounds of Jesus Christ, "6" as 2x3, a reflection of the most Holy Trinity in man (Mary), "7" in relation to the holy order of things and times, "12" in relation to the Patriarchs, the tribes, later on the apostles and finally the 12 gates of new Jerusalem. This is a simple example for the Spiritual importance of number in the Mosaic-Christian world.

pose of numbers in the construction of the temple and liturgical prescriptions.[64] Numbers in liturgy are the visible expression of order in the universe and divine liturgy, celebrated by the angels before the throne of God.

One: One God.

The number "one" always refers to the one God. There is only one God. *"Hear Oh Israel, the Lord Our God is one..."*[65] Our great brother, and Prince of the heavenly host, teaches us with his "Who is like unto God!" to orient and concentrate our every action on the one God. Only in God can we become "one," only in Him can our unique vocation be fulfilled. Our hearts must be ever restless until they rest in Him.[66]

Every day, in our evening examination of conscience, we are called to give an account before God and to question our fidelity to the "one" important mission of the day. Did we seek out and find the one idea of the day? Did we accomplish that one thing necessary or did we lose ourselves in unimportant details?

Our Guardian Angel is ever eager to assist us through the confusion of this world, orientating us to the greater honor and glory of God and the salvation of souls. As our personal representative before God, he knows our particular needs, and by grace is ordered to assist and strengthen us with the necessary graces, helping us to avoid distractions and deviations on our way to our "one" necessary destiny: God.

The number "one" reminds us of our call to be one, in its integrity only found in Christ. It is the sacred number pointing to and assisting our journey to the eternal goal: union with God.

---

[64] Liturgy should not only reflect something of the order of the universe (The fallen angels know more about it than we do, so be careful to discern gnostic from true wisdom!), but is the inspired and conscious response of man and his praise and thanksgiving to God Who has allowed the faithful to live in a world of order and harmony amidst all the confusion of a world drowned in sin. Maximos, the confessor, knew more about "cosmic liturgy," Teilhard de Chardin knew better about the cosmic dimensions of Holy Mass! God's wisdom has hidden precious pearls even in the humble prayer of the holy rosary!

[65] Dt 6:4-5 and Mk 12:29-30

Two: two natures of Christ, two natures of man.

The number "two" refers to the person of Jesus Christ: God and man, *"the image of the invisible God."*[67] Misunderstandings and reoccurring heresies, under the guise of attractive new titles, continuously arise with respect to the dual nature of Our Lord. Even our own unconscious participation and emphasis of one nature of Christ to the exclusion of the other reveals our failure to correspond to the profound mystery of the Incarnation.

One of the great dangers of liberation theology, as well as other "modern" theologies, is the overemphasis of Christ's humanity. There have been periods in church history when the opposite was the trend. Only once or twice a year, and in great fear, did the believer approach the communion rail. Christ's "Godhead" was so over-emphasized that the common man hardly conceived approaching God by way of His humanity. Both extremes are faulty and lack proper understanding of the Incarnation of Our Lord Jesus Christ. What we need more than television (literally "far vision"), knowing about everything in a superficial way, is the "real and perfect vision" of things and man by Our Lord in the most blessed Sacrament. It is before the tabernacle that our human understanding and eyesight will be corrected, reach a greater depth and so consequently become more humble and serviceable.[68]

---

[66] cf. Confessions of St. Augustine

[67] Col 1:15

[68] Before the fall of man, the cultivation of the earth was a blessing: *"The Lord God then took the man and settled him in the garden of Eden, to cultivate and care for it."*(cf. Gen 2:15) But after man's disobedience the Lord God cursed the ground. *"Cursed be the ground because of you! In toil shall you eat its yield all the days of your life...."* (Gen 3:17-19) and only by the "sweat of his brow" would he earn his living.

Unfortunately most of the profit of man's scientific discoveries has only helped him to grow proud and more self-sufficient. Today's man is almost self-reliant, he "does everything himself." It is the extreme realization of the "homo faber," the "working man," constructing his own world. This loss of balance (in all respects) can only be remedied with a humble return to the feet of the Lord. Like Mary of Bethany, we must "choose the better part." Whatever we think, speak or do should be put at the feet of Our Lord.

There are quite a number of big heresies to be corrected, not only dogmatically, but moreover in their consequences down to our daily life. Our Lord Jesus Christ is not simply to be considered "our best friend" or "brother." He is and will always be the only begotten Son of the eternal Father. He is the only One capable of breaking the vicious circle of our lives in all His utter impotence in the most sacred species in the Holy Eucharist. In His humility and abnegation He is a continual challenge for our faith. Without the preparation by the angel of Portugal the shepherd children would have been unable to fulfill their mission in and with Mary. The first thing they had to learn was: more faith, hope and love, but first of all more faith in union with the adoration of the angel of the Eucharistic Lord![69] The Angel of Fátima teaches us that only through adoration, sacrifice and reparation can we come to a true and holy fear of God with respect to this Sacrament of love.[70]

"Two" also refers to the duality of our human nature: we are Spirit and flesh, man and woman, will and senses, intelligence and sentiment,[71] but wholeness as human beings is reached only when these apparent oppositions are brought together. Schizophrenia and other mental illnesses are only symptoms of the fatal disease of the loss of God as the center of humankind. Calling man "a bundle of nervous reactions," sentiments, or other psychological "identifications" of man show how much man has lost his center of crystallization. Only in virtue of the unity of the God-man, Jesus Christ, can we attain wholeness.

---

[69] "My God I believe, *I adore…*!"

[70] Recall the words of the Angel to the three children in his third apparition: *"Take and drink the body and blood of Jesus Christ, horribly outraged by ungrateful men.."*

[71] These four most important faculties of man form another cross: will to the East, because it is the most important faculty in order to reach God; sentiment to the North, intelligence to the South, senses to the West.

Three: refers to the Most Holy Trinity.

God is one, but God at the same time is three.[72] God is *"family."*[73] Unlike the dictatorial and predetermining God of Mohammed, God invites us and calls us by way of His Son in His Holy Spirit to participate in His life of union. The church, as the bride of Christ, is to reflect the trinitarian life of God. It is to be an image of the Holy Family of Nazareth: St. Joseph, Our Lady and the child Jesus. It is then that she will be that "city on the mountain top," it is then, even in silence, that she will proclaim the greatness of the First Commandment.[74] Our Lord never established His church to be a mere institution, organization or administrative unit. The church was born out of the love of His Sacred Heart on the cross, and by

---

[72] Correlate Gen 1 with the Prologue of St. John's Gospel so as to appreciate this unity of persons in God.

The first allusion to the Most Holy Trinity is found in this first chapter of the Bible: "God created man to his similitude, He created him as man and woman. The "opposition" of man and woman, reflecting that of the Father and the Son, will be solved by the "third person" of the child! Only in a community of "three" can there be true happiness. Man must lose himself as the Son loses Himself to the Father — before the eyes of all men on the cross, when he cries: *"My God, my God, why have you forsaken me?"* Into the darkness of this utmost abandonment will pierce the light of the Holy Spirit, to break the prison of death!

[73] Genesis initiates the creation of the world with God in the third person "He" and verbs conjugated for the third person. In verse 26, we find the first mention of a plural identity in God, and it is in direct relation with the creation of man. *"Let **us** make man in **our** own image...."*

[74] It is quite significant that during the miracle of the sun on October 13th the shepherd children have three visions which seem to deal with the future of the church, purified by the fire of the love of God, coming on it like a storm of light:

  • The vision of St. Joseph with the child Jesus blessing;
  • The vision of Our Lady of Sorrows;
  • The vision of Our Lady of Mount Carmel.
    This is a possible interpretation:
  • Church must become a "Holy Family";
  • it will have to follow the Lord on the way of cross to Golgotha; only then will an apocalyptic word of St. Francis be realized: *"at the end the whole church will be a Carmel!"*

the merits of His sacred passion, it should give a home and be a family to all those born in His name.

Four: the four directions of the cross

"Four" is the symbolic number of the holy cross. Referring to creation as a whole, it denotes the four directions of the wind,[75] the four elements, the four most important faculties of man, and the four Spiritual directions.[76] It is not by coincidence that the church recognizes the four living creatures inspiring the four evangelists, as they inspired before the four main prophets in the Old Testament[77] and the "fours" of the Book of Moses.[78] Christian living is a call to live in four dimensions and to contemplate things from more than one, two or three perspectives. Only by way of the cross will man come to "the fullness of truth" in the person of Our Savior.

Five: the five wounds of Christ

The number "five" recalls the Sacred Wounds of Our Lord. Indeed, *"By his wounds we have been healed."*[79] The naked cross is nothing but an instrument of diabolic torture. The "four direction of the cross" point to Him Who redeems us. The pierced limbs of Our Lord transform this cruel and torturous instrument into a means of salvation. "Five" tells that we must look out for the center of the cross: the pierced heart of Our Lord. In order to share in the benefits of His Redemption we must make up in our own flesh

---

[75] Our Lord Himself refers to the *"four winds."* (cf. Mt 13:27)

[76] Here we can discover something of the "analogy of being," starting from the four directions of the wind: east, north, south, and west, the four elements: fire, water, air and earth, by the four major faculties of man: will, sentiments, intelligence and the senses we arrive at the four Spiritual directions: adoration, contemplation, reparation and mission, in which man should realize his Spiritual destiny.

[77] Isaiah, Daniel, Jeremiah and Ezeckiel

[78] Exegesis speaks about the four "codices": that of the priest, that of the jahwist, the eloist and the deuteronomist with their different theological point of view on the history of salvation.

[79] Is 53:5

what is lacking in His sufferings.[80] This is not to infer that His sufferings were not complete, but by the Holy Spirit He continues to live in His Mystical Body the church and in every soul and continues to give His life for the salvation of souls.[81] Our Lord not only extends his limbs in compliance with the Father's will. In His death, He gives birth to His church with the opening of His Sacred Heart. This fifth wound of our crucified Lord becomes for the faithful the open door to heaven. Our captivity by way of the five-pointed star is broken by the five wounds of our Lord on the cross.[82]

Praying the rosary in view of the middle mystery of each of the major Mysteries will enable us to understand better the Spiritual birth of man in Christ by way of His pierced heart.

Six: Our Lady perfect reflection of the Most Holy Trinity

In the symbolic language of numbers, "six" is a product of "two" and "three" ("two" — the number of reflection, of the dual nature of Christ, image of the Eternal Father and "three" — the number symbolizing the Most Holy Trinity). In this context, "six" helps us to understand something of Mary's place among the other creatures; she is the most beautiful "image" of the "Most Holy Trinity." The ornamental and symbolic use of mirrors in Baroque architecture, especially within the Marian sanctuaries, reflects the beauty of Mary in likeness to the triune God. The number 666 is the veiled pretension of the fallen angels to substitute the reign of

---

[80] cf. Phil 2:8 and Col 1:24 sacrifice and reparation are Spiritual realities canceled in the catalogue of modern life. We are accustomed to "help ourselves…" out of any situation. Technology seems to give the necessary means to do so. This is why more and more the Protestant heresy that faith alone is sufficient, He has done everything for us … is entering more and more in our catholic way of living; redemption becomes a hieroglyphic figure, nobody really understands it anymore!

[81] The only way out of a shallow understanding of the Mystery of Redemption is our interior participation in it by the Holy Spirit. Again, He wants to live His life in us, He wants to make His suffering present in us for our personal salvation and that of our brothers. The more we let him do so, the more we have, in and by Mary, part in co-redemption.

[82] If man puts himself thus: his arms outstretched, lifted up a little bit, his head right up (in pride and self-confidence!), his legs apart in the form of a triangle, he is a living representation of the five point star, symbol of Satan the prince of this world who has everything under his power!

God by the reign of Satan: making the most out of the triple consequence of original sin.[83] The devil is nothing but the "ape of God,"
trying to build his own "creation" against God. Reflection in Mary
is always for the greater glory of God! This is why God will let her
rise as the "great sign" in the heavens of last times against the
counter sign of the dragon, the old serpent.[84]

Though the apocalyptical use of the number may refer to Satan's
reign over the world's sophisticated commercial and political systems, we must never forget that the number first points to "Mary"
in her perfect reflection of God. She will help us to escape all demonic seductions and enslavements to this world: she will crush
the head of the serpent and this first of all in the image of Apocalypse 12, perfectly represented in the image of Our Lady of
Guadalupe.

Seven: The Holy Trinity united with creation

"Seven" is three and four ($3 + 4 = 7$): God the Most Holy Trinity united with the four directions of creation. It is the number that
points to the gifts of the Holy Spirit as well as the general rhythm
and order of God's work in creation, by way of the Holy Spirit
Whose instruments are the holy angels. Having passed their trial,
the good angels are perfectly and eternally united to God. In the
realm of creation, they are God's engineers, and with respect to
salvation, they are Christ's servants and our best helpers. In view
of the consummation of all things they are the army of Mary which
will definitely push the fallen angels to their eternal hell. The more
we are united with them, the more we can collaborate in the plans
of the mercy of God.

Eight: the perfection of creation through the cross

"Eight" is two times four ($2 \times 4 = 8$). It is the number used in
the construction of the churches of the Carolingien epoch (Ravenna).

---

[83] cf. Rv 13:18: the number "666" is making fun of the Most Holy Trinity and
Mary as perfect image of the triune God. In these last times, Satan promises
man more than only heavenly beatitude, he offers him all the riches of the
world. He presents himself as the "true god," the one who will fulfill all our
earthly desires of the flesh (concupiscence), the blood (purely earthly existence), of domination (power). The final end of these "gratitudes" is the final
destruction of the universe. (cf. Jn 1 and 1 Jn)

[84] cf. Gen 3:15

The octagon is also frequently found in sanctuaries of Our Lady, because in Our Lady the triple creation, material, angel and man, has already reached its perfection. This is best seen in the *Recamara* — the chamber of Our Lady in the Basilica of Ocotlan, Tlaxcala. It is an octagonal structure within the basilica behind the main altar and the miraculous statue of Our Lady. On the ceiling of this same chamber is a painting of nine angels. These three symbolic details speak about the birth (9) of a new creation (4) by way of the cross (2 x 4) to the similitude of the triune God.

Nine: The Most Holy Trinity reflected in the nine choirs of holy angels

"Nine" is three times three (3 x 3 = 9). The hierarchy of the nine choirs of holy angels. Nine is not only another reflection of the Most Holy Trinity, it is a number of plenitude: the triune God is glorified in His angels. Only by way of them, ascending the "ladder" of the nine choirs can we approach the mystery of the Most Holy Trinity. The revelation of the Most Holy Trinity is a progressive one. The Old Testament reveals more of the Father, the New Testament the Son, the mystery of the Most Holy Trinity is the last step of revelation, and it is to this third revelation that the holy angels are most related. All four evangelists make references to the angels,[85] but it is really in the Book of the Apocalypse that we find "the book of the angels."[86] Its center (of interest!) is *"the Great Sign"* (ch.12), *"the woman clothed with the*

---

[85] This is only a short selection:
   St. Matthew: 1:20, 1:24, 2:13, 2:19, 4:6, 4:11, 13:39, 13:41 13:49, 16:27 18:10, 22:30, 24:31, 24:36, 25:31, 25:41 26:53, 28:2, 28:5; **St. Mark**: 1:13, 8:38, 12:25, 13:27, 13:32; **St. Luke**: 1:11, 1:13, 1:18, 1:19, 1:26, 1:28, 1:30, 1:34, 1:35, 1:38, 2:9, 2:10, 2:13, 2:15, 2:21, 4:10, 9:26, 12:8, 12:9, 15:10, 16:22, 20:36, 22:43, 24:23; **St. John**: 1:51, 5:4, 12:29 and 20:12

[86] 1:1 and 20, 2:1, 8, 12, 18, 3:1, 5, 7, 14, 5:2, 11, 7:1, 2, 11, 8:2, 3, 5, 6, 7, 8, 10, 12, 13, 9:1, 11, 13, 14, 15, 10:1, 5, 7, 8, 9, 11:1 and 15, 12:7 and 9, 14:6, 8, 9, 10, 15, 17, 18, 19, 15:1, 6, 7, 8, 16:1, 3, 4, 5, 8, 10, 12, 17, 17:1 and 7, 18:1 and 21, 19:17, 20:1, 21:9, 12, 17, 22:6 and 22:16. It is in the Apocalypse that we find "groups of angels" with a specific apocalyptic action: like those of the seals, the trumpets, of "thunder," the cups of wrath. Groups of seven are an indication of their being apocalyptic instruments of the Holy Spirit Who will make all things new!

sun." The correlation with the Virgin of Guadalupe confirms the apocalyptical dimension of the first important revelation of Our Lady at the beginning of modern times. Necessarily, these two, Mary and the holy angels, are inseparable in the preparation of the reign of the triune God!

Ten: The omnipotence of God

God alone is almighty. He veils His power in the inanimate substance of bread, placing Himself at the mercy of Man, so as to be present with us till the end of times. He depends on His priests to consecrate the sacred species to distribute Him to all those who hunger for the "Bread of Life." He suffers innumerable abuses in silence, offering His mystical passion in the church for our conversion.

Nevertheless, the power of His omnipotence will come forth one day from His Eucharistic impotence, helped by the holy angels.[87]

Twelve: three times four

The number "twelve" speaks to us of the patriarchs of the Old Testament, of the twelve apostles of Jesus, the twelve stations of the cross (up to His death) and the twelve gates of the new Jerusalem, coming down from heaven as the consummation of this creation.[88] The cross (4), symbol of the passion of Our Lord, has brought its final fruit for the greater glory of the Most Holy Trinity (3). The splendor of the new Jerusalem (3 x 4) is the eternal glorification of the Most Holy Trinity.

Example of Holy Order: the Construction of the Cathedrals in the Medieval Age

By way of numbers, related to the basic numbers, we get a glimpse of the hidden secrets of construction in the cathedrals of

---

[87] This is best seen in the third spoken apparition of the Angel of Portugal before the shepherd children at Loca do Cabeço in 1916. The children are the first asked to help the Lord out of the impotence of His Presence in the Holy Eucharist — and this in union with their angels.

[88] cf. Rv 21:12-23

the Middle Ages, especially in the Roman and Gothic styles. In every respect, these houses of God were a living gospel for those who would open their eyes to the parables of faith in order (construction), sculpture and image.[89] They continue to silently speak of the order of the universe and the invisible order of the reign of God. The three most important principles of construction are a silent testimony of man's vocation to be an image of the invisible triune God. The first principle: weight (statics) corresponds to the Father; the second: right measure corresponds to the Son; and the third: number corresponds to the Holy Spirit. These principles together with the laws they imply relate back to Yahweh's revelation to Moses in the construction of the Ark of the Covenant, the tent of encounter and the prescription on liturgical instruments.

A basic number can always be found with respect to the construction of the great cathedrals. It is a number which serves as the numeric foundation of its construction, and most often is found in the measure of the apse. As a constructive principal, it is employed in various ways (mostly through multiplication with other basic numbers). It is the "key" that allows a particular church to reflect the beauty, harmony and order of God and that which makes the great cathedrals "living houses of God." Upon entering these sa-

---

[89] Although western art seems less bound by constructive laws than that of the Eastern church, up to the end of Medieval Age whatever had to do with religious instruction was in full accordance with the religious tradition of the epoch. The different styles, like roman and gothic, constitute a doctrinal edifice of order, harmony and beauty, and give testimony of the unity of the church looking up to the one God in Jesus Christ.

The great cathedrals rose up by the dedication of those who belonged to the "Order of Construction." Like all religious, entrusted with the eminent mission of evangelization, its members made the vows of poverty, chastity and obedience so as to be worthy instruments of the Gospel in and through construction.

Up to today, the Eastern church has conserved this doctrinal unity of laws governing religious art, and is best seen in the icons. Normally only monks or consecrated persons, bound by strict laws governing the art of icon painting, are allowed to paint the icons. Fasting and strict silence is a requisite. Only void of self, of personal aspirations and ambitions can man truly be open for divine inspiration.

cred temples, anyone with a pure and open heart can immediately sense the mysterious presence of God, because the whole construction is prayer — become stone![90]

Weight

Of the three important principles observed by the Christian architects in the construction of the cathedrals, only the first one, weight, is still applied today; the other two have practically been obliterated. Weight (statics) is the principle which enables an edifice to remain standing. Modern churches have "weight," but are primarily functional buildings. They are mere places of assembly. Self-glory and the feeble "inspiration of the architect" are the principles which have been substituted for "right measure" and "number."

Measure

The second element is measure. All proportions and correlations must express harmony. No part is to dominate or be lost in the whole. All elements of the edifice combine such that the overall construction becomes a pure reflection of the beauty of Mary. Church is her "mystical womb" because she is "Teotokos": she will bring God to birth. She does the same in the "house of the rosary" with its manifold mysteries.

Number

The third principle of construction is number. The key number for a particular construction is related to one of the holy numbers in

---

[90] Unfortunately it is almost impossible to find any literature on this subject. The activity of the "Orders of Construction" ended with the Medieval Age. Whatever documents were conserved seem to have been intentionally destroyed by those who, beginning with the 18th century, century of rationalism and illuminism, proclaimed "free masonry" in opposition to the "bound masonry" of the Christian cathedrals. Today this "free construction" of churches has come to its climax: reflecting the sometimes scurrilous "inspirations" of the architect — glorifying himself!

the Bible: three, five, seven, nine or twelve. It becomes the point of reference for all the proportions of the construction. This is what gives the entire edifice its harmony. The house of God is not only a living prayer, it is also a silent sermon of the Order of God. Order is harmony, and harmony is just measure. Little by little we will learn more about this triple order in the "house of the rosary." The deeper we meditate the mysteries of the rosary, the more perfectly will we enter into the *order*, the rhythm and the "movement" of God. If persecution forces the church of tomorrow to become a "church in tents," then this holy order must become incarnate, individually and socially, by a Christian life entirely orientated unto God.

The "free principle of construction" of the freemasons took over when man lost insight into the order of God.[91] He thought he could arrange the order of life by himself. Our modern "self-made" world is largely constructed on the principle of the first fallen angel: "I will do everything myself." Because of our sin and consequent blindness to God, the devil also takes over in the religious realm.[92] Confusion, syncretism (the mixing of elements of different religions) and imminentism are the outstanding symptoms of a world where "God is dead."[93]

---

[91] cf. Rv 12

[92] The holy order of liturgy, so jealously conserved by the Tridentine Council, has given way to an "aggiornamento" for pastoral reasons, certainly most necessary, because God is waiting for the living answer of man in this time. But we should not forget that liturgy is first of all orientated to the "holy God!" We are in great need of the holy angels to help raise up the vertical beam of the cross once again!

[93] The so called "mission" of Elisabeth Prophet, with her poetic *"Rosary of St. Michael,"* in the luxury hotels of the world is an example of this. She is one of the closest collaborator of Maitreya. The esoteric science presented on the first page of her pamphlet is enough to discern that it isn't the handwriting of Mother church. Man's curiosity is enticed about the "secrets of the hidden life of Jesus" and "the healing power of the Seven Archangels," etc., all used as bait to catch even those with true religious aspirations. What is missing though is the Gospel: *"deny yourself, take up your cross and follow me."* (Mk 8:34, Lk 9:23)

The depth of the rosary as the interior house of God can be seen in the three perspectives of every message of God image, word, light.[94] If we try to pray the rosary with our Guardian Angel, we will become aware of the trinitarian order of the prayer in its formal construction. Even the fine chord that links the pearls is part of the message:

- The pearls, normally of wood, should remind us of the mystery of the cross. Together with the material element of "wood" they take in the whole of material creation. As "image," symbol of the invisible Spiritual world, they are "Bible of the Father's infinite love for the prodigal son."
- The words we pray are part of the good news of the Son. They begin with the message announced by St. Gabriel to Mary: *"Hail, full of grace..."*
- The light of understanding will come to us if we enter ever more deeply into the correlations between the image (mate-

---

[94] cf. Here we refer to the first of the seven gifts of the Holy Spirit: the Gift of Understanding, which necessarily includes the other six gifts. Here, the six help the first to unfold in wisdom, counsel, science, fortitude, fear of God and piety. They are like the colored spectrum of light. Our way of perceiving things always starts with the perception of our senses (of the "image" of things they give us). The more we have some part in intuitive understanding, the more we come to understand about the image already initially perceived. In the beginning man had this Gift of Intuition, otherwise he would not have been able to name the things God presented to him. (cf. Gen 2:19)

This gift was lost by the first sin, but by grace it can return if the heart of man is purified. Normally we must take the way of analysis (that's where we need the word!) to finally be able to make a judgment about the essence of a thing: to see it in the light of God. Only then our judgment is true! Children still have something of this gift, and this explains why they have a natural preference to look at pictures.

Given: image of a circle. Task: analyze. After finally reaching some kind of understanding we return to it. Conclusion: image is a spiral, because the light of understanding has brought the object meditated closer to the light of God. This is the simple way we will bring the things of this world "home" to God. Necessarily, understanding must be in love and not a pure rational exercise. In the end light and love will be one!

rial creation) and the word directed to us. This is primarily the work of the Holy Spirit in us.

Necessarily, every message of God has these three perspectives:

- In relation to the Father it is the image which can be understood only by the word and in the light of the Spirit.
- In relation to the Son it is always a message by way of the word, because the Son as the word, the second person of the Most Holy Trinity, is the message of the Father to each of us in the Holy Spirit.
- Only in the light of the Holy Spirit will we really understand this word of the Father spoken to us in the Holy Spirit. He will also help us to see these three dimensions in one.

Image and Parable

The great modern civilization, the "City of Man,"[95] has very little to do with nature. Constructions and architectural progress no longer have symbolic meaning and even less religious attraction or appeal to the interior man.

Man, primarily orientated to the word,[96] is tempted to discover God only by way of the word. But if we do not look up to the Father, and at the same time beseech the light of the Holy Spirit, our understanding of God and the world He created becomes evermore reduced to the letter, as was that of the Scribes and Pharisees.

If evangelization is limited to announcing the word of God, then it is a deficient means of revealing the reality of God. It must be correlated with the bounty of the Father revealed in nature, and meditated in our heart in the Holy Spirit, for only in a trinitarian

---

[95] *The City of Man* is no longer in print. It glorifies man's achievements in this modern world. It is like the counterpart to the "City of God" of St. Augustine, he who initially exposed the opposition of the "two cities."

[96] ...as the angels to the Holy Spirit and material creation are correlated to the Father

light can we probe the "great things God has done for us" in His Son, and thus come to a deeper vision of our salvation.

We should not underestimate or disregard the value and use of the image in our religious instruction.[97] The devil doesn't. He knows its value and uses it day and night as a type of brainwashing tactic to deviate our senses and understanding from the right path of truth. The pedagogy of the Master was simple: show the reality of the kingdom of God by way of symbols and parables.

Image and Rhythm of Nature

Jesus is the good news of the Father's infinite love for us poor sinners. He addressed his listeners in parables, using creation as an image of the invisible realities of the kingdom of God. It really isn't that difficult to recognize the bounty of God's love for us in the visible creation. It is never too late to be born again, to become a child. What may seem to be insignificant exterior circumstances can open our interior vision to the message of God. Listening to or reading the Gospels is a call to enter into the time, place and the environment surrounding Our Lord as He speaks. Whether Our Lord speaks at the shore of the lake or on the mountain are not casual details, they are part of the good news. Our Lord Jesus Christ is the wisdom of God, and He takes in all of nature to communicate the message of the Father's unconditional love.

No external reality is of insignificance for our speaking and or interacting with others. Being in a room, a church or amidst nature influences our thought and speech. Again and again the Lord uses the parables of nature to help us understand more about the invisible reign of God. Here also our good angel can help us to be closer

---

[97] Remember that in the Medieval Age up to the time of St. Francis, when the friars started preaching the word of God, evangelization was done by means of the "image": the example of saint men and women and their deeds and achievements: building "Houses of God," monasteries, cultivating the land, opening the first schools, as did the Benedictine monks. An evangelization by life rather than by the word! (Life is deeply related to "image." According to a word of Our Lord to Catherine Emmerich, "His Gospel are the God loving souls"!)

to Him in words and deeds. Each bead touched, while praying the rosary, should be a prayer in union with the beauty of nature that surrounds us. This is one of the best ways to break our mechanical rhythm of prayer "in the void," prayed without really looking up to God, not taking in anything, forgetting the presence of our good angel who always wants to pray with us. St. Ignatius recommends that we place ourselves in the presence of God before we pray. This is the simplest way of transforming our "words in the air" into true prayer.

We are to seek out fresh avenues to enrich and assist our approximation of God. If there is nothing to support us in our prayer on the outside, why not listen to the living rhythm of our heart, and try to follow this rhythm in our prayer? Sometimes it is just a matter of opening our interior eyes to see the banquet the Lord has placed before us. Praying should be a way to get away from the vicious circle of our ego. Living in the hustle and bustle of city life is not an excuse for losing the interior rhythm of the rosary. We ought to recognize its rhythm as our lifeline to God, but when this "lifeline" seems difficult to find, we need to: stop, step into the beauty of nature and begin to pray the rosary in union with the movements of nature. Nature helps us to re-encounter our own vital rhythm and so find the way back to the "rhythm of God."

Look, listen, feel and sense the "movements":

- of a landscape,
- at the shore of the sea in the rolling of the waves,
- in the whistling of the wind in the trees,
- in the gliding clouds of heaven.

Let this rhythm pass through you, take it into your heart, walk and breathe the movements of nature and then try to conform the rhythm of your prayer to it. The outward rhythm will enter even deeper in us if we remember the angels of nature about us, because there is nothing in God's bountiful providence which is not protected and guided by the angels, for His greater honor and glory! This will enable us to pray in union even when we are completely alone; we will be in union with creation around and in us.

If it is impossible to take refuge in nature for a while, look for a silent place, close your exterior senses and concentrate on the image of Our Lady in your heart.[98] As our good Mother wants to be with us always in the dispersion of this world, she will help us not forget about the "one necessary thing." Her image within helps us to remember better that we should be continually in prayer.

The "Full" Word

Whatever prayers Holy Mother the church has given into our hands, we are to remember that the words are sacred and thus we should respect them, making every effort to accept them in the Spirit of good children. We should not only take them into our hearts, but also try to pronounce them slowly and correctly and pray with others in unison. The light of our Guardian Angel will enable us to "see" and contemplate the words we speak. He helps us to "weigh" our spoken words. In his light, we will learn of the "tone" of words, their "color," their implications and their depth in relation to the word of God, the second divine person.

We should remember to pray consciously in the presence of the Holy God; any careless way of praying is an offense to God's majesty. The more we are conscious of Whom we address, the better our prayer will reach God's hearing. Our prayer, like the pearls of our rosary, should become smoother and rounder by our frequency with them. With and by way of Mary, our praying will become smoother, as if gliding in "oil" (another symbol for the action and "unction" of the Holy Spirit Who helps us pray "in truth," adoring the only true God). We have to pray the rosary interiorly, filling it with all our love for God and Our Lady. Silent interior prayer is the source from which all exterior and community prayer will be renewed.

---

[98] This is why we have to learn to look up to her continually while praying. It is a practice that will also help us to be better prepared in our reception of Holy Communion, a bridge that will finally enable us to carry Our Lord in our heart from one communion to the next, another trinitarian relation to the Father, the Son and the Holy Spirit!

Word and Light give a deeper understanding of things in the Holy Spirit. The encounter of the two disciples with the risen Lord on the way to Emmaus is a perfect example of Our Lord taking advantage of natural circumstances, to tell them better about the ways of God.[99] The disciples reach the end of their human knowledge and understanding of "the Christ" before they finally allow Jesus to speak. They are so engrossed with their political illusion that their senses are closed to Our Lord's mysterious real presence. By way of the Prophets, the Lord occasions the opportunity of explaining His passion and Resurrection, but His explanation only reaches their ears, not their hearts.

As nightfall draws near, an inexplicable fear enters their souls. Their self-confidence fades, the first ray of understanding concerning "the Christ" falls upon their ignorance. At that moment Jesus feigns to continue His journey alone. Only now they sense that He is "different" and implore Him to remain with them through the night. Their anxious plea causes Him to remain with them. For the first time their interior uncertainty prompts them to seek help. It is probably their first consciously pronounced word since having left Jerusalem. Their fear of "night" forces them to open their hearts to the light of the Lord, it helps them to invite the Lord to remain with them. The natural darkness becomes a symbol for the deeper reality of the darker "night" ahead, the last night of life when a definitive decision for light or darkness has to be made in the presence of the Lord. Beforehand they were unable to hear His words, because they were yet filled with the "noise" of all their spoken and unspoken words. Now that their hearts have been opened by the silent message of nature they are ready to receive the deeper message of the love of God.

---

[99]   cf. Lk 24,28-33: This pericope can also help us recognize how far away we are from the Lord at times, because of our own way of looking at things. We have a lot of words, even for holy things, but they are in the air. This pericope tells us that meditation is a "coming closer to reality" — to look at things as they really are and not as we want them to be.

Resuming the Three Dimensions
of Every Message in Another Perspective

"All was created through Him, all was created for Him. He is before all that is...."[100] These words of St. Paul help us to understand that the entire created world was made in view of the word of God, and therefore is at the service of His message of love for us. This is another reason why every revelation of God should be seen in the context of its trinitarian correlations. We will discover them in the light of the Holy Spirit by way of our angel in the three dimensions: length, in reference to time; breadth, in reference to place; and mode, in the way it is accomplished. Again, this refers back to the three persons of the Most Holy Trinity.

The hidden dimensions of the rosary open our eyes to the holy order of the kingdom of God, which is an order hidden from the eyes of this world. We will discover more about the "house of God" in the interior of our soul as we enter more into the depths of the rosary in its correlations of form and structure. God is always the greater God. At the hand of our good Guardian Angel and with the rope of the rosary we will be allowed to climb peaks which before we did not even suspect! What we need is only the admiring curiosity of children. God's love will lead us from one surprise to the next!

The Four-Times-Five Mysteries of the Rosary

The four-times-five mysteries are the constructive part of the "interior house of the rosary." The three traditional Mysteries, the Joyful, Sorrowful and the Glorious, related to the triune God, together with the "angelic rosary," form that "interior house" where with God, already here on earth, we may dwell.[101]

---

[100] Col 1:16

[101] The "five mysteries of the angels" in the rosary open the door for a deeper meditation of the rosary in its formal construction.

What is the "Angelic rosary"? Five of the fifteen mysteries specifically manifest the intercession of the holy angels in salvation history, helping us to:

- build the house of the rosary,
- understand better the formal structure of the rosary,
- have an idea of the "apocalyptic" importance of the prayer so recommended by Our Lady in her apparitions.

The Five Mysteries of the Angels in the Rosary

Today, there exists quite an erroneous concept of the holy angels. They are painted as lovely feminine creatures with wings floating in the air or as baby cherubs with hearts and arrows. They are an inseparable element of salvation history. They are bound to the person of Jesus Christ. They prepared His coming, accompanied Him, and will bring all things to consummation by way of Him. This is best exemplified in the five angelic mysteries.

As the rosary is a synthesis of the salvation history, we must recognize that each mystery, including the angelic ones, has its place in the edifice. Within the Joyful Mysteries, the Annunciation and the birth of Our Lord clearly speak of angels. The Sorrowful Mysteries present Our Lord's agony in the garden as an angelic mystery. The Glorious Mysteries also present two angelical mysteries, the Resurrection and the ascension. Removing the angels from their God-given role in salvation history would make the house of creation and salvation crumble. Looking closely, we find that the angels intervene at key points of salvation. Associated to the mission of Christ and Our Lady at the foot of the cross, the angel is mediator between God and man. It is his mission to interiorly explain in the Spirit what exteriorly takes place. He reveals the underlying realities and helps us to recognize the Spiritual significance of God's actions.

The holy angels represent the hierarchical order of things, and their transparency as symbols of the reign of God, therefore, is our best assistance to discover more about the deep link of sign and Spirit — symbolic dimension of things. Our Lord's choice of the conditions and way of life of a Mediterranean culture by His birth in Galilee are not relative. It is not ours to exchange the symbolic reality of bread and wine for cake and coke. Inculturization does not imply: "While in China, use rice cakes and tea or if in Mexico, use tortillas and pulque."

The Importance of the Number Five in the Rosary

In the normal construction of a house, the cornerstones or columns provide a certain sturdiness of foundation for the rest of the structure. This "rule of four," the cross, is even reflected in the fundamental construction principles of the atom. If "four" is the principle of construction, where then does "five" come in? The first step is discernment: to know better about the right form and the significance of the cross! We must be careful to discern the evil of one's use of the things of God for the sole purpose of misleading man.[102] The devil no longer hides his face. He has removed his mask and shows his face in the daylight. In the hustle and bustle of this world we have become so blind as not to really look at things anymore, we just take them in like babies who put everything in their mouth. This is why even "silly things" can appear wholesome to some,[103] and so become the delighted target of the devil's wiles. A true cross will always bear a Corpus Christi.[104]

Our Lord's four limbs are extended and pierced, and where vertical and horizontal come together we encounter the pierced heart of Our Lord Jesus Christ. The wound of the Sacred Heart of

---

[102] There is a form of cross where the vertical and horizontal proportions are of equal measures. It takes man's eyes off his vertical duty to love God above all. It is a subtle tactic, because the aim is not to increase our love for our fellow-man, but primarily to belittle the "First Commandment." The "love of neighbor" is a virtue, but it should never overshadow or be placed on the same par as the love of God. We lose the light of discernment when our love of God becomes philanthropy. We must beware of any form of neopaganism accepting sin as an innate human condition. (Recall the Kinsey Report and other "statistics" — "go with the flow"; it is a flood of amorality that is killing the youth!)

[103] A cross with a serpent on it can only find its relation to the staff on which the Lord told Moses to make and mount a bronze serpent so that whenever anyone bitten by a serpent looked upon it, he would be healed. The devil killing our Lord proclaimed his own sentence of eternal condemnation. This is the message of the cross: Christ has overcome the power of hell!

[104] With the exception of the bare crosses of the contemplative communities of the Trappists or Camaldalese monks. Their intentional consideration of the bare cross is to recall it as cruel instrument of chastisement, suffering and martyrdom so as to inspire them to a life of greater reparation and sacrifice.

Jesus is what gives the number "five" its deeper dimension. It implies interiority with respect to the construction of our interior house. It is not sufficient to lay down the foundation and raise up walls. Our interior dwelling needs to be furnished, for an interior culture of life is essential in order that a house be called a "home," a place of dwelling. The fact that a majority of the modern churches are purely functional is one of the factors that fault our liturgies of interiority. Another negative factor is our mechanical mentality and our modern instability and superficiality. Sacred rubrics are dropped or exchanged because we do not understand them any more in their symbolical significance; they are adapted to our shallow way of living. If we learn to consciously pray the rosary with our angel we will find our way back to a deeper understanding of the order of liturgy in all its beauty and healing power which is no other than that of Our Lady: "tota pulchra"!

The Lost Center in Life: Return Through Suffering

When Our Lord Jesus Christ is accused of casting out the evil Spirits by the power of a certain devil, He responds *"a kingdom divided against itself will fall."*[105] The fallen angels have lost God as the center of life, and therefore live in an disorder only organized in a hatred of God. The growing anarchy in our days is a replica of their situation. Hell's effort is to deviate man from a response to God and drown him in this flood of disorder. This is so much easier for the enemy, because man's heart is empty and increasingly filled with the rubbish of the world. It is not that every new fashion, conquest or success of man is bad in itself, but the influence of the evil one's pride causes man to believe that he himself is a "god." Therefore, what may be good becomes a path to

---

[105] Mt 12:25-27 By this statement Our Lord does not infer that there is no unity amongst the devils, but that their only "togetherness" is found in their hatred against God, their "non serviam." Jesus refers to the fact that the devils battle amongst themselves, because each devil wants to be first and only brutal violence on the part of the higher devils guarantees some kind of unity in the combat against God and man. Our human sphere reflects the same type of unity by suppression. Hitler and Nazism are the best example of how a dictatorship seems to unify anarchy!

perdition, leading him and his brothers further away from God, the only true center of life.

Against this growing disorder of the reign of Satan we have to put the untouchable order of the reign of Mary, representing the reign of God.[106] Among the five mysteries in the rosary which expressly deal with the angels, the center is the agony of Our Lord and His being comforted by the angel. This center of angelic mysteries makes us realize that the suffering of Our Lord Jesus Christ should be the motor of our Christian living. Only in and by the power of His most precious blood are we freed from sin, made new men and enter into the reign of Mary. Wherever the cross is removed from our churches, the structure of the church is crushed. It becomes like a house built upon sand.[107]

Already in 1950, a study of modern art by Professor Sedlmeyer[108] reveals that our age has lost its center. The work of Picasso is an example: Man is dismantled and remantled according to the "artist's" inspirations: man creates man. This is not too far from being a reality with our present genetic engineering and "scientific" efforts to produce genetic geniuses and computer programmed supermen. Only with our eyes and heart fixed on the cross will we find our way in and through the growing confusion of this world. But where do we find the cross? Even the modern Basilica of Our Lady of Guadalupe in Mexico lacks a crucifix. The only crucifix to be found is the one almost destroyed in the bombing of the portrait of Our Lady, but it's a relic/museum piece exposed under glass. The only other semblance of a cross is above the main altar: a composition of many fragments. It may be "modern art," but it is hardly a cross, and less a crucifix.

---

[106] The liturgy should represent the harmonious order of Mary. In the Middle Ages only the best, most beautiful and most precious things were good enough for the praise of God in liturgy. Today, one steps right from the street into the celebration of Holy Mass ... and wonders why there is little difference!

[107] See the end of the Sermon on the Mount with St. Matthew, chapter 7, also St. Paul reminds us there is no other foundation but Christ. (cf. Cor 3;10,12 and EPH 2:2O)

[108] cf. *Loss of the Center*, 1950; it was a famous book when it first appeared and a clear sign that after the war we had come back on the solid ground of reality again, which today again seems to be lost in the rush for gold!

Our Lady of Guadalupe Announcing
the Second Coming of Her Son in Silence

Every copy of Our Lady of Guadalupe is different, because each is a living image. Mary's message is a personal one, and therefore every person will see her image in the uniqueness of her maternal love for him. A dramatic example of this image variance is seen in the two images in the state of Veracruz, Mexico. The first is an image in a chapel in Antigua, Veracruz where the Spaniards first celebrated holy Mass upon their arrival in Mexico (1519). The large image of Our Lady of Guadalupe is completely dark. In another image, found in a nearby village, only Our Lady's throat remains in light. The darkness of the image in Antigua is a sign that her message has been darkened, it no longer radiates the light she wants to give to those lost in sin. The "lighted throat" of the other image reminds us of Mary's mediation of grace.[109] Anyone straying from Our Lady is already in the darkness although he does not note it. The living light of the Gospel is fading, darkness will cover the earth as in the beginning.

The beautiful European cathedrals, once a visible representation of the Spiritual order of the reign of God, have become museum temples for tourists. With the constant milling of people, there is little time and space for the holy liturgy. This is a negative, yet clear sign of the "devastation of the holy."[110] We need another "purification of the temple"; this time by the Holy Spirit and His

---

[109] It can be likened to Our Lady of Grace in the Rue de Bac in Paris where she appeared to Catherine Labouré, 1830. Already on this image, the dark spots on her fingers remind us that there are many graces we do ask for.

[110] cf. Mt 24:15 In the new Basilica of Our Lady of Guadalupe in Mexico there are other details which reveal that this temple with a few more changes will become the "temple of the New Era" — as is gloriously announced in one of the pamphlets of the "metaphysical workshops" of Guadalajara. The blessed Sacrament is reserved in the chapel of the Holy Spirit with a representation of "Christ" bringing down the light from God (as Prometheus did!). This is the satanic strategy of "inverting the poles." The tabernacle, in the same chapel, looks as if there are hidden freemason symbols represented. But in all the darkness the merciful light of the image of Our Lady is undiminished. Our Lady's portrait is the unconfoundable promise in our "babylonic captivity" that Our Lady remains present with us as Our Sorrowful Mother. She will not forsake us; she suffers imprisonment on behalf of us her children.

instruments the holy angels.[111] They will help to re-establish the invisible and holy order of the reign of God present in their hierarchy. The more the exterior order of the reign of God is lost, the more it must become an interior reality in our souls. The assistance of the holy angels can best be understood in likeness to the help Our Lord received in His agony in the Garden of Gethsemane: in order to be able to give His last drop of blood for the salvation of sinners. "This is the hour of the angels!"[112] does not mean that we have to wait for an external intervention of the angels, but we should join up with them right now to help in the Spiritual battle for the reign of God in and with Mary. This battle for the moment is not so much an active one, but is that of His agony in the beginning of His passion.[113]

Centering Our Life in God

"What can man give as price for his soul, what would it avail him to conquer the whole world if he would lose his soul?"[114] These words of Our Lord truly characterize modern man's situation. He is scattered in a thousand directions; in manifold activities and global service, but his productive plurality has robbed him of his center. He no longer has an interior into which he can retreat and be rejuvenated in and with the Lord. The Eastern esoteric religions attract his innate need for wholeness, because they offer him what seems to be a "solution" to his unsolvable difficulties. TM suggests that by going inside oneself, one can find the

---

[111] cf. Jn 2:13-22 and Mt 13:39,41 This purification is alluded to in Our Lord's words.

[112] Title of a little book on Padre Pio de Pietrelcina; He lived not only close to the sanctuary of St. Michael on the Monte Gargano, but first of all was a good "friend" of the prince of the heavenly hosts.

[113] Our Lady appeared in Marienfried, near Augsburg, southern Germany, shortly after World War II. Her message confirms the necessity to help her with our prayer and sacrifice: "It is not yet the time for my star to rise, but I will give crosses as deep as the sea to my children in order to help save souls before the time is over!"

[114] Mt 16:26

center of life.[115] As offspring of Adam and Eve we are inescapably branded by original sin and its consequences. Subliminal "journeys"[116] bring us into regions where man has lost any control of himself and becomes prey to "powers" he is not able to discern. He is victim to the falsities of the tempter who in this case again is inverting the poles: making black shine white! St. Paul reminds us that the fallen angels remain "creatures of light," and have the capacity to manifest themselves as creatures of light.[117]

We will never find the "center of life" by entering the ambiguity of our interior. We ought to aim our deeper centering on the mysteries of Christ present in us from the moment of our baptism. As long as we are found in grace, the mysteries of salvation continually grow in us. Our lost center is found in and through Our Lord Jesus Christ. Focusing on His life in us unfolds the mystery of God within. This is quite different from TM ... "a discovery of self."

The lives of the saints are perfect examples of "living" a particular mystery of Christ or the Blessed Virgin Mary. Some of them centered in one of the Joyful Mysteries; a saint of social welfare, like St. John of God, is a beautiful reflection of the mystery of the visitation of Our Lady to her cousin Elizabeth. Sacrificial souls like Little Therese can be seen in the mystery of Mary's offering of Our Lord in the temple. Other saints have a primary center in one of the Sorrowful mysteries. Padre Pio reflects a life of continual crucifixion with Jesus. Benedict Labre, a man despised by everyone, exemplifies Our Lord's flagellation. As he never bathed, he

---

[115] TM - Transcendental Meditation, offered as high school, university and clinical courses. Already Pascal remarked that man's soul is an "abysm" — how much we need discernment by our good angel not to fall into the false abysm!

[166] We have already lost so much ground under our feet that we are prey to the most absurd "solutions" of our problems. It is no difficulty for the fallen Spirits to make us believe in fantastic extra-terrestrial voyages, in flying saucers and other "thrillers." If already normal man has a power of hypnotizing, how much more these powerful Spirits!

[117] cf. II Cor 11:14. The light of the fallen angel is always a glittering, a nervous light — kindling our curiosity and bad instincts, making us run away from our duties, from the reality of this world — the light of God gives us peace and joy and helps us to take up our cross in generosity.

was called the "dirty saint," but interiorly he was so full of the glory of the Lord that his prayer caused him to levitate. There are saints of misunderstanding, "crowned with the crown of thorns," and there are other saints who must go their steep way of the cross day by day until they break under its weight. Saints of the Glorious Mysteries are persons like Don Bosco, in whom the power and the force of the Resurrection is almost tangible. These saints of glory, having passed through the narrow door of the cross, irradiate glory of God and the eternal praise of the angels already here on earth. Praying and taking the hand of our Guardian Angel we approach the central mystery of our own life in relation to Christ. We only need to go deeper, to plunge our soul into the "abyss," not as an adventure but as an effort of fidelity to our unique vocation!

The Formal Structure of the Rosary by Way of the Three Central Mysteries

The central mysteries of the rosary are of special importance in the life of Our Lord and for our imitation. In our meditation we should give them more weight than their "surrounding mysteries." They are:

- The birth of Christ in Bethlehem
- The crowning with thorns
- The descent of the Holy Spirit

Each of them, as the third mystery within its respective grouping can be likened to the center of the cross: the pierced heart of Our Lord framed in by the four other mysteries that surround it. These mysteries are full of the promise of new life:

- The birth of life in Bethlehem is a promise to lead us out of the darkness of this world;
- The crowning with thorns is a promise of the King of Peace;
- The descent of the Holy Spirit on the Blessed Virgin and the apostles is a promise of the final sanctification of all things in the Holy Spirit.

The central mysteries act as a synthesis of the life, suffering and glory of Christ. The four sister mysteries serve as the columns of our interior house where the triune God will live and grow. They reflect the deeper reality of the cross and of the church's call to become more cruciform, so as to make of it the "third ark" for these times of great darkness and confusion.[118]

By way of these mysteries we are to be reborn, in joy and in suffering, to new life in Christ. Passing through the humiliations and misunderstandings that are part of life, we become progressively purified of our sins and might even be admitted to repair in and with the Lord and Mary. Our heart, like that of the Immaculate Heart of Mary, must be opened by the sword of suffering so as to receive the Holy Spirit as Mary and St. John did under the cross. The Lord crowned with thorns is the promise that we will overcome and finally reign with Him.

The Four Mysteries Surrounding the Central Mystery

The three central mysteries, reflecting the life of the Most Holy Trinity in Christ, will help that same life grow and develop in our hearts. This growing life must be protected, sheltered in a "Spiritual house," formed by the sister mysteries, representative of the four pillars corresponding to the four greater attributes of God: holiness, wisdom, justice, and omnipotence. In this way, every rosary is a "house" in and of itself in which we can dwell with the triune God. The Joyful Mysteries, with the central mystery of the birth of

---

[118] The "first ark" is that of Noah; it reflects God's union with creation. The "second ark" is the cross of our Lord Jesus Christ on Golgotha. It represents the salvation/union of God with man. The "third ark" is the sealing by the holy angels of the faithful in their communities so that the hatred of the enemy will not touch them. Outside of these communities, life will progressively decay in amorality and self-destruction. Within the communities Christian life in, by and with Mary will blossom forth greater than in the beginning.

Our Lord, correspond more to the Father, the Sorrowful with its crowning of Our Lord with thorns more to the Son. The Glorious, with its central mystery of the descent of the Holy Spirit, relates with the Holy Spirit.

In the Joyful Mysteries

The Annunciation reflects the presence of Holy God, and therefore His sanctity, entering the Immaculate womb of Our Lady, and thus becoming present among men. The Visitation of Mary to her kinswoman Elizabeth beautifully illustrates the union and inseparability of the two great commandments. It is an act of neighborly love, she cannot keep the Son for herself! While yet in her womb, He prompts her first mission! It is here also that we will encounter the inscrutable plans of God's wisdom. Like Mary, we must be prompt to obey.

The presentation of the Lord in the temple reminds us that God will never become our possession; He became man in order to lead us to the Father. The presentation in the temple represents the justice of God, because only in Christ do we who are lost in sin again find our way back to the Father.

Visitation
Wise God

**Finding in
the Temple
Omnipotent God**

**Annunciation
Holy God**

**Presentation
Just God**

The finding of the Child Jesus in the temple shows us that our offering is never complete. Time after time we will lose the Lord, so as to seek and find Him more deeply in our hearts. *"Unless the grain of wheat falls to the earth and dies, it remains just a grain of wheat; but if it dies, it produces much fruit.* "[119] The omnipotence of God is revealed most in His impotence among man, i.e., his willingness to be powerless and at man's disposal and mercy, especially in the Holy Eucharist.

In the Sorrowful Mysteries

Our Lord sweats His most precious blood in the Garden of Gethsemane as a willing submission to the "price" of man's Redemption from sin, death and the devil. Though Jesus never stopped being God, His human will, in relation to the Father had to be fortified by the angel.[120] This "chalice of strength" enables Him to overcome all the obstacles and attacks of the enemy and thus extend this grace of fortitude to all mankind. This is the action of Holy God.

In His scourging at the pillar, Our Lord takes upon Himself all the sins of the flesh so that we might be able to overcome the temptations in our own flesh by the power of His suffering. He pays for our concupiscence, which wants to dominate us in everything, by becoming so poor that even His skin and His flesh are torn away by the terrible lacerations of the scourges. This mystery of Our Lord's scourging has been a source of strength for the ascetics, monks and penitents throughout the church's history. It is the wise God who permits us to be tempted in order to prove our greater love to Him.

The fourth mystery is a daily invitation to participate in the mystery of salvation with the Lord. The more the cross is pushed aside in our time, the heavier it becomes for those yet faithful in following Our Lord in His dolorous ascent of Golgotha. This is the justice of God: that we are called to collaborate in our Redemption — it has to enter deeper and deeper in our body and soul.[121]

---

[119] Jn 12:24

[120] Remember here the central mystery of the angelic rosary; it is the "motor" of salvation!

[121] We are not Protestants saying: "Christ has achieved Redemption, we only have to believe in this truth!" This makes the "truth of Redemption" exterior to us, and it must become incarnate!

Scourging
Wise God

Crucifixion
Omnipotent God

Agony in the Garden
Holy God

Carrying the Cross
Just God

The crucifixion and death of Our Lord on the cross has brought Redemption to its consummation. If we die with Christ, our sins are taken away and we will participate in His Resurrection. "Oh death, where is your victory? Oh death, where is your sting?"[122] By his death on the cross, Our Lord Jesus Christ has overcome the death of sin. The omnipotence of God has achieved what the impotence of man was unable to achieve!

In the Glorious Mysteries

Ascension
Wise God

Coronation
Omnipotent God

Resurrection
Holy God

Assumption
Just God

Christ's Resurrection from the dead is the victory of the Holy God over the power of hell. His ascension into heaven is God's wisdom; He takes "captivity captive," that is, he conquers sin. (cf. Mass of the ascension) If we look up to Him, sin no longer has

---

[122] I Cor 15:55

power over us. "And when I am lifted, I will draw all things to Myself." The Assumption of Mary into heaven is the first visible fruit of the Lord's Resurrection for mankind. The justice of God dictates that having

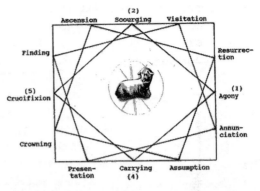

borne the Savior of the world, Her inviolate body would not suffer corruption. The coronation of Mary as "Queen of Heaven and Earth" is the supreme act of the Omnipotent God. It is the promise of the final transfiguration, even of the material world, into the "precious stones" of the new Jerusalem. the Holy Spirit will continue Christ's work of Redemption!

The 3 x 4 Mysteries of the Holy Rosary

Each rosary forms a house, and together, with the "triple birth of Our Lord" in the center, we have a beautiful image of the new Jerusalem (the 3 x 4 mysteries representing the twelve gates).

RESUMING:

The cross, our interior "house" with its four "walls," conceals the greatest treasure God has given us: His only begotten Son present among us in the poverty of the cradle of the tabernacle, suffering for us and with us as the despised Lord, crowned with thorns, and continuing His presence among us to the end of the world through the action of the Holy Spirit.

Is it necessary to go into the catacombs to rediscover the order of God? God will take His faithful remnant the way of Golgotha. Christ crucified is the center of our faith. St. Paul encountered this truth and writes to the Galatians: *"The world is crucified to me, and I to the world."*[123] He found the center, and no one or thing

---

[123] Gal 6:14

could tear him from Him. This "reason for living" seems quite absurd to the world, but remains the reason why we should commemorate the passion of Our Lord each week on Thursday night and Friday afternoon.[124]

A well-conditioned athlete is one who by constant and faithful training performs the same exercises over and over again such that they become second nature. Being a Christian is no different. We are to repetitively "exercise the way of the cross" now, on this side of eternity![125]

First, in relation to the Father: *"Deny yourself."* It is only through self-denial that we become new creatures in God. In relation to the Son: *"Take up your cross."* Our cross is a unique one, different from all others. It is not an abstract science to be hidden in some forgotten corner to collect dust. It must live in us; in our shortcomings, in our difficulties and in all of our sufferings, it will be crystallized in the one word which will be our name for all eternity in heaven.

In relation to the Holy Spirit: *"Take up your cross, and follow Me."* This requisite for the Christian is hardly lived today. So many times we run in circles oblivious to the rhythm of the focus which ought to be ours.

---

[124] The "holy hour": 9 to 12 p.m. on Thursday and 12-3 p.m. on Friday are times of special graces from the passion of Our Lord.
[125] cf. Mk 8:34 and Lk 9:23

"Follow me."

The "little way" of St. Therese should encourage us. Her physical frailty did not enable her to accomplish or aspire to great sacrifices, but she learned and profited from the numerous opportunities of daily living to exercise self-abnegation and sacrifice. Moreover, her little way of sacrifice holds the great advantage of being hidden from others. As it is a hidden way, it does not focus on one's accomplishments, but on doing all out of love. We must seek to remain beneath the veil of Our Lady and come closer to our Guardian Angel. He will help our awareness of the many hidden offers of God's sacrificial love to join Him on the way of the cross.

The Rosary: A Help to Find the Lost Center

We must begin to count every cross and tribulation as the true grace that they are. The church is already in the persecutions of "tomorrow," but only by them will her members be purified and begin to image Mary Immaculate. Like Mary, they will become invincible to any and all attacks of the devil.

Like her Lord, the church will also need to be comforted by the angel as she enters her agony. We must not close the door to these graces because of our abhorrence of suffering. The success and prevalence of the Eastern cults and religions in the West is filling this void in our soul, they have no relation to the sacrifice of the cross.[126] As the rosary revolves about the sacrifice of Christ, it helps us to come closer to the center: to the pierced heart of Our Lord. The Sacred Heart of Jesus pleads with us to unite ourselves to his sufferings, and to offer ourselves in union with his sacrifice.

---

[126] St. Bonaventure tells us that even if man had not sinned, the Son of God would still have incarnated so as to bring man, and though him the whole creation, back to God! We go even further with St. John (cf. 10:18ff); even then man had to be "crucified" but not in the violent and bloody passion of

The Third Meditation on the Rosary

The "Movements" in the Rosary

Part of the integral construction of the rosary is its "movement." The term may initially sound foreign to our ears, but it is a term also used by St. Ignatius in his spiritual exercises. The saint tells us that the retreat master must watch for the "movement of spirits" in the soul of the retreatant." The image of Our Lady of Guadalupe, with its "movement of ransom," is a precious help in understanding what "movement" is.[127] In the rosary this "movement" is unfolded in a triple way. The image of Guadalupe shows more the third, the "glorious" movement, because even with the Aztecs she is recognized as the "glorious woman."

The Blessed Virgin is the final word of the Father to mankind and all creation: "Come!" Spoken with all the attraction of the pierced heart of Our Lord and the incomprehensible love of the Father for the Prodigal Son in the Holy Spirit.[128] Whatever is gold in the image is symbol of the final glorification of creation. Here the "word" of the Spirit: "Come home!" has come to its completion. The dark shading of the "movement of ransom" symbolizes the passion of the Mystical Body of the church following the Son on His way of the cross — as St. John shows it as a way to glory!

---

[126] (cont.) Golgotha — he needed to become cruciform. God's love revealed in the passion of the Son is a sacrificial love! (This truth is revealed by the symbol of the fire on the shore with "bread and fish on it") (cf. 21:9) As man is made according to the image of the triune God he necessarily must grow up to the full age of Christ on the cross: the complete submission to the holy will of the Father. But note the difference: if man had not sinned, denying yourself would not have been difficult — as it is the nature of the Father and the Son to lose themselves in another in the love of the Holy Spirit!

[127] cf. Book IV: "The Movement of Ransom in the Sign of the Lamb of God."

[128] In some way or another we are all "prodigal sons." The angels are like the "elder brother," they always remain faithful in their service of God, but they are not called to share in the banquet as we poor sinners are!

The Trinitarian movement in the Holy Rosary

- The primary movement of the Joyful Mysteries is "acceptance." It is not predominant, but it is emphasized more than any other.
- "Giving — surrender" is the movement of the Sorrowful Mysteries.
- In the Glorious Mysteries, it is the movement of "receiving again."

This triple movement is explained in the word of the Lord: "Unless the grain of wheat falls to the ground and dies, it remains a single grain. But if it dies it will bring forth a rich harvest."[129] We are all called to participate in this "movement" of all life, founded within the Most Holy Trinity. Whatever is "light" in the image of Guadalupe is a symbol for the "first movement." It corresponds to the Incarnation, but we must remember that this "light" of God, for our human eyes, may be dark … just as the earth is dark for the grain that falls to it. The beginning of this "movement of light" is the loving glance of Our Lady, and we should learn to follow it as we pray the rosary. If we find ourselves in the darkness, we must never lose hope, for the net of God's apocalyptic love is already cast out. We must not run away. We must remain tranquil and fervent in prayer: God is love.

The Father always gives, because He is the fountain of life. The Son is the offspring of the Father, begotten of the Father from all eternity. It is from Him and with Him that we accept all gifts, first of all the gift of new life in the Son, on condition that we deny ourselves, *"Unless the grain of wheat falls to the ground...."* The earth is dark.... The Mystery of new life is hidden....[130]

---

[129] Jn 12:24 This parable is another confirmation of the truth that man is "projected towards sacrifice"!

[130] This precisely was the trial for the angels in the beginning of times: to say "yes" to the incomprehensible will of God in relation to His Son! As we do now: we want to understand, we know better … and so we fail to die and have part in God's life!

We are called to give away in the Son what we are, as well as the new life we receive. We are to take up the cross and die to self as does the grain of wheat: *"... and dies...."* We will receive again: life in plenitude through the Holy Spirit, only when we follow Jesus up the hill of Golgotha, when we share in His death; then our life in Him *"...will bring a rich harvest."*[131]

The Trinitrian Rhythm in God Himself

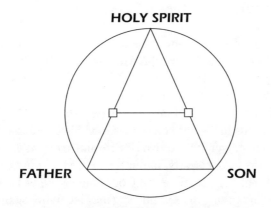

HOLY SPIRIT

FATHER   SON

The Father is complete donation of Himself to the Son. The Son enters in this movement of donation — having Himself surrendered completely He will receive Himself back in the love of the Holy Spirit.

As the Most Holy Trinity wills to live in us, we must enter into the movement of divine life: the Father giving Himself to the Son, the Son giving Himself back to the Father and receiving Himself anew in the Holy Spirit. This same trinitarian rhythm will be fully realized in the church after her purification.

---

[131] There are many ways to express this trinitarian rhythm. We can observe it in nature: darkness, dawn, daylight; in our body: respiration — inhalation and expiration; in our perception: perceive, discern, understand; in the Spiritual life: the rhythm of "via purificationis," iluminationis, unionis (purification, illumination, union). The more consciously we live these three stages, the more we can already participate here in the rhythm of trinitarian life.

The praying of the rosary should make this rhythm ever more profoundly lived in our hearts, not only in relation to God, but also with respect to our neighbor. In the last times, the church will attain a greater measure of love than that which she experienced in the beginning, because of the final outpouring of the Holy Spirit so that Our Lord's command: *"Love one another as I have loved you"* will be brought to perfection.[132]

The "Trinitarian Rhythm" of the Rosary

The "trinitarian" rhythm of the rosary is the rhythm of all life in the likeness of the life of the Most Holy Trinity. The Father completely gives Himself up to the Son, and the Son responds by passing His life over to the Father in His sixth last word on the cross: *"Father, into Your hands I commend My Spirit."* Our Lord Jesus reminds us in his Sermon of the Good Shepherd that the Son of God has the power to lay down His life and to take it up again![133] This rhythm is in our hearts, in our respiration and in everything that has part in the life given by God. Pausing between the two movements of "giving oneself up" and the "receiving again" is the promise of the "eternal rest" we will one day find in God. In union with the angels in adoration and contemplation of God we are already allowed here on earth to participate in this sacred "rest."

The first movement of "giving" in the Joyful Mysteries is centralized in the adoration of the angels and the shepherds God gives His Son. It is a "giving" that resonates into the Sorrowful and Glorious Mysteries in the bowing down in the dust of our sins in contrition and adoration *"de profundis"* and in the waiting with Mary and all the apostles for the coming of the Spirit! Looking more closely, we find that the three "movements" are really one: the one

---

[132] This promise was a firm conviction of Pope John XXIII, but it will not be consummated in a confused or general way. It is a promise which brings the holy angels to earth as our assistance in this final combat for the reign of God!

[133] cf. Jn 10:15-18

movement of the triune God Who is eternal giving, inviting mankind, by way of the Son, to join in this never ending giving of love! It is the Father Who first gives.

Like Mary at the Annunciation and Incarnation, we enter His giving through the Holy Spirit. Every step in this way of giving in Mary is a visible sign of the invisible surrender of the Son to the Father. The Father's giving is extended in us when like Mary we go in assistance to our neighbor. But that is not all, we have to go on giving: not to just one person, but to all, to the whole world: that's what Mary did when she gave birth to Christ in the humble cave of Bethlehem. Her giving doesn't stop with the birth of Christ, she must give her Son back to the Father in fidelity to the prescriptions of the law and must experience losing Him when He is twelve years of age. Above their comprehension, but part of their humble resignation to the plans of God, both Mary and Joseph become aware that Jesus has to go His own "way of giving." The finding of Jesus in the temple acts as a "bridge" over to the Sorrowful Mysteries.

The Sorrowful Mysteries present Our Lord as the "sole" and exclusive center of our meditation. Mary is invisibly present with Him in holy union, but only at the foot of the cross is she visibly presented for all the world to behold and accept as "Mother."[134] It is the exacting love of the Father which presses out the last drop of the precious blood of His Son. The Father wills the complete and unconditional surrender of the Son, His complete and total oblation of self in the name of whole mankind, and this infinite surrender in love of body and soul is consummated by His death on the cross!

- Our Lord's agony in Gethsemane calls for the total submission of Jesus' will with the incomprehensible will of the Father. Jesus must surrender the last drop of his proper will, of self defense.
- In this surrender, the skin and flesh of Our Lord is torn from His Sacred body as He is scourged.

---

[134] *"...behold your Mother."* Jn 19:26-27

- Our Lord becomes the object of diabolical cruelty and mockery as He is crowned with thorns. *"Ecce Homo"* commands Pilate. Our Lord is *"a man despised and rejected."*
- The taking up of His cross and ascent of Golgotha entails an expenditure of His last ounce of strength so as to reach His goal: the consummation of the Father's will.
- In His crucifixion and death, Our Lord not only entrusts His most treasured love on earth, Mary Most Holy, to us, but He must now surrender, "give up," His breath in a most painful suffocation.[135]

Here, the "movement of giving" reaches its zenith: Humanly speaking, there remains nothing ungiven, but His love extends even in death, for in the piercing of His most Sacred Heart, water and blood are given, the church is born in the power of the precious blood and life giving spirit of her Lord! It is Jesus' unconditional abandonment to the will of the Father that will strengthen us whenever we find ourselves in the impossible and incomprehensible will of God. He is the way also for those who have lived before Him. By his descent to the just souls He opens again the doors of "paradise."[136]

The Joyful Mysteries still allow an active participation on our part, but the more we enter the way of the cross, the more the force of the passion of Our Lord has to carry us along. The passion of Our Lord is an irresistible current. It is the current of the victorious love of God!

- The movement of "giving" on the part of the Father has completely taken over in the Glorious Mysteries. God will do All by way of the Holy Spirit. All resistance, the weight of our bodies or our will, has been overcome. It is a movement which

---

[135] cf. *Doctor at Calvary*, an analysis of the death of Jesus based on the studies of the Holy Shroud of Turin

[136] This is the beginning of "purgatory": man recognizing in Christ his real destination is allowed to enter in this way of truth, to be completely purified of the "old Adam."

will free us from the heavy burden of our sins. It can be likened unto purgatory, when the purified soul rises, lifted up by its own desire to join with God for all eternity!

- Resurrection is overcoming the earthly heaviness of our body.
- In ascension we enter into the never ending attraction of God's love.
- The coming down of the Holy Spirit is the gift of the One Who has given Himself up completely!
- Assumption is the promise for our body and the material world to enter in this eternal giving of God.
- Coronation of Mary: creation has found its way back to God, it is found in the eternity of God's life.

In this perspective of giving, the one movement is differentiated by the different degrees of "giving = surrender." As seen, the Joyful Mysteries are more of an active surrender; there is a progressive takeover on the part of God in the Sorrowful Mysteries and finally, it is God alone Who is the surrender in us in the Glorious Mysteries.

The Inter-permeation of the Three Movements

The divine persons are three yet one, and just as their life, love and being are interpermeable, so also are the three movements that come forth from their Godhead.

Joyful Mysteries

The predominant movement in the first Joyful Mystery is the "acceptance" of Mary. She gives her "Yes" to the incomprehensible "offering" of the triune God as "acceptance" to God's merciful Plans of salvation. Her *"fiat mihi"* is a surrender of self and provides the disposition of her being "overshadowed by the Holy Spirit." She receives the Son of God and in return received herself in Him Who is conceived in her womb.

Application:

- We must learn this openness to the Father. We are to rid ourselves of all obstacles and excuses so as to receive the gift of the Father.
- But this gift is not meant to be retained for ourselves; we must give it away again.
- Every giving away opens us for a deeper and fuller receiving. In this way we enter the spiral of the life of God.

There are three parallel steps in the pericope of the Annunciation:

1) The angel is sent to the Virgin Mary; she is silent. She must open her heart to the greater love of God, considering the message of the angel in her heart. With her heart she must look up to the Father.
2) To confirm her surrender she asks: *"How can this be?"* This in relation to the Son Whom she will conceive.
3) Assured that "the promise" will be accomplished in the Holy Spirit, her *Fiat* is consummated.

Although "acceptance" is the predominant movement in the Joyful Mysteries, as we advance, we see Mary having to give away Him Whom she has received. This "acceptance-giving" reaches its climax in the fifth Mystery when she loses her Son in Jerusalem, and then again receives Him. It is the Mystery which already points over to the Sorrowful, where the movement of surrender will reach its climax.

The third movement of "receiving again" will climax in the Glorious Mysteries, but in a hidden way it already permeates into the Sorrowful Mysteries.

In the second Joyful Mystery, Mary is prompt to give away Him Whom she has received, not only to God, but to Elizabeth and her Son's precursor.

In the third Joyful Mystery, Mary receives but at the same time she must surrender herself in complete material and Spiritual poverty, because she is not able to provide anything for the birth of her Son.

In the fourth Joyful Mystery, Mary must offer her Son back to the Father. It is not only a liturgical form, but the expression of this movement of life.

This is visible in the fifth Joyful Mystery when Mary loses her Son and finds Him again more profoundly as the Son of the eternal Father.[137]

Sorrowful Mysteries

The movement of "giving/surrender" is predominant in the Sorrowful Mysteries. In the first Sorrowful Mystery, we see Our Lord's complete surrender to the incomprehensible will of the Father. He is the unblemished Lamb of God Who must be sacrificed to repair the sins of all men. All the attacks of hell fall upon Him. He must receive the painful grace of His Father's will, abandoned not only by His apostles, but seemingly also by His Father. He is only left with the invisible presence of His most faithful disciple, Mary.

He has received His mission from the Father, and now He must return it in the very same Holy Spirit by Whom He has received it. This is so painful, because the devil shows Him clearly that His entire mission apparently was in vain: everyone has abandoned Him, everything He has taught and accomplished, all the miracles He had worked are seemingly for nothing! He is in utter despair. His question, *"Father, why hast Thou abandoned Me?"* is already present in His agony. Yet, as He surrenders Himself, He also receives in the angel's chalice of strength and comfort the grace to continue in fortitude. Here the "movement of "receiving again" penetrates.[138]

In the mystery of the scourging, we witness the Lord giving up His own flesh. His poverty is so complete, that He looses possession of His own body. He gives away His dignity, hiding the Omnipotence of His Godhead, as He allows Himself to be crowned with Thorns. His strength has been so drained that He cannot carry His own cross. (It is also a great act of love on His part to allow the

---

[137] *"Did you not know that I would be in my Father's house?"* (Lk 2:49)
[138] cf. "Rosary of the Agony" at the end of this book.

burden bearers, in the person of Simon of Cyrene, to assist in His sacred ascent of Calvary.) Finally, in all His impotence, He gives Himself to be nailed to the cross, He is crucified amongst two criminals.[139] Most people use less than forty percent of their potential energy. The remaining sixty (plus) percent is wasted, scattered or tossed to the dust of the earth. Our holy angel wants to enkindle a greater generosity of surrender in our hearts so that we will be sufficiently fortified in reaching a complete surrender with Christ in this life. Only then, in absolute abandonment to the divine will, will our earthly purgation be complete, making an immediate entry into heaven at the end of the earthly sojourn assured.

Glorious Mysteries

The movement of "receiving anew" breaks through in the Glorious Mysteries. It is like a great flood or tornado that takes along everything found in its path. *"When I Am lifted up, I will draw all things to Myself."*[140]

In the first Glorious Mystery we see that the ultimate "surrender" of the Son in the Sorrowful Mysteries is reciprocated by a "receiving anew" from the Father. The Introit to the Easter Mass beautifully expresses this with "Admirabilis scientia = admirable science." The more the Father allows our participation in the suffering of His Son, the more He will also teach us of this *"admirable* science" of Resurrection. Together with the Son we will receive new life from Him.

The ascension continues in the movement of "receiving anew," only now it reveals that it is life with the Father for all eternity. As a magnet attracts metal, so also should the cross attract us in the depths of our souls. And as iron filings are attracted to the magnet

---

[139] The mystery of the dolorous passion of Our Lord found its concrete expression in Padre Pio of Pietrelcina. Like Our Lord, and as priest, he gave away his last drop of blood. The stigmata he bore for 50 years disappeared at his death. The wounds closed at his death, because Our Lord lived and completely fulfilled His surrender in the saint. Although he is not officially canonized he is recognized as the "exemplification of the priesthood."

[140] Jn 12:32

in a wondrous order, so also should our lives be ordered by the victorious cross of Our Lord.

We can see its action in the fourth chapter of the Apocalypse: when the seals are opened by the four living beings: the four riders go forth spreading the cross over all creation.[141] Whoever accepts the cross and is ordered by it will find his way to heaven; whoever rejects the cross will fall into darkness and condemnation. We must allow the holy cross to conquer and overcome every "private" sector of our lives. There should be no "private apartment" where God is not welcome. The apocalyptic mission of the trumpets is to wake us up, to shake us in the depths of our being that we stretch open our arms to be crucified! In this way, like the Son, we will find our way to heaven.

We will receive the Holy Spirit if our hearts, like the heart of Our Lady, is pierced by the sword of suffering. In the "folly of the cross," the piercing of our heart is not a losing force, but gaining supernatural force. It is a chalice of strength enabling our participation in the saving of souls from the clutches of the devil. This was the great grace of Padre Pio, that in the Resurrection force of the Holy Spirit, in union with Christ, he was able to save innumerable souls.[142]

The Assumption of Our Lady is an apocalyptic mystery, because it encompasses all of material creation, and demonstrates the repatriation of all material creation! Contrary to the oriental religions which depreciate the body and material creation, we must consistently grow in our appreciation of it. Nothing is purely external. Rubrics and exterior rituals are important in sacred liturgy for

---

[141] Rv 6:1-8 In the end, all creation must be cruciform. The sending out of the angels in the *"four direction of the wind"* (cf. Mt 13:29ff) does not only connote the four directions of the wind in a material sense, but first of all signifies to those who are signed by the cross. Only in this sign the Father will accept us as "sons in His Son"!

[142] It is worthwhile to remember the presence of the two other "movements": we receive our life as a pure gift out of the hands of the Father; in the dolorous passion of the Lord we surrender it again into these same hands; in Resurrection we receive new life by the force of the Holy Spirit; and this only if we remain united with Mary, waiting for this promise of the Father.

the end of assisting a maximum of interior participation. We are worshipping God from the inside out.

The more man is purified the more his exterior face will express an interior reality. At the end of times, the Holy Spirit will bring about the identity of the exterior representation with the interior: the interior and the exterior will be identical. This will be the consummation of "truth" as adequation of word and thing.[143]

"Acceptance" entails passing through the "fire of purification" of the sacred passion, but leads to the beatific vision promised in the "coronation of Mary."

It is then, at the end of the sixth day that we will be invited to participate with Our Lord and heavenly Mother in the wonderful knowledge of God: *"God saw everything He did and it was very good."* (Gen.1:31)

Scholion: "The Discipline of the Cross"

The power of the Spirit is a power of discipline, one that should attract us to Christ's love on the cross. The material aspects of our life should reflect this discipline of Spirit so that "right measure," even in the little things of every day life, be attained. We have much to learn regarding "right measure" and food. Our celebrations of the great feast days have become occasions of good food orgies to the point that our Spirits are smothered, we lose our frail balance as well as the graces particular

---

[143] Lies, especially when we are swept along by our words, do not reflect reality, but change and destroy it. The Holy Spirit is the Spirit of truth, and in the end, all will be found in His truth. Man's efforts to "cover up" his defects are reflected in his extravagant use of cosmetics. He doesn't realize that his efforts to cover up his major defect is an effort to hide from his sin. Everyone presents him or herself as a king or queen, and thinks self better than one's proximate. Death seems to mirror this "lie" and thus becomes the reality man tries to avoid. Many have the corpses of their loved ones painted up so as to appear alive, but we must humbly recognize and accept our being poor sinners and leave it to God to reform our bodies in the power of the Resurrection of Christ.

to the day. Again, it is only by attentive listening to our angel that we can learn right measure.

The Eastern religions are ahead of us with respect to the discipline of food. They distinguish three classes of food. The first is reserved for those who work hard and need heavy food (sole existence in this class stifles the Spirit). The second class of food is neutral. The third class consists in food which helps lift up both body and Spirit. It supplies the body with the necessary energy, but is not a burden to it.

Right measure in food teaches us that our entireties are to be reformed. What may apply to food is also true for anything else "ingested." We are not to burden ourselves with the "thousand things" that are of no use,[144] because indigestion can also be a Spiritual ailment that can bring one to die the "second death."

Our earthly pilgrimage is destined for heaven, but like mountain climbing, we need to "pack lightly" and take along only what is necessary to be able to reach our final goal. The cross (in the vertical beam of discipline) is our secure "landmark" on return to God.

"Tota Pulchra est Maria, et macula originali, non, non est in te..." we sing, because Mary is the perfect and most beautiful example of living completely in the harmony and order of God. This refers to her immaculate soul and body. Bearing the Son of the eternal Father was enough to grant her being assumed into heaven body and soul, but her perfect compliance to the order of the reign of God here on earth is another reason that her most pure body was not subject to corruption.

The coronation of Our Lady as Queen of Heaven and Earth is the final victory of "receiving anew." Mary fully "receives anew" the life she gave away throughout her earthly existence. St. John tells us: *"They will find life, and they will find the fullness of life."*[145]

---

[144] Mt 6:28-34 *"Consider the lilies of the field.... Tomorrow has worries of its own."*
[145] Jn 10:10

The patriarchs who died in the fullness of life also had a presentiment of this "fullness of life." They experienced the riches of life in joy as well as in sorrow. It is a "fullness of life" offered to us in Christ if we persevere to the end. In order to enter this fullness we have to break out of the bourgeois narrowness of a life of "piety" that forgets about the thirst of Our Lord.

The doors and windows, opened wide by Vatican Council II, were left unguarded and unattended. It is not by coincidence that we are experiencing the Spiritual battles St. Paul refers to in his second letter to the Corinthians.[146] To fight well we must learn both strategy and discernment. The Father wants all men to be saved, so we must keep the doors open, but fidelity to Our Lord Jesus Christ on the cross does not condone or grant "everything" a permit of entrance.[147] The first application is to all that is sin in us, and then to all that is sin in the world, remembering always the distinction of St. Augustine: "love the sinner, but hate the sin." The "movements" in the mysteries advance, as if growing in the knowledge of God.

The Forth Meditation:
The Rosary and the Holy Angels

We are not alone in this world. We are not self-sufficient nor is it ours to dispose of material creation according to our human indulgences or lusts. We are part of a threefold creation. Our Lord Jesus Christ is God the Father's gift to mankind. By the Incarnation of Jesus man becomes the "Benjamin" of God's creation, that is: the theme of central importance in creation and salvation history. We must humbly and gratefully accept that we are surrounded on one side by material creation (the visible), and on the other by

---

[146] cf. II Cor 10:4

[147] There is another Trinitarian distinction we should observe:
- The Father speaks to creation: "Become"
- The Son speaks to sin from the cross: "Depart"
- and in the end, the Holy Spirit will speak in the name of the Father and the Son: "Come."

Spiritual creation (the invisible), that of the angels. In reality, God created them first, on the first day. Man was brought forth from the clay of the earth at the end of the sixth day.

The holy rosary has dimensions beyond our human comprehension, but we are called to reach out for its fullness. With each bead, with the assistance of the holy angels and in deeper meditation with Mary, we are to take in all of material creation. We must call out to our own Guardian Angel, St. Gabriel, and all the other holy angels to help dispose us for the reception and incarnation of the word of God in us! *Every* baptized Christian is called to this mystical incarnation of the indwelling presence of the Most Holy Trinity.

The Seven-fold Help of the Holy Angels in Respect to the Incarnation of the Word of God in Our Souls

In view of the Incarnation of His Son, the image of the immaculata was carried in the heart of God from all eternity. The word would encounter something of the immense love of the Father in her Immaculate Heart. In her God would find a worthy dwelling place. The Father eternally begets the word, but in Mary He begets His Son. In the fullness of time, Mary conceives the eternal word of the Father and gives birth to the Only begotten Son of the Eternal Father.[148] The mission of the angels with respect to man and his unique place in salvation, is to prepare man's heart in likeness to the Immaculate Heart of Mary.

- The angels help rid us of attachments which bind us to the earth and our sinful condition. Like the crystalline *"Fiat"* of the Virgin at the Annunciation and incarnation, they help us to give an ever clearer "yes" to the incomprehensible will of God.
- They will assist the birth of the new Man in Christ in us such that we will seek the will of God in all things.

---

[148] cf. Gal 4:4

- Ever more consciously, they will help us give our personal answer of love to God.[149]
- They will make of us a "throne" of God, a living tabernacle like Mary, a place where the Most Holy Trinity can come to dwell.[150]
- They will mediate the Gifts of the Holy Spirit, making us conscious of our royal vocation as Sons of God! We are *"a holy nation, a royal priesthood, a people set apart."*[151]
- They will help us to respond better to all the graces of God's unique love for us.
- They will open our interior eyes for the glory of heaven, and make us forget about the passing pleasure of earthly life and fill us with the joy of the children of God.
- They will bring us deeper into the Loving HEART of the Lord, pulling us higher with them into the eternal adoration, praise and glory of God.

The Rosary: Sign of the Eternal Covenant[152]

Just as the angels were the mediators of the law of God in the Old Covenant on Sinai, and as, in the person of St. Gabriel, an

---

[149] cf. Jn 18:34 Recall Jesus' words to Pontius Pilate: *"Do you say this of yourself or because others have told you!"*

[150] Jn 14:23

[151] cf. Rv 20:6 In the end, by the sacrifice of the cross, we will all be "priests forever" — sacrificed in Christ to the greater glory of the Father!

[152] Here we link up with the first meditation, where we first spoke about the "Rosary as a symbol of the covenant of God with man." In a simpler way this truth is expressed by the image of the rosary as "umbilical cord" or as "climbing rope." As long as we do not let loose, we are unspeakably bound by Mary and the precious blood of her Son to God!

This tie will be even stronger if we pray the rosary with the angels, the mediators from God to man after Jesus Christ and Mary. This is best seen again in the image of the "staircase to heaven."(cf. Gen 28:12)

Remember also the parallel word of the Lord to Nathanael in his vocation. (Jn 1:51) As the angels are intimately related to the salvation of Christ (cf. Mk 1:13) — after the temptation Satan left Him and "angels came to serve Him." (Lk 1:13) and this certainly in a very individual way — we can relate them to the different mysteries of the Rosary as the "steps of the stairway." The "stairway of the angels" is a frequent vision with the saints.

Angel served as the mediator of the new covenant in Christ Our Lord, so also in the end will we experience the angels as the instruments of the justice of God consummating this eternal covenant. The faithful angels passed their trial at the beginning of time. Now, both individually and collectively, we have to decide for or against God. This is the reason why the holy angels want to help us make a mature decision for the greater glory of God. Like theirs, ours also is a decision that must be rooted in the fear of the Lord: *"Who is like unto God!"*

They mediate the theological virtues of faith, hope and love, helping to bind ever firmer our union with the triune life of God received at Baptism. They are not abstract virtues received once, but a very personal expression of God's unique call to each one of us. In Christ Jesus, we see that God is not like the "gods" of other religions. In no way does He resemble the self-sufficiency of earthly dictators. The deepest essence of God is overflowing love, "God is love."[153] It is His nature that He wants to share His love with all His creatures through His Son in the Holy Spirit.

The neo-platonic philosophers already had a clear idea about the necessity of mediation between the one inaccessible God and creation, and this is the idea of mediation with respect to the hierarchy of the holy angels: they are the channels by which the graces of God descend to earth and to men. The angels are not stagnant bystanders of our prayer. It is they who carry our prayers before the throne of God and mediate God's response with special graces unique to our prayer or unique to the mysteries of Our Lord or Our Lady prayed and meditated. Such it is that the rosary is like a luminous chain of mediation from earth to heaven and from heaven to earth, binding together what no man before Christ would ever have thought to be compatible.

[152 (cont.)] (i.e. St. Romuald, the founder of the Monks of Camaldoli) The rosary is to help us to be more in Christ; so if only we "are in Christ" the angels will help us the same as they did with Our Lord. Here the common disbelief in the holy angels is revealed as a lack of union with the Lord!

[153] Jn 4:8

What Christ has done for us in the humility of his Incarnation is a treasure both in the sight of God and with in the church. There is no sin of man, no problem, no tribulation which cannot be counteracted by a mystery of the life, death and Resurrection of the Lord. Through the mediation of the Virgin Mary and holy church God has entrusted these treasures into our hands, and with them we can open the merciful heart of the Father to help us in this vale of tears.

The mysteries of the rosary, representing the infinite number of mysteries of the life of Christ, are all related to the one mystery of the cross. It is only through this mystery that we can enter into their contemplation. Little by little and in like manner, all the moments of our life must be integrated into these sacred mysteries, because Our heavenly Father seeks out the image of His Son. This likeness will only come about in, with and through Mary. It is to this end that the praying of the holy rosary becomes a most effective and transforming prayer. Prayed meditatively and with devotion, trying to relate the events and circumstances of our life with the life of Christ, it is a powerful means of entering deeper into the life of Christ. This is also the means by which we will receive the necessary force and strength to solve our problems as He has solved them on the cross. No one can render greater or more effective help than our own Guardian Angel in establishing these correlations with the life of Christ. He will help us to recognize, incorporate and unite ourselves to Him. In this union with, in, and through Him, our life must become a continual offering to the Father. This is the challenge of our baptism: to be co-priest, co-altar, co-victim with Christ, saying in union with each Holy Mass: *"This is my body... This is my blood...."*

The Fifth Meditation: Interpretation of the Individual Prayers of the Rosary

The Sevenfold Structure of the Our Father

The "Our Father" as "Bread"
in the Hands of the Father

As the Son has become and daily continues to become Bread of Life in the hands of the priest, representing the Father in heaven, so also we, through our continual offering, must become the Bread of Life in Him, for the salvation of the world. This is possible only if, together with our angel, we become one in adoration of God, the way the Angel in Fátima taught the children. For this reason, and before all else, we must pray the Our Father in the Spirit of adoration, contemplation and intercession.

The Three First Words Constitute
The Triple Adoration of God: "Our Father,"

This address in and by the Son should immediately lift our hearts up into the life of God. By and through Christ we really are sons of God, but it is a reality that must become incarnate in a life worthy of the royal vocation — this is best realized in adoration!

"Who Art in Heaven"

Already in Gen.1:1, the word "heaven" is a symbol for the first created world, the angels. Their clear vision allows them to experience, perceive and know things which we poor humans must experience in blind faith, hope and love. Their adoration of God is perfect and therefore their power of prayer is of greater efficacy. They can help us to love and adore "Our Father," rendering a more perfect prayer from us.

"Hallowed be Thy Name"

A perfect praise of God will only come about with the union of the three creations: the material world, man and the angels. This ardent desire to worship God worthy of His dignity is what underlies the use of the best materials for the Eucharistic liturgy. We beautify the church and altar with clean linens and fresh flowers to call in the participation of the material world. By way of our singing we lift up our hearts and souls to unite in the angelic praise of God. *Psallere cum angelis* — to sing with the angels — was the effort and practice of the monks from the earliest centuries. Their conscious orientation should help us to begin, already here on earth, participating in the eternal heavenly liturgy. On the basis of this unity and triple adoration we can genuinely proceed beseeching the sevenfold Bread of Life:

The seven petitions in the Our Father to become "bread"[154] in relation to the "sevens veils" of the Virgin of Guadalupe[155]

1. "Thy kingdom come" — We ask for the bread of salvation so that we ourselves become "bread of salvation" for our brothers.

   Salvation started in the immaculate soul of Mary: likewise the kingdom of God has to begin in the depths of our soul.

2. "Thy will be done on earth as it is in heaven" — We ask for the bread of union of will between God and creature. Meditate how in Mary's most pure body the word has become flesh: God's will must permeate us completely such that it will even become the expression of our body.

3. "Give us this day our daily bread" — We ask for the Bread of Life, for both body and soul. Inner white gown: Nobody is more interested that we receive daily the Bread of Life (the Holy Eucharist) in pureness of heart than our Guardian Angel.

---

[154] Here, "bread" has the symbolic meaning to "take in, to incarnate," the bread becomes part of our flesh (in opposition to "prayer of lips"!).

[155] cf. "A Little Catechism on the Holy Rosary in Relation to the Image of Our Lady of Guadalupe," Appendix. Here we begin with the innermost veil: the Soul of Mary Immaculate.

4. "And forgive us our trespasses" — We ask for the bread of pardon[156] Earth-toned gown: Every day is a combat with sin, we get "dirty," so we need the grace of forgiveness.

5. "As we forgive those who trespass against us" — We ask for the bread of salvation and mercy.
   Turquoise mantle: It is by forgiving that our relations to our neighbor come to order and peace.

6. "And lead us not into temptation," — We ask for the Bread of dark faith. God will not permit to have us tempted above our forces.[157]

   Golden rays: We will be able to resist temptations when we are protected by Our Lady's mantle of rays — symbol of the victory of Christ.

7. "but deliver us from evil" — We ask for the bread of ardent desire.

Clouds: No devil dares to touch the ardent desire of being hidden in the mystery of God, the "burning bush."

Petition	Veil	Bread
1. "Thy kingdom come"	Mary's Soul	of Salvation
2. "Thy will be done on earth as it is in heaven"	Mary's most pure body of union	of will between God and creation
3. "Give us this day our daily bread"	Inner white gown	of life
4. "Forgive us our trespasses..."	Earth-toned gown	of pardon
5. "... as we forgive those who trespass against us"	Turquoise mantle	of salvation and mercy
6. "And lead us not into temptation,"	Mantle of golden rays	of dark faith
7. "but deliver us from evil."	Clouds	of ardent desire

---

[156] Sometimes it is extremely difficult to forgive with one's whole heart, to remove even the last movement of hatred, anger or spirit of revenge.

[157] cf. Jn 1:13

"The Hail Mary as a Triple Address

In the Our Father, the Lord speaks on our behalf. In the Hail Mary, Mary is silent for all of us, but is addressed in a triple way:

by the angel — as a messenger of the promise

"Hail, Mary, full of grace, the Lord is with you!"

by men — as heir of the promise

"Holy Mary, Mother of God, pray for us sinners now and at the hour of our death" — and

by God — as the giver of the promise

"Blessed are you among women" — He addresses Her in a personal way, giving Her the promise: Jesus

At the moment of conception, Mary becomes the bearer of the promise.[158] In her, God addresses Himself to the whole of creation, to all of humanity, to the church, and finally to all souls open to Him, to all who desire to give themselves to Him. In each mystery of the rosary, we see that Mary, always in a different way, carries the life of God for all of us, and then returns it back to God in silence, listening, obedience, poverty, sincerity, and fidelity. She is the mediatrix of all graces!

The Seven Parts of the Hail Mary in Relation to the Seven Gifts of the Holy Spirit and the Image of Our Lady of Guadalupe

1. "Hail Mary, full of grace" — To the depths of her soul, Mary is "full of grace." By the first part of the address of the angel,

---

[158] Mary is honored as conceiving the Son of God in her soul before she actually conceives Him in her body.

Mary is lifted up unto the light of God. More than any other saint, she receives the Gift of Understanding.

2. "the Lord is with you." — As Mary's soul is in her body, even more so is the triune God in her. The second word of the address symbolizes the union of God and man first realized in Mary. Here is concentrated all the wisdom of the love of God.

3. "Blessed are you among women" — Mary is the purest of all women, and is even "purer" than the angels. In the third part of the address, Mary is exalted above all women. It is the counsel of God bidding us to enter with her in this unique grace.

4. "and blessed is the fruit of your womb Jesus" — By way of her Son, she will crush the head of the serpent. The center of the Hail Mary is the Incarnation of the Son of God in the womb of the ever Virgin Mary. This is the science of all sciences. Only in the light of the Incarnation can we understand the deepest mysteries of creation, Redemption and consummation.

This four-fold address of Sts. Gabriel and Elizabeth constitute Mary, the "house" in us, wherein Christ is to grow in age and wisdom before God and man. In the following three parts we plead Our Lady's help and intercession.

5. "Holy Mary, Mother of God," — Our heavenly Mother must hide us under her mantle as in her womb. She is Mother of God and Our Dear Mother in Christ. It is with the Gift of Fortitude that she will bring us forth in a new birth. As the "new Eve" she is to give birth to all those who are to be born in her Son. Being the Immaculata, she does not suffer a physical labor, but she suffers the Spiritual pangs of birth more than any other woman.

Part	Veil	Gift
1. "Hail Mary, full of grace"	Soul	Understanding
2. "The Lord is with you"	Body	Wisdom
3. "Blessed are you among women"	Inner gown	Counsel
4. "and blessed is the fruit of your womb Jesus"	Gown	Knowledge
5. "Holy Mary, Mother of God"	Mantle	Fortitude
6. "Pray for us sinners"	Rays	Fear of the Lord
7. "now and at the hour of our death"	Clouds	Piety

6.   "pray for us sinners" — In her glory she is our most powerful intercessor before God. She intercedes through her Son before the throne of God for us poor sinners, that we will not be lost in the darkness of sin. More than any living creature she had part in the fear of God and knows better than any Saint of the untouchable majesty of God. She helps us avoid sin, recognizing that it is an offense against God's majesty.

7.   "now and at the hour of our death." — She will be present in our last hour and bear us in the mystery of God. It is to our eternal advantage to have Our Lady's intercession, especially at the hour of our death.[159] This last trial of our life will be the real proof of the piety we are called to, but we are not to wait for the last hour of death to begin living it. We must look up to and learn from Our Sorrowful Mother standing beneath the cross of her Son.

One day the rosary will enter into the never ending life of God, and all creation will have returned to God by way of the mysteries

---

[159] Even St. Bernadette was so aware of Our Lady's valued intercession that over and over again she prayed "pray for me a poor sinner, now and at the hour of death." These were her last words.

of life, passion and Resurrection of Our Lord Jesus Christ. This will be the consummation of the salvational work in Christ, when, through and with Mary, full of praise and gratitude, we return to God all the graces which have come to us through her, and in likeness to her seek only to be a channel of His merciful love and glorification.

The Participation of the Angels in the Rosary

The angels have a glorious perspective of the mysteries of the life, passion and Resurrection of Our Lord. With each mystery, the Angel sees the corresponding grace Our Lord has merited by His submission to the will of the Father. Our perspective is more earthly and dolorous, but when we pray the rosary, our perspectives should come together and complement each other for the greater glory of God. The angels can be likened unto a living *sanctus*, and they comport to our *sanctus* the power of their adoration. This is why we should end every mystery with the *sanctus*. In a special way, this grants them the grace of joining us in the Trisagion of the "Glory be to the Father...."

At the end we should pray with them, because it is their earnest desire to intercede on our behalf with the "Holy God, Holy Mighty One, Holy Immortal One, have mercy on us and on the whole world."[160]

Conclusion

"The flower of the rosary"[161] is a life renewed in God in wisdom, beauty and harmony. Suffering is one side, the glory which

---

[160] cf. Chaplet of divine Mercy

[161] Here we link up with the beginning of this book, where we started to speak about the "four steps of construction/growth" in life. (pp. 25) We spoke first about the "root" and then about the "stem" in the similitude to the growth of a tree. Now we come to the last two steps: "blossom" AND "fruit." Again these steps of growth are subdivided in three "virtues."

helps one to suffer is the other. Many times only the outward side of suffering is apparent, the interior side remains hidden. No saint can suffer without the support of the glory of God. The glory is already a fruit of the Resurrection. We could not carry the cross without the power of the Resurrection. We should remember this in all humility. No one is able to go the way of the cross with the Son except in the power of the Resurrection. Only this truth is a truth of the wisdom of God, hidden from the eyes of the world and revealed only to those who take up the cross in Christ!

A life in the rhythm of "accepting, giving away and receiving anew" is being continually renewed in the Spirit as well as in the body. As we approach the end of times, the mysteries of the Resurrection will become more powerful with those who really believe in Christ. Let us remember the saints whose bodies haven't suffered physical corruption. There are many such saints throughout the world. With them incorruption is a sign of a life lived in just measure, giving testimony of the power of the Resurrection of Christ. The face of Bernadette irradiates something of the unspeakable beauty of heaven.

As true flowers of grace, just as Mary was the purest lily ever to blossom on this earth, we should reflect something of the beauty of God. It is thus that we contribute to the glories of Mary here on earth. We should strive for a life of harmony and so be vigorously on guard against any kind of excess. When we work too hard, we lose our stability and fall into disharmony.

Harmony is not, in a bourgeois sense, cutting everything to a middle measure, but trying to keep a balance, living in harmony with the rhythm of God. It is not always in our power, but we should strive to find this balance. (i.e. If we are awoken during the night with the thought to get up and pray, we should first discern if it is prudent. If we have to work hard during the day, it might be a temptation, so praying for five minutes is the best way to discern; if we remain awake for those five minutes, then we should get up, pray, and trust that God will give the strength to fulfill our duties during the day.)

The Fruit of the Rosary

The fruit of the Rosary is Found in the Six Virtues of Our Lady.

The silence of Our Lady is of primary importance, but it is the most difficult to attain. The closer we come to God the more we must bow down in adoring silence before His majesty. First of all, silence means being empty. If we always have something to say, God can't speak to us. With so many prophecies of the "end of times," chastisements and purifications to come, we see that only by shaking up the world can God silence man.

Silence, in the apocalyptic sense, is humbly acknowledging the greater God. No longer will our arguments have value, only our repentance and adoration of God in silence. If we follow the attraction of the Lord from the cross, God will separate us more and more from the turmoil of the world. In the beginning it is a bitter experience, but it will heal us. Out of silence blossoms *listening*. We must learn to listen to our Guardian Angel, who is the first to transmit to us the very personal call of God. We shouldn't expect locutions, visions or extraordinary events; anything extraordinary is still "outward bound." We must learn to hear the quiet, almost imperceptible "voice" of our angel.[162]

"Listening" may be a matter of life or death in the persecution that is to come. The angel can always find an opening even though all the doors have been locked, but if silence isn't found within us, we will be unable to hear or listen to his inspirations. Silence is also a most beautiful virtue in relation to our neighbors; it enables us to be more sensitive to their apparent or even their hidden needs. Our Guardian Angel will teach us to be a visible Guardian Angel for the others!

Listening implies prompt *obedience*. The seer of St. Michael in San Miguel del Milagro received a hard lesson in obedience.[163]

Twice, Diego Lazaro was severely punished because he did not obey. The first time he fell gravely ill and almost died. St. Michael

---

[162] The noise of our modern world with all its machinery is the negative sign of the importance of silence. The devil wants to destroy our sense of hearing. He does it very successfully with our youth. The music of the age is not music, it is noise to throttle the outcry of their conscience. Many of them have this experience: "something is crying, shouting in them," but they are afraid to hear it, so they try to kill it with noise and drugs!

[163] cf. Book III: "The Message of Our Lady of Guadalupe and St. Michael"

the Archangel appeared to him and told him that the cause of his illness was his disobedience. The humble Indian feared making the message known, because he thought that the Spaniards would not believe him. During the second apparition St. Michael again asked Diego Lazaro to go to the authorities with the message about the healing waters, but again he hesitated. He suffered his next chastisement while attending a Holy Mass.[164] The severe beating he received helped him to overcome his fear; he finally obeyed by taking the blessed water to the bishop, and found that the bishop was quite disposed to receive the message. The shepherd children of Fátima also demonstrate a beautiful example of prompt obedience. They had to pass through a crowd of thousands of people, many of whom pleaded favors, but the children clearly understood that their first obligation was to be with Our Lady at twelve o'clock sharp. They always managed to make it to the place on time. We must learn to discern the voice of the angel within us or by a little outward sign. The angel speaks in silence, by signs and by light. Theirs is a world of silence, there is no audible word. If we want to grow closer to them, we must learn their language of light.

The next virtue is *poverty*, primarily spiritual poverty. *Soli Deo* — God alone suffices! Difficult situations are not to be avoided with "Christian white lies." We need only humbly prostrate ourselves before God, confess our sins and admit that in and of ourselves we cannot make it. God would immediately come to our assistance. Unfortunately this is the one solution we shy away from. We continue on with our endless conferences, meetings, programs and plans without ever finding real solutions to our problems. We need dialogue, but particularly in the "vertical," with God!

The virtue of *sincerity* teaches us that we must become as *transparent* as the angels. They are transparent before God, completely empty of self, but full of God, ready to speak in His name without presumption, without cutting off or adding anything of their own.[165] Sincerity helps us to be empty vessels, tubes and

---

[164] At times we also even try escaping our duties with "pious disguises."

[165] In the Old Testament, many times it is difficult to distinguish if God Himself or an angel is speaking. We clearly see a sober completion of mission with St. Gabriel at the Annunciation: after having brought God's message to Mary he leaves.

instruments which allow the grace of God to flow. "Little white lies" are an easy exit out of our difficulties, but they leave a "black mark" on our soul and cut down our willingness to serve God only! The more we add from our purely human part, the more the light of God becomes mixed with the darkness of the one who is a liar from the very beginning. The Holy Spirit is extremely severe regarding the "little lie" of Ananias and Sapphira.[166] The giving of "everything" in the early church sounds horrendous compared to the ten percent tithe today. If we had been the judges of Ananias and Sapphira we would probably excuse them for having given something, but their "something" was not good enough for the Holy Spirit, it was a lie, and they fell dead on the spot because of their sin against sincerity.

The sixth virtue of Our Lady is *fidelity*. This virtue of Our Lady is so urgent today and offers all Christians the opportunity of being great saints. We live in times of continual change. We can even be misled in the church by an undiscerned readiness to adapt to different trends that have nothing to do with Catholicism or Christianity. We have already suffered many fashions[167] in the church and God asks for our faithfulness. In and of ourselves, it seems an impossibility, but God is faithful and on Him we must build.

Helping Construct the New Jerusalem

If we pray the rosary daily, humbly, in union with our Guardian Angel and with all the angels, then together with the angels we participate in the construction of the new Jerusalem. The new Jerusalem will be the union of God with men.[168] God will be with men as the light and the temple. We will enjoy the beatific vision for all

---

[166] cf. Acts 5 — There is no "bargaining" with God. Also Rv 18:11ff — "Commerce" is intimately connected with Babylon, the whore, who has her ships over all the waters. World unity by means of commerce is a reality of our days, tomorrow the antichrist will use this "false unity" to bring his "one world religion": the religion of easy living already prepared by "world commerce"!

[167] Our Lady, speaking to Jacinta, says that there are "no fashions in the church!"

[168] *"I saw a new Jerusalem coming down out of heaven...."* (Rv 21:2) We won't renew the church; God, by way of the holy angels, will do it! This is what the book of Revelations tells us.

eternity, every one united with his angel for all eternity in the praise of God day and night.

Meditating the mysteries of the rosary should help us enter into deeper union with God each day. Being a humble prayer, it is not adequately appreciated in today's world, but in the eyes of God it is a prayer of great value, by way of its mysteries we partake in the life of Christ!

With Mary we meditate and contemplate the life of Christ so that again He is made incarnate in our lives for the salvation of the world. Blessed Elizabeth of the Trinity encourages us to plead the Lord to utilize our bodies as "another body of the Incarnation" allowing Him to mystically continue His life here on earth.

The truths and mysteries of the faith contained in the rosary will be made a reality in our lives in the measure that we truly pray them. Indeed, the rosary holds the means for the church to become "in truth and fullness" the Mystical Body of Christ.

What was once dead through lack of interior participation in the recitation of the rosary will, with the breath of the Holy Spirit, will be given new life: the life of Christ within us.

Let us first of all ask for the grace of the *humility of Mary*. Only that which is humble will be lifted up to God's heart. May the most Holy Virgin with all the holy angels, especially St. Gabriel and the Archangels, help us in this apocalyptic mission for the renewal and final consummation of the church.

Scholion (Example for Unfolding a Mystery)

The Rosary of the Agony of Our Lord

In the love and light of the Holy Spirit each mystery of the holy rosary has an unfolding potential. Each is like a diamond with many facets. The Mystery of the Agony of Our Lord in the garden, for example, can unfold into many new mysteries. The following meditation is one such unfolding prayed on Thursday night. It is prayed with the specific intention of accompanying Our Lord in His abandonment; now suffered in His Mystical Body, most in particular for His priests and those consecrated to Him.

First Mystery: After having celebrated the Pascah, giving His body and blood as Eucharist for the first time,[169] Our Lord leaves the Cenacle and proceeds with the apostles to the Garden of Gethsemane. The apostles sing psalms, but Our Lord is silent and His solemn demeanor begins to disturb their "hallelujahs" and vain hopes of overturning the imposed Roman government. They do not "understand" Him.[170]

Second Mystery: From the eleven apostles, the Lord chooses three to participate in His Agony.[171] It is a grace to be allowed to share in the mystery of the Agony of the Lord. It is not to be taken, only received and then reoffered into the Father's hands through the Son. Participation in the redemptive work is not a personal accomplishment. We are to be prudent about our sacrifice making. Our sacrifice doesn't conquer God, only the sacrifice of His only begotten Son is worthy of His Godhead; we must try to share in His sacrifice. Attentiveness to our angel is the best and surest means of knowing how to enter the sacrifice of the Son. The sacrifice of obedience is of greater value than that of our own choosing, for even satanic cult members have their "sacrifices," which often call for a greater self-denial than Christians are willing to endure. To their great loss, their sacrifices are in vain, for nothing of their practice is found in the will of God. The sacrifice of the Son is part of the incomprehensible "wisdom" of God.

Third Mystery: This mystery depicts right distance. Although three were chosen to participate more intimately in Our Lord's agony,[172] they must yet remain a "stone's throw" from Him.[173] The suffering of Our Lord is a divine mystery, one beyond our human comprehension. The mere taking upon Himself the sins of all mankind, from the beginning to the end of time, would have been enough

---

[169] cf. Mt 26:20-28, Mk 14:18-25 and Lk 22:14-38

[170] cf. Mt 26:30-36, Mk 14:26-31, Lk 22:39-40 and Jn 18:1

[171] cf. Mt 26:37-38, Mk 14:33-34 and Lk 22:40

[172] The three chosen are also the three allowed to witness the raising of Jairus' daughter and Our Lord's transfiguration. Cf. Mk 5:37, Lk 8:51 Mt 17.1, Mk 9:2 and Lk 9:28

[173] cf. Mt 26:39 and Lk 22:41 A group of pious pilgrims once asked Padre Pio to let them share in his suffering. P. Pio smiled at them and then responded: "If you would take only a tiny part of it … you would die right away!"

to kill Him as man, but He is not only man; He is God! The "councel" for us is: if in some way in union with Our Sorrowful Mother we are called to share in His suffering, we should recall that it is first of all He Who suffers in us.

Fourth Mystery: As the Mystery of the Agony unfolds, we find Our Lord pleading with the Father: *"Father, if it be possible, take this chalice from me...."* Jesus does not show us how to escape the cross, He shows us how our submission is perfected when He adds: *"not my will, but Your will be done."*[174] God respects our free will to accept suffering. He will not reject us if we argue with Him in humility. We must *"ask, seek and knock,"* but always submit to His will. This "science" of the cross will always be a science of opposition.

Fifth Mystery: The Lord is completely abandoned by His apostles. Their Spirit is willing, but as Our Lord experiences, their flesh is weak.[175] He is comforted by the angel because He is left alone in His humanity and this battle against the devil and against despair is so great that His humanity reaches its limit of endurance.

The presence of the Father is hidden, because the sins of all humankind cause Him to feel less than human, something the psalm seems to capture: *"I am a worm, not a man."*[176] The justice of God dictates a Redemption by the oblation of a perfect humanity. Christ never loses His Divinity, only humbles Himself, *"becoming of human estate."*[177]

Though Our Lord invites His chosen ones to partake in His passion, *"pray, lest ye enter into temptation,"*[178] He has already told them that He will be betrayed by one of them,[179] and that they will be scandalized and scattered.[180] The chalice of fortitude offered Him by the angel is like an injection of strength to continue

---

[174] Mt 26:39,42 and 44, Mk 14:36, 39, and 41 and Lk 22:42
[175] cf. Mt 26:40-41,43 and 45, Mk 14:37, 40 and 41 and Lk 22:45
[176] Psalm 21:7
[177] Phil 2:7
[178] Mt 26:37,40 and 43 Mk 14:32, 34 and 36 and Lk 22:40 and 46
[179] cf. Mt 26:21, Mk 14:18-21 and Lk 22:21
[180] cf. Mt 26:31 and Mk 14:27

suffering to the utmost. It is a Marian grace because Our Lady keeps vigil with her Son, thus giving us the example of fervent fidelity.[181]

Sixth Mystery: The struggle of Our Lord's prayer is so great that he sweats blood. Here, His precious blood becomes a symbol for His ardent desire to gather all poor sinners into the heart of the Father. If our fear of God were in a just proportion we would have nothing else to fear. It is only then that our intercessory prayer has the potential of liberating souls from the clutches of Satan.

Seventh Mystery: Our Lord is betrayed by the *"kiss of a friend."*[182] Our Lord surrenders to His enemies stretching out His hands to be bound: this is piety: *"there is no greater love than this, to lay down one's life for one's neighbor."*[183]

There is a predominance of the movement of surrender in these seven mysteries, first and foremost to the incomprehensible will of the Father. These mysteries should be prayed and offered in particular for priests, especially for those priests who betray Our Lord, selling Him in exchange for the riches and pleasures of this world.

---

[181] St. Luke's account of the agony in the garden is the only one that recounts the presence of the angel and Our Lord's sweating blood. Unlike Sts. Matthew and John, who were present in the garden, he is the evangelist who writes on Our Lady, and it wouldn't too far from conjecture to infer that her union with her Son allowed her to eyewitness the extremity of His sufferings and assistance by the angel.

[182] Mt 26:47-50, Mk 14:53-45 and Lk 22:47-48

[183] Jn 15:13

The Seven Veils of Our Lady of Guadalupe

Book Two

The Extension of the Cross Over the World

Just as every baptized Christian receives a Guardian Angel as a proof of God's very personal love for him or her, and as a certitude of salvation if one collaborates with the heavenly companion, so also does every Christian nation receive an Angelic Guardian, one who in a very special way expresses the unique God-given mission to that nation. As the "angel of peace" preceded the apparitions of Our Lady of the Rosary to the three shepherd children in Fátima, Portugal, so also did an angel precede the arrival of the "good news" in the pagan nation of Mexico.

The princess sister of Moctezuma, Papantzin, received an angel visitor in a very peculiar way. She was believed to have died, and was already entombed, when the angel came to her in a vision, telling her about the coming of the bearers of the faith in the true God. Valeriano, the author of the Nican Mopohua, the first written relation about the apparition, was her nephew.[1] Here again, the light of God proves itself, breaking forth out of the deepest darkness, which in this case was also present in the family of Moctezuma II, the last "chief" of the Aztecs. The princess had been prepared by

---

[1]   As Valeriano was the "nephew" of both Papantzin and Moctezuma it makes them both hold the position of "aunt" and "uncle," a position which in the Nahua world is of great lineal importance. In the Nahua society, the "uncle" inherited his nephews. In the writings of Sahuagun, the great historian, "uncle" was the most respected expression of honor. "Uncle" is the center and the root of society. Cf. *Mi Nina Duena de Mi Corazon*, pg. 47.

the angel and therefore it is to no wonder that she was amongst the first persons baptized in Anahuac.[2]

We recall that the angel is a pure spirit, a person, the first of God's creation, a species in and of himself with a definitive mission for the glory of God. A person who at all times enjoys the beatific vision even when he is with us as Guardian Angel, having powers and intelligence far beyond that given to man. It is because of God's tremendous love both for them and for us that they touch our lives and become intimately involved in our salvation. Rather than deny them, the wise person cultivates an intimate relationship with his Guardian Angel and with all other angels with whom God may choose to put him in contact either for his own good, or for the good of others, and always for the glory of God.

"Ave Crux Spes Unica"
"Hail Holy Cross Only in You There is Hope"

The Father gives us His Son as Bread of Life
The Son is His word of love to us poor sinners
The Holy Spirit will raise up the sign of the cross
as the sign of victory of the light of God *over all darkness.*[3]

---

[2] This is the name of the valley on the high plain of Mexico where the Aztecs arrived, coming from the North.

[3] The Gospel is essentially a trinitarian message, cf. Book One, not only, as we are inclined to think, simply a message of the word.

The First Four Crusades[4]

Just as Jesus' historical way of the cross is the foundation of all other stations of the cross, so also is "His Crusade" the foundation and basis of all the Crusades. Our Lord did not save us by His thirty hidden years, nor by His three years of public ministry. He redeemed us by His three hours of supplication, agony and death on the cross.

The "Crusade of the apostles" was initially oriented in all directions of the wind, but was only successful in the west. To the east it failed by the closure of China, to the south (Africa) by the counter-attack of the Moslems, and to the north by the eastern division (the Orthodox church) and much later the treason of Protestantism. The "Crusade for the Holy Land," as an attempt to reconquer the lost portions of Palestine, also failed. These crusades gave Catholicism a "military" character and the dynamism of conquest.

The "Crusade of the Spaniards and the Portuguese in the New World" really began with the reconquest of their own peninsula, a land occupied by the Moslems for eight hundred years. Their "Crusade" was both religious and militaristic. They were the only two European nations who took up the mandate of evangelization. More and more, the other nations of Western Europe lost themselves in secular, political and national interests. This is when the "wars between the nations" began, the first apocalyptic sign to be realized, according to St. Matthew 24:7, with respect to the second coming of Christ. The battle against heresy, particularly in Spain, gave rise to the Inquisition and helped to close the door to Protestantism, which took over the greater part of northern Europe. The intimate union of power and cross continued in Iberia until the end of Franco's regime, but in the progressive well-being of the present age, Spain is in danger of losing its religious mission.

---

[4] This is an attempt to better understand the historical/theological background of the apparition of Our Lady of Guadalupe. For more extensive information consult any historical manual on the history of the conquest of Mexico. In the Spanish language we recommend *Flor y Canto del Nacimiento de Mexico*.

The XVIth century in Spain is considered a "golden age" for its literary contributions. Historically, it marked the end of Spain's eight-hundred-years conflict of the Moslem occupation. Military victory became the rampart, but unfortunately, with all its post-war consequences. Even so, religious fervor prevailed in the widespread anarchy and disorder. Religious vocations flourished and with the Carmelite reform, a serious renewal of religious life began. This fervor of faith was also the flame of impetus in bringing the faith to the New World!

The "cradle" for the mission to the New World:
Guadalupe in Estremadura

Enthusiasm, even in matters of faith is not sufficient. Holy ardor needs orientation from above and concretization from below, and the river valley of Guadalupe of Estremadura, Spain, seemed to be the place of realization for these two points of foundation. It was here that a relic statue of Our Lady was miraculously found. According to the legend, the Virgin appeared to a shepherd, Gil Cordero, in 1284. She told him to return to the city, bring the Priests and to dig in the very spot of her apparition. Her sacred image, along with its documentation of authenticity, was found in the very place the Virgin had indicated.

The statue was believed to have been carved by St. John and painted by St. Luke, having been chosen by the latter from amongst his favorites for his tomb in Asia Minor. It was later found and preserved in Constantinople where it is credited with saving the capital of the Roman Empire from an earthquake in 446 AD. In 582 AD it was given to the future Pope Gregory the Great, and then was given by him to a Spanish friend, later known as St. Leandro, Archbishop of Seville. During the reign of Don Rodrigo, 793 AD, in order to protect it from the Moslem invasion, the statue was hidden in the valley of the river of Guadalupe of Estremadura, only to be excavated five hundred years later.

The Moorish translation of Guadalupe is "River of Light"/ "River of love." Considering the deeper significances of this name, as well as the finding of this statue in the hidden valley of Guadalupe, we begin to appreciate the beauty of divine providence in the evangelization and the mission of the New World. Mary is the "river of light and love" through whom we receive the mercy and love of God in the person of her Son. She can be likened unto the spring in the Garden of Eden (cf. Gen 2:6) that gives moisture to the entire garden (this spring of life is sheltered and hidden as if in the cloister, participating in the most sublime union with God). Wherever Mary appears, we can also make a correlation with the "tree of life" that gives its fruit twelve times a year.[5] In the end, her presence in all the places where she has appeared will have penetrated the depths of the earth, bringing about its final transformation into the new Jerusalem.[6]

Three great Spanish monarchs, Alfonso XI, Isabel de Castilla, and Ferdinand and Isabel, all had great devotion to the "Virgin of Guadalupe." The latter couple reunited Spain, when by their marriage, the kingdoms of Aragon and Castilla came together (October, 1469). They were the chosen ones for the financing of the voyages of Christopher Columbus, and thus his discovery of the New World.[7] It's interesting to note that the Portuguese also maintain that the legendary statue was found in a cave in the rocks of Nazaré on the Atlantic coast where King Rodrigo came by on his flight from the Moslems. Here, the name "Nazaré" reminds us that the church first of all starts in the life of the Holy Family, the hid-

---

[5]   cf. Rv 22:2

[6]   We get a beautiful glimpse of this transformation of nature upon her coming to the Hill of Tepeyac. cf. Book III or the Nican Mopohua.

[7]   Spain, with the defeat of the Moslems at Granada, was again a proud nation. It was Queen Isabel who really assisted Columbus in his venture in the New World. This Catholic Queen actually hawked her royal jewels to provision Columbus' journey, but she also asserted that he dedicate his journey and discoveries to the Holy Mother of God. It is for this major reason that Columbus changed the name of his mother ship to Santa Maria ... a name which together with the Pinta and the Niña will serve the deeper essence of God's plan for the New World and the "new evangelization." If we consider the transparent correlation with the Gospel of St. Luke 2:39-56, we begin to appreciate the relation of the inspired action of this holy Queen with the role of Elizabeth (a name which translates to Isabel in Spanish), and the role of Our Lord's "precursor." Isabel lays her entirety at the disposal of the Queen of Heaven, and it is thus that heaven can do "great things" by way of Columbus, namely bring the "good news" to the New World.

den and humble family of Nazareth. Both Guadalupe of Estremadura in Spain and Nazaré in Portugal served as points of departure in the conquest of the New World: although beneath the banner of Mary, it is a conquest in the same military Spirit that had inspired the reconquest of the Iberian Peninsula.

The Discovery of the "New World" by Columbus:

When we consider the names of his three Spanish ships, the "Pinta," the "Niña" and the "Santa Maria," we note a hidden providence with respect to the miraculous image of Our Lady of Guadalupe. The Spanish word "Pinta" is a derivative of the verb "pintar" meaning to "paint;" "Niña" means "young girl" and "Santa Maria" is "Holy Mary." These names, when translated, tell us that God is about to paint the portrait of His most beloved Daughter, Mother and Spouse. Literally these three names say: "He (God) paints the young girl, Holy Mary.[8] This beautiful detail, together with many others,[9] underlines how divine providence used these frail instruments to bring the light of the Gospel to America. Five-Hundred years had passed in 1992 since Christopher Columbus entered the new continent. The Holy Father John Paul II came to Mérida (Yucatan, Mexico) to celebrate this memorable date for the evangelization of the New World.[10]

---

[8] For the Aztec, the verb "to paint" expresses the reality of creating or of causing a thing to be.

[9] If divine Providence had not been with the Spanish adventurers, the conquest of the Aztec kingdom would have been virtually impossible. Moctezama's mortal misinterpretation of the person of Cortéz as the god Quetzacóatl, the help of the only native interpreter Malintzi, the assistance of the Tlaxcaltecas and other Indian tribes, the political difficulties with the rivals of Cortéz always resolved — and many more other "impossibilities" — give a clear testimony, how much heaven was interested in this "enterprise." God soberly reckons with our sins and frailties: did He not deliver Himself in the most cruel hands in the person of His Son! José Guerrero's book is a beautiful exposition of this divine providence on Mexico!

[10] Twenty years after Columbus' arrival in the New World, the Spanish had already fixed installation in the Antilles, the Atlantic Coast from Canada to Argentina was already known, and by "chance" a group of fifteen Spaniards escaped shipwreck and in this way discovered the Mexican coast of Yucatan.

"Conquering" the New World for Faith:

Putting things in their historical perspective,[11] it is easy to see that the "Conquistadores" acted to the best of their knowledge and abilities. With the war against the Moslems over, it is quite natural that the adventure of the New World attracted the adventuring types that the "picaresque novel" portrays. We can compare Columbus and Cortés to the Old Testament figures of Moses and David, but now in the drama of the New World conquest. As they went forth in faith, with a religious ideal, and under the banner of Mary, they knew that there would be no lack of assistance. In the end really, the Virgin took care of everything by her miraculous apparition. In the final battle for the reign of God, she will do the same!

---

[11] This is not the place to enter into the discussion of the historical facts of the "conquista." However we should remember some basic historical facts, briefly exposed in José Guerrero's book: *Flor y Canto*, Libr. Claveria, Mexico D.F., 1990, pp. 21-25. As an extract:

- Fr. Francisco Aguilar, participating in the expedition with Cortés recalls that there were all kind of nations in the "army" of Cortés, except people from Aragon, which at that time was already an organized reign. Spain as a nation, in the literal sense of the word, did not exist, it was only coming to birth by way of Castilia. The political situation of Castilia was chaotic. The "Catholic Kings" were of different reigns which only came together in the person of Carlos I. (We should remember even in our days there is "battle" between different nationalities!)
- Only in one point they came together: they were all Christians, and this in a fanatic, military way they had learned in the fight with the Moslems. The best illustration of this truth is the three first points in the "Spiritual Exercises" of St. Ignatius on " the temporal and eternal king." That the question of "military intervention" in matters of faith was "in the air" is testified by the convocation of a meeting of theologians by the catholic King Fernandez 1512 in Burgos where this matter was openly discussed. Military interventions for taking possession of foreign territory were denied; only in the case of defense should arms be used. But at the same time they underlined the obligation of catholic sovereigns, explicitly recommended by the Holy Father, to evangelize the pagans.

*The Providential Role of St. James the Elder
for the Construction of the Church on the Pillar of Mary*

In his television film "The River of Light," John Bird points out the role of importance of St. James the Elder in the foundation of the church upon Mary. He builds his thesis on the transparent correlation of the Patriarch Jacob being the first to erect an altar for God at Bethel, the Apostle St. James the Elder (a name which is equivalent to the Hebrew Jacob) being the first to erect the first Christian temple in Europe in Zaragoza, Spain, the same St. James as the patron of the first church in Mexico and then again the patron of the church in Medjugorje.

Ordered by his father to search for a wife, Jacob the Patriarch (son of Isaac, the son of Abraham, our father in faith) wrestles with the angel of God throughout the night. Later, in Haran, in his sleep "he saw a ladder standing upon the earth and the top thereof touching heaven: the angels also of God ascending and descending by it, and the Lord leaning upon the ladder saying to him 'I am the Lord God of Abraham thy father and the God of Isaac, the land where in thou sleepest I will give to thee and thy seed.'" (cf.Gen 28:10-22)

This biblical account of Jacob's mission reminds us that it is God Himself Who lays the foundation, and he does it with those who step aside, with those who unconditionally follow the call of God as later on Mary will do for all of us, giving her "yes" to the angel. It is also important to underline that in this first preparation for the later "foundation" of the church, the angels are an integral part, because to them is entrusted "the blood circulation" between God and His creation.

Later, King David is denied by the Prophet Nathan to build a temple for the Lord, because he is a man of action and whose hands are stained with blood. The foundation of the church, already in its preparation in the Old Testament, is first of all a matter of contemplation, and not of action. This is so much more difficult for the modern man to understand, as he proclaims himself the one to build his own world, who will do everything by himself. This fundamental heresy has entered deeply into the church, giving little or no more place to God's action. Man is not able to step aside and let God do the first step. This idea that God is first is emphasized also with Jacob in the statement "that the land wherein thou sleepest, I will give to thee and thy seed."(Gen 28:13) It is in this passive attitude of sleep that this great promise is given to Jacob, that God will be with him on all his ways. This is already pointing out to Mary, who is the only human creature in which all of the plans of God came and will yet come to their consummation.

As related by Maria Agreda, the Spanish mystic, it was because of the utter impotence and desperation of St. James that Our Lady appeared to him in bilocation at the bank of the Ebro River, asking him to build a house for God in this place where she appeared. The angels brought a column of jasper as a foundation stone of this first temple of Christianity in Europe. This is to tell us that God Himself, already revealed at Pentecost, wants to build His church on the "column of Mary." There is no other fundament on earth for His Son as in Mary, with Mary and through Mary. This is something which we have to deeply ponder in our hearts in this time of confusion in the church, that the church will have its fundament in God also in this time, only if we are a hundred percent Marian. Only in this way will the church be able to receive the Lord in its womb when He comes to judge the living and the dead.

The mission of St. James, preparing the way for a church fundamented in Mary, continues in the foundation of the church in Mexico. It is in the first church in Tenochtitlan dedicated to St. James by the Franciscans that Juan Diego receives his catechism and goes to holy Mass. It is here also that the first bishop of Mexico, Juan Zumárraga, after all his hesitations and doubts fall prostrate before the image of Our Lady imprinted on the tilma of Juan Diego, adores the only true God in Jesus Christ.

We recognize the providence of God in this "church fundamented in Mary," in Medjugorje, where again, Our Lady appears in a church dedicated to St. James, one where thousands of souls are reconciled to God by the grace of penitence, the virtue especially related to the Apostle St. James. The seashell is the best symbolic expression of penitence, for it not only symbolizes the unquenchable desire of man for God, but also that the void of his heart can only be filled if God will completely take possession of him. This again is only possible if he will recognize himself before God as a poor sinner.

It is this fundamental idea of penitence related to St. James which the fallen angels try to eliminate in the hearts of the Christians, substituting it for the illusion of "progress." More and more, the desire of man for God has starved in our hearts, no longer leaving any room for the living God. God really has to address Himself to this little remnant of the faithful who respond to the incessant plea of Mary for penitence in all her apparitions. As even the larger majority in the church has lost this treasure, God has no other way than to shake the fundaments of this man-built world in order to give room again to the unconditional "yes" of Mary which in the end will be the consummation of the church in the new Jerusalem.

The call to penitence, transmitted by Mary, is different than the call of the Lord when He came to this earth, because it is the call of a mother who suffers immensely for the sins of her children. This reality of the suffering of Mary is best expressed in Apocalypse 12, where the "woman clothed with the sun" cries out in the pangs of birth. The presence of the passion of Our Lord in Mary is another reality which modern rationalism, even in the church, will not accept. But already in the apparition of Our Lady in Zaragoza, the passion of Our Lord is symbolically present in the jasper column which, as it is believed, is no other than the column to which Our Lord was bound in His flagellation.[12] This same flagellation Mary has suffered together with all the other atrocities of the passion, not stepping away from her first "yes" at the Annunciation. Only by way of this deepest trial of her life has she become Mother of the church and of all mankind, and only by this passion

---

[12] The promise given to St. Peter in Cesarea Phillipi: "Thou art Peter and upon this rock I will build my church and the gates of hell will not prevail over it" must be seen in the context of this pericope to which also belongs the harsh word to Peter: "get behind me Satan, that art a scandal unto me, because you do not think the things of God, but the things of man." (Mt 16:18 and 23) Here we see that the promise is not without condition, there is no rock of the church in St. Peter if he takes the ways of man, he is only rock if he follows the Lord on His way of the cross where only Mary and later St. John kept Him faithful company.

In the new Jerusalem, among the precious stones, the first foundation for the first gate is this mysterious jasper, symbol for a church built on the "fiat" of Mary. As this fiat, which Mary had to continue in the three hours under the cross, is the Spiritual reality of the jasper so also the church of the end of

present in her can she be the unshakable fundament for a church which is called to climb up with the Lord the steep hill of Golgotha.

This reality of Golgotha is also present in the place of apparition, the hill of Tepeyac, even though there she appears as "the glorious woman." She is thus only because she has gone through the pangs of death of Her Son and this is why there cannot be any renewal of the church other than in the passion of Our Lord, which we are only allowed to enter by way of Mary at the hand of our Guardian Angel.

Brief Chronology of the Birth of Mexico and the Apparitions of Our Lady

1325 — The arrival of the Mexicas to Lake Texcoco. The eagle devouring a serpent over a nopal cactus was the sign that made this nomad people settle in the Valley of Anahuac.[13]

1492 — Christopher Columbus arrives at the island of Guanahaní.

1505 — Moctezuma II became the emperor of the Aztec nation: Tenochtitlán was built during his reign.

---

12 (cont.) times has to live it in its integrity, it has to become "jasper," that is, not only "cornerstone," but also stone of contradiction which will smash those who will stand up against it.

Curiously, Gate I, Gate V and Gate X form a triangle. The common idea of this seems to be precisely this so much forgotten idea of penitence. It has three different perspectives according to the three different gates.

- In relation to Gate I it recalls that only by denying ourselves completely do we let God Himself be "cornerstone."
- In relation to Gate V, it recalls to man that we are poor sinners that can be saved only by the greater grace of God.
- In relation to Gate X, that of St. Thomas, the idea of penitence must be directly related to the passion of Our Lord. Only by acknowledging the wounds of Christ, St. Thomas comes to recognize Jesus as "My Lord and God." In this way, St. Thomas represents a church which has lost the deeper understanding of Christ suffering and will find its way back to God only when it will suffer these same wounds as His Mystical Body. This again is a clear demonstration that the consummation of the church can come only by way of the passion of Our Lord mediated by Mary.

13 The eagle was a symbol for their warrior god Huitzilopochtli who had led them here, the serpent was a symbol of his opponent, Quetzacóatl. The nopal cactus is a typical plant of Mexico. The three signs have entered the coat of arms of Mexico.

1509 — Princess Papantzin, sister of Moctezuma, has the vision of the angel with the cross on his forehead announcing the arrival of the "bearers of the true faith."

1519 — February 2, the year "Ce Acatl" for the Aztecs begins (it is the year of Quetzacóatl).

1519 — April 22, Good Friday, Hernán Cortés disembarks on the shores of Antigua, Veracruz. He officially erects the cross on Mexican soil and meets with the chiefs of Cempoala. Moctezuma, yet in Mexico/Tenochtitlán, hears of Cortés' arrival, believes him to be Quetzacóatl, and out of fear sends him a message of welcome accompanied with the flesh of human sacrifice. Naturally, the Spaniards are horrified, and the error, along with the fact that the tribes oppressed by Moctezuma see in him their immediate liberation, make it possible for Cortés to conquer the Aztec nation with a small number of adventurers.

1519 — August 16, Cortés begins his journey to the capital, Tenochtitlán.

1519 — September 23, Victorious entry of the Spaniards to Tlaxcala. The Tlaxcaltecans, those living East of the Great Popocatépetl and Ixtacihuatl, are the first native noblemen to be baptized. In fact, as a group of Spaniards ascended the smoking and trembling Volcano, the Tlaxcaltecans feared that indeed these white men made the "gods" tremble. They would become the most powerful allies in the conquest of Mexico.

1519 — Cortés enters Tenochtitlán on November 8 and is peacefully received by Moctezuma II.

Cortés, even more horrified at the sight of the "slaughter houses" of temples, puts a cruel end to the cruel worship of human sacrifice; his soldiers kill all the pagan priests. Moctezuma is deposed and soon after dies, but an upheaval of the nation causes the Spaniards to be cast out of the city.

1521 — New attacks by the Spaniards assisted by the Tlaxcaltecans; after ninty-three days of defense, the last of the Aztec Emperors, Cuauhtémoc, is captured and with the assistance of their Tlaxcaltecan allies, Tenochtitlán is definitively retaken by the Spaniards.

1522 — Papantzin is baptized Doña Maria, in the parish of Santiago de Tlatelolco. This church of St. James is the same parish where Juan Diego will receive his religious instruction and go to Mass.

Saturday, December 9, dawn, 1531 — on the way to Holy Mass, Juan Diego encounters Our Lady on the hill of Tepeyac. She sends him to the bishop with the request for "a sacred little house."

Saturday, December 9, afternoon, 1531 — Juan Diego returns to Tepeyac to tell Our Lady of his unsuccessful meeting with the bishop. He implores her to chose some one else for the task, but she convinces him of her favor towards him.

Sunday, December 10 — Juan Diego returns to Bishop Juan Zumárraga to beseech him to comply with the Virgin's wish; but after much interrogation, the bishop asks for a "sign." Juan Diego returns to Tepeyac in the afternoon and tells Our Lady of the Bishop's request. Our Lady accepts and tells Juan to return the following day for the requested "sign." Upon reaching his home in Tulpetlac Juan finds his uncle gravely ill and remains nursing him the following day, thus making it impossible for him to keep his "rendezvous" with Our Lady of Guadalupe.

Tuesday, December 12, dawn, 1531 — As the death of Juan Bernardino seems eminent, Juan tries to respond to his last wishes by bringing him a priest. As he approaches Tepeyac, he thinks that he may be detained by the beautiful Lady and decides to go about a different way. His effort of avoidance is shamed when "She who sees everything" comes down the hill to meet him. She consoles him for his concern for his uncle and promises to heal him and then gives him the promised sign, castilian roses, to bring to the bishop. Upon opening his tilma before the bishop the miraculous image of the Virgin appears.

Tuesday, December 12, 1531 — At the same moment the Virgin promises Juan Diego that she will heal his uncle, she herself goes to the death bed of Juan Bernardino and heals him. In this fifth apparition of the Virgin, she entrusts to Juan Bernardino her name, "Tlecuauhtlacupe," with the mission of relaying the same to the bishop.

December 26, 1531 — There is a solemn procession of the image from the cathedral to the first chapel on Tepeyac. During the festivity, an Indian dancer is pierced by an arrow, dies and is miraculously resurrected. This is the first recorded miracle of the Virgin of Guadalupe.

1538 — Eight million are converted during the first seven years following Our Lady's apparition. The real "Guadalupan miracle" is the conversion of an entire nation to the living God.

May 15, 1544 — 84-year-old Juan Bernardino dies in Tulpetlac.

1545 — The "Nican Mopohua," relation of the apparition by Don Valeriano, nephew of Moctezuma, is written.

1548 — 74-year-old Juan Diego dies on Tepeyac. (After the image of Our Lady was first brought to Tepeyac on December 26, 1531, Juan Diego remained on Tepeyac as her sacristan and messenger for the rest of his life.)

1556 — Don Alonso Montufar, second bishop of Mexico constructs the third chapel, where the image of the Virgin stayed for sixty-six years. It is he also who sends a copy of the image of the Virgin of Tepeyac to the King of Spain, who in turn gifts the Admiral, Andrea Doria, to carry it in the naval battle against the Turks. This victorious Battle of Lepanto on October 7 of 1571, with the copy of the image of Our Lady of Guadalupe present at sea, saves Christendom from the Moslem threat. The Holy Father at that time honors Our Lady with the title "Queen of the most Holy Rosary" and adds a new advocation to the Litany of Loretto: "Help of all Christians."

1667 — After the first official inquiry on the apparition of Our Lady of Guadalupe, Pope Clement IX officially decrees the 12th of December as the Feast of Our Lady of Guadalupe.

1754 — Pope Benedict XIV declares Our Lady of Guadalupe as Patroness of Mexico, applying to her the words of Ps. 147, "God has not done such with any other nation."

1810 — Don Miguel Hidalgo, a Catholic priest, uses the image of the Virgin of Tepeyac as the banner in the insurrection against the Spaniards. This is the initiation of the war of independence.

1895 — First papal coronation of the image by Pope Leo XIII (It is he who gives the church the official exorcism prayer of St. Michael the Archangel.)

1910 — The Pope Pius XI declares Our Lady of Guadalupe as the Patroness of Latin America.

1955 — It is officially announced on the radio that one of the figures discovered in the eyes of the image of Our Lady of Guadalupe is Juan Diego.

1976 — Consecration of the new Basilica.

1979 — First papal visit of Pope John Paul II to Mexico.

1990 — Beatification of Juan Diego and the three martyred children of Tlaxcala.

The "Fifth Crusade" and the Mission of Our Lady in the "New Evangelization"[14]

Mary Most Holy, Mother of our America,
by the preaching of the gospel
our people know that they are brothers and
that You are the Immaculate One, "full of grace."
With loving certitude we know
that in your ear is the Annunciation of the angel,
on your lips, the Magnificat,
in your arms, God become a child,
in your heart, the cross of Golgotha,
on your forehead, the light and the fire of the Holy Spirit,
and beneath your feet, the crushed serpent.
Oh Most Holy Mother,
in this hour of the new evangelization,
pray for us to the Redeemer of mankind;

---

[14] *The Seven Veils of Our Lady of Guadalupe* proposes that the term and meaning of "the new evangelization" can only be truly understood if we look up to Our Lady of Guadalupe, for already in 1531 she demonstrates its deepest meaning. The perspective of the seven books is an apocalyptic belief in the universal importance of the apparition of "the woman clothed with the sun and the moon under her feet."

that He save us from sin which so enslaves us;
that we unite by the means of fidelity to the church
and to the shepherds that guide it.
Show your maternal love to the poor,
to those who suffer and to all those who seek
the reign of Your Son.
Animate our strength in building the continent of firm hope,
in truth, justice and love.
We gratefully thank you for the Gift of faith
and together with you we glorify the Father of mercies,
through your Son Jesus, in the Holy Spirit. Amen[15]

The Fifth Crusade has to do with what Our Holy Father John Paul II calls the "new evangelization." Everyone makes reference to it as to some sort of "new" preaching method, but few really understand what this "new evangelization" means. Shortly after becoming pope, John Paul II made his first papal visit to Mexico. He entrusted his papacy to the Virgin of Guadalupe. Had she not been given the title "Help of all Christians," along with the title "Queen of the Rosary," by Pope Pius V after the victory over the Turks at the Battle of Lepanto, where she was also present with Admiral Doria? In this first visit to Mexico, Pope John Paul II epitomizes and gives us a first light as to what "new evangelization" means. By way of Mary all the mysteries of life, passion and Resurrection will come to their fullness.

The "new evangelization" should be a conscious continuation of her mission, which began in 1531, where she first addressed herself to the hearts of the Indians. Through her, with her and by her the word of God, carried by Marian priests, must touch again the hearts of men to bring about the final conversion to the living God. Here already we should throw a first glimpse on Her special messenger, Juan Diego, because responding to this Marian call is a mission which necessarily follows his footsteps. In order to realize His plans, God needs, among men, instruments who correspond to His inscrutable will as perfectly as the holy angels who

---

[15]   This prayer is given us by Pope John Paul II at the initiation of the V Centennial of the Evangelization of the New World.

always hang at the face of God. This instrument, in the case of Mexico, is Juan Diego, a poor Indian who certainly best represents this important nation before the throne of God. One could dare to say that he is like the human Guardian Angel of this nation, corresponding perfectly to the invisible Guardian Angel God has given this nation in order to become "totus tuus."

Mexico at the Threshold of Modern Times

Not far from Mexico City, in the direction of Vera Cruz, in Antigua, where the Spaniards first entered the country, can be found San Miguel del Milagro. It is in the state of Tlaxcala, the smallest province of the United States of Mexico. It is situated opposite the two volcanoes of Popocatépetl and Ixtacihuatl, which are considered to be the geographic symbols of this country.[16]

Its central position can be summarized in a triple yet seven-fold manner:

- The first with respect to Mexico's central position — its "natural cross"
- The second with respect to the country at the "Crossroads of modern times" — its cross in salvation history
- The third in respect to its mission in the "plan of salvation" through Mary and the help of the holy angels — the cross of its mission

In the Nahuatl tongue the word "navel" is part of the word Mexico. This can be explained in a seven-fold manner.[17]

1) In a global perspective, Mexico lies between east and west, between Asia and Europe.

---

[16] They are considered symbols of man and woman and so according to the Aztec idea, a perfect image of Ometéotl who was also, at the same time, male and female.

[17] cf. Book III, The Virgin appearing on the "middle of the moon" — "metzli-xicli-co"

2) Within the continent of America, it also lies in a central position, between North and South America.

3) With respect to the races, it is also a cross between east and west, north and south. The Mother of God appeared as a "Mestiza," and in this manner she closes the gap and links the descendants of Cain and Abel. *"And Cain went out from the presence of the Lord and dwelt in the land of Nod, to the east of Eden."*(Gen 4:16)

4) The Virgin of Guadalupe, appearing in 1531, has become the "center" of this people. Only through her has this people of such diverse backgrounds constituted a nation. She is the point of "crystallization" for Mexico, and this "crystallization" will continue until the entire nation is declared "totally of Mary."

5) By means of the Virgin, Mexico was "born" out of the "modern age," which began with her apparition and coincided with the Reform of Luther in Europe. The "modern age" signifies the beginning of the Spiritual and apocalyptic battle for the reign of God in Jesus Christ!

6) This is what causes Mexico to be eminently "religious" — the esoteric speculators state the very same. Although the Mexicans haven't yet realized the mission which is theirs, the Spiritual battle for this mission already seems to have been won by the enemy. As always, "he has been raised up an hour before" us Christians!

7) An image of this mission is the "child" at the feet of the image representing Juan Diego with his total and complete disposition to the mandate of the Virgin, to carry this "Fifth Gospel" to the world: as "sons in the Son" (a child), in his sacrificed love (red garment) and with the wings of testimony of the angel: through the *"water, the blood and the Spirit!*[18]

---

[18] I Jn 5:6-9

The Beginning of "Modern Times" in Mexico

The prominent sign over Mexico: the "woman clothed with the sun" (Rv 12:1) and the *"countersign"* of the "dragon" (Rv 12:3, 7 & 13): There are three decisive steps of the enemy to prepare the reign of the "dragon":

- In 1317: the "nominalism of Occam,"[19] maintains that the manner in which man names things is purely exterior and artificial. Names are given by mutual agreement; we aren't capable of arriving at a knowledge of reality, and even less of God, the supreme reality! In a certain sense he's right. Sin has marred man's intuitive knowledge, that capacity which the angels yet preserve: "by species!" They can see the reality of this world through the "spiritual image" that God has in His mind. The "Realism of St. Thomas Aquinas," adopted by the church, is the counterpart of nominalism. Knowledge of reality is attained by abstracting from sensible impressions, which in essence is the beginning of all human knowledge. By the effort of his intelligence, man can arrive at the understanding of the spiritual realities of things and thus at least approach the intuitive knowledge of the angels!

  The technological world of today has reached the ultimate consequences of the nominalism of Occam: man builds his "own world" — of skyscrapers, computers, missiles and spaceshuttles, world commerce, and a "world religion" common for all! "Real" is the term given to that which is man-made, fabricated, or produced: in the end, all has to be a "man-made product," including his very being! The idea behind the "self-made man," the "superman" of the Nazi regime, is a pure inspiration of the pride of Lucifer.
- In 1517, the "Protestant reform" of Luther in Europe. By means of this "protest," doubt in matters of faith stand up. Little by little, subjectivity, religious nominalism, corrupts all "security of faith." All becomes relative according to the

---

[19] a Franciscan philosopher

viewpoint of the "spectator!" All of the past and present "Protestant" sects and ideologies are faith substitutes, including the "idealistic German philosophy," springing up from this root.

- In 1717, the first Freemasonry Lodge was founded in Paris by an apostate Cistercian priest. Here the two extremes of rationalism and "illuminism" (esoteric knowledge) come together imperceptibly, preparing the "one world government" we are heading for in our times.

    "Capitalism" and "socialistic communism" are but two sides to the same coin. The plan of the "Illuminati," published at the beginning of this century by Ford, reveals the intentions of the enemy: the progressive domination of the world by the destruction of Christian Europe, the corruption of religion and morality, and extermination of the church. Today, a great part of this infernal plan has been realized.

- In 1917, the October Russian Revolution. It has as its pretext the "reformation of the face of the earth!" From the beginning, the heresies have surged forth from the very "womb of the church." The "mystery of iniquity," already present with Judas, continues, unfolding universal dimensions: the militant denial of God in imitation of Lucifer, the first created angel. It aims at establishing the "reign of anarchy," which is the "human" face of the "reign of Satan," the "prince of this world" as Our Lord Himself refers to him. Today, the devil is unmasked, he works openly, not only having the right of "publicity" but more and more the dominion of the governing bodies of the entire world.

The reaction of the church is late and feeble: with the Thomistic Philosophy (realism), the church maintains that although intellectual work is necessary, it is possible to know reality, and to arrive at a natural knowledge of God. The "counter-reform," fomented by the Council of Trent, defends the "treasure of faith," the Sacraments, and the hierarchical structure of the church against the heresies of Protestantism.

Against "rationalism," which insidiously infiltrated the church (indirectly by the "sciences" and the "arts," which have reanimated

Roman and Greek paganism,)[20] a few "lucid spirits" like Pascal entered the battle, and it was only later that a true defense began. Pope Leo XIII discerned the infernal attack against the church and reminded the faithful of the value of "spiritual arms": prayer of St. Michael and exorcism.[21] St. Pius X[22] unmasked "modernism" and opened the door to frequent and childhood reception of the Holy Eucharist.

In our days communism forced its way into the church with its "liberation theology." We can concretely see the consequence of the "Warsaw Plan" of 1945: "to destroy the church from the inside." Separation and division (sectarianism within the same church), fanaticism, "spiritual and moral liberty," democratization, mysticism, and traditionalism are the "fowl fruits" of the fallen angels. In Mexico, the priest and "national hero" Hidalgo, with his "yell of independence" (and this while offering Holy Mass), started the liberation of the country from the oppressive Spaniards. "Simplification" with the falsification of "historic dates" is part of the strategy of the enemy. We can't deny that oppression, injustice, and brutality existed; it is "Christian realism" to recognize that we live in a world impregnated by sin and that it enters the poorly protected doors of the church.

The Help of St. Michael and of the Angels for this Mission of Mexico in and for the Virgin

Mission and Cross

If we would only realize the desperate state of the church; *"will the Son of man still find faith?"* (cf. Lk 17) and recognize its "babylonic captivity" by the same enemy, then we would understand the im-

---

[20] The "Renaissance" even left its imprint on the "face of the Roman Catholic church" as you can see even in St. Peter's — the representation of the angels is a speaking symbol!

[21] In 1895, Pope Leo XIII authorized the first pontifical coronation of Our Lady of Guadalupe.

[22] Known for his famous "To restore all things in Christ" — "Restaurare Omnia In Christo."

portance of the help of the holy angels in this Spiritual battle in which we presently find ourselves! Just as each of us will one day have to pass crucified through the "narrow door of death," so also must every nation have to give an account for its particular "mission" in God's plan of salvation. Many times, the "special grace" which we receive from God is also our cross. This applies to the individual as well as to the nations, and it's for this same reason that God gives each country a Guardian Angel, to help it in its hidden mission. The enemy, as a Spiritual creature, intuits each man's mission and has the advantage of attacking us even before we are conscious of God's will for us. At least for our benefit, the attacks can serve as a means of waking us up!

Conscience of this Mission

The cross of Mexico's mission is concretely encountered in its modern history. It's curious that a predominantly Catholic country is totally under a "lay" government; up to 1992 the church has been denied its right as a "citizen." Why does God allow the daily burden and suffering of this people? It seems that the Spiritual mission of this country is still hidden.[23] The church has the responsibility of "opening our eyes" for our mission here on the earth! As we haven't yet woken up, the enemy astutely gives us "another mission," not only purely terrestrial, like that of "liberation," but authentically diabolical, one that misguides us, orientating our vocation to this earth and not toward heaven!

"Acceptance in sacrifice," without Christian discernment, already a pagan inheritance, impedes the Mexican people from seeing their mission in the light of God. The enemy has already taken advantage of the "illusion of liberty" in establishing his regime of the minority! Who will open the eyes of the Mexican people so that they see and believe? In a certain way, Mexico can be likened unto the Apostle Thomas, who was last among his brothers to believe in the Resurrection of Jesus; he was only convinced by the pierced limbs and side of Our Lord. Only crucified will it finally recognize its mission in our crucified Lord.

---

[23] Only Concepción Cabrera, "Conchita," seems to have caught a glimpse of Mexico's true mission.

Suffering and Co-redemption in and Through Mary

There is a "sea of suffering" in the country of Mexico, and mostly through the egoistic exploitation of the "few." This sea must be entered into the sea of suffering of the passion of the Lord, because only then will it have Spiritual and redemptive value. The Virgin wishes to harvest this suffering by means of the church, and let us have part as co-redemptorists in this last and most efficacious mission of the church. The devil tries to destroy what little understanding we have of the necessity of uniting our sufferings with those of Christ, denying flatly the necessity of sacrifice with respect to Redemption.

The coming of the Blessed Virgin to Mexico was of deepest consolation to all those who had suffered the base demoralization of the pagan domination. The suffering of our day is no less. Why is it that we hesitate in calling upon her presence and that of St. Michael the Archangel to comfort and fortify us? As Our Lord Jesus Christ was comforted by an angel in His passion, so too can we count on the comfort and assistance of the holy angels, that is, on the condition that we suffer with Him for the salvation of souls! This is the first thing we should understand about this mission of Our Lady of Guadalupe in Mexico: it is a mission for us now, in this very moment of salvation history: God cannot give a greater and more valuable help than that of His Own Mother, "the Queen of Heaven"! We only need to bow down, confess our sins and the help is right at hand!

The Mission of the "Fifth Gospel":
"The Harvest has Begun!"

This mission of suffering, united with that of Christ, explained in the image of the "apocalyptic woman, who suffers labor pains" (cf. Rv 12), is the best preparation and the most solid foundation in announcing the good news that the harvest has begun! The "gathering of flowers"[24] and bringing them to the bishop as proof of the

---

[24] The symbolism of the roses has various dimensions; we will speak about them later on. In the context of "harvest," they signify the souls who have "ripened" in the "winter" of the diabolic occupation of the country (remember the human sacrifices!). The most precious "rose" — also the purest soul — is certainly Juan Diego, the seer.

authenticity of the apparitions is significant for the mission of Mexico in the church and in the world today. By her apparition in the beginning of "modern times," the Virgin announces that the time of the harvest has begun. In the person of St. Michael, appearing 100 years later in Capula, Tlaxcala, the angels are sent to help in the gathering of the harvest!

The Testimony of the Purified Church

Only a church purified to the likeness of the image of the Immaculate Heart of Mary will be able to enter the unmatched battle against the infernal powers which presently occupy the entire earth. In this "way of the cross" with Our Lord Jesus Christ the church will finally be purified from all worldly contagion and will be, by the pure grace of God, that "ideal" church, such that even the most ferocious enemy will "want to see in us"!

As Juan Diego received his mission from the Virgin, on behalf of the Mexican people, so also does Mexico receive its mission of announcing the apocalyptic harvest, in the sign of the "woman clothed with the sun," on behalf of Holy Mother the church. As the Lord tells us in St. John's Gospel, 4:35–36, *"Well I say to you, lift up your eyes and behold that the fields are already white for the harvest. And he who reaps receives a wage, and gathers fruit unto life everlasting, so that the sower and the reaper may rejoice together."* Those whom the Lord sends for this final reaping are only the "apostles of this last time" in union with the holy angels! Thus speaks the Lord to the first "angel of the harvest."[25] *"The harvest is the end of the world, and the reapers are the angels."*[26] We are the "personnel of the earth" (in the airport of life), opening to them entrance so that they may work. The purer the heart, the quicker we are to obedience the easier it is for them to enter, as by way of a "clean landing strip." The

---

[25] Rv 14:15
[26] Matt. 13:39

purity of heart of Juan Diego, Diego Lázaro of Capula, Tlaxcala and of the "remnant" church is like unto the anawim before the first coming of Christ. Only the "pure of heart" will be allowed to enter this final way of the cross for the reign of God beneath the sign of the apocalyptic woman! The promise of Her Immaculate Heart's triumph is the banner under which we have to fight in union with the holy angels. Has it not already opened the doors of Russia? Most Christians today do not even know that she has already accomplished part of Her promise![27]

One reason why we understand so little about the help of the holy angels, is that we have the tendency to look for something extraordinary, as if a lightning bolt from heaven would clear up all our difficulties in a second. On the last day, this lightning will fall on us,[28] as the light of judgment. Heaven still looks for an opening for our deeper conversion. As it is a "silent chance," out of the incomprehensible mercy of God, we must open ourselves and our Spiritual senses so as to recognize it and take advantage of it.

The Apparition of St. Michael in St. Bernabé
— Capula, Tlaxcala 1631

The apparition of St. Michael one hundred years after Our Lady of Guadalupe is another sign that God is sending His heavenly hosts to help complete the work done by Our Lady of Guadalupe in casting out the demons from their most clandestine recesses from

---

[27] We must become more acutely aware of what the "triumph of the Immaculate Heart" really means. Many stagnate themselves, limiting the concept to: "Russia should become Catholic!" It is pharisitical to ask for "extraordinary signs." We must first learn to humbly bow down so as to see things in the light of God and not as we want to see them. God's miracles are not to run over man's free will or decisions. The conquering of man's heart and soul by external stupefying miracles is the tactic of the antichrist, Maitreia.

[28] Mt 24:28 — it will really reveal the deepest darkness — nothing will be hidden any more! We have to confess before Him ... and be saved or condemned for all eternity!

which they continued their malicious activity.[29] The ancient pagan sanctuary of Cacaxtla can be found at a distance of only about 400 yards west of the actual Sanctuary of St. Michael. A tunnel has recently been discovered which leads directly from the place where St. Michael appeared to this pagan "sanctuary," where human sacrifices were offered.[30] Diego Lázaro de San Francisco was the recipient of this 1631 apparition of St. Michael. He was born at the foot of the hill of the present day village of San Miguel del Milagro. As was the custom of his day, he married very young, seventeen. The first apparition took place while he was participating in a Eucharistic procession, in honor of St. Mark, at the parish of Santa María Nativitas, on April 25 of 1631. St. Michael the Archangel spoke to him:

"Know, my son, that I am St. Michael, the Archangel: I come to tell you that it is God's will and mine, that you tell the inhabitants of this village and of its surroundings, that in a ravine, which is made of two hills, and is in front of this place, there can be found a spring of miraculous water for all infirmities. It is the one which is under a big boulder. Do not doubt that which I tell you, nor put aside that which I command you."

---

[29] Again it is help in the sense of "offer of more help," if we only would ask for it. What the Lord has done in this place by St. Michael, he would do anywhere else, if we only would believe in this help and ask for it. In this sense it is an important offer to the New World, to avail itself of the help of the holy angels after having received the immense grace of faith directly out of the hands of the Virgin Mary. As in many other cases the help was taken at the moment, but as in the multitude of heavenly visited sanctuaries, the offer is readily forgotten! Out of every one thousand Christians, "who knows really about the price of faith?" How many are ready to respond like the merchant who finds the "pearl of great price," selling everything else so as to purchase it!

[30] Evidently the place of opposition of St. Michael had something to do with the pagan worship. Maybe it was the place where the victims of sacrifice were kept captive.

Diego remained perplexed and confused after the vision, and reasoning that no one would believe him because of his humble Indian origin, he decided to keep quiet and to forget the mandate. On the eve of May 8, Diego fell deathly ill. His family and friends were gathered about his bed, praying for a happy death, when all of a suddenly a bolt of lightning burst through the window. All but the dying invalid fled for their lives. Diego remained alone to greet the heavenly visitor. For fear that the straw hut was being burnt, his family members waited before they returned to Lázaro's side. When they reentered the hut, they expected to find him dead, but to their surprise he was quite alive and ready to tell about his vision. "Don't be afraid for me, St. Michael has appeared to me and has given me back my health. He took me, I don't know how, to a ravine near here. He went before me taking huge steps. At the ravine he told me:

'Here where I touch with my staff is the fountain which I told you about while you were in procession. You must make it known or you will be gravely punished.

"Then a great light from heaven descended and bathed the place of the spring."

'This light which you have seen descend from heaven is the virtue which God is giving to this spring for the health and healing of all infirmities and necessities. Make it known to all!'"

To prove that the vision wasn't a dream, Diego jumped from his bed, completely cured of his previous state. He made haste to Tlaxcala in hopes of communicating the message of St. Michael to the governor of the Indians. His initial fear was realized when his story was disbelieved and the governor reprimanded him with the stern warning of punishment if he persisted in spreading the account of the vision. Diego was not discouraged by the negative response. His family encouraged him to seek out the gorge of his vision which had been so blessed by St. Michael. The place was a hill parted by a great ravine which the ancient Indians called Tzopilotitlan and Tzopiloatl, the place of the turkey vultures and of the back water. A little beyond the gorge was the place St. Michael had designated with his golden staff. The spring was covered by a huge slab of sod. Diego and his family arrived at the spot. However, all four of them together could not remove the huge slab.

Then from out of nowhere there appeared a handsome young man to offer his assistance. With the visitor's touch, the slab moved with ease. The four of them began to dig, and their efforts were blessed with great joy, for the spring of crystalline water began to well up before their very eyes.

During Holy Mass of November 13 Diego Lázaro had another painful experience. He felt an invisible hand beat him with such force that he left the church doubled over. Once in his small hut St. Michael came for the third time. "Why are you a coward and negligent in fulfilling that which I entrusted to you? Do you wish me to punish you by yet another means for your disobedience? Get up and make known that which I commanded you!"

Diego returned to the place of the spring, filled a container with water from the blessed spring and then took it to the Bishop of Puebla. The bishop listened to his story and promised to investigate the apparition. He furthered decreed that the "blessed water" be distributed among the sick of his household and hospital. All who drank of it recovered their health.

Before the apparitions were officially approved by the church, the local Franciscan priests from Nativitas already considered Diego's account favorably. They referred to the apparitions in their sermons and organized procession to the miraculous fountain. Holy Mass was frequently offered on the sacred grounds. From the beginning, devotees took relics of the sod slab and clay from the spring. The small pieces of earth were sent all over the Spanish Empire. The small cake-like relics were then put into large containers of water and distributed to the sick. The water was used not only for the relief of physical infirmities, but also for Spiritual maladies, including the dispersion of the evil one.[31]

The church made three official investigations of the apparitions in 1632, 1643 and 1676 . The outcome of each investigation was positive. The visitations of St. Michael were approved by Holy Mother church. It was determined that the apparitions were inte-

---

[31] The water has been experienced as being extremely sensitive to the Spiritual order, such that if it isn't respected or used properly it can bring more of a chastisement than an apparent blessing.

rior in nature and that only Diego experienced them. In the three apparitions, with those of the Virgin of Guadalupe and Our Lady of Ocotlán and of St. Michael, curiously, all the seers had the name Diego. It is said that the last three years of Diego Lázaro's life were spent at the spring, completely dedicated to the service of St. Michael. Many say he spent his time serving the sick and crippled who came to the spring in hopes of a cure. He was the first sacristan at the little chapel which was constructed. At the same time, his life of austerity and penitence gave testimony to the veracity of the apparitions.[32]

Summary

The Angel of Portugal, in his second spoken apparition with the children, told them of the "plans of mercy of God on them." Something of this plan of mercy we can also see on Mexico, geographic center of the world and at the crossroads of modern times. Only in this larger perspective on the apparition of Our Lady of Guadalupe can we better intuit something of the apocalyptic dimension of this apparition, underlined by the apparition of St. Michael in San Bernabé, Capula, a hundred years later.

---

[32] The apparition of St. Michael is unique in all of America. Among the other apparitions of the archangel in Europe, it is one of the most well-documented. The fame of this apparition went all over the known world, but naturally first of all to the part of the world under the Spanish domination. Water and mud from the well were sent to many places. The pulpit in the actual sanctuary is a gift from the Philippines in the beginning of the 18th century and is an abiding proof of this statement. The Spiritual presence of St. Michael is today more a provincial phenomenon, even though to the feast of St. Michael in the months September/October thousands of pilgrims are coming, especially from the nearby regions. Its strategic importance for the whole country and all America needs to be "excavated" so as to parallel what is presently being done with the ruins of the old pagan "sanctuary" of Cacaxtla and its surrounding pyramids, insidiously preparing "the return of the gods of Mexico." The present government has fomented more than a thousand excavations of pagan sanctuaries all over the country.

The New Evangelization as "Reform of the Church"

According to the Image of the "Seven Communities of Asia," in the Likeness of the Apparition of the Most Holy Virgin Mary Apoc. 1:20-3:22

The preceding historical outline, together with the following, will help us to understand better about the relation of the apparition of Our Lady of Guadalupe to the Apocalypse of St. John, received while on the island of Patmos. The "Beloved Apostle" is the "faithful one," chosen by the triune God, from all eternity, to be at the foot of the cross. It is there that he receives the Last will and testament of Our Lord, and witnesses with his own eyes, on behalf of all humanity, the consummation of the great sacrifice of the Lamb of God. The words of Our Lord, directed to him and Our Lady,[33] represent his apocalyptic mission with, in and through Mary Immaculate, which permeates time and enters eternity. He is prototype of fidelity to the hearts of Jesus and Mary, "taking Mary into his home," passing with her the remainder of her earthly life in Ephesus. He learned to meditate with her and in her the mystery of the cross as the axis of all human history. This "lesson in wisdom" by Mary, is the fundament for his apocalyptic vision in which he is allowed to see salvation history with the "eye of the eagle."[34]

In order to better understand the trinitarian correlations in this vision of St. John, we will make a triple correlation of the seven communities;[35] with the days of creation, with the seven words of Our Lord on the cross and thirdly with the seven gifts of the Holy Spirit. The works of Most Holy Trinity in creation must be seen in one, but at the same time can be attributed to other persons. In this way the days of creation reflect more the work of the Father, the

---

[33] cf. Jn 19:26-27

[34] Of the four living creatures, it is the clear and farsighted sight of eagle that influences St. John and his scriptural writings.

[35] In a unique way, each of the seven communities is an image of the church for the final times.

seven words of Our Lord, the salvation of the Son and the Gifts of the Holy Spirit the consummating work of the Holy Spirit. This trinitarian relation is a permanent "rhythm" in the whole of the Apocalypse.

The entirety of human history is an act of creation, not only in the beginning and going on unto the end of times, but also in view of salvation by Our Lord Jesus Christ and finally in the consummation of history in the new Jerusalem. The triune God ... *"will make **all** things new."*[36] All material creation, all men, even the hierarchy of the angels will be brought to its ultimate perfection. This is why the "new creation" will be a perfect mirror of the glory of the triune God. God will recognize Himself in this creation, created in view of, redeemed by, and consummated according to the image of His Son by the Holy Spirit.

We should keep this Apocalyptic perspective in mind when we hear about a "new evangelization" in view of the third millennium. It certainly should not be limited to a program elaborated by man, enlightened by the light of the Holy Spirit, but it should correspond to this renewal of all things. This Trinitarian perspective is the necessary correction of all our plans on the renewal of the church. It is not we who will do it, but it is God Who will fulfill this deepest desire of man to come to perfection. This is also why necessarily Mary, as the most perfect creature, will enter into the scene, and first of all as the "apocalyptic woman clothed with the sun," and together with her the holy angels as instruments of the Holy Spirit.

The "seven letters" to the respective Asian communities give us the clearest idea of what Our triune God intends with respect to what we call the "new evangelization." Our only obstacle is not having yet learned the entrance to or the understanding of this last book of the Bible, one which is laden with images, to the degree that our rationalistic mentality necessarily feels lost. This is the first reason why we must learn to "read the images" of the Apocalypse with the eyes of our Guardian Angel.

The seven apocalyptic letters will help us to give a fuller re-

---

[36] Rv 21:5

sponse on our part in view of the apocalyptic times we are living in and so approach more Our Lady "Spouse of the Holy Spirit" who is the patroness of these last times. The image of Our Lady of Guadalupe, is truly "a summary of the Apocalypse" seen in the light of the holy angels in which the church is that of the seven communities of Asia guided and governed by their angels in the breath of the Holy Spirit.[37]

- Each community, judged according to the image of Mary Immaculate, has to give an account for how it has answered the specific call of the Lord. If it does not respond, the angels will take away its "lampstand," for no longer will it be worthy to stand before God.[38] The letters can be likened unto a Magna Charta of the "new evangelization" in view of the renovation of the church in Mary Immaculate.

  "As for the mystery of the seven stars that thou sawest in my right hand, and the seven golden lampstands; the seven stars are the angels of the seven churches, and the seven lampstands are the seven churches."

We must become golden lampstands, reflecting the perfection of heaven. Gold, as we understand from the icons of the orthodox church, symbolizes eternity. St. John's vision gives a true idea of God's will of a final reform of the church in order to represent the perfect beauty of Mary. Anything in the church which is a human by-product will be eliminated. Above the seven Churches are seven

---

[37] Why communities of Asia? The Apocalypse here geographically refers to what we call today the Near East, originally evangelized mainly by St. Paul, but later on lost to the Moslems. This is to symbolically tell us that these communities will have to grow in barren land and probably under persecution (as referred to in the second community). Another perspective of "Asia" is the promise that at the end of time, when the church will live the perfection of love … the multitude of pagans will come in. This is also a promise in the image of Our Lady Guadalupe in her coming from the east and going to the west.

[38] cf. Rv 1:20 and 2:5

stars which the Lord has in His hands. They are symbols of the angels, the faithful and pure servants of God, who, like the stars, helps the mariners orient themselves on the immensity of the seas, and will help us not to lose our way to God. The number seven refers to the Gifts of the Holy Spirit, but is also a symbol of plenitude. Each of the seven communities has to realize its personal vocation in Mary. Only in this way will it become a living reflection of the Most Holy Trinity. Each person, at the latest, the final hour of his or her life, will have to account for his or her unique vocation. We will meet Christ as He lived in us. In Him we will see what we should have become, and by the grace of contrition we will be accepted to purgatory so as to make up for our deficiency.

The seven letters to the seven churches remind us how much God wants to see His image in each man. In this perspective the Apocalypse can be considered the "book of reform of our soul." As all of mankind has to go through this final purification in the fire of the love of God, so also must each soul go this way in order to reach the heavenly gate. If we do not match up to the image of the Lord, as is given to the community, He will not know us! This truth is exemplified in the parable of the last judgment in St. Matthew.[39] In this way, each of the seven letters is also a judgment over the respective community for not answering God's urgent call. Each man is "church," and in this way he has to find himself in one of these seven images in order to concur with the plan of God on his life.

Every letter has these three parts:

- Image of the Son of God corresponding to the particular vocation of this community,
- Praise and reprimand with respect to how it has corresponded to the Son of God,
- and promise of an eternal inheritance.

---

[39]   25:31-46

I. To the Church at Ephesus
(Apoc 2:1-7)

Be Children of Light!

- Day I: the soul created by God is light of the light of God similar to that of the angels. The call of God to each of us individually and then to the whole church is to become "Light"!
- "Father, forgive them...."(Lk 23:34) It is by the passion of the Lord and the force of the Precious Blood that our souls will be washed of all their sins and become again "light" in God. More and more, these first of the last words of Our Lord on the cross must penetrate all those who belong to the community of Ephesus. These words of Jesus must be prayed ever stronger with the heart of Mary; with her, at the foot of the cross, we will again find our vocation. The words of the Son became her own. She could live and relive the sacred passion by living the last will and testament of her Son. Over and over again in Ephesus, she would recall and intercede for all of human kind, pleading with the Father to forgive us for we know not what we do. Mary's heart has the power to bring us back to our "first love."
- Only by the Gift of Understanding, given by the Holy Spirit, are we better able to understand our vocation in the "light of God."

    "To the angel of the church at Ephesus write: Thus says he who holds the seven stars in his right hand, who walks in the midst of the seven golden lampstands."

This community must correspond to the image: The Lord holding the seven stars (angels) in His hands. This is to say: He wants to be recognized as the Lord of the angels. Only if we look up to Him in adoration will we avoid making the church a human invention.

This community is judged first on its positive conduct:

> *"I know thy works and thy labor and thy patience, and that thou can'st not bear evil men; but hast tried them who say they are apostles and are not, and hast found them false. And thou hast patience and hast endured for my name, and hast not grown weary."*

But it is also reprimanded:

> *"But I have this against thee, that thou hast left thy first love. Remember therefore whence thou hast fallen, and repent and do the former works; or else I will come to thee, and will move thy lampstand out of its place, unless thou repentest."*

We yet find another note of positive judgment in verse six:

> *"But thou hast hatest the works of the Nicolaites, which I also hate."*[40]

The threatening of the removal of their lampstand symbolizes that this community is in danger of losing its place in God, falling out of the plan of God. If persecution were to hit this community, the wind would take it away with the chaff.

The following schemes will help the reader understand the deeper correlations present in the meditations, and will also serve as a means for new contemplations.

---

[40] The Nicolaites were a sect.

The Days of Creation

Relation to the Theological and Cardinal Virtues and to the Sacraments of the Church

Day I	Day II	Day III	Day IV	Day V	Day VI	Day VII
Gen 1:3-5	Gen 1:6-8	Gen 1:9-13	Gen 1:14-19	Gen 1:20-23	Gen 1:24-31 & 1:28	Gen 2:1-2
Light/Darkness (creation of the angels - separation of the same)	Water/Air	Earth	Cosmos	Fish/Fowl	Animals/Man	Rest
Hope	Fortitude	Love	Just Measure	Wisdom	Justice	Faith
Baptism	Holy Orders	Confirmation	Holy Eucharist	Matrimony	Penance	Extreme Unction

The Seven Gifts of the Holy Spirit

Day I	Day II	Day III	Day IV	Day V	Day VI	Day VII
Understanding	Wisdom	Counsel	Knowledge	Fortitude	Fear of the Lord	Piety

The Seven Last Words of Our Lord

Day I	Day II	Day III	Day IV	Day V	Day VI	Day VII
Father, forgive them, for they do not know what they are doing! Lk 23:34	Amen I say to thee, this day thou shalt be with me in paradise Lk 23:43	Woman, behold thy son... Behold thy Mother Jn 19:26-27	I thirst! Jn 19:28	My God, my God, why hast thou forsaken me? Mk 15:34, Mt 27:46	Father, into thy hands I commend my spirit. Lk 23:46	It is consummated Jn 19:30

The Seven Communities

Ephesus	Smyrna	Pergamum	Thyatira	Sardis	Philadelphia	Laodicea
Light He who holds the seven stars.	**Eternal Life** The First and the Last	**Word as Sword** The One Who holds the sharp two-edged sword	**Burning Justice** Who has eyes like to a flame of fire	**King of the Angels** He Who has the seven spirits of God.	**The Faithful One** Who has the key of David	**He Who Consumes** The Amen, the faithful and true witness
...works, labor and patience... have endured for My Name	...tribulation and poverty	You are faithful to My Name	...charity, ...faith, ...spirit of service, patience		...guarded My Word	
You have lost your first love		permits false doctrine	permits immorality	reputation of being alive, but is dead		...neither warm nor cold
...to eat of the tree of life.	...not be hurt by the second death	...the hidden manna, ...a white pebble ...a new name	...authority over the nations ...the morning star	...arrayed in white garments, ...name in the Book of Life	Column in the Sanctuary of My God, ...engrave the Name of My God upon him	...seat him beside Me on My throne

How do we then find the place that God has destined? love is the only way. We must have a holy zeal, the kind of zeal that brought the Spaniards to the New World. We must live with the zeal of the saints, because the church of tomorrow calls for Saints (with a capital "S"!) If we aren't or don't become saints we will remain outside, there's no other option! It is for this reason that returning to "our first love" is the most important thing. The angels, having passed the first trial in the beginning of times will help us to this end.

Finally, the letter concludes

"He who has an ear, let him hear what the Spirit says to the Churches; Him who overcomes I will permit to eat of the tree of life, which is in the paradise of my God."

If we are faithful to the call of the Lord then we will receive the reward that He has in store. To eat of the "Tree of Life" is to receive the Most Sacred body of Our Lord Jesus Christ in the Holy Eucharist. In Genesis, man tried to take the fruit of the tree of knowledge, but he was deceived by the devil and his deception brought death to the world. As a remedy the Lord gives us the fruit of the tree of life, which is His very body and blood, because the Holy Eucharist is "the remedy to immortality."

II. To the Church at Smyrna
(Apoc 2:8-11)

"He who perseveres unto the end will be saved"

- Day II: Creation of the two elements: water and air.[41]
- *"This day you will be with Me in paradise."* (Lk 23:43) Our place at the cross should be with the good thief, begging the Lord to remember us in His kingdom. "Paradise" here is not

---

[41] Air is implicitly included by the establishment of the firmament over the waters. The firmament is symbol of the cross and its separating power. The waters below are symbol of creation incapable of ascending.

heaven. It is a symbol for purgatory, where we will be re-formed according to the measure of the cross of the Son.[42] We are offered to have our purgatory here on earth, going the way of the cross so as to fulfill the will of God.

• This community correlates with the Gift of Wisdom resumed in the symbol of the cross. Only those who: "deny themselves and take up the cross" are allowed to follow the Lord on His royal way of the cross. The folly of the cross is the deepest wisdom of heaven, and therefore its learning is a prerequisite for all those who want to enter heaven.

"And to the Angel of the Church at Smyrna write: Thus says the First and the Last, who was dead and is alive:"

This is the image by which this community will be judged: "...who was dead and is alive." Here the call of the Lord to us is of white martyrdom, the daily death to our personal ego and pride and interests. Only if again and again we die to ourselves will we also experience Resurrection.

"I know thy tribulation and thy poverty, but thou art rich; and that thou art slandered by those who say they are Jews and are not, but are a synagogue of Satan."

The Lord blesses their poverty and helps us to understand what it means to be truly rich, for only those who are poor can reflect the riches and wealth of the Lord.

---

[42] One can't live a disorderly life and then go straight to heaven. When the Lord descended into the "bowels of the earth," He opened the door for all in the Old Testament who looked forward to the Redeemer. In this context, "Paradise" is "purgatory," because even if man had not fallen into sin he would have had to pass the narrow door of trials in the same way as did Mary Immaculate. We will also meet the Lord, face to face, in our last hour, and in Him we will recognize all our sins. Hopefully, we will ardently desire to be purified from them and their consequences ... this is the theological meaning of paradise.

We are also surrounded by synagogues of Satan, but we must hear:

> *"Fear none of those things that thou art about to suffer. Behold, the devil is about to cast some of you into prison that you may be tested, and you will have tribulation for ten days."*

We do not find a reprimand directed at this community because it corresponds to that which the Lord wills of it. It bears the life of the Lord. He consoles the community, because it will have to endure more tribulation. The "tribulation of ten days" signifies a suffering that can only be endured in the omnipotence of God. The Lord then gives the counsel:

> *"Be thou faithful unto death, and I will give thee the crown of life."*

In our weakness and decadence we seek out more life, but this life can only be acquired through self-denial and death.

> *"He who has an ear, let him hear what the Spirit says to the churches: He who overcomes shall not be hurt by the second death."*

The second death is condemnation in the Last Judgment. We must take advantage of time for the sake of "life" and not death. In the end, our pietistic masks will be taken away, because they do not emulate life. Already now, we should become crystals reflecting the life of God, not only at the hour of our death, because there is always the danger that the grace of contrition might be found lacking at the last hour.

III. To the Church at Pergamum
(Apoc 2:12-17)

"On this rock I will build My church."[43]

- Day III: the earth, as the fourth element in the creation of this world, is separated from the waters. The firm soil is symbol of the holy church, but also of our unique vocation in the Mystical Body of Christ. If we fulfill it, we can never be lost.
- *"Woman, behold, thy son. Behold thy Mother."* (Jn 19:26-27) The church is our rock in the roaring waters of this world when it reflects its original image, Mary Immaculate. This is why Mary appears in so many places in these end times (a reminder that it is given to her to crush the head of the serpent). Like St. John, if we are truthful, we will we be able to bring Mary into our home. There is a lot of false devotion and piety hidden behind devotion to Mary. Our devotion must be a true devotion like St. John's, who, of the twelve, remained faithful to Christ and to Mary at the foot of the cross and continued to care for her for the rest of her life. True devotion is seen and measured by our readiness to suffer with Christ and to share in His sacrifice. This is the true doctrine which so many have left today, not a doctrine of paper, but it should be a doctrine of life as it is in Mary, who has overcome all heresies by standing under the cross.
- The Gift of Counsel is first of all a light of God on our personal vocation in the reign of God. This same light will help us to find our place in the church, to become a "living stone" for its construction. Any true vocation is necessarily a con-

---

[43] The rock should be understood in a triple way:
- first of all the rock is God Himself.
- Only because Peter has received the light from the Father he is able to recognize in Jesus the Son of God. (Mt 16)
- The third rock for the church of these final times is the help of the holy angels as depicted in the Apocalypse. Their power will overcome the domination of Satan in this world.

fessor of the true doctrine of the church and so also a sword against all heresies which try to tear us away from the true way of salvation.

The image of the Lord for this community is:

"And to the angel of the church at Pergamum write: Thus says he who has the sharp two-edged sword."

signifying that the Lord surely cuts although we may try to hide behind our false piety. He perceives to the depths of our souls.

"I know where thou dwellest, where the throne of Satan is; and thou holdest fast my name and didst not disown my faith, even in the days of Antipas, my faithful witness, who was slain among you where Satan dwells."

Pergamum reflects the world in which we live, dominated by Satan.

"But I have a few things against thee, because thou hast there some who hold the teaching of Balaam, who taught Balak to cast a stumbling-block before the children of Israel, that they might eat and commit fornication."

We don't even have to try and imagine the perversities and immoralities that have entered into the religious realm. Religious prostitution is something that has its roots in pagan practice, and the Jews are not exempt from the infiltrating contamination which threatens the very fibers of the church of our modern age.

"So thou hast also some who hold the teaching of the Nicolaites. In like manner repent, or else I will come to thee quickly, and will fight against them with the sword of my mouth."

The promised reward:

"He who has an ear, let him hear what the Spirit says to the churches: To him who overcomes, I will give the hidden manna, and I will give him a white pebble, and upon

*the pebble a new name written, which no one knows
except him who receives it."*

We receive the "hidden manna" by doing the will of God. The
more we do the will of God, the more our vocation will become
firm, will be a "rock" and so approach the "pebble" with our new
name, representing our mission here on earth.

IV. To the Church at Thyatira
(Apoc 2:18-29)

*"Do not think that I have come to destroy the law and the
Prophets, I have not come to destroy, but to fulfill...."*[44]

- Day IV: Cosmos: The luminaries of the fourth day always have
  been for mankind an indelible sign of the wonderful order of
  creation. Behind the order, we discover the justice of God,
  which gives everything its right place and the right mutual relation, which mankind is losing more and more in the anarchy
  of modern times. But wherever order is lost, the warmth of
  love is lost. This is why we will find our way back to the love
  of God and of neighbor only if God graciously will bestow us
  again with the order of the reign of God.
- *"I thirst."* (Jn 19:38) The thirst of the Lord is not only for
  saving souls from the clutches of Satan, but it is also, and
  first of all, to reestablish the order which has been disturbed
  and sometimes destroyed because of the sin of the fallen angels and man. This "thirst" is most apparent, but at the same
  time veiled, in the presence of Our Lord in the Holy Eucharist. In thousands of tabernacles all over the world He makes
  present His "thirst" for saving our souls into the order of the
  reign of God and to enkindle in generous souls the fire of
  following Him on His way of the cross.
- The Gift of Knowledge is not a worldly science, but a "science" of the cross, which will transform those who turn the

---

[44] cf. Mt 5:17

cross towards themselves.[45] Only by way of the cross will we find our right relation to the only center of our life, which is God. This is why, necessarily, these three entities: the Holy Eucharist, the word of God and the cross, should always be in the center of our Christian life also exteriorly, first of all in our Churches, but also in our homes. By this testimony of life we will help those who are far away from God to find their way back. Our Lady, as the "morning star," formerly indispensable orientation for the mariners on the vastness of the sea, will indicate us the way to the heavenly harbor.

"And to the angel of the church at Thyatira write: Thus says the Son of God, who has eyes like to a flame of fire, and whose feet are like fine brass."

This image of the Lord speaks to us of the penetration of the eyes of the Lord who intuits the deepest recesses of our heart and will set our souls on fire. His fiery eyes will to purify us, already in this life. His feet like fine brass tell us that there is nothing which will resist him.

"I know thy works, thy faith, thy love, thy ministry, thy patience and thy last works, which are more numerous than the former. But I have against thee that thou sufferest the woman Jezebel, who calls herself a prophetess, to teach, and to seduce my servants, to commit fornication, and to eat of things sacrificed to idols."[46]

This community, above all else is judged for its immorality, and like the previous community, for its belief in false doctrines. Our

---

[45] The Latin and the Spanish word for this gift is "ciencia," i.e. science ... not to be confused with the natural sciences. We refer here to the Science of the cross, the knowledge of a right relationship with God.

[46] This community has fostered a Jezebel Spirit, the Spirit of sexual indulgence, of seduction and of immorality. This Spirit brings death to the body, as Jezebel died for her misdeeds. (cf. 2 Kings 9:36-37)

times are filled with false prophets who bring confusion, often in the guise of humanism.[47]

> *"And I gave her time that she might repent, and she does not want to repent of her immorality. Behold, I will cast her upon a bed, and those who commit adultery with her into great tribulation, unless they repent of their deeds. And her children I will strike with death, and all the churches shall know that I am he who searches desires and hearts, and I will give to each of you according to your works. But to you I say, to the rest in Thyatira, as many as do not hold this teaching and do not know the depths of Satan, as they call them, I will not put upon you any other burden."*

The sects offer their followers false wisdom and the promise of hidden and secret "science," such that the many believers, lacking depth and true roots, even in the church, fall "hook, line and sinker" into these pits. The angels will help us to acquire discernment in this time of confusion. Satan is sly and shrewd, offering "subliminal trips" and "out of the body experiences" so much so that the great majority of youth are easy prey to his deceptions.

> *"But that which you have, hold fast till I come."*

We cannot be with Christ and at the same time search for new religious novelties. Once we find a secure road and good rhythm in Christian living, with frequent confession and daily rosary, we should be faithful to it. We needn't chase after new revelations.

---

[47] God has allowed man to unravel many of the secrets of science and medicine. Unfortunately, worldly man has chosen to abuse this knowledge and the medicines and drugs that should be used for healing and growth are allowed to become a tool of Satan. Here again we find the tactic of inverting the poles: actions intrinsically sinful are condoned as enlightened, while those who oppose them are treated with contempt.

> *"And to him who overcomes, and who keeps my works unto the end, I will give authority over the nations. And he shall rule them with a rod of iron, and like the potter's vessel they shall be dashed to pieces, as I also have received from my Father and I will give him the morning star. He who has an ear, let him hear what the Spirit says to the churches."*

The morning star is the symbol for understanding through Mary, a knowledge from on high, because she is the morning star. She is the "Tota Pulchra," the perfectly beautiful One. We too must learn to walk this way of beauty of the Most Holy Virgin for it is she who will triumph over all heresies. Mary should continue to be for us the source of wisdom as she was for the apostles.

V. To the Church at Sardis
(Apoc 3:1-6)

> *"For at the Resurrection they will neither marry nor be given in marriage, but will be as angels of God in heaven"* [48]

- Day V: Fish and fowl. The fish are more prisoners of the element they live in than are the birds, this is why the fish can serve as a symbol of a life more imprisoned and the birds for a life open to the wider horizons. Our Lord, as the King of the angels, as He is presented in this community, soberly reminds us that we cannot orient ourselves only on a purely human social level, but that we have to look up to those first created creatures who represent the Spiritual order of the reign of God. The angels, first of all coordinated to the Holy Spirit are living "in the air" (in the breath) of the Holy Spirit. The

---

[48] Mt 22:30.

Spirit of God is not a Spirit at random, but it is the Spirit of the order represented by the hierarchy of the holy angels.

- *"Eloi, Eloi, lama sabacthani?" "My God, my God, why hast thou forsaken me?"* (Mk 15:34, Mt 27:46) The utter abandonment of Our Lord on the cross, not first His physical suffering, is His deepest passion. Man has gone away so far from God that he has not only forgotten about Him, but also has put himself on the throne of God as was the intention of the first fallen angels. Christ has to suffer by his abandonment the judgment of the Father on human pride and arrogance, to bring back those who are lost in the darkness. Whoever will reach out for this deepest light of Christ will one day be vested with the "white garment" and not be canceled out of the book of life.

- The Gift of Fortitude: Fortitude is not bravery in a human sense, but it is relying on the greater help of God in circumstances where we are at the end of our human forces. We must climb higher (like the birds ascending in the air), in the upward breeze of the Holy Spirit. In a church where the Spirit of sacrifice has been lost there is not even an idea of what fortitude is. It will need purification by persecution to restore the fire of surrender to the Greater God.

> *"And to the angel of the church at Sardis write: Thus says he who has the seven Spirits of God and the seven stars: I know thy works; thou hast the name of being alive, and thou art dead."*

The Lord Himself is with His angels to guide His church on the path of light. There is a perfect parallelism between the "seven Spirits" (representing the angels who govern these communities) and the "seven stars" (representing the communities). This is to remind us that there are not only Guardian Angels for each individual Christian, but also for all the entities of the church which make up its Mystical Body. The holy angels, light from the light of God, are sent to help the church, such that our hearts remain steadfast, detached from all earthly attraction. Here we find a community that looks pious exteriorly, but is dead interiorly because it has lost its orientation to the light of God.

> *"Be watchful and strengthen the things that remain, but which were ready to die. For I do not find thy works complete before my God."*

Many of our churches and cathedrals have become religious museums. They are full of the things of the world, and there is no life of God.

> *"Remember therefore what thou hast received and heard, and observe it and repent. Therefore, if thou wilt not watch, I will come upon thee as a thief, and thou shalt not know at what hour I shall come upon thee. But thou hast a few persons at Sardis who have not defiled their garments (white garment is symbolic of baptismal innocence), and they shall walk with me in white; for they are worthy.*
>
> *"He who overcomes shall be arrayed thus in white garments, and I will not blot his name out of the book of life, but I will confess his name before my Father, and before his angels."*

This is the promise: If we testify on His behalf, He will testify on ours, at our judgment, before the Father. What the Lord asks of this community is to give witness to their faith, to be "confessors"! Becoming a confessor starts with little things in the home. The children bring home pornographic literature and the parents do nothing. Little by little they graduate to films and videos of the same nature and when those don't fill their obsessions they move on to drugs and even suicide. If the parents had nipped the problem in the bud, it would have sufficed to stop it right away. Many things have infiltrated the church, because the priests and the bishops were not responsible, dealing with the problem at the inception. This is why the devil has had free entry at all levels.

VI. To the Church at Philadelphia
(Apoc 3:7-13)

"Do not be afraid, little flock, for it has pleased your Father to give you the kingdom."[49]

- Day VI: creation of animals and finally of the "Benjamin" of creation: Man. Man is meant to become the "crown" of creation, because he is the center between the material and Spiritual creation, partaking of both. This is why the second divine person, in order to bring back creation from the fall of sin, had to incarnate in man. We are not yet at the end of the sixth day, but the effort of hell to destroy man in our days is a clear sign that we are approaching the end. Man can become the "crown" of creation only in intimate union with the two other parts of creation. Instead of exploiting material nature, and despising and forgetting about the angels, which at the end signifies his destruction, he should collaborate with the forces and wealth of nature and with the help of the angels to come closer to the image of God he should bear.

- *"Father, into thy hands I commend my Spirit."* (Lk 23:46) Everyday, the church in the liturgical hour of Complines, repeats praying these four last words of Our Lord on the cross, because she wants to remind us that only by complete surrender we will enter the narrow door of heaven. This is the grace of this sixth community to have faithfully preserved His word. This is also why they will be able to go through "the trial" which will come over the whole world. It's precisely the trial we have entered in our days, marked by the cry of St. Michael: "Who is like unto God!" Only if we surrender body and Spirit into the merciful hands of God are we already here sheltered against the growing confusion and violence of a world governed by the powers of evil.

- The Gift of the Fear of God — With this gift, God will always be first in our hearts, minds and souls. Modern man has lost this precious gift. Soon, God will reveal Himself in His

---

[49] Lk 12:32.

Omnipotence and will demolish the babylonic construction of this modern world if only there is a little flock of the faithful left on the earth, filled with the fear of God, and crying out day and night amidst all tribulations for the justice of God to put an end to the reign of Satan.

"And to the angel of the church at Philadelphia write: Thus says the Holy One, the True One, He Who has the key of David, he who opens and no one shuts and who shuts and no one opens."

We know and understand this power of the church to open and close, to bind and unbind. If we confess, the priest, with the power of "the keys," is able to absolve ours sins. Many times we prepare poorly for the sacrament of penance. Padre Pio sent home those penitents who where not well prepared, to re-examine, repent more fully and then return to the confessional. Here the "key of David" symbolizes the power of Christ Himself to help us out of the prison and slavery which is due to our sins. Church has lost so much of the liberty of the children of God that she finds herself today in a "babylonic captivity" like the Jews after all their infidelities with God. But God's greater grace can open the gate of the prison like He did with St. Peter when he was taken prisoner,[50] but we should not forget that the whole community was praying for his liberation. This is again in our times the obligation of the little faithful flock, symbolized in this community of Philadelphia. As the name signifies, this is also the community where the love of the brother will come to its fullness, because they are first of all full of the love of God (which will help them to overcome the "trial").

"I know thy works. Behold, I have caused a door to be opened before thee which no one can shut, for thou hast scanty strength, and thou hast kept my word and hast not disowned my name."

---

[50] Acts 12:1-11

With this community, the Lord emphasizes that although they have little strength and are despised in the eyes of the world, they have guarded His word.

> *"Behold, I will bring some of the synagogue of Satan who say they are Jews, and are not, but are lying — behold, I will make them come and worship before thy feet. And they shall know that I have loved thee."*

This is the great promise if the church of tomorrow is found in the truth: the Jews will convert in the victorious sign of the cross.[51]

> *"Because thou hast kept the word of my patience, I too will keep thee from the hour of trial, which is about to come upon the whole world to try those who dwell upon the earth."*

That we are already in those times we will see more clearly when the antichrist will present himself to the world as the "true Christ" and will try to destroy the church. Many will follow him, because he proclaims "the right of the world," and this against God.[52]

> *"I come quickly; hold fast what thou hast, that no one receive thy crown. (The crown is symbolic of our vocation) He who overcomes, I will make him a pillar in the temple of my God, and never more shall he go outside."*

Our faith has to be as firm and solid as a column, reflecting the cry of St. Michael, "Who is like unto God!" Only then will we be

---

[51] cf. Rom 9 -11

[52] "The right of the world" comprises a life of comfort, pleasure and unlimited liberty already lived in our times with complete disregard of the commandments of God. This is why the presentation of the antichrist is only a final point to an evolution of mankind ever since the end of the Medieval Age, when man began to take over his own government.

able to withstand persecution, and so become the fundament of a church renewed in the fire of God.

> *"And I will write upon him the name of my God, and the name of the city of my God — the new Jerusalem, which comes down out of heaven from my God — and my new name."*

We can only become columns if we are not only exteriorly carrying the name of God, but if really God lives in us, if we irradiate Him in our actions and build up families in the likeness of the Holy Family. Only by God also will we come to participate in the graces of the new Jerusalem, because we will become "living stones" in its construction. This is the greatest of the promises to the communities.

VII. To the Church at Laodicea
(Apoc 3:14-22)

> *"...but as for seating at My right hand or My left, that is not mine to give, but it belongs to those for whom it has been prepared."*[53]

• Day VII: Rest of God: The rest of God in the "folly of the cross" begins with the passion of Our Lord. The cross was the only place poor mankind offered to Our Lord that he stay with us. This is why, at the end of times, mankind will have no other place to rest in all the travail of chastisement we merit than the cross. According to a charismatic seer, the only secure place for us will be "the shadow of the cross." Whoever will take refuge there is already saved; whoever is outside of this "shadow" is under the curse of God on sin and so is given into the hands of Satan. This is why, soberly, the holy

---

[53] Mk 10:40

church, in Matins, reminds us everyday to struggle "to enter in the rest of God."

- *"It is consummated."* (Jn 19:30) The consummation of the church as the Mystical Body of Christ will come only when the church has equaled the passion of Our Lord, because necessarily "the disciple is not over the master." This is why, at the end, the little flock of the faithful will have to walk up with the Lord the steep hill of Golgotha and suffer with Him His crucifixion.
- The Gift of Piety is almost completely lacking with this community, because it has overlooked the "signs of the times." Like many Christians of today, we are so much blinded by the false lights of human progress (even in the church) that we think that we will go like this forever. This blindness for our actual situation is one of the outstanding symptoms that we have lost the living God. We have put up our "own house of God" where God "is reformed to our image.[54] St. Michael's battle cry reminds us that "true piety" has almost nothing to do with sentiments and emotions, but it is primarily the act of bowing down before God's majesty, recognizing Him as the reality on which the reality of the world is founded.

"Thus says the Amen, the faithful and true witness, who is the beginning of the creation of God."

St. Michael fits the description of the faithful and true witness. His cry was one that hurled the unfaithful host from heaven and opened the beatific vision of God to the good and faithful angels.

"...Who is the beginning of the creation of God."

---

[54] This is one of the blasphemous words of the German philosopher Feuerbach who inverted the word of Genesis: God created man according to His image.

All of creation is in view of Our Lord Jesus Christ and in Him all will come to its fullness.[55]

"I know thy works; thou art neither cold nor hot."

What the church needs are fire souls, like those for whom St. Louis M. Montfort prayed for.[56] This is at least partly the situation of today's church. Life is easy-going, filled with pleasure and party.

"I would that thou wert cold or hot. But because thou art lukewarm, and neither cold nor hot, I am about to vomit thee out of my mouth."

The words of the Apocalypse are not sweet to the hearing. They are direct and to the point.

"...because you say, "I am rich and have grown wealthy and have need of nothing," and dost not know that thou art the wretched and miserable and poor and blind and naked one."

Materially speaking, today's church is rich, but in the eyes of God it is poor and has become a disgrace. Because it seeks the glory of this world it has fallen poor, blind and naked to the Lord. The Lord's reprimand:

"I counsel thee to buy of me gold (symbol of eternity) refined by fire, that you might become rich, and might be clothed in white garments and that the shame of thy nakedness may not appear, and to anoint thy eyes with eye salve that you might see."

---

[55] cf. Col 1:16-17
[56] cf. his prayer asking God for the "apostles of the last times."

Many priests live with their concubines in plain day and are accepted by the congregation as living blameless; the blindness for the true God is more and more apparent. There is no piety without the fire of truth!

> *"As for me, those whom I love I rebuke and chastise. Be earnest therefore and repent. Behold, I stand at the door and knock. If any man listens to my voice and opens the door to me, I will come in to him and will sup with him, and he with me."*

Again, intimacy with God necessarily means, in the light of St. Michael, readiness to serve God unconditionally. It calls for blind faith, hope and love: "the whole man must move at once." This holds true also for piety!

> *"He who overcomes, I will permit him to sit with me upon my throne; as I also have overcome and have sat with my Father on His throne."*

Many times we sing that we are a kingly people and a royal priesthood for the Lord, but what we proclaim with our lips is not witnessed by our lives. If we march with St. Michael, resisting the temptations of the world, then the Lord will sit us with Him on His throne.

> *"He who has an ear, let him hear what the Spirit says to the churches."*

This is the great challenge and call for the church of today and so necessary also for the Mexican church, who had this privilege of the Virgin's constant presence, as well as St. Michael's binding offer of assistance: the great help to those who are willing to awake from their slumber. More than in any other country, God wills to lift up His throne there, but it is a throne that will only rise in the sign of the cross. With God's grace and the intercession of the blood of the martyrs, the Gospel of Our Lord Jesus Christ will reflower and come to fruition. May we never be found lukewarm, because then we are lost. This is why it is good to look up to our Guardian Angel, who is a "fire soul" next to us. Little by little, he will help us overcome the heaviness of this earth and our sins and stretch out with our forces to the holy will of God, Who wants us to be holy as He is holy!

Summary

The seven communities are an x-ray of the church of our days, in seven different perspectives. Whoever is not blind to its reality, will find out that the letters to the communities are the most sober analysis of our present situation. Only two communities: Smyrna and Philadelphia, those under the gifts of wisdom and fear of God, are exempt of reprimand. This again tells us how much we need today these two gifts to understand better the inscrutable ways of God. The Apocalypse is also an examination of conscience for each of us; we will find in the septuple image of the church our own image with its positive and negative traits.

As Our Lady is the primitive image of the church, according to which the church will be reformed in these last times, the Seven communities must also be found in her image of Guadalupe in a symbolical way

We can discover them in a triple way.[57]

- In relation to the Father we can discover them in the seven veils surrounding the mysterious Presence of Our Lord in the womb of Mary.[58]
- In relation to the Son we can see them in the three and six flowers on the gown of Our Lady.
- In relation to the Holy Spirit we can discover them in the constellations represented by the stars on her mantle.

---

[57] Certainly there are more symbolic references to the seven communities. These three are only the most outstanding. We encourage the reader to pray with the seven communities by way of the seven veils of the Virgin of Guadalupe.

[58] cf. Book III for a deeper unfolding of the seven veils.

Ephesus	Smyrna	Pergamum	Thyatira	Sardis	Philadelphia	Laodicea
Light	Life	Order	Burning Justice	Angels	Fidelity	Who like unto God
1. Clouds	Rays	Mantle	Gown	Inner gown	Body	Soul
2. First three flowers[59]	2nd flower	3rd flower	4th flower	5th flower	6th flower	7th flower
3. Virgo Boötes, Comma[60]	Ursa Major, Canis Venatici, Draco	Auriga, Taurus	Orion, Sirius, Procyon	Crux, Hydra, Centaurus	Victima, Libra, Scorpio, Ophiucus	Corona, Gemini, Leo

[59] cf. placement of the large golden flowers, also correlation with "movement of ransom" to be further unfolded in Book IV, pg.11ff
[60] cf. Book IV for a deeper understanding of the constellations and their correspondence with the Image of Our Lady of Guadalupe.

The Four Living Creatures

Spreading the Cross to the Ends of the World (cf. Apoc 6)

The call St. John hears from Heaven[61] is like the sound of a trumpet, opening the way for the apocalyptic message. It comes from "behind," unexpectedly, as the "thief in the night": man must be alert so as to recognize the "time of visitation" (kairos). When the beloved apostle is finally allowed to look up to this vision of the triune God, he falls prostrate at His feet.[62] St. John's experience is one which the whole world will experience when the "seals" are finally broken.

The four living creatures[63] are those who call out for the breaking open of the seals. Through them the Gospel, with the sealed treasures of the suffering of Our Lord Jesus Christ (those reserved for the end times), is meant to extend in the four directions of the wind, over the entire face of the earth. Throughout salvation history and the evangelization of the good news, we recognize unique ways in which the cross "goes out." In the Benedictine way, for example, the cross became the symbol of all order and discipline. For the Franciscans, the cross became the means of recalling the life and passion of Jesus and approximating His life on earth among us. There is a third and apocalyptic way of participation in Christ's passion. It is not a subjective recalling, but the living out of that which the

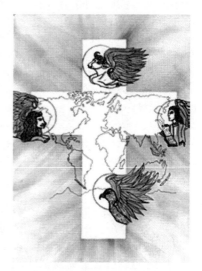

---

[61] cf. Rv 1:10

[62] cf. Rv 1:17

[63] The same to whom we attribute the inspiration of the four evangelists.

four living creatures are doing in the Apocalypse: spreading the cross over the entire world!

Nothing will escape the cross, no one, no material reality, no man nor angel, because the cross is the sign of union and only in the cross will there be consummation. This truth is visually manifest in the image of Our Lady of Guadalupe. The "nahui ollin," the cross flower in the center of the Virgin's image, immediately over her womb, will bring the cross to fruition.[64] It is the promise of heaven of the final victory of Christ, born again in pangs of birth (cf. Rv 12) in His Mystical Body, the church.

When the seals break open, the power of the cross will be released. Its force of thrust will make the entire earth tremble. This Spiritual reality is easily visualized when we consider the extreme pressure and temperatures needed in the production of jewels. Our Lord Jesus Christ, never ceasing to be God, allowed Himself to be pressed down into nothing. The force of compression acquired from His suffering is far greater than that of an atomic explosion. He suffered all torments without opening His mouth, without returning the evil we inflicted on Him.[65] The power of His cross is an accumulative force and treasure which He deigns to open for the church, in the Spiritual combat against the powers of hell.[66]

Unsealing is not only giving free run to the positive force of the Lord's suffering to those who will receive it, it also means unleashing the negative forces of evil. By way of the passion of Our Lord the power of hell has been repressed and withheld. More and more, man leaves the protective power of the cross aside, giving

---

[64] Will be further treated in Books III and IV, cf. any references on Nahui Ollin.

[65] cf. Isaiah 53:1-7

[66] In a very concrete way, we can participate in Christ's Agony and way of the cross by commemorating the hours of His passion. (Thursday night, 9:00 p.m. — Friday afternoon, 3:00 p.m. It is a unique way of the cross with twelve stations extending over the eighteen hours, each station opening a corresponding gate of the new Jerusalem.

free reign to the devil to extend his "cross"[67] of non-submission over the whole earth. More and more, those who love the Lord will gather under the shadow of the cross and those who run away from or fight the cross will suffer the negative consequences of the "unsealing" as the Apocalypse tells us.

Modern man experiences this progressive infiltration and satanic domination of the world; it is the camp of influence of the "first four seals." The three last seals depict the destiny of this unsealing: the destruction of life, except for those who are sealed in the cross.[68]

These are the First Four Seals,
Loosened by the Four Living Beings

The first living creature says:

> *"'Come!' And I saw, and behold a white horse, and he*
> *who was sitting on it had a bow, and there was given him*
> *a crown, and he went forth as a conqueror to conquer."*[69]

He represents all the sins of pride. These are the sins against the Gospel of St. Matthew, orientated to the east, "Soli Deo": "Who is like unto God!" Man's folly is his: "Who is like unto man!" Loosening the seals is a releasing of the power of the cross for those who want to receive it, but it is also an opening of hell and damnation for those who lack the grace of humility. Those who don't reach out in humility will become a victim of their own pride.

---

[67] Already, in Book I, we meditated true opposition as being fundamented in God Himself, and false opposition as revolt, unsubmissiveness and the anarchy which enters the world by the denial of Lucifer to serve the Greater God.

What is true for opposition is also true for the crosses we have to carry. We must learn to discern what is a cross coming pure out of the hands of God (as Francis de Sales describes it beautifully!) and what is a cross we have fabricated ourselves by our sinfulness or negligence. Poor as our fabricated crosses may be, in the cross of Our Lord, they can become instruments of sanctification if we but take them up with contrition and humility!

[68] Rv 6:1-8:1

[69] Rv 6:2

> *"And when he opened the second seal, I heard the sec-
> ond living creature saying, 'Come!' And there went forth
> another horse, a red one; and to him who was sitting on
> it, it was given to take peace from the earth, and that
> men should kill one another, and there was given him a
> great sword."*[70]

The Gospel of St. Mark, reflecting the living creature of the
lion, reveals truth as consuming fire. love and truth can not be separated. With the loss of one there is a consequent loss of the other.
This is the deepest reason of anarchy. Man lacks orientation and
there is massive confusion, at times with the only outlet being the
violence of war. "War" surrounds us on all sides: within us, within
our families, communities, and between nations. The second seal
counsels us to truth. We must bow down before God and adore
Him in silence, only then can we escape the door of violence which
so readily offers a quick solution.

> *"And when he opened the third seal, I heard the third
> living creature saying, 'Come!' And I saw, and behold,
> a black horse, and he who was sitting on it had a bal-
> ance in his hand. And I heard as it were a voice in the
> midst of the four living creatures, saying, 'A measure of
> wheat for a denarius, and three measures of barley for
> a denarius, but do not harm the wine and the oil.'"*[71]

The first consequence of war is the third plague of poverty and
hunger. sacrifice and self-denial are the sure counsel to avoid the
"solution" of violence, when unheeded "sacrifice" is imposed without mercy. Our falling out of God's wisdom is an inexorable consequence of sin. We are already experiencing something of the
plague of poverty and hunger today. Things have become increasingly more expensive. Inflation, often artificially produced, makes
man's misery ripe for other violent "solutions."

There is a way out for those who accept the chastisement of
poverty in humility and contrition, because the wine and the oil

---

[70] Rv 6:3-4
[71] Rv 6:5-6

will not be touched. Both are symbols for the sacraments: the wine for the precious blood, the oil for the healing sacraments. The poverty inflicted upon the church will enable its unity and healing power to grow! The church of tomorrow will be poor exteriorly, like the Israelites in their "exodus" from Egypt, leading a nomadic life, but it will be rich in interior treasures the world will have completely lost.

> *"And when he opened the fourth seal, I heard the voice of the fourth living creature saying 'Come!' And I saw, and behold, a pale-green horse, and he who was sitting on it — his name is Death, and hell was following him. And there was given him power over the four parts of the earth, to kill with the sword, with famine, and with death, and with the beasts of the earth."*[72]

The final consequence of violence is death. Justice is the virtue that we correlate with St. John. If we relinquish the decalogue, the teachings of the church, and do not heed the voice of our Guardian Angel, then we also will die, because hell will spread its confusion over the entire world. This confusion urges modern man to be in constant movement until he reaches a breaking point. Only in this triple obedience can we find the door of life. Our obedience must reflect Our Lord's, He Who was obedient even unto His death on the cross.[73] This obedience will make us "cruciform" — as the Lord, as Our Lady. Before the cross the devil finds himself powerless in his efforts to break us. Even if he were to dare to try, he would fail, because the cross is the sign of victory and therefore of his eternal damnation.

---

[72] Rv 6:6-7

[73] In a very concrete way, we can participate in Christ's Agony and way of the cross by commemorating the hours of His passion. (Thursday night, 9:00 p.m. — Friday afternoon, 3:00 p.m. It is a unique way of the cross with twelve stations which extend over the eighteen hours and every station opens a new gate of the new Jerusalem.

Summary

Where the living being, the Angel, is looking, there is clear sight. There you find the word of God in faith and faithfulness in the beginning as in the end, be it sealed or not. This is where you can rest, if you are tired. Here is your mission to teach, to admonish, to bless. Here the white linen of victory covers the word.

Where the lion is looking, it is bloody red. Here is the wall against the armies of hell. It is there that the word will be proved in blood; there the sacrifice of love and obedience is flaming up. This is where the church has to go its way of the cross. There you find strength. There you have to go to harvest what you have sown. Here the red linen covers the word and thousands are buried under the word." (The word of God is a sword, meant to fight.)

Where the bull is looking, there is the word of separation, the balance of justice. There you find peace and healing, hope and mercy against confusion and the false gods of the world. Keep up the word and conserve it in pureness and humility till the time of judgment. It should be for you prayer and intercession under the black linen of contrition and penitence.

Where the eagle looks, there is the word and the look over time and space, over the earthly and Spiritual hunger, the earthly and Spiritual death, the earthly and Spiritual pestilence, the earthly and angelical war. Over this word the angel will spread the golden linen and the name of God, Who will stand on it, calling the nations from the four directions of the wind. Here you can expect your recompense.

Under you are the reigns of those who wait for your help. You must bring them with you, they have to speak with you: "Here I am Lord." (Isaiah 6:8) And around you are the reigns of decadence, destruction, of trial, of the last time. Collect what is sane, separate what is infected. Work hard! The fields are vast. Over you is the silence of Heaven, holding their breath because the time of trial has come.

A Broader Perspective on the History of America

The Part of the United States in this Mission
A Plan of Mercy for the New World

Recent research has shown that while some historians have tried to write history as purely the achievements of man in relation to his environment and his fellowman, ignoring all Spiritual values and motives, religious historians, through the mercy and light of God and through the obvious help and light of the angels, have given us a more complete picture. The celebration of the fifth centenary of the evangelization of the New World has served as an impulse in the uncovering of the religious histories of all of America, of those countries both to the north and to the south of Mexico. The religious history of these lands, the "Americas," shows that God's dispensation to the New World has truly been through Our Lady and that only in, with and through her can the "New World" reflect God's mercy for these times.

In 1898 a Minnesotan farmer found a stone of great historical interest. The inscription: "Hail Virgin Mary, save us from evil" and the year 1362 on the stone have been carbon-dated as authentic and correspond to a Norwegian historical record. King Magnus of Norway, a Christian, had sent an expedition to what is now northern Minnesota, USA. The expedition sailed into the Hudson Bay, up to the Nelson River to Lake Winnipeg and into the Red River of the north. They encountered difficulties with the Indians and fled, but before leaving, they left a proof of their presence as well as of their faith. The stone has become the oldest historical artifact left by Europeans on the North American continent.[74]

From the beginning, Mary has intervened and shown a special love for the Americas. Some religious historians would propose that God gave the Americas to Mary so as to console her weeping heart. The church, in the onset of the XVI Century, was being shaken to the foundation. She was witnessing the abandonment of the faith all over Europe. Christianity had been blocked to the east by the

---

[74] Cf. article from Caritas

Chinese, the Turks etc., to the north by the developing Russian ideologies, and to the south by more religious wars. It is only logical that the Church's apostolic movement westward, to lands fertile and receptive, would be chosen. The Americas were not only fertile land with material wealth, but God had Spiritually prepared them for just such a moment in history.

In 1492, Columbus, unable to secure funds for his expedition, discouraged, weary and tired, spent the night at the monastery of Our Lady of Arabida. The prior promised him to speak to Queen Isabela on his behalf. (Here began the recorded series of events that would change the world, all through the intervention of Mary, God's Mother and our own Mother.) Despite the strong opposition from her council, Queen Isabela gave her consent on the condition that his voyage be undertaken under the auspices of none other than Our Lady of Guadalupe of Estremudura. Columbus not only consented, but changed the name of his mother ship to "Santa Maria," and had all his men confess and receive Holy Communion in a chapel dedicated to Our Lady. The ship's records show that they sang hymns to the Blessed Virgin every evening and that the first official words uttered in San Salvador after erecting the cross were: "Hail, Holy Queen, Mother of Mercy…," the Salve Regina.

Gratitude for Our Lady's protection caused the Spanish explorers to name many places in her honor: Our Lady of the Sea, Holy Mary of the Immaculate Conception, Star of the Sea, Port Concepcion, etc. They also delighted in teaching the Ave Maria to the Indians. Cabeza de Vaca, of the ill-fated expedition under Panfilo de Narvaez, 1528–1536, writes: "Our method was to bless the sick, breathing on them, and to recite a Pater Noster and an Ave Maria.… In His clemency, God willed that all those for whom we prayed should tell the others that they were sound and in health, directly after we made the sign of the blessed cross over them."[75]

Religious historians are again calling our attention to the names of his ships: The Niña, the Pinta and the Santa María. Some of these scholars join the names to form the phrase: Santa Maria pinta (la)

---

[75] The Narrative of Alvar Núñez Cabeza de Vaca, edited by Frederick W. Hodge. Spanish Explorers in the Southern United States 1528–1543. (New York, 1097), p. 53.

Niña; while others form Pinta la Niña, Santa María. Either arrangement tells us that Mary has been painted for us. Yet for all this, when Columbus discovered America, little did he realize how masterfully the hand of the Father was consummating prophesy. Surely he had not heard of the princess Papantzin's dream and of the Aztec prophesy of the return of Quetzacóatl, dealt with elsewhere in this book.

Juan Diego was an eighteen-year-old pagan when Columbus landed in America. He was in his mid forty's when he saw his first white man. He was turning fifty-one when baptized. Six years later the image of the Virgin of Guadalupe would be miraculously painted on his tilma. Thirty-nine years after Columbus discovered America and ten years after Cortés had captured Mexico, Our Lady was again an active factor in the spread of Christianity in the Americas.

Further north, the English settled the thirteen colonies, which later became the United States of America. At the same time the French settled in Canada, claiming the Mississippi Valley. The French sent out Father Marquette, acting both as a government agent and missionary. He discovered a mighty river which would show up on all maps as the backbone of the United States. He gave it the name: "The River of the Immaculate Conception." Later, however this name was changed to the Mississippi River.

The Spanish and the French, under the banner of Our Lady, went to a large part of the country, preaching to the Indians and spreading Christianity. Many suffered and were martyred. It was the English, however, who gave our country its customs, laws and, for the most part, its language. Sadly, the greater majority were Protestants, and no longer held Mary in their hearts as their Mother. Those few colonists who did were greatly feared and persecuted both by the English and by the Puritan colonists of New England and the Anglicans to the South. This "remnant" banded together to form a colony with a hidden intent. Under the pretext of having chosen it in honor of Queen Henrietta Maria, they named it "Mary"land. Mary had once again claimed the western hemisphere as her own. In Maryland, those English Catholics, who had suffered so much, instituted a policy soon to be followed by the nation as a whole. In Maryland there would be freedom of religion. A century and a half later, Maryland citizens took the leading role in making this tebet a part of the first amendment of the Constitution of the United States of America.

A century later, the nation was immersed in the French and Indian War. The colonists sided with the British, while the Indians and the French fought together. thirteen-hundred British and American troops were headed to Pittsburgh when, seven miles outside the city, they were ambushed by the French. The English and American forces attempted to fight European fashion, while the French and Indians employed guerrilla warfare. The British and Americans lost seven-hundred and fourteen men, and out of eighty-six American and British officers, only one remained on a horse. The French and Indians suffered few casualties.

The only officer left on his horse was a twenty-three-year-old, who the next day wrote to his mother and brother: "…By the all powerful dispensations of Providence (God), I have been protected beyond all human probability or expectation for I had four bullet holes passed through my coat and two horses shot out under me, yet I escaped unhurt, although death was leveling my companions on every side of me…."

In 1770, fifteen years later, this officer returned to this woods with a doctor friend. An old Indian chief, hearing that the officer was returning, traveled a long distance to speak with him. As they sat facing one another over a council fire the latter said: "You don't know me. Fifteen years ago you and I were in these woods, although on different sides. I was the chief in charge of the Indian forces. We saw you riding and knew that you were one of the leaders and if we could kill you we could scatter your men. So I told my braves to single you out and fire at you. I personally shot at you seventeen different times. When we saw that the bullets were having no effect on you, I told my braves to stop shooting at you. I came all this way to meet the man God would not let die in battle."

This young officer was none other than George Washington, the future Father of the United States, and it is evident through his letters and records that the hand of God was upon him and that he responded in kind to God; and that He believed that God had led and built this nation. He believed that it was called to be a Christian nation and that all its laws were to be based on biblical foundations.[76] Henry Knox has said that it was Washington's character,

---

[76]   First Inaugural Address and Farewell Address

and not the recently signed Constitution, that made it possible for the thirteen colonies to unite as one and that it was his cohesive personality that held the newly formed union together.

Washington was not a Catholic and so some may ask what has all this to do with Mary? First, Jesus Himself has said: *"Anyone who is not against us is with us"*(Mk. 9:40). Let us not make the mistake of stereotyping our Christian brothers; many love Mary as much as we do, and some put us to shame, because we are the children to whom so much has been given and we have not known how to appreciate it, let alone be grateful. Mary is Mother to all God's children and is interested equally in all. She loves us all.

In a recent research an incident in Washington's life was discovered that shows decisively just how interested Mary has been in the United States, even from its earliest beginnings. The story was told by Anthony Sherman in 1859 to Wesley Bradshaw and originally published in the *National Tribune*, Volume 4, #12, December 1880. It is all the more remarkable when one considers Washington's dignity, the awe and respect which surrounded him, and his impeccable honesty, which would indicate that he would be little inclined to divulge such an event unless it were fact.

> The last time I saw Anthony Sherman was on the Fourth of July, 1859, in Independence Square. He was then ninety-nine years old, and becoming feeble. But though so old, his dreaming eyes rekindled as he gazed up Independence Hall, which he came to visit once more.
>
> "Let us go into the hall," he said. "I want to tell you an incident in Washington's life — one which no one alive knows except myself; and, if you live, you will before long, see it verified.
>
> "From the opening of the Revolution we experienced all phases of fortune, now good, and now ill, one time victorious and another time conquered. The darkest period we had, I think, was when Washington, after several reverses, retreated to Valley Forge, where he resolved to pass the winter of 1777. Ah! I have often seen the tears course down our dear commander's careworn cheeks, as he would be conversing with con-

fidential officers about the condition of his poor soldiers. You have doubtless heard the story of Washington's going to the thicket to pray. Well, it was not only true, but he used often to pray in secret for aid and comfort from God, the interposition of whose divine Providence brought us safely through the darkest days of tribulation.

"One day — I remember it well — the chilly wind whistled through the leafless trees, though the sky was cloudless and the sun shone brightly. He remained in his quarters nearly all afternoon alone. When he came out I noticed that his face was a shade paler than usual, and there seemed to be something on his mind of more than ordinary importance. Returning just after dark, he dispatched an orderly to the quarters of an officer, who was presently in attendance. After a preliminary conversation of about half an hour, Washington, gazing upon his companion with that strange look of dignity which he alone could command, said:

"'I do not know whether it is owing to the anxiety of my mind, or what, but this afternoon, as I was sitting at this table engaged in preparing a dispatch, something seemed to disturb me. Looking up, I saw standing opposite a singularly beautiful female. So astonished was I, for I had given strict orders not to be disturbed, that it was some moments before I found language to inquire the purpose of her presence.

"'A second, a third, even a fourth time did I repeat my question but received no answer from my mysterious visitor, except a slight raising of her eyes. But this time I felt sensations spreading through me. I would have risen, but the riveted gaze of the being before me rendered volition impossible. I essayed once more to address her, but my tongue had become useless. Even though I thought it had become paralyzed. A new influence, mysterious, potent, irresistible, took possession of me. All I could do was to gaze steadily, vacantly at my unknown visitor. Gradually the surrounding atmosphere filled with sensations and grew luminous. Everything about me seemed to rarefy, the mysterious visitor herself becoming more airy and yet more distinct to my sight than before. I now began to feel as one dying, or rather to experience the sensation which I have sometimes imagined accompanies dissolution. I did not think, I did not reason, I did not move. All alike, were impossible. I was conscious only of gazing fixedly, vacantly, at my companion.

"'Presently I heard a voice say, *"Son of the Republic, look and learn!"* while at the same time my visitor extended her arm eastwardly. I looked and beheld a heavy white vapor rising, at some distance, fold upon fold. This gradually dissipated, and I looked upon a strange scene. Before my eyes lay spread out in one vast plain all the countries of the world — Europe, Asia, Africa, and America. I saw rolling and tossing between Europe and America, the billows of the Atlantic Ocean, and between America and Asia lay the Pacific. *"Son of the Republic,"* said the mysterious voice as before, *"look and learn."*

"'At that moment I beheld a dark, shadowy being, like an angel, standing, or rather floating in mid air between Europe and America. Dipping water out of the ocean with his right hand, he cast it upon America, while that in his left hand went upon the European countries. Immediately a cloud rose from these countries, and joined in mid ocean. For a while, it remained stationary, and then it moved slowly westward, until it enveloped America in its folds. Sharp flashes of lightning gleamed through at intervals; and I heard the smothered groans of the American people. A second time the angel dipped water from the ocean and sprinkled it as before. The dark cloud was then drawn back to the ocean, in whose heaving billows it sank from view. A third time I heard the mysterious voice say, *"Son of the Republic, look and learn."*

"'I cast my eyes upon America and beheld villages, towns and cities springing up one after another until the whole land, from the Atlantic to the Pacific, was dotted with them. Again I heard the voice say, *"Son of the Republic, the end of the century cometh. Look and learn."*

"'And with this the dark, shadowy figure turned its face southward, and from Africa an ill-omened specter approached our land.

"'It flitted slowly over every town and city of the land. The inhabitants presently set themselves in battle array against each other. As I continued to look I saw a bright angel, on whose brow rested a crown of light on which was traced the word 'Union', place an American flag between the divided nation, and say, *"Remember, ye are brethren."* Instantly, the inhabitants, casting from them their weapons, became friends once more, and united around the National Standard.

"'Again I heard the voice say, *"Son of the Republic, look and learn!"* At this, the dark shadowy angel placed a trumpet to his mouth and blew three distinct blasts; and taking water from the ocean he sprinkled it upon Europe, Asia and Africa.

"'Then my eyes beheld a fearful scene: from each of these countries arose thick black clouds that were soon joined into one. And throughout this mass there gleamed a bright red light, by which I saw hordes of armed men, who, moving with the cloud, marched by land and sailed by sea to America; which country was enveloped in the volume of cloud.

"'And I saw dimly these vast armies devastate the whole country and burn the villages and towns, and cities that I beheld springing up.

"'As my ears listened to the thundering of the cannon, the clashing of swords, and the shouts and cries of millions in mortal combat, I again heard the mysterious voice say, *"Son of the Republic, look and learn."* As the voice ceased, the shadowy figure of the angel, for the last time, dipped water from the ocean and sprinkled it upon America. Instantly the dark cloud rolled back, together with the armies it had brought, leaving the inhabitants of the land victorious.

"'Once more I beheld villages, towns and cities springing up where I had seen them before; while the bright angel, planting the azure standard he had brought in the midst of them, cried in a loud voice, *"While the stars remain and the heavens send down dew upon the earth, so long shall the Union last."* And taking from her brow the crown on which was blazoned the word "Union," she placed it upon the standard, while people kneeling down, said, "Amen."

"'The scene instantly began to fade away, and I saw nothing but the rising vapor I had at first beheld. This also disappeared, and I found myself once more gazing upon the mysterious visitor who said, *"Son of the Republic, what you have seen is thus interpreted. Three great perils will come upon the Republic. The most fearful is the third, but the whole world united shall not prevail against her. Let every child of the Republic learn to live for God, his land, and the Union."* With these words the figure vanished from my sight.'

"Such, my friend," concluded the narrator, "were the very words I heard from Washington's own lips; and America will do well to profit from them."[77]

The following may seem to be somewhat of an apparition litany on Mary's behalf, but we briefly mention them to confirm our initial statement with respect to the divine dispensation for the New World: only in, with and through Mary can the "New World" reflect God's Mercy for our times.

Mary was seen as Our Lady of the Rosary by several persons in Peru in 1535. In 1544 she was seen as Our Lady of Andacollo in Chile. In 1555 she was seen by many persons as Our lady of Chiquinquira in Columbia. She appeared as Our Lady of Copacabana in Bolivia in 1556. In 1586 she appeared as Our Lady of Quinche in Ecuador. In 1594 she again appeared in Quito Ecuador. In 1600 Mary appeared to many people as Our Lady of Altagragia in the Dominican Republic, and in the same year an

---

[77] The *National Tribune*, Volume 4, #12, December 1880

image of Our Lady came to life before the Araucani Indians in Concepcion, Chile. In 1603 she appeared as Our Lady of Caacupe in Paraguay. In 1604 Mary came to Cuba as Our Lady of Cobre. Many people of Santa Fe, New Mexico, USA claimed to have seen her in 1625 and called her "La Conquistadora."[78] In 1634 Mother Maria de Jesus Torres saw Mary as Our Lady of Good Success, and in 1696 the Bishop of Quito, Ecuador was cured by Mary when she appeared to him as Queen of Heaven; in 1714 Our Lady appeared to three priests as Our Lady of the Cape, and in 1717 many people saw her appear in Brazil. Uruguay was visited by Mary in 1825 and there have been many more apparitions in South America to our present day.

Prayer

Oh Merciful Lord, we are poor sinners,
lost in both earthly and Spiritual pleasures,
unable even to intuit what true beauty is.
In the poverty and humility of Mary
let us approach Your unspeakable beauty,
for only in and through her
is Your beauty most perfectly reflected.
She helps us to find the beauty of cross and sacrifice,
for only if 'the grain falls to the ground and dies
can it spring up and bring forth fruit.'
Be merciful to us Oh Lord
and give us the grace to take up all the little crosses of every day,
so as to be prepared to take up Your Cross for us,
when the final hour has come.

---

[78] Poorly translated as "Our Lady of the Conquest," a better translation would be "She who conquers."

Book Three

The Message of Our Lady of Guadalupe and St. Michael the Archangel

The Message of the Image
According to the Spanish Background

It is natural that the Spanish, who didn't understand the language in which the Virgin communicated with Juan Diego, would hear her name according to their understanding, i.e., as "Guadalupe," especially after having entrusted themselves to her as the patroness of their mission.[1] They also had to interpret the entirety of her words, as well as the message of her image according to their mentality: that is to say as a confirmation of the origin of their mission from Guadalupe, Estremadura, at least for those who accepted the divine origin of the image, because there were others who did not!

Their acceptance came from an already defensive background. They had battled with the Moslems for their country and had been forced to struggle for the orthodoxy of the faith against the Protestant heresies. The anarchic situation in Spain fomented the concept that the apocalyptic reign of Christ was approaching. The Franciscans, idealistic in their aim of helping to build up the reign

---

[1]   cf. Book II, "Fourth Crusade"

of Christ in the New World, as did the Jesuits later in Paraguay, well resonated the speculations of Joaquim Fiore of the "three ages" of the Father, the Son and the Holy Spirit. This is why in the image of Our Lady of Guadalupe they recognized the "apocalyptic woman": *The woman clothed with the sun!*[2] Those who joined in with Cortés certainly also in some way were affected with the illusion of this apocalyptic reign even though it was mostly understood in terms of a reign more of this than the other world. Certainly this militaristic idea was an important factor in the conquest of the reign of Moctezuma, a kingdom so much more powerful than the insignificant "armada" of Cortés.

The Aztec View

The natives to Meso-America, those especially of Nahuatl-Toltecan background, had legends of white bearded men-gods with blue eyes who had come from the sea of the east and who had promised to return one day from this same direction.[3] Though the name given to these "white gods" was not the same in all cultures, there were many similarities. The following is the ethnological and archeological description of one such man: He wore a long white robe, sandals and a mantle embroidered with crosses. He covered His head with a type of miter and carried a staff in His hand. With respect to "Quetzacóatl," the "white-bearded man-god" of Meso-American legend, and a psychosocial description, we find this: "He was considered to be a powerful warrior and legendary king of spartan character as well as being a priest of austere and ascetic customs. Something rare among the indigenous, he had no wife or children, but frequented out of the way and solitary places in the mountains.

---

[2]   Rv 12:1 This is also why the first attack of "demystification" against the image of Our Lady of Guadalupe was directed against the authenticity of the rays, the stars on the mantle, the flowers on her robe and the boy at her feet — four attributes indispensable for an interpretation of the image in the perspective of Apc. 12.

[3]   Some see in this person Eric the Red or another member of the early Viking expeditions.

Quetzacóatl, having given the Nahuas their religion, their laws, the foundation for their calendar, and having taught them artisan and agricultural techniques, is considered amongst the outstanding characters of the Meso-American religions. He also was an enemy to human sacrifice. When he disappeared from among the Aztecs, he was replaced by Huitzilopochtli, the "sun god of putrification." The Aztec sage-poets wrote optimistically of the return of Quetzalcóatl. The arrival of Cortés on the beaches of Antigua, Veracruz, April 22, 1519 of the Julian calendar, corresponded perfectly to the judicial return as it was prophesied by the Aztecan solar calendar.

The legend of Quetzacóatl helped prepare the way for the Gospel, for his teachings served somewhat as a foundation for and or a pre-gospel to the Gospel of Our Lord Jesus Christ. He had won the hearts of the Nahuas and Toltecans and it was thus that he predisposed Meso-America to Christianity. Historically, by the conquest of Mexico in 1427, the Aztecs initiated the "mystical mission of warfare," a religious devotion to the sun god Huitzilopochtli, the god of war, because it was he who helped them conquer the other Meso-American tribes in what is now Mexico.

Their understanding of history in the terms of different "Suns"/ epochs, was orientated toward the coming of Christ. The Meso-Americans attribute to Quetzacóatl the discovery of their "daily bread," the corn for their tortillas as well as the teaching of the one god, Ometéotl. Before the arrival of Columbus in 1492, an idea and practice of sacraments very much like those known only to Christendom, penance/confession and communion, existed.

In the epoch of the "second sun" we find in their religious tradition something very similar to the Tower of Babel and in the "third sun" that of the great flood. The passing from the "third sun" to the "fourth" is likened unto the destruction of Sodom and Gomorrah. Someone had to have prepared this people, be it prophet or saint, God alone knows. Certainly the doctrine of Quetzacóatl served as a launching pad for the Spanish conquest and a ground work for the "new evangelization" by the "River of Light," the Virgin of Tepeyac.

To understand and appreciate the Aztec vision of the apparition of the Virgin of Tepeyac, one must be willing to enter more fully into their world and experience. We must consider the entirety of the intervention of heaven on the "cerrito" of Tepeyac as well as the lasting proof of heaven's interest; the miraculous image of the Virgin of Guadalupe.

The Symbolic Meaning of the "Ayate"

Our interpretation of the image has to begin with the tilma itself. It is made of what the natives call "ayate," because even this crude material is like the sign of the sacraments: God constructs His reign on the most humble thing, here with the Aztecs on the raw cactus fiber of the maguey. It's a course burlap material. Normally it has a life span of twenty years: but four hundred and sixty-two years have passed and still the ayate tilma has not yet disintegrated. It is of two pieces sewn together by a crude seam. It is a sort of blanket used by the natives not only for keeping warm and sleeping, but also for the carrying of things. For this purpose it was tied about the back of the neck, and the object to be carried was placed in the quasi-basket formed by the holding of the loose ends. The crude ayate was not used by the nobleman, but by those of humble origin, and it was this that made it a symbol of the man who bore it. It is for this reason that we conclude that the sacred tilma represents Juan Diego. In a symbolic way, the two joined pieces of the ayate represent the union of two persons, Juan Diego and Our Lady, of "Cuauhtlacupeuh" and "Cuauhtlatoátzin."[4] It represents something of a mystical bond between these two entities. It can also be seen as a symbol of the old man, Adam, who is made out of the dust of the earth, but is designed to be transformed according to the similitude of God.

"I Will Make all Things New."

From the historical point of view, the apparition of Our Lady is something so absolutely new that it can be interpreted as a "new

---

[4] cf. "The Bearer" and "Our Lady's Name," pg. 8

creation," the ayate being a symbol that it had to start "from the bottom," and this is why it reminds us also of the words of the Apocalypse, *"I will make all things new."*[5] This reality in the Nican Mopohua, is expressed by saying that *ten* years after the conquest of Mexico by the Spanish, there was peace among the two nations. This peace, from an Aztec perspective, even though there was no longer any war, was really a peace of death, because all their culture and religion that gave support and meaning to their life had been put to death.[6] Before her apparition, many tribes throughout Mexico vowed to be chaste so as not to bring offspring into the chaos of the "new regime." Looking up to Our Lady, their understanding of man as that of "Macehualli" — "he who merits through suffering" — helped them to start a new life.

It is a false belief, in some way fomented by the Spaniards, that the Aztecs were crude heathens with no concept of God. Their hearts had been pierced by the sword of suffering so as to receive the heavenly message. Only in this way can the fruit of the "new evangelization" — eight million converts — be explained. Our Lady did what St. Paul says in his discourse to the Athenians, *"I see that in every respect you are extremely religious. For as I was going about and observing objects of your worship, I found also an altar with this inscription: 'To the Unknown God.' What therefore you worship in ignorance, that I proclaim to you...."* (Acts 17:22-24). She did not come to destroy, but to bring to fullness the sparklets of light that this people already had. They had a concept of a "Nelli Téotl," a true God, which ontologically speaking equaled that of

---

[5]   Rv 21:5 This promise of the Apocalypsis we should have always before our eyes to understand better that "New Evangelisation" really *must be a new creation* — this is why our part in it is humbly that of Mary in Cana: confess that we have no "wine" anymore (all our talking is nothing but plain water!) and then, like her wait humbly and in faith: God will do it!

[6]   cf. *Flor y Canto*, pp. 277-280; Fr. Guerrero poetically states: "On August 13, 1521, heroically defended by Cuauhtemoc, Tlaltelolco fell into the power of Hernán Cortés. It was neither triumph nor defeat, but the painful birth of the mestizo nation that is Mexico today."

the European. This "Nelli Téotl" was He Whom they referred to as "Ometéotl," the One and Only True God.[7]

Because of His awesomeness, Ometéotl was not depicted in images. However the very names used by the Virgin of Tepeyac in her presentation on the occasion of her first apparition to Juan Diego corresponded perfectly with those used by the Mexicans in reference to him, as well as his attributes.[8]

She says:

"Nehuatl . . . . "I am
in Nizenquizca Zemicac Ichpochtli . . . . . the ever perfect Virgin
Santa Maria in Inatzin . . . . Mary Most Holy
in huel Nelli Téotl Dios . . . . Mother of the true God
in Ipalnemohuani . . . . of Him for Whom we live
in Teyocoyani . . . . Creator of persons (both self and others)
in Tloque Nahuaque . . . . God of salvation history
in Ilhuicahua . . . . Lord of heaven
in Tlaltipaque" . . . . Lord of the earth"[9]

The coming of the Holy Virgin reinstated everything that seemed to have been lost by the Spanish conquest. The Mother of Ometéotl had come and offered to be Mother of all those who loved Her and who willed to be one.[10] We do not confuse here what the esoterics try to insinuate i.e., that the Aztecs saw "Cuauhtlacupeuh" as "Tonantzin," the mother of the gods. The apparition of "Cuauhtlacupeuh" on Tepeyac was not a coincidence. The fact that this very mountain had been the place where the mother of their sun god had previously been venerated was the very reason why heaven chose it.

---

[7] cf. Book I, page 25

[8] *In náhuatl, "Ipalnemohuani," "Moyoloyani Y Teyocoyani," "In Tloque in Nahuaque" and "Totecuio in Ilhicahua in Tlalticpaque in Mitlane" are all names and titles that refer to Ometéotl, the One and Only True God...."* Cf. *Flor y Canto*, pp. 273-274.

[9] cf. Nican Mopohua, vs. 26

[10] cf. Nican Mopohua, vs. 30

The natives surely felt betrayed by the Spaniards. Not only had their "gods" been destroyed, but the Spaniards had disregarded all that was precious and beautiful to them as being of lesser value. To the Aztec soul, "in xóchitl in cuícatl," "flower and song," comprised all that could be considered a precious and authentic experience of God. Gold, silver, bronze and other precious stones were not sought after for their monetary value, but for their beauty. Whatever was precious to them, like feathers, had little real value to the western mentality. When the Aztecs gave the Spaniards gold and feathers, the Spaniards seized the gold and tossed the feathers. What an unfortunate insult to the Aztec! Flowers, like feathers, were considered as the "embodiment of God on earth." They mirrored a beauty of God that could only be properly appreciated by the poet. "In xóchitl in cuícatl" really was a means and access, for the Aztec, to a deeper understanding and union with Ometéotl. Both the Nican Mopohua and the image itself were profound instruments of evangelization. The Most Holy Virgin, with and through the cultural experience, gave new birth to a dying people. She not only offered them access, through the "in xóchitl in cuícatl" of the apparitions,[11] but she, as Mother of Ometéotl offered further access, by opening to them the door to the One and Only God.

Virgin, Mother and Mother of God

"Ichpochtli" — "Nantli"

Already, a first glimpse of the miraculous image brought the Aztec to three basic conclusions: She presented herself as Virgin, Mother and Mother of God. Though "virgin" in Náhuatl is "ichpochtli," the Aztec used another word to express a fuller meaning to what they saw: "Xihuitl."[12] She appears wearing a mantle, of color that only nobility dared wear. Her tunic is superimposed with golden vegetation. The "Cihuapilli," Noble Lady, is "Ichpochtli," because she is the essence of beauty. As "Amoxtli," she represents

---

[11] cf. Nican Mopohua, vs. 8-21
[12] Xihuitl has four basic connotations: 1) herb, 2) year, 3) fire, and 4) turquoise.

everything that is precious and virginal as well as all that is fruitful and fecund. Maternity is the natural and supernatural fullness of virginity. Only in and through the Most Holy Virgin can the Gospel of the Son of God be conceived in the right way. The virginal purity of "Cuauhtlacupeuh" is manifest in her maternity, and vice-versa. She is the perfect virginal representative of the virginity of all creation, "Immaculate Conception," and it is this purity that attracts the Author of life.

To the Aztec, the sash is a symbol of motherhood, that the bearer is with child. The purity of virginity necessarily reaches out to motherhood, so motherhood is in no way an opposition to virginity: virginity is consummated in motherhood. The black sash that she wears forms a "greater" or "less than sign" (i.e., 5 > 4, 4 < 5) depending on the angle in which the image is perceived. It points out that what is below is something that asks for our consideration. The Aztecs as well as the other heathen religions have a great respect for virginity. They surround virginity and motherhood with all the necessary ritual defense; whoever touches it infringes upon a law of God and is severely punished. This fact is underlined in the legend as to the conception of Huitzilopochtli, the sun god: Tonantzin conceived him in a most virginal way.

As the black sash is found over the four petalled flower, she necessarily is "Nantli" of "Téotl," Mother of God. The four petalled flower is called "nahui ollin." It has over eighty meanings referring to divine attributes. It represents a flower called "uilacapitzxóchitl" and translates to the "thin flower that crawls" as does ivy. Scripturally, it can translate to the *"The stone rejected by the builders has become the cornerstone,"*[13] because the verb to crawl in Spanish is "arrastrar." It encompasses different meanings: that which pulls or that which debases itself. Thus, the flower representing Christ in the womb of His Mother, represents His abnegation and self-debasement as the necessary price of our Redemption. This interpretation follows perfect suit with the three modes of fishing that are noted in the image. The net is hurled out to bring in the catch. Christ is at the same time the hook and the light, He is the true fisher of men. By way of Mary, He will bring in the catch.

---

[13] cf. Ps 118:22, Mt 21:42, Mk 12:10, Lk 20:17, Acts 4:11, I Pt 2:7

By her apparition she shows that He Whom she bears is the One and Only God Who also is the Creator of the sun. In the image, she seems to be proceeding from the sun, as if she were her divine Son. But she herself is not a goddess, because her hands remain folded in reverential prayer and her head is inclined. The black cross of her golden brooch manifests the union of the two cultures. The symbolic beauty of gold for the Aztec was lifted to a higher value, because it now bears the emblem of Christianity, the cross.

Bearer of Christ Through Mary

We see in the person of Christopher Columbus a glimpse of the mission of the New World. His very name is a gesture of mercy on God's part with respect for His dispensation of the Gospel. Christopher means "Christ bearer," and we know that Columbus did not get support for his journey to the New World until he first promised Isabela of Spain to dedicate his voyage to the Holy Mother of God, and it was thus that he changed the name of the third ship to "Santa Maria." This indeed is the bridge over from the fourth Crusade to the fifth.

When the Virgin sent Juan up the hill of Tepeyac to cut and bring the flowers as a proof of the authenticity of her presence, he brought them back to her and she rearranged the flowers and sent him to the bishop.[14] Juan Diego, carrying the flowers — "embodiment of God on earth" — and through the intercession and mediation of the Blessed Virgin, became a "Eucharistic minister." He was sent as a St. Tarsisus, a bearer of Christ, to bring the Lord, veiled by the roses and later by the image of Our Lady, to the bishop. This point is especially important to underline in view of the evangelization of Mexico: it is not so much a direct message, but always in and through Our Lady, veiled by her personal presence. So here, two hundred years before Louis M. de Monfort, God Himself emphasized that we should receive His Son, in, through and with Mary. This mission to bring Christ through Mary is the apocalyptic mission of the Christian in modern times. This is the "new evan-

---

[14] Let us recall the value of "in xoxitl in cuicatl," flower and song, cf. pp. 29-30.

gelization" first realized in the New World and it is the same that will bring about the consummation of all creation.

The "Serpent Lifted Up"

Another important symbol, the moon under the Virgin's feet, is also liable to different interpretations. To the Aztec, the crescent moon was a symbol of Quetzalcóatl, the "plumed or feathered serpent," also identified as the "white god" who had an important role in the conquest of Mexico. His coming back dethroned Huitzilopochtli, and his human instrument, Moctezuma II. Both Moctezuma II and Malinche, the Indian Princess and translator of Cortés,[15] were born under the sign of Quetzalcóatl, another important sign to the Indians to discover the hidden plans of divine providence. Cortés himself was considered to be Quetzalcóatl. This deception was discovered by the Indians only when Mexico had already been conquered by Cortés and his soldiers.

Now this "woman transformed in the sun," standing upon the moon, really was the true victor. Huitzilopochtli (symbolized by the sun) and Quetzalcóatl (symbolized by the moon) were only the vehicles of bringing her to the place God had foreseen from all eternity. The eagle, also a symbol of Huitzilopochtli, had brought them to the valley of Mexico from the northern part of the country. Here he made himself seen with the serpent in his mouth hovering over a nopal, up unto this time the symbol of Mexico in its national banner. Now Our Lady, by way of her true name, also revealed herself as an eagle, and her messenger, Juan Diego, was called the "speaking eagle": so only now really the initial symbol of the eagle with the serpent revealed its deepest secret. The land God wanted them to dwell in was the "land Mary." Here again this symbol acquires a deeper meaning, not only for Mexico, but for the Christian world in these apocalyptic times. Only in Mary we will find our true home here on earth.

---

[15] Malinche was a Toltecan princess who was sold by her own mother because, having been born in the year Ce Malinalli (Uno Grama), her birth date marked her as being in direct opposition and danger to the reign of Huitzlilopochtli. Cf. Pg. 33, *Flor y Canto*

The serpent, which the Aztec considered the beholder of all the values of the earth, is here lifted up from the dust of this earth and so liberated from all the heaviness of the material world. Only in and through Mary will we be able to give the right value to the things of this world, in the light of the Holy Spirit, which so strongly irradiates from her image. In the light of the Book of Genesis the serpent on the staff is another symbol for Christ, Who so much humbled Himself to be mistaken as the worst of criminals, but lifted on the cross He precisely became victor over the serpent who wanted to tear Him down to the dust to which he was condemned from the beginning of time.[16] In light of chapter 12 of the Apocalypse, the serpent is identified with the "dragon," the counter-sign. Only by way of the "woman clothed with the sun," can we recognize the overwhelming power of Lucifer, who in these times, beginning with the modern times of the fifteen hundreds, makes his last effort to overcome the power of Christ to be constituted as "prince of this earth." Here again we see how important it is that we come to the "deeper sense" of the word and also of the image as language of heaven. Already the fathers of the church insisted that the Bible could only be understood if we would penetrate "the fuller sense" of the word of God. The same naturally is true for all the details in this image of Our Lady, not made by human hands.

The Virgin Appearing on the Middle of the Moon

Remember: in Náhuatl, "On the middle of the moon" is, **Metzli**-moon, **xi**cli-umbilical, center and **co**-one. By way of this image-language they came to: ME — XI — CO! Mexico as a country, with this name, did not exist; it received its name silently by Our Lady of Guadalupe — as in a similar situation the Israelites did,

---

[16] cf. Num 21:8-9 and Jn 3:14

after the "fight of Jacob with the angel."[17] This country, ravished by the hellish fire of human sacrifices, "liberated" by the military violence of the Spaniards, like the moon, was a burnt out earth, but as St. Paul reminds us in his letter to the Romans, *"Where sin abounds, grace abounds all the more."*[18] So here, in this geographically central point in the world God starts the apocalyptic mission of Our Lady to bring us back to the only Savior, His Son Jesus Christ. At the same time, when the Old World had lost its religious and Christian impetus, God chose a new center for the Gospel. It is here then that the deeper significance of "the new evangelization" manifests itself. Juan Diego became the first missionary of this "new evangelization" in, with and through Mary. After the miraculous appearance of the image on his tilma, he remained on Tepeyac, until his death, teaching and instructing, "evangelizing," as a true "Cuauhtlatoátzin," Speaking Eagle. His living presence, as well as his permanent testimony to the authenticity of the image, became the instrument of conversion for more than eight million Indians.

Evangelization and Dialogue with God

Through original sin man fell out of the friendship and dialogue with God. When man was sent out of the Garden of Eden, he became more and more lonely. This loneliness would have finally killed him if God had not foreseen salvation in His Son Jesus Christ. Hell is the place of absolute and unconditional loneliness. The devil, in the eyes of God, has lost his personality, he has lost

---

[17] cf. Gen 23:28 Clearly, our real name with God is a mission we have to accomplish. We are only truly "Mexican" if we can stand with her on the middle of the moon, this is to say if your foot is right on the head of the serpent, so it cannot bite you anymore. In order to finally stand on the moon you have humbly to start below as the "boy"! In one of his "Angelus adresses" the Holy Father John Paul II has pointed out this deeper understanding of "Mexican"!

[18] Rom 5:20

his name, he is non-existent. Out of revenge toward God, hell's strategy with respect to man is to isolate him, more and more, until in everything he becomes as "alone" as the fallen angels.

When God sent His Son to the earth through Mary, Mary's answer to the mission of St. Gabriel was the first decisive step to renew the lost dialogue with man. Whatever response to God that had been before, in the Old Testament, was only preparation for this decisive new beginning. Whoever, in Christ, is called to share in the friendship of God necessarily has to give his response in, through and with Mary. This also holds true, not only for the individual, but also in the social dimension for a tribe and a nation. Naturally, it always has to be one person, prepared in a special way, like Mary; all the saints were to give this answer to the love of God. This person, in the case of Mexico, was Juan Diego, whose soul was so crystalline and pure that he really was destined to be the representative of the Aztecs before the face of God.

Looking at the image with the eyes of a child and the understanding of the Aztec for symbols, we see that the vertical line of dialogue starting at the mouth of Our Lady passing through the "nahui ollin" terminates at the right ear of Juan Diego, who is represented in the child at the feet of Our Lady. The fact that the dialogue necessarily had to pass through and by way of this four-petalled flower, symbol of the One and Only True God, shows us that dialogue is possible only in, with and through Christ, the Son of God. The placement of this jasmine is doubly symbolic for it appears superimposed on the womb of the Virgin. Not only is Christ the reason why we can once again speak with God, He is also the center of interest in the person of Our Lady. She is the catechist, the "Cuauhtlacupeuh," "who comes from the region of the sun singing a new song." Later on she will echo the song through the "speaking eagle." Juan Diego has really become so much one with her in this mission, that he himself is another living image of her. He really is her master catechist chosen to announce the new Gospel in integrity responding to heaven's mandates. It is this call on the part of Ometéotl and in the person of His most Blessed Mother and in her messenger, Juan Diego, that resounded in the hearts of all the Aztec listeners and viewers.

"Cola y Ala" – "Tail and Wing"

Only now the preaching of the Franciscans, "God has given us His Mother to be our own," began to make sense. The same words had now been retranslated into a language and context that they were able to fathom. Surely Juan Diego, one of them by birth and culture, yet a baptized Christian, was Mary's choice. Although, after his first unsuccessful encounter with the bishop, he tried to convince Our Lady to choose another "more worthy" for her mission, his very excuses seem to be the same ones that make him her "chosen one." The natives can recognize themselves and associate with the person of Juan, because they also would say, stunned by the glamour of Our Lady: I'm a nobody, a "mecápatl" and "cacaxtli," I'm but a "cola y ala." Each of these terms have profound significance, both to the Aztec mind and to the modern, namely because they reflect the true mission of Juan and all those who truly enter into the call of the Most Holy Virgin. Juan is simple in his essence and recognizes that he is but a "burden bearer," but what he doesn't recognize at the time is that he is to be the bearer of a most "wondrous burden"!

There has been much discussion with respect to the presence of the angelic creature at the foot of the image. The Aztec could write a separate book with respect to that part of the image filled with imagery and symbolism. It spoke to them of angels and beauty, sacrifice and union. It also spoke to them of him who was entrusted with Mary's call. For the Aztec, this boy had "huel ixe" and "huel cacace," "big eyes" and "big ears," and as the image is an "amoxtli," a type of hieroglyphic codex, he is also easily identified as a messenger, as one who is to transfer and communicate a certain information. So, even though they did not have an image of the angel represented as a person with wings, their understanding of this boy as a messenger did coincide perfectly with the western concept of angel: messenger of God.

Important for their interpretation of the boy are blessed Juan's terms, "cola" and "ala," "tail" and "wing." The right hand of the child is holding the "tail" of Mary's mantle and his left the "wing" of her tunic. Though the child is somewhat hanging from the ends of her garments, he is a "mecápatl" and "cacaxtli," a burden bearer, he is bearer of the "Cihuapilli," the "noble lady." This is the portrait of the seer. The term "cacaxtli" translates to a ladder type instrument used to bear heavy burdens and reminds us of the image of the ascending and descending of the angels of Jacob's dream, Gen 28:12, the promise of Jesus to Nathaniel, Jn 1:51 and to the wood of the cross: the key to heaven.

The Apostle Simon, whom holy church remembers on October 28, is considered in a special way as a burden-bearer. He represents all Christians, who in a humble and hidden life take up the burden of the cross day after day, becoming as Simon of Cyrene, a "burden bearer" called by the Lord on the way to Calvary. The burden bearers, like the martyrs of Christ, are "pillars of the church," called to give new life to the veins of the church. Recognizing Juan Diego amongst their ranks gives us another glimpse of this Christian country in the whole of the church. Already, the Mexican Christian by nature is orientated toward sacrifice, and thus is called in a special way to help by his life of sacrifice and burden-bearing to renew the church in its eagerness to follow the Lord up on His way to Our Lady of Guadalupe. In a special way, Our Holy Father, Pope John Paul II, in his never tiring apostolate for the crucified Lord, is another a burden-bearer. He, like Juan Diego, is a sign that the church of these times is called on the way of the cross up to Our Lady of Guadalupe, because only there will the church find its consummation.

The feathers of the wings of the angel-child are another important message. Because they are pointed like swords they symbolize sacrifice and warfare. Being short and sharp, they are likened unto the feathers of an eagle, "cuauhtli," and the fact that the owner of these wings is in the upright position spoke to them of

"Cuauhtehuamitl," the eagle that ascends. The "ascending eagle" was correlated to Huitzilopochtli as patron of the "caballeros aguilas y tigres."[19] The presence of "Cuahtehuamitl" at the feet of the Noble Lady — "Cihuapilli" — helped the Aztecs regain some of their lost esteem as warriors. In their Floral Wars — "xoxhilyaoyotl" — the essence of the mystique of war was constituted in the image of eagle and jaguar. Now, together with Juan Diego, they were called to be warriors and ambassadors of the Mother of Ometéotl, the One and Only True God. The Bourbon Codex gives us another reference for the red and white wings. It presents the image of an angel, in the form of a butterfly, with red and white wings: a deity of sacrifice and penance, Itzpapalotl, having the mission of carrying the sacrifice of human hearts and blood to the gods. The concept is christianized in changing "gods" to God. The greatest manifestation of piety, the concept of offering themselves, their hearts and lives, was not obliterated. Through the intercession of "in huel Nelli Téotl Dios" their sacrifice has been integrated in the sacrifice of Christ Who offered Himself to God the Father for our Redemption. We have then, a first synthesized catechesis on the value of the sacrifice of Christ on Our Lady of Guadalupe and consequently also on its unbloody repetition in Holy Mass. Lastly, the outstretched arms of the boy at the feet of Our Lady represent the common priesthood of the Christian. Only if we are crucified in, with and through Christ can this common priesthood come to its consummation and we will be able to, as St. Paul says, *"...make up for what is still lacking in the suffering of Christ for His body, the church."*[20]

---

[19] cf. *Flor y Canto*, pg 268
[20] Col 1:24

The "Whereabouts" of Our Lady

Our manner of showing direction is:	The Aztec had a similar form, but it looked like this:

According to Valeriano's description of the image,[21] "the angel comes forth from a *cloud*,"[22] giving us an overlapping interpretation with the Hebrew culture. Cloud for them was the mysterious presence of God. For the Aztec, it was a symbol of Tlaloc, god of water and rain, but also symbolic of the One and Only True God —

---

[21] It is believed that Antonio Valeriano wrote the Nican Mopohua before 1545, during the lifetime of Juan Bernardino (1458–1554), Bishop Zumárraga (1468–June 3, 1548) and Juan Diego (1474–1548). The Epilogue of the Nican Mopohua, contained in Book Three, is a description of the image of Our Lady.

[22] cf. Epilogue of Nican Mopohua

Ometéotl — with the title, "Tlallichcatl," "he who covers the earth with cotton." These few details made the world of difference for the Aztec. Their interpretation was different from that of the Spaniards, but what they were experiencing reflects St. Paul's letter to the Galatians 3:24-25 when he states that the old law served its purpose and now has to be left behind, because it has come to its fullness, which is Christ. The Gospel of Jesus Christ was new to the Aztecs, but the Aztec concepts of truth, beauty, sacrifice and man's destiny were preparing its way. This "Cuauhtlacupeuh" not only gave her name to Juan Bernardino, but demonstrated it on the "Amoxtli" of Juan Diego's tilma of ayate.

The Mountain of Revelation

Although no topographical maps of "New Spain" existed in 1531, a recent correlation has been made with the golden flow-

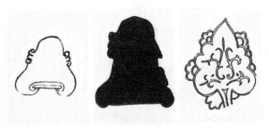

ers of her gown and their relation to the different significant mountains looking from east to west. As already stated, Our Lady of "Cuauhtlacupeuh" comes from the east, the region of God. Placing the image of Our Lady of Guadalupe on a topographical map of Mexico or superimposing the map on the image, and using a scale of one million/one we will note a correlation of outstanding dimensions.[23]

---

[23] We note that the large golden flowers have somewhat of an heart-like shape (depending on viewing perspective). When the form is placed next to the hieroglyphic marking for hill/mountain we note that they are quite similar. The Aztec codices demonstrate the use of "Tépetl" whenever a city or village was to be depicted. The form was only customized so as to portray a note-worthy element of the place.

The large flower of her left side, beneath the folded mantle of her left arm, is symbolic of Tepeyac. It is made up of two parts: **Tépet**l (hill) and **yac**atl (point or nose). Taking the underlined elements of the above terms, we arrive at the name Tepeyac. When we consider the flowers on the sleeves of the Virgin's tunic, noting of course that they are topped with the white of her inner gown (symbolizing snow) and in a further eastern direction, we would be surprised to note on the topographical map a correspondence to two of Mexico's highest points of elevation, the great Popocatépetl and Iztaccihuatl (home of Tlaloc, god of water and the rain).

Superimposed on the breast area of the image is another large golden flower with the form of a mountain. Moving eastward from the two great volcanoes we encounter the beautiful Malinche, named after Dona Marina, Cortés' interpreter and partner in the conquest. Mountain or Tépetl elements correspond to accidents that denote specific peaks of the mountains that cross Mexico from east to west. The portion of the Eastern Sierra which is closest to the Gulf is located over Mary's head. The Pacific Ocean may be found in the region of the angel. The Virgin's left hand also has the shape of a heart. We would be blind not to conclude a correlation with the Immaculate Heart of Mary. Geographically, between the two great volcanoes and Malinche, we find the humble hill of the miraculous apparitions of St. Michael in 1631. This correspondence is not a coincidence, it is a clear manifestation of St. Michael's mission in the triumph of the Immaculate Heart of Mary and a further concordance with the appearance of St. Michael after the "great sign."[24] We mustn't forget either the "ascending eagle"

---

[24] cf. Rv 12:7 and 12:1 respectively

at her feet. The previous relationship made with Huitzilopochtli and his patronage over the mystical warriors can also be made with both Cortés and St. Michael, the great Spanish warrior and Prince of the heavenly host.

A Combined Perspective

The Spanish and Aztec!

The greater a "work of art," the more it represents the universal values of man, beyond any specific culture or religion. As the image of Our Lady of Guadalupe is a "masterpiece" of the divine Artist, it merits the credit of having something to say to all mankind, to each man and culture according to their unique experience and perspective. For the Spaniards the apparition of Our Lady of Guadalupe was: the fulfillment of all their hopes!

This is why the Aztec interpretation does not exclude a "further interpretation" in the light of faith. To the contrary, the image needs this deeper interpretation so as to correspond to the truth that we come to know in and through revelation in Jesus Christ. The different interpretations of the moon in the two perspectives is a good example to show how two different point of views do not exclude each other but help to a deeper interpretation in the light of faith. The moon for the Aztecs was a symbol of this earth, of what is "below" as the sun, for what is "above" us. In the light of our faith we know that the earth in which we live has been "burnt" by the sin of the fallen angel and by the sin of men who follow him. Another example is the interpretation of the figure of Our Lady of Guadalupe. From an Aztec viewpoint the image is that of a "glorified woman," but then what about the shadows in her dress? According to the data of our Christian faith, Mary will only be fully "glorified" when all of her "children" enter heaven with her. Here again, we are only able to arrive at a deeper comprehension of the image in the light of Christian truth. The Aztec perspective should help us Christians to develop a deeper sensibility for the symbolic character of signs and for their transparency to the reality of the invisible world we have lost in the technical endeavor to dominate and control nature for personal profit, to be used and plundered for human ambitions, consumption and a life of comfort on earth.

The next "controversial" point is that of "sacrifice." Why did our Lady not say a word about the abominable custom[25] of the human sacrifices of the Aztecs? Studying soberly the religious background of these pagans, we can not do otherwise than admit that they were contrived in "erroneous conscience"[26] They did not have the clear vision of the truth we Christians received through revelation. Behind this truly horrible cult, more developed with them than with other pagan religions, was the idea which modern man has almost lost: life necessarily has to do with sacrifice. The significance of what sacrifice really is only becomes clear in the fuller light of the sacrifice of Our Lord Jesus Christ on the cross. Only through the Blessed Virgin, Our Mother of Sorrows, are we able to actively or passively participate and profit in the passion of her Son.

For the Aztec, humility and purity were a prerequisite to the participation of sacrifice.[27] This truth is fully expressed by the position of the "angel" at her feet. The dimension of the cross, which seems to be lacking with the "glorified woman," can be seen in the

---

[25] We could go further and ask: why did she not blame them in anything bad they had done before — as we are so much blamed in "messages" — because as "Christians" we should know better? (The neo-pagans will not listen anyway!) The answer is simple: the deeper we are in the darkness of sin the more we need the pure light of mercy. Not preaching hell will help those who are already with one foot in hell on earth, by directing their eyes towards the glory of light! This is another reason why really the Guadalupan way of evangelisation is the only adequate one in this time of darkness!

[26] Only in the cross of Christ we are allowed to know what sacrifice really is. The Mexicans with a deeper understanding for the necessity of sacrifice to "keep up with their gods" have a deeper "natural" basis for the folly of the cross than we modern Westerners do. Their mission in the sign of the cross (see Book II) purifies and transforms this deficient concept, distorted by the snares of the fallen angels.

[27] For the Aztec, purity of heart was necessary for being worthy to offer sacrifice. This is why there were as many strict rules regarding observance in liturgical sacrifice as there were in the preparation for war. These rules of observance were believed to have been revealed by their own gods! This also is why they were unable to match the purely pragmatic warfare practiced by the Spaniards.

outstretched arms of the messenger as well as in the upright position of Our Lady — crossed by the horizontal bar of the position of her arms. She is really a living sermon on the reality of the cross. The small cross on her brooch is a clear sign that we can only enter into a new life by the narrow door of the cross. The cross is the sign of transformation of the old Adam into the new man in Jesus Christ. Seen from this viewpoint, Mary standing on the moon has a double meaning. The Aztecs recognized her as having an earthly origin like our own. By the cross, the old man is lifted up from the dust of sin and transformed through the five wounds into a new creature. Man is likewise extended in the four directions of the cross; the fifth dimension is the pierced heart of Our Lord, the unique entry into the reign of God.

In the boy at the feet of Our Lady of Guadalupe recognized by the Aztec to be one of them.[28] With eyes illuminated by faith, they could recognize that he represents a messenger in war: the eyes of the boy are intent and concentrated on his mission, his heart is really with God. His black hair enters into the black color of the crescent moon; for the Aztec symbolizing Mexico, the place on earth given to them by God. In the Christian perspective the moon is symbol of the fallen, the "burnt out" angels, and all earth affected by sin. We have to carry the burdens of sin as Christ took them on Himself on the cross and so could not be distinguished from us poor sinners!

His eyes almost appear closed, looking out as does the eagle upon his prey: in the Aztec perspective a typical attribute for the "eagle fighter" sent out to bring back sacrificial souls for their warrior god. In the Christian perspective he is looking out for souls to be saved from the clutches of the devil. The "dark eye of faith" sees deeper and clearer than our carnal eyes in the light of the day! The depth of his eyes are a sign of the depth of his soul. As a messenger he is meant not only to carry a message in an exterior way, but to become one with it in body and soul.

Another forgotten Christian truth is revealed in the Aztec perspective of the image of Our Lady of Guadalupe. That is the fact that God's creation is threefold:

---

[28]   According to Fr. Mario Rojas he is the "most Mexican part" of the image.

- It is made up of the visible material world, in the beauty of nature that surrounds us and the luminous splendor of the stars above us: "Bible of the Father"
- It is present in the invisible world of the Holy Spirit, comprising the world of the angels, present wherever we go, wherever we look, revealed in the picture by everything that is white and gold. This precious metal is a symbol of eternity. The Aztecs considered it "the excrement" of the gods, something which they let fall on the earth as the "least" of their splendor, yet retaining its "brilliance"!
- Finally, man is in the middle of the two worlds, he is surrounded by the visible and the invisible creation. Jesus, present visually in the Nahui Ollin, is brought to us by Mary: and it is she who continues to bring Him into our lives through the action of the Holy Spirit especially in the sacramental life of the Mystical Body.

"The angel," holding onto the garment of Our Lady with his right hand, clings to the visible world of the cosmos. With his left hand he holds on to the word of God represented by the fold of her robe, which looks like a book. The left side of the book has the most light and therefore can be interpreted as the last book of the Bible: the Apocalypse.

The Message of the Cross in the Revelation of Our Lady of Guadalupe

The Beauty of Sacrifice

The beauty of this revelation of Our Lady of Guadalupe is first of all that it is a trinitarian Revelation, one that helps us to better understand the "beauty of sacrifice," not as something imposed by violence, but as an invitation to share in the surrender of God in His Son by way of the Holy Spirit.

This also helps us to understand better about the human sacrifices of the Aztec: blood was given to their gods to help them in their battle for the world's equilibrium. They were convinced that man himself lives from the blood of the gods which helped man to resurrect after the catastrophe of the "fourth sun."[29] It isn't in vain that archeologists speak about the "cruel beauty" of Aztec art. Only the blood of Christ was able to liberate them from their profound blindness and this fundamental error, a condition of fallen man. They were on the right way thinking; sacrifice is absolutely necessary, to give birth to life, to make it continue, but they were wrong thinking that man, in his poor condition could contribute something on his part.

Only God Himself, by the sacrifice of His Only Begotten Son, can give man the grace of new life; and He did it by the sacrifice of the blood of His Son! They were close to this truth with their belief that in the matter of sacrifice the most important thing was the "blood of the gods." On the other hand they were not completely wrong when they desired to "help the gods" — here the Christian discernment will tell us: yes, we are even allowed to help, on condition that we know that in incomprehensible condescendence God invites man to give his little contribution to the only necessary and fundamental "part" of God in Christ His Son. And we are not only allowed, but we must collaborate in order to have our personal part in salvation.[30]

---

[29] Remember that as with the Stoics every epoch of the history necessarily had to end in catastrophe; the only thing man, with the help of the gods, could possibly influence was to prolong a little bit the time of the respective "sun" — before it would crush. This was what they tried to do with their sacrifices: fortifying the gods with the blood of human sacrifices, because the gods themselves were in this battle.

[30] This is the "Protestant conflict" admitting that Christ has done all in salvation — man has no possible part in it. Consequently he will lose interest, and go his own ways (creating his own world where he has no need of God!) — this is the necessary dead end of Protestantism, revealed in our days. But we should remember humbly that Protestantism was the necessary "protest" against a false Catholic position in which the part of man in salvation was overemphasized "by his works." Here again: just measure in between the extremes is a matter of pure grace — and so we will be in the battle all of our life.

It was Tlacaélel, the Aztec wiseman, who brought up the "ideology of the blood."[31] It was he who found and gave the Aztecs the most profound root of his "warring mysticism," a new mystical-warring vision of the world and of man which became the root of the great future of the people of the sun.[32] It was necessary for them to correspond to the sacrifice of the gods by offering them the same precious liquid that fortified and impeded death; to better realize the blood offerings, Tlacaélel initiated the practice of the "floral wars."[33] The pulsating hearts were literally ripped out of the living victims and offered to Huizilopochtli, enabling his fortification and the indefinite conservation of the life span of the sun.[34] The young war-god is identified with the sun himself, as we may see in many of their sacred hymns. The Aztecs were the "chosen people" of Huizilopochtli and by nature of that mission were to collaborate with him in circumventing the end of the epoch of the sun's movement. According to the ancient myths, this epoch began its existence with the self sacrifice of the gods, who with their blood — chalchíhuatl — reengendered life.[35]

Looking at it from this perspective we can derive a deeper sense of the Aztec vision of the world. The Aztecs are situated on the side of the sun, Huizlipochtli. They considered themselves to be on the good side, in a battle without reprieve, against the powers of death and of the night. This carries with it the justification of all its conquests; the persuasion that the submission of other tribes, mak-

---

[31] *Estudios de la Filosofia en Mexico*, 1980, pg. 46 ff., Tlacaelel was one of the Aztec "tlamantini = wisemen"

[32] "People of the Sun," because Huitzilopochtli , the "god of the sun," had brought them to the region of the lakes, and thanks to him they had contemplated the eagle devouring the serpent at the end of their long pilgrimage.

[33] The "Floral Wars" were the arranged periodic battles with the neighboring states of Tlaxcala and Heuxotzinco, entered into for the sole purpose of obtaining sacrificial victims

[34] Huitzilopochtli appears in the mind of Tlacaélel, fulfilling his extraordinary mission of cosmic resonance: he is holding back the cataclysm that could bring to an end the epoch in which we live.

[35] Blood is the precious water (chalchíhuatl), wherein the vital energy that maintains human life is confined.

ing them tributaries, is fulfilling his supreme mission. It is thus that Tlacaélel proportions a philosophy of action to his people, rooted in the concept and in the reality of battle, so as to give a definite visage and power to the previously unknown Aztecs. It is this that broadens their dominion from sea to sea and to the distant regions, which today are known as Honduras and Nicaragua.[36]

The cross is inseparable from the Christian concept of beauty, apparent in Our Lady of Guadalupe — this is the static view. Next we need to see the cross in its dynamic dimension as crusade and message of the cross. The cross should be, as we understand it, the nucleus of what is spoken of as the new evangelization. We cannot separate it from the Mission which started with Our Lady of Guadalupe in 1531.

---

[36] Nicaragua comes from two Nahuatl words signifying the termination of the Aztec Empire: "Nican" — here or up to this point, and "Anuahuac" — the valley of Anuahuac.

Hitler also wanted to extend "his reign of thousand years" beyond all borders, not afraid to enter into war with the whole word and eliminating in his own country whoever was against him or not useful for his plans of conquest. He also had his model idea in the philosophy of action of a "Schopenhauer, Nietzsche," that the "strong," by their "excellence," would have the power and competence over all those who are weak. His ideology also was based on "blood," almost in the same sense as the Aztecs: through the blood of the weak the "destiny" of the strong is fortified so as to establish the "apocalyptic reign of the thousand years" for the Aryan race.

Whoever contemplates the parallelisms of "today and yesterday," of the paganism of before and the neopaganism of today, will easily find the same demons. They were invoked, even celebrated by Wagner ("Götter-dämmerung!") and other "modern prophets" of the antichrist, gloriously returning to take the reins of the nations into their hands. Because of this, we should not be surprised if the sacrifice of Christian blood is required in the future to avoid "another catastrophe": "the annihilation of the age of Aquarius," so openly proclaimed by those of the "New Age"!

Even we Christians forget that which man lost through original sin has more than been recompensed by The Blood of Christ. The image of man, which should reflect the image of God, has been restored. The image of Our Lady of Guadalupe not only reflects this reality, being God's masterpiece in creation, but also in salvation.

The Sign of the Cross in the Apparition of The Virgin of Ocotlán[37]

"Virgin Mother of the Byways"

In the spring of 1541, in the present-day capital of Tlaxcala, another native American, also named Juan Diego, became the privileged recipient of the message of the Most Holy Virgin. The young Tlaxcaltecan was bringing water for members of his epidemic-stricken family when he was encountered by a heavenly visitor. Stopping him in his tracks, she said, *"God bless you my son, where are you going?"* After telling her his plight, she replied, *"Follow me, I will give you water that will free them from their ailments, but also heal not only your relatives, but all who drink of it, of the contagion; because my heart is always disposed to help the helpless..."* Leading Juan Diego to a spring, she said, *"Take as much of the water as you wish, and know that even contact with the smallest drop will bring complete health to the sick."* She also told him to go to the Franciscans, and to tell them that they would discover an image of her, one not only manifesting her perfections, but her tenderness and compassion.

Juan carried out her request in complete obedience, telling the Franciscans that he would be shown the designated place. Unbeknownst to himself, he was followed into the ocote woods that night. The eye witnesses were amazed to see a XVIth century version of "the burning bush"! The entire forest seemed to be aglow, but only a particular tree seemed to be on fire without being consumed. The following day, with many eye witnesses present, a miraculous carved image of the Virgin was found within the desig-

---

[37] Even though Ocotlan is a "minor apparition" in line with so many others, some of them mentioned at the end of Book II, it should be seen in synopsis together with that of Our Lady of Guadalupe and the one of St. Michael, all three close to each other in time and space: in a region of less than 70 miles. The reign of Our Lady as the apocalyptic woman must be prepared by the cross (the tree in which she appeared is a symbol of the cross). The fire which surrounds her in her apparition in the oak tree certainly is a symbol of our purification and of the necessity of our ardent love of Our Crucified Lord.

nated ocote tree. To this day, this very image is venerated in the Basilica of Ocotlán, Tlaxcala.

There is ten years between this apparition of the Blessed Virgin (1541) and that which took place in Mexico City (1531). A beautiful parallel between these separate apparitions can be found in Genesis 2:5-6. The "Apocalyptic Virgin of Tepeyac" can be correlated with the "rain" which comes from above, for she brought with her the promise of the new Jerusalem, descending from heaven as the consummation of the church. The Ocotlán apparition is more like the "mist" which "rose up from the earth and all the surface of the ground."[38] The Virgin of Ocotlán associates herself with man's humble way of life; his work, his sufferings and his aspirations. Her availability to serve her children makes it easy to call her the "Virgin of the Byways." In both apparitions, it is her maternal heart that wills to accompany us on our pilgrimage through this "valley of tears," until at last we reach our heavenly homeland. How appropriate that the first recorded words on this continent were directed to her and were the Salve Regina, when Columbus landed in San Salvador.[39]

This visitation of Our heavenly Mother at Ocotlán does not call one to gaze heavenward, as does the glorious Virgin of Guadalupe. Here rather, Our heavenly Mother reminds us that she

---

[38] cf. Gen 2:6

[39] There is a beautiful parallelism we should meditate more deeply on between the visit of Our Lady to the New World and her frequent visits to old Europe beginning with 1831. To both continents she is sent as the "Mother of the Byways" — in a mission that recalls the first mission she fulfilled when she went from Nazareth to visit Elisabeth. By way of HER Son she wants to kindle in our hearts the fire of St. John the Baptist. He should help us prepare the way for her Son. At the same time we should keep in mind that she is the last prophet — so what she wants to awaken in our hearts is her own mystical presence: only if she is in us, her Son can be born in our soul!

is very close to us. Even as she is sheltered in the wood of the cross, she wills to do the same for us. The wood of the cross is the message of the sober love of God which she desires to share with her children. We are to find our shelter in it, our earthly home! It is thus that we discover the silent message of the apparition of the Most Holy Virgin in Tlaxcala: the proclamation of our salvation through the cross. Like Mary, we need to embrace the cross. In so doing, in union with Jesus and Mary, our cross will become enveloped in the "fire" of glory.

We humbly recognize that the Most Holy Virgin is the "woman of sorrows," whose crowning glory is found in the sufferings of her Son, united to Him, on and beneath the cross. For this reason, the 1541 apparition of the Virgin has an important element to add to that of her glorious apparition of 1531. We can only be true "children of Mary" if we follow Christ Crucified![40] Both apparitions of the Virgin's exact complete surrender and perfect obedience, even to death on the cross if necessary! Any veneration of the Most Holy Virgin, which does not lead to the cross of Christ, is not true devotion.[41] More than ever in this "modern times" we are call to look up to the cross, unique sign of salvation, to "adore God in Spirit and truth"

This invites us to consider the relationship between Jesus at the well of Jacob and Mary Most Holy at Ocotlán, their parallels and symbolisms. Keep in mind that any secondary revelation only finds value to the degree that it reflects the first; as the moon does not shine of itself, but reflects the light of the sun. If we were to put chapter 4:1-42 of St. John's Gospel and the words of the alleged apparition at Ocotlán side by side, we would soon realize that the latter is a reflection of the former. Our Lady, in her profound humility, is the purest reflection of her Son. And it is thus that her apparition at Ocotlán finds its just place in the light of Holy Scripture.

We must consider the settings of both revelations: Samaria and Mexico. The inhabitants of Samaria were descendants of Jacob,

---

[40] cf. *True Devotion*, St. Louis Marie de Montfort
[41] cf. *Friends of the cross*, St. Louis de Montfort

and so the woman says, *"Are You greater than our father Jacob who gave us this well."* As we know, the Samaritans were not exactly the people most accepted by the Jews. They had intermarried with pagans. The Mexican people were not any more accepted by the Spanish conquistadors. They were pagans with many gods! Recall also that the seer at Ocotlán was named Juan (John), as is the evangelist of this chosen text, who calls himself the "disciple whom Jesus loved." It is the same who receives Mary into his home at the foot of the cross (cf. Jn 13:23 and 19:27). With respect to the two accounts, we have a reversal of roles, Jesus addresses a woman; Mary addresses a man. Both recipients were of lowly states; beautifully manifesting the infinite mercy of heaven toward us poor sinners.

In both revelations, heaven initiates the dialogue. Both speak of a "water" of unique properties. One that heals and another that "lives" and springs up to life eternal. Mary actually says "Follow me, and I will give you..." JESUS' manner of dealing with the Samaritan is different, it is a call to self recognition, trust and conversion. Mary at Ocotlán gives us the "living water," Who is her Son, but we must be converted as was the Samaritan. We must heed Mary's invitation to follow, for only then will we be able to receive the "water" that heals all our impediments and will bring us to conversion.

Jesus says, *"Woman, believe me, the hour is coming when neither on this mountain nor in Jerusalem will you worship the Father.... But the hour is coming, and is now here, when the true worshippers will worship the Father in Spirit and in truth. For the Father also seeks such to worship Him. God is Spirit, and they who worship Him must worship Him in Spirit and in truth."* Here it is that we find the core of this Gospel passage. We hear the echo of this "Spirit and truth" in Our Lady's request to Juan Diego. She later tells him to go to the Franciscans, the church authorities, and to tell them that she wishes to leave an image of herself that would not only manifest her perfections, but would be a means of conveying her clemency and mercy.

She insists that the gift be taken and placed in the church. Mary first of all directs her lowly son to the church of her Son, the true church with the One God. Though Juan Diego was already a bap-

"...Jesus therefore, wearied from the Journey, was sitting at the well. It was about the sixth hour. There came a Samaritan woman to draw water. Jesus said to her, 'Give me to drink....' The Samaritan woman therefore said to Him, 'How is it that thou, although thou art a Jew, dost ask drink from me, who am a Samaritan woman?' For Jews do not associate with Samaritans. Jesus answered and said to her, 'If thou didst know the gift of God, and who it is who says to thee, Give me to drink, thou, perhaps, wouldst have asked of him, and he would have given thee living water.... Everyone who drinks of this water will thirst again. He, however, who drinks of the water that I give him shall never thirst, springing up unto life everlasting.'"

Juan Diego, bringing water on behalf of his epidemic-stricken family members, was suddenly intercepted by the "beautiful lady." She greeted him, asking, *"Where are you going my son?"* Juan was awestruck at the heavenly vision, but responded, "I'm taking water from the river to my sick ones, who are dying without remedy." She responded with, *"Follow me, and I will give you another water that will not only heal your relatives, but anyone who takes even a drop of it will be completely healed."*

tized Christian, she confirms his faith in the True God. With her request of being brought to the church, she sets herself up as an ambassador and missionary of her Son. As Jesus, from the altar of the cross, gave His Mother to the "beloved apostle," so also here does He give her to Juan at Ocotlán as Mother and Mediatrix. To this day, 450 years since her initial visitation, she has remained the same, a missionary of the true God Who wills to be worshipped in Spirit and truth.

Both encounters end jubilantly. The Samaritan woman hurries off to Sichar, informing the town's people of the man who has just told her of her past, ending with the line, *"Can he be the Christ?" Many believed because of her testimony, but after hearing Jesus themselves, they believed Him to be the Savior of the world.* (Jn 4:39-43) Juan Diego takes his "gift water" to his sick ones and they are miraculously healed. They also believe through Juan's testimony, thoroughly convinced by the healing results. The Franciscans listen to Juan's testimony and are duly moved by the clarity and conviction of the seer. The lack of faith which might have remained was transformed upon the opening of the ocote tree, following the direction of the Mother of God.

Not only do the revelations deal on a personal level of conversion, but many people have been, and continue to be, converted even to this day, not so much a result of the "healing water," but of Our Lord's promised "living water." Jacob left a well to his son Joseph at Sichar, thus remaining a blessing to his descendants. The people of Tlaxcala, the first to actually receive the faith of the Spaniards, were also left a lasting legend by Providence in the miraculous wooden image of the Mother of God.

Our Lady, Messenger of the Cross

Ours is the duty to delve beyond the external. We must enter the deeper and interior message of these revelations so as to truly appreciate that which God has revealed in and through the word. Only a disposition and readiness to conversion can prepare our hearts for the grace of the "water" Who is life and to a worship which is true. As the apparition of the Virgin of Tepeyac lets us see our heavenly destiny, so does that of Ocotlán (close to that of the Tepeyac in time and distance) let us espy the course for this destiny: the cross! She comes forth from an ocote, the tree being a symbol of the wood of the cross on which her Son died to redeem us. Only by the cross are we able to achieve the glory of heaven which is revealed in the apparition of the Virgin of Guadalupe.

It is as if she wants to teach us that we also have to grow in the wood of the cross, in "image and wisdom before God and man."[42] Here is seen the value of sacrifice, as it issues from the cross of Christ. Only if our sacrifice is integrated in the sacrifice of Christ on the cross will it help us on our pilgrimage to heaven. Here is the answer to Guerrero's question: "Why, at the initiation of its history, was the annihilation of the Mexican people so necessary?" Why was it necessary for them to lose the entire order of their life and their culture before the Virgin could show them the "new way," which miraculously justified all that was genuinely authentic in their own culture and religion?

Guerrero, himself, gives us the answer. It is simple, and at the same time inscrutably profound: *"...unless the grain of wheat falls into the ground and dies, it remains alone. But if it dies, it brings forth much fruit."*[43] This people, so oriented toward sacrifice, was able to enter the reign of God only through the greater sacrifice of all their values, which will later resurrect purified and in greater glory. Here again we recognize the parallelism with the people of Israel: the old covenant through the law of Moses yielded the way to the new covenant in Jesus Christ. The law, as St. Paul explains, was the *"tutor unto Christ"*;[44] by itself, without this orientation, it was the *"law of death."*[45] The clearest expression of this reality, was with the sacrifice of animals of the Jews; with the Aztecs, the sacrifice of men. Both tell us that there is no way of escaping death. It was a theme that also troubled the tlamantines, the wise men amongst the Aztecs.[46] Moctezuma's rule would sooner or later have led to sui-

---

[42] cf. Lk 2:52

[43] Jn 12:24

[44] Gal 3:24

[45] Rom 6:9-16, 7:6-10

[46] cf. "The contribution" of Miguel Portilla, especially Ch. VI: "The Thoughts of Nezahualcóyotl," pp. 38 ff.

cide. Was it then the wisdom of God that did away with it, replacing it with another rule, that of the faith of the Spaniards!?

Our God is a God of reality, soberly reckoning with our weaknesses, even our vices. The Old Testament is filled with stories of man's wickedness, his cruelty and violence. Man, each of us in our own way, by nature, bears the mark of original sin. This same principle applies to the nations. There is an approximation to the plans of God, but there yet remains a final separation of light and darkness. *"God looks from heaven upon the children of men, to see if there be one who is wise and seeks God. All alike have gone astray; they have become perverse; there is not one who does good, not even one...."*[47] Only the blood of Christ can break the chains of sin. With the apparition of the Virgin this knot of confusion, concerning the concept of sacrifice, is dissolved in pure and unadulterated harmony, which we are able to admire even today in the image. Before the coming of Christ, the intuition was valid: only through struggle, by the sacrifice of blood, would man be able to save himself from the eternal death that threatened him. More sublime yet was that the gods themselves had to give their own blood so that man, after the final catastrophe, would once again rise from death.

God always surpasses even the most sublime intuitions of man and his nostalgia for salvation. Who would have been able to imagine that the Father was going to sacrifice His own Son to redeem us from the bondage of the devil? It is necessary that we kneel down and adore, and that we forget the horrible sacrifices of the Aztecs or the cruelty and greed for gold of the Spaniards. Whoever is born into the eternal life of Christ, in truth, has to be a *"new man,"* the *"old has passed away."*[48] The fact that Christians are not yet capable of this manifests ever more lucidly the necessity of the reign of Mary, of her Immaculate Heart, in which we all will be "new men" in Christ, her Son: the triumph which the apparition of the Virgin in Mexico already prophesies!

In Ocotlán, the Virgin comes forth from a tree; in Fátima, she appears above a tree, a small holm oak (of which not even a fragment remained!). This difference enables us to intuit the distance in

---

[47] Ps 13:2-3
[48] cf. 2 Cor 5:17

time of these two apparitions of the Virgin: We are closer to the end of all things! Having appeared as if floating over this small tree, the Virgin of Fátima reminds us that in the beginning of the world the Spirit of God hovered above the waters, above the chaos ("tohu-wabuho," symbolic expression that the world was going to be created from nothing!). The world is a creation of the love of God, because God wishes to encounter Himself in it, in His own Son. In this sense, the small holm oak in Fátima is also a symbol of the "small flock," "the remnant" that will have faithfully passed the final proof that the Apocalypse speaks of.[49] It will crystallize amidst the chaos of the "last days" (a correlation to the "beginning") and they will already bear the face of Christ. Thus, the irrevocable meaning of the apparitions of the Virgin is that Christ should be formed in us as He was first formed in the womb of the Virgin.

The abiding presence of the Virgin, by means of her image in Mexico, is a clear sign that the Lord, in a very special way, desires to imprint His face on this people, in the same way He willed to do with the chosen people of Israel, who already by its natural disposition, was "predestined to sacrifice…," unlike those nations where the dollar and ego are the new "gods." Here the antichrist will completely do away with sacrifice, demonstrating that Lucifer never submitted himself, because he wasn't capable of denying himself before the greater reality of God. With the assistance of the fallen angels he prompts the glory of the "city of man." Here, in Mexico, God wills that by means of sacrifice, something of the heavenly Jerusalem, as man's last destiny, may be made visible. Each and every one of us, from whatever nation we may be, must pass this most difficult proof, revealing the value of all things by the fire of divine love.[50] Let us console and fortify ourselves in the words of the letter to Philadelphia: *"He who overcomes, I will make him a pillar in the temple of my God, and never more shall he go outside. And I will write upon him the name of my God, and the name of the city of my God — the new Jerusalem, which comes down out of heaven from my God — and my new name."*[51]

---

[49] cf. 3:10

[50] cf. I Pt 1:7, 2 Pt 3:7

[51] Rv 3:12

The Relationship Between the Apparition of Our Lady on the Hill of Tepeyac (1531) and the Apparition of St. Michael in San Bernabé, Capula (1631)

*The Hill of St. Michael symbolized in the
left hand of the Virgin of Tepeyac*

The angelic trial at the beginning of time was a proof of blind faith, hope and love. These first creatures entered "three days of absolute darkness." Within this darkness their only reliance was the natural light of knowledge of God before the trial. This natural ray of light had to be converted into the flame of faith, hope and love, into that which we call theological virtues: the only bridge from man and angel to God in Jesus Christ. In this terrible darkness, the "I" of the angels, a symbol of their self-reliance, had to be completely consumed, burned to ashes. Only thus were they able to follow the cry of St. Michael: "Who is like unto God!" The Immaculate Heart of Mary is found shadowed on her left hand as if burnt to ashes. Symbolically it speaks of Her total consummation in the love of God.

The holy angels, especially the archangels, prepared the way of Our Lord Jesus Christ. This is true in His first Advent, recognized in the mission of St. Gabriel, preparing the first coming of Our Lord Jesus Christ. This is also true for the coming of the Gospel to the New World. As Our Lord Jesus Christ had to break the resistance of those whom he called *"...a synagogue of satan,"*[52] so too, in coming to this new continent, He had to break the satanic domination of the country. Sometimes, when speaking of evangelization, we tend to forget that bringing the word of God to man is first of all a Spiritual battle between the good and the bad angels. As one can see clearly in the parable of the sower, the devil is always at hand to take away the word of God before it arrives to our heart.[53]

---

[52] cf. Rv 2:9
[53] cf. Mk 13

Necessarily, a Spiritual fight must have preceded and accompanied the conquest of Mexico by Cortés, because the devil never easily lets go of that which is already in his hands. It is thus that we conjecture with certainty that the Spanish missionaries very consciously took advantage of the help of the seven archangels as the leaders of the heavenly hosts. A clear proof of this fact is the presence of the images of the seven archangels in Latin America, particularly in Tlaxcala, the first diocese of the New World, where we find their images, together with their names, in several churches.

The mission of the archangels seems to be to prepare the Reign of the Immaculate Heart of Mary, preparing her Son's second coming. This is confirmed when we seriously consider the apparition of St. Michael in 1631, in the small of town of San Bernabé, Tlaxcala. Folklore amongst Tlaxcaltecans has it that the final Spiritual battle for the reign of God will take place where St. Michael appeared. Whether that legend comes to be or not, we are reminded that this diocese of Tlaxcala, the cradle of evangelization in the New World, will most certainly have a primary role in the battle of the triumph of the Immaculate Heart of Mary. The healing of mankind from sin and the consummation of creation has to come through the passion of Our Lord Jesus Christ. Soberly seen, the end of the world will only come when the church as the Mystical Body of Christ will have consummated the measure of the passion of Christ. The apparition of Our Lady in Mexico in 1531 is the counter-sign to the reformation of Luther in Europe, which made three million Catholics fall away from the true faith. The apparition of St. Michael in 1631 corresponds perfectly with Chapter 12 of the Apocalypse. The appearance of St. Michael, the Prince of the heavenly host, is to follow the "great sign" and the "counter-sign." It is his mission to open the battle against the dragon. (Rv 12:7-12)

> "A great sign appeared in the heaven: a woman clothed with the sun, and the moon was under her feet, and upon her head a crown of twelve stars. And being with child, she wailed aloud in pain as she labored to give birth." (12:1).

The counter-sign follows:

> *"And another sign was seen in heaven, and behold, a great red dragon having seven heads and ten horns, and upon his heads seven diadems. And his tail was dragging along the third part of the stars of heaven, and it dashed them to the earth; and the dragon stood before the woman who was about to give birth, that when she had given birth he might devour her son."* (12:3 ff.).

In this final combat of the Spirits, man is the booty. For a long time the devil has been preparing this decisive stroke against the church of Christ. Only if she will cling to Our Lady and call out for the help of the angels will she be able to overcome the last furious attack of the devil. Unfortunately, most of the faithful are blind to the signs of the times.

Every action of God, irrespective of who executes it, has different layers of meaning. There are different layers of meaning in the apparition of St. Michael:

- it was an immediate help against the continuing diabolic infestations in this place during the time following the apparition of Our Lady. The older people from San Miguel still remember when people were afraid to pass by certain places because they were known to be infested by the evil one.
- this apparition certainly was meant to help people in the various human ailments caused by a life of poverty, especially the natives, who had suffered so much at the hands of the Spanish government.
- it was a means of rehabilitation and affirmation for the poor Indians in the person of the seer, Lázaro. One of the reasons Lázaro did not immediately fulfill St. Michael's mandate was because of the poor self-concept held by the Indians, who considered themselves inferior to the Spaniards, and hardly dared to meet them.

However, this apparition of St. Michael still has a deeper significance. It is not merely an historical event. The site of the second apparition is located in a deep gorge, probably produced by an earthquake, where there was a hidden fountain of crystalline water which collected a little further away into a muddy pond at which vultures used to quench their thirst. This detail can be interpreted symbolically: the muddy waters of this pond represent mankind, slave to sin and prey to the devilish thirst of the fallen angels who want to make man fall deeper and deeper into sin until he finally falls into the abyss. The ray from heaven which descended into this fountain when St. Michael touched it with his staff is a symbol for God's grace descending on poor mankind, helping all those who seek the light in order to escape the darkness of sin.

The Prophecy of Daniel in Relation to St. Michael

Over the main entrance to the sanctuary at San Miguel del Milagro, a quotation from the Book of Daniel is displayed:

At that time there shall arise Michael, the great prince, guardian of your people; (DAN 12:1)

It is this prophecy that will help us to enter into a more profound interpretation of this apparition of St. Michael. This prophecy is part of other apocalyptic prophecies in the Book of Daniel. The first is found in Chapter 2, describing King Nabuchodonosor's dream of a statue composed of various materials, with the head of pure gold and feet of clay. The interpretation is simple: the secular governments, approaching the end of times will become increasingly earthly, until finally they will be destroyed by a stone falling down from the mountain, a symbol for the rock of God, Who in the end will take over the government of this universe.

The second vision in Chapter 7 describes four beasts, symbol of the devil's domination over the entire earth, the fourth and last being the worst one:

"It had great iron teeth with which it devoured and crushed, and what was left it trampled with its feet. I was considering the ten horns it had, when suddenly another, a little horn, sprang out of their midst, and three

of the previous horns were torn away to make room for it. This horn had eyes like a man, and a mouth that spoke arrogantly." (7:7-8)

The little horn seems to be a clear reference to the antichrist.

The third vision is of the "ancient one" and the Son of Man follows: *"His dominion is an everlasting dominion that shall not be taken away."* (7:13,14) At the end of the citation we find an explanation of the fourth beast:

> *"The fourth beast shall be a fourth kingdom on earth, different from all the others; it shall devour the whole earth, beat it down and crush it.... He shall speak against the Most High and oppress the holy ones of the Most High, thinking to change the feast days and the law. They shall be handed over to him for a year, two years, and a half year. But when the court is convened and his power is taken away by final and absolute destruction, then the kingship and dominion shall be given to the holy people of the Most High."* (7:24-27)

This again is an allusion to the final battle between Christ and the antichrist.

The fourth vision in Chapter 8 speaks about the ram and the he-goat. Beyond the concrete relation to the Jewish people in the two centuries before the coming of Christ, we also perceive here an apocalyptic sense. The he-goat, triumphant over the ram, can be interpreted as another mask of the devil conquering by violence the government of a world lost in commercial affairs and sinful life. It seems to be telling us that one day the violence of communism will put an end to the world-wide power of capitalism run rampant as described in the Apocalypse:

> *"The waters that you saw where the harlot sits, are peoples and nations and tongues. And the ten horns that you saw, and the beast, these will hate the harlot, and will make her desolate and naked, and will eat her flesh, and will burn her up in fire."* (Apoc 17:15-17)

The fifth prophecy is the prophecy of the "seventy weeks" (Ch. 9). As interpreted by St. Gabriel, it signifies the time of chastisement for the holy people:

> *"Then transgression will stop and sin will end, guilt will be expiated, everlasting justice will be introduced, vision and prophecy ratified, and the Most Holy will be anointed."* (9:24)

Again, this vision applies apocalyptically to the last times when Christ in His second coming will put an end to the dominion of the devil on earth.

The last vision, (Chapters 10 to 12), already mentioned in the beginning of this chapter, is referred to as the "great vision" and deals with the history of the Hellenistic wars and the occupation of the holy land by the enemy. Already in Chapter 10, St. Gabriel appears to Daniel and explains why he did not come sooner:

> *"But the prince of the kingdom of Persia stood in my way for twenty one days, until finally Michael, one of the chief princes, came to help me...."* (10:13).

The "prince of Persia" is one of the fallen angels who dominates this pagan country. Michael, as the prince of the heavenly host, is called to enter into battle with the enemy.

The quote from the beginning of Chapter 12 with which we began our interpretation of Daniel continues in verse two:

> *"Many of those who sleep in the dust of the earth shall awake; some shall live forever, others shall be an everlasting horror and disgrace. But the wise shall shine brightly like the splendor of the firmament, and those who lead the many to justice shall be like the stars forever."* (12:2-3).

This prophecy refers to St. Michael in his final mission of separating darkness from light by his battle cry, "Who is like unto God?" Whoever hears it and follows him is assured of eternal salvation and will awake from the death of sin and participate in eternal life.

The words of the prophecies of Daniel were to be sealed "until the end of time." As they are for the most part the words of an angel, they can be explained only in the light of the angels.

The First Apparition — April 25, 1631

To the Feast of St. Mark, The "Hidden" Word

The fact that the first apparition of St. Michael in Capula-Nativitas coincides with the Feast of St. Mark gives us another clue to a deeper interpretation of this event.

The Gospel of St. Mark uniquely presents Christ as the Son of Man whom we have already met in the visions of Daniel. He is not seen as the Messiah that the Jews expected to come from the root of David. It is God's Son Who will descend from heaven to accomplish the final judgment. This vision of Our Lord Jesus Christ is not one from "below" as the Messiahs, but from "above" but they complement each other. "Messiah" is the title of Our Lord in the line of the Incarnation, the "Son of Man," descending from heaven is the title for Christ returning to judge the living and the dead. As we know from the Gospels, He will return seated upon a cloud accompanied by all His angels.[54]

Because of the preeminence of the "Son of Man," St. Mark is considered the apocalyptic Gospel among the four Gospels. This Gospel is Spiritually orientated to the west, where the sun sets,[55] symbolizing the final judgment: *"He who believes and is baptized*

---

[54] cf. Mt 24:30, 26:64, Mk 13:26, 14:62, Lk 21:27 and Rv 1:7

[55] The gospels, as word of the Lord are directed to the four directions of the wind. According to their predominant perspective on life and mission of Our Lord Jesus Christ it is not difficult to find out to which special direction they should be related. St. Matthew as the evangelist of the holiness of God is related to the East, St. Luke with the perspective of the mercy of God to the north (never we needed so much this Mercy of God than in our dark times — and God has responded to our cry in the beatified Faustina with her revelation about the merciful Lord), to the south the clear sight of St. John on the justice of God and finally to the east in St. Mark the revelation of the omnipotence of God. For a deeper interpretation of the Synoptics see the lectures on the Synoptics (not yet published).

shall be saved, but he who does not believe shall be condemned."[56]
It is also the shortest Gospel with the most concise expression of
the Christian Kerygma. Mark does not tarry over the human details
of the person of Christ or enter into meditation as does St. Luke.
Unlike St. Matthew who uses many references to the Old Testament, St. Mark is direct, thus making the word of his Gospel action. It produces what it says. There is no room for discussion, we
can only accept it in blind faith and obedience. The Gospel of St.
Mark represents the fourth main quality of God: omnipotence. The
end of the world will only come when the gospel of the kingdom
will be preached again, and for the last time, through the apocalyptic mission of St. Michael, together with the other archangels as
leaders of the heavenly hosts in line with the Omnipotent God. The
archangels certainly also had accompanied Cortés and the first missionaries[57] in the conquest of this country and the New World. This

---

[56] Mk 16,16 — This grave sentence is often omitted in liturgical texts — we are
too much "humanistic" — but in the light of the dawning sun there is no "in-
termediate" solution. We have to respond to St. Michaels cry: "Who is like
unto God!"

[57] The first 12 Franciscan missionaries arrived to Texcoco in 1523, but did not begin
evangelizing until the following year after they had studied the language of the
nahuas. It is significant that in the small diocese of Tlaxcala we find seven churches
with the images of the seven archangels with their names, the oldest in the actual
cathedral, where the first nobleman of the Tlaxcalenses were baptized.

is one of the reasons why images of the seven archangels can still be found primarily in the Latin American countries, and especially in Mexico.[58] The whole world, in the omnipotence of God, present in the Gospel of St. Mark.[59]

The Second Apparition — May 8, 1631

To the Apparition of St. Michael
on Monte Gargano, Italy, IV Century (same date)

The second apparition of St. Michael in Capula coincides with the date of the most important apparition of St. Michael in Europe. In a book on St. Michael, Rosenberg[60] enumerates almost two hundred apparitions of St. Michael that took place up until the Medieval Ages in Europe. Most of them have been practically obliterated. Mount St. Michel in northwestern France is not much more than a museum. The only "living" place of apparition is that of Monte Gargano in southern Italy, very proximate to where Padre Pio lived at San Giovanni Rotondo.

It is told that a nobleman was in pursuit of a runaway bull. He followed it into a cave where it had fallen and there, St. Michael

---

[58] The first sanctuary to the seven archangels was consecrated by Cardinal Sim a few years ago in Manila, on the common decision of the conference of bishops of the Philippines. Although there is an age-old tradition of the veneration of the seven archangels in the Philippines, it is only an oral tradition. The images of the seven archangels in the sanctuary of Manila are reproductions of images from Mexico, most probably of those of the basilica of Our Lady of Ocotlán in Tlaxcala.

[59] cf. Mt 24:14 It will be a word enlightened and enforced by the power of the Holy Spirit by way of His instruments, the holy angels. The human instruments according to St. Louis Marie Montfort will be "the prophets of the last times." They will accomplish this mission in the omnipotence of God so that no force of the devil nor any obstacle of the enemy can hinder the word of God in reaching the hearts of those who in these dark times still look up to the light of God (cf. the "signs" that will accompany them: they will expulse demons, speak in new tongues, they will lift up serpents, if they will drink something poisoned it will not harm them, they will put their hands on the sick and make them sane" (16:18). These five signs are another scriptural confirmation that the power of the five wounds of Our Lord will be given to them — first of all against the hellish fiend and his grip on man. Remember what we wrote about the number five in relation to the five mysteries of the rosary!

[60] This book is no longer available.

appeared to him.[61] This marked the first of four apparitions of St. Michael, the first in the VIIth, the last in the XVIth century. News of the apparition was transmitted to church authorities, and it was soon acknowledged by the church. Monte Gargano became a famous shrine to which thousands of pilgrims came. Here, St. Michael put an end to the black death. He asked that the villagers gather in the grotto to pray and that they take home relics of the rock of the cave. The black death was one of the worst plagues of the Middle Ages. It has always been considered a "religious disease of chastisement," such as leprosy was in the Old Testament and as some might consider cancer and AIDS today. That being the case, only God can take away these plagues. As God sent His angel to free Peter from his chains, He can once again liberate the church from its babylonic captivity.

During the Middle Ages, pilgrimaging to St. Michael on Monte Gargano was second in line of importance after the pilgrimage to Santiago de Compostela in Spain. This fact alone shows the important role of St. Michael in his mission to help the church to overcome the obstacles and the attacks of the devil against the good news. The last important apparition of St. Michael must have been that in Rome, on occasion of a terrible plague which came over the Holy City. The place where he appeared is the Fortress of St. Michael on the right bank of the Tiber River, not far away from the Vatican.[62]

---

[61] Is not the bull which fell into the cavern, according Greek mythology, a symbol for the continent of Europe which at that time urgently needed help from the angels to be delivered from the clutches of the devil? Here again we must look for a deeper understanding of this apparition. Later, meditating on the constellation on the mantle of Our Lady, we will find another correlation to the bull in the constellation Taurus, represented by three stars where her mantle cuts through the moon.

[62] Here we also find the image of the seven archangels — their names, by order of the church, have been erased. As this was done in Rome it is significant for the whole church — we have to pray for the "comeback" of the heavenly warriors. In the Philippines, Cardinal Sim took the first step on behalf of his flock in their strenuous fight against communist infiltration, by dedicating the former Procathedral of St. Michael to the seven archangels. Only when we know (by suffering!) that we are in a Spiritual fight without pardon, will we be able to appreciate the help of the "heavenly army"! God does not impose His graces — they have to be asked for in contrition and humility!

In the apparition on May 8 in Bernabé, Capula[63] a ray of light from heaven descended into the muddy waters of Cacaxtla, the ravine where the seer was miraculously transported after having been healed from his grave illness. In this apparition, St. Michael explained: *"The light that you have seen descend from heaven is the virtue which God is giving to this spring for the health and healing of all infirmities and necessities. Make it known to all."*

In the first apparition on April 25, Lázaro had an interior vision of the angel who told him to make the apparition known to the corresponding Spanish authorities. St. Michael broke the chains of sin which held the poor native captive enabling him to fulfill his mission. His strictness with the seer is a mandate of the concentration of his entire will so as to accomplish his mission. The heavenly mandate had to profoundly penetrate the seer's heart thus making him capable of that which he was asked.

The Third Apparition — November 13, 1631

Related to the Apparition of Our Lady of Fátima in 1917

Another relation is indicated by the date of the third apparition in Capula on November 13. The number thirteen is considered by many to be an "evil" number. Many people become anxious about doing anything important on days which fall on the 13th of the month. The truth behind this superstition is that the number thirteen is the number which the first fallen angel has arrogated for himself. For this reason Our Lady chose the 13th of each month to appear in Fátima as a reminder to us Christians that it is She Who will crush the serpent! By appearing on this date, one month before the anniversary of the apparition of Our Lady on the 12th of December, St. Michael certainly wants to remind us that faith overcomes all fear: *"This is the victory that overcomes the world, our faith."*[64] But faith will grow strong only through sacrifice, as can be

---

[63] Formerly, May 8 was the official feast day of St. Michael on Monte Gargano; as more and more the importance of the apparition for the church in Europe was obliterated, it was officially suppressed by the church at the end of the last century.

[64] 1 Jn 5:4

clearly seen in the children of Fátima who, in order to confirm the mission of Our Lady, sought all possible occasions to offer any kind of sacrifice. On September 13, 1917, Our Lady even had to curtail their eagerness for sacrifice because they were harming their health by wearing a rope around their waists.

This third intervention of St. Michael was while Lázaro was attending Mass in Nativitas[65] with the Franciscans, he was severely beaten by an invisible being, so much that he could hardly make his way home. At home, he met St. Michael who soberly explained to him that this chastisement was necessary to remind him of his duty to continue trying to make the apparition known. At last, Lázaro found the courage to present himself to the bishop of Puebla, Monsignor Palafox, who received him with open arms. He listened with interest to his story, and asked for the water and mud which Lázaro had brought along as testimony of the authenticity of the apparition. The bishop promised to investigate the apparition and to send him the results of his findings. When Lázaro had gone, he distributed the water to the sick in the hospital. All who drank the water were cured.

It was only fifty years after before they began building the Sanctuary of San Miguel del Milagro, which remains standing today. In the beginning Lázaro, the same as Juan Diego in Mexico, served as sacristan for the small chapel which had been erected, but died soon thereafter. The lesson of this last apparition is that of sacrifice, the same lesson given to the children at Fátima. The most difficult sacrifices are not the physical restriction we impose upon ourselves, but the sacrifice of submitting our own will to the greater and wiser will of God. Man can be used as an instrument in God's plan of mercy only if he dies to his own ideas and desires. This is true not only for Lázaro, for the Fátima children, but is equally true for every Christian. In order to surrender ourselves, we must ask God for a greater and deeper love, a love that helps us to forget ourselves in order that we might lose our hearts and minds in God.

---

[65] Another "Marian coincidence" — this major village to which San Bernabé-Capula is subordinated, is dedicated in a special way to the birth of Our Lady. This reminds us that Christ Her Son can be born in our hearts only if Mary is born there first.

The Angelic Obedience of Diego Lázaro, the Seer

"Obedience begins where human reason ends." The entire story of St. Michael's apparition to Lázaro is a beautiful example of this bitter truth to which we have to submit. The way St. Michael speaks to and treats the seer is quite in line with the Gospel of St. Mark: no explanations, no consolations, no exterior help! The seer must look up to God alone and ask for His help; only in this way can he fulfill the difficult mission received by the angel. He needs dark faith, dark hope and dark love in order to enter deeper into his mission. God leaves him time to discover the urgency of his mission and grow into it, but He will not remove one iota from the original mandate given him by the archangel in the first apparition.

This is also the sober way God wants to educate us in our union with our angel. Only if, little by little, we learn to follow our angel in silence, listening, obedience, purity, sincerity, poverty and fidelity in imitation of Mary can we become instruments of the mercy of God. The angel explained this to the children in the second apparition in Fátima in 1916 when he told them: *"The hearts of Jesus and Mary have designs of mercy for you."* The severe challenge of the angel will always be a hindrance for the majority of Christians in submitting to God's plans of mercy. So we will necessarily be singled out from the "multitude" and must follow the incomprehensible ways of God's will for salvation. This is possible only at the hand of our good Guardian Angel, helped and accompanied by all the angels.

The last apparition parallels not only the apparition of the angel of Portugal to the three shepherd children in Fátima but also the mission given to Juan Diego by Our Lady of Guadalupe. Again, as in the beginning, we see that the help offered and given to us by Mary and the angels in these last times is one. Wherever we meet Our Lady we also meet the angels; and wherever we meet the angels, there Our Lady is present. And wherever Mary is, we can know that her Son is also there. For this is her one objective: to cause her Son to be known and loved and through Him to make better known and loved the Most Holy Trinity.

The Prophecies of the "Two Witnesses"

In the eleventh chapter of the Apocalypse, an angel gave St. John a rod and told him, *"Rise and measure the temple of God and the altar and those who worship therein. But the court outside the temple, reject it, and do not measure it; for it has been given to the nations, and the holy city they will trample under foot for forty-two months. And I will grant unto my two witnesses to prophecy for a thousand two hundred and sixty days clothed in sackcloth."* (11:1-4) In the last times, the church will be reduced to a small flock following Christ on His way of the cross.[66]

The only riches left to her will be the house of God in relation to the Father, the altar in relation to the Son, and worship in relation to the Holy Spirit. Everything else the church has acquired throughout the centuries as part of the world in which she lives will be progressively taken away from her. In exchange God will give her the immeasurable treasures of His love, primarily by way of the two hearts of Jesus and Mary which are here represented as the "two witnesses" of God's love before the church and the world. The prophecy of the forty-two months is a prophecy wholly in and by Mary, because the number "42" added horizontally equals 6 which is Our Lady's number.[67] The church must be reformed according to the image of the Immaculata in order to represent Christ. The time of prophecy, 1,260 days, is also symbolic. Added horizontally, it equals 9, the number of the choirs of angels. The angels are the help of Our Lady in her last mission with the church.

What is described in Chapter 11 of the Apocalypse is the final call of God's love by the two hearts (also designated as the "two olive trees" and the "two lamp stands" that stand before the Lord of the earth (11:4)). But there will come a time when their mission will end: *"The beast that comes up out of the abyss will wage war against them, and will conquer them and kill them."* (11:7) This is a symbolic indication that the church in the last times must follow the Lord on the way of the cross to Golgotha. Only in dying on the cross with Him will she rise with Him:

---

[66] The devotion to the two hearts of Jesus and Mary has already, in our days, been reduced to a few faithful souls.

[67] 2 x 3 indicates that she is the most perfect mirror of the Most Holy Trinity.

"After the three days and a half, the breath of life from God entered into them. And they stood up on their feet, and a great fear fell upon those who saw them. And they heard a great voice from heaven saying to them, 'Come up hither.' And they went up to heaven in a cloud, and their enemies saw them. And at that hour there was a great earthquake and the tenth part of the city fell; and there were killed in the earthquake seven thousand persons; and the rest were affrighted and gave glory to the God of heaven." (11:11-13).

The earthquake is a symbol for the purification that the church must undergo: *"the tenth part"* of the city points out the omnipotence of God to which man has to submit. We need to be shaken awake so that we find our way back to the Fear of GOD[68] and to true sober Piety. The number "7,000" indicates that this chastisement is an act of the Holy Spirit, eliminating all those who instead of letting themselves be guided by the Spirit of God are guided by the Spirit of the fallen angels.

Summary

The Apparition of St. Michael as a Message of Light

A confirmation of the apocalyptic mission of St. Michael is that in the second apparition of May 8, 1631, a beam of light descended into the muddy pond where the vultures gathered to quench their thirst. His mission was not only to cast out the demons in Cacaxtla, a former pagan sanctuary, and to promise cure to the sick and assistance to the dying, but he also prophesied in a veiled way his final intercession on our behalf in the Spiritual combat at the end of time. This is confirmed by an "insignificant" detail: In his apparition in Capula, St. Michael carries neither a sword nor a balance as he usually does when shown in pictures. But he carries a golden staff with a small cross on top, the same way that St. John the Baptist is usually represented. The distinctive sign of this staff is that here the vertical bar in comparison with the little horizontal

---

[68] Here meaning "right measure" or awe.

bar is overemphasized, proclaiming that his mission is first of all to point up to God alone. With St. John this staff is of wood — remembering that Our Lord will die on the wood of the cross. With St. Michael the staff is of gold, indicating that He will come again in glory to judge the living and the dead! As creation began with God's words *"Let there by light,"* and as at the birth of Christ, the fields of Bethlehem were inundated by the light of the angels singing "Gloria,"[69] so too at the end, this world will be immersed in the light of God descending by the angels.

St. Michael is the angel of faith indicating that which is most necessary in order to enter into the heavenly mansions. Because in these last times the devil has managed to remove much of the external support of faith, it has become imperative that we rely on "pure" or "blind" faith, because the outward structure and order of Christianity has been increasingly lost or secularized. As the outward structure of the church poorly represents the heavenly order of the angels, we must root ourselves in the immutable order of the angels that we might be able to hold fast during this storm of evil. The angels, and in particular, St. Michael, Prince of the heavenly hosts, are sent to help us in this crisis of faith.

In Fátima, the angel of Portugal, St. Gabriel necessarily had to prepare the children for the subsequent apparitions of Our Lady. In San Bernabé, St. Michael's apparition is subsequent to that of Our Lady of Guadalupe: he will open the eyes of those who want to see for the Spiritual combat which necessarily will have to follow the apparition of Our Lady of Guadalupe as the "woman surrounded by the sun" and so free her mission of any purely national and local interpretation, which unfortunately because of our human sinfulness was inevitable.[70] The angel living in the face of the triune God can tell us better not only Who God is, but also what precisely

---

[69] cf. Gen 1:3 and Luke 2:7-14

[70] The same thing happens with our traditional Christian truths, thanks to God, so well guarded by Mother church. If we are not stirred up again and again in a more direct way — which always directly or indirectly has to do with the special mission of the holy angels in the work of salvation of Christ. They must help us to a deeper interpretation of Holy Scripture — if we do not arrive, in the light of the Holy Spirit, to the "profounder sense" of the word of God, we are easily tempted, as largely demonstrated in today's exegesis, to adapt it to our contemporary way of understanding the things of God!

He is asking us for! Even these pure souls, as we see with the three children of Fátima necessarily need to be "stirred up," in order to receive the message in the depth of their soul and not as something they are just given, as is today the case with so many "messages."[71]

In her memoirs, Lucia writes about the second apparition of the angel in the Loca de Cabeco:

"Only now we knew Who God was, how much He loves us, and how much He wants to be loved."[72]

By means of the apparition of the angel they came to know more about the greatness and majesty of God and learned something about the fear of God, which is increasingly lost in our times. In Fátima the angel had the important mission of placing the children into the "right distance" in relation to God.

Only thus were they guarded against the temptation of adapting the apparition and the message of Our Lady to the human perspective. Unfortunately the importance of the angel for the apparition in Fátima has almost been forgotten; the consequence is apparent: here as in other places of Our Lady's apparitions a kind of "religious tourism" has taken over. Consequently the message loses the "force of light," becomes sentimentalized, "provincialized," and minimized; we are adapting Our Lady and her message to our "religious standard of living."

---

[71] The enemy's acute psychology is aware of all our frailties and uses them to turn us away from God. This is unfortunately true also with our technical means today, by which we want to get more hold on what heaven has to tell us (charismatic "network").

[72] cf. *Fátima in Lucia's Own Words.*

Book Four

The Movement of Ransom in the Sign of the Lamb of God

A Eucharistic Vision of the Image of Our Lady of Guadalupe

The Mystery of the Lamb of God

Another Sign for the Trinitarian Mystery of the Holy Eucharist

"Lamb of God" is the expression used by St. John to introduce Our Lord Jesus Christ in his gospel. St. John the Baptist first points to Him as the *"Lamb of God, who will take away the sins of the World."*[1] The "Lamb of God" is also St. John's center of focus for the Apocalypse. The four petalled flower on the womb of Our Lady of Guadalupe should in turn be understood in light of the Lamb of God, He Who is preparing his second coming, in, with and through the "woman clothed with the sun."

In God's wisdom, everything is foreseen and nothing happens outside His providence. The more we explore the depths of His words, His parables and His deeds, in and with Mary, the more we

---

[1]   Jn 1:29

begin to see an interrelatedness throughout the spectrum of time up to and inclusive of His final coming. This "exploring the depths" is also necessary for the image of Our Lady of Guadalupe,[2] when we see her as "the great sign," the apocalyptic woman. Her continued presence through her image is as much a sign of consolation as is the book of the Apocalypse, already called by the fathers "the book of consolation." In like manner, considering this perspective of the second coming of Our Lord Jesus Christ, it holds true that the image of Guadalupe is like the roof on the House of Revelation, it is "The Fifth Gospel."[3]

The Eucharistic Presence of Our Lord is yet a deeper veil about His Incarnation. In the sacred species of bread and wine the Lord becomes the fundamental sustenance of our life. This mystery can be seen in a triple way:

- in relation to the Father, He is the foundation of our life IN God. We are fundamented in God and have to construct our lives on God. (static)
- in relation to the Son, the Eucharist is the force which will help us to extend ourselves towards God more and more, seeking Him until we are finally home with Him. (dynamic)
- in relation to the Holy Spirit, the Holy Eucharist is promise of consolation: our life must become "round" according to the eternal plan of God (realization).

---

[2] Rv 12:1 calls Mary the "Great Sign," but if we were to examine the entire book, we would find that St. John's vision surrounds "the sign" of the lamb: cf. Rv 5:6, 5:8, 5:12, 5:13, 6:1, 6:16, 7:9, 7:10, 7:14, 7:17, 12:11, 13:8, 13:11, 14:1, 14:4, 14:10, 15:3, 17:14, 19:7, 19:9, 21:14, 21:22, 21:23, 22:1, 22:3

[3] As a pictorial message, a message of silence and light, resuming the four written gospels.

A sign of the trinitarian presence of God in the Holy Eucharist can be found in the image of Guadalupe:

- in the four-petalled flower (the very center of the person of the Virgin of Tepeyac)
- in her heart burnt to ashes (visible on the outside of her left hand)
- In her golden colored shoe (on the right side below her gown)

For the Aztec, the Mother of God, by way of her word, her messenger and her image, is the Gospel. She brings her Son, not in the image of the Child of Bethlehem, which the Aztec would have hardly understood, but precisely in the sign of the four-petalled flower.[4] From this starting point, a symbol comprising all their ideas about the transcendent God, they will understand all the other signs and thus little by little enter more deeply in the good news of Christ.[5] Maize (corn) is the grain from which the "daily bread" (tortilla) of the Mexican nation is made. Even the poor, many of whom have but a tortilla with a little salt for a meal, can afford this humble sustenance. Corn has multiple significances within the culture and religion of the Meso-Americans. Historically, it was even rendered as having a sacramental relation to God. Even today, the corn tortilla remains the daily sustenance for the Mexicans. It seems that faith has not yet made a bridge between wheat and corn, between bread and tortilla. Certainly, this is a deeper reason for the lack of the enrooting of this mystery of the Holy Eucharist in the Christian people. Only Our Lady can help make the bridge. So as to understand more fully, we have to meditate "in Spirit and truth," and therefore, we need the light of the angel through the Holy Spirit. In the following meditation we try to point out how this relation between wheat and corn could be established by way of a deeper understanding of the Eucharistic signs in the image of Our Lady.

---

[4]   A symbol pointing to Ometéotl, the one and only true god who is the fundament for all created things

[5]   The four-petalled flower, "nahui ollin," has more than eighty meanings ... all divine attributes, and was therefore a most perfect symbol for the Aztec of the divine presence in the womb of His earthly Mother.

The Triple Sign for the Eucharistic Presence of Our Lord in the Image of Our Lady of Guadalupe

The First Sign: The Four Petalled-Flower

The Sign of the Cross with its Four Directions

This flower certainly is another sign of the cross and its four fundamental directions, pointing out that the mystery of the Holy Eucharist will unfold only in living faith: by adoration, contemplation, reparation and mission.[6] They mysteriously recall the presence of the Most Holy Trinity in this sacrament:

- of the Father, Whom we come to know deepest in adoration,
- of the Son, Whom we should come to know better through contemplation in and by Mary, and
- of the Holy Spirit, Who more and more asks us, especially today, for reparation, because of all the outrages and sacrileges against this Holy Sacrament. (recall the third apparition and the prayer of the angel in Fátima asking for this reparation).

Only if the triune God is present in us in this triple manner, will we be ready for our mission.

The Rounded Cross

The cross is the "iron law" of creation and salvation, and only by way of it can we grow, unfold and be consummated. Whoever stands up against the law of the cross will, like the rebellious an-

---

[6] Remember that the Aztec had a different way of pointing to the north, cf. Book III; pp 7 and 14

gels, fall out of God and destroy oneself. As a hieroglyphic sign, we find the "rounded cross" in all pagan religions and ancient cultures. Deep in his subconscious, man knows that life is fundamented on sacrifice, but being seduced and misguided by the devil, he invents his own ways of sacrifice, many of which lead to genocide and an outright annihilation of the genuine idea of sacrifice, of helping man to realize himself.

By way of meditation in the loving heart of Our Lady, the cross loses the rough edges which make it an inexorable sword. It becomes a jewel of the wisdom of God and a key for all deeper understanding in the Holy Spirit. The pearls of the rosary are a beautiful external expression of this truth.[7] The fact that we find this "rounded cross" with the pagans, as a religious sign, is an indication that man guided by the Holy Spirit is orientated towards Mary in whom creation and salvation comes to its consummation.

The Four Fundamental Directions of the
Cross in the Mission of Juan Diego

- Adoration we find in his admiration for the beauty of light falling on him through Our Lady: it is light from the light of God.
- Contemplation is found in the manner in which he takes up his mission deeply into his heart, until finally he is completely identified with it. Mary lives in him and by way of her Son.
- He partakes in reparation by silently accepting all rejection of the bishop and his servants.
- After the apparition he consecrates his entire life to continue the mission Our Lady has entrusted to him. It is a mission hidden in the Immaculate Heart of Our Lady, we can see as a hidden sign on the outside of her left hand. In serving her, his heart will also become ashes.

---

[7] cf. Book I

The Second Sign: the Immaculate Heart of Mary Burnt to Ashes as Veil around the Presence of Her Son

This Heart of Our Lady is another sign for the seven veils surrounding the presence of Her Son in her womb.[8] Every veil, unique and different from the others, is a veil of pure love! How could it be otherwise with the love of a mother for her son, ever so much more with the holy Mother of God! And again, we have to see the presence of her Son in a triple way; in the sign of the four-petalled flower, the Lamb and the Holy Eucharist: a triad of symbols again in relation to the most Holy Trinity:

- The four-petalled flower is the distinctive sign of this apocalyptical apparition, in relation to the Father, because it is the Father who wants to see the cross flourish in our hearts before, by way of the Immaculate Heart, we return home in the Holy Spirit.
- The lamb is the sign proper to the Son, of Him Who has given His life, to free us from the captivity of sin.[9]
- The Holy Eucharist is the sign for the heavenly food given to us on this pilgrimage home. It is a sacramental "Sign," truly the Body, Blood, Soul and Divinity of Our Lord Jesus Christ, it helps us to be more and more transformed into the Son by the Holy Spirit, so that when we arrive at the door of heaven, the Father will recognize us in Him!

It is the Mother Who Wants to Give us
Her Son, as Mother of the Holy Eucharist

Only with, in and through Mary, the *"woman clothed with the sun,"* will we, little by little, find out about the depth, the greatness and the beauty of this sacrament of love. Only by way of the "imi-

---

[8]   Recall the seven veils presented in Book III.
[9]   cf. Isaiah 53:7

tation of Mary" in her burning surrender for God will we arrive at this deeper understanding, because it is a mystery which can only be understood with her at the foot of the cross.[10] Here we will come to know why the Lord has instituted this Holy Sacrament already before His suffering: by way of His Eucharistic Presence in us, He wants to continue His sacrifice for the church as His Mystical Body.

Living Tabernacle of God

It is not by chance that the joined hands of Our Lady of Guadalupe are in the upward direction. The white of her ermine cuffs and her undergown, shaped like an alpha[11] and a small omega, are another sign for the Most Holy Sacrament of the altar hidden in her womb as in a tabernacle. Only by way of her can we begin to understand the desire of little St. Thérèse of Lisieux; that the Lord would abide in her in the sacred species from one communion to the other. Here also, we should remember this special grace given to the holy bishop, St. Anthony Marie Claret. By this "real presence" of Our Lord in the soul of the first faithful, the church will be fortified and remain constantly under the guidance of the Holy Spirit.

---

[10] The mystery of Eucharist is already unfolding at the Annunciation when the Angel tells her that He Whom she will conceive will save his people from their sins, when in Bethlehem, "House of Bread," He is born in utmost poverty, but hailed the same by the "Gloria" of the heavenly hosts, the Wisemen of the Orient and of the humble shepherds, when at His circumcision and presentation to the Father He is prophesied to be the cause of the rise and fall of many and the reason why the Immaculate Heart of his Mother will be pierced. The Child Jesus lost for three days reminds us that we can meet Him in this Holy Sacrament only at the foot of the cross. Openly, at the Wedding Feast of Cana of Galilee, she gives her Son as Eucharist: she says "they have no wine.," as if telling her Son to be "wine," to be drink, to satisfy the thirst of those invited to the wedding feast.

[11] It is a styled A, like the point of an arrow, pointing upwards to her Immaculate Heart, saying: this is the new beginning.

Key for all knowledge

Between Our Lady's joined hands, one might recognize a shadow likened unto a key: a silent sign for us that this holy sacrament holds for us not only the key to eternal beatitude, but also the key for all mysteries of our faith and all knowledge of God already here on earth. Only by way of God can we come to know God. This is what St. Paul points out to the early Christians.[12]

If we only understand the Holy Eucharist as the presence of Our Lord in His church in an exterior way, then we run the risk of misinterpreting it in a magical way, and trying to manipulate it according to our religious desires. This is not only a temptation in those countries where the faith has not been more deeply rooted, but more and more also in "Christian countries" where the living faith is lost: the pious reception of frequent communion can also become a practice of an "eternal life insurance."

It is by Her That This Sacrament Will be Unsealed.

This greatest of all mysteries of our faith will unfold only in the apocalyptical light of the holy angels in those "who adore the Father in Spirit and truth."[13] In the image, the seven seals are indicated by the seven folds of the black sash, for the Aztecs a sign of her maternity. In our perspective, they are seen in light of the central sacrament of our faith. Our Lady of Guadalupe is holding her hands, joined in prayer precisely over these seals. By this gesture, it is as if she is interceding for us with the Father and the Son, that they yet have patience with us poor, blind sinners. In many of the contemporary Marian visitations, Our Lady, weeping, pleads a conversion of man, because she can no longer hold back the arm of justice of the Father at the sight of His Son outraged in the holy sacrament of the altar. The sign of the Lamb of God is not only the sign for His meekness and infinite mercy, one day, as the Apocalypse announces, it will become the sign of final justice!

---

[12]   cf. I Cor 2:12
[13]   cf. Jn 4:23

The Sign of the Lamb with St. John as Two Edged Sword[14]

In the vision of the Gospel of St. John, "the historical Jesus" is identified by way of the "Lamb of God" with His Eucharistic presence in the church. This is why his Gospel has no institution of the blessed sacrament as we find with the Synoptics. Two words are used by St. John to designate the *"Lamb"*: in 1:29 and :36 the term is *"amnos tou theou"*: only twice again in the New Testament do we find the same term used. In the Apocalypse, he uses the term "arnion" twenty-seven times and only once in chapter 21:12 of his Gospel. The term *"amnos tou theo"* refers to the "Lamb led to slaughter."[15] The apocalyptic use of *"arnion"* translates to "horned-Lamb," and symbolizes the power of Resurrection irradiating from this symbol of Our Lord. By way of adoration, St. John sees Our Lord transparent to His Eucharistic presence in the church until the end of time. By His Eucharistic presence, the Lord aims at becoming present in the sacred species in the hearts of all the faithful. It should be underlined: not only by a merely Spiritual presence, but as previously pointed out with St. Thérèse and St. Anthony M. Claret, a presence by the sacred species.

This Eucharistic presence in the heart of the faithful has to make the church invincible in the apocalyptic battle against all the powers of hell. Only by "this presence" will the church overcome the infernal enemy. And only when this Eucharistic presence, will have conquered the hearts of the faithful of the last times, the end of things will come: the Lord coming on the clouds of heaven will recognize Himself in His Mystical Body the church.

---

[14] One edge is the call: "come, blessed of the Father...." This edge will prepare those called to eternal life a "holy way" through the red sea of sins of this time so that no enemy can do them harm when they have to leave "Egypt"; that which is already given to the wrath of God. The other edge is the sword: "depart..." to those who denied themselves to the love of God and now are thrown to eternal fire. The unsealing of the Holy Eucharist is the beginning of the last judgment, starting when the communion in the hand was officially allowed.

[15] cf. Isaiah 53:7, Jn 8:32 and I Pt 1:19

The Third Sign: A Sign of Mission - The Holy Eucharist in the Symbol of the Golden Colored Shoe: Sign of the Last Announcing of the Good News

Gold Colored Like Corn

The shoe of Our Lady is the only part in the entire ayate that has absolutely no coloring. The fiber of the ayate in itself has a golden hue, close to that of the color of a grain of corn. The point of her shoe is also in the form of a grain of corn. Remembering that the moon, as symbol of

Quetzacóatl, the feathered serpent, is a symbol for the values of the earth, then the fact that her shoe/foot touches a particular point of the moon silently tells us of the most important fruit of this earth. An overall view of the image of the Virgin (within the veil of the golden rays) not only has the form of an ear of a corn, but that of a kernel of wheat.

Out of the Material of this Earth

Is not the Eucharistic Bread, synthesis of the earth, serving us men and conserving our life such that we can fulfill our mission? More and more, in the same way that Our Lady was imprinted on the ayate of Juan Diego, we also must receive the form of Christ. As the "grain of corn" is a symbol of Mexico as "the umbilical cord" of the world,[16] so also the Holy Eucharist is the fruit in which the whole creation will finally be presented in the heavenly banquet where the Father will celebrate with the Son, in the Holy

---

[16] cf. Book II, pg. 8 and Book III, pg. 10 The shoe is a symbol of promise, that in this country the Holy Eucharist has to come to its fullness. The grain of wheat will enter into the gold colored corn. The grain of wheat is less gold in color than the corn. The shoe of Our Lady is precisely this lesser color of gold. How hidden is the message of the symbols.

Spirit, the consummated union of God with creation. In a certain way, the color of Our Lady's shoe can be likened unto the gold trimming of her gown, but it is not the same. Our Lord is not yet recognized in this sacrament of poverty and thus waits for His final glorification. As He sent the angel of Portugal to teach us Eucharistic reparation, so also by way of Our Lady's golden shoe does He teach us the same.

- The Last Announcing of the Gospel in the Sign of the Lamb.

Her shoe is also a sign that she is walking. It is a sign:

- Of her coming from the east and going to the west.
- Of her dancing pace, representing the prayer of the Aztecs, and their liturgical order.[17]

Her foot is the promise that again the Gospel will be announced over the whole earth, announcing the victory of the LAMB as St. John has seen it: a symbol of the Holy Eucharist in the sign of the Lamb.

The Movement of Ransom in the Nine Large Flowers on the Gown of Our Lady of Guadalupe

(An Interpretation of the Nine Big Flowers in View of the Prologue of St. John)

Introduction:

*The Movement of Ransom as a Silent Call of "I Thirst"
Out of the Eucharistic Heart of Our Lord*

The "Nahui Ollin," the four-petalled flower superimposed on the womb of Our Lady of Guadalupe, is Our Lady's geometric

---

[17] The holy rhythm of the dance is always a mirror of the order and the harmony of the universe and thus a sign of the justice of God.

center. It is the center, together with the two other centers: the sign of her heart burnt to ashes and the sign of her gold-colored shoe.

Recalling the movements of the rosary about the center of the triple birth of Our Lord in the soul,"[18] we can make the following correlation:

- The joyful birth related to her heart burnt to ashes; only being absolutely empty of herself can she receive her Son in her heart. She is really only a veil (of seven veils!) around His incomprehensible presence as God and Man.
- The sorrowful birth in the crowning with thorns corresponds to the Nahui Ollin, another sign, of the Lamb of God.
- The glorious birth in the descent of the Holy Spirit on the apostles in the sign of the golden colored shoe, as sign of mission in the Holy Spirit.

Already in the rosary we have seen that the movements of the other surrounding mysteries should not be seen as closed but as "open circles = spirals." This is precisely what we will discover in the image of Guadalupe: There is a movement with the large flowers starting below her Immaculate Heart, ending in the last of the nine flowers which is most in the light on the left side of her gown under her sleeve. It is this sleeve, like unto a fishing net, that will lift captive souls into the Sacred Heart of Our Lord, symbolized by the Nahui Ollin and the star Regulus, "Little King," of the constellation Leo which is directly in front of it.

- There is the second movement of the stars on her mantle, again mysteriously related with the two hearts: the Immaculate Heart of Mary and Our Lord's SACRED HEART.[19]
- There is a "third" invisible movement - corresponding to the silent call of "I thirst" to the heart of the faithful ... to your heart, if it is open for this call!

---

[18] cf. Book I
[19] to unfold in "The heavens Proclaim the glory of God"

The first movement, symbolized in the flowers, offers man, now become the "prodigal son," a new home in the "garden of Mary."

The second movement, symbolized in the movement of the stars, englobes the whole of creation, including the holy angels. There will be a new order reinstituting "paradise lost."

The third movement is a call to each man of good will. Only when the last man called to Eternal life will have entered the pierced Heart of Our Lord, creation and salvation will have come to its consummation.

The Currents in the Image

As expression of the life of the Most Holy Trinity, we can also recognize the three "currents" in the image, coming down from God through the mediation of Our Lady. We distinguish three different currents of graces:

- The current of life, attributed first of all to the Father, because He is the origin of all life. It is He Who engenders the word from all eternity and has brought creation into being in view of His Beloved Son, and sustains it in the love of the Holy Spirit until it will finally return home.

This current can be best seen on the turquoise mantle of Our Lady. Looking more attentively at the image, one will recognize like a flow of the waters of graces, especially on her left side. Water is the symbol for all created things, life has its origin in the water and will come to its perfection by the water of Grace in Jesus Christ in the love of the Holy Spirit. It is important to remark already now, that this current of life, in the image, is identical with the mantle of Our Lady, enveloping also the creation of man represented in her earth-toned gown and also that of the angels in the white undergown of Our Lady. Before God created anything, He first created space and time as the two dimensions in which the three-fold creation would come to its perfection. Here again we have the image of a house before our interior eyes: the house of space and time.

- The current of word and force correlated primarily to the Son, the word, the second divine person, is symbolically represented in the multiple lines we recognize on the gown of Our Lady. Practically all of them participate in what we call the "movement of ransom," having its origin in the descent of the Son of God into the darkness of this world and His ascending again to the Father after resurrecting.

This "movement of ransom" takes in the material world and avails itself of the holy angels, called to collaborate in bringing home "the prodigal son:" mankind lost in sin. In this movement of the word we can distinguish quite clearly four major lines of different size and mode. They can be compared with the four-pillars in the house God wills to construct, so that man has a home to live in on this earth.

They are like a presymbol of the house of the church and they have their parallel in what the ancients called "the columns of creation," comparing the immensity of creation, the space in which all created things are contained, with a house with four columns. Also, the hierarchy of the angels must have a mysterious relation to these columns, because in the history of salvation, they are called to help man build this house.

Their invisible participation in building the house of God on earth: the church can be seen in the construction of the great cathedrals of Christianity, so crystalline in their structure, that they make us see something of the admirable order of the reign of God. In them the three principles of construction: weight, just measure and number portray the presence of the Most Holy Trinity in a mystical sense. It is in these houses that the Holy Spirit wants to gather the faithful, those who follow the attraction of the pierced heart of Our Lord on the cross. Remember that church (Greek: ekklesia: Hebrew: quahal) signifies: "those who are called out of the world to constitute the little flock."

- The current of love cannot be limited to material details on the image. It is present all over, everywhere, as it is the mission of love to penetrate everything, even the depths of the abyss to attract those souls who still have a sparklet of desire of light. But necessarily there must be a sign in the image where this current of love has its offspring: this sign is the Immaculate Heart of Our Lady on her hand and the point where this movement emerges into this world are her loving and merciful eyes.

Again, this current of love embraces the three creations, each one in its peculiar and corresponding way. love always has the last aim to "form family," to bring together, to unify. This can be best seen in the mantle of rays surrounding Our Lady. With respect to the icons, this is what we call the mandorla. Geometrically, the ellipse, with its two foci, is the most eloquent symbol for the union of God and creation. The simple contemplation of the wonder of an egg gives us an idea of how some of the deepest secrets of God's love are hidden in the smallest and most insignificant things. It is a property of the Holy Spirit to hide the secrets of God from the eyes of the proud and reveal them to those who are bowed down.

The veil of clouds, the most exterior wrapping of the mystery of God in the womb of Our Lady, was our entry point and it is with this veil that our contemplation should resume. Only by bowing down in adoration before the Greater God can we begin to understand the things of God. Just as at the occasion of the transfiguration of Our Lord, the disciples had to enter into the cloud of the mystery of God, so also those who look out for God in Our Lady must be plunged into the waters of grace, symbolized by the clouds.

At the end, everything will be grace, outside and inside, and those who have found their way to God will find God not only in the deepest recesses of their heart, but also all around them. God will permeate them in His breath of love and at the same time will wrap them up with His love so that wherever they go, inside or outside, they will meet only God, Who at the end will be *"all in all."*[20] He will fill the space of creation, and time will be drowned in eternity.

Penetrating the word of St. John: *"This is eternal life, to know the One True God and Jesus Christ Whom You have sent"*[21] we can already experience on this earth something of the "breath of eternity" and come to know *"what no eye has seen what no ear has heard what God has prepared for those who love Him."*[22]

The Movement of the FLowers

The first three flowers being one

The golden flowers are the most enigmatic signs on the gown of Our Lady, this is one of the reasons why they can be seen in different perspectives and relations. They can be related to the days of creation, taking the first three as "one flower." representing the first day in which the triune God, by the angels, creatures of light, is best reflected. Creation has not come to an end, mankind still is in the process of growing and has not yet reached the end of sixth day. salvation history and creation permeate each other: the more man returns, in the light of God, the more he is on the way to become a new man in Christ. In history also, we can speak, as already the fathers of the church, especially St. Augustine did (in reference to the prophecies of Daniel), of the seven epochs of mankind. Again, these epochs should be correlated with the "days of creation" of the Gospels.[23]

---

[20]   I Cor 15:28

[21]   Jn 17:3

[22]   I Cor 2:9

[23]   The word of God is a creative word, not only in the days of creation in Gen 1, but also in the four Gospels which can be divided in seven epochs or steps: the last one being the passion and the Resurrection of Our Lord Jesus Christ.

We first contemplate the movement of these flowers as they descend into the obscurity and darkness of the sin of the world (right side of Our Lady's earth-toned gown) and as they ascend into the light (left side of her gown). This dynamic movement also reflects the growth of the church and each soul in the mystery of the Incarnation, until we enter into the open light of the last flower representing the battle cry of St. Michael, "Who is like unto God." This movement has been characterized as a "movement of ransom," of "fishing" and "bringing home, of harvesting." It can be understood also as a "litany" of advocations of Our Lady, which like a climber's rope will help us to find our way out of the darkness into the light of God. The flowers are like battlefields, breaking deeper into the fortress of darkness of the fallen spirits and it is thus that they also constitute like dominions, empires of Our Lady, each one alike yet very different from the other.

Following the Prologue of the Gospel of Saint John, which most eloquently speaks about the descent of light into the darkness of this world, we will be able to see more clearly this "movement of ransom" in relation with the nine large flowers on the gown of Our Lady of Guadalupe with the creative word of the triune God: *"Become."*

"In the beginning was the word, and the word was with God and the word was God. The same in the beginning was with God. Everything came into being through Him, nothing came into being without Him.[24]

The first three large flowers in the movement of ransom are as one. Mary's Immaculate Heart reflects the life and unity of persons in the Most Holy Trinity: necessarily all new life in the church has to come out of the inhabitation of the Most Holy Trinity in our hearts. The more the triune God will live in us as in Mary, the more the church

---

[24] Jn 1:1-3

will be able to give the testimony of Christ's presence in her. It is here, together with Mary as mediators of graces, that the mission of the angels is most apparent. This is why adoration with the angels[25] is the response of love on our part for the gift of the indwelling presence of the Most Holy Trinity. More and more, God will impregnate His divine countenance on the face of the man who adores Him, *"in spirit and truth."* Indeed, nothing helps more in our personal transformation than the "continual hanging at the face of God." The fathers of the church called it "walking in the presence of God." The first three flowers, corresponding with the "Gift of Understanding," remind us that we can only understand God if He lives in us and makes Himself understood by us. Only God can recognize God.

The Fourth Flower

"in Him was life and the life was the light of men. And the light shines in the darkness; but the darkness grasped it not."[26]

The fourth flower, the second[27] in the descent, is likened unto the call of God to man such that he may participate in His light. This Light may come to man in many ways, but as the light of God, at the end it is always a dark light. It is a veiled light, deep down in the soul of man, not only because "man is an abyss," as Pascal says, but also because sin has pushed it down, covering and hiding it. St. John recalls that in the beginning this light was one with the life of man. He did not need any exterior explanations to understand things, he had part in the wisdom of God.

---

25   They are those who "like hang at the face of God" because of their perfect and constant adoration.

26   Jn 1:4ff

27   In this meditation, remember the first three flowers are considered as one.

Throughout history we see that God does not leave man in the darkness of sin, but over and over again attempts to bring him into the brightness of His light. St. Paul points this out in his letter to the Hebrews 1:1, *"many times and in varied ways God has spoken to our fathers through the prophets, but in these last times He has spoken to us through His Son."* Any light received by the pagan cultures before Christ: with the Chinese, Mesopotamian, Egyptian, Greek, Roman culture, unto the chain of light of true revelation beginning with Abraham, is coordinated with this fourth flower, and is looked upon as part of the saving love of God on behalf of all mankind. In the image we can see something like a stream of light piercing the darkness, where near the bottom it finally forms an "L." The horizontal bar here is substituted by a triangle symbolizing: this light is of the triune God. At a distance from the image, one can hardly see the fourth flower. The shadows seem to swallow the glimmer of the gold. Man, in sin, has forgotten that the deepest revelation of God is in life.

The Fifth Flower

"The true light, which shines into the heart of every man, came into this world. He was in this world and this world has been created by Him, but the world did not recognize Him. He entered His property, but they did not accept Him."[28]

The mystery of the rejection of God's Light is reflected in the fifth flower. It is with this flower that the dark shadowed background is most dense. Hell had already taken hold of mankind, even of the elect and religious authorities. The attempt of Yahweh to create a "people peculiarly His Own" seemed to have been in vain. The temple had become a place of thieves.

---

[28] Jn 1:9-11

[29] Remember the fourth apparition when Juan Diego tries to avoid his encounter with Our Lady, thinking that by turning at a certain point, "she who perfectly sees everywhere would not be able to see him." Nican Mopohua, vs. 104.

Our Lady of Guadalupe, seeing with the eyes of God,[29] pierces all darkness. Although the Virgin was born in time, she was already in the thoughts of God before all times in view of the Son of God. Whenever the Father looks down on creation he looks through the specter of Mary. She is the perfect form of this world, the plan according to which it was created in order to be able to receive His Son.

The Sixth Flower

"But to all who received Him He gave the power to become children of God, even to those who believe in His Name, who are not born out of the blood, nor the will of the flesh, nor of the will of man, but of God."[30]

The sixth flower is part of the horizontal fold of Our Lady's gown at her feet, forming something like a book, "the Bible." In this fold the revelation of God is unfolding, opened like a book before the eyes of the world; first in the Old Testament, but as seen in the sixth flower, opening towards the seventh flower, representing the New Testament. The blood of the just, of the prophets, has prepared the way for Christ. They are light of His light piercing the darkness. In the image of Our Lady, the darkness is pushed aside where the two flowers cover the fold.

---

[30] Jn 1:12ff

The Seventh Flower

"And the word became flesh, and dwelt among us, and we beheld His Glory, the Glory of the only begotten Son of the Father, full grace and truth."[31]

The seventh flower comes forth from, as if blossoming forth from the sixth one. With respect to the "book," it correlates to the second half, the New Testament, specifically the Book of the Apoca-

lypse, proclaiming that the light of the angel will take over and cast out the last shadow of darkness. Here, being the fifth flower in the "movement of ransom,"

the Incarnation of the Son of God is related with the Gift of Fortitude.[32] This is to remind us, that in order to become a new man in Christ, we have to deny ourselves, take up our cross and follow Him. It is a trinitarian condition, because following the Son is only possible in the force of the Holy Spirit Who will help us to become "sons in the Son." "Glory" for us poor sinners here on earth is first of all experimented in this force to overcome the old man and look over to the "other side."

---

[31] Jn 1:14

[32] The order of the gifts with the large flowers is the same as presented in the rosary of the seven veils, cf. Book III, Appendix III; understanding, wisdom, counsel, knowledge, fortitude, fear of the Lord and piety. Many other correlations with other groups of seven can be made as well.

The Eighth Flower

*"Out of His plenitude we have all received grace
upon grace. For the law was been given by Moses,
but grace and truth came by Jesus Christ."*[33]

The eighth flower is only touched by the enigmatic dark figure in the middle of the "U," which seems to be fading in the light surrounding it. *"Whatever is put into light will become light"*[34] or will be dissolved in the light.[35]

More and more light will reveal its glorious splendor and take home all those who have stretched out their arms to the light of God. This is the promise of the great times we are living in: whoever submits in fear of God and poverty of Spirit (remember the sixth community of Philadelphia)[36] to the greater plans of God will receive this abundance of graces to overcome darkness.

The Ninth Flower

*"No one has ever seen God, the only Begotten Son, in the bosom
of the Father has made Him known."*[37]

Mankind, now in the maturity of time, is in the same situation as were the angels at the beginning of time when they were called

---

[33] Jn 1:16

[34] EPH 5:13

[35] In this vespertine light for a last time the ugliness of darkness will have to appear, indicated in "the hieroglyph of a man without a face, arms outstretched and as if falling into the abyss." It is a symbol of the fallen angel cast out of heaven together with his fellow companions

[36] Meditating you should also establish the relation to the seven communities of Asia, beginning with that of Ephesus!

[37] Jn 1:18 The eighth flower can be likened to the unfolding of the reign of Mary. The eighth flower is most exuberant in growth and almost out of the darkness.

into their "night of trial." They had to freely and consciously decide by themselves for or against God. It was St. Michael, with his cry "Who is like unto God" that brought about the separation of the good and the bad angels. Whoever has woken up from the dream of progress looking out for the "signs of the times" knows that general defection from God is the clearest sign that mankind is in the trial, having become "adult." As with the angels in the beginning, we have to decide in blind faith, hope and love. Happy those who hold on to their good Guardian Angel. He will help them persevere in the trial already announced to the sixth community.

If we follow St. Michael and his battle cry "Who is like unto God!" we will help the church come to its consummation. Many are yet tottering, filled with doubts and caught up in self pity. Lukewarmness gives the devil free entry into our lives as well as into the community of the church. Therefore, the Lord recommends to the seventh community of Laodicea the fervor of faith. In the last flower there is a sign which points out that Satan is really falling to the depths in the hieroglyphic which looks like a five-pointed star: where light has come to its fullness there is no room for darkness.

The Message of the Big Flowers in Relation to the Communities of Asia

It is not difficult to relate the seven communities of Asia to the seven large golden flowers. The following is only a short synopsis of the "dark side" of this glorious message.

Ephesus Apoc 2:1-7 loss of light	1. first three flowers
Smyma Apoc 2:8-11 persecution	2. forth flower
Pergamum Apoc 2:12-17 presence of false teaching	3. fifth flower
Thyatira Apoc 2:18-29 immorality	4. sixth flower
Sardis Apoc 3:1-6 activity of illusion	5. seventh flower
Philadelphia Apoc 3:7-13 worldly pride	6. eighth flower
Laodicea Apoc 3:14-22 lukewarmess, blindness	7. ninth flower

1. Unfortunately, people no longer live with an eternal perspective, that is, looking up to God: light as a goal. Even within the church, the Spirit of adoration is fading. Man is losing his orientation. Confusion persists as part the of demonic tactic of abhorrence for God. *"First love"* (pure, holy, catholic and apostolic) for God and the things of God even among religious is rare. Love for the church and for Mary is lost. Many are unable to understand the call of the Immaculate Heart which is that of the triune God for conversion. The church will become poor, a "little flock."

2. Defection of faith will soon be followed by persecution, so as to put an end to the Church's existence in this world. The persecution will help to purify the church, allowing the life of God to once again irradiate through her into the darkness of sin.

3. Within the church, the word of God will be mingled with atheistic wisdom and therefore lose its strength. The mystery of the Incarnation is no longer believed, gnosis, pure rationalistic knowledge will try to substitute the sobriety of faith.

4. Discipline, morals and the interior life no longer correspond to the commandments of God, because the attraction of the world is stronger. Only in the folly of the cross will we find the way back to truth. Only in repentance and sacrifice will the church be renewed.

5. Man is incapable of coming to a standstill. He is drowned in the illusion of a better man-made world. He forgets about the eternal life of his soul and thus falls into Spiritual death, ever forgetful of his responsibilities.

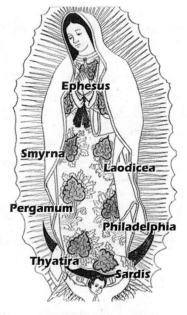

6. The pride of human sciences, of building a new "tower of Babel," will bring about the last trial of the world and lead to the catastrophe of its destruction. Only a holy "remnant" of faithful will be saved from this ever more apparent chastisement.

7. Man seeks only earthly goods and thus is blinded, naked and sterile. Only passing the hardest trials will he be able to reach the wedding feast of the Lamb.

The cry "I Thirst"

The first three flowers symbolize the call of the triune God Who is light and Who wills to share His divine Light with us. As each community so also each man is called to become like unto a flower in the garden of God, exhaling his unique perfume of praise and glory owed alone unto God's majesty. Although the fourth of Christ's last words on the cross is an "outcry of love," it is a silent cry which can only be heard with the "ears of our heart," it is a word "through a flower," one which respects our liberty of response and decision.

The outcry of the Lord pierces the deepness of our darkness. It unfolds where the "book" represents the Old and the New Covenant. If we were to truly read Holy Scriptures with our hearts and hold on to its promises, as does the boy with his left hand to the gown of Our Lady, then also, will we be taken into the movement of ransom at this turning point of ascension unto the greater light of the Lord's victory on the cross. With the last flower, representing St. Michael's cry, "Who is like unto God," we will reach the fullness of the light. The *"Sitio,"* "I thirst" of the Lord," will save us into the fold of her mantle and lift us up to her Immaculate Heart. She will help us to pass through the narrow door of the cross (on the brooch at her neck). Only through her will we truly be home!

The Nine Steps of Birth into Eternal Life

In the natural order, man is born into this world after having spent nine months gestation in the womb of his mother. In the Spiritual order, man must pass through the nine choirs of the angels before reaching the throne of God.[38] It is in this perspective that the large golden flowers should also be considered as a symbolic way of "birth" into eternal life in and through Mary and the holy angels. Every choir of the angels has a special mission in helping to purify and sanctify man on his way to God. Purification

---

[38] cf. book of Cardinal Danielou "La Mission des Anges," part of his patrology, where this doctrine of the fathers is exposed. Dantes "Divine Comedy" gives another perspective of this belief.

should already start here on his pilgrimage over the earth, because at the last moment, if there is not at least a small opening to the light in his heart, it will be too late.

Being *"born again"* is a Spiritual reality and has apocalyptic dimensions.[39] We must necessarily have to go through the pangs of birth, but we mustn't ever forget that at the foot of the cross, Our Lady, in union with her Son, already suffered these labor pains for each one of us. We need only avail ourselves of these graces of Redemption. In relation with the flowers we should recall the help of the seven sacraments on this earthly pilgrimage:

First the Sacraments of "Life":

- Baptism into the triune life of God is the door. (Here again we should relate it to the first three flowers)
- The Holy Eucharist is food and medicine for our body and our soul.
- Confirmation will help us to overcome the attacks of the enemy.
- The Sacrament of Confession purifies our soul when we fall into sin.
- Extreme Unction helps us to stand in the final battle in the hour of our death.

Then the Sacraments of State:

- Matrimony helps to continue and sanctify life on earth.
- Ordination to the priesthood helps us to find our way to heaven.

The order of "seven" is never stagnant, it is variable according to the point of view or perspective; because the order of things in the reign of God is always a living order. It is like the "principle of variation" we observe in nature assuring that life is never changing, but always "new."

---

[39] cf. Rv 12

"Evangelizo Vobis Gaudium Magnum"[40]

"In the beginning God created the heavens and the earth...
God said, 'Let there be light,' and there was light. God
saw that the light was good. God separated the
light from the darkness...."[41]

"And God said, 'Let there be lights in the firmament of the
heavens to separate day from night; let them serve as signs
and for the fixing of seasons, days and years; let them serve
as lights in the firmament of the heavens to shed light
upon the earth.' And so it was."[42]

The Movement of Ransom in the Stars in the Mantle of Our Lady of Guadalupe

The Heavens Proclaim the Glory of God[43]

The following meditation is an effort to join with the heavens in the eternal praise of God. One might ask, "How do the heavens and the world of the stars relate with nine large golden flowers, a "movement of ransom" or a blossoming rosebush, for that matter?" Let us call to mind the magnificent words from Psalms 147 expressed by Pope Benedict XIV on his first encounter of the miraculous image of the Virgin of Guadalupe, *"Non fecit taliter omni nationi!"*[44]

It is no coincidence that in this very psalm, we also encounter the testimony of the psalmist when he refers to God as He Who names the stars, *"He calls each by name."*[45] Genesis tells us how God gave man the task of naming the birds of the air and the beasts

---

[40] Lk 2:10
[41] Gen 1:1-4, Day I of creation
[42] Gen 1:14-19, Day IV of creation
[43] Psalms 19:1
[44] Psalms 147:20
[45] Ibid., verse 4

of the field,[46] but the Psalms tell us that He retained the naming of the stars for Himself.[47] The image of Our Lady of Guadalupe is, as this meditation will show, a "rosebush" that blossoms also in the silent proclamation of the Gospel by the heavens.

St. Paul's letter to the Romans,[48] quoting himself from Psalm 19:4, confirms: *"Their voice has gone forth into all the earth, and their words unto the ends of the world."* This "least" amongst the apostles testifies that the heavens indeed do declare the glory of God! From the earliest ages man has recognized something of the silent proclamation of the Gospel through the unspoken voice of the stars, for even before the arrival of the three Magi to Bethlehem the chosen people had marveled and ordered their lives according to the seasons established by the heavens.[49]

*"Let them be as **signs** and **seasons**...."*[50] Here we note the Hebrew root for "sign" — "avah," meaning a "mark." This is the same word used in Exodus 4:9,17 when Moses performed *"signs"* to convince Pharaoh to let Israel go. The "signs" performed were for the purpose of letting Pharaoh know that Moses was God's instrument, speaking His message. "Sign" then is a mark of something other than itself, and it is thus that we conclude that the "signs" in the heavens are "marks" of God's message to man.

In Hebrew, the word "season" is "moed" and signifies an appointed or fixed time. In sacred scripture, a different word for the

---

[46] Gen 2:19-20

[47] The year was 1754 AD, also cf. Isaiah 40:26

[48] Rom 10:18

[49] cf. * *Mazzaroth*, 1863, Frances Rolleston; *The Gospel in the Stars*, 1884, J. A. Seiss and *The Witness of the Stars*, 1893, E. W. Bullinger. The above studies will help us to better understand the names and meaning of the stars as well as their survival throughout history. There are basic ideas underlying different languages and cultures with respect to the names of the stars and constellations: curiously enough, they go back to single sources recalling that God used them for His prophetic revelation.

    * Mazzaroth: a word occurring only twice in Sacred Scripture in Job 38:32 and II Kings 23:5, means *the separated, the divided or the apportioned and it refers to the allotted spaces given to the twelve signs in the circle of the zodiac.* Job encounters the voice of God from the whirlwind which questions him, *"Can you bring forth Mazzaroth in its season?"*

[50] Gen 1:14

seasons of spring, summer, autumn and winter was used. "signs" and "seasons," used by God with respect to the mission of the stars, were to indicate "happenings" and the "periods of time" pertaining to them, specifically for prophetic reasons especially that of signifying historical incidents at chosen times as the plan of salvation unfolded.

"The heavens proclaim the glory of God!"[51] They foretold and continue to tell the eternal plan of God. They prophesied and continue to prophesy the great drama of Redemption. God's promise of Genesis 3:15 was one that never left the posterity of our first parents without hope. The "signs" of the heavens remind man that the disastrous consequences of original sin are remedied and that we will be saved from our bondage by the promised Redeemer.

> *"God, who at sundry times and in divers manners spoke in times past to the fathers by the prophets, last of all in these days has spoken to us by His Son, Whom He appointed heir of all things, by Whom also He made the world; Who, being the brightness of His glory and the image of His substance, and upholding all things by the word His power, has effected man's purgation from sin and taken his seat at the right hand of the Majesty on high...."*[52]

can also be interpreted in this way: the Lord, being the fullness of light, was already prophesied by the light of the stars; the stars being "silent prophets"! The fullness of the "glory of God" is radiated in the Only Begotten Son as II Corinthians 4:6 proclaims:

> *"For God, Who commanded light to shine out of darkness, has shone in our hearts, to give enlightenment concerning the knowledge of the glory of God, shining on the Face of Christ Jesus."*

---

[51] Psalms 14:4
[52] Hebrews 1:3

The beloved apostle St. John, in his prologue states: *"And we saw His glory — glory as of the Only Begotten of the Father, full of grace and of truth."*[53] As *"The heavens declare the glory of God!"* they necessarily also declare *Jesus Christ!*

How then do the heavens proclaim Jesus Christ and this in, with or through a blossoming rosebush? Eighteen of the twenty-four brightest stars, seen from earth, directly seem to correspond to the stars on the mantle of the Virgin of Guadalupe. This inspired intuition of Fr. Mario Rojas Sanchez was seriously deliberated by Drs. J. Cantó Ylla and Armando García de León in 1981. Their studies have been published under the title *Las Estrellas del Manto de la Virgen de Guadalupe*, by Fr. Mario Rojas Sanchez and Dr. Juan Homero Hernandez Illescas.

The "woman clothed with the sun, and the moon under her feet" is really the "new evangelization"! It is She whom Our God of creation has chosen to herald not only the first coming of His Son, but also to announce His second and glorious coming. She, the Virgin of Tepeyac, is the blossoming rosebush, the *"Tree of Life,"* spoken of in the Apocalypse, giving its fruit twelve times a year,[54] with her the roses that bud forth are the fruit that proclaim the glory of God in His Only Begotten Son, Jesus Christ.

The Winter Solstice of 1531

The investigations made by the aforementioned scientists show that the winter solstice, normally occurring on December 22, happened to occur at 10:36 a.m. (90W of Greenwich) on December 12, 1531, the exact day and perhaps the exact time of the actual miracle on the ayate in the presence of Bishop Juan Zumárraga. The sky of the winter solstice at 19 degrees latitude, the geographical correspondence of the present day Mexico City, held a most wondrous sight! It testified the *"glory as of the Only-Begotten of the Father, full of grace and of truth,"*[55] leaving a physical evidence of their testimony in the ongoing apparition on the holy tilma.

---

[53] Jn I:14
[54] cf. Rv 22:2
[55] Jn I:14

The primary inspiration proved successful, when the image (as seen in the diagram) was inverted with respect to the star map. It

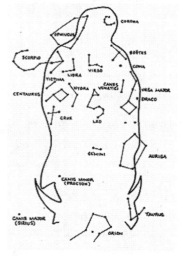

was only then, almost at the moment of abandonment, that the correlation was found. What we see on the image is the position of the stars as seen from above: God looks upon all of creation through Mary, the Immaculate One. He gives us the Gospel through her.

The image of the Virgin of Guadalupe speaks to us of how God would want to find all of His creation. According to directionality,[56] we recall that in the image, Our Lady comes from the east, but She looks to the west. East has always, by way of the rising sun, been a symbol of God the eternal light.[57] Our Lady brings not only the Gospel from the east to the west, but She comes from God, bringing the Gospel of Her Son, symbolized by the "Nahui Ollin" superimposed on her womb.

---

[56] cf. Book III, The "Mountain" of Revelation, pp. 13-16
[57] The Garden of Eden was in the east, cf. Gen 2:8

The Eighteen of the Twenty-Four Brightest Stars corresponding to the Image of Our Lady of Guadalupe

STAR	Constellation	Meaning	Reference
1. Sirius	Canis Major	Prince	Isaiah 9:6
3. Toliman	Centaurus	The Heretofore and the Hereafter	Apoc. 1:8
5. Capella	Auriga	She Goat	Ezek. 37:22-24
6. Arcturus	Bootes	He comes	Psalm 96:13
7. Rigel	Orion	The Foot that Crushes	Gen. 3:15
8. Procyon	Canis Minor	The Redeemer	Isaiah 59:19-20 Isaiah 49:24-26
11. Agena	Centaurus	unknown	
12. A-Crux	S. Cross	unknown	
13. Betelgeuse	Orion	The Coming of the Branch	Isaiah 4:2 Malachi 3:1-2
14. Aldebaran	Taurus	The Governor	Psalm 22:28
15. Pollux	Gemini	He Who comes to suffer	I Pet. 1:11 Psalm 22
16. Spica	Virgo	The Branch	Zechariah 3:8 Zechariah 6:12
17. Antares	Scorpio	Wounding	Isaiah 53:5 Zechariah 13:6
20. Regulus	Leo	Treading Underfoot	Isaiah 63:3 Gen. 3:15
21. B-Crux	S. Cross	unknown	
22. Castor	Gemini	Ruler or Judge	Acts 7:27,35 Deut. 18:15
23. Alioth	Ursa Major	Goat or Sin Offering	Lev. 16:15,27
24. Bellatrix	Orion	Swiftly Destroying	Ezekiel 28:16

The Proto-Gospel (Gen 3:15) as the Point of Entry into the Zodiac!

The word zodiac comes from the Greek "zodiakos" meaning circle. Its primitive root is "zoad" meaning "*a way or a path or going by steps.*" Its pertinence here is the apparent path the sun seems to journey amongst the stars during the course of twelve months. The journey is marked by the appearance of twelve major constellations, each of which have three other decans or faces, three other smaller constellations associated with the major one. Each of the twelve constellations, along with their three decans, can be seen as prophetic pictorials of unfolding salvation history events. E.W. Bullinger goes so far as dividing the twelve into three major groups of four: The first group of four depicting Christ as the Suffering Servant, the second as the Glorified Blesser and the third as the Reigning Judge.[58]

Going back to ancient cultures like China, India, Babylonia, Persia, Egypt, Israel, Greece, Rome, Scandinavia and Central America we recognize the common denominator of a knowledge in the tradition of the stars. Unanimously they recognized the same twelve signs of the zodiac as well as the same names and or meanings of names associated with the constellations. There is no explanation of this shared knowledge other than that it comes from one original source: God.[59] We must put to ease the mind of those who initiate this meditation with a fear of astronomy simply by stating that it is a science and quite different from the distortion of the astrological cult. Astronomy considers the wonder of the cosmos whereas astrology is a distortion of those truths so as to distract man from the true orientation that the heavens proclaim.

On the other hand we should acknowledge that what seems to be a cluster of stars, a constellation, is really an earthly perspective of stars that at times are lights years apart from each other. Even though for thousands of years, so as to help him study the groupings, man has drawn lines to connect the stars in a grouping. This connecting of stars in a group happens to create something like human and animal forms, much like the simple "dot to dot" exercises for children. From the time of the Ancients, forty-eight such

---

[58] cf. page 30

[59] Fr. Jean Danielou, in his book *The Angels and Their Mission*, Ch. II, p. 19, quote Origen "The [religion of the stars] was given by God to all people who are under heaven, except those whom He wished to be set aside for Himself as his chosen part."

forms have been counted with the human eye.[60] As the earth revolves around the sun, the position of the sun seen from the earth, during the day, also seems to change, but really it is the earth that is moving about the sun, and about its own axis. In the course of twelve months, thirty degrees per month, the earth completes a 360 degree revolution of the sun, a full circle. The apparent path that the sun seems to make in the sky is called the ecliptic.

During a one year cycle, while the earth is revolving the sun, the earth's moon also makes twelve revolutions about the earth, and it is this heavenly region, distinguished by our twelve months, that is called the Zodiac. Each month is recognized by the particular major constellation and her sub-signs that are visible in its season; each decan has a ten-degree endurance, that is, within the thrty-degree (days) length of a major constellation, each of her subdecans has ten degrees (days).[61] The question where to enter this heavenly cycle is not something to be jumped into without first seriously considering "how?" or "where?" As with the ancients, we must discern according to and with a Christian perspective. "Modern astrologers"[62] propose that the entry is with the "sign" Aries. However archeological findings as well as salvation history as related in the Bible point to that sign that corresponds with the divine promise of the "seed of the woman"[63] and its climax,[64] prophesying the "triumph of the Lion of the tribe of Judah."

---

[60] These 48 are the 12 major constellations, each with their 3 subdecans (12x3=36)

[61] See E. W. Bullinger's constellation chart

[62] The distortion of the names of the stars may have arisen through foolish corruption by ancient rulers and biblically insensitive astronomers, many times influenced by the evil one, because he is most interested in the misinterpretation of the message of the stars. This is why the original terms many times have lost their meaning. This is why it is advisable to go back to ancient cultures and civilizations which conserve the original form: exposed by Bullinger.

[63] Gen 3:15

[64] Rv 5:5

The twelve signs corresponding to the twelve months of the year beginning with January are as follows:

January	Aquarius	May	Gemini	Sept.	Libra
February	Pisces	June	Cancer	October	Scorpio
March	Aries	July	Leo	Nov.	Sagittarius
April	Taurus	August	Virgo	Dec.	Capricorn

(We must realize that the correspondence with the given months is not exactly perfect. The major constellations begins during the given month, but extend into the following month, i.e. Aquarius begins in January, but extends into February, etc.)

The biblical correspondence and Christian perspective along with the enigmatic "riddle of the Sphinx" brings us immediately to Virgo and Leo.[65] Already here, we find a celestial proclamation of the "glory of God," Jesus Christ, born out of the Virgin, destined to overcome as Lion of Judah. The entire zodiac prophetically  reveals a salvific pageant with Our Lord Jesus Christ in the spotlight! He and his adversary are the two main characters that are represented by numerous names and symbolic figures. As Our Lord Jesus Christ is the main theme in the written word of Holy Scripture, so too do we find Him to be the main theme in the unspoken, but brilliant, heavenly evangelization.

---

[65] The Dendereh Zodiac, dating back 2000 B.C., was found on the ceiling of an Esneh temple in Egypt. Between the "signs" of Virgo and Leo is found a picture of the Sphinx (an Egyptian monument having the head of a woman and the body of a lion). In this sign which unites "Virgo and Leo" beginning and end of the zodiacus mysteriously come together. Many scholars discern this placement on the Esneh temple as the key of entry into the understanding of the zodiac.

Immovable Order of the Stars

"When you see all these signs, lift up your head
because your liberation is near"[66]

The recent discovery of a correlation of the stars on the mantle of Our Lady of Guadalupe with the heavenly constellations must be seen as an act of love on God's part as well as an extension of the maternal love of Our Lady, when we relate it more closely with all the problems rising with the beginning of "modern times." Because of the discoveries of new continents, vast dimensions in space research, but first of all the loss of the geocentric system, man began to lose his "home" and sense of security on earth. The stars in this respect play an important role, because without astronomy, he would have never dared to undertake the search for "new continents."

Although no one discovered or noted the constellations on the image of Our Lady of Guadalupe at the time of her apparition, Spiritually, they are a counter-weight to all the revolutionary discoveries "on heaven and earth" which constitute the "human glory" of the "modern times." These "new horizons" were, in the beginning, quite a menace to faith, because up to the "new times" the Ptolemaic system was unseparably linked with the Christian vision of this world. Galileo was considered a heretic when he announced that the earth was not the center of the universe. All these and many more questions raised by the surgence of the natural sciences put man into an state of anxiousness: Where then is man's place?

This disequilibrium which more and more brought the church into a situation of defense has lasted up unto our times and prepared the way for the "kings of the east"[67] to bring death to mankind, in a

---

[66] Lk 21:28

[67] Rv 16:12 It is the sixth angel which pours his cup of wrath on the "River Euphrates" so it will dry and open the way of the "kings of the east." This is a symbol for all the eastern religions entering, but also for the rise of militant atheism since the last century. The river Euphrates is symbol for the current of life coming from God: God sustains all life! Today on a large scale mankind has optioned for "suicide," not only by admitting more and more abortion in a legal way but because the whole trend of life of modern civilization is against life, as it is given by God!

hidden or an open way. Whoever in faith and trust will look up to our Lady will recognize in the stars on her blue-green (turquoise) mantle (green being the sign of life!) a silent promise, that with God everything is order: "Heaven and earth are full of your glory," even though we do not yet see it with our human eyes. The starred heaven instead of threatening us should make us recognize better the vastness of God's creative hand, if only we recall that this universe has the Only Begotten Son of God as its center. Although the earth may be the smallest of all stars, in the Spiritual perspective, it is the center all of creation, redeemed and sanctified by the life, passion and Resurrection of the Son of God, Who will, at the end, bring it home to His Father as the most precious booty of His passion.

The Mystery of Figures and Signs in the Heavens

It really takes the pure eyes and ingenuous heart of a child to find out that there really are figures in the heavens which can also be interpreted as "signs" of God. Objectively speaking, star figures in the second dimension certainly do not exist. The stars of a constellation are not as we see them from the earth "in one line/ plain," constituting a perfect image. What is it then that has caused man to see certain figures? It cannot be pure fantasy, otherwise there would not be an almost unanimous concordance amongst the major ancient cultures of the world. There must be an element of faith involved with its origin in God. Mankind, even in its downfall into the dust of the earth, did not forget to look up to heaven; the stars have always been a luminous promise to him, that one day God would again establish order to the chaos of this world.

In the coming of Our Lord Jesus Christ to the earth, bringing down the fullness of the light of God, the prophetic light of the stars necessarily had to be eclipsed. But as faith, in the approximation of the "modern times," again diminished, and darkness became more dense, man again began to look up to the light of the stars. Without the advances of modern technology, the present discoveries of the cosmic dimensions would never have been thought to be real. The vastness of the universe is not so much a consoling sign as it is a threat to insignificant man in his nothingness. Here, in this critical situation of "modern times," "the mantle" of Our Lady extended to mankind is a sign of consolation, as much as the Apocalypse is considered to be a book of consolation.

But again we must emphasize: this is so only for pure souls with the ingenuousness of children, courageous enough to follow divine inspirations. This is true with respect to all discoveries. Just when Europe was getting too small for enterprising men, God inspired the few to look for Him beyond the "known," beyond the "comfortable," beyond the "limit" of the horizon. These few are never the curiosity seekers, but those impelled by a living faith to seek and find God in all and to the farthest bounds of the known world. It took a faith-filled courageous soul like Christopher Columbus to initiate the future findings of Copernicus (1543) and Galileo, making them a living reality before they were ever brought to the forefront. And so it is, in this childlike spirit, that we also endeavor to look Heavenward, at the stars, so that through Our Lady's maternal care, we may not be swallowed up in the confusion of modern discoveries, but find ourselves in the embrace of God, looking up in to the immensity of a universe "without limits."

The Constellations and their Decans

E.W. Bullinger divides the book of the stars in three parts, corresponding to the three divisions of the liturgical year:

BOOK ONE
The Redeemer - His first coming
"The Sufferings of Christ"

The Prophesy of the Seed of the Woman

Virgo — "The Virgin": A woman bearing a branch in her right hand and an ear of corn in her left.
1. Coma — "The desired one": The woman and child.
2. Centaurus — "The despised sin offering": The double nature Centaur holding a spear piercing a victim.
3. Boötes — "He cometh": a man walking bearing a branch called Arcturus, meaning the same.

The Redeemer's Atoning Work

Libra — "The scales": The price deficient balanced by the price which covers.
1. Crux — "The cross endured."
2. Lupus or Victima — "The victim slain."
3. Corona — "The crown bestowed."

The Redeemer's Conflict

Scorpio — "The scorpion": seeking to wound, but itself trodden underfoot.
1. Serpens — the serpent held by Ophiucus.
2. Ophiuchus — "Serpent handler": man wrestling with the serpent.
3. Hercules — "The mighty man": a man kneeling on one knee, humbled in the conflict, but holding aloft the tokens of victory, with his foot on the head of the dragon.

The Redeemer's Triumph

Sagittarius — The two-natured conqueror going forth "conquering and to conquer": the archer.
1. Lyra — "Praise prepared for the conqueror": the harp.
2. Ara — "Consuming fire prepared for His enemies": the altar.
3. Draco — "The dragon" cast down from heaven.

BOOK TWO
The Redeemed: "the Result of the Redeemer'sSufferings"

Their Blessings Procured

Capricornus — "The goat of atonement slain for the redeemed": fish-goat.
1. Sagitta — "The arrow of God sent forth": the arrow.
2. Aquila — "The smitten one falling": an eagle.
3. Delphinus — "The dead one rising again": The dolphin.

Their Blessings Ensured

Aquarius — "The living waters of blessing poured forth for the redeemed": the water-bearer.
1. Pices Australis — "The blessings bestowed": the southern fish.
2. Pegasus — "The blessings quickly coming": the winged horse.
3. Cygnus — "The Blesser Surely Returning": the Swan.

Their Blessings In Obeyance

Pisces — "The redeemed blessed though bound": the fishes.
1. The Band — "Bound," but binding their great enemy Cetus, the sea monster.
2. Andromeda — "The redeemed in their bondage and affliction": the chained woman.
3. Cepheus — "Their redeemed coming to rule": the king.

Their Blessings Consummated and Enjoyed

Aries — "The lamb that was slain, prepared for the victory": the ram or she-goat.
1. Cassiopeia — "The captive delivered and preparing for her husband, the Redeemer": the enthroned woman.
2. Cetus — "The great enemy bound": the sea monster.
3. Perseus — "Delivering his redeemed": the breaker.

BOOK THREE
The Redeemer His second coming:
"The glory that should follow"

Messiah, The Coming Judge of all the Earth

Taurus — "Messiah Coming to Rule": the Bull.
1. Orion — "Light breaking forth" in the person of the Redeemer.
2. Eridanus — "The river of the judge": wrath breaking fourth for His enemies.
3. Auriga — "Safety for the Redeemed in the day of that wrath": the shepherd.

Messiah's Reign as Prince of Peace

Gemini — "The twins": The two-fold nature of the king.
1. Lepus — "The enemy trodden under foot": the hare.
2. Canis Major — "The coming glorious Prince of Princes": the dog.
3. Canis Minor/Procyon — "The exalted redeemer": the smaller dog.

Messiah's Redeemed Possessions

Cancer — "The possessions held fast": the crab.
1. Ursa Minro — "The lesser sheepfold": the smaller bear.
2. Ursa Major — "The fold and the flock": the big bear.
3. Argo — "The redeemed pilgrims safe at home": the ship.

The Winter Solstice of 1531 and "The Movement of Ransom"

One cannot escape the marvel of God's majesty in the contemplation of the miraculous image of Our Lady of Guadalupe! The Artist of this "masterpiece is none other than the same Who created the Pleides and Orion[68] and gave them their place in the heavens. As Author and Origin of the universe He now, in a mere reflection of His Being, gives us an image so as to guide and orient us once again through the darkness and obscurities of these difficult times. As the pillar of cloud led the Israelites by day and

---

[68] cf. JOB 9:9

the fire led them by night out of the slavery of Egypt[69] so too, in the pillars of clouds and fire (recognized in the image of Our Lady of Guadalupe as the first and second veils), God leads us from this world to Himself through this blossoming rosebush, who wrapped in the heavens, proclaims "the glory of God"!

The eyes are mirrors of the soul, this even more with the merciful eyes of Our Lady; they reflect her most pure soul as mirror of God's wisdom. She was with God in the beginning when He made the world.[70] Now, as She is with God with her body and soul, we can also assert that the loving glance that her eyes manifest is the very love of God Whom She not only bears, but with Whom her soul is eternally united. When we speak of the love issuing forth from the heart of God, permeating the created world, like fountains of eternal grace and radiation, we can also conclude that the same merciful love of God is that which is seen flowing forth from the eyes of the Blessed Virgin. Her eyes are not the first cause of the "movement of ransom," but here it becomes visible. She is the vessel from which that eternal plan of "ransom" is poured out upon the world.

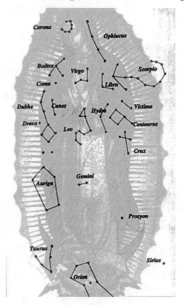

Following the "movement of ransom," we would necessarily begin with the first constellation appearing in Our Lady's direct view, Boötes, but as she herself is not the first cause of the "movement," we will begin with a constellation not visibly present on the tilma, but is part of the winter solstice and coordinates perfectly with the left hand and shadow of the Immaculate Heart of Our Lady: representing Virgo, beforehand determined as the entry into the cycle of the zodiac. We gaze upon the star map of the holy tilma throughout the mediation of

---

[69] cf. Ex 13:21, Num 14:14-15. etc.
[70] cf. Wisdom 9:9

the Immaculate Heart of Mary. The proto-gospel of Genesis 3:15 finds perfect residence in this key of understanding and "sign" of God's plan of Redemption.

The Forty-six Stars on the Mantle of Our Lady of Guadalupe

Boötes	Coma	Ursa Major
Arcturus - Alpha Mirac - Epsilon Lambda, Zeta	Diadem - Alpha	Dubhe - Alpha Merach - Beta Phaeda - Gamma Megrez - Delta Alioth - Epsilon Mizar - Zeta Benet Naish - Eta Kappa, Omicron
Canes Venatici Cor Caroli - Alpha Asterion/Chara - Beta	**Draco** Thuban - Alpha	**Auriga** Alioth/Capella - Alpha Menkilinan - Beta
Taurus Aldebaran - Alpha Theta Gamma	**Canis Minor** Procyon - Alpha	**Crux** A-crux, B-crux, Delta, Gamma
Centaurus Toliman - Alpha Xi, Eta, Theta, Iota	**Hydra** Pi	**Libra** Zuben al Genubi Zuben al Chemali Sigma
Victima Alpha Beta	**Scorpio** Antares - Alpha Graffias - Beta Dschuba - Delta Pi	**Ophiucus** Ras al Hagus - Alpha Kappa Lambda Yed Posterior

Virgo

The "sign"/constellation of Virgo has the three decans: Coma Berenices, Centaurus and Boötes, all of which are beautifully represented in the image of Our Lady of Guadalupe. Three stars of the aforementioned constellations are amongst the twenty-four brightest stars seen from earth.[71] In order of brightness they appear in Centaurus (third-Toliman), Boötes (sixth-Arcturus) and in Virgo (sixteenth-Spica).

With the help of the Ancients we can begin to ponder the silent gospel spoken by the stars which constitute the constellation. To begin with, the name "Virgo"/"Virga" comes from the Latin and signifies both "virgin" and "branch" respectively. The Vulgate uses both as references to Christ.[72] In Hebrew, the constellation has the name "Bethulah." This is the most commonly used word for virgin in the Old Testament. "Adarah," also meaning virgin is the Arab name for Virgo while "Parthenos" is the Greek. It is this latter term that is used for "Virgin" in the New Testament writings. The profound understanding for the unfolding of virginity in motherhood[73] can also be found in many of the ancient cultures. They not only recognized the virginal attribute of this "sign," but they also saw "Virgin-Mother." Egypt's name for Virgo was "Aspolio" meaning "the seed." Here we note a recognition of the unique relationship between the Virgin and her Son.

Spica, the sixteenth brightest star seen from earth, exemplifies this unity. Its ancient meaning was "the branch" and marks the ear of wheat (hidden symbol of the "Bread of Life," the Holy Eucharist and the seed) which she holds in her left hand (symbol of the passivity and impotence by which the "branch" will allow Himself to descend out of love for mankind). The promised "seed" of Genesis 3:15 is now linked to the prophecies of the "branch." The star "Spica" in Hebrew was called "Tsemech." Although there are over twenty different words used for branch in the Old Testament, Tsemech is specifically used as a messianic reference. It is only used four times; in Jeremiah 23:5,6[74] denoting king, in Zechariah

---

[71] cf. chart on page 25

[72] cf. Isaiah 11:1 as the "branch" and Matt. 1:23 in His "virgin-birth."

[73] cf. Book III, pg 7

[74] Jer 23:5,6: "Behold, the days come, saith the Lord, That I will raise unto David a righteous branch and a king shall reign and prosper."

3:8[75] denoting servant, in Zechariah 6:12[76] denoting man, and in Isaiah 4:2[77] denoting God. These four messianic uses of "Tsemech" in the Old Testament correspond perfectly with the fourfold character of Christ given by the four Evangelists: Matthew, Christ's Kingship, Mark, Christ's servanthood, Luke, Christ's manhood and John, Christ's Godhead.

Zavijaveh, found on Virgo's head, is the Hebrew word for "gloriously beautiful," the exact word found in the Isaiah 4:27 reference. The star on the Virgo's right arm, is Chaldean for "the son who comes or the branch who comes." In Arab, the star is called civilization and signifies "who shall come down." Virgo's right hand is marked with the star Subilon, Hebrew for a "an ear of corn." The same star in Arab is called Al Azal and means "the branch."

These major stars of the Virgo constellation told the ancients, and tell us as well, that the Virgin was to have a Son (her seed) and He would be called the Branch of Jehovah. God would appear in human form, the Child of a Virgin mother. The Incarnation of the Son of God, the "glory of God," was first proclaimed through the constellation of Virgo! Correlating with the image of the Virgin of Guadalupe we note that the merciful love of God, made manifest in the "movement of ransom," flows forth from the loving and merciful heart of His Virgin Mother.

It would only seem proper that we should correlate Virgo's decans as they appear with her in the night skies; but as her second decan, Centaurus, correlates with the left side of the Virgin of Guadalupe's mantle, we will discuss it later in this meditation.[78]

---

[75] Zech 3:8: "Behold I will bring forth my servant the branch."

[76] Zech 6:12: "Thus speaketh the Lord of hosts, saying, Behold the MAN whose name is the branch."

[77] Isaiah 4:2: "In that day shall the branch of Jehovah be beautiful and glorious." So that this Branch, this Son, is Jehovah Himself; and as we read the record of John we hear the voice from heaven saying, "Behold your God." Isaiah 40:9

[78] cf. page 50

Boötes

The "sign" Boötes is the first constellation in the "movement of ransom." It is Virgo's third decan. The shape the constellation takes on the holy tilma is one of a "T" or "tau" in Hebrew, the letter which also signifies "cross" and it is such that the "movement of ransom" initiates with the holy cross.

 Boötes is depicted as a herdsman or even a prince with a sickle in one hand and a staff or spear in the other. This  "sign" of "the coming one" (Greek) prophetically speaks of the second and final coming of Christ, although we find it as the first "sign" in the glance of the Virgin of Guadalupe. This perfectly corresponds with the Virgin's role as "harvester." Boötes comes from the Hebrew root "bo," the coming.[79] Arcturus, the brightest star in this constellation and the sixth brightest seen from earth, also means "He Cometh." This name is spoken of in the Book of Job 9:9. The ancient Egyptians called this constellation both "Smat" and "Bau," the first signifying "one who governs or rules" and the second "the coming one." Two-hundred seventy years before Christ, a famous Greek poet, Aratus, wrote about Boötes as being the *"The Guardian of the flock of the Greater Fold;"* this we know is the former name of Ursa Major, also present on the holy image.[80]

The symbolic reality of Boötes holding a sickle in hand as well as being the first constellation in the "movement of ransom" of the Virgin of Guadalupe tells us something of the silent yet profound proclamation of the heavens concerning the mission first proclaimed in Mexico with respect to the "coming harvest." Apocalypse 14 speaks to us of *"one sitting like to a son of man, having upon his head a crown of gold and in his hand a sharp sickle"* as well as two

---

[79] Bo the Hebrew root meaning "to come" or "the coming" referred to in Psalm 49:13, *"For He cometh to judge the earth; He shall come to judge the world in righteousness, And the people with His Truth."*

[80] cf. Ursa Mayor, pg 36

other angels of harvest.[81] This constellation of Boötes gives us an idea that the apocalyptic mission of the harvest has started in this country.

Mirac, "the coming forth as an arrow," Mizar and Izar, "the preserver, guardian" all represent the same star. This star is also represented on the mantle of the Virgin of Tepeyac. Two other stars of this "sign," not represented on the tilma, but having great importance in the understanding of this constellation are that of Nekkar or Merga and Al Katurops. The first is the Beta star of the constellation.[82] It is Hebrew for "the pierced"[83] or "who bruises." Al Katurops marks Boötes' spear-head and translates to "the branch, treading under foot." Indeed, this constellation spoke very clearly to the ancients of the triumphant return of the Christ as the judge of the earth.

Coma

Coma is Virgo's first decan. Looking at a modern "dot to dot" star map, we would see Coma depicted as a woman's wig.[84] This has nothing to do with the ancient name or understanding of this second "sign" in the "movement of ransom." The ancient Hebrew name for the constellation was Coma, "the desired." The ancient Egyptian name for it was Shesnu, "the desired son." In the temple of Denderah, where the zodiac goes back 2,000 years before Christ we find the draw-

---

[81] cf. Rv 14:14-20

[82] A beta star in a particular grouping refers to the star of second greatest magnitude.

[83] cf. Zech 12:10

[84] The wife of Ptolemy III, after her husband had gone off on an dangerous expedition, vowed to consecrate her hair to Venus if he returned safely. Her vow was kept, but later her hair was stolen from the temple. To comfort her, an Egyptian astrologer told her that Jupiter had made a constellation of it.

ing of a woman and a child. The proceeding figure is that of Shesnu which dates 4,000 years.

Many studies concluded that it is most probable that "the star of Bethlehem" appeared in this constellation. Abulfaragius, an Arab Christian Historian, says that Zoroaster, the Persian, predicted to the Magi, the astronomers of Persia, of the appearance of *a new star*. This star would notify the birth of a mysterious child whom they were to adore. The *Zend Avesta* also states that a new star was to appear in the "sign" of the Virgin. The tradition of a new star appearing in the heavens is well supported by ancient Christian writers, amongst them St. Ignatius of Antioch, 69 AD, and Prudentius, 4th century AD. St. Ignatius says, "At the appearance of the Lord, a star shone forth brighter than all the other stars." It is quite obvious that he is recipient of eye-witness testimony.

An Arabian astronomer of the eighth century says, *"There arises in the first Decan, as the Persians, Chaldeans, and Egyptians, and the two Hermes and Ascalius teach, a young woman, whose Persian name denotes a pure virgin, sitting on a throne, nourishing an infant boy (the boy, I say), having a Hebrew name, by some nations called Ihesu, with the signification Ieza, which in Greek is called Christos."*[85] The Virgin mother depicted both in Virgo and Coma speak to us of Mary, the Virgin mother of the "the desired of all nations"[86] and the infant son in Coma is correlated with the "Seed" and the "Branch" of Virgo. Isaiah 9:5-6 announces quite later what the heavens were already proclaiming from the creation of the world:

> *"For a child is born to us, a son is given; upon his shoulder dominion rests. They name him Wonder-Counselor, God-Hero, Father-Forever, Prince of Peace. His dominion is vast and forever peaceful, from David's throne, and over his kingdom, which confirms and sustains by judgment and justice both now and forever."*

---

[85] *The Witness of the Stars*, E.W. Bullinger, Kregel Publications 1967, pp.34-35
[86] cf. HAG 2:7

Ursa Major

As we follow the "movement of ransom," having passed through Boötes and Coma, we next encounter the constellation better known today as the "Big Dipper." Its representation on the mantle of the Virgin of Guadalupe by seven stars, speaks to us of the unfolding action of the Holy Spirit in this heavenly production of the Gospel of Our Lord Jesus Christ.

A modern diagram of the "sign" Ursa Major is that of a bear. Unfortunately the name appears to have been a mistranslation of the word Dubeh, a herd or flock. It is believed to have been confused by the Greeks for the Persian *Dob*, bear, and therefore we now have the Latin, "Ursa." A true depiction of this star group is that of a herd of sheep gathered around their shepherd. It is most likely that it takes its name from its alpha star, Dubhe, "a herd or flock."

 The name bear really has no resemblance to the name of any of the constellation's stars. All the names of the stars of Ursa Major reflect  something of an assembled flock and thus it is believed that the ancients' understanding or view of this constellation was a pastoral scene of a gathered flock. Job 9:9 and 38:32 both make reference to this constellation, but modern translations appear to have ignored the root of the Hebrew word "ash" as "Arcturas" which means to hasten or to assemble together (as sheep in a fold), in fact, the seven known stars of this "Big Dipper" were interpreted by the old Jewish commentators as "ash."

A consideration of the seven better-known stars of this constellation, those also most recognizable from the earth, can easily be compared to "blossoming roses" of the beautiful image of Our Lady of Guadalupe. They act somewhat as a confirmation of one of the possible interpretations of the roses: the souls of those which have ripened in the suffering of a pagan domination, such that when Our Lady came, they were ready to be harvested into the barnyards of heaven. The beta star, below Dubhe is called Merach, Hebrew for "flock." The star Phaeda means "visited, guarded, or numbered as a flock." Alioth, a name also found in the constellation of Auriga, means a "she goat." Mizar means "separate or small," close to it is Al Cor, "the lamb." Benet Naish is Arabic for "the daughters of the assembly" and is also called Al Kaid, "the assembled."

There are many other stars within this constellation, and they all repeat the same idea: sheepfold, multitude, many assembled, the assembled, separated as the flock in a fold, protected, covered redeemed and ransomed. The pastoral role of the "branch who is to come" is also echoed in Jeremiah's words, *"Hear the word of the Lord, O nations, proclaim it on distant coast, and say: He who scattered Israel, now gathers them together, he guards them as a shepherd his flock."*[87]

Long before St. John wrote on the "Good Shepherd,"[88] the "seven stars" of Ursa Major inspired the prophets and the star gazers alike in their teachings. Ezekiel 34:12-16 is a beautiful passage exemplifying what the heavens proclaimed through this apocalyptic "sign."[89] The fact that Ursa Mayor occurs so early in the order of the "movement of ransom" begets something of the Merciful and tender love of God for all those who long for His second coming.

Draco

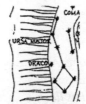 Draco is the third decan of the constellation Sagittarius, "The Triumphant One."[90] In Greek, Draco means "trodden on." The Hebrew word is Dahrach and means "to tread." In the star  charts, the head of Draco is under the foot of Hercules. It is yet

---

87 Jer 31:10
88 cf. Jn 10
89 *"As a shepherd seeks out his flock in the day that he is among his sheep that are scattered; so will I seek out my sheep, and will deliver them out of all places where they have been scattered in the cloudy and dark day."*
90 Sagittarius is a centaur like Virgo's second decan, only he is not "The despised one," he is "the triumphant one."

another heavenly pictorial of the seed (Hercules) crushing the head of the serpent (Draco).The correlation with the image of Our Lady of Guadalupe is the Alpha star, Thuban. Over 4,000 years ago, this star, "the subtle," was the Polar Star, the North Star of orientation. On the mantle of the Virgin of Guadalupe, we see it as if falling off. Apocalypse 12:9 tell us, *"And the great dragon was cast out, that old serpent, called the Devil, and Satan, which deceiveth the world:...."* All the stars of the constellation portray Draco as the original tempter and eternal enemy of God.

Just to name a few:

Rastaban - Beta star: "head of the subtle, Ethanin: "the long serpent or dragon"
Grumian: "the Subtle," Giansar: "the punished enemy,"
Al Dib: "the reptile," El Athik: "the fraud,"
El Asieh: "the bowed down"

Thuban, as the North Star of orientation, lost its place to Polaris of Ursa Minor just as Satan lost his place as "light bearer." It is now to his great shame that he must give testimony of his eternal fall on the mantle of the Virgin of Guadalupe.

Auriga

"Who may abide the day of His coming?"

"Behold, the Lord God will come as a mighty one, And His arm shall rule for Him: Behold, His reward is with Him, His recompense before Him. He shall feed His flock like a shepherd, He shall gather the lambs in His arm, and carry them in His bosom, And shall gently lead those that give suck."[91]

Auriga is Taurus' third decan, but within the "movement of ransom" it is presented even before Taurus or its other decans. The

---

[91] Isaiah 40:0-11

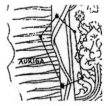 

"movement" itself is consistent though in portraying the merciful love of God. As a member of the "Taurus clan" it should manifest something of power and glory or of the unbearable fire of Christ's second coming, but like its predecessor "Duhbe," Auriga manifests the gentle love of the Good Shepherd, and why not, its Hebrew root meaning is shepherd. Auriga is seated upon the Milky Way, holding Alioth, "the she goat" (Alpha star), upon his shoulder. She, together with the newborn kids, clings to him out of fear looking down at the on charging bull, Taurus.

The Beta star Menkilinon, means "the band or chain of the goats" signifying that the lambs will no longer be separated, but eternally bound to the shepherd. The star in Auriga's right foot is El Nath, Arabic for "wounded or slain." Here, we have beautiful correlations with He Who was once bruised or wounded in the heel. He is the "Good Shepherd" who lays down His life for His sheep[92] and He is the "Great Pastor of the sheep brought forth from the dead."[93] In the Denderah Zodiac (2,3000 BC), Auriga does not hold sheep, but holds a scepter called "trun," meaning scepter or power. The hieroglyphics show the "trun" to be unusually different. The top of it has the head of a goat and below the bearer's hand it is a cross. The cross for the Egyptians, without knowing about the "death of Christ on the cross," was a symbol of life. In both considerations of Auriga, we find "life and salvation for the sheep of His flock when He comes to reign and rule in His judgment."[94]

Taurus

We find the "sign" Taurus on the lower left-hand side, or "tail" of the Virgin's mantle, which the angelic boy at the foot of the image is clinging to. According to Fr. Mario Rojas, these three

---

[92] cf. Jn 10:11
[93] cf. Heb 13:20
[94] *The Witness of the Stars*, E.W. Bullinger, Kregel Publications, pg. 136

stars represent the Aztec year 13 caña (3 entities over olive green/ 10 is equivalent to 13 caña). Taurus seems to be the same in all ancient star studies. He is a bull in the act of charging. Tor is the Chaldean name, Al Thaur the Arabic, Tauros the Greek and Taurus the Latin. Shur is the Hebrew, meaning both coming and ruling. Though there are many Hebrew terms for bulls and oxen, the most common poetical use is "reem," connoting loftiness, exaltation, power and pre-eminence. Even the name of Our Father in faith, Abram, pre-eminent/high father, is traced to this poetic term.

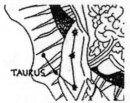 Taurus' Alpha star is Al-debaran and is found in the "bull's eye!" It means "The leader or governor." Its beta star is shared with  Auriga's right foot, El Nath, "the wounded or slain." The Pleiades are found on Taurus' back and signify "the congregation of the judge or ruler." The brightest of these stars is Al Cyone, "center," and has long been conjectured by many astronomers as being the center of the universe. Here we can suggest that the year 13 caña,[95] of the Aztec calendar, and 1531 of the Julian Calendar, the year of the apparitions of Our Lady of Guadalupe, being one and the same, must definitely have a central and focal point in salvation history. Let us be like Juan Diego and say, "I'm nothing more than a "tail" and a "wing." We must hold tightly onto the Virgin's mantle so as to have part in the "Parousia" of Jesus Christ.

Taurus also has another group of stars on his face called the Hyades which also signify "the congregated." This group, together with their sisters, the Pleiades, tell us that the saints will be secure with their mighty Lord when He comes to rule. I Thes 4:17 echo the "glory" already proclaimed by this constellation:

---

[95] Remember that the tail end of Our Lady's turquoise mantle, that "cola" with three stars, also represents the year 13 caña, and therefore a transparency for the message of Taurus, the stars of its constitution and its decans.

"Then we who live, who survive, shall be caught up together with them in clouds to meet the Lord in the air, and so we shall ever be with the Lord. Wherefore, comfort one another with these words"

We might also consider the symbolism of the bull as also being an animal of sacrifice, that the Lord would first be One slain in sacrifice (El Nath). The fact that the horn of Taurus coincides with the foot of Auriga tell us that it is the "Shepherd" Who lays down His life for his sheep.[96]

Orion

The constellation Orion is not represented by stars in the image of Our Lady of Guadalupe, but was definitely present in the winter solstice of 1531, and has a most glorious role for the proclamation of the heavens of the "glory of God." Orion proclaims that the "coming one" of Taurus is no Bull, but a man: a mighty and glorious prince! The poet Aratus says:

"Eastward, beyond the region of the bull
Stands great Orion.
And who, when night is clear,
Beholds him gleaming bright,
shall cast his eyes in vain
To find a sign more glorious in all heaven."[97]

The Denderah Zodiac depicts Orion (Hagat — this is he who triumphs) as coming forth pointing to the stars, Rigel, Bellatrix and Betelgeuse as belonging to him. In the hieroglyphics his name is Oar, a spelling from the ancient Oarion coming from the Hebrew root meaning "light."

---

[96]   Cf. Jn 10:11
[97]   "Diosemeia" (The divine signs), Aratus, 270 B.C.

"Coming forth as light" is Orion's Hebrew name. Urana, "the light of heaven" was the Akkadian name. Orion was a well known constellation in the eastern sky. In sacred scripture we find reference to it in Genesis 3:15, JOB 9:9, 38:31 and Amos 5:8.

 Orion's Alpha star is found in his right shoulder and is called Betelgeuse. It corresponds with Malachi's reference to the day of his "coming."[98]  Rigel, the beta star, is found in his left foot which is placed on the head of his enemy. It translates to the "the foot that crusheth." Rigel bespeaks or signifies its essence. (Its name is its mission.) Bellatrix, found in Orion's left shoulder, signifies "quickly coming or swiftly destroying." The delta star, found in Orion's belt, is called Al Nitak ("the wounded one"), and tells us that this "glorious one" was once wounded. Together with the hilt of his sword, in the form of a lamb, it tells us that "the glorious one to come" is the "lamb that was slain."[99] The kappa star in his left leg, Saiph, means "bruised" and thus connects Orion with the Genesis 3:15 prophecy. Later, with our consideration of Ophiucus, we will see that both have one leg bruised and one foot crushing the enemy.

There are other stars and other names that confirm all of the former conclusions with respect to Orion, for example: Al Rai, "Who bruises, who breaks" and Thabit, Hebrew for "treading on." Some Arabic names include: Al Gianuza, "the branch"; Al Gebor, "the mighty"; Al Mirzam, "the ruler"; Al Nagjed, "the prince"; Niphla (Chaldean), "the mighty"; Nux (Hebrew), "the strong." Heka is Chaldean for "coming" and Meissa is Hebrew for "coming forth." Along with the Pleides, Orion's testimony is also found in Sacred Scripture. Isaiah beautifully manifests the truths that Orion proclaimed for centuries.

---

[98]   cf. Mal 3:2
[99]   cf. Rv 5:9,12

"Arise,
Shine; for thy light is come,
And the glory of the Lord is risen upon thee,
For, behold, darkness shall cover the earth,
And gross darkness the people;
But the Lord shall arise upon thee, and His glory
shall be seen upon thee.
And the Gentiles shall come to thy light
And kings to the brightness of thy rising."[100]

The "glory of God" which the heavens have been declaring is that glorious time when all creation will be filled with His glory.[101] As Isaiah says when *"the glory of the Lord shall be revealed, and all flesh shall see it together."*[102] Seeing that the constellation of Orion corresponds with the child at the feet of the Virgin, and remembering that we have consistently made a correlation of this angelic child with the person and mission of Juan Diego, so now then do we point out the beautiful correlation with "the saints of the latter days," prophesied by St. Louis M. de Montfort, who will take the Gospel again over the whole world. It is in them that the word of St. Paul will be fulfilled: *"I live no longer I, it is Christ Who lives in me."*[103] They will truly be "alter Christi" as again Louis M. de Montfort points out in his "Fire Prayer" asking God for these saints of the last times. It is they who will put the light of Christ "on the table," they will make the church shine in the darkness of a devastated world in the glory of the new Jerusalem.

We note that the star Betelgeuse, "the coming," is superimposed on the seventh large flower, that flower which represents the New Testament of "The Book." We know that the New Testament is the written word concerning the Word, the Only Begotten Son, the "glory of God." Here we see the convergence of the written and the silent word, proclaiming the same Gospel.

---

[100] Isaiah 60:1-3
[101] cf. Numbers 14:21 and Isaiah 11:9
[102] cf. Isaiah 40:5
[103] Gal 2:20

The star Bellatrix, "quickly coming, swiftly destroying," corresponds with the blue coloring of three-toned wings. In one relation made with the three witnesses of earth, as found in I John 5:8, we can easily coordinate this color with the testimony of the "water," but as St. John says, *"the Spirit, and the water, and the blood; and these three are one."* We see a beautiful correspondence with the three creations: angel, man and material creation brought to its consummation in this apocalyptic appearance of the Virgin. Here also, we might recall the significance of the "ascending eagle," attribute of Huitzilopochtli, as the patron of the mystical warriors. Bellatrix, as well as the entire constellation, corresponds perfectly to the mission of the archangels, the warriors of God, in bringing about the reign of Mary as a precursor to the establishment of the reign of Christ the King.

Canis Major (Sirius)

Gemini's second and third decans are Canis Major and Canis Minor. Though the "big dog" does not correspond with any stars on the holy tilma, it does appear in the 1531 Winter Solstice. Canis Major is known by its brightest star, the very brightest star in the heavens (from earth's perspective), Sirius, meaning "prince." It gives witness to Christ Who is the "Prince of princes."

The Akkadian name for this constellation is Kasista, "the Leader and Prince of the heavenly host," a name which Holy Mother the church attributes and advocates St. Michael the Archangel. The Sacred Books of Persia contain praises of Sirius with names Tistrya or Tistar, "the chieftain of the East." The beta star of Sirius is Mirzam. It also means "prince or ruler." All of Sirius' stars give the same testimony, not to the Greek picture of a dog or the Egyptian hawk, Naz, "swiftly coming down," etc., but to "the Prince of princes"[104] and the "King of kings and Lord of lords."[105]

Canis Minor (Procyon)

 The Denderah Zodiac manifests Canis Minor as a human figure with a hawk's head and what appears to be a small tail. Here it is  called Sebak, "conquering, victorious." Its alpha star is called Procyon, "the redeemer" and tells us that the previous Sirius, "the glorious prince," is the same one who was slain. In a certain way, both being in Gemini (the twins, one victorious and the other wounded), so also do its decans, Canis Major and Canis Minor reflect the dual character of the prince: the victorious and the wounded Redeemer. Gomeisa (Arabic) is the beta star meaning "the burdened, loaded, bearing for others."

Canis Minor corresponds with the lone star in the upward "movement of ransom." It is next to the point on the "hook."[106] Our Redeemer wants to catch each and every man individually. As it is also next to the eighth of the nine large golden flowers and corresponds to the eighth Beatitude, *"Blessed are they who suffer persecution for justice' sake, for theirs is the kingdom of heaven."*[107] Procyon gives testimony to the wounds Christ bears for the sake of the Father's justice, the price of our redemption. We might also note that this star of Canis Minor is within a triangle. The redeeming love of God is Trinitarian!

---

[104] cf. Dan 8:23,25

[105] Rv 19:16

[106] We see this "hook" in the stream of light which descends on Our Lady's right side and ascends on her left side.

[107] Mt 5:10

Crux

The easiest constellation to recognize on the mantle of the Virgin of Guadalupe is that of the Southern Cross. It is Libra's first decan, but appears in the "movement of ransom" before its mother constellation.

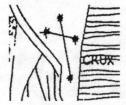 Adom is its Hebrew name and it literally means "cutting off."[108] "Adom" was visible in the Jerusalem latitude at the time of Our Lord's death, 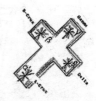 but due to the recession of the Polar Star (Thuban of Ursa Major) it moved to the southern latitudes. It was only within the dawn of expanding empires and missioning that the Southern Cross was rediscovered, that's why Dante writes, "the four stars never beheld but by the early race of men." Crux comes from the last letter of the Hebrew alphabet, "tau." It means mark and can be found on coins as an "x" or "+." Some of the ancients lost the true meaning of "crux," but the Persians and the Egyptians worshipped it. Cakes marked with "+" were made and eaten in honor of the Queen of Heaven. The mantle of the Queen of Heaven is marked with a "+," thus Mary is she who brings her Son, the Bread of Life, to all who will to receive Him.

When we look at the constellation of the Southern cross on the image of Our Lady of Guadalupe, we see that its Gamma star is in perfect alignment with the "Nahui Ollin," the four petalled flower superimposed on the Virgin's womb. *"How beautiful on the mountains are the feet of him who bring good news, announcing peace, proclaiming news of happiness!"*[109] As Crux belongs to Libra, we must be ever grateful for the "price" the Lord paid for our ransom.[110] The Denderah Zodiac depicts this second decan of Libra differently: a thirsty lion, with his tongue hanging out of his mouth. It is being given to drink by a female figure. A symbol of running

---

[108] cf. Dan 9:26
[109] Isaiah 52:7
[110] cf. page 53

water is found under its fore paws. The Egyptian name for the lion was Sera, "victory." There's no harm in making a correlation of a thirsty lion with a cross. The "lion of the tribe of Judah," Christ, (also present in the sign Leo corresponding with the "Nahui Ollin") was brought down "into the dust of death" and as Psalm 22:13-18 elaborates, *"I am like water poured out; all my bones are racked. My heart has become like wax melting away within my bosom. My throat is dried up like baked clay, my tongue clings to my jaws, … they have pierced my hands and my feet; I can count all my bones."*

Centaurus

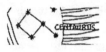 

Centaurus is Virgo's second decan, but as part of the upward "movement of ransom" it partakes in the passive element of Our Lord's saving love. Centaurus comes from the Hebrew "Bezeh" and means "despised." It is the same name used by Isaiah when he is prophetically speaking about Christ as the suffering servant. *"He is despised and rejected by men"*[111] Another Hebrew name for the "sign" was "Asmeath," "sin-offering." Belonging to the constellation of Virgo, and being a creature of two natures, the ancients deduced that the "the branch," the "desired one," "Who was to come as the seed of the Virgin" would have two natures: human and divine. He would be "despised," but as the Alpha Centauri star, Toliman (the closest star to our solar system) when translated, tells us, He is also *"The Heretofore and the Hereafter,"* He is the Christ of Apocalypse 1:8, *"the One who is, who was, and who is to come,"* the Alpha and the Omega.

The connection of the alpha star with the "sign's" name silently proclaim the dual nature of Our Lord Jesus Christ. In His human nature He is the "sin-offering" and as God, He is the Eternal One, the Alpha and Omega. On the image of Our Lady of Guadalupe, Centaurus corresponds with the third instrument of "the

---

[111] Isaiah 53:3

catch," the fishing net, created by the fold of Our Lady's mantle. It is also situated above the Crux, thus proclaiming His own death. For us to be in the safety of the "net" guarded from the constant attack of the evil one is a tremendous grace for which we should be most grateful to Our Lord and Savior.

Hydra

 To the ancients, Leo's first decan proclaimed "The old serpent is destroyed." It  is the role of the "lion of the tribe of Judah" to trample the "serpent," the arch-enemy of God, underfoot, and this is exactly what we see when looking at Leo's forepaw.[112] Hydra is portrayed as a female serpent, the mother of all evil, and retains the significant translation "he is abhorred!" All of its dim stars announce its eternal doom: Al Pharad, "the separated, put away"; Al Drian, "the abhorred"; Minchar al Sugia, "the piercing of the deceiver."

Leo's second and third decans also show the end of Hydra in this manner. The Crater is a cup of wrath being poured out upon Hydra as she represents the life of all evil. Psalms 11:6 and 75:8 as well as Apocalypse 14:10 and 16:19 all speak of the cup of wrath which awaits the eternal destruction of all evil. Corvus, Leo's third decan, is a raven which is devouring Hydra. The name found for Corvus on the Denderah Zodiac is Her-Na, meaning "the breaking up of the enemy." Only one of Hydra's stars, Pi, is noted on the mantle of the Virgin, and it is found near the end of the Hydra's tail. Since this star corresponds to the left arm of the Virgin, we can make the correlation with Virgo's left arm, it has the star Spica, "the branch" and the promised seed of Genesis 3:15. The Virgin of Tepeyac is the very same woman represented in Virgo for the past millions of years. It is her seed, "the lion of the tribe of Judah" Who will crush the head of the serpent.

---

[112] cf. pg 56

Victima

Victima is Libra's second decan. The modern version of this constellation is the "wolf" Lupus, but the ancients saw the constellation as a figure that had been wounded and was dying as it fell to the ground. Victima is Latin for victim and this follows with the Hebrew "Asedah" and the Arabic "Asedaton," both meaning "to be slain." As the sketch illustrates, Victima is being slain by Centaurus, by a figure that represents the same person, Our Lord Jesus Christ. We recall the words of St. John, *"I lay down my life for the sheep.... No man takes it from me, but I lay it down of myself. I have power to lay it down, and I have power to take it again,"*[113] and St. Paul in his letter to the Hebrews, *"He put away sin by the sacrifice of Himself."*[114]

The Denderah Zodiac gives a picture that corresponds perfectly with Isaiah's words *"He was brought as a lamb to the slaughter; And as a sheep before her shearers is dumb; So He opened not his mouth."*[115] A little child called Suru, translated as "lamb," is depicted with one of his fingers to its lips. It seems that the mystery of the cross was present to Jesus even in His youth, He would be led like a lamb to the slaughter without opening His mouth. The same concept is brought to our attention in the image of Our Lady of Perpetual Help. The Child Jesus, upon seeing the instruments of His Sacred passion, looses his sandal out of fright.

As Victima corresponds with the left side of the Virgin, the passive side, we can logically imply the necessity of passivity and sacrifice in the upward "movement." Note, all of the constellations of the left side, save Hydra, all show Christ as the passive and suffering servant. The upward "movement" is one that derives its inertia from the passive grace of the suffering Servant. The passive participation goes deeper than the active one.

---

[113] Jn 10:15-18
[114] Heb 9:26
[115] Isaiah 53:7

Libra

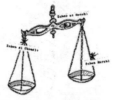

Libra follows Virgo in the celestial production of "signs" and prophecies. Virgo was the presentation of the "desired one" coming forth as the "seed" of the "Virgin." Libra manifests the price of our Redemption paid by Our Lord. As we've already encountered Libra's first and second decans, Crux and Victima, we've glimpsed something of Libra's gospel. The Hebrews call the sign Mozanaim, "the scales or weighing"[116] Al Zubena is the Arabic name and translates to "purchase or redemption." We see that salvation is considered in the same line of purchasing. Lambadia is the Coptic name and it means "station of propitiation." The root words here have the literal significance of "the grace of the branch."

Libra has three stars of greater brilliance. They are Zuben al Genubi (the price which is deficient), Zuben al Chemali (the price which covers) and Zuben Akrabi (the price of the conflict. "Zuben" is the key word that speaks to us of the great price necessary and paid for our salvation. "The deficient price" is that which man attempts as his payment. "The price which covers" is that which St. Paul tells us, *"Not with corruptible things, as silver and gold,... but with the precious blood of Christ"*[117] "The price of the conflict" accentuates this truth. Even St. John's vision of the *"things to come"* tell us that the ancient ones sing in praise *"Thou wast slain and hast redeemed us to God by Thy blood."*[118]

The constellation Libra soberly speaks of the just price required by a just and loving God. The shedding of Christ's precious blood on Calvary is the meeting point of God's justice and love. Located on the left side of the Virgin's mantle, it also reminds us that man is incapable of making just restitution for his own ransom. Redemption, and the "price" of Redemption is a gift.

---

[116] cf. Isaiah 40:12 and Dan 5:27
[117] I Pt 1:18-19
[118] Rv 5:9

Scorpio

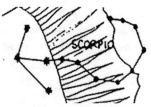

The "sign" Scorpio tells of the conflict that the "seed" will have to endure in order to merit our Redemption. In He-

brew, Arabic and Syriac, Scorpio has the name Al Akrab, meaning "scorpion" as well as "wounding him that cometh," "conflict," "war." In Coptic the "sign" signifies the "attack of the enemy." Antares is the alpha star and heart of Scorpio, it also means "the wounding." The star, Lesath, in Scorpio's sting means "the perverse." Victima is Libra's second decan.

The modern version of this constellation is the "wolf" Lupus, but the ancients saw the constellation as a figure that had been wounded and was dying as it fell to the ground. Victima is Latin for victim and this follows with the Hebrew "Asedah" and the Arabic "Asedaton, both meaning "to be slain." As the sketch illustrates, Victima is being slain by Centaurus, by a figure that represents the same person, Our Lord Jesus Christ. We recall the words of St. John, *"I lay down my life for the sheep…. No man takes it from me, but I lay it down of myself. I have power to lay it down, and I have power to take it again."*[119] and St. Paul in his letter to the Hebrews, *"He put away sin by the sacrifice of Himself."*[120]

The written word frequently shows the enmity between the "seed" and the serpent. Exodus 1:16, 22 shows how Pharaoh was induced by the evil one to destroy every male seed of Abraham. I Kings 11:1 tells how Athaliah was prompted to destroy the "royal seed." The book of Esther also portrays Haman as wanting to destroy all the Jews while in their exile and Matthew 2:16 also records the action taken by King Herod at the birth of Jesus.

When we study the star charts as well as the correspondence with the image of Our Lady of Guadalupe, we see that the stinger of Scorpio is aimed at striking Ophiucus, the serpent holder, and

---

[119] Jn 10:15-18
[120] Heb 9:26

Ophiucus is in the process of crushing Scorpio's heart. Four stars on the mantle of Our Lady Guadalupe correspond with the constellation of Scorpio, but not on the image are the nine stars which make up the tail and stinger. Symbolically, they have fallen off the mantle of Our Lady. These nine stars may not say a thing to most people, but symbolically speaking they do have a correspondence to those angels from the nine choirs that fell from heaven and no longer are found in the grace of God.

Ophiucuso

Ophiucus is shown as a mighty man wrestling with a serpent

 and at the same time crushing the heart of Scorpio. The snake with which Ophiucus wrestles is apparently trying to grab the "co- rona," the crown, and this seems to be the object of their struggle. Ras El Hagus, "he who holds," is the name of the star on the head of Ophiucus. It almost translates to the meaning of Ophiucus, "the serpent held." As was earlier noted in Orion, Ophiucus also has a star on one leg which means "bruised," Siaph, while at the same time the other foot is "treading underfoot."

Four of Ophiucus' stars are found superimposed on the mantle of the Virgin of Guadalupe. They can be found in the head region and appear to bend with its incline. The number "four" symbolically calls to mind the image of the cross. Both the first constellation on the mantle (Boötes) and the last reflect something of the mercy and power of the cross. The Virgin who brings forth the "Seed" as well as Her Reign are well protected. Although we see that "Corona" falls perfectly on the forehead of the Virgin we must constantly be on guard with Ophiucus. We must protect Her reign for the serpent is still desirous of Her crown.

Corona

Corona is Libra's third decan. Its Hebrew name is Atarah and translates to "royal crown." In the heavens, it follows the work of the cross, the "price of the conflict" and therefore is the reward of those who follow in the Master's footsteps. St. Paul's letter to the Hebrews tells us that the cross is followed by the crown, *"Jesus, crowned with glory and honor because of his having suffered death...."*[121] As beloved children of the "Queen of Heaven and Earth," we are called to participate in a yearly Coronation of the Virgin of Guadalupe, even as God crowned her on that December 12, 1531.

Corona is the crown which the Son gives to His Mother. The Alpha star, Al Phecca means "the shining" and beautifully portrays Mary as the morning star and the One *"who comes forth as the morning, fair as the moon, bright as the sun, terrible as an army set in battle array."*[122] The "movement of ransom" springs forth from the heart of God, manifests itself in Virgo, leaves the Virgin through her loving glance, descends with the harvester Boötes, spirals with Taurus, Orion and Sirius, begins an upward passive movement and then spirals again with the crowning of the Virgin.

Gemini

Gemini is really a "sign" which speaks of the Messiah's peaceful reign, for there is no confrontation, even with the duality within Gemini:

---

[121] Heb 2:9
[122] cf. Cant of Cant 6:20

Lepus (crushed beneath Orion's foot), Canis Major and Canis Minor. The alpha and beta stars are those represented in the diagram of the winter solstice. They correspond with the fifth of the nine large flowers and the fifth Beatitude, *"Blessed are the merciful, for they shall obtain mercy.."*[123] Jesus is the perfect example of heroic mercy. This was his mission as the God-Man.

Leo

 Leo is the last of the twelve "signs." As part of the winter solstice of 1531 (90W of Greenwich) it coincides with the  womb of the Blessed Virgin Mary. Regulus, its alpha star (sometimes called Cor Leonis — heart of the lion), falls exactly in concordance with the "Nahui Ollin" of Our Lady. Apocalypse 5:5 puts it clearly, *"Behold, the lion of the tribe of Judah, the root of David, has overcome."* Our "movement of ransom" returns to its source. This "sign" is not only in the center of the person of Our Lady, it marks the "Nahui Ollin," the center of all existence as being as Our Lord Jesus Christ.

Conclusion

The "movement of ransom" is a movement of love. Flowing forth from the Virgin's heart, we realize that it really precedes from the very heart of God. He, Whose infinite love is manifested in the sending of His Only Begotten Son, has invited us to an intimate union with Him. We see that from the very beginning, from the dawn of creation, God has given us hope of living in this union. He not only gave a verbal promise of our Redemption, Genesis 3:15, but He placed the same proclamation in the heavens. Man has for-

---

[123] Mt 5:7

gotten to look up, he has forgotten to take advantage of the orientation that his Creator has written in the skies, for the most part, he has placed the gospel of the stars on the backshelf of bygone years. Indeed, *"The heavens proclaim the glory of God."* They proclaim Jesus Christ!

God's merciful love is eternal and throughout all times He allows the fruit of His work to glorify Him in new and wonderful ways. As His word never returns to Him void, It must come to fruition in us. Just as the heavens declare no "entry," except through the Virgin Mary, so also in His masterpiece of Her in the Holy image of Our Lady of Guadalupe. Mary is that "Tree of Life" that always gives fruit in due season. It is She who makes sure that the flow of merciful love, "the movement of ransom," reaches all the children of God. In her, by action of the Holy Spirit, with, in and through Her Son, we are called to become that Alter Cristus, that image of Christ the Father seeks, that "new Adam," who is a proclamation of the "glory of God"![124]

---

[124] Lumen Gentium, 55 ff.

Book Five

The Way of the Cross of Blessed Juan Diego

Foreword

There is no better way to understand the significance of the help of the holy angels in the miraculous sign of the "woman clothed with the sun" than in the light of the holy cross, the only authentic sign of God's infinite love. In like manner, the revelation of Our Lady of Guadalupe, despite the fact that she appears as the glorious woman of the Apocalypse, can only be understood if we see her in and through the sign of the holy cross.

The following the "way of the cross of Blessed Juan Diego," based on the document of the Nican Mopohua, the authentic relation of this wonderful happening, reveals exactly fourteen stations of the cross in perfect harmony with the historical stations of the cross of Our Lord Jesus Christ in Jerusalem. Just as Our Lady accompanied her Son on the sorrowful way of the cross, Juan Diego also had to enter into this only authentic way of salvation from the moment of his first encounter with Our Lady on the hill of Tepeyac. We can announce salvation only if we are "burden-bearers" like Simon of Cyrene, Juan Diego and all the saints of the church who in a special way were called by God to carry the cross of Our Lord Jesus Christ.

There is a glorious perspective of the way of the cross in, with and by mediation of Our Lady. Because each station of the way of cross has merited a special grace for man, considering that the twelve first stations are the most important, we are certainly allowed to make a relationship of the stations of the cross with the corresponding gates of the new Jerusalem.[1] She, as the "great sign" of Apocalypse 12:1, and more than any of the saints, is "the burden-bearer," who through the pearls of the rosary is entitled to dispense the saving and healing power of the holy cross to all those who look up to her as the Great Mediatrix of graces.

In the image, Our Lady of Guadalupe is not simply hovering in the air. She stands on the inclined head and outstretched arms of the seer. Like the Gospel of St. Luke, giving the all the necessary details for what is to follow, the Nican Mopohua also beautifully portrays that precisely this "standing upon" becomes the clearest

---

[1] Remembering the twelve tribes of the chosen people of God, the twelve apostles, there necessarily must be a correlation to the twelve gates of the new Jerusalem, especially if we recall that the number of those who will be saved is one hundred and forty-four thousand. This is to say 12 x 12,000. It is a symbolic number telling us about the consummation of the plan of God for the salvation of mankind, which came into existence already with the twelve tribes. This is why each gate of the new Jerusalem is not only related to the corresponding station of the cross, but also related to the twelve tribes and the twelve apostles. In a symbolic way, God has prepared twelve ways of salvation in all the tribulations of our earthly existence. These ways are characterized by the specific character of the apostle to which each door is correlated, but we should not forget that we find the number twelve also in the material creation, for example the precious stones above the gates, (cf Apoc. 21:20) in twelve planets and the twelve major constellations. Moreover, the Apocalypse tells us about the presence of the elders and the apostles over each gate (cf. Apoc. 21:12), likewise of the presence of an angel over each gate. In order to more deeply understand these multiple relations of twelve, we certainly would need more light. One thing is certain, it is not a matter of pure speculation in an gnostic way, because finding out about the correlations we would have a deeper insight into man's relation with the visible and invisible world. Besides, it would be a very concrete interest to know to which apostle we are correlated in a special way, because this would help us to walk more securely on our way of salvation.

symbol for her historical encounter with Juan Diego. Time for the Aztec was part of the essence of man and of all creation. This is why the suffering of Juan Diego, of always having to wait a long time before meeting with the bishop, is not just a moral suffering, but an ontological one.

The prologue of the Nican Mopohua gives us the historical background: exterior peace after all the horrible blood shed and destruction caused by war. As previously pointed out, it was more a "peace" of death. As part of his mission from the Virgin, Juan Diego, as a "burden-bearer, had to take this "death" upon himself, so as to bring new life to his people. In the following stations we have first placed the reading from the account of the apparitions, a short commentary and then a larger one which includes a deeper interpretation of the Nican Mopohua document.[2] You can meditate on it in the manner best fitting: reading only the text corresponding to each station or reading it together with the first commentary or together with the second one.[3]

First Station

Jesus is Condemned to Death
(Nican Mopohua, vs. 1-9)

Only because Jesus accepted His condemnation could peace come to the earth.

The coming of Our Lady Guadalupe to Mexico:

- brought the knowledge of the True God to the pagans,
- gave them a house for the True God,
- and opened a new era after all the bloodshed of the human sacrifices by the Aztecs and the destruction of the war caused by the Spaniards, bringing peace to this suffering, smitten country.

---

[2]   The entire Nican Mopohua is available in Book Three; Appendix I
[3]   The second commentary always begins with a (*).

The Lord pronounces over them, by way of His Mother, His first word from the cross: *"Father, forgive them, for they do not know what they are doing!"* [4]

"A new begining" can best be seen, in that the three laws lost by man through original sin, are fulfilled: the law of the right time, the right place and the right mode.

The law of the right time: Whatever God does is done at the right time, forseen by His wisdom from all eternity. The hour of the encounter, it is dawn, symbolically pointing out to a new beginning, like the "very early morning" when Mary Magdalene went out to see the grave of the Lord. In fact it is still night, when Juan Diego left his home to go to Mexico (the sunrise in winter is some time after 7 a.m.). The night time he is leaving is symbol for the blind faith in which he must proceed. It is a Saturday, the day of Our Lady, the only person who really consciously participated in the passion of Our Lord, and who knew, even in her deepest suffering under the cross that He would resurrect. Walking towards the light of the dawning morning Juan Diego is already approaching her, because she is the dawn preceding the light of the sun, her Son Jesus Christ.

The law of the right place: Rationalism, even in the church, has forgotten about this truth. Not every place is apt as a "place of God." [5] God, by way of the Mother of His Son, chose the right place, which was exactly the place where before the mother of all

---

[4] Lk 23:34

[5] There is a knowledge about hidden things which is given to man in a charismatic way, mostly by the help of the angels, be it of the good or the fallen angels. In our days this charismatic knowledge is a powerful arm in the Spiritual fight for the reign of God. The more man looses faith in the Only True God, the more he is liable to be guided by the fallen angels. There is a geography of grace, according to which there are places less or more apt for building a house of God. The fallen angels know about it, and this is why they try to take hold of these places, neutralizing the special grace present in these places. In the beginning, the Christians knew well about this fact and so most of the churches were built where formerly a pagan temple had been.

gods was venerated. The mountain in general[6] is not only a symbol of firmness, it is also a place closer to heaven, and also closer to the "gods"; this is why the Aztecs were horrified and filled with awe at the same time, when they heard that some of the Spaniards had climbed up to the crater of Popocatepetl, the Holy Mountain, and this during a time of rumbling and issuing of smoke.[7]

The law of the right mode: The "how" something is being done is so very important: we say "the tone makes the music" — it is important how you say things. Whatever God does is always done in the best possible way. In May of 1524 the first Franciscan missionaries arrived to Juan de Uloa. They prepared themselves for one year by studying the language of the Aztecs, and before embarking with the evangelization of the Gospel they made a retreat. The first harvest of converts is attributed to their zeal. Among the first were Juan Diego and his uncle Juan Bernardino, who certainly had been prepared by God's greater grace beforehand to receive Baptism with an open heart. Although the apparitions became the starting grace for many of the millions to be converted, it was not thus with Juan Diego. Knowing about the Mother of God is normally not the first thing one starts with in catechism, but he certainly knew well of her, for immediately before she presented herself he already recognized her as the Virgin, Mother of God.

The questions Juan Diego asks himself[8] when he meets Our Lady first in a transfigured ambience, go out to the "four directions" of

---

[6] Recall the great revelations of God in the Old Testament. In the New Testament also, there is a trinity of revelations on mountains: the Sermon on the Mount, the Transfiguration and the hill of Golgotha, where the Eternal Covenant of God with man was sealed by the death of the Son of God.

[7] *Flor y Canto Del Nacimiento de Mexico*, XV, pp. 76-77

[8] "Where am I? Where do I find myself? Is it possible that I am in the place that our ancient ancestors, our forefathers spoke about, in the land of the flowers, in the land of corn, of our flesh, of our sustenance, possibly in earthly paradise?" (Nican Mopohua vs. 7-10)

the wind. It is only by the cross that he can identify *where* he is. In the image, it will become even clearer through the four-petalled flower, the "nahui ollin," signifying the presence of the Lord in Our Lady's womb. Necessarily the whole of nature together with the four directions of the wind, the "four elements" as the ancient Greek philosophers taught, are part of this revelation, and need to be considered in the deeper understanding of this revelation.[9] The Aztecs saw paradise with the properties of all that is already beautiful and necessary on this earth: the flowers and the singing of the birds and the corn. We recall that the daily sustenance was recognized as a gift to man. On the other side of the coin, Huitzilopochtli demanded the sacrifice of human lives as admittance into paradise. Here it is that we approximate the deeper truth of Christ: only His sacrifice of life and death reopened the doors of paradise.

Step by step, by his questions of admiration, he comes closer to truth: there are four steps he takes which can be related to the four qualities of God:

- Sanctity — is represented by the flowers.
- Wisdom — has given man the corn to nourish himself.
- Justice — has made man a creature of mortal flesh.
- Omnipotence — gives him the goal to reach. With the fifth step he is closest to truth. Again and again, looking up to the image or meditating the word of the Nican Mopohua we discover the divine pedagogy of the sages: not imposing the truth but letting man find it, as if by his own effort.

Second Station

Jesus Takes up the Cross
(Nican Mopohua, vs. 10-30)

Jesus, taking up His cross, reopened the doors of paradise. Remember Our Lord's second word from the cross: *"Amen I say to thee, this day thou shalt be with me in Paradise."*[10]

---

[9] The elements: air, fire, water and earth, also have a beautiful correlation with the first four of Our Lady of Guadalupe's seven veils.

[10] Lk 23:43

Our Lady coming from the "region of the sun:"[11]

- Caused nature to be transformed into the splendours of the new Jerusalem.
- Opened the eyes of Juan Diego to the glories of heaven and renewed the dialogue of God with man through her intercession.
- Acknowledges Juan Diego's dignity so that he can approach her and converse with her as an equal.[12]

Where God (here by way of Our Lady) begins to speak to man, the voices of the creatures have to stop. Only in the deepest silence can we hear the words of God so that they penetrate deeper into our hearts.[13] The words of a mother always go deeper into the child's heart than those of a father. The Aztec sages had recognized both a masculine and a feminine principle in God. God's wisdom ties up with this light of truth. It is really the Father Who addresses Himself to Juan Diego by way of the Mother of His

Son, because the Aztecs needed a father in order to become a new people in the Son. This is why the modern tendency of doing away with Mary, more than man realizes, is the putting aside of our Heavenly Father, and the void created by this negation leaves the soul open as prey for the fallen angel: the "father of iniquity."[14]

By faith we know that God is love, overflowing bounty (already realized by Plato, the pagan philospher), but this love

---

[11] "Tlacupa" — region of the sun. Part of the overall make up of the Virgin's name: TleCuauh**tlacup**euh.

[12] The term "equal" is used because of the intimacy of words and expression between Mary and Juan Diego.

[13] I Kings 19:12

[14] Jn 8:44

needs the face of a person in order to touch the heart of man. Through Mary, this bountiful love of God was not only able to heal the wounds suffered through the destruction of their religion and culture, but to engender new life in the Son of God. In a man-made technological world there is no place for the living God. Already, Pascal cried out against the rationalistic theologians of his day, "God is not the God of philosophers," He is not an abstract idea. He is person more than any other person and so adresses Himself personally to each of us. It is His call which awakens man for the mystery of God. This is best expressed in the loving call of Our Lady of Guadalupe to Juan Diego.[15] Remember the Lord's call to the young Samuel who was destined to save the priesthood from utter disintegration.[16] God's love is the distinction of christian priesthood, always in danger to degenerate in a pagan ritualism. How can a priest, as good shepherd, respond to God for his flock if he does not respond to Him for himself?

Like any word of God, this call which goes deeper into our heart is a life-giving word. It awakens man from the slumber of his own "glories" and opens him for the only reality: God. Normally it is easier for the Asiatic people to address God than for us cool-hearted western technicians. By nature, they are more child-like. This natural disposition provides an easier entrance to prayer along with the challenge to "walk in the presence of God day and night." Juan Diego, in the deepest part of his soul, is a child. He is transparent and crystalline, like water from a mountain spring. He is tuned to the "waves" of the Immaculate Heart, certainly more than any other Mexican of his time. Nevertheless, because of an innate fear in approaching Our Lady, Juan Diego has to overcome a moment of hesitation. We mustn't forget: he is entering into the adventure of his life. God is always the greaterGod, even in the mediation of Mary. She is not only the humble handmaid of the Lord here on Tepeyac, but at the same time she is the *"woman clothed with the sun,"* representing the victorious glory of God. Man has to refind the just distance to God, between

---

[15] cf. Nican Mopohua, vs. 12, "Juanito, Juan Dieguito"
[16] cf. 1 Sam 3

the love which attracts us, and the fear which holds us back. He who courageously takes up his cross is he who approaches just measure. There are two opposing "movements" in his heart: the more he approaches her the more he is attracted by her beauty beyond human measure.[17]

Third Station

The First Fall of Jesus Beneath the Weight of the Cross
(Nican Mopohua, vs. 14-28)

By virtue of the fall of Christ to the dust of the earth, man was once again elevated to his primary dignity to dialogue with God. Our Lady, as messenger of her Son, the personified love of God, when appearing to Juan Diego, draws this pagan people, lost in the darkness of idolatry, nearer to Him.

- She calls him to come close to her that he might admire her supernatural glory.
- The nature around her is also formed in the same glory apparent in her apparition.
- She reminds man that his only goal is God and that as a permanent sign of this, a house should be built for her on the hill in which she, as Mother, wants to give "…Him in my personal love, my compassionate glance, my help and my salvation.[18]

* For the Aztecs, vestments were considered a symbol of the person and his state. The glorious vestment of Our Lady of Guadalupe tells us where she is really coming from: out of the sun, always a

---

17 cf. Ibid., vs. 16 ff.
18 cf. Nican Mopohua, vs. 28.

symbol for God, not only with the Aztecs.[19] Already by her exterior, as later in her image, she was marked as messenger of God, even more so than the angels at her service in this mission. The winged child at Our Lady's feet has many layers of interpretation, but a forefront is the symbol of Juan Diego, Our Lady's chosen ambassador.

The fact that God sends the Mother of His Son to us is a clear sign that in these last times He wants to meet us first of all in and through His Mother. Following the Protestants in their direct approach, we are on the wrong way; this is one of the deeper reasons for the crisis in the church today. One day, individually as well as collectively, we will have to meet Him in His Son as the One Who will judge the living and the dead. The fact that Mary is given to us in a special way as mediatrix is an apocalyptic grace, which those who live in the illusion of progress, like the Saducees, or by the letter of the law like the Pharisees and Scribes, can not grasp. Both of them forget that we are called to approach God in a personal way, as the God of Abraham, Isaac and Jacob, as the God of Our Lord Jesus Christ. This unique call of God to each and every one of us is a grace for the "adult Christian," "adult in heart." It is particularly evident in Juan Diego, who at the time of his "call" was fifty-seven years old.

As this God is so far away from us, declared dead by the theologians, and this because of our sins, we will only find Him as a "child" of Our heavenly Mother, who in a special way reminds us that she is close to us every moment of our life by way

---

[19] The sun was, even amongst the Jews a symbol of God, remember Zechariah's Canticle, *"In the tender compassion of our God, the 'dawn' from on high shall break upon us, to shine on those who dwell in darkness and to guide our feet into the way of peace."* (Lk 1:78-79)

of our good Guardian Angel, who in the trial at the beginning of time has become an "adult" and thus is capable of being a sure guide to heaven in the trials of our day. There exists a beautiful complementation between the apparitions of the Angel of Fátima and those of Our Lady: the angel teaches about the greater God and of His outraged Majesty, and Our Lady shows the children how to respond to this challenge. In Mexico, the angel is in Our Lady, irradiating in the glory sourrounding her. This glory, also reflected in the transformed nature, is for those who look out for God's help in all tribulations, like that of the new Jerusalem for those who are blind to the signs of the unbearable glory of the Last Judgement.

The precious stones irradiating their light are also part of the new Jerusalem.[20] Material creation is seen in the symbol of the precious stones whose molecular structure can no longer decompose. (The fundamental difference between carbon and a diamond is their molecular structure.) The transformation of nature partaking in the glory of heaven is a sign that transformation in this creation has already begun. Another sign of this is the incorrupted bodies of many saints. The beauty of St. Bernadette's face is a promise that "repatriation" of the material creation, in which we partake in our body, starts with the humble, with those who have gone barefoot over the soil of this earth. Remember: our mission as Christians is not only with our fellowman, it is also with nature.[21] In Christ we are called to bring it home to the Father.

In a special way, among the precious stones, the emerald symbolizes purity, and thus also for Mary Immaculate and her glorious assumption of body and soul into heaven. A noble woman among the Aztecs, after having given birth, was given an emerald necklace. The nobility were also buried with emerald/turquoise masks on their faces. We note here the intuition that life in its essence is pure. The Aztecs noted this immediately in the turquoise color of the mantle — representing the purity and virginal life in nature. Gold for the Aztecs,[22] as with the icons of the east, was for them a

---

[20] cf. Rv 21:19-21

[21] cf. Rom 8:22

[22] Gold was thought to be "excrement of the gods."

sign of eternity. For us Christians there is no other way to enter eternity than by the cross. This is evident already in her word. Four are the qualities of her word,[23] a humble sign that the word of God announced to the world should represent the four qualities of the triune God; it should be glorifying His sanctity, in its amiability it should be sign of His wisdom, it should have the attraction of the justice and love of God and exalting the omnipotence of God.

The way he adresses her[24] manifests that she not only represents the triune God, but that he also is child to God, and so conscious of his dignity as a Christian disposed to the things of God: this is why he invites her to "come to her house," but she does not answer this invitation, she asks him for a "greater house" (even though it will be smaller for a long time), a house for "Him," in order to reveal the "triune God."[25] Her mission is a trinitarian mission: She wants to "show, exalt and reveal Him,"[26] and this precisely in the place where she appears. It is from Tepeyac where the "new evangelization" should begin in the Franciscan church of Santiago, where Juan Diego invites her, down on the plain,[27] even though for the moment, the center of all missionary activity is indirectly subordinated to this place indicated by God — not by words, but in the Spirit. Here we encounter the hidden opposition of the whole narration: it is in similitude to that of the Beatitudes of Our Lord according to St. Matthew, proclaimed on a mountain, to that of St. Luke.[28] Here the apocalyptic perspective of the good news, in the light of the living being, the "angel" precedes that of the "bull."

---

[23]   cf. Nican Mopohua, vs. 22, "extremely glorifying, most amiable, as if drawing him to her, highly esteemed him."

[24]   cf. Nican Mopohua, vs. 24

[25]   cf. Nican Mopohua, vs. 26

[26]   cf. Nican Mopohua, vs. 27: the word for "pantlaza" — "to exult" — in Nahuatl has a variety of meanings; to magnify, to exult another, to put above, to discover a secret, to publish or make known, even "to give birth to."

[27]   cf. Nican Mopohua, vs. 24, "…there I will arrive, at your house of Mexico Tlatilolco…"

[28]   cf. Book VI

The Son exalted on the cross, Who wants to attract everybody to His Pierced heart, is the ONE she wants to make better known[29] — and we must see Him

- as the One Whom the Father has given into our hands.
- obedient to the Father's will, up to dying on the cross.
- to be revealed in the hearts of the faithful by way of the Holy Spirit.

Here again, the Trinitarian character of the revelation of Guadalupe becomes apparent. The revelation of the triune God is the center of the message of Guadalupe.[30]

In the same way Our Lady first received her Son in Nazareth, in Bethlehem and then under the cross, so also does she will to give Him to us. According to Our Holy Father, Pope John Paul II, this is what makes all the difference in a "Marian Kerygma," as the essence of the "new evangelization": "tota in Maria." In the title "Mother of the Church, given to Our Lady at the end of the II Vatican Council, the Holy Spirit has clearly pointed to Mary as the help of all Christians: confirmed by the first visit of John Paul II to Mexico. She is the Mother of the byways preceding and accompanying the church on her last steep way to Golgotha. In Mexico, this "meeting on the way" has become part of its personal experience with God: 1531 on Tepeyac, 1541 at Ocotlan, and 1631 inTlaxcala when St.Michael reveals himself to Diego Lazaro during a Eucharistic procession.

In a fourfold way, as only a mother can do, she wants to give her Son to the people[31]

- through all her personal love: the Mexicans, by the total destruction of their religion and culture, had almost lost ther identity. By way of her image — "amoxtli" — she looks at each one

---

[29] cf. Jn 12:32

[30] This is beautifully protrayed in the phylological study of the Nican Mopohua by Fr. Mario Rojas in his translation from the Nahuatl text.

[31] cf. Nican Mopohua, vs. 28

in a very personal way, there is no other way to explain the conversion of the eight million Indians. Truly, the Virgin of Tepeyac became Mother to each one. She takes us up into her Immaculate Heart by way of her merciful eyes. Modern technology opens our dullened faith with photographic magnification of Our Lady's eyes, showing the reflection of Juan Diego, the bishop, even an entire family in the pupil of her eyes.

- By means of her merciful glance she takes on herself his miseries and ailments.
- By her assistance she prepares the way of her Son so as to enter into the hearts of people.
- By the power of her Redemption she wraps us in the plenitude of graces she has received through her Son.

Fourth Station

Jesus Meets His Beloved Mother
(Nican Mopohua, vs. 29-32)

Our Lady of Guadalupe makes herself known as the Mother of the One and Only True God. It is by way of her that the people of the Americas should come to know more about God.

- "Truly, I am your compassionate Mother, yours and of all those who in this land are one."
- Her words testify that She is present "for all races of men, for those who love me, who cry out for me, those who seek me, those who confide in me."
- She wants to be the first missionary to bring the faith to this people.

Here we find a relationship with the Lord's third word to His Mother and his disciple: *"Woman, behold thy son. Behold thy mother."*[32]

"Truly, I am your compassionate Mother." This sentence, translated into an image, easly brings to mind the icon "Eleusa," the Merciful Mother with her Child close to her heart who wants to embrace us all in her mercy. She really is the "help of us Christians," because whenever we have merited the wrath of God, she will intercede for us and hold back the "arm of God's justice." It is by way of her mercy that she becomes the Mother of all those who look up to her, and through her to God. Only in the mercy of God, can man, dispersed by sin, find his way back to union. This is why Our Lady of Guadalupe can also be called the "Mother of the last times." In the mercy of God, she has been sent to overcome all heresies, schisms and barriers which sin has placed between men, even among Christians. The is the "great sign" countering that of dispersion, distraction and destruction. As she must always be seen in the sign of the cross, so also those who look up to her must be orientated toward the cross. This is symbolically exemplified in the four verbs: "who *love* me, who *cry* to me, who *seek* me and who *confide* in me."[33]

Our Lady of Guadalupe comes forth from the fire, iconized in her mantle of rays (the Aztecs going so far as seeing "the woman transformed in the fire"). As Yahweh spoke to Moses by way of the burning bush, so do we recognize the Virgin of Tepeyac as an icon of the Mercy of God. God, sympathizes with the misery of Israel in captivity, promises to lead them to the promised land and to redeem them by the intercession of Moses. The Virgin of Tepeyac confirms the word of the Lord: "Only love can save the world." This promise of "liberation" is not only limited to the Mexican people. Through Mary, the mercy of God wants to heal man to the deepest roots of original sin. The good news of salvation which Our Lady brings to Mexico, as when Our Lord an-

---

[32] Jn 19:26-27
[33] cf. Nican Mopohua, vs. 31

nounced His Gospel, should be accompanied by the healing of infirmities and ailments of the people.[34] As the the Lord wants to heal mankind, covering us with His five wounds, so also does Our Lady want to cover the whole world with the precious blood of Our Lord coming out of the five wounds: this is the deeper sense of the five apparitions.[35]

Fifth Station

Simon of Cyrene helps Our Lord Carry the Cross
(Nican Mopohua, vs. 33-40)

Like Simon of Cyrene, Juan Diego is called to become a "cacaxtli," a burden-bearer. His cross, first and foremost, is the mission given him by Our Lady.

- He must tell the bishop about his encounter with her and that the bishop should erect a house in which she will assemble the Indians as her family.
- She promises to recompense him abundantly.
- Juan Diego bows down before her as a sign of submission and immediately sets out to fulfill the mission she has entrusted to him.

Here the relation is with the fifth word of Our Lord: *"I thirst."*[36]
Immediately following the mandate of Our Lady is the realization of her desire. The word of God through Mary is a creative

---

[34] cf. Mt 4:23
[35] cF. Short Chronology of the Apparitions, Book II
[36] Jn 19:28

word which will consummate what it promises. The more the seerer is one with Our Lady, the better and the sooner he will be able to fulfill his mission. This is why only a man pure in heart like Juan Diego is able to correspond: He must be a faithful servant, not adding to or subtracting from that which Our Lady asks of him.[37] The promise of a recompense in Nahuatl refers back to a "recompense coming from God Himself": God is our greatest wealth and happiness, He is the "one denarius," in Him we will receive payment for our mission which is always a mission in and through the Son.[38]

The mission of Juan Diego is a mission in the sober love of God: there are no sentiments, no longer indulging in Mary's loveable presence, but immediate obedience. This is the angelical obedience which will be more and more necesary in these last times if we don't want to fall prey to the wiles of the fallen angel. Also the Spaniards, in their more militant way of propagating the faith, are requested to humbly submit to the mild government of the Immaculate Heart. Remember the opposition between the "house" she asks for in the beginning (vs. 26) and the "temple" on the plain (vs. 33) she asks for at the end of her first encounter with him. The "temple on the plain" should be like a bridge over to the little house on the top of the hill which we might call with St. Augustine "the house of the Spiritual saints" who already live in the light of God in poverty and ingenuity, those saints who continue the mission of St. John, close to the heart of Our Lord, but not less close to the Immaculate heart of Our Lady who he took into his "house" according to the words of the Lord.[39]

The "temple down on the plain," closer to the world, many times is in danger of being confounded with the world. This is why, again and again, God has to send His saints, who are/must always be saints in Mary, to remind the "church on the plain" that it should look up to Mary as the beacon of sanctity. In the history of the church, it has been at the Marian shrines and sanctuaries, many times outside the cities of man, where faith has been con-

---

[37] cf. Nican Mopohua, vs. 30
[38] cf. Ibid., vs. 34-36
[39] Jn 19:47

served when everywhere else it has lost, being the *"salt of the earth"* and the *"city on the hilltop."*[40] This "sanctuary on the plain" is another mediation to the hierarchical church where after the miracle, the image of Our Lady was brought for a short time before a little chapel was built. This double mediation is a symbol for Our Lady being the "stairway to heaven." The more the church will grow closer to the Immaculate Heart of Our Lady, the more it will approach the heavenly Jerusalem coming down from heaven.

Juan Diego will deeply have to suffer this opposition, but at the same time, by his suffering in, with and through Mary, he will become part of the "staircase" to heaven. In this perspective, the roses which finally cover the gap between Our Lady and the hierarchical church are symbols for the white or red martyrdom, in the cold of this world. They become points of crystallization for a church closer to the heart of Jesus. The church up on the hill, built on the place of the first apparition, is the home of a Carmel which has the special mission to keep alive the memory of the apparition. No order is more apt for this than that of Mt. Carmel. Like unto the dolorous way of the cross of Juan Diego these contemplative sisters, in the midst of the hustle and the noise around Tepeyac, were called to keep open the door for this "Staircase," which is Our Lady. Fidelity to her "Noteocaltzin"[41] is that which extends the "thirst" of Our Lord on behalf of the salvation of souls, especially those ever farther away from God.

Sixth Station

Veronica Wipes the Face of Jesus with her Veil
(Nican Mopohua, vs. 40-47)

The bishop does not yet accept this message as humbly as Juan Diego has received it.

---

[40] Mt 5:13-14

[41] The word used by Our Lady in her apparition to signify the "sacred little house" she wanted.

- He has many doubts about it.
- Juan Diego is greatly saddened by the Bishop's apparent rejection. Nonetheless, he returns directly to the hill with deep confidence in Our heavenly Mother.
- Jesus rewards Veronica's efforts by leaving his face imprinted on her veil; Mary imitates her Son by leaving her image on Juan Diego's tilma.[42]

*Don Juan de Zumarraga, the first to witness the miracle of Guadalupe, was quite a noble character. Though he had newly been appointed as the "governing priest," he had not yet been consecrated bishop. It was he who first brought printing to Mexico; in negotiation with Toledo, he founded the first American University; he established the Hospital of the love of God and brought many fruit trees from Spain. He fostered teaching the Indians the cultivation of silk and wool and the weaving of fabrics, carpets and tapestries. In the Nican Mopohua, he represents the hierarchical authority of the church, to whom, in the person of Juan Diego, Our Lady humbly also submits.[43]

Down on the plain, Juan Diego again becomes a poor Indian without any importance, overlooked by the bureaucracy. He is simply a "nothing" in the eyes of those who are the superiors. It is quite a different world which seems to have nothing in common with the "paradise" he comes from. How different is his relation to the bishop in comparison to that with Our Lady! But nothing will deviate him from his mission, he wills to accomplish it in perfect fidelity. In the "Informaciones" of 1666, the indigenous witnesses testify that in the first encounter, the bishop and his companions made fun of Juan Diego. He in no way found the comprehension he was hoping for. For the Aztec "tlamantine" — wisemen — "time" was part of the being of man. Separating "time" from things or persons will cause them to fall into nothing. The Greek word for time, "kairos," translates: "just time/moment" in accordance with the holy will of God. We find it in the word of Our Lord to the

---

[42] The name "Veronica" signifies "true icon-image."
[43] cf. Nican Mopohua, vs. 40-42

Jews: "Your time is always, My time has not yet come."[44] Juan Diego has made the experience of the fullness of this time on the hill with Our Lady, but now on the plain, he meets quite a different, even opposite concept of time, that of administration.

This is why Juan Diego's suffering is not just a personal, transitory sentiment, it is metaphysical, because there is a total lack of understanding with respect to what he has just experienced in the presence of Our Lady. With her there is fullness of life, light and love. "On the plain" he finds himself as if in a desert. As he returns to the mountain, he is a broken man. Night is approaching and the only hope he has is to once again find Our Lady.[45]

Seventh Station

Jesus Falls Beneath the Cross the Second Time
(Nican Mopohua, vs.48-67)

Juan Diego, anxious, discouraged and heartbroken, is virtually devastated by the weight of the bishop's initial denial.

- In the first meeting he met Our Lady with his dignity intact, as if on equal terms, but now with the weight of the cross on his shoulders and the frustration suffered in his first mission he throws himself down at the feet of Our Lady. Here, the mission of the burden-bearers is clearly seen: to repair the lack of faith on earth.
- He wants to give back his mission, because he thinks himself unworthy and unable to accomplish it. He expresses this using five terms: common man, "mecapal," "parehuela," "cola" and "ala." The five attributes point to the open heart of Our Lord.[46]
- Our Lady lifts him up from the dust of his despair and with all the love and tenderness of a mother and yet, with the firmness that begets obedience, asks him to continue his mission. With filial love Juan Diego can only reply, "Yes."

---

[44] Jn 7:6
[45] cf. Nican Mopohua, vs. 43-47
[46] Nican Mopohua, vs.55

Juan Diego has to experience the abandonment of Our Lord on the cross, the Fifth word of Our Lord. *"Eloi, Eloi, lama sabacthani?" "My God, my God, why hast thou forsaken me?"*[47] If it wasn't for Our Lady's help he would have given up.

*The way he addresses her, in five terms, shows that he is really crucified, he has lost all enthusiasm and asks her to take back the mission, not only for his sake, but first of all because he doesn't want to grieve her any more.[48] Verse 52 is a perfect rendition of verse 45. Juan Diego, verbatim repeats the bishop's words, but he omits the bishop's words "my son." Perhaps he considered this pure protocol on the bishop's part. The fact remains, the bishop's distrust has robbed him of all self-confidence. He does not have the five properties necessary to be recognized on the level of the Spaniards. (to be a "noble," esteemed, known, respected or honored, vs. 54). Excusing himself, with what he thinks are the typical properties of a poor Indian: commoner, mecapatl, cacaxtli, cola and ala, he unknowingly defines his mission. He really is "macehualli" — "a poor man who must earn his living by penance." Above any of his fellow Aztec brothers, with the mission he received, he is the "burden bearer," and as the image of Our Lady portrays, he is really hanging with one hand to the "cola," "the tail" of her mantle and with the other to the "ala," the "wing of her tunic."

This pictorial definition of his mission, out of his own mouth, is most symbolic. Really, he can only fulfill his mission, conscious that he is only a poor sinner. Now, he must concentrate the entirety of his forces to carry the burden of his mission and only then does he find himself lifted up by the movement of Our Lady's Assumption. The right hand, clinging to the "tail" of her mantle, takes hold of the constellation Taurus,[49] an animal of sacrifice: this again is to say that

---

[47] Mk 15:34 and Mt 27:46
[48] cf. Nican Mopohua, vs. 50
[49] cf. Book Four, *The Heavens Proclaim the Glory of God*; Taurus

he can only accomplish his mission in sacrifice. Clinging with his left hand to the "wing" of her gown he is grasping in someway for the help of the holy angels indicated in this extreme left fold representing the Apocalypse, the last book of the Bible. This is emphasized by the fact that his right hand touches the golden trim of the "tail," the gold being symbol of eternity and so also of the angels sent to help free us from the captivity of Satan. With his left hand he touches not only the golden trim of her gown, but his finger enters onto the earth-toned gown, pointing to the inside to this "last book" of the Bible, symbolically present in this left angle of the book. With this almost imperceptible gesture, he points out that with the apparition of Our Lady in Mexico, the apocalyptic times have begun.

In his position as messenger at the feet of Our Lady he is in total conformity with Our Crucified Lord: not only Our Lady is "cruciform" (the cross has become the essence of her being), but her messenger has also taken up of the cross, not only in an outward manner, but into his being. And the taking up of the cross in this fashion gives wings so as to overcome not only the gravity of this earth, but the heaviness of sin (both of them signified by the crescent moon weighing on his head). In this perspective the crescent moon becomes a "cup of sacrifice": the first sacrifice is that of Mary and the Lord in her womb. We poor children of Adam can partake in the benefits of this sacrifice only by way of her. Having no way to escape the cross, Juan Diego has to participate in the abandonment of Our Lord on the cross: the burden on Him is too much for his poor human forces.[50]

As Our Lord, only in the power of His Divinity, is able to carry the burden of the cross, so also Juan Diego is supposed to carry his mission not by his own forces, but by the graces he receives from Our Lady. Only now, conscious of his nothingness, is he capable of entering into this divine mission. Our Lady stretches out her hand to lift him up from the dust, thus enabling him to fulfull the mission she initially conferred.[51] Again she expresses her will and emphasizes that it is "she personally" who is sending him to the bishop. Juan Diego consequently has to further deny

---

[50] cf. Nican Mopohua, vs. 56
[51] cf. Ibid., vs. 57-60

his human way of thinking so as to be "another Mary." This is the most important point of a true mission in Mary; just as it is for the priest, who is called to be "another Christ" (alter Christus), those called to be a servant of Our Lady must become "another Mary." More and more, the mission of Our Lord Jesus Christ in these apocalyptic times becomes a mission veiled in Mary, the Spouse of the Holy Spirit.

This is what gives the mission in Mary the character of "mysterious," incomprehensible and even unacceptable in the eyes of the world. In wanting a direct grasp on the things of this world, man has the tendency to cling to the earthly, but the mystery of Christ never was given into the hands of man to be disposed of according to his meagerness. Subjectively we Christians have lost the "real presence" of Our Lord in our churches because we have not given Him a true space in our hearts. Faith has been substituted by man-made ideologies. Only by repentance and through the loving hands of Our Merciful Mother can we receive our Our Lord once again: veiled in the incomprehensible mystery of God's infinite love for us poor sinners.[52]

In the loving farewell with Our Lady, unison is reestablished: the harmony of two hearts in perfect consonnance. All dissonance of disappointment has disappeared. The night into which both enter is a symbol of the mystery of God Who has sent both of them: for His greater glory, in His love and for the salvation of souls.[53]

Eighth Station

Jesus Meets the Women of Jerusalem
(Nican Mopohua, vs.68-92)

The next day, Sunday, after attending Holy Mass and catechism, and after some difficulties, Juan Diego, comforted by his childlike confidence in Our Lady, again meets with the bishop. The interrogation testifies that his faith has grown.

---

[52] cf. Ibid., vs. 63-65
[53] cf. Ibid., vs. 66-67

- In detail he again explains that she really is the "ever perfect Virgin, the loveable and admirable Mother of Our Savior Jesus Christ."[54]
- The bishop asks for a sign.
- Juan Diego responds, "governing bishop, think about what the sign you will ask for will be, because then I will go and ask for it." Here he really shows himself the perfect mediator between the two "columns of the church": the hierarchy and the charisma. This is the most sober way that we can console Our Lord and heavenly Mother on the one hand, and the people of God suffering from the consequences of sin on the other.

*The bishop, in his juridical position, has to ask for some sign of confirmation, because he has no idea of the interior heart-to-heart relation that this ingenious messenger has with Our Lady. God is very aware of our frailty and sinfulness, but the more we approach the end of all things, the more He is asking for a deeper faith, hope and love: witnessed with the Angel of Fátima, who from the very beginning taught the children the prayer, "My God, I believe, I adore, I hope and I love You...."[55] The manner in which Juan Diego addresses the bishop, "Governor," betrays how much this poor Indian recognizes in him the union of the ecclesiastical and secular authority. He represents the new order of things after the reign of Moctezuma, supported and guarded by the military force of the conquerors. Juan Diego accepts it in the attitude of a loving burden bearer.

Administration almost necessarily is subject to the laws of this world and so is prone to distrust. The bishop has to investigate this unusual Indian, this is why he sends some of his "best servants" to follow the "enigmatic Juan Dieguito," *"where he went, who he saw and with whom he spoke,"*[56] forgetting that Juan Diego, as a messenger of Our Lady, is hidden under her mantle and therefore is out of human reach (similar to Our Lord up to the time

---

[54] cf. Nican Mopohua, vs. 75
[55] cf. Ibid., vs. 75-79
[56] cf. Nican Mopohua, vs.82

of His passion). The Pharisees were unable to take hold of Him before "His hour" had finally come. Exactly at the bridge, close to the hill of apparition, ecclesiastical and secular jurisdiction loose ground. Here it is that the "country of the liberty of the children of God" begins. We lose this sacred ground when we grasp for the securities of the world. Distrust and negative thoughts are part of this insecurity and many times violence is called to help support this frail security which never lasts long. Recall the arguments of the Sanhedrin against Our Lord, that He was guilty for the upheaval of the whole country.[57] Juan Diego finally met with Our Lady on the hill and conveyed the bishop's response. She consoles him: "Know, my dear Son, that I will reward your attention and the efforts and fatigue that you have undertaken on my behalf." Already now, on the face of Juan Diego you can see the face of the burden bearer, Jesus Christ.[58]

Ninth Station

The Third Fall of Jesus Beneath the Weight of the Cross
(Nican Mopohua, vs. 93-122)

In Our Lady's promise to cure Juan Bernadino, we recognize her power of intercession with the people of the Americas. It is her will that all be healed from the consequences of original sin, as well as to rise into the light of God. At that time thousands of Mexicans were suffering from the smallpox brought by the Spaniards. The healing of Juan Bernardino is a promise that Our Lady wants to help all these Indians to be healed from this mortal disease.

---

[57] cf. Lk 23:2
[58] cf. Ibid., vs. 88-92

Juan Diego, wanting to avoid an encounter with Our Lady, comes to know her as "the one who sees everywhere."[59] Because of her purity, Our Lady is close to God and shares in His omniscience. Patiently she listens to him and reassures him in every way:

"Am I not here, I who am your Mother? Are you not beneath my shadow and protection? Are you not beneath my loving glance? Are you not in the hollow of my mantle and in the crossing of my loving arms? Do you have need of any other thing? Let nothing afflict or perturb you."[60] The same way that he is asked to carry her in his tilma, symbol of his personal dignity, so also does Our Lady want to carry him. Here we should remember the sixth word of Our Lord on the cross: *"Father, into your hands I commend my Spirit."*[61] The more faith we have in God's omnipotence, the more God can help us. Because of her fidelity at the foot of the cross, Mary is our most powerful intercessor before the throne of God.

*One reason why he was so preoccupied about the disease of his uncle[62] was that among the Aztecs, the uncle was the supreme authority in a familiy. This is why the heritage was given to the nephew. Many historians believe that the plague the Indians were suffering was not really smallpox, but a venereal disease; sad consequence of a life not worthy of Christians who were supposed to bring faith to this indigenous people, not only by words. Here again Our Lady mercifully intervened to help this poor people in all its afflictions. We recall that at both Ocotlan, Tlaxcala (1541) and Capula (1631) heaven gave "healing waters" to remedy those infested with disease and Spiritual ailments.[63]

Original sin brought three consequences: disease, concupiscence and death. Truly, only heaven can directly intervene in putting an end to these plagues like smallpox, so frequent in the medieval age. The healing of his uncle points forward to the

---

[59] cf. Nican Mopohua, vs. 104
[60] cf. Ibid., vs. 118-120
[61] Lk 23:46
[62] cf. Ibid., vs. 95
[63] cf. Book III

promise in the charismatic revelation of our Lady in our days to bring to an end abortion. As the devil is the "murderer" from the beginning, abortion is a sign that he has arrived to kill life at its very inception. The only real remedy to this mortal disease is to put an end to the first cause of all sin: the revolt of the fallen angels. The fact that Our Lady herself wills to put an end to this venereal disease is another sign that she wants to heal man from the mortal disease of sin. She truly is the promise of new life.[64] In his dilemma, of being called by Our Lady yet on the other hand obliged to help his uncle, we witness Juan Diego's struggle in relation to the first two great Commandments: Love of God and love of neighbor must become one. We can only prove our love for God if we really help our neighbor. As a true child, he necessarily chooses the "next thing": to help his uncle. Only God's greater grace can resolve this conflict: the deeper we trust in God, the better we can help our neighbor.

The darkness of his uncle's disease is the second shadow which falls on this "way of light" which Our Lady has opened to him. It is she who will help cast away the last trace of shadow so that her light will finally enter this country, as well as the whole world, like a "river of light," healing the last consequences of sin. Thinking like a child, truly unaware of the wonderful light he has taken in by meeting Our Lady, he tries to avoid meeting her, but it is exactly this that secures the unwanted rendezvous. When he changes his direction from west to east, way up on the hill, he symbolically returns to the direction of the stronger light, a light which also moves towards him in the person of Our Lady.[65] Her genuine comprehension and loving concern for his anxiety make him feel ashamed. Like the three disciples with Christ on Mt. Tabor, he also hides behind his ingenuous greeting, "My young lady, youngest of my children, my child, I hope your are happy, how do you feel this morning, are you in good Spirits, how is your health, My Lady, my little one?" She gives him all the time to speak himself out, because what he says is so much the "condition of man" on this earth.

---

[64] cf. Nican Mopohua, vs. 95-96
[65] cf. Ibid., vs. 97-105

She is not imposing, the mission she has given him should be realized in "dialogue."[66]

The answer she gives him certainly reached the deepest of his heart. These are the most beautiful words of the entire message of Our Lady and we should make the effort to learn them by heart. These words are spoken throughout all time and especially in our day, so close to apocalyptical events: we must trust completely in Our heavenly Mother, she who will take all of us under her mantle so as to share with her "the fountain of joy," her Son, Jesus Christ. These words are truly creative words, which effect what they say. As Juan Diego came to know later on, his uncle was healed at that very same hour.[67] Here again a word is fulfilled, which he himself spoke without knowing what he said when he compared himself to "cola" and "ala." Here Our Lady promises to take him like the Indian women do with their children in her "mamalhuatli," the fold of their shawl in which the child is placed for protection, as if yet in the womb of his mother.

But there is a second significance in this loving word: mamalhuatli: "to make fire." Protected by Our Lady, Juan Diego will grow up to be the "fire eagle," he who apocalyptically announces the final mercy of God with us poor sinners. He represents all the "fire souls" the church so urgently needs in this last combat for the reign of God. The five promises of Our Lady open up an even deeper perspective. The epochs of the sun, according to the Aztecs, are over. Juan Diego is presented as the "new man" of the fifth sun. If the four dimensions of the cross signify the totality of creation then the fifth dimension points to the pierced heart of Our Lord, signifying the depths of the love of God in which, in the end, man should realize his destiny. This is also why the fifth apparition of Our Lady with Juan Bernardino is the final message of Guadalupe. The blood coming from the heart of Christ will heal mankind from the last consequences of original sin.

"And when Juan Diego heard the lovely words, the lovely breath of the Queen of Heaven, he was greatly comforted and his heart came to peace."[68] Indeed, he has placed everything into Our Lady's

---

[66] cf. Ibid., vs. 110-116
[67] cf. Nican Mopohua, vs. 203
[68] cf. Ibid., vs. 122

hands. He no longer has need of preoccupation and is once again perfectly disposed for his mission. We can learn from his growth in "poverty of Spirit." Whatever mission heaven may confer upon us, "poverty of Spirit" remains the most important condition. He partakes in the peace of the word of Our Lord, *"Into Your hands I commend My Spirit."*[69]

Tenth Station

Jesus is Stripped of His Garments
(Nican Mopohua, vs.123-146)

- By giving the sign, Our Lady covers the nudity of sin of this poor people who are called to share in the light of God.
- Our Lady asked him to go to the top of the hill where she saw him for the first time, because this is the place where she wants to have her house. The hilltop where she first appeared to him is a sanctified place. Ascending the hill makes Juan Diego like unto the Aztec priests who ascended the pyramids in the offering of their sacrifices to their gods. In this case, the sacrifice he has to offer is his own understanding of things: in blind faith, hope and love he is to ascend, because one could not expect to find a single flower on the top of Tepeyac in the middle of winter. The sacrifice of his own intelligence allows him to partake in the priesthood of Christ, He Who in the garden of Gethsemane called out to the Father to take away the chalice of His Holy will. Just as Our Lord, at the tenth station, is stripped of His garments, so too does Juan Diego have to strip himself of any pure human way of thinking.
- She tells him to cut the flowers, to gather them, put them all together and to bring them to her presence, because she wants to impress her holy face upon them, putting them in a beautiful order.[70] In this way the roses are not only a symbol of our very personal vocation in God's love, but also a sign that by Our Lady's

---

[69] Lk 23:46
[70] cf. Nican Mopohua, vs. 126

intercession and help each one of us will find his definite place in the Mystical Body of Christ. As she is the most beautiful of all roses: "Tota Pulchra," so also in the end, the church has to reflect her unspeakable beauty which is no other than the beauty of God Himself.

- She sternly tells him to be careful, that nothing fall nor be lost. Again the priestly mission of Juan Diego is apparent: not one of the articles of the faith should be lost in the church.

*Remember that for the Aztec, the place where God reveals Himself, the place of truth, was always "flower and song." For this reason the hilltop has already been designed to be the place of the truth of God, not only for the Mexicans, but for the whole church. Only by way of parables and similitudes are we able to understand the things of God. This is the other characteristic of the Marian kerygma: it is a message through the flower, a message of the veiled beauty of God, it is not abstract truth exposed by intellectual theologians, but always mystery, hidden in the zealous veils of God's love.

Again, we find five indications; three for what he has to do upon the hill, in view of the triune God and two in view of Our Lady who represents by His veiled presence in her womb the two natures of Christ. So the sign he has to bring to the bishop in relation to the Aztec understanding of the number five will be an "overwhelming sign" which recalls the words of the Apocalypse 1:7, *"They will look up to Him, Whom they have pierced."* Just as St. Thomas was only convinced by the wounds of Our Lord, so also in the end will the church penetrate the depths of faith as she participates in the passion of the Lord in His Mystical Body the church. For the most part, roses are red, and it is thus that they best recall the price of our Redemption: the precious blood of Our Lord.

What is done on the peak of Tepeyac should be seen in a trinitarian perspective, in view of the last coming of Our Lord, as judge of the living and the dead and Lord of the harvest. In this way Our Lady, sent to prepare His way, is also identified as Our Lady of the harvest. This is the trinitarian relation:

- The Father determines the time, already prophesied by the Aztec "tlamantine."
- The Son, in the sign of the cross, gathers those who are ripe for the harvest.
- The Holy Spirit, by way of the angels, brings home the harvest to the heavenly barnyards. No other is the fruit of this harvest than Mary alone! In her purity is enclosed the totality of those who are called to eternal life with God.

Just as Our Lady grew up amidst the sin of a pagan world, without, in the slightest way, touched by the stain of sin, so also do we find with Juan Diego. Indeed, the reception of the roses manifests that he alone is worthy to receive this message of love, and better than anyone else, he certainly will understand. As the sign of the roses is multiple, even those who are yet faraway from Our Lady will understand something of the living miracle offered to the bishop.[71]

The admonition of Our Lady, to keep secret what he is carrying in his tilma, ties up with the "arcunum" of the early church; the rule of not speaking outside the circle of believers of the mystery of the Holy Eucharist, for fear of being misunderstood or beeing misinterpreted by those who had not yet by faith found the way to approach this mystery. Here again we meet a peculiarity of the Gospel of St. John who doesn't mention the institution of the Holy Eucharist as do the synoptics. With him, the mystery of the Holy Eucharist is present in a different and more profound way than with the others. In his Gospel, the Lord is present from the beginning as the Lamb of God: this term designing His Eucharistic presence which makes Him present in His Mystical Body, the church, and finally bring about the perfection of the church in the new Jerusalem.

Together with the German mystics of the 12th century and in parallel to them, we could say: "What use are the Sacraments, and especially the Holy Eucharist, if they do not help us to enter deeper into the life of Christ?" It is first of all this interior dimension of the Holy Eucharist we find with St. John and in a similar way in

---

[71] cf. Nican Mopohua, vs. 127-134

the narration of the Nican Mopohua and the image: It is a veiled mystery of deep intimacy with God, the outward sign of which is the "nahui ollin." So as to better understand the dimension of this miracle we should emphasize that they are both children: Our Lady and her seer. Only as children, in the purity of their hearts, can they accomplish the mission God the Father has given into their hands: to bring His Son, as light, into the darkness of this world. Here again we see the relation to the Gospel of St. John. Remember that "child" in the Greek word "pais" not only signifies child, but also servant. They must penetrate each other: because the servant is only a good servant if he is a child in his heart, and he is only a good child if he humbly submits to whatever is told him. This interpretation is confirmed by the image of the boy at the feet of Our Lady.[72]

This mission, to take the "sign" to the bishop, is given in full confidence that he will fulfill it with his entirety. Not only a kind of responsibility is put on him, as many times unfortunately we experience in church, but it is in loving care that Our Lady gives to him that which is most dear to him: *"I place absolute confidence in you."* The order is strict and clear, but as we will see later, it is not an order he has to accomplish by the letter, but much more in free will, full consent and the collaboration of all his faculties. Only by totally being himself can he give a living testimony, because he himself, and not only the roses and later on the image, are an integral part of the miracle of Guadalupe.[73]

He descends in peace of heart, because in the roses he feels not only her presence, but also the presence of God Himself. He truly has a priestly mission: to bring the Lord in the veiled mystery of Our Lady to his beloved people. He is like St. John running to the tomb of Our Lord and arriving before St. Peter: he does not enter, because the priviledge belongs to St. Peter. The privilege of first announcing the message of Our Lady is not his, it belongs to the bishop. He is not preoccupied, because the fragrance of the roses blows away any thought contrary to his mission.[74]

---

[72] cf. Nican Mopohua, vs. 135-139

[73] cf. Ibid., vs. 139-142

[74] cf. Ibid., vs. 143-146

Eleventh Station

Jesus is Nailed to the Cross
(Nican Mopohua, vs. 147-160)

- In this mission to the bishop, Juan Diego, like Jesus, is extended to the furthermost limits of endurance on the cross of his mission, because he has to break through the wall of sin which keeps man from looking up to the light of God. On this day, he has already risen shortly after midnight in order to accomplish his uncle's wish of obtaining a priest for his last confession.
- Again he has to wait because of the servants who don't want to let him in; he is exposed to the mockery of the world.
- Only at the end, when he cannot hinder the servants seeing something of the flowers, do they run to tell the bishop that he has arrived with the requested sign. Even though they tried to grasp the roses, they are unable to take the flowers from him, for as soon as they tried, the flowers appear as if painted on the tilma.
- Finally, he who is "nothing" in the eyes of the hierarchical authority, is admitted into the palace of the bishop.

*The meeting with Our Lady on this day was yet in the darkness of night, or at least at dawn. This is another sign that we best meet the light of God if we go towards it in blind faith, hope and love.[75] One of the witnesses of the information process speaks about a one-and-a-half-hour wait before he was admitted to the bishop. Again it is a deep suffering for Juan Diego to see how the order of things is disturbed through the arbitrariness of man. Again, we can see through to the passion of Our Lord, Who after having been taken prisoner, was put into a dungeon and then only in the morning was presented before the high priests. Other times of waiting followed, precisely the painful wait before being nailed to the cross. It is a typical sign with the "laws of this world" to make one unjustly wait for the sole purpose of demonstrating superiority. Many times, as in the case of the bishop, this is not intentional or conscious, it is only part of the system established out of our human

---

[75] cf. Nican Mopohua, vs. 147-148

frailty and miserableness. In the measure that we humbly accept this injustice, as did Juan Diego, the more we will help to bring down the order of the reign of God.[76]

The persistance of the servants became more and more outrageous until Juan Diego no longer knew how to push them back. Interiorly, he retained Our Lady's strict mandate of not letting anyone else know what he was carrying, and certainly it cost him a deep interior battle to let them see something of the secret he was commissioned to carry. The decision on his part was not disobedience, but simply adapting to the conditions. If he had been scrupulous, he would have followed the mandate to the letter. That he made the right decision is proved by the outcome: finally the servants became aware that he really had a special message for the bishop and thus went to tell him about it. So also in this difficulty he proved to be a faithful missionary; deciding more according to the Spirit than to the letter of his mission. The reaction of the servants, as later that of the bishop, is the first sign of conversion. In going to the bishop and relating their experience, they indirectly confess their maliciousness.[77]

Twelfth Station

Jesus Dies on the Cross
(Nican Mopohua, vs. 161-178)

- The great sign of our faith, the blessed sacrament, is Our Lord Jesus Christ sacrificed on Golgotha. The sign given by Our Lady in the red castilian roses (remembering the blood of Christ shed for us) is identical with the sign of the cross, delivered by one who is a "burden-bearer."
- He repeats, to the letter, the mission given to him by Our Lady before showing the roses as a definite proof. The bishop should not only be convinced by this extraordinary sign, but first of all by the message delivered in all faithfulness. The miracle is only the final confirmation of the message.

---

[76] cf. Ibid., vs. 150-152
[77] cf. Nican Mopohua, vs. 157-160

- Juan Diego wants to awaken the Bishop's faith. In blind faith he ascended the frozen soil of the hill to look for the roses. Truly, it was his faith that opened "the Doors of Paradise" for the Mexicans.[78]

The sign given to him by Our Lady is the sign of the precious blood of Christ Who takes away all sins. This sign is what makes the bishop fall to his knees and to ask forgiveness for his having doubted. At last, hierarchy and charisma are on the same level: poverty — man recognizing his nothingness before God.

Here we should remember the last word of Our Lord on the cross: *"It is consummated."*[79]

*Juan Diego, throwing himself down before the bishop, gives clear witness that he is nothing more than an instrument of divine providence, as also the bishop and all those who have responsibility in the church should be. At the end, the bishop also falls to his knees before Our Lord incarnated in Mary. The wounds of Our Lord Jesus Christ as with St.Thomas finally have overcome all distrust. At the end of time, the whole church — hierarchy, charisma and the people of God — will have to acknowledge that only He is the Lord. This is the apocalyptical dimension of the encounter of Juan Diego and the bishop as it links up with the initial encounter of Juan Diego and Our Lady. The circle of this wonderful apparition is almost closed.[80]

Now, as he is reaccounting the apparition and its details, he is different from the person he was in the beginning. In his first interview with the bishop he gave testimony, first of all, of his admiration at this marvelous encounter with Our Lady, but it had not yet

---

[78] cf. Ibid., vs. 175-176
[79] Jn 19:30
[80] cf. Nican Mopohua, vs. 162

totally permeated him, although from the very beginning he had taken Our Lady into his heart. His first encounter with her was yet something exterior to his life. Proof of this is his decision to avoid an encounter with her so as to bring a priest to his sick uncle more quickly. In this last encounter with the bishop, he is not only speaking of something that happened to him, but he himself has become the same message conferred to him by Our Lady. Indeed, as much as the image on the ayate later will be, he is her living presence. His recapitulation of the apparition, but in particular the miracle of the roses, manifests that in all truth he was only carrying out the bishop's request. In this way he shows himself to be completely not only under the authority of Our Lady, but also under that of the bishop and therefore of the hierarchical church. His person is the bridge over this gap, so much so that if the bishop would now follow him to the place of apparition he would not lose him again at the foot of the hill. The place of apparition on top of the hill and the place of the bishop, down on the plain, have become one.[81]

The aim of his extensive narration is to convince the bishop more by the fact of the encounter with Our Lady than by the miracle to follow. The bishop for his part should be able to judge things objectively and give his assent not only to the message, but also to the person of the messenger, and through him to all the poor Indians whom he represents. Here we can discern the criterium of a true Marian miracle: it does not overwhelm by its extraordinariness, but by the depths of its truth, even those truths which at the onset seem unapparent. Authenticity can only be experienced by those who with Our Lady *"ponder it in their hearts."*

If it hadn't been for the delay caused by the servants, the bishop would have received the message at dawn; an exterior sign for the mystery of this message which was now confided to him, because in the bright light of the day things are more critically analyzed by reason.[82] We should remember: "the dark eye sees deeper." This is

---

[81] cf. Ibid., vs. 164 ff.

[82] Man unfortunately can reduce God's merciful intervention. As Lucia testifies in Fátima. If it had not been for the intervention of the Freemasons on August 13th, 1917, the miracle in October would have been greater and so more convincing. So also the message in Mexico delivered at dawn might have avoided the continual attacks against the authenticity of the image.

like an indication that the depths of this message of Our Lady of Guadalupe will only be revealed when the night of persecution has come upon the church, when she will have to leave all her earthly administration behind. Only in dark faith, hope and love will she look up to the light of the Lord. The bishop can receive the message in the right way only if he is approaching the confidence of Juan Diego, because the message should not be received like a matter of fact, but as a personal gift of God's infinite love. He should not only meet the messenger, but is called to recognize Our Lady herself in him. She wants to be identified with him.

The roses of Castile are another detail which binds this message for the New World back to Spain. It has to help the Spanish Franciscan missionaries to consider the message as their own so as to carry it on with their own blood. Are not the red roses of Castile a beautiful symbol for the fervor of this nation propagating the faith? They should give courage to the bishop in the mission for the conversion of this country, a mission which only recently has been conferred upon him. In bringing the grace of the faith to this country, he is asked to transform it into "a paradise" like unto that which Juan Diego found on the top of the hill. The top is a sign that we will only reach this paradise if we lift our hearts up to God and overcome the heaviness of the attraction of this earth. Doesn't Our Lord Jesus Christ speak of the church as "a city on hilltop?"[83] This is to remind us that the church will only come to its consummation if it has completely become a church in Mary Immaculate.[84]

He not only found castilian roses but this is to say that the consummation of the church will bring forth the greatest diversity of the beauty of souls. It is like a little correction in relation to the "castilian roses" representing the perfection of faith with the Spaniards. The "castilian roses" are an invitation to the bishop to understand a little better the Aztec mystery of "flor y canto."[85]

The word of Our Lord Jesus Christ, *"it is consummated"* presupposes for the church, His Mystical Body, that it will have con-

---

[83] cf. Mt 5:14
[84] cf. Ibid., vs. 175-176
[85] cf. Ibid., vs. 177-178

summated in, with and through Him the way to Golgatha. Only if the old man will have died completely, Christ will come to life, and so He will be the one Who finally will submit Himself to the Father and so God will be *"all in all."*[86]

Thirteenth Station

Jesus is Taken Down from the Cross
(Nican Mopohua, vs.179-194)

- Our Lady, standing under the cross with St. John, is the first to receive the legacy of Christ: His precious blood. In handing over the flowers to the bishop, through the person of Juan Diego, representative of St. John, Our Lady gives him the legacy of her Son.
- For the Aztecs, the tilma symbolized the person who wore it, and now, before the eyes of the bishop, it is transformed into the image of Our Lady. In a pictorial way (language of the Aztecs), this tells the bishop that by way of the blood of Christ, he has to transform this nation of pagans into the image of Our Lady of Guadalupe: every Mexican, in a certain way, like Juan Diego should resemble the features of Our Lady.
- This transformation, intended by God, starts with the bishop and with those who surround him. Finally Our Lady, by this acceptance of the hierarchical church has found her place in this new country.

*In a wonderful way the image painted on the tilma meets the deepest concept of God and his creation. In a poem of the "tlamantine" one can read:

> *"He lives in our interior.*
> *He writes and creates in our interior,*
> *He through Whom we live.*
> *By way of flowers He paints all things.*

---

[86] cf. I Cor 15:28

You Who give the light,
You Who paint thtough sun and colors
Whatever is living on earth.
We live only in what You paint on earth. "

Here we find in a certain variation the platonic idea grown in the light of revelation that all things are in some way an image of the invisible Father by way of His Son. If God "paints" the creation, Mary necessarily is the most perfect image painted by God. The image of Our Lady of Guadalupe collects all the sparklets of light of the Aztec wisemen in the one center, the "nahui ollin" superimposed on her womb, showing that she is expecting and that she will bring the Son of God into the world and that in Him all of creation will find its consummation. What she did here, she wants to do with each and every soul if we but open our heart in faith. She wants to do it with each family, community and each nation. This is an apocalyptic secret which will be fulfilled in the Holy Spirit in the end times.[87]

Again we recall the similitude in the conversion of St. Thomas, the last of the apostles to acknowledge Our Risen Lord. It is like an apocalyptical sign for the final "conversion of the church" by and through Mary, who encloses the mystery of her Son veiled by seven veils. Only in deep conversion, where the heart of man is open, will these Veils reveal the deepest of all mysteries. Something of this is happening today in the places where Our Lady appears: it is like a presign of this greatest of miracles which God will grant in the end through the intercession of Our Lady: the conversion of sinners.

This moving scene mirrors the first encounter of Juan Diego with Our Lady where also he bowed before her.[88] It is not an adoration of Our Lady, but of her Son, veiled in the deepest part of her womb. This adoration reminds us of the adoration of the shepherd children together with the Angel in Fátima. Here, the deepest meaning of her mysterious expression, "her breath and word," is being revealed. The bishop confesses with contrite heart that he is sorry that he has not immediately fulfilled her "will," her venerable

---

[87] cf. Nican Mopohua, vs. 183
[88] cf. Ibid, vs.22

"breath" and "word." He literally repeats what Juan Diego has done from the beginning when he first brought the message. He is finally identifying himself with the poor Indian who was the first to receive this message as her "will, her breath and her word." This trinitarian expression recalls again that the message of Guadalupe is through and with Mary, a message of the triune God. It reveals

- The holy will of the Father, before all times.
- The Spirit of the Son Who expired his breath on the cross to give us part in God's life.
- The word in the Holy Spirit, which the church should carry again and for a last time over the whole earth.[89]

In a similar way, as Our Lord was taken from the cross by the help of Joseph of Arimathea,[90] the converted bishop takes the tilma from the shoulders of Juan Diego who has been crucified with Him. In this way he "becomes Mary" and recalls the "Pieta" — Our Lady receiving her dead Son again in her womb. The more the image will come to life, in the heart of the bishop, the more Jesus Christ will come to life in this country. This is henceforth the mission of Juan Diego: to help by his prayer and sacrifice as a sacristan of Our Lady that by way of Mary, Christ will grow in the hearts of his compatriots. It is not only by way of her image that Our Lady wants to stay alive with us, but more and more in our hearts.

We should ponder the beauty of this narration as another image of Our Lady in her miraculous apparition: word and image are one as soon as we look to them in the sign of the cross — the only true sign of salvation. The part of the angels is emphasized when Our Lady reveals herself as "Queen of Heaven." This word is again and again repeated at the end of the narration; it reminds us that in this apparition she is really coming as "Queen of the angels" with all the angels to prepare the second coming of her Son in glory![91]

---

[89] cf. Ibid., vs. 187

[90] cf. Mk 15,34ff

[91] cf. Nican Mopohua, vs. 189 and Book Three, Beauty and Order, a Structural Analysis of the Nican Mopohua: the Keywords in the Vocabulary

Fourteenth Station

Jesus is Laid in the Tomb
(Nican Mopohua, vs.190-218)

In the fifth apparition of Our Lady to Juan Bernardino, we can symbolically see how, by the grace of God, this Aztec people is released from the captivity of sin by the blood of Christ.

- Our Lady of Guadalupe appeared to Juan Bernardino as she did to his nephew.
- He also received the mission to go to the bishop and to give testimony of her apparition.[92]
- To Juan Bernardino she reveals her name as "a name that heals" in which the blood of her Son is present and able to remit all our sins.

The testimony of Juan Bernardino is the last confirmation of the authenticity of the apparitions of Our Lady, sent to bring about the conversion of this people through the sacrifice of Jesus Christ.

- By accepting the testimony of the cure of Juan Bernardino, the bishop, as a good pastor of this people, takes to his heart all the misery of this people which sin has caused.[93]
- When the bishop exposes the image for the veneration of the people, the entire city is moved. Just as when the three wise men of the Orient revealed in Jerusalem that they had seen the star of the "new-born Savior."[94]
- It is the Aztec belief that God, the Most High, creates things by painting them, so by painting this miraculous image of Our Lady of Guadalupe, He wants to create for Himself a people according to His own image so that they might fall down and adore Him, bringing to Him all their prayers that they might experience and marvel at the greatness of His love.

---

[92] cf. Nican Mopohua, vs. 205
[93] cf. Nican Mopohua, vs. 209
[94] cf. Mt 2:1-3

*It is a curious reversion. While there is a falling out of faith in Europe, there is an implantation with those who are "from afar" — the pagans. This reminds us of the coming of the wisemen from the East, but here there is another reversion: Our Lady *first* comes to them, to attract them by her presence. It is like a a "new Bethlehem" in the New World: Our Lady is the star who indicates the place where her Son is being born.

The coming of Our Lady to the New World, already with Columbus, can also be understood as her flight from Europe, where she is more and more removed from the churches. She is brought over by the Spanish and the Portuguese, the only two nations which resisted the attacks of protestantism. In this sense her coming to the New World can be related to the apocalypse where she is fleeing the dragon: she receives the two wings of a big eagle to hide for sometime in the desert, far away from the dragon. There are three concordances:

1. The wings of the eagle, seen also with Juan Diego, he who is "Cuahtlatoatzin" — "He who speaks like an eagle."
2. Her flight into the desert: certainly has to be understood as "the desert of the pagans."
3. "To her place," we have already characterized as the "place of the center." No doubt that also there the persecution goes on, because the serpent throws water after her like a river and began war with the rest of her seed.[95]

Certainly, this text should not only be referred to Mexico, but to all those Our Lady wants to hide under her mantle in this time of persecution.

By way of the apparition of Our Lady, Mexico has become a nation. In her image, Our Lady has given them a "constitution." Here also, as with the Jewish people, this extraordinary grace is a promise which has to be realized step by step by all those who want to follow the example of Juan Diego. Soberly speaking, it will be "a remnant" of the faithful, as it was with the chosen people,

---

[95] cf. Rv 12:17 ff.

because the attack of the enemy against this nation is a hard trial which only those deeply rooted in faith will be able to withstand.

Our Mission in the Common Priesthood

The mission of lay people so much emphasized in our time is a another sign that the church is entering the Spiritual battle of the last times, which will require of each Christian to be a confessor or even a martyr. Here Juan Diego is a beautiful example how we are called as Christians to live our faith, and this especially in view of this last time, which has to be a Marian time. He is a shining example for the common priesthood to be lived by every Christian, and this also in a liturgical way. Ordered by Our Lady to go up to the top of the hill to bring down the roses, he has the function of a deacon or of a Eucharistic minister (remembering that the roses are symbols of the mysteries of the life, passion and Resurrection of Our Lord Jesus Christ). At the same time, the roses are a symbol for the suffering of his people during their pagan era. Now, theirs is a suffering which has been assumed into the suffering of Christ on the cross.

Is it not precisely the passion of Our Lord Jesus Christ which is most easily forgotten in the church? This is true with the Spaniards also. They were far too conscious of it having been their privilege to bring the true faith to the New World. Let us remember with St. Paul that if we are to boast, let it be in the Cross of Our Lord Jesus Christ.[96] In our times, by the apparitions of Our Lady of the Rosary in Fátima, this truth has once again been brought to the attention of the church. The Cova da Iria is called the paten of the world. Behind this image is a deep understanding of the significance of the Apocalyptic dimension of the apparition of Our Lady in this place. What makes the three shepherd children "little saints" is their fervor for sacrifice as reponse to the call of the angel in the beginning ("in everything you can, offer sacrifice as an act of reparation to God for the sins by which He is offended and pray for the

---

[96] cf. Gal 6:14

conversion of poor sinners.")[97] In this sacrifice the whole church has to enter more and more, called with the Lord to share in His way of the cross to Golgotha. For Mexico, this truth is clearly expressed in the position of the boy with arms outstretched under the feet of Our Lady.[98] It is a call and invitation for all Christians to participate in the "general priesthood of Christ." It is emphasized by the person of Juan Diego and after him by all the other seers of Mary in the last two centuries. It can also be understood as a challenge to the hierarchical priesthood: to remember its primordial mission (so clearly seen in Padre Pio de Pietrelcina) to share in the sacrifice of Christ, not only in a "liturgical" exterior form, but with the entirety of their being.

The Holy Rosary

In the Light of Our Lady of Guadalupe

Our Lord Jesus Christ did not save us by the thirty years of his hidden life, nor by the three years of his public ministry, but by the three hours He hung on the cross. This is to remind us that we should not put so much importance on our activity. The greater activity is that of the Holy Spirit, and that He be active in us, we need to be passive and receptive to what God wills to do with us.

We should learn to pray the Rosary with the mysteries interpermeating, that to say that within the Joyful Mysteries we encounter both the the Sorrowful and the Glorious. The descent of Our Lord, into the womb of Mary, is already a mystery of suffering. Relating the idea to our lives, it would be something like being taken from our beautiful homes and put into a dark isolated prison cell. Our Lord Jesus Christ, in the plenitude of the presence of the Father, descended into the darkness and narrowness of the womb

---

[97] cf. *Memorias da Irma Lucia*, 2nd Edition, pp. 56, second apparition of the Angel of Portugal

[98] cf. Book Seven: more about the call of the church in joining in the passion of Our Lord as a deeper relation of the consummation of all things in the heavenly Jerusalem

of Mary, and mystically, everyday He descends into our hearts, which for the most part are not yet sufficiently purified. This is the passion of Our Lord in us. If with Mary we wait in faith, hope and love for His Resurrection, He will also resurrect in us, the sign of His birth in glory.

Our Lord Jesus Christ, though being God, renounced being superior. He became like unto us, He humbled Himself, and we must follow in His footsteps. We, the church, must enter with Him into His passion and ascend with Him along His way of the cross up Calvary. We cannot be like the modern theologians or what progressive theology professes: a false illusion of a world that is "improving." We must accept the stark realities that things are becoming worse. For those who are faithful to the Lord, it is a sober entering into the passion of the Lord.

In the Perspective of the Passion of the Lord

We begin these meditations in union with the holy angels and pray:

> *"Holy, Holy, Holy Lord, God of power and might. Heaven and earth are full of your glory. Hosanna in the highest. Blessed is he who comes in the name of the Lord. Hosanna in the highest."*

The Joyful Mysteries

The Annunciation: We recognize the Annunciation in the mystery or the veil of the clouds which surrounds Our Lady. The image of Our Lady of Guadalupe is a mystery. We can only understand it if we enter into the clouds. In the Old Testament, clouds are a symbol of the mystery of God.[99] This sense of mystery is something which the devil has tried to take away from the church. We try to understand our faith in a rationalistic way and so lose the perspec-

---

[99]   cf. Ex 13:21, 14:19, 20, 24, 16:10, 19:9,16; I Kings 18:44.

tive of mystery and follow the false light of the devil, because he is the most intelligent of all creatures. We must humble ourselves and be willing to go the dark way of faith, hope and love so as to be admitted into the most profound mystery of salvation: the Incarnation of Our Lord Jesus Christ.

We also recognize the wonderful correspondence between Our Lady and the little messenger at her feet. We are only able to bear Our Lady if we stretch open our arms as does the child. Only if we are crucified with Our Lord do we find ourselves in agreement with Our Lady who was also Spiritually crucified when She participated in the passion of her Son beneath the cross. This is also symbolized in the red vestment he wears. We must be crucified with Christ. With Her we must take part in the sacrifice of her Son. In the Annunciation, our reception of the Lord is the first step in our participation in His passion. In this mystery, we ask for the painful grace of having our hearts opened by a sword, the same sword that Simeon prophesied would pierce Mary's heart.[100]

The Visitation of Mary to Elizabeth: Our Lady visits us as she visited her cousin Elizabeth. She does this by means of her loving glance. We see this as the most important aspect in the image. She looks down on all human misery. The dark shadows on the right hand side of her gown are a symbol of the battle between the powers of light and darkness. There is something like a movement of mercy in her eyes that goes out, descending, in order to lift us up. We have called this the "movement of ransom."[101]

Modern photographic studies initially revealed that Juan Diego and others were present in the left eye of Our Lady. Later, and with more sophisticated equipment, they found her right eye also reflected personages: Juan Diego, the bishop, his translator, Juan Gonzalez, even an indian family within the pupil of both her eyes. Moreover, oculists who have studied the image have declared that when examined with an opthalmoscope the pupil of Our Lady's eye reflects light in the same manner as a living eye, that is, in a diffused manner, giving the impression of hollow relief. Normally

---

[100] cf. Lk 2:35
[101] cf. Book Four

this is not possibly in two-dimensional objects, nor is it found in other two-dimensional paintings studied.[102] None of this should surprise us. We should only say

> *"Oh Holy Mother of God, who so mercifully looks upon all mankind, grant that we too may be found within the pupil of your eye. Come visit us and let us be transformed by this wonderful glance of mercy so that in our pilgrimage through this dark valley, we, too, may ascend into the light of God!"*

We can identify three instruments of fishing in the image. We must be attracted, first of all by the light of Our Lady. Let us remember her arabic name is "Guadalupe," "River of Light." She attracts us by the light which comes from her eyes. It is the pure light of God, because She is but His instrument. The next instrument is a hook which is aimed at lifting us up. Everyone must be caught individually. We call this lifting up "conversion." We must enter more deeply into the mystery of God and this is done by the hook. The third instrument for fishing, found in the fold of her mantle under her left arm, is the net. When Our Lady goes to Elizabeth, She is really going out for the "first catch"! Her catch is the precursor of her Son, St. John the Baptist. We must be like him. We must be touched in the deepest recesses of our hearts so we can be with Her and by Her like the little messenger at her feet: messengers of the second coming of Our Lord Jesus Christ Who is to come in glory with all the holy angels.

The Birth of Our Lord Jesus Christ: Our angel will help us see through the mysteries of Christ's life and to recognize them in the life of the church. One of the great German mystics of the Middle Ages, Eckhart, gave us a most profound challenge: "To what value is the solitary historical birth of Our Lord in Bethlehem if He is not born in our hearts. "The modern world has commercialized Christmas. Its commemoration has become an exterior expression. There

---

[102] Drs. Javier Torroello Buene and Rafael Torifa Lavoignet, 1951 and July 23, 1956, 1979.

is little left for the interior life. So much of what is the mystery of God has become a show and a propagation of the exterior. We have no time to prepare for Christ's coming into our hearts, because silence, the veil of creation wrapping the mystery of His birth, has completely disappeared from our lives. This fest of joy has become a deep suffering for Our Lord.

In Our Lady, we see that the birth of Christ is the deepest and the focal point of her life. It is symbolized by the "nahui ollin," the four-petalled flower. It is a symbol of the mystery of God, not only for the Aztecs. By way of the four cardinal directions of the wind, the four basic elements and the four faculties it symbolizes the mysterious presence of God in His creation: expressed in the form of the cross. His presence in her womb, symbolized by the "nahui ollin," is in the center of her person. It tells us that She is even now pregnant, suffering the pangs of birth to bring Our Lord Jesus Christ again into the world for a second time, and we are called to share in this life-giving suffering. It is in the church that the Lord must be born again in His fullness, so that when He comes in the power of the holy angels, He will recognize Himself in His Mystical Body, the church.

This is the deeper understanding of Advent. It is not a sentimental recalling of Christ's first coming, but the awareness that He will come again, to each of us individually as often as we accept Him and at the end of time as the victorious Christ! By "end" here we refer to that apocalyptic coming when time shall be for us no more. This too is both individual and collective, for any one of us, if we should die, would experience our personal apocalypse tomorrow. He will come for us whenever He decides to do so. We must be prepared, at all times, with the whole of our lives centered on Him. And, of course, He will come at the final judgment for all mankind.

Christ is, and must always be the center of the church, of the world and of our lives. This is what the "nahui ollin" teaches us in the center of the person of Our Lady. But this mystery of His humble presence is veiled in a seven-fold way: the clouds, the rays, the mantle, her gown, her white gown, her body and her soul. Our lives, including our activities, should should also be veiled around this mystery of the indwelling of the Most Holy Trinity in our heart.

In this mystery we ask that Christ the King will become the king of our hearts so that when He returns in power, with all His angels, He will recognize Himself in our hearts.

The Presentation of Jesus in the Temple: In His trial before the Jews, Our Lord Jesus Christ was accused of saying that He would destroy the temple and rebuild it in three days. This was used as a reason for demanding His death. But we know that He was referring to the temple of His body. We must be ready to accept the scourging reality that our temples may be destroyed in the near future. The Lord is not looking for the temples made of stone or by human hands. The Lord tells His disciples in the synoptic gospels that *"not one stone will be left upon the other."* Something similar may happen to the church, because God wills to recreate it, to renew it. This is a key phrase of the Apocalypse, *"I will make all things new."*[103] Many things that are purely human have entered into the structure of the church and blur the face of Christ in her; this is why the church urgently needs purification in order to irradiate again the face of Christ to all the world.[104]

Although our temples may be destroyed, we will have a place to gather to pray and worship in common. We must be priest, altar, and victim, we must be sacrificed with Him and we must adore God together with our angel. Our Lady is the real temple of these last times. Even within the early church, within her lifetime, she appeared to St. James in Zaragosa, Spain. As she wanted to be the fundament of the church in western Europe, so also in the New World. It is she who took these orphaned pagan children into her heart. She is the real temple in whom we will always find our home and our shelter. We ask this Grace for all those who live under persecution, that they will find shelter in the Immaculate Heart of Mary: the indestructible temple of God.

The Finding of the Child Jesus in the Temple: Here we particularly recognize that the Joyful Mysteries are also sorrowful, because they are a pre-Annunciation of what Mary has to suffer be-

---

[103] Rv 22:25
[104] cf. Rv 11

neath the cross. She had to lose her Son in order to give birth to Him in heaven. The fathers of the church say that Christ was only really born in glory at the hour of His death. This is also the reason that we celebrate the feast days of the saints, not on the day of their birth, but on the day of their death. Everyone must make this offering. No one will or can escape this reality. It shows no partiality or exemption for creed or race. Everyone must give up his mortal life. This hour is the most difficult, the most important and the most dangerous of our life, and the devil astutely tries to make us ignore it or to put the thought out of our mind. We are so naive that we think that we can escape our death by scientific means, as those who freeze their bodies in hopes of future cures.

As Christians, we must be sober and realistic. We have been given a clearer vision, not only with respect to the things of this world, but also those of the other world. We must go through the narrow door and live the seven last words of Our Lord Jesus Christ on the cross. In a certain way, we must also suffer that abandonment suffered by Christ. Our Lady has gone through this same abandonment when she lost her Son in Jerusalem. One thing She never lost, and one thing we also will not lose if we remain united with our angel is the conscious awareness that God is. This truth must become firm in our hearts so that even if we lose all support in exterior things we will never lose the support that God is. Because God is, He will never forsake us. We must all undergo abandonment. God wills to prepare us by sacrifices and renouncements, voluntary or involuntary, so as to be able to go through the last hour.

In this mystery, we pray for the grace: that in and through all abandonment, we leave behind all that separates us from Christ in order to be a new creature in Him.

The Sorrowful Mysteries

The Agony of Our Lord in the Garden: Our Lady cries out in the pangs of giving birth,[105] but She stands firm beneath the cross. She even smiles, because She knows light will triumph over darkness.

---

[105] cf. Rv 12:2

The Scourging of Our Lord at the Pillar: One can see an image very much like Our Lord tied to the pillar of flagellation on the lower part of the Virgin's left sleeve. By this sign, She invites us to shelter her Son from the three-fold scourging that tears away his flesh. Who cares for Him when He is thrown in the dirt in the particles of the Eucharist lost by Communion received in the hand?

The Crowning of Our Lord with Thorns: The crown Our Lady of Guadalupe wears is almost invisible, because She herself wants to hide it; her crown is the glory of her Son penetrating her whole being.

The Carrying of the Cross: Look at her right foot: She is walking, "coming from the region of the sun," She precedes Him as the morning star, She will not stop until the light of God has driven out all darkness.

The Crucifixion: We notice a line down through the middle of her garment and we note her folded hands: She herself is cruciform; She will carry us up to Golgotha if we only stretch out our arms like the boy at her feet, who is clinging to her vestments. She is first on the way up to Golgotha; She is the first to be crucified with her Son.

The Glorious Mysteries

As the image of Our Lady of Guadalupe is the image of the "glorified woman," the *"woman clothed with the sun"* the Glorious Mysteries cannot exclude, but must necessairly include the combat which has caused Her to be the "glorious woman."

The Resurrection: As we have already seen, the moon can have different meanings. In relation to the first mystery, the moon reflects the darkness of the tomb of Our Lord Jesus Christ. The black of the moon covers all of the immense suffering endured by Our Lord Jesus Christ because of the fallen angels and their human instruments. Only Our Lady and St. John, by the prevenient grace of the Resurrection were able to stand upright under the cross. And so Our Lady in the image is Herself the symbol of the Resurrection of Her Son from the dead. Her right shoe standing on the decrescent moon is also a symbol of the Holy Eucharist, the Bread of Life which She was the first to receive in her heart. The fathers of the church also call the Holy Eucharist "the Bread of Immortality," because the risen Lord has overcome the power of death. The fact that Her foot is put forward is another symbolic sign: only in the power of this Bread can man realize his pilgrimage to heaven.

The Ascension: The fact of the Ascension can best be seen in the person of the boy at her feet, by way of Christ and Mary, those who spread out their arms in the form of the cross will also partake in the power by which Christ has "led captive captivity."[106] But ascension can also be seen in the "movement of ransom" starting with her merciful eyes, lifting up all men of goodwill in the power of the ascension of her Son. The more the power of the ascension will be effective in us, the more we shall leave behind the earth burnt out by sin. In the same way that Our Lord blesses the apostles when departing, so also shall His blessing come down upon us through the folded hands of Our Lady, and it is an apocalyptic blessing, for we see the "omega" in her white hand cuffs. This blessing will have the power to lead the children of God through the Red Sea of the sins of these times to the blessed shores of the Promised Land.

The Descent of the Holy Spirit: The black hair of Our Lady is said to have the form of a dove. This dove is black, because black here symbolizes the inscrutable mystery of God. Man on his part can do nothing to bring down the Holy Spirit if it isn't through the purity of heart of Our Lady. The descent of the Holy Spirit is symbolized in the image through Her folded hands on the outside of which we can recognize her Immaculate Heart. But the coming of the Spirit is as an apocalyptic (white hand cuffs "omega") coming, a coming in

---

[106] cf. Introit of the Mass of ascension.

the seven black seals beneath her hands. This is to say that the coming of the Holy Spirit in these last times will be restricted to the seven sealed communities of the Apocalypse.[107] Whatever is outside of these communities is under the wrath of God.

The black of the seven folds is as dark as the black color of her hair: again an indication that the last coming of the Holy Spirit is an inscrutable mystery hidden to the eyes of the world. The fourth sign for the descent is the black decrescent moon. Finally the fire of the love of God will burn all our sins and even those of the angels to ashes. So this third mystery of the Rosary in the image of Our Lady of Guadalupe has clearly an apocalyptic accent and thus it is different from the coming down on Pentecost on the apostles. This time, the Holy Spirit will come down on those, who together with this boy, are burden bearers, carrying not only the heaviness of the cross, but without knowing, the glory of Our Lady: symbol of a renewed creation.

The Assumption of Our Lady into Heaven: The clearest sign of the Assumption of Our Lady into heaven is the upward movement already described several times. Our Lady, Assumed into heaven, wants to take all her children, and with them, the whole of creation, into this "movement of ransom." This is why also the constellations of the stars on the mantle of Our Lady partake in this upward movement.[108] This upward movement is also seen in the boy as the "ascending eagle" as well as he who carries the hearts and blood of those sacrificed to heaven.[109] This is to remind us that no one will have part in the ascension if he does not partake in the pierced Hearts of Our Lord and of Our Lady. Signs of the coming home of creation are not only the golden flowers on Our Lady's robe, but also the golden trim of her mantle. It is even a sign that the glorification of creation has already begun with the Resurrection of Our Lord Jesus Christ.

---

[107] cf. Rv 2-3
[108] cf. Book IV
[109] Itzpapalotl, Aztec deity who was believed to present human hearts to the Gods; Tob. 12:12; Our Lady of the Light.

The Coronation of Our Lady as Queen of Heaven and Earth:
The coronation of Our Lady as queen of heaven and earth is the
mystery best seen by the fact that Our Lady is surrounded by the
rays of the sun. There are one hundred and thirty-eight rays that
can be seen. When added together in horizontal order, (1+3+8=12)
their sum equals twelve, the symbolic number for the new Jerusalem with its twelve gates. So in reality with regard to Our Lady of
Guadalupe, the new Jerusalem has descended to earth not only in
the sign of the natural environment that was transformed, but also
in Her person. This is a clear sign that beginning with Her apparition in 1531 we have begun the "last times" on earth.

> *"Then I saw a new heaven and a new earth. The first
> heaven and the first earth had disappeared now and
> there was no longer any sea. I saw the Holy City and
> the new Jerusalem coming down from God from heaven
> as beautiful as bride adorned for her husband."*[110]

The Apocalypse speaks clearly of a new heaven and a new
earth, in the symbol of the new heaven the reign of the angels will
suffer transformation. This is something we cannot yet understand,
because we have such a static comprehension of the angels as being in heaven continually singing the praise of God. They are sent
from heaven not only as our Guardian Angels but they must take
part in the final combat for the reign of God and for the renewal of
all things. Only then will man, angel and material creation sing the
eternal praise of God together with, in and through Mary. This praise
is already present in the image of Our Lady of Guadalupe "as the
one coming from the east singing a new song." As soon as we will
come closer to our angel will we also participate in this new song,
because its one tone is our vocation in Jesus Christ Our Lord.

---

[110] Rv 21:22

Book Six

Proclaiming the Good News

cf. Mt 24:14

Foreword

If we have really understood the silent call of Our Lady of Guadalupe in our hearts, then Book VI is a challenge for mission; to follow her in the footsteps of Juan Diego.

Part One will tell us more about this "silent mission: with Our Lady of Guadalupe." As we contemplate the image more deeply in our hearts, we will understand that it is a call of reparation in and with Mary under the cross. We are invited by her to enter into the apocalyptical dimensions of the Holy Mass," which will finally bring about the consummation of Redemption in the sign of the Lamb of God.

Part Two will tell us more about the beauty of this mission in which we should participate in order to become "all beautiful" as Mary. Like the Beloved Apostle, St. John, and Juan Diego, we must take her into our hearts, so that we can reflect something of her beauty. Only if we first become "word of her beauty" will our word of mission participate in the light of God, and irradiate from her image.

- The measure of this beauty is the cross and on the cross the beauty of the wounds of the Lord, the price of our Redemption;

- As seen in her standing upon the decrescent moon, as if on a paten, its essence is sacrifice;
- As it is best revealed in the golden rectangle, its order is harmony;
- Its promise are the beatitudes: we really have to become "city on the hilltop;"

Only thus will we, in union with the holy angels, help to prepare the reign of Mary and the final coming down of the new Jerusalem.

Part One

Introduction: Word and Light

The revelation of Our Lady of Guadalupe, first of all by her image, marks a new epoch for the proclamation of the word of God. "Evangelization by Light," first apparent with Our Lady of Guadalupe, has to penetrate the so called "new evangelization" which is exclusively conceived as a proclamation of the word. Only if the word will light up again, as it was in the beginning with Our Lord and the apostles, in the Light of the Holy Spirit, will it be able to touch the hearts of those who are called to eternal life. Otherwise the word will simply be lost in the inundation of the many words in which man threatens to drown in these times.

Wherever word and light come together, a new creation begins. This is so clear in the intervention of Our Lady in this poor country of Mexico. The Mexican nation, like unto the Jewish, in a special way, is a particular creation of God. This creation is according to the image of Our Lady of Guadalupe, which as we have seen before, is in a veiled way, the image of the triune God to Whose similitude man was created in the beginning. Here we intuit a little more about the "sacramental character" of the image of Guadalupe, something already mentioned in the Eucharistic presence in the image.[1]

---

[1]   cf. Book IV

Although Our Lady's unique manner of proclaiming the good news, even up to our day and age, has never really been studied, even less practiced, it continues to be an orientation which heaven wants to give us so as to better understand what the "new evangelization" really should be. If we would only probe deeper into the Book of the Apocalypse we would find a very similar manner of announcing the good news in view of these last times. This is precisely the most important distinction of this evangelization by Mary in relation to our traditional way. It is an apocalyptic way of proclaiming the good news. In the fuller sense of the Lord's words: "Convert, because the kingdom of heaven is close."[2]

We rely on the traditional means of simply proclaiming the good news, because we don't have the discerning eye of recognizing the "signs of the times." In the world of today, the word of God is shadowed by the "the good news" of the newspapers. This is why also the word of God, in this "flood of words," is drowned.[3] Whoever meditates the Apocalypse more profoundly, in the manner shown for the contemplation of the image of Our Lady of Guadalupe, will soon discover that the "word" of this last book of the Bible is really a "last word of God" and this much more than any of the current charismatic messages which many times, in-

---

[2] Practically, with these words, Our Lord starts His mission. This is best seen in the beginning of the Gospel of St. Mark, in the words of St. John Baptist: "Make ready the way of the Lord, make straight His path." cf. 1:3 Remember that this word of St. John is considered as "the beginning of the Gospel of Jesus Christ, the Son of God. (1:1) The parellel citation can be found in the other synoptics.

[3] In order to make up for this "loss of weight" of the word of God, we employ all the technical means of our day to make it better heard and seen, but this again is a deception, because as soon as the sound of the word has passed and the show is over, most people forget what they have heard or seen, there is no time to let it enter deeper, pondering over it in our heart as did Mary. The confusion of words and images is so dominating that it really needs the light of our angel to bring again to our conscience the word of God as word of God and not as something beautifully arranged by man. Although we may understand this, we yet employ brainwashing, even in Spiritual retreats, repeating things over and over again instead of helping people to find a personal entry in the word of God by contemplation.

stead of helping man to orient himself in all the confusion of this time, help to increase the same.[4] The Apocalypse, as a word of light, provides us a means of discerning spirits in the general confusion of words and signs in our days. We need only take advantage of the light of our angel and all the angels to better understand it.[5]

The Apocalypse as "word-image" and the "image-word" of the image of Our Lady of Guadalupe complement each other. Although the message of the Apocalypse is word, it is much more image than word. We are incapable of understanding this if our good angel will not help us to interpret it in its symbolic significance. Just as Our Lord used parables to announce the good news, so also does the Apocalypse use them, only the parables therein are not so much taken from the ambiance of daily life as in the Gospels, but are much more symbols on a Spiritual level which is that of the angels. Simplifying, we could say that "these parables" give us the perspective of how the angels look down on the things of this world.

- If we follow the evolution of the word of revelation, we will discover that there are three different levels we have to consider. The announcing of the good news in the Old Testament is first of all by images which constitute the fundament/root of human life. These images always have "a taste of earth."
- Our Lord Jesus Christ helps us lift up our eyes from this earth without taking away the soil from beneath our feet. By the Light of the Holy Spirit, He makes transparent the things of this earth, especially that of nature and our human environment in order to make us understand better about the reign of God.

---

[4]   Here, the right and the obligation of the church to judge and coordinate these messages according to the orientation we receive from the Apocalypse is apparent. Unfortunately, this unique valid criterium for a "new evangelization" has not yet been discovered by the corresponding authorities in the hierarchical church. This is why people continue to be exposed to an ever growing confusion even in the religious realm.

[5]   Already in the interpretation of the image, we have pointed out how important it is to interpret the symbolism of any message in the light of the holy angels.

- In the Apocalypse, as in the image of Our Lady of Guadalupe, this light from above is so much stronger that the things of this earth, used as parables/symbols, acquire an even greater transparency for the invisible realities of the reign of God. It is precisely this Spiritualization of the word of God which we need for proclaiming the good news in an apocalyptic perspective.[6]

The icons of the Eastern church are a beautiful example of what an "image-word" in the Spiritual perspective means. They are like windows into the invisible world of God and this, first of all, because the painting of icons is governed by Spiritual laws which empower the artist to be an instrument in the expression of eternal realities. The governing Spiritual laws are realities of the world of the angels as much as are the laws of construction of the great cathedrals of Christendom. Having lost these laws, living more and more in a world of lawlessness, we need to enroot in the invisible order of the reign of God as it is represented by the hierarchy of the holy angels. The icons representing things of heaven, ac-

---

[6] A little help for understanding the different character of the word-image of the Apocalypse comes from studying the evolution of traditional painting, where things are represented in a realistic way (more or less as they are), towards painting in an abstract way, where things no longer appear in an outward way, but according to their essence or constructive pattern. Consider the evolution of a painter like Picasso or Klee, who started in a traditional way, but more and more arrived at an "abstract level," where the painting tries to bring us closer to a Spiritual perspective of the things of this world. Unfortunately, most abstract painting ended up in the blind alley of an inspiration from "the other side." This is why modern abstract painting many times gives us a very clear image of the destruction of human values and order. Modern abstract art is a realistic view of our "human condition" in these modern times, because it helps us to "see through" the surface of things. Witnessing the entry of this destructive art even in our churches, we should know that the "time of desolation" has come (cf. Mt 24:15). On the other hand, the Apocalypse shows us the positive way of "abstract painting." If we consider the first chapter, for example, St. John gives an image of Most Holy Trinity. Here, the Spiritual properties of God are exposed by way of attributes which seem to have lost any relation to their earthly background. This is why also, if we would try to combine these attributes in a logical way, the result would be absolute nonsense. Here only, the analogy of all creation, climbing up to the highest level, will help us to an understanding in the Holy Spirit.

cording to the laws of heaven, necessarily have an apocalyptic perspective, because they tell us how we will be one day when we arrive at the other side.[7]

What we do not realize right away is that the icons are also part of the history of salvation and this is why we must not only consider them in a static but also in a dynamic way. This we have explained already with the foremost icon, the image of Our Lady of Guadalupe. In the Apocalypse, the dynamic perspective is overwhelming. The "word-image" of the Apocalypse is like an ark from the beginning to the end of time. If we look more intensely on the image of Our Lady of Guadalupe will find out the same. This revelation is beyond the historical moment of her apparition, extending like the Apocalypse over the limits of place and time. This is the first reason why we try to meditate the Apocalypse as "an apocalyptic Mass" in relation to the image of Guadalupe.

The "Apocalyptic Mass"
as Consummation of Salvation History

Introduction

The apparition of Our Lady of Guadalupe, as the "great sign in heaven," is announcing that the time of the final transformation for the world has come. This is already seen in the transfiguration of nature in her first apparition and in the mantle of rays surrounding her.[8]

The "motor" of transformation in this world is the sacrifice of Christ present in the church by the Holy Mass. Even a small understanding of the Spiritual power of the sacrifice of Christ will

---

[7] Western Christians have little understanding or appreciation of the icons. What may seem to be distortion or abstraction to an untrained gazer is part of the deeper entry into the eternal. Every material detail in an icon, especially the form in which the icon is painted, is part of the message from the "other side" and must be interpreted in a symbolical way.

[8] cf. Rv 12:1, Nican Mopohua and the image of Our Lady of Guadalupe

help us to recognize the Apocalypse as an "apocalyptic Mass" with the seven typical parts of the Holy Mass.

At the end of this Mass we will hear the "Ite missa est" — "The mass is ended, go in peace." And so the "sixth day of creation will enter definitively into the seventh: when God will rest of all His Works in the glory of the new Jerusalem. The rays surrounding Our Lady of Guadalupe are not only a mantle of glory, they are part of the eternal perfection of things in the Holy City coming down with Mary and with help of the holy angels to take us up to the Heart of God.

Outline

The following outline, together with the Seven Gifts of the Holy Spirit, will orient us on our first way through this most angelic book of the Bible.

I. **INTROIT**: Invitation to the dialogue with God. God is love and expects our answer in love. (Chapt. 1)

Gift of Understanding: to understand God and to love Him, we must know Him better in the Light of the Holy Spirit Who is the author and principal of the Apocalypse.

II. **READINGS**: In a special way, the church should reflect the image of the triune God (Chapt. 2 and 3), only then will it perfectly be like the holy angels: light of the light of God.

Gift of wisdom: meditating the seven letters to the communities of Asia we will know more about the wisdom of the ways of God.

III. **OFFERTORY**: God sends His holy angels to make the church an acceptable gift to the Father in the Holy Spirit. (Chapts. 4-7) (The mission of the angels with the seals):
- Sealing the good ones in the sign of the cross. (4)
- Impregnating on them the Face of God in fire. (3)

Gift of Counsel: we must be living stones in the edifice of holy church, we have to live our specific vocation; we have become "cruciform" so as to be conformed to the image the Son of God Who died for her on the cross.

IV. **SANCTUS**: The THIRST of God for the sanctity of the church as an ever more urgent call for conversion:
    A. The call of the trumpets as the last call for conversion
    B. Mary is the "apocalyptic sign" of the beginning battle
    C. The counter-sign is the dragon and his dominion: the whore of Babylon (Chapt. 14)

Gift of Knowledge, which is no other than to be able to deny ourselves, to take up our cross and follow Him. Knowledge as "science of the cross" is the kind of knowledge that the church will learn in the final battle for the reign of God,

V. **CONSECRATION**: The angels of judgment and harvest are sent to bring about the final transformation of the creation. (Chapts. 15-20)

Gift of Fortitude: this is the most needed gift of the Holy Spirit in these times of Spiritual warfare.

VI. **COMMUNION**: "Therefore whoever eats this bread or drinks the cup of the Lord unworthily, will be guilty of the body and blood of the Lord." (I Cor 11:27) This is the action of separation and judgment by the angels with the cups of wrath. (Chapt. 16-20)

Gift of the Fear of God: mankind will learn it again when this earth will begin to tremble under the wrath of God; it is the foundation for our relationship with the Holy God.

VII. **END OF MASS**: The descent of the new Jerusalem (Chapts. 21-22)

Gift of Piety: those who persevere to the end will be saved. When man finally will cry out, he will be able to respond to God's call of love: Marantha, come Lord Jesus!

Note The division corresponds as follows:

I	II	III	IV	V	VI	VII
7 pts.[9]	7 pts.	2 pts.	3 pts.	2 pts.	7 pts.	3 & 7 pts.
Introit	Readings	Offertory	Sanctus	Conse-cration	Com-munion	End

In the Apocalypse, the triune God, as with Our Lady of Guadalupe, is inviting us to participate in His eternal dialog of love. Read the beginning of the Nican Mopohua, and you will find a reflection of this dialogue in the first encounter of Juan Diego and the Virgin of Tepeyac.[10]

Interpretation of the Apocalypse as Apocalyptic Mass

I. **INTROIT** (Chapt. 1:1-20)

  A. Invitation to the dialogue: (1:1)

    1. The entire cosmos has to participate in the sacrifice of Christ. *"The things that must shortly come to pass,"* (1:1)

    2. A triple testimony is required:
- The angel,
- The servant John,
- Jesus, *"of whatever he saw" (1:2).*

The church will come to its consummation only when man, angel and God are one in the consummated testimony!

3. The receiver is blessed: (1:3)
$$\left\{ \begin{array}{l} \text{in reading with his eyes,} \\ \text{in hearing (heart to heart),} \\ \text{in conserving (in his heart).} \end{array} \right.$$

These are the three steps taking up the message.

---

[9]   pts. = parts, divisions, note the wonderful harmony in the construction of the Apocalypse.

[10]   cf. Book III, Appendix II

B. Salutation (1:4-6)

Receiver: *"...to the seven churches that are in Asia..."* as representatives of one church beneath the direction of the seven angels, instruments of the Holy Spirit. Only in the Holy Spirit will it encounter *"...grace and peace..."*

From: *"...Him Who is, and Who was and Who is coming ... and from the seven Spirits who are before His throne ... and from Jesus Christ. Who is:*
- *The first begotten of the dead*
- *The Prince of the kings..*
- *Who has loved us, and washed us from our sins in His own blood, and made us to be a kingdom, and priests to God His Father." (1:5)*

"To Him be glory and empire for ever and ever." (1:6) The Apocalypse reveals the glory and sanctity of God by means of Jesus Christ, Who, in His holiness, is at the same time both Son of God and Son of man. This revelation is brought forth through the holy angels, the first representatives of the light of God. Looking up to the image of Our Lady of Guadalupe we see a parable of this mystery of Son of God and Son of man in the big golden flowers imposed on the earthen-colored gown of Our Lady of Guadalupe. They are "imposed" in a way that you cannot separate them from the underlying gown. This way they represent not only the unity of God and man but also the presence of God in the history of salvation by way of His Son Jesus Christ. In Him all things will receive their ultimate form: the face of God.

C. Announcing the Son of Man (1:7-8)

The Lord is revealed in all of His Omnipotence out of the impotence of the Holy Eucharist, the Lamb of God.

"He comes with the clouds and every eye shall see Him,
and they also who pierced Him.
And all tribes..." (1:7)

> He is the revelation of the triune God
> "'the alpha and the omega,
> the beginning and the end,'
> says the Lord God." "'Who is…'" (1:8)

The coming of the Lord is always in the mystery, indirectly veiled by the seven veils as are found in the image of the Virgin of Guadalupe.

D. St. John represents the "answer" of man to God and serves as the "deacon" in the apocalyptic Mass! Representation is the privilege of the Christian: as Jesus Christ represents us with the Father, so each one of us must represent also his brother before God. Here St. John, as the disciple closest to the Lord, is called to represent all mankind called to eternal life. (1:9-12)

John is called to this representation as: *"brother and partner in tribulation, in the kingdom and patience in Christ."*

We are "brothers of Jesus" only in as far as we also share in his "way," which is triple:

- it has part in His suffering,
- in His mission to erect the kingdom of God — everyone of us will have his/her special part in it,
- to be acquired in patience.[11]

Already here is emphasized the importance of a more "passive, suffering attitude" towards the things to come. We can-

---

[11] Four times we find this keyword of the Apocalypse: in relation to the patience of Jesus Christ (1,8) together with the effort (erga) and the trouble (kopos) the community of Ephesus takes on itself for the sake for Jesus Christ (2,2); as "word of patience" that the community of Philadelphia has conserved; finally as an absolute necessity for the church in the coming persecutions (13:10), repeated in 14:12, as "patience of the saints, that is of those who observe the commandments of God and the faith of Jesus." Patience is seen in relation to the Holy Spirit — it requires a more passive, suffering attitude, corresponding to the passion of the Lord to be repeated in the church, His Mystical Body. This way it will help build the new Jerusalem (remark the relation of the quotations to the four qualities of God).

not do it by ourselves. The Holy Spirit has to help us with the patience which is that of Christ in His passion.

Location *"on the island of Patmos..."*
for the word of God
and the testimony of Jesus."

Again, there is a threefold determination: in relation to the material creation, to man and to the Spirit.

Time *"I was in the Spirit on the Lord's day*

Here is given the perspective in which we must look on whatever is revealed in this book: it is that of Resurrection (1:10); it is the perspective "from above," not anymore that from below, as we find in the synoptic Gospels. The Gospel of St. John already has part in this "glorious perspective." This is also why no one will understand if he or she is not "in the Spirit." Let us remember that this is also the preponderant perspective in the image of Our Lady of Guadalupe, as the "glorious woman" (Aztec view), as the "woman clothed with the sun." (Rv 12:1)

"...and I heard behind me a great voice, saying, 'What thou seest write...'"

Destination of the message "'...and send to the seven churches(1:11).'

"Turning to see the voice, I saw seven golden lamp-stands."

The communities are represented by the "lamp-stands," e.g.: the only thing God expects of them is to receive His light and put it on the lamp-stand, so that anybody can see it. In order that it be "golden" lampstands,[12] it has to be purified in the

---

[12] Compare with the golden lining of Our Lady's mantle, her gown and the aura of golden rays. Although Mary was conceived without original sin, among all creatures, she was most tried by God. It was thus, that under the cross, she became Mother of all who are called to eternal life.

fire of the jealous love of God. The lampstand is, as is the whole message, a challenge to become new in Jesus Christ by way of the Holy Spirit.

E. The "face" of the most Holy Trinity is revealed in nine perspectives, related to the nine choirs of the hierarchy of the holy angels, as reflection of God, Who is Spirit.
1. The triple essence of God *"in the midst of the golden lampstands One..."*
   • ...like to the Son of man,
   • ...clothed with a garment...
   • ...and girt about the breast with a golden girdle." (1:13)
     This "Son of man" is an image of the most Holy Trinity.

1. *"and His head and His hair were white as white wool, and as snow, (1:14)* (symbolizing the Father)

2. *"...and His eyes were as "flame of fire"* (Son)

3. *"His feet like fine brass, as in a glowing furnace"* (symbolizing the Holy Spirit: in His essence), *"and His voice like the voice of many waters."* (1:14-15) (The Holy Spirit in His action)

This symbolic representation of Most Holy Trinity corresponds to the three big flowers on the chest of Our Lady of Guadalupe.

2. The Work of God:
"And He had in His right hand seven stars.
And out of His mouth came a sword;
and His face was as the sun."* (12-16)

F. Reaction of St. John: *"I fell at His feet as one dead and He laid His hand on me saying: fear not...."* (1:17)[13]
Here, we can see a remarkable difference with the revelation on Tepeyac, mediated by Our Lady. In this perspective, the image of Guadalupe is not yet the "apocalypse in action," but announcing that the apocalyptic time has begun with this first apparition of Our Lady. By way of her we have time to better meditate this last message of the love of God and so prepare ourselves to stand firm when the apocalyptic events will come over us.

G. The Son of man and His mission
In another perspective, the four divine attributes are revealed:
His sanctity - *"I am the first and the last,*
His wisdom - *"and is alive and was dead,*
His justice - *"I am living forever...*
His omnipotence - *"...and I have the keys of death and of hell."* (1:18).

"Write therefore the things that thou has seen..." The mission of writing for St. John is to open man's eyes to God's perspective on the history of salvation. He should not look on it with the eyes of the carnal man, but from above, with the eyes of his angel. Then only, whatever is announced will not come on him like an inevitable fate, but will be an invitation to look at it with open eyes: here

---

[13] Here is the "place of the Confiteor — the confession of our sins" — which should not be omitted in the celebration of the Holy Mass if we will not presume to be "on the same level" as God, as it is unfortunately many times done in today's liturgical practice. God is always majesty and man has to bow before him acknowledging that he is His creature and besides a poor sinner.

the will of God is being executed and this by the Son of man Who calls man to enter already here in the vision of eternal life.[14]

"...*the mystery of the stars and the seven candle-sticks*" (1:19-20) is that of the inseparable relation of the seven communities representing the church of the end of times with their angels. Here again, we are reminded that we should not look at the church only in a social dimension. In the end, she has to enter in the glory of God, already present in the holy angels who have passed their proof in the beginning of time. This intimate relation of whatever happens on earth, especially in the church, with the angels, is necessarily a mystery which man can intuit only if he bows down before the greater majesty of God and His plans. The Apocalypse is, even for the church, a book closed with seven seals as long as she will not look up to the hierarchy of the holy angels as the primitive image she is called to represent in a visible way.

II. **THE READINGS**[15]

The Seven Letters of the Apocalypse:

The letters to the seven communities are the "call of God," through the word, to reform us according to the sanctity of God. This sanctity is to be reflected in us, in the Holy Spirit, in a septuple manner. It is thus that each of the seven communities are to reflect something of the face of God in Christ Jesus, that which uniquely corresponds to it, in order that it truly be an image of God.

The face of God is always threefold, because God is Trinity. This triple face of God must be reflected in each of the communities as well as in the whole church. In the horizontal addition, $3 \times 7 = 21$. Three signifies that in the end, the church, purified and crystallized in the fire of apocalyptic love of God,

---

[14] "This is eternal life that they know you...." The Apocalypse as revelation of the victorious light of God (not the one anymore which descended into the darkness — now it is rising, as in the "movement of ransom" in the image of Our Lady of Guadalupe.

[15] cf. Book II; Seven communities.

will perfectly represent Mary, and in Mary, the divine and triune countenance of God.

For this reason, the judgment of the church is not only with respect to its septuple mission in the Holy Spirit, but also in its representation of the triune face of God. Each of the communities is judged according to the face of the Son of God which the Father wills to see in it. The Son is, at the same time, the praise of the community as well as the mission that it should faithfully fulfill; He is admonition in that which it fails to fulfill, and advice as to how it may amend. The face of the Holy Spirit is seen in the promise of consummation which is given to those who are faithful to their vocation.

I. The Father shows in the face of His Son how the community should be.

II. The Son is the sword of separation from evil.

III. The Holy Spirit will fulfill the plan of God on this community if it faithfully heeds the admonition.

	LIGHT	ETERNAL LIFE	SWORD
I. **The Image of the Lord**	He who holds the seven stars Ephesus	The First and the Last Smyrna	He who holds the sharp two-edged sword Pergamum
II. **Praise of the Community**	...works, labor and patience... and have endured for My Name	I know your tribulations and your poverty	You are faithful to My Name
Admonishment	You have lost your first love		have permitted false doctrine
III. **Promise for those who overcome**	He who overcomes I will permit to eat of the tree of life	He who overcomes shall not be hurt by the second death	...I will give the hidden manna ...a white pebble ...a new name

Burning Justice	King of the Angels	The Faithful One	He Who Consumes
Who has eyes like to a flame of fire Thyatira	He who has the seven spirits of the God Sardis	Who has the key of David Philadelphia	The Amen ...The faithful and true witness Laodicea
Your charity, your faith, your spirit of service, your patience		You have guarded My Word	
permits immorality	reputation of being alive, but dead		You are neither warm nor cold
...I will give authority over the nations ...and I will give him the morning star	...shall be arrayed in white garments ...name in the Book of Life	Column in the Sanctuary of My God ...I will engrave the name of My God upon him	To the victor, I will seat him beside Me on My Throne

The "readings" are symbolically present in the image of Our Lady of Guadalupe by way of the lower fold of her gown forming like a book, but not only this fold is "a book," she herself is the living response to the Gospen and so is "Gospel" herself. In her we can see how God wants to see the church in these last times: beautiful as she is, overcoming the darkness of the fallen angels by the greater power of the light of God, which in the "movement of ransom" penetrates the densest shadows.

III. **OFFERTORY** (Chapts. 4-7)

The sign of the cross is spread over the earth as a challenge to join in the Sacrifice of Christ

A. *A door opened in heaven* (Chapt. 4-5):

1. Vision of the throne of God (4:2).
2. Jasper-stone and a sardius, and a rainbow round about the throne, in appearance like to an emerald. (4:3)

The jasper represents God's immobility, sardius — sacrifice, and the rainbow — the union of all things in God. Symbolically again, they also represent the Most Holy Trinity. Jasper, the Father Who is the beginning, sardius, the Son Who is the sacrificed one, and the rainbow, the Holy Spirit Who consumes the order of creation and Redemption.

3. The twenty-four ancient ones (4:4) are representatives of the Old and New Testaments.
4. The Seven Lampstands (4:5-6) (symbols that the church, governed by the Holy Spirit) and in the midst of them, the Lamb, symbol of the Lord in His church in the Most Holy Eucharist, the life of the church.
5. The opening of the book (5:8) signifies that in the end times, by means of the holy angels, God will reveal the most hidden mysteries of His life, to those who, like Mary, live a hidden and abnegated life in continual adoration and contemplation of God. Revealing these mysteries is at the same time setting free their power of Redemption which, for those who do not accept, is condemnation.
6. Adoration (5:8), like the angels and with the angels, must be the response of all Christians to Holy God.
7. Praise of God (5:9-14) is always the last step in the progressive development of the Apocalypse. The Lamb is the offering, thus, only in Him are we an acceptable offering to God the Father.

B. *The opening of the seals* (Chapts. 6 and 7):
   • by the action of the living beings, who spread the cross over creation, God is taking possession of the universe
   • The Four Apocalyptic Horses revenge (6:2-8).
      - The white one avenges the Holiness of God (6:2) violated by man's pride (behind which is the intellectual pride of Lucifer) = relation to St. Matthew.
      - The red one avenges the depreciated wisdom of God (6:4). Not accepting God's providence, men, in their blindness, kill one another = relation to St. Luke.

- The black one avenges the hurt justice of God (6:5), giving space to the violence of murder, anarchy and hunger = relation to St. John.
- The pale one avenges the unacknowledged omnipotence of God (6:8), the ultimate result of man's violence, pestilence and the beasts of the earth = relation to St. Mark.
- The three following seals are action of the triune God, unfolding His power which up to this moment has been hidden in the impotence of Our Lord in the Holy Eucharist.
- The fifth seal (6:9-11) The souls under the altar call for revenge in the name of the Father. More and more the whole of heaven with all its saints is entering in the final battle for the reign of God.
- The sixth seal (6:12-17) Resume of the chastisement in the name of the Son.
- The sealing of the faithful (Chapt. 7) amidst total destruction.

At the offertory, we should remember the offertory prayer of the Mass of the Most Holy Trinity: "let us become ourselves a perfect offering (sacrifice)…" — not in a general, but in a unique way corresponding to our special vocation, because only thus can we help the church to become a *"living structure,"*[16] *"a light on the lamp-stand, a city on the hilltop"*(Mt 5:14) for the greater praise of God's name. Only in being built with "living stones" will the church resist the ever fiercer attacks of the devil. God will seal her through His holy angels, in the sign of the cross extended over creation as a whole.[17]

The relation of this "offertory" part of the Apocalypse to the image of Our Lady of Guadalupe is first of all in the "moon as cup of sacrifice." It is the boy below her who is

---

[16] cf. Eph 2:19-20.
[17] cf. Book II; The four living creatures.

"offering" her not only to his brothers as the last gospel, but he is also offering her to God, and this in the "cup of the moon." Here the moon acquires a third dimension.[18] The "non serviam" — "I will not serve" — of Lucifer, which has brought about all the immense suffering in the world (to all three parts of creation in a congenial way!), is overcome in the suffering of the Lord on the cross. The mystery of sacrifice, which is the very mystery of the triune God in the mutual surrender of the three divine persons to each other. After Christ (in His humanity) it is Mary who was the first to give her consent to total sacrifice by way of her "Fiat" to St. Gabriel.

In the boy, representing this time St. John, God wants us to offer this "yes" of Mary, witnessed in her standing under the cross of her Son, as the of all mankind to God! In this unique and all comprising answer of Mary we are saved! This is the greatest grace of God's inscrutable love in these last times: whoever enters with his frail and stumbling "yes" in the "yes" of Mary, pronounced in the power of the Holy Spirit, will have part in the "sealing of the angels" and be saved in one of the communities, which will find their consummation in and through Mary.

IV. SANCTUS

The Revelation of the Holy God (Chapts. 8-13).

A. The trumpets (Chapt. 8)

The seventh seal with the call for conversion by the fire of the apocalyptic love of God.

- Silence in heaven (8:1) … symbolic of absolute adoration of God.

---

[18] The first is from the Aztec point of view: earth. The second is apocalyptic: symbol of the fallen angels ("burnt out, ashes!") The third is the moon as cup of sacrifice. The "no" of the rebellious angel has served in the wisdom of God as the "sting in our flesh," "as cup of sacrifice": in resisting the "no" of Lucifer we have ever better learned to say "yes" in Mary.

- Incense and the golden altar (8:3) = fire … not only a symbol of the prayers and sacrifices of the saints, but also of the consummation of the earth in the fire of God's love.
- The seven angels sound the trumpets (8:6) to prepare creation to be an offering pleasing to God. There are always three possible responses to the triune God. The first is that of those who have already decided on behalf of God; the second, of those who have not yet decided; and the third, of those who decided against God. The "louder" the trumpets will sound the "Who is like unto God!," the more those who have not yet decided will be forced to make a final decision for or against God. The "trumpets," on the human level, can be understood in many ways: in the beginning they are the loving call of Our Lady and her ever-urgent invitation to conversion. Later, mankind will be shaken by catastrophes of many kinds, which should remind man that he is not as he thinks himself to be, the absolute "lord" of this earth and life.

The First Four Trumpets

1) Hail destroys (8:7)
$$\begin{cases} \text{earth (woman)} \\ \text{trees (man)} \\ \text{all green grass (youth)}^{[19]} \end{cases}$$

The first day in Genesis is that of the creation of the angels with their foremost mission to give "form to all life." The more we lose their guidance, the more things will become formless, chaotic, drown in the "tohuwabohu = chaos" of the beginning of all things.

---

[19] The symbols of the Apocalypse sometimes almost leave the material reference behind. This is best seen in the "description of Most Holy Trinity in the beginning. Here the symbols denote the very essence of "woman": to bring forth life; of man; to stand up in witness; of youth: to give testimony to the abundance of life.

2) Mountain of fire — sea of blood (8:8).[20]

3) Star — Wormwood (8:8) St. Margaret Mary of Alacoque gives us the word of the Lord: "At the end I will surround them with My sanctity. If they will not accept it, they will die in their sins." This challenge of sanctity for every and each Christian is "bitter" for most of us, so we better turn to the sweetness and pleasures of life. The angels are the first reflection of God's sanctity.

4) As the message of Our Lady to Juan Diego starts in the deepest silence of nature, in the dawning morning, announced by a wonderful singing of the birds, so also here, the trumpets break out of the deepest silence of heaven (8:1). The deepest love of God is always the silent love which the Son suffered in all its heaviness, by dying on the cross, expressed by the fifth word, "My God, My God, why have You forsaken me?"

This silence of God is getting heavier and heavier in our times. Those who think themselves to be just cry out "Why does not God interfere?" Like the Pharisees who were about the cross, they think: "If you are the Son of God, get off the cross!" The modern Sadducees, on the other hand, try to make up for the insupportable silence of God by endless discussions, modifications and new plans of evangelization, causing man to be further drowned in a deluge of words. The world is so much hammered by noise that it no longer knows what silence is. Only those of pure heart, like Juan Diego, will not be shaken by the trumpets, because their heart is

---

[20] In a certain way, all life comes out of the water, thus making the sea a symbol of the abundance of life. Water turned to blood signifies that it has lost all its "upward movement" (best symbolized in the clouds!). So "blood" here stands for a life which is only earthly, nothing but "earth," dust — linking up with the beginning, when man was formed out of the dust of earth. It has not entered into the attraction of the Holy Spirit (hovering over the waters) (Gen.), so it will fall back into dust! What brings about this final separation is the "mountain of fire" falling into the waters, symbol of the lust and most powerful call of the love of God for conversion … before it is too late. This call is carried by the angels of the trumpets; each one will add to it his special "note"!

already with God, they are already beneath the mantle of Our Lady, in Her Immaculate Heart where the silence of God is like an armor which will not permit the noise of the world to enter.

The Three "Woes!" The Fifth Trumpet
(Chapt. 9)

The fifth trumpet is the chastisement for the domination of the five-pointed star, symbol of satanic domination in a world governed by man's arrogance, trying to destroy man's call to share in God, smothering any interior life. Remember, the relation to "five" as symbol of interiority, the lost interiority is chastised by five steps of chastisement and five month of torments.

* key to the bottomless pit (1-2).
* locusts (3).
* torment of five months (5).
* Their hope (7-9).
* Their king (10)

The appearance of the locust can very easily be likened to the powerful and deadly weapons of today.

In the image of Our Lady of Guadalupe, all suffering is resumed in the shadows on her gown. Not only the glorious light of resurrection breaks the darkness, but the golden flowers superimposed on her gown are also a firm promise that amidst the darkness of this world, the reign of God is irresistibly growing.

The Sixth Trumpet

Voice from the four horns from the golden altar:
* *"Loose the four angels...."* (9:14) The altar, here seen in its form as *quadrangle,* is a symbol of creation, projected in view of the cross and finally consummated in the cross. It can be seen in the beginning in the Garden

of Eden, encircled by the four rivers, and finally in creation consummated: the holy city, new Jerusalem.

The Euphrates is symbol of the current of the life of God, from which all life on earth depends. The action of *letting loose of the four angels* removes their assistance from creation, as they support it in the structure of the cross, and thus it will collapse.

- by three plagues one third is slain (9:17). The fire, the smoke and the sulfur are symbols of the chastisement that humanity suffers. The fire represents the unrestrained passion of both body and Spirit, the smoke signifies growing confusion, and the sulfur points to the growing dominion of Satan's reign on earth.

St. Gabriel and the Seventh Trumpet
(Chapt. 10:7; 11:16)
Last Prophecy
(Chapt. 10)

- Seal the message of the seven thunders. (4)
- *"...there shall be delay no longer."* (6)
- *"...the mystery of God shall be fulfilled."* (7)
- Eating the book — its taste is bitter. (9)
- St. Gabriel is recognized by the rainbow, the sign of the covenant of God, by means of the Incarnation of Our Lord Jesus Christ. *"His face like the sun"* reminds us of the light of the Lord in the Most Holy Eucharist; *"...his feet like pillars of fire"* are a sign of the justice that God asks through him for revenge on all who maltreat and sacrilegiously disgrace the sacrament of love. *"His right foot upon the sea but his left upon the earth"* are symbols that He is the Lord of all life that has been formed according to the plans of God (the earth) or that which is yet without form (water).
- St. Gabriel announces the judgment (10:5): *"...lifted up his hand to heaven, and swore by Him Who lives forever and ever ... that there shall be delay no longer; ... in the days of the voice of the seventh angel, when he*

begins to sound the trumpet, the mystery of God will be accomplished." Lastly, the mystery of God is His Incarnation, His presence with us in the Holy Eucharist. St. Gabriel, the Angel of the Incarnation will asks accounts of all we do with this sacrament of love. If St. Gabriel could be identified as the angel of Portugal, preparing the apparitions of the Virgin of Fátima, his apparition would announce the beginning of the judgment upon the world.[21]

Another Perspective of the Judgment of God is the Measuring of the Temple with the Reed.

The Measuring of the Temple: as Judgment over the Church (Chapt. 11)

A Triple	The Temple	represents The Father
Measure of	The Altar	The Son
the Temple	The Adorers	The Holy Spirit

The relation of these three entities to the three divine persons tells us of the necessity of a "trinitarian faith":
- The Father asking of a holy place, according to the measure given to Moses for the construction of the ark;
- The Son asking for sacrifice,
- The Holy Spirit for adoration![22]

---

[21] There are three indications for this "identification": comparing the pericope of Annunciation with the message of Fátima (see "Fátima, Message of the Cross," manuscript). According to Sr. Lucia it very well could have been the date of his former feast on the 24th of March. "Standing with one foot on the earth and the other on the land" recalls us that Portugal has about 7OO km of coastline and is only 200/250 km broad.

[22] This is also emphasized in the trinitarian prayer the angel of Portugal teaches the children. In this prayer faith is related first of all to the Father (together with adoration, which we can give only in union with our good Guardian Angel!), Hope to the Son, love to the Holy Spirit. This is also to counteract all the hidden heresies in relation to the Son of God and the Holy Spirit.

The Testimony of the Two Witnesses (3-6)

- 1260 days/horizontal addition = 9
- The two witnesses are symbols of the hearts of Jesus and Mary, Who announce the final mercy of God with us poor sinners. (11:4-6)
- There is war against them and they are killed (7-10). Above all, this is a battle by means of man's intellectual pride which has been contaminated by the superior intelligence of the fallen angel, one that aims ever more to destroy our heart-to-heart relationship with God, exchanging it for a purely intellectual ideology.
- Their resurrection (11-12).
- Earthquake of the "*city*" (13) that destroys a tenth of the city. The "city" this time seems to be a symbol of the church. It has to acknowledge the omnipotence of God (10) so much forgotten today in the impotent presence of Our Lord in the Holy Eucharist; that seven thousand are killed is a symbol that first of all the sins against the Holy Spirit are punished.

The Seventh Trumpet Announcing: *the Lord has Taken Over the Reign of the Universe* (14-19)

- It also announces the apparition of the apocalyptic woman, symbolized in the *"Ark of His Covenant"* in the temple (11:19).

   Pride has hardened their hearts, making them like unto stone. Those who have pushed Mary out of the churches, making them cold assembly halls, will be incapable of looking up to the great sign of hope in all tribulation.

B. The center of the Apocalypse: The apparition of the great sign, the "woman clothed with the sun." (Chapt. 12).

   The sanctity of God is veiled in the appearance of the apocalyptic Virgin. Here on the earth, we would be unable to bear it unveiled:

- The sign and the countersign (1-3) In these end times, all the evil of the bottomless pit, of Satan's arrogance and rebellion against God, will be revealed.

- The fury of the dragon toward the "woman" (4-6) Mary, by her humility, has assumed the place of the first created angel. This is the very reason that Satan pursues her with unending hatred and together with her, all her children.
- The battle in heaven, the dragon cast out unto the earth. (7-9) The battle in heaven reaches its climax on the earth and it terminates beneath heaven when all material creation has been destroyed.[23]
- The "woman" pursued (13-18)
  (and all those that remain faithful to the testimony of Jesus in the church).

---

[23] The concept of "time" and consequently the sequence of events cannot be simply seen according to our concept of time. We must always keep in mind: the Apocalypse is a book of the angels, passed on by an angel to St. John. The angels live in a different dimension of time. Remember that they were created in the beginning of this world, millions and millions of years before man. They are not in the "space" as we are with our body, even though they are not out of space. Their relation to both time and space is Spiritual, difficult for us to imagine. Because of this fundamental difference with us men, they see things differently. St. Thomas tells us: "by species," that is in some way as God sees them, according to their essence, their truth. The closer they are to God, the more they approach something of the omniscience of God, without ever reaching it (as Lucifer tried to do!). The events in the Apocalypse certainly have some sequence, because they are related to time and space in which we live, but at the same time, they copenetrate each other and copaginate with each other. Again the image of the spectrum, the rainbow, breaking up the white light in the seven colors, will help us understand better about the groups, the rhythm, the rows of "seven": in the first are included the other six, each following links up with the one before him, joining his part, the last "returns" to the first — they form a "spiral"; out of the last many times springs forth another row of seven; the last is the first of the next row; always they are orientated towards the center of the spiral: the triune God, because their mission is in the movement of ransom: to bring the whole creation back to God. (What we have learned with the rosary can help us understand better!). They always reflect something of the infinite harmony and beauty of God, even in their actions of chastisement: God's justice is beauty (naturally a beauty quite different from that of our times, and even beyond that of any piece of art). Only in the image of Our Lady of Guadalupe we can find something of this "beauty beyond." Here also we recognize that the justice of God is love — whoever looks up to her merciful smile, will be saved!

C. The two other beasts (Chapt. 13):

The dragon has already been mentioned as the counter-sign (12:2-3), but two other beasts, as representatives of hell, also emerge.[24]

• The beast out of the sea (1) *"And the dragon gave it his own might...."*(2)

Above all, this beast represents all the material and carnal power of man, all of its wonder-working (the good life of today) to bring man to the worship of the dragon in him: *"They worshipped the dragon...."* (4)

This same beast opens its mouth so as to blaspheme *"...against God, to blaspheme His name and His tabernacle, and those who dwell in heaven."* (5-10) Our modern means of communication are recognized here. It is the greatest tool of confusion and corruption of the mind and heart of man.

• *The beast out of the earth* (11-12)

"...and it had two horns like to those of a lamb, but it spoke as does a dragon. And it exercised all the authority of the former beast in its sight; and it made the earth and the inhabitants therein to worship the first beast, whose deadly wound was healed.

It performs great wonders to deceive and seduce the inhabitants of the earth, telling them to create an image of the beast, and then it was permitted to bring the image to life, *"...that the image of the beast should speak...."* Behind this image, we can detect an allusion to the television, the primary means that the devil employs in his ploy to dominate the earth.

It performs great wonders to deceive and seduce the inhabitants of the earth, telling them to create an image of

---

[24] The more God will reveal his sanctity, in this first of all by the angels, "his created sanctity," the more the fallen angels have to reveal their true "face." (In reality they have not "face" anymore, they are nothing before God, pure lie, pure no). In these days we observe that the devil has openly entered on the "stage" of this world. This is frightening for those who do not believe in God's greater power. The more this brutal power of "no" will reveal itself, the more we will wake up to the call of the trumpets and finally understand: it is "the hour of the angels"!

the beast, and then it was permitted to bring the image to life, *"...that the image of the beast should speak...."* Behind this image, we can detect an allusion to the television, the primary means that the devil employs in his ploy to dominate the earth.

The satanic domination succeeds in that *"...all ... will have a mark on their right hand or on their foreheads, and it will bring it about that no one may be able to buy or sell, except him who has the mark, either the name of the beast or the number of its name."* (16-17): Predominance of commerce in the modern world.[25]

- A reference to the antichrist also follows; he hides himself behind the number 666, a mockery of the Most Holy Trinity. According to the first letter of St. John (cf. I Jn 2:18-22 and 4:4), this number is applicable to all the antichrists that have passed through history as well as those who are yet to come in this infernal battle against Christ Jesus.

It is in relation with the "Sanctus" that we have to look first of all to the image of Our Lady of Guadalupe. Her presence on Tepeyac transforms even nature around her into the splendor of the new Jerusalem. It is in her that God wants to show man what the response is to His word to Moses: "be holy as I am holy...."[26]

As holiness has been first of all a gift to Mary (a gift which she had to collaborate, ascending Golgotha), so it will be in the end of times: the whole church will be holy in, by and with Mary; this is why Mary is the last sword of separation!

---

[25] The world commerce unified, to the detriment of all those "little ones" who can not keep up with this iron pattern worked out in computers, is the first important step for the domination of the world. The second will be "the one religion" propagated by the antichrist (Maitreia?), fundamented on the economic welfare: the religion of "easy life." Therefore persecution of those who will stay faithful to the "testimony of Jesus" is coming closer and closer. For those who have not lost the clear sight of things it is already going on in "a cold war," and this even inside the church and its communities.

[26] Ex 2:19, Lev 11:44

V. **The Consecration/Transubstantiation** (Chapt. 14)

The Lamb, the angels of harvest and of judgment.

All the world must be transformed by means of the sacrifice of the Lamb of God as are the one hundred and forty-four thousand, *"having His Name and the Name of His Father written on their foreheads."* (1) A horizontal addition of 144,000 gives us 9. It signifies those born in God, *"the sons of God"* Jn 1:12.

Once again, the action of God, the mission of the judgment and harvest angels, is preceded by the praise of God. (2-).

The angel with the last call for conversion (6-7).

A. The angels of judgment

> This conversion is an unconditional adoration of God. It is the last chance for conversion. We can relate this first judgment angel with the apparitions of the Blessed Virgin since 1830 in Paris, France.

The angel of chastisement over Babylon (8)
The third angel announcing the cup of wrath (9-12) over all that adore the beast and its image.
"Here is the patience of the saints." (12)
The vision of the Son of man is the center: (13-14)
He is the measure of God's justice.

B. Angels of harvest

> Another angel: *"Put forth thy sickle and reap for the harvest of the earth is ripe"* (15-16) *"And another angel came forth out of the temple...."* (17) *"And another angel came forth from the altar, he who has authority over...."* (18) *"Put forth thy sharp sickle and gather the clusters of the vine of the earth; for its grapes are fully ripe."*

The sickle is one of the communistic symbols; here it represents the impending judgment. Communism is nothing other than an instrument of chastisement for us who have lost communion with God. The message of the Virgin of Fátima confirms this.

As God began His creation of the world with light = energy = hydrogen, so too will it be consumed in the fire of the incandescent love of God.

The mantle of rays with Our Lady of Guadalupe is symbol for this incandescent love of God, which does not permit man to touch her. She will help us to enter in this burning thornbush so that the flames of the fire of chastisement will not harm us, but consume our purification already here on earth.

VI. **COMMUNION** (Chapt. 15-20):
The action of the angels with the cups of wrath reforming the earth to the image of Mary, Virgin Most Holy.

These angels, along with Mary, are "another sign in heaven, great and marvelous,"[27]

A. The first three angels with the cups of wrath.
  1. A sore and grievous wound *"...upon the men who have the mark of the beast, and upon those who worship its image."* The sign of the devil is disorder, anarchy and confusion, destroying all organic, physical or Spiritual growth.[28]
  2. Sea of blood *"...like a dead man;"* The sea is a symbol of life, and blood "like a dead man " signifies a purely terrestrial life, of carnal pleasures, which in itself bears the germ of death.[29]
  3. Fountains of water — blood; The fountains are symbols of both natural and religious families; the rivers are symbols

---

[27] Ibid., 15:1 It is to be referred back to the "great sign" of the "woman clothed with the sun." In these angels the immaculate beauty of Mary will burn to ashes all those who glorify themselves in the ugliness of the beast.

[28] Ibid., 16:2 The "ulcers" are an image of this chaotic growth so much abundant in many modern diseases, especially in cancer.

[29] Ibid., 16:3

of the generations: as time goes on, life itself poisons and destroys itself.[30]

The bloodthirsty belief of the Aztecs could be remedied and even transformed into the faith in the redemptive force of the sacrifice of Christ. The purely earthly life of the new pagans of this time has no opening any more for the transforming light of God.

> *Praise of God -"Yes, O Lord God Almighty,*
> *true and just are Thy judgments."*[31]

B. The second Three angels with the Cups of Wrath
1. On the sun...*" and he was allowed to scorch mankind with fire."*[32] The fire that burns them is a symbol of the unbridled passions that destroy man: passions of the flesh, ambition, money and power.
2. On the throne of the beast *"...and its kingdom became dark."*[33]

> The reign of Satan has to reveal itself in the light of the Holy God as a reign of obscurity. Man is so confused by the false light of the fallen angels that he does not even know anymore what is truth. *"For they have not received the love of truth that they might be saved. Therefore God sends them a misleading influence that they may believe falsehood, that all may be judged who have not believed the truth, but have preferred wickedness."*[34]

---

[30] Ibid.

[31] Ibid., 5-8: God is not simply a "revenging God" — the chastisements are part of a heavenly liturgy — to the greater glory of God — this is why again and again there is an interruption in what otherwise would seem pure causality by the praise of God. The more we learn already now this praise of God in daily life, always adoring the greater God in all the incomprehensible trials we have to pass, the more we will be able to participate in the glorious part of chastisement, which is coming closer and closer.

[32] Ibid., 8-9

[33] Ibid., 10-11

[34] II Thes. 10-12 — how much is this sinister prophecy already realized in our days!

3. On the great River Euphrates *"...that a way might be made ready for the kings from the rising sun."*[35] More and more we testify the entrance of the eastern religions and heresies, trying to substitute the lost faith in Christ.

C. Admonition: *"Behold, I come as a thief! Blessed is he who watches and keeps his garments, lest he walk naked and they see his shame."*[36]

Here the Battle of Armageddon is mentioned. It symbolizes the arrogance of the leaders of the earth who dare to rise up against God.

The seventh angel with the cup of wrath upon the air ... earthquake.

It is a consummation of the judgment of God, above all symbolized in the destruction of the "great city of Babylon," representing now not so much the gentiles who have not yet been touched by the light of true faith but those new pagans who rise up against God.

Unfolding of the chastisement of the "great harlot."

Her universal dominion.[37]

Explanation of the angel.[38]

E. The fall of Babylon

- Announcement of the fall by the angel.[39]
- The necessity to *"Go out from her...."*[40]
- chastisement = revenge of God. [41]
- Wailing of the kings and merchants.[42]

---

[35] 15:12 It is curious to observe that most of the heresies have come from the "east," where the enemy has established himself to obscure the light of living God. Remember: "Abel went to the east...."(Gen. 4:16)

[36] Ibid., 15-16

[37] 17:1-6

[38] Ibid., 7-18

[39] 18:1-3

[40] Ibid., 4-5

[41] Ibid., 6-8

[42] Ibid., 9-19

By means of commerce and modern technology, the world is becoming one, not as it should, one in the spirit of the love of God. Modern man, with his technological advancements and his immeasurable pride, is a Babylon. The apparent unlimited power of man is one which is assisted by hell itself.

Praise:[43]

> *"Make merry over her, O heaven,*
> *and you the saints...*
> *...like a great millstone...*
> *...found no more..."*

F. Christ's Victory
Praise[44]
"Adore God"[45]
The *"white horse"*[46]
just chastisement[47]

G. Satan Bound: The Last Battles:
The angel with the key of the abyss.[48] The first judgment, *"The reign of one thousand years"* signifies the power of God over Satan by means of the saints, which have always existed in the history of the church, and many more will be in the end times of persecution, when the entire church, in union with the holy angels must be a holy church. The sanctity of God in us is the only remedy of conquering the impurity of the evil one.[49]

After the 1000 years there will be the last battle and judgment. [50]

---

[43] Ibid., 20-24
[44] 19:1-9
[45] Ibid., 10
[46] Ibid., 11-15
[47] Ibid., 16-21
[48] 20:1-3
[49] Ibid., 4-6
[50] Ibid., 7-15 The 1000 years again have a multiple signification. They signify the reign of Christ by way of His saints throughout all the histories of the church. They point to the reign of Mary, preparing the second coming of Christ and finally are a symbol of God's omnipotence in all His impotence on earth and even in the church.

As Our Lady of Guadalupe of Guadalupe first of all reveals the apocalyptic bounty of God with us poor sinners and lost sheep in these last times of confusion, the part of chastisement can be seen only in some more hidden signs: as the "cut-off leaves" (the devil himself has cut himself off from the living God!) and some dark stains, which, seen with a magnifying lens, seem to be like skulls. The positive part of communion is in all the signs of "union" — in the union of the three parts of creations mantle as the material creation, gown as representing mankind, her white gown the angels. In the signs of union of God and man — the golden embroidery. In the sign of union of Our Lady and her messenger.

VII. the END of the MASS: the new Jerusalem
(Chapt. 21-22).

New heaven and new earth (Chapt. 21).
The holy city coming down (1-4).
   "Behold I will make all things new!" (5-8).
   Vision of the holy city (9-27).
      "Twelve gates" (15).

Measure (16-17).[51]
Material 18-21).
"No temple" (22-27).
"The river and the tree of life" (Chapt. 22)
- River and tree (1-2)
- Throne in the middle (3-5)
- "These words are true" (6-7)
- Adore God (8-9)Promise (10-12)
- "I am the alpha and the omega" (13-16)
- "Come, Lord Jesus!" (17-21)

The Apocalypse, like the image of Our Lady of Guadalupe, is as an admirable picture of light, order and harmony. Unlike the image of Our Lady, it is a "picture painted by words." Considering more closely, we will find the close relation of word with light: word as means of communication among man, light as communication among the angels. At the end they have to come together to link up with the beginning: "in Him the word was life and life was the light of man."[52] This is also why in the end — as the enemy has understood better than we do — "message" will be conferred more and more by light.[53] It is thus that we are enabled to contemplate their "pictorial message."

Recalling the prologue of St. John's Gospel: *"in Him (the word) was life and life was the light of man,"*[54] we have an

---

[51] 21,17 "and he measured the wall ... a measure of man and at the same time of the angel" in most translations this explanation is left out or translated in the wrong way — because it is difficult to understand, even though the sense is simple: in the end when angel and man will become one in Christ together with material creation — this is it what the new Jerusalem wants to tell us — so they will have the same measure which is no other than Christ!

[52] John 1:3 — the same thing in other words, in relation to the "unction of the Spirit (Who is light!) is remembered in the first letter of St. John when he says "you have no need to be taught.... 2:20,27. Life was crystalline — not as it is now: opaque as it has become by sin.

[53] As it is technically already today: by radio, television, computers.. even on this technical base word and light (electricity) are coming closer together: we can see words not only written in books, but on the screen, transformed by electronics; this is a silent parable for man to understand, that he should come closer to the angel, his invisible companion who is light!

[54] Jn 1:2

indication that life and word penetrate one another as does life in the most Holy Trinity ("Perichorese"). Words do "paint" and colors "speak," they even "cry"! This is also why a word penetrates deeper into our soul if it is accompanied with a loving smile. This is the way we have to understand the few words of Our Lady of Guadalupe transmitted by the Mopohua as words of light, because at the same time they do come out of the loving, merciful eyes of Our Lady of Guadalupe.

The call of God, by means of his servant John and the holy angels,[55] has finally brought a response of love on the part of man: "Come, Lord Jesus!" This answer should be as simple and spontaneous as that of Juan Diego: even after the disillusion of the first meeting with the bishop, willing to quit, it is not difficult for our Lady to bring him back. Who could resist her loving words!

The promise, announced by St. Luis Marie Grignon de Montfort, over three hundred years ago, will soon be accomplished: the church will be renewed by the living witness of holy priests. These priests, apostles of the last times, like unto St. John the Evangelist, living in the finest union with the holy angels, are those who will carry the word of God for the last time around the word, and only then the end of all things will come.[56]

Remember that each of us, participating in the common priesthood, is sent out at the end of every Mass. And who more would like to accompany us, if we keep the Lord warm in our hearts, than Our Lady! She so much would like to join Her love to whatever we think, say and do. Whether in silence, by words or in deed, it is our mission to announce God's love in Jesus Christ to the world. In this respect, Padre Pio of Pietrelcina is a living promise of the future renovation of the priesthood.

---

[55] cf. the first three chapters of the Apocalypse
[56] cf. Mt. 24:14 It will be a word filled with light and life (the sanctity of these apostles) which will pierce the deepest darkness of a world which has lost the light of God.

Part Two

The Beauty of Revelation in Mary

Introduction

The most difficult thing for the angel is that God, Creator and Lord of heaven and earth, should bow down to the dust of this earth to lift up man from the abyss where he fell because of his sin. Only if by suffering we come to measure the incomprehensible distance between heaven and earth, between God and man, between the Holy God and us poor sinner, and the even greater distance from heaven to hell, then we will approach the dimensions, the measure, of the cross.[57]

Only then also will we be able to appreciate the dimensions of the image of Guadalupe depicting the most glorious fruit of the Redemption, which is no other than Our Lady. Only then we will know that it is really the only true icon of Our Lady and as such her "real presence" with us here on earth. Only then the glorious image will become the banner under which all children of Mary will unite in the battle against the dragon. The more her beauty will light up in us, the more she will be with us and make us invincible in the combat against the enemy whose outstanding sign, so openly revealed, in our days is ugliness.[58]

The following six meditations on the beauty of Revelation should help us to understand a little better about the folly of the cross, which is the nucleus of all beaut, best intuited in Our Lady of

---

[57] For us traditional Christians the mysteries of Redemption, by way of our education and the feasts we celebrate or commemorate, have become something we are so much used to that their their dimension of mystery and awfulness have been lost to us. We need a "shaking up" so as to better understand that they have not been entrusted to us as occasions of "worldly feasts." It seems that not even the trumpets of the Apocalypse will be able to convert us, cf. Apoc. 9:20 ff. "...and they did not convert — and this after the most terrible plagues...!

[58] Wherever there is disorder, anarchy, putrification, ugliness, even though it be hidden by a brilliant deceiving makeup, we easily are able to recognize the presence of the hellish foe.

Sorrows.[59] Even though the image is first of all that of the "glorious woman," looking deeper, we will also discover Our Lady under the Cross. The cross, as we explained before, being not only her center (in the Nahui Ollin) but also her interior form. Relating the six meditations to the six outstanding qualities or virtues of Mary will help us understand, that the Beauty of Our LADY is a powerful weapon in the combat for the reign of God. We are called to be soldiers in her army; this is why we have to acquire them and put them on like an armor.[60]

- The first meditation, *the Measure of the Cross*, is related to the first quality: SILENCE, so difficult to acquire that hardly can it be found even in religious and contemplative life of the church of today. The Beauty of the cross must be discovered, not first outwardly, but in our heart, more concretely, in Our Lord's suffering in us. Only this suffering will help transform us, little by little, in the glorious beauty of Mary. This beauty we can admire already in this time with so many, in the outside world, completely forgotten victim souls, who are allowed to share with body and soul in the sufferings of Christ for His Mystical Body the church.[61]
- The second meditation, *the Decrescent Moon as Cup of Sacrifice*, is related to the second virtue of Mary: listening. The thing

---

[59] Only those who suffer with Christ in His passion in the Mystical Body of His church will not laugh at this statement, which is the absolute opposition to the concept of beauty we find among man. Only they are able to speak of the "beauty of His wounds of His precious blood" by which we have been saved. It is the beauty of His immense love for us poor sinners.

[60] They have first been exposed in Book I as "fruit of the rosary" We have to ask again and again for the grace to have our Spiritual eyes opened for the incomprehensible beauty of Mary, which is not an outward but first of all an interior one, mirror of her being cruciform.

[61] Remember there are three degrees of suffering: the lowest is if we suffer like the animals, without knowing why and what for; the second suffering, much more valuable, is when in our sufferings we look up to Jesus CRUCIFIED and try to unite our sufferings to His; the third is when we are so void of ourselves that Christ Himself can suffer in us — this is what the victim souls are allowed to experience.

most despised and rejected in this world of ours is sacrifice. Modern man, following the inspirations of the fallen angels who did not want to deny themselves before God, has done and still is doing everything to make suffering disappear from this earth in order to establish himself in an integrally comfortable life, no longer threatened by pain. Heaven has given us a beautiful lecture on the beauty of sacrifice in the sacrificial life of the shepherd children of Fátima, who inspired by our Lady and their good angels, would not miss any occasion to "fill their cup of sacrifice to the brim."

With them, as any victim soul, we intuit a hidden quality of sacrifice which is even more folly to the world. They enjoy suffering. Their suffering therefore is not less than that of the children of this world, it might even be more acute, because they open their heart to it (they "listen" to it). But at the same time it is joy because it will unite them more intimately with Our Lord, suffering with them. They will even come to better know that it is really His suffering that they are allowed to share in.[62]

- The third meditation, *the Golden Rectangle*, related to obedience, can help us understand better that only by true obedience will we enter deeper into the order of the reign of God. As this order, built up by Christendom, is more and more consciously destroyed by the fallen angels and their human collaborators, we are called to an heroic obedience which tomorrow might even lead us to martyrdom. The real and beautiful order of the reign of God is that of the resurrection from the dead, another folly of the children of the world. Only this order of resurrection, so beautifully mirrored in the image of Our Lady of

---

[62] A beautiful story will explain this better: a group of pious pilgrims came to Padre Pio asking him if he would not let them take some part in his continual suffering in order to alleviate a little bit his burden. Smiling P. Pio replied : "If I were to give you part in them, but for a second, you would die immediately.

Guadalupe, is capable of withstanding the anarchy of hell poured out on the earth.[63]

- The fourth meditation, *the Beatitudes,* is related with the virtue of poverty (this also being the first of the Beatitudes). The church of our day has almost completely lost it, not only material, but, even more so, Spiritual poverty. We are to be open to the inspirations of the Holy Spirit, wherever we are, whatever we do, trying to be a docile instruments in His hands. If we know everything better, if we do everything by ourselves, then the angel who is called to teach us this first most-important beatitude, is made to be a stranger in our world and in the church. Only poverty will bring him back.

- The fifth mediation, *preparing the reign of Mary,* makes us look up to her Immaculate Heart, so pure, so crystalline that it is able to pass through all the graces she receives out of the heart of God. We so greatly need her virtue of sincerity to come closer to her angelical beauty! But how difficult is it to live in this time where Satan has come back on his throne as Prince of the World helping those who build up their reign of power and lie, dominating this world of ours. Are we not accustomed, still being children, to the "little lies" which help us to get out more easily of the difficulties of daily life? We even tell "pious lies" not realizing that by them we help the enemy build up his reign ever more solidly. We are all in need of purification!

- The last meditation should help us to "raise our eyes to heaven," looking up to *the new Jerusalem* coming down as the last perfection of this creation. How much we need the help of our good angel who always hangs at the face of God, even in the deepest darkness of this earth, in order to persevere looking up to heaven; how much we need FIDELITY in a world which offers new at-

---

[63] Pope Leo XIII, instituting the exorcism against Satan and the fallen Spirits and the prayer to St. Michael after Holy Mass, was the first to officially come to know about the last and most decisive attack of hell against the church and mankind. Since Vatican II, we have forgotten to defend ourselves against our mortal enemy, and the open doors leave free entry to the enemy whenever he wants. Hell has been unleashed, and if we haven't yet realized, World War I and II have the same author as does the establishment the "one world government" of our day.

tractions every day, which artificially tries to increase our hunger for new things, for change. How much we need to learn from Our Lady to remain faithful under the cross, even though the whole world wants to tear us away from this only secure place in all the chaotic order of things. Do not forget to look up to her, try to hide in her loving and merciful eyes and you will learn!

The "Measure" of the Cross

Although the Apocalypse, like the Gospel of St. John, starts in heaven, it should unfold already here on earth, in the victorious glory of the "seven communities of Asia."[64] The church is the first to be called before the tribunal of God[65] and then, as in concentric circles which reach out over all of creation and mankind, the Judgment will extend to the whole world. No one will escape, not a single community nor a single person: all will have to meet the fire of a zealous God, Who wills to see His Son wherever He looks upon the earth; a will and a search that first of all aims at seeing Mary. This is the preeminent reason why the church of the last times and each member of it must become "one hundred percent Marian." He wants to see in us her celestial beauty. Only in, with and through Mary under the cross will we find favor with God.

Mary as the created "criteria of God's beauty" is the measure God will apply to His church. This measure is given into the hand of St. John, so close to Our Lady in the symbol of the rod: "to measure the temple, the altar and those who adore in it."[66] Even though the angels are sent to execute the judgment of God, it is not they who do the measuring. It is given to the disciple closest to

---

[64] We recall from Book II that the seven communities are images of how the church of the last times will be.

[65] "the judgment will begin with the church" cf. 1 Pt 4,17 , and it seems that it has started precisely in the moment that Communion in the hand started. We need the help of the angels to understand better, that the "last judgment" is not only in "the last moment," but it has a dynamic dimension, precisely that which is exposed in the Apocalypse.

[66] Rv 11:1f

Our Lord who has come to know the measure of the Lord, he who lay inclined on his Sacred heart. In a glorious perspective, this measure is that of the new Jerusalem.[67] The first time St. John discovered this glorious measure was when he looked at the "measure" of the linen cloth telling him about the mystery of the Resurrection of Christ.[68]

It is the measure of the cross by which man, material creation and angel will become one. It is present in a veiled way in the image of Our Lady of Guadalupe, apparent in the "golden proportion."[69] Only by the way of the cross and crucified with Our Lord will creation come to its consummation, and so reflect the beauty of God. This is what the apocalyptic Mass wants to tell us: only by this measure will we enter into the house of the eternal Father.

The Decrescent Moon in the Image as a Sacrificial Paten

Another common denominator between the Apocalypse and the image of Our Lady of Guadalupe is the symbol of the decrescent moon at her feet. Mary is standing on the non-visible part of the moon, that crescent which is dark in the night sky, because it does not reflect the light of the sun. Figuratively, Our Lady herself is compared with the moon: the fourth day of creation tells us of the creation of the two great lights, the sun and the moon, to serve as "signs, seasons, days and years," so also

---

[67] The measure of the wall of the new Jerusalem is a measure by man and angel: all things will be measured according to the ORDER of INCARNATION in Christ. In a mysterious way, the angel must have his part in it! cf. Rv 21:17 "And he measured its wall of one hundred and forty cubits, man's measure, that is angel's measure."

[68] John 20:8 He really has the "measure of the Lord" in himself, so wherever he looks "with the eye of the eagle" he discovers Him. Juan Diego received the same "eye": he is Our Lady's messenger as eagle. It is the "eye of justice" who will not only see reformed according to the order of the reign of God but by seeing will help to establish it amidst a chaotic world.

[69] cf. Book VII.

are Our Lord and Our Lady likened unto to these two great lights respectively.

As the moon reflects the light of the sun, so does Our Lady reflect the light of God. In this case, the dark decrescent moon is a symbol that the light of the sun reflected on the moon has yet to cover this last dark element, because only then will the glory of Mary, already so much visible in the image of Our Lady of Guadalupe, have reached its fullness. This is another hint to remind us of the apocalyptic dimension of this image, because in this perspective the decrescent moon becomes a symbol that the last times, those of the battle of the "woman" against the serpent, have definitely begun in 1531.

The "open book" is covering part of the decrescent moon. In the icons, the "open book" in the hands of the Pantocrator is a symbol that He is the One Who will come to judge the living and the dead, and the fact that it is open tells us that this time is already upon us. So the "book" at the feet of Our Lady signifies clearly that she is preparing the way for the last coming of the Lord, Who by the sword of His word, will definitely cast the devil into hell, because in this perspective the moon is the symbol of the enemy of God who, by the force of the light of God, will disappear.

There is another symbolism of the moon which gives us a bridge over to the Apocalypse as "an apocalyptic Mass." The decrescent moon can also be seen as a paten, and Our Lady, "Teotokos," is offered to God by the child who is found beneath her, clinging to the hem of her gown and mantle. Together with Juan Diego and all the saints in heaven, we should continually offer Our Lady to God, remind-

ing Him that He should not wait any longer and send Our Lady to put her foot on the head of the serpent who holds mankind captive in these last times.

We should soberly recognize that the dark hair of the boy touches the decrescent moon; this tells us that only by the sacrifice of our intellect can we make such an offering to God. If we only look deeper in the image of Our Lady, we will discover a glorious perspective of the Holy Mass: Mary is the perfect fruit of the sacrifice of Christ on Golgotha. The combat of light and darkness on her robe, her position in the form of a cross, the aura around her all corroborate this symbolic interpretation.

Once we have this intuition with the image, as well as with the Book of the Apocalypse, it is no longer difficult to accept this last book of the Bible as representing: "the Mass on the world"[70] which will finally transform the entire creation into the glory of the new Jerusalem depicted in chapter 21 of the Apocalypse. It is the "sacrifice" of Our Lady under the cross which has to be consummated in a mystical way by the Church[71] and all its members. The proclamation of Mary as "Co-Redemptrix" will come only when a larger part of the church will recognize that our most efficient part in our salvation is in these times, not in the evangelization by the word, but in the hidden sacrifice of reparation for the sins of the world, and this: with, in and through Mary.

In the western perspective, the boy at Our Lady's feet represents an angel, and it reminds us that the holy angels also have their part in this final "Mass on the world," and this not only in their mission as Guardian Angels at our side,[72] but precisely in

---

[70] This recalls "La Messe sur le Monde" of Teilhard de Chardin, certainly also an apocalyptic intuition of this so-often misinterpreted Jesuit author.

[71] cf. Col "...make up what is lacking in the sufferings of Christ" for His Mystical Body, the church.

[72] The accompanying of us Christians, so often far from God on our earthly pilgrimage, is really a way of cross for the angels, by which they are previleged to participate in the mystery of salvation in Christ. We should also note that both hands of the boy stick to the golden hem of her mantle on one side and of her gown on the other. The part of the mantle he clings to by way of the presence of the constellation of Taurus speaks clearly about the necessity of sacrifice. The other part of the gown, again pointed like an arrow, tells us about the victory in this final combat. Remember that we symbolically interpreted this part precisely as the Book of the Apocalypse.

their apocalyptic mission as we find it in the Apocalypse. The consummation of this world will come only if mankind will have exhausted the measure of the sufferings of Christ on the cross. Just as the angel brought the chalice of strength to Our Lord in agony in the garden of Gethsemane, so too does it belong to the angels to give us strength to bear the burden of the sacrifice in this last combat.[73]

The Golden Rectangle

Fibonacci's law in the image

The finding and attainment of the perfect balance and symmetry of composition, the "golden rectangle," can be considered "the great artistic quest" which has pervaded the world's cultures. Although particularly true of western art, it is also noted with the Mesopotanian, Egyptian, Greek and Roman Art forms. It has the same importance as the number 6, the Greek letter *Phi*, and Fibonacci's law.[74] The scope of this "golden aesthetics" extends itself to the ends of creation, marveled at in the astronomic photo-

---

[73] This multiple interpretation of symbols is another example for the depth of the message of Our Lady of Guadalupe.

[74] The "golden section" is a line segment that has been divided into two parts in such a way that the ratio of the longer part (a) to the shorter part (b) is equal to the ratio of the entire segment (a+b) to the longer part (a). a/b = (a+b)/a = *Phi* = 1.618 . The "golden rectangle" is based on the same principles, its adjacent sides with lengths in the golden ratio.

graphs of far-off galaxies and the beauty of precision in the most basic biological expressions in nature: in plants, shells, even the human form.

In the course of the centuries, primarily for the purpose of ac-commodating it to a variety of frames, the tilma of Juan Diego has been stretched and cut, such that it no longer forms that "perfect rect-angle"; but the properties of the "golden rectangle" help us to once again find the original position of the image on the tilma. It is be-lieved that the adjustments made, fitting the tilma to its various frames throughout history, is that which gives it the impression of leaning forward. It has been sug-gested that the vertical seam unit-ing the two pieces of hemp of the tilma may very well in fact be the true vertical center. This hypothesis as a base, along with the appli-cation of simple geometrical principles, assists in finding what are believed to be the original dimensions of the image.

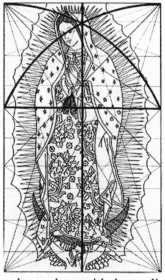

A perpendicular and equi-distant line from the vertical seam center to the right and left sides allows the construction of the first side of a perfect square (lower part of the image). Using the lateral mid-point and a compass, a rectangle in the upper region is then made, thus making it possible to identify the original real dimen-sions of the tilma, those which amazingly correspond to the crite-ria of the "golden rectangle." Another corresponding golden rect-angle in the lower region of the image can also be made by apply-ing the initial measurements. All the lines formed by the dimen-sions of "golden rectangle," with a little attention, are noted as passing through important details of the image. Diagonals of 15, 30, 45, 60, 75, and 90 degrees can be made from each of the four corners. The same, in turn, are intercepted horizontally and verti-cally, meeting their corresponding point and confirming the per-fect and overall harmony of the entire image.

Many geometrical figures are formed: triangles, circles, curves north to south and east to west, all having corresponding and symmetrical counterparts. Not only will the trained eye recognize the balance of the corresponding geometric proportions, corroborating the unity that exists between the upper portion of the Virgin, and the lower portion with the combined values of the angel, the moon and the horizontal portion of the tunic, but all who begin to enter into the appreciation of the beauty of God will recognize that, "Indeed, the image of Our Lady of Guadalupe reflects the beauty and perfection of God." With Pope Benedict XIV we can echo Psalm 147: *"God has not done such with any other nation!"*

There exist nine divisions on the central seam that seem to serve a unique function, perhaps even correlate in the Spiritual dimension to the hierarchy of the nine angelic choirs. Unaware of the presence of the "golden rectangle," it is easy to overlook them or not even recognize them. They show up on the image as little dark spots. The first can be found near the center of the angel's forehead, above the angel's left eye. The second is located in the next shaded area where the horizontal fold of Mary's tunic and the central seam meet, just above the seventh of the nine large flowers. The third is near Our Lady's left knee. The fourth is determined by

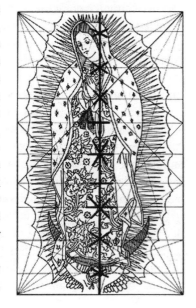

a dark point visible both on the original and in copies. The fifth, seemingly to be the center of the entire figure, corresponds to the shape of the five-pointed star. The sixth, less noticeable, is found on the central fold of Our Lady's mantle, beneath her left sleeve, the large dark region of the left-hand ermine cuff marks the seventh. The eighth is a black mark where the seam and her ermine collar meet. Finally, the ninth correlates with the first star on Our Lady's head.

The actual figure of Our Lady on the tilma is 56³/₈ inches, however lighting gives the impression that she is taller. Her bearing is that of a demure young lady, her complexion is suntanned, her cheeks rosy, her eyes down-cast, but so alive that one might expect them to move at any moment. Her hair is like ebony and her hands have an aspect of gentility. In the rock home of Our Lady in Ephesus, within the chamber believed to be Mary's bedroom, one will encounter a painting on a broken tile dated around the 4th century. It is said to have been painted from a description by St. Epiphanius, quoted by Nicephorus. This description, sketched in the fourth century, from traditions now effaced, and in manuscripts no longer possessed, is the only one that has come down to us:

"The Virgin ... was not tall of stature, though her height was a little above the middle size; her color, slightly bronzed, like that of the Sulamite, by the sun of her country, had the rich tint of ripe ears of corn; her eyes lively, the pupil being rather of an olive color, her eyebrows perfectly arched and black; her nose, remarkably perfect, was aquiline; her lips rosy; the shape of her face a fine oval; her hands and fingers long. She was utterly full of divine grace and loveliness."

The resemblance between these two paintings thousands of miles and over a 1000 years apart is amazing! We found that superimposing transparent overlays one on the other, all facial features correspond exactly. Finally, we have the simple comment by St. Bernadette: *"My Lady is beautiful, beautiful beyond compare; so beautiful that when one has seen her once, one would wish to die so as to see her again: so beautiful that when one has seen her, one can no longer love anything earthly."*

Meditating more on structure of the golden rectangle it is possible to transcend the geometrical details in their symbolism; we only enter more deeply in one significant detail: the vertical line, coinciding with the seam of her robe with nine points of intersection that we interpret as *nine steps of growth towards God.* The nine points can certainly be interpreted in different ways as we did with the large flowers. Here we recognize them as nine steps towards the Spiritual birth of man into heaven. They also remind us of the three-times-three circles of the Rosary, as seen from the central mystery of the rosary: the crowning with thorns, the Lord despised as "Ecce homo" — "Behold the man!" It is this "hidden king" who will defeat Satan and make him fall from his throne as "prince of this world.[75] This is why the most important intersection is the fifth. It coincides exactly with the falling five-pointed star, symbol for the rebellious angels being cast down from heaven. The last intersection over the head of the boy coincides with one of the stars of the constellation Orion, "glorious light," and the first one with the last star of the constellation Ophiucus, "the Serpent Holder." By way of her true and humble servants, the "saints of the last times," represented in the boy under her feet, Our Lady really comes to crush the head of the serpent. This is the glorious promise of the image of Our Lady!

Here, let us remember again our meditation on the harmonious construction of the rosary, parallel to the golden rectangle. Both of them make visible a holy rhythm of construction in continuation with the instruction of Yahweh for the construction of the Ark of the Covenant. Here we should remember the Lord's word with St. John: *"This is eternal life, to know the One True God...."*[76] It is only by way of the Holy Eucharist [77] that we will come to this knowledge of God and grow into eternal life.

It is important to recall that there are "two centers" of the image: the first in the four-petalled flower is the center of the person of Our Lady, the second is the center of the image — the falling five-pointed star, rresuming the drama of the history of salvation. In the image the solution of this drama is already indicated: "the lion of the tribe of Judah has triumphed," "the Prince of Tyre" (image for Lucifer's pride) is definitely thrown into hell.[78]

We should remember soberly that the "line of birth" to heaven passes through this central point. Each man in the power of the Incarnation of Christ has to overcome the power of hell present in us by sin. This is why our birth towards the triumph of the lion of Judah is necessarily a painful one. We also need to pass the central mystery of the sorrowful mysteries of the rosary: the "Ecce Homo." Christ did not overcome the enemy with the weapons of this world,

---

[75] cf. Book Six

[76] Jn 17:3

[77] cf. Book IV

[78] cf. Ez 28:1-10, *vs. 8

but by His suffering present in the history of salvation, in the impotence of the Holy Eucharist. Only if we are "burden bearers" like the boy at the feet of Our Lady will we have part in this victory of the Son of God over the first created angel and his followers. The heaviest burden which we have to carry is the Lord Himself in the species of the Holy Bread. It is Mary, who is sent as the first burden bearer to help us carry this precious treasure.

Finally, this birth into heaven can also be understood as an image of the way of purification in Purgatory. The smallest inkling of the knowledge of God is all that is necessary for the grace of a perfect contrition and entry into Purgatory.[79] Contrition is the most powerful weapon against Satan. The tiny spark of an ardent contrition, of not having loved a most loving God, will become a flame burning out all the darkness of the soul, transforming the whole man into the knowledge of God: Who is burning fire. Only in this fire the creation will come to its consummation and awake in eternal beauty in the new city of Jerusalem, symbol for the creation definitely united with God. The triple creation of angel, man and material creation finds its consummation in the beauty of Our Lady which can already be admired here in her image of Guadalupe. The reign of Mary, revealed in the apparition of Our Lady, should already begin here on earth. We are called to collaborate in it according to the measure of our purification, because only if we have overcome the enemy in us, will we be able with and through Our Lady and the holy angels to incarnate this reign of beauty, which will bring an end to the domination of Satan and his reign of ugliness.

---

[79] Indicated by the star on the head of the boy.

Another Interpretation of this Way of Growth into God is:

The Beatitudes as "Convenant" with the Heart of God

The Beatitudes are another way of birth to God. They can be seen in the vertical line of the golden rectangle. The first beatitude corresponds with the first intersection on the head of the boy at the feet of Our Lady: In order to serve the plan of mercy of God in Our Lady we must be *"poor in Spirit."* The last beatitude, coinciding with the ninth intersection on Our Lady's head, is our victory over the serpent. Relating them to the nine large golden flowers, they follow the "movement of ransom." They are like a vine which has its roots not on earth, but in the heart of the triune God. In this way the Beatitudes are like an organic growth in sanctity, but it is a growth first into the depths, into darkness and incomprehensibility, a way in complete opposition to the world.

- The first three Beatitudes correspond to the three flowers superimposed on the solar plexus of Our Lady. They are like the roots of our sanctity in the triune God, especially in the Father.[80] The first, *"Blessed are the poor in Spirit, for theirs is the kingdom of God,"* reminds us that our way to sanctity begins in complete self denial. It begins in God Himself. Any other fundament will not suffice, *"the house must be built on the rock."*[81]
- The second Beatitude, *"Blessed are those who mourn, for they will be consoled,"* is the challenge to enter the way of the cross of the Lord. This is why we will mourn in the beginning, but the Lord promises that His *"yoke is easy and His burden is light."* (Mt 11:30)
- The third Beatitude, *"Blessed are the meek, for they will inherit the earth,"* reiterates the law of "non-violence." There is no way "to conquer the earth" with the arms of this world because they are arms of injustice and murder.

---

[80] Also correlated to the first of the three classical stages in the Spiritual life — "purgative."

[81] cf. Mt 7:24-27

- The second three Beatitudes should be related to the Son in a trinitarian way. They tell us of the sentiments of the Son of God in His humble mission to bring us back to the Father. The three flowers corresponding to these Beatitudes descend into the darkness of the right side of the gown of Our Lady. This is a clear sign that this stage of growth into the sanctity of God is especially painful and dark; we will find our way only if we are leaning on the staff of the cross.[82]

- The fourth Beatitude, *"Blessed are they who hunger and thirst for justice, for they will be satisfied,"* soberly tells us that on this earth there is no way of arriving at complete justice. Justice is a promise that will be fulfilled only when we have reached "our mansion" in the Father, when finally we are, after all the confusion of this world, in the right place.

- The fifth Beatitude, *"Blessed are the merciful, they will know mercy,"* is a continual challenge to never rely on whatever we are or what we did, to never judge anything accept in the light of the mercy of God; only if we become children of mercy in the Son are we sure that we will find the door to the heart of the Lord wherever we may be.

Here, at the center of the nine Beatitudes, we should recall that the preceding Beatitudes are always part of the following: not to judge and to rely only on the mercy of God presupposes "poverty of Spirit," signifies "mourning," because nobody will understand us; it is a challenge to renounce any violence and is an unquenchable "thirst for the justice of God."

- The sixth Beatitude, *"Blessed are the pure of heart, for they will see God,"* is the promise that even in the darkness of sin and the confusion in the reign of Satan, we will always find a path of light following the steps of Our Lord Jesus Christ Who has crossed over this "vale of tears" and with His cross has opened the gates of heaven. This sixth Beatitude is already the turning point where the "movement" into the depths, crossing the dark-

---

[82] Also correlated to the second classical stage in the life of Spiritual growth — "illuminative."

ness of sin on the right side, is turning over to the side of light on the left side, becoming an upward "movement."

The last three Beatitudes have their correlation first of all to the Holy Spirit Who will bring salvation to its consummation in the fullness of the light of God.[83]

- The seventh Beatitude is *"Blessed are the peacemakers, for they will be called sons of God."* The peace of God is not that of the world, a peace secured through violence and suppression. It is the peace of Our Lord Jesus Christ Who has overcome and so won the victory over the powers of darkness. This can also be seen in the flower found on the left side of what we call the "book." The cross has become a sword piercing the wall of darkness and breaking into the light of God.
- The eighth Beatitude, *"Blessed are those who suffer persecution for the sake of justice, for theirs is the reign of heaven,"* has the same promise as the first Beatitude. Again we must remember that in the sequence of the Beatitudes, all the antecedents form part of the following: only in poverty of Spirit, the justice of God will find its right place in our hearts. This justice of God is the clearest sign of the presence of the reign of heaven here on earth. It is like an oasis in the desert of injustice and violence. Here again, especially in and with Christ, we are lifting up the cross on the soil of this earth as the sign of the incomprehensible justice of God. This justice will push out the last shadow of darkness which is seen at the right side of the eighth flower, making the enigmatic shadow fall.[84]
- The ninth Beatitude, *"Blessed are you when men reproach you, and persecute you, and, speaking falsely, say all manner of evil against you, for My sake. Rejoice and exult, because your reward is great in heaven; for so did they persecute the prophets who were before you..."* is a three-fold Beatitude and therefore

---

[83] Also a correlation with the third classical stage — "unitive."

[84] The shadow looks like a man, with hands thrown up, falling into the depths. He has no face, because Satan has no name before God anymore; he is only negation, nothing.

a sign that we have obtained the peak of sanctity: the Heart of the triune God.

Looking up to God with the face of an angel while being stoned to death by the Jews, St. Stephen irradiates this last Beatitude. If we reach this point we are already in the "net" of Our Lady, formed by the fold in her mantle. We are part of the "135" fish caught on the occasion of the last apparition of Our Lord on the Lake of Tiberius.[85] This is the symbolic number of the saints as Adrienne Speyer explains: The triune God (1=3) by way of the five wounds of the Son of God is the last cause of our sanctity, only He is holy.

Preparing the Reign of Mary

The following interpretation recapitulates the "combined perspective" of our meditations on the apparition of Our Lady of Guadalupe, that is, beyond the traditional European as well as of the Aztec comprehension of the image. As the fathers of the church, with respect to sacred scripture, it has been our aim to enter the "sensus plenior," the deeper sense of the image, so as to make this apparition more transparent to the second coming of Christ, the Son of God, in view of Whom everything has been created to the greater glory of the Father.

The interpretation is based on the Apocalypse. The word "apocalypse" specifically means revelation. It is thus that everything in it has part in the transparency of the visible world to the invisible world of God and His angels: the "outward face of things" has become sign for the invisible reality of the Spirit which otherwise could not be understood. This "fuller interpretation" is the angelic way of perceiving this world as image of the triune God. The more we come together with our angel, the more we will be able to participate in it and so learn what the angel calls: "to look through." This is why we were able to profit even from the "discoveries" of modern science in relation to the image of Our Lady and tried to embody them in an integral interpretation of the whole of the image.

---

[85] cf. Jn 21:11

Let us remember:

**The ultimate goal of the new evangelization
is to establish the reign of Mary.**

*This is why we have to look out for the invisible
helpers for this reign: the holy angels.*

In our day and age, man is in the center. He thinks himself autonomous and self-sufficient, forgetting about "the two major companions" at his side: material creation and the angels. Without the assistance and collaboration of the other two created worlds he cannot realize himself according to God's plan. This is why, in this fifth centennial of evangelization to the New World, it is a matter of gratitude to remember the invisible help of the holy angels who, with the Spaniards and their conquest, partook in the liberation of the New World from the captivity of the devil.

They will help to bring about the final liberation of the whole universe from the plague of the fallen angels. They are the first created creatures, called after the trial in the beginning of times to collaborate in the construction of this universe; they were called to prepare the way of Our Lord Jesus Christ and to accompany Him; they prepare the way for Christ the King, coming as the judge of the living and the dead.

*TLAXCALA - "Tortilla" -
House of Bread*

The most tangible proof of their presence in the conquest of Mexico is the presence of their images in several different churches in the Diocese of Tlaxcala,[86] the "cradle of evangelization." Not only can the oldest pulpit of the New World be seen in the cathedral of Tlaxcala, but its very name, "Tlaxcala," is a transparent correlation to Bethlehem, the "House of Bread" from which came forth Jesus, the Bread of Life. This is to remind us that

---

[86] The first Diocese in the New World was in Tlaxcala, Tlaxcala.

the final intercession of the angels is by and through the Eucharistic Lord.

Even as the holy angels helped in the conquest of the continent for the Christian faith, so also can we count on their assistance in the new evangelization through Mary, simply in beseeching their assistance. This is their apocalyptic mission: to prepare the reign of Mary on earth; a prerequisite of the second coming of Our Lord Jesus Christ! This is why the image of Our Lady, *"clothed with the sun and the moon under her feet and the crown of twelve stars,"* is a symbol of the reign of Mary and the consummation of the church on earth. Symbolically this reign is present in the large flowers on her robe. As these flowers are in the form of a heart this reign of Mary will be the triumph of her Immaculate Heart by: non-violence.

We do not use this word in the political sense, hiding the strategy to weaken the enemy in order to overcome him more easily. The non-violence of Ghandi proved to be a powerful arm against the English domination and rule in India. Non-violence can never co-exist with injustice. As we understand it, non-violence lines up with the laws of creation as well with those of salvation. As spring draws near, we see the little snowbell piercing the cover of ice, opening its blossom to the sun. As in contradiction, we might say: "non-violence is the way of the violence of God." Its most glorious expression is in the "Magnificat" of Mary, reflection of the impotence of the Lord on the cross, bringing the final victory over all injustice and violence. God respects the poor, the feeble and the sinner; this truth is emphasized in many of the parables of the Lord, especially with St. Luke.

The reign of the Immaculate Heart is a reign of love symbolized in the merciful glance of Our Lady of Guadalupe. It is the last offer of the mercy of God in the first of the angels of judgment who cries out *"Fear God, and give Him honor, for the hour of His judgment has come...."*[87] The angels who follow him are already angels of inexorable justice. "reign of mercy" means a reign in which all traces of unjust violence have vanished, because violence as

---

[87]   Rv 14:7

expression of the power of sin is the most outstanding characteristic of the reign of Satan.

St. John points to this reign of mercy when he says,

> *"But to as many as receive Him He gave the power of becoming sons of God; to those who believe in His Name: who were born not of blood, nor of the will of the flesh, nor of the will of man, but of God."*[88]

The family of Lazarus in Bethany was the hearth that Our Lord Jesus Christ chose as a place and moment of rest before entering into His passion. It is a most lucid expression and promise of the reign of Mary. It is a reign not propagated so much by the word, as by the example of a life in the love of Christ. It is to this reign that one should apply the words of Our Lord:

> *"A new commandment I give you, that you love one another: that as I have loved you, you also love one another. By this will all men know that you are my disciples, if you have love for one another."*[89]

The "new evangelization" should make present this reign of love, not so much by the word, but by the example of a saintly life. It is only the love we receive from God that will discover and lift all human values into the light of God. In the reign of Mary, the holy church will incorporate all the genuine values of all religions and cultures throughout the world, for the greater glory of God! This is the deeper aim of what today we call, in a very technical and abstract way, inculturization. It is not an adaptation of the Christian truths to a particular culture as some purport, but rather *a lifting up of the truths of religion and culture into the light of God where they will show their particular splendor.*

It is in the reign of Mary that the most profound promise of Our Lady of Guadalupe will be fulfilled in its zenith: "I am the Mother of all those, in these lands, who wish to be one."[90]

---

[88] Jn 1:12-13
[89] Jn 13:34
[90] cf. Nican Mopohua, vs. 30

Ecumenism is not primarily a matter of theologians of different religions coming together to create a new uniform religion. This is precisely what the antichrist will try to do: offer us a religion adapted to the welfare of this world. Union in the truth of Christ is only possible in the *"great sign"* which is Mary. *"great sign"* refers to its radiance, splendor and the presence of all the holy angels helping her to fulfill the ardent desire of the Sacred heart of Our Lord:

> *"...that all may be one, even as thou, Father, in me and I in thee; that they also may be one in us...."*[91]

The New Jerusalem

> *"Then I saw a new heaven and a new earth.*
> *The first heaven and the first earth had disappeared now*
> *and there was no longer any sea.*
> *I saw the holy city and the new Jerusalem*
> *coming down from God from heaven*
> *as beautiful as a bride adorned for her husband."*[92]

The "new heaven and new earth" is already present in the image of Our Lady of Guadalupe.

• The "new heaven" is reflected in the constellations of the mantle of Our Lady, as a gospel of light, singing the glories of God in His universe. Here, the stars are also symbols of the angels, the "engineers of creation," the invisible helpers of Our Lord Jesus Christ in salvation and the loving Spirits under the command of the Holy Spirit who prepare the triple creation for the "the heavenly banquet."

The "New heaven" is first of all an order of light and love, best symbolized in *"the sea mingled with fire;"*[93] water as symbol of creation and fire as symbol of God's love have united.

---

[91] Jn 17:21
[92] Rv 21:22
[93] cf. Rv 15:2

This is already indicated in the golden stars of the blue mantle of Our Lady, because she is the synthesis also of the "new heaven" coming down from God as the "new Jerusalem."

- The "new earth" is indicated by her earth-toned gown. In particular the left side where the light has overcome all darkness, where the ninth large flower is the most eloquent symbol of the consummation of the covenant of God with man. The nine large golden flowers again remind us that the covenant of God with man is something that has to grow in our hearts. The superimposed flowers are a clear sign that man's last perfection is a work of grace, a pure gift of God which in no way can be obtained by man's earthly existence.

Being a symbol of the action of the angels with man, the flowers are like the "brick stones" for the building of the new Jerusalem by means of the material of this world. As beauty, they give form to all seeming chaos on the brown gown of Our Lady. The holy angels will help everything and every man find his right place in the pattern of the love of God.

The book at the feet of Our Lady, opened up by the boy who holds it, is an eloquent symbol that at the end the deepest mysteries of the love of God will be revealed to those who stretch out their arms in surrender and adoration to God. The book with the two golden flowers imposed, representing the old and the new covenant, is to remind us that Our Lady is the Gospel of the love of God in which the four other Gospels become one:

Mary is the consumated gospel of God,
in the new Jerusalem. In her the Beatitudes
have come to life and glory.

Here we should admire the immense patience of God
preparing the coming down of the new Jerusalem
There are seven steps:

- The first image of the new Jerusalem is that of Our Lady in the heart of God in view of His Son to be incarnated.[94]

---

[94] cf. Gen 3:15

- The second is that of the Garden of Eden surrounded by the four rivers[95] which symbolize the three currents of life, force and love. The fourth current is that of salvation.[96]
- The third image is that of the ark of Noah.[97]
- The fourth image is that of the ark with its measures as they were given to Moses.[98]
- The fifth image is that of the temple of Jerusalem.
- The sixth is that of the house of the church on its pilgrimage over the earth.
- The seventh is that of the Holy City Jerusalem coming down from heaven.

As it is with all Christian truth, being truths of incarnation and thus necessarily of opposition, we are reminded that the new Jerusalem is not only coming down from heaven, but at the same time, attracted and formed by the Holy Spirit, is slowly coming forth from this earth, precisely as response to the call of God's love, received in its fullness in Mary in the plenitude of time. This is why it has to grow also in the souls of the faithful and in the church as a whole, until it will finally become visible in all its glory, here on this earth, as seen in the ninth large flower: the entire church will be totally penetrated by the Gift of "Piety," a "piety" now to be called "beatitude." The church has become "Corpus Mariae Mysticum" and so is ready to receive in her womb Christ; the Son of God, in His fullness ("Pleroma").

The large golden superimposed flowers are symbols of the forging action of the Holy Spirit. By means of the holy angels, God will have carved out the face of Christ on the face of every man, and mankind as a whole, so as to enter into heaven. Here the promise of the prophets, that God will put his law into the hearts of men[99] has been fulfilled. The holy city is to be a reality in every heart as well as in mankind called to share in God. By way of the

---

[95] cf. Gen 3
[96] cf. Ez 40-42 and 47:1-12 the four currents in detail
[97] cf. Gen 6:14-16
[98] cf. Ex 25:10-11
[99] cf. Jer 31:33 and Ez 36:26-27

Beatitudes the Holy City has always lived in the saints, but now, at the end of times, has to live integrally in each member: only "beatified" will we enter heaven.

The Beatitudes as the Structure of the new Jerusalem

Our Lady comes from the east, the region of the rising sun, symbol for the light of God and His never ending love. She has her face turned to the west, to bring the gospel to all those millions in Asia who still lack the light of the word of God. The dark side of her gown is orientated to the north, symbol of combat against the powers of darkness. The light side of her gown is merged in the victorious light of the south, the region of most light. This way she represents the holy city of new Jerusalem as described in the Apocalypse.[100] The following relation of the nine Beatitudes to the new Jerusalem is nothing else but a simple coordination of the Beatitudes, according to their significance to the corresponding corner or walls of the holy city.

St. Matthew, with the eyes of the living being, the "Angel," lets us see through the words of the Sermon of the Mount to the glorious promise of consummation in the new Jerusalem. If we look up the beginning of the Sermon on the Mountain[101] we should fix our attention to the following significant details:

- The Lord ascends a mountain — practically going away from the multitude.
- He sits down (certainly on a stone like a throne).
- He is surrounded only by His disciples.
- Only then He starts to speak to them: announcing the "Magna Charta of the New Testament."

---

[100] 21:13 — Not the sequence from the east to the north then to the south, finally to the west. The three doors on each side corresponding to the twelve apostles represent always the three Divine Persons, in a trinitarian "rhythm" — four times the triune God looks out into the corresponding direction of the wind — and looking through the eyes of God will bring creation home!

[101] Mt. 5:1 ff

In this way it is clear that this is a "law" not for everyone, but first of all for those who by pure grace of God are called to follow the Lord as closely as possible. As with St. Matthew, the Lord being seen in the perspective of the angel, necessarily is the Lord of the angels. This imitation is challenged to be a angelical one, symbolized also by the mountain where Our Lord ascends. This is also revealed by the "angelical structure not only of the Beatitudes but the whole Sermon on the Mount,[102] moreover the whole Gospel in its "systematic way" of exposing the good news.

As the message of Guadalupe is like the "promulgation" of the "third covenant," already realized in Our Lady, the image and the Nican Mopohua alike must reflect this "angelical structure," not by words but this time by the image, e.g. in its full realization. It is the final invitation to mankind to enter in Mary in whom the whole of salvation is already consummated.

How is this house of glory constructed? Following the sequence of the Beatitudes, we have to remember that the most important elements of a house to be constructed are the four corners. So it is with the city of God: the city of God in the church, and the City of God in the little "church" of our hearts. This is why necessarily the first four Beatitudes should be related to the corners of the new Jerusalem. They are really cornerstones, on which the whole weight of glory should rest.

The first Beatitude *"Blessed are the poor in Spirit for theirs is the kingdom of God"* best fits into the northwest corner. Spiritually, here is the place where the last battle (therefore: west) against the enemy (therefore north) is waged by those who want to become one with the will of God. God can use them in His Son as "souls of sacrifice," ready to be even martyrs for Christ like the protomartyr St. Stephen. Only in sacrifice will we be able to realize the deepest union with Our Crucified Lord. "Poverty of Spirit" is a disposition for any sacrifice God may ask of us. It is a total dependence on the guidance of the Holy Spirit by way of our good Guardian Angel. By way of the sacrificial souls the light of God shines a last time (west) into the darkness (north).

---

[102] cf. Lectures on the Synoptics, Anapolis 1986, manuscript of Miguel Guadalupe.

In the human heart, this will be the final separation of light and darkness: those who receive this "last word of God" will enter into the light (south); those who do not renounce the infertile works of sin will definitely fall into the abyss of darkness. This is the way the Incarnation of the word is explained in the Prologue of St. John: The word became flesh (east), but man did not accept it (north), so he could not enter into the light of God and so become "sons of God" and stand up in the final combat for the reign of God in the west.

The next Beatitude according to the way indicated by the description of the holy Jerusalem[103] is to the southeast: *"Blessed are those who weep, for they shall be comforted." "They are those who come out of the great tribulation, they have washed their garments in the Blood of the Lamb. This is why they now stand before the throne of God and serve Him day and night in His temple."*[104] They have left the darkness of sin and violence behind, with all the suffering they had to go through in the north, now they are comforted in the light of God in silent adoration before the Holy God. Man bows down before the majesty of God, inclined by the power of the cross, of suffering, in adoration and silence. It is not the "mourning of the world," which loudly cries out in self pity, it is the silent mourning of those women who with Our Lady and St. John persevered under the cross in the power of the Holy Spirit.[105] The deeper suffering is born in the depths of our hearts, the greater the merit. The silent tears of man enter deeper into the Heart of God.

---

[103] cf. Rv 21:13

[104] cf. 7:14f

[105] We should remember that the gift of the Holy Spirit extends over the whole time of the Lord's apostolate, becoming more and more powerful in the time of His passion, and finally poured out on the whole church on Pentecost. Not only blood and water came out of Our Lord's opened heart, but invisbly already the Holy Spirit, especially on those who did not forsake the Lord. It is this same Spirit who through Mary and John little by little brought the apostles together again and made them understand by the words and the apparition of Our Lord the deeper "why" of the suffering of Christ.

The presence of the Holy Spirit is symbolically indicated by the south. He is the One who will little by little enlighten our hearts to overcome all "mourning."

These first two beatitudes form a diagonal in the quadrangle of the holy city. The following two must follow the same "rhythm." The "X" structure, by means of the first four Beatitudes, is one of fortification, making the corners immovable. It is thus that they become "towers," resisting all attacks.[106] The walls have only to be filled in by bricks or other material.

The third Beatitude then is found in the northeast: the light, the fire of God, expects the answer of the whole man in truth. We recall the harsh sentence on Ananias and Saphira.[107] We will only be able to enter heaven when we are purified like God. Truth is never a mere matter of fact. We must fight for it. It must first be conquered from the powers of darkness/untruth (north), and then we are to defend it by remaining faithful to God (east). As truth is God's privilege, man can have part in it only if he is humble and meek, willing to be taught by God. Therefore: *"Blessed are the meek, for they shall inherit the earth."* For the time being it is quite the opposite: all heritage of this earth is to those who retain power and violence, armed with all the arms of death.

Humility is the only real approach to reality. Imposing our own view of things, our ambitions and desires, we deform reality, according to our image — and this even with God.[108] Our modern civilization of technology has the tendency to deform reality. We say, "This world is our world, and we can do whatever we want with it!" We build our skyscrapers, and take from the earth whatever resources we need for our purposes, but it's lack of humility and hinders our discovery of reality. All human "super-structures" of man's pride will come tumbling down with the touch of the finger of the Holy God. On his own, man cannot find his way to God; he is prey to the powers of darkness, the more he trusts in himself. This is symbolically his situation in the "north." He needs the light of God, the guidance of his good Guardian Angel, the motherly help of Our Lady. But pride and the insane self-conscience of the modern man do not admit a need for assistance.

---

[106] In Spanish the vertical concrete construction is called "castillo=castle."

[107] cf. Acts 5:1-11

[108] Feuerbach, a German philosopher of the last century, gloriously proclaimed: "Man forms the face of God according to his face!" This is becoming more and more true, even inside the church.

The first step in receiving help is to repent and then to hear, to listen, to obey. Only then can we find our way out of the confusion of this world and enter into the ways of the justice of God. We have to look out for the just God (south) and remember that we have to give account to Him, at the latest: the moment of our death (west). There is no way to escape the justice of God, even the fallen angels in hell have to submit. Justice requires obedience. Christ conquered the kingdom of God not primarily through His humble life or by His preaching but by dying in the justice of God. This is why at this corner we have the Beatitude: *"Blessed are those who hunger and thirst for justice, they will be satisfied."*

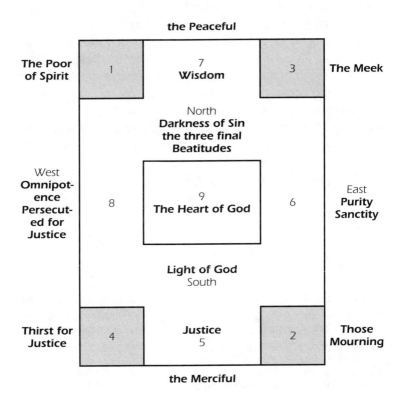

When the "pillars" of the corners stand up the walls can be filled in. This is done with the following four Beatitudes which will indicate us the way to follow;[109] we are invited to go on in this very light of God, which is no other than that of the infinite mercy of God. This is why we have to remember continually that we are only worthy of the infinite grace of salvation (being saved out of the darkness of the north!) if we are children of mercy. Mercy is the most genuine way to pass on the love and the light of God. Therefore: *"Blessed are the merciful, for they shall obtain mercy."* Only conscious that we are to be servants, as abnegated as the angels, can God use us together with the angels as messengers of His light in the darkness of the world.[110]

There is never an end with God. More and more, we must take Him up in our souls. The vessel of our soul must be filled to the brim. This is why we now move from the south to the east: to meet the Holy God: *"Blessed are the pure in heart, for they shall see God."* We have to enter more deeply into the pure heart of Our Lady. During an apparition at Marienfried in Germany, at the end of World War II, Our Lady said: "Exchange your maculate heart with my Immaculate Heart and offer it to God." We should make it a daily practice to do such, for our hearts are yet full of sin, pride and evil. God indeed will heed our prayer when He looks first upon Mary: Her "Immaculate Heart should be our refuge."[111] According to Our Lady's words at Marienfried, "in this way you will draw down torrents of grace." And this will be her final triumph — when it will have substituted the stained hearts of her sons!

---

[109] There is no way of following Christ if we do not first: deny ourselves and take up our cross. This the Lord has repeated to His disciples again and again. It is the fundamental law of Imitation of Christ. The old man must become a "new man in Christ." This is first done by self-denial. Then we have to be assimilated to the crucified Lord — and then only we can follow Him in the Holy Spirit.

[110] Here again we have to remember: the light we received is not a possession; we have to give it on, as Mary did, going to Elizabeth, offering the Lord in the temple. We have to go back into the north to bring His light to those who are waiting for it. Our Christian growth, as we have seen it in the rosary, should be an upwinding spiral, so we have to go through the "same stations" again and again, always a little closer to God.

[111] Words of Our Lady to Lucia on June 13, 1917; second apparition.

Filled with God we dare to go back to the north, where God's greater grace has already touched our hearts. It is here that we receive the mission of bringing peace to a world full of war and violence: *"Blessed are the peacemakers, they shall be called sons of God."* In the midst of quarrels, hatred and war, like St. Francis of Assisi, we must be instruments of *peace*. This peace is to be a wall erected in our hearts, such that no devil can overthrow it and behind which the many God has confided to us may find shelter.

The western wall is the last one to be lifted up. It is the direction of the wind where the sun sets, symbolically where the "final battle" will be waged. Only those who are ready for martyrdom, together with the holy angels, will be allowed to erect this wall. We must remember: It is not by our force, but God's merciful help that we will overcome. It is here that we will encounter the omnipotent God. It is He Who will give the victory against the abundance of evil trying to throttle us.

"Blessed are those who are persecuted for righteousness, theirs is the kingdom of heaven." Only in the poverty of Spirit we will inherit the kingdom of God: the last Beatitude links to the first. Naked we have come to this world, naked we will leave it.[112] Blessed those who build "their house" in God alone! In these times, there is no alternate solution for Christian living than to become saints; this is the call of Our Lady to Juan Diego at the beginning of modern times.[113] Only God in us can overcome the abundance of evil in this world. The process of beatification for Juan Diego has proven that he is a saint,[114] and this always implies that he has lived the beatitudes in an heroic manner.[115] Remember that together with the martyr children of Tlaxcala he is the first saint of the New World, and so also indicates what kind of sanctity God is expecting from this biggest Christian continent:

---

[112] cf. JOB 1:21

[113] In Juan Diego in a special way laity is called to sanctity. The more we near the end of times the closer religious and lay people will come to each other under the one challenge: "Be holy as God is holy"!

[114] cf. Los Dos Mundos de Un Indio Santo, Fr. José Luis Guerrero

[115] Part of our participation in his beatitude is reflected in his "way of the cross," cf. Book Five.

- It should be a sanctity in, through and with Our Lady!
- It must realize more and more the common priesthood of Christians by sacrifice!"
- It should be in union with the angels as the first messengers of the good news.[116]

The surest way therefore to become a saint in these days of confusion and disorder is to keep close to our Guardian Angel. Day by day, moment by moment, we are to walk the way of the cross which is our life, never forgetting his precious company. If we do not let loose of his hand, he is our firm promise that we will reach heaven.

The way to holiness or beatitude is not by fasting or special works, but rather by continual self-denial: "I don't know how to make it, but my good angel knows!" This disposition is to be remembered every second. In the person of one's Angel the unique call of God's love is present all the time! We must only listen to it and obey. We must get away from the "easy solutions" of the world: simplifications destroy, mutilate, and obliterate. The "Holy Angel" is not an easy pious solution, so seemingly solicited these days. God wants us to become saints without mutilation or elimination of essentials.

The last Beatitude necessarily has its place in the center of the new Jerusalem. It shines in the fullness of light of the Sacred Heart of Jesus, inviting us to enter into the furnace of love. If we only believe in this love, with St. Paul we can proclaim: *"what can separate us from the love of God...? Therefore: "Blessed are you when men reproach you, and persecute you, and, speaking falsely, say all manner of evil against you, for My sake. Rejoice and exult, because your reward is great in heaven; for so did they persecute the prophets who were before you."*

Everything must lead to the one center of the world: the heart of Jesus, the luminous sign of the love of the triune God. It is for this reason that the final Beatitude is fourfold and threefold at the same time;[117]

---

[116] cf. Lk 2:4 ff — the angels announcing to the shepherds in Bethlehem.

[117] In the Greek original we find four terms — the last two in most translation are combined in one.

- as fourfold it speaks us of the necessity of being crucified with the Lord;
- as threefold it is the promise of union with the triune God for all eternity: here "piety" will come to its consummation.[118]

Resuming

Our understanding of the image of Our Lady of Guadalupe, even though it is an understanding in mystery is a responsibility before the church and the world. We have to be confessors in our faith, otherwise we will drown in the confusion of these times.

Beauty, as revealed in the golden mantle of rays as in the entire image is an unrefutable proof of its authenticity. No human hand, as a whole and in all details, is capable of producing a like image. The presence of the "golden rectangle" is the best proof here. Man can not match the wisdom of God.

Contemplating the turquoise star-studded mantle of the Virgin, we receive this counsel: our journey on this earth should be a birth into heaven. We will be best able to give an accounting before the Lord in the degree that we find order in our life.

As the image of Our Lady of Guadalupe is an image painted by God Himself, the "greater perspective" perceived should be that of our angel. He is "at home" in the reign of light, the reign of God and Reign of Our Lady. The science to be learned at the hand of our good Guardian Angel is to evermore see all things in the perspective of light, more than with our human and carnal eyes. We applied technological discoveries in our defense of the image, remembering always that the grace of faith and "knowing better" should never

---

[118] Remember the different ways to pray the rosary: in six steps, in nine, in seven — according to the perspective we chose. This way we should also pray the Beatitudes, so that more and more they will become steps of birth into Eternal life. As Our Lady of Guadalupe and Fátima manifest, the only way to reach the heart of God is by way of the Immaculate Heart of Mary. We can look at the construction of the new Jerusalem also as representing a heart with its four chambers, where the current of blood is passing through in an order similar to that which we followed with the Beatitudes in relation to the corners and walls of the new Jerusalem. God is love, and there is no better way to reach Him than by love!

make us proud. Like the earthen-colored gown of the Virgin, we are from the dust of this earth and to the same we will return.

Because of man's sin, our world is ever becoming a Spiritual desert. But the little flock of the faithful is not abandoned. Our loving God and Father sends His holy angels as help on the steep way up to consummation by the cross. This is the message of the white undergown of Our Lady. In the purity of Her Immaculate Heart and with the help of the angels we will have part in the Gift of Fortitude. The currents of grace coming down from God will meet us more than half way!

The beauty of the image of Our Lady of Guadalupe is not only to be admired, it is to be incarnated in our life as Christians. We are called to follow Our Lord on His way up to Golgotha. It is our humble human condition to be part of this material world by our body, but at the same time the Beatitudes are the challenge of God to overcome all hindrances and obstacles in the grace of fortitude. the new Jerusalem is our destination. It is there that the Lord Himself will wipe away all our tears. We need the Gift of piety, acknowledging and accepting the "Sober love of God."

> *Sober Christian piety is to share in,*
> *through and with Mary Immaculate*
> *the veiled mystery of God's presence*
> *in her Immaculate Heart*
> *on the way of dark faith, hope and love,*
> *at the hand of our good Guardian Angel*
> *whose eyes penetrate all darkness*
> *to bring us into eternal light. Amen.*

The Seven Veils of Our Lady of Guadalupe

Book Seven

The Seven-Fold Candelabra

Learning More About Contemplation

Introduction

In this last reflection of *The Seven Veils of Our Lady of Guadalupe* we should consciously enter deeper into the ascending spiral of meditation with its manifold dimensions. This will help to go ever deeper into the meditation of the other six books. A practical help to do so is the "chaplet of the seven veils" as another "instrument of harvest." Should we not bring everything to the feet of Our Lady so that she will put it all into the heart of her Son for the greater glory of the triune God!

It will help us not only to understand deeper the marvel of the image of Our Lady of Guadalupe, but also to embrace the reality of one's life, to take into one's meditation whoever and whatever surrounds one; all one's joys, sorrows and glory. This way, meditation will become "harvesting with and by Our Heavenly Mother," such that at the end we will not appear alone before the throne of the eternal judge, but in company with our brothers and that part of creation we are called to repatriate with and through Christ Jesus.

Three Orders of "Seven"

There are three perspectives on the Sacraments which help us to penetrate deeper into the order of seven:

- One with the days of the week, adapted to the order of the votive masses as they were found before in the Tridentine Missal.
- Another adapted to the order of the days of the week in relation with the different hours of the Divine Office.
- A third adapted to the "seven days of creation" of the Gospel of St. John.

They can be correlated to the Three Divine Persons respectively.

These orders will help you to see every day of the week under a special light, e.g. the corresponding item of one of the three orders. We recommend starting with the first order, concentrating alternately each week: first on the days of creation, then the corresponding votive mass, then on the Sacraments.

Always, this living order of things should help us to praise God, to thank God, because it will guide us in the disorder and confusion of the world. Praying the Liturgy of the Hours according to this order of seven will make us conscious that we are called to participate in the creative order of the seven days of creation, salvation and repatriation.

A good counsel for the beginner: do not take too much at a time, otherwise instead of helping you to find order and peace in your soul it will confuse you. Before you pass on to another order of the "seven," you should really be at home in the previous one. This will also help you to more easily find out about the correlations with the other orders of "seven." Remember always St. Ignatius of Loyola's fundamental counsel for meditation: "not the many things will satisfy your soul but plunging deeper!"

Always, we start the week with its first day: Monday, because Sunday is, in relation to the days of creation, the "last day," the same it is looking on the life of Christ as we find it exposed in the "days of creation of the Gospels," the same it is for the order of the Apocalypse: the coming down of the new Jerusalem. In the Liturgy of the church Sunday is the first day because the Resurrection of Christ is our birth to new life.

There are other coordinations possible than these exposed in the three orders of "seven," because the order of life is always richer and more abundant than we really are able to understand. Little by little we will discover that the art of meditation is to enter deeper in the multiple relations of things which one day we will be able to appreciate as the perfect harmony and beauty of the reign of God.

First Order: in relation to the Father

Mon.	Tues.	Wed.	Thurs.	Fri.	Sat.	Sun.
Most Holy Trinity	Angels	St. Joseph	Holy Eucharist	Passion	Mary	Resurrection
Baptism	Holy Orders	Confirmation	Holy Eucharist	Matrimony	Penance	Extreme Unction

The Seven Veils of Our Lady of Guadalupe

Second Order: in relation to the Son[1]

Clouds	Rays	Mantle	Gown	Inner Gown	Body	Soul
Under-standing	Wisdom	Counsel	Know-ledge	Fortitude	Fear of the Lord	Piety
Father forgive them for they know not what they do	This day you will be with me in paradise	Behold your Mother	I thirst	My God, My God, why have You forsaken me?	Father, into Your hands I com-mend my spirits	It is finished
Ephesus	Smyrna	Perga-mum	Thyatira	Sardis	Phila-delphia	Laodicea
Day I	Day II	Day III	Day IV	Day V	Day VI	Day VII
H. Eucharist - Matins	Marriage - Lauds	Baptism - Terce	Penance - Sext	Holy Orders - None	Confir-mation - Vespers	Extreme Unction - Comp-lines
Introit	Readings	Offertory	Sanctus	Conse-cration	Com-munion	Ite Missa est

Correlated with St. John's Gospel - Order of the Holy Spirit

Day I	Day II	Day III	Day IV	Day V	Day VI	Day VII
Marriage	Baptism	Offertory	Holy Eucharist	Confir-mation	Com-munion	Holy Orders

---

[1] This is the order we will refer to (except, with respect to the Sacraments, we will use the order of the Father), the same order as structure for the praying of the seven veils. The other two orders remind us that we should look at things not only in view of the Son, but only looking up to the Father and asking for the help of the Holy Spirit.

The Seven Steps of Trinitarian Interpretation

In the Light of the Gifts of Holy Spirit[2]

It is according to the order of seven of the Gifts of the Holy Spirit that we will best understand the particular intention of each item of the order of seven.

The Gift of Understanding

We can only arrive at a truth if:

- we first investigate its reality as the Father created it in view of the Son;
- we search for the word of the Son which explains it to us;
- in the end we intuit in the Holy Spirit the significance of that which God desires to tell us through this reality, i.e., His message!

United and penetrating each other in this way, the three steps of revelation become one as God in Three Persons is One!

The Gift of Wisdom

In the Wisdom of God:

- The image is referred to creation,
- The word to man,
- and the concept to the angel.

The Gift of Counsel

This is the Counsel of God for an organic sequence of the understanding, whether for each person or for humanity as a whole: it is only that "modern" man has inverted it by his "isms!"

---

[2] The order of seven we use for the Gifts is a little different from the traditional one. The reason we use it is that it better corresponds to the rhythm of seven as a fundamental instrument of meditation.

- The image corresponds to comprehension through the senses,
- The word to discursive comprehension,
- The concept to the intuitive comprehension which engulfs and penetrates to the most profound essence of things.

These three forms need to be "one" just as the most Holy Trinity is One in the Three Divine Persons. One form of comprehension is always linked to the other and complements the other.

The Gift of Knowledge

To these three forms, there simultaneously correspond three movements of human understanding which apply to every true science.

- to the image: the movement toward the exterior to discover reality
- to the word: taking in by the word that reality we wish to understand,
- and to the concept: the movement towards the heart, like Mary who meditated all words within her heart.

The Gift of Fortitude

These three means of comprehension relate also with three attitudes which we must live in the spirit of fortitude.

- For its comprehension, the image demands total openness on the part of man, in both body and soul, and with all his faculties of comprehension. It is because of this that man must learn to keep silence, so that the image may be integrally impressed in all its details.
- The word demands intellectual work in order to find just expression.
- The concept implores a profound contemplation of the image, not only externally, now, but also from within, so that

---

[3] "Terminus a quo y ad quem"

the image might become an interior reality, part of my life. The process of understanding the image is both its beginning and its end.[3] The image, we intuit from the beginning, something of the idea of God which the word explains to us and the concept deepens and so it becomes our own.

The Gift of the Fear of God

- Any trinitarian comprehension in the fear of God is necessarily orientated to the contemplation of God, face to face, orientated towards the beatific vision which the angels and saints already enjoy.
- In this sense, it is already an apocalyptic knowledge, as may be discerned in the Book of the Apocalypse. Man usually only arrives at this level of surrender in his final hour, when in an instant, his entire life passes before him like a movie.
- Meeting the Son of God, face to face at the hour of our death as He has lived in us, will help us to discover the mission God has entrusted us here on earth and so also to acknowledge how much we have failed to do so.

The Gift of Piety

Contemplation, after our active input, must lose itself, and at the same time, find its repose once again in God, so that He, in the Holy Spirit, may complete it in us.

- True contemplation will engender new contemplations, until it is completely consumed in the contemplation of God Himself at the hour of our death. In the same face of God, which will be revealed before us at this blessed hour, we will realize that all the contemplations made during our life are as stones in the great mosaic, which are now made one in the face of God which we will reflect for all eternity.
- Only if all our contemplations are open to the greater God, will our knowledge become, here on the earth, truly trinitarian, and thus have part in the fertility of the knowledge of the triune God in His Son. The Father, knowing His Son, engen-

ders Him for all eternity: because, in God, to know is to engender.

- The only condition necessary to come close to this knowledge is:
- to desire that our sinner's heart be purified and thus brought closer to the Immaculate Heart of Mary

The reality of this world is not yet complete. We have not yet arrived at the end of the sixth day of creation; not the material world, not that of man, not even that of the angels' has reached its consummation, which will come only when all things are restored in Christ: *"And when all things are made subject to Him, then the Son Himself will also be made subject to Him Who subjected all things to Him, that God may be all in all."* (I Cor 15:28)

Thus it is that true piety is
when the same triune God
is our first and final thought.

Three Perspectives of life in a Trinitarian Way:

- The static aspect of things is when we arrive to understand the idea of things that the Father had from all eternity,
- The dynamic aspect of things is when we look at them in the process of being created, of growing towards the Son!
- The aspect of multiple correlations: there is no created thing which finds its total meaning alone in and of itself; it depends on all that surrounds it, in the two dimensions of time and space. At the last judgment, the Holy Spirit will reveal these multiple correlations for all the world to see!

Again, only the three interrelated perspectives will give us an integral vision of reality! Therefore, contemplation is "work in piety" and will help us yield eternal fruit through its practice. It is thus that we fulfill God's idea (concept) for us. This is true in our personal lives, but is equally true for nations, and for the people of God as a whole. In conclusion, every true contemplation, if brought forth from a pure heart, tends to the vision of the triune God, of the

Father through the image, of the Son through the word, of the Holy Spirit through the concept.

Thus, different "attitudes" are demanded of us in the Holy Spirit, in relation to the Three Divine Persons. To know is to give oneself to God, so that He can see His Son in us. This knowledge of the Son, in a pilgrimage state, is yet imperfect: we cannot yet repose in Him definitively, as we shall one day, when we arrive at the other shore. It is a dynamic knowledge, and at the same time, in the Holy Spirit, a knowledge in all things, persons and circumstances.

SUMMARY

These are the seven "activities" necessary to reach a true comprehension of reality:
1. The orientation of all our knowledge toward the triune God.
2. The three "modes" of knowledge of reality: through image, word, and concept.
3. The three steps of comprehension: sensitive, discursive, and conceptual.
4. The three movements: towards the external by means of the senses, entering in us by the word, penetrating into our heart by means of the concept.
5. The three attitudes: silence, intellectual work, and meditation.
6. Contemplation of the triune God "in all things of creation."
7. The fruit of this contemplation: the birth of God in our soul.

The Movement of the Spiral
in the Seven-Fold Candelabra[4]

Practical Hints

Always begin with prayer. Ask especially for the gift of the Holy Spirit which corresponds.

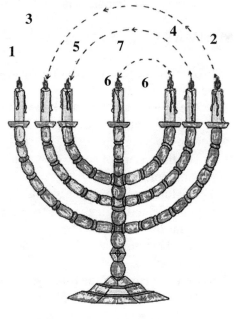

1. Look at the image of Our Lady of Guadalupe and the corresponding veil in adoration and admiration.
2. Ask the Lord to let you have part in the purification promised to the corresponding community of Asia.
3. Remember the corresponding word of the Lord on the cross.
4. Recall that you are under the "shadow" of the Holy Spirit who wants to make you a new man in Christ (relation to the corresponding day of creation),
5. Whom you should meet in the corresponding sacrament.
6. Finally refer to the corresponding part of the "apocalyptic Mass" which is meant to transform the world according to the face of Christ.

Always, our meditation should start with and lead us to the Eucharistic Lord of the apocalyptic Mass. It is in the Holy Mass where

---

4   Note that this seven-fold candelabra of spiral dimension is based on the spiral of four centers.

the "movement of ransom" initiates and to the same where it comes to rest. We end where we start: in adoration and admiration of the beauty of God, a beauty always hidden under seven veils, hidden in Mary Immaculate, so much present with us in her image of Guadalupe. Always refer to the Image of Our Lady of Guadalupe as a very concrete presence of her among us. She is the Mother of meditation, the Queen of the angels and the Spouse of the Holy Spirit. It is the Holy Spirit Who has to guide us by our angel to the contemplation of the triune God, Face to face. This is a practical way to repeat and to bring to deeper meditation the six books. As we started with the rosary, so we do here.

The Seven-fold Candelabra of Book One

The Hidden Dimension of the Rosary

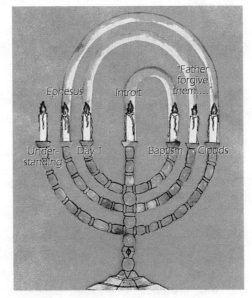

1. Gift of the Holy Spirit: Prayer for understanding
2. Veil: Clouds
3. Community: Ephesus
4. First of Christ's last words: "Father, forgive them, they know not what they do."
5. Day one of creation
6. Sacrament: Baptism/Holy Eucharist/Matrimony[5]
7. The Holy Mass : The Introit

[5]   We always list the sacraments in relation to the three different orders of "seven," the first in relation to the Father, the second to the Son, the third to the Holy Spirit — concentrate on the order of the Father!

Prayer for Understanding

"Holy Spirit of God, only in Your light can we understand the marvels of the reign of God. Look down on us poor sinners and help us to lift our eyes from the dust of this earth to the eternal glories shining through the Image of Our Lady of Guadalupe. Help us to better understand, that God is always a veiled God. He is a never-ending mystery, even when we will come to see Him, face to face."

The light of understanding which we are lacking is basically received from Our Lord Jesus Christ in Baptism, and it is preserved and augmented by His true presence in the Most Holy Eucharist. This light will not only help us to become one in Him, fulfilling our unique vocation, but it should also help us to form one family, one community according to the image of the Most Holy Trinity.

We can easily relate the three Sacraments to the three rosaries: Baptism to the Joyful Mysteries, the Holy Eucharist to the Sorrowful Mysteries and Matrimony to the Glorious Mysteries. The light we receive in Baptism is no other than that of Most Holy Trinity Whom we are called to share eternally by the Son of God, Jesus Christ. It is this light which will help us to adore Our Lord Jesus Christ in this sacrament of love together with all the holy angels already here on earth. It is by adoration that finally the whole creation will return to the heart of God.

The First Veil — The Clouds

In our exterior or interior contemplation of the image of Our Lady of Guadalupe, we should approach by way of her first veil: the clouds. They are the first of the seven veils surrounding the invisible presence of Our Lord Jesus Christ, indicated by the sign of the four-petalled flower on the Virgin's womb. There is no possible understanding of the image if we do not place ourselves within these clouds. The clouds are a veil about the mysterious presence of the triune God, an insupportable mystery for us if not first hidden by this veil.

Water, in the form of clouds, seems to be exempt from the force of gravity and it is thus it becomes a symbol of the life which ascends to God. As rain, it returns to the earth, making it fertile and then again it ascends to heaven as vapor. Likewise, in the holy rosary, our prayers, by way of our angels, ascend to God and bring back to us the blessings and graces we pray for, but always, whatever we ask for is hidden in the mystery of the Greater God Who knows better what we really need. This is why he who prays the rosary in view of the greater God puts himself also into this cloud of the mystery of God.

In the Old Testament, the cloud was symbol of the mysterious presence of God among the Israelites.[6] This "cloud of God" wants to envelope us both from within and from without, until we have totally entered into Him. This is also recognized in the column of cloud which covered the Israelites when they left Egypt. Only in God and by God were they able to break the chain of the Egyptian slavery. Creation will have reached its consummation when at the same time God is the most outward and most inward of all creation. God is not only that which is in our innermost self, but He is also the most exterior, *"because in Him we live and move and have our being."*[7]

Symbolically, the cloud is the expression of the natural and supernatural life of Mary. She appears in the midst of clouds.[8] She not only carries in herself the mystery of God, but this very mystery also veils her. Clouds can take many forms, just as the Virgin has appeared in many ways and in many places. The common denominator is that she is *mediatrix* and *messenger* of God. Through her, more than through any other creature, God pours forth His graces over the arid soil of life; and many times the rosary is the tube by which these graces will come to us. Always, the Virgin, in her concern for her children, entrusted to her by God, enwraps us in these clouds, not only for our protection, but also to separate us form the grip of the world. It is by this mystery of God, in us and

---

[6] cf. Ex 13:21, Nm 9:15, I Rom 8:10
[7] Acts 17:28
[8] cf. I Kings 19:12b

around us, that we become "invisible" for the world, they will not understand us anymore, because they do not know the waters of graces which sustain our lives.

The seven communities of Asia in the Apocalypse are an image of what the church should be in these last times: she must reflect the face of the Son of God in a seven-fold way (that is: in the Holy Spirit) in order to approach the image of Mary Immaculate, the only one worthy of receiving the Son of God. As the image of Our Lady Guadalupe represents Mary in her apocalyptic perfection, as the woman clothed with the sun, so also does it represent these seven communities. They are challenged to reach out for their perfection in Mary, who at the end must be the perfection of each Christian and the whole church. This is why we must pray the communities like we pray the rosary of seven, because each community represents a mystery of the mystical presence of Our Lord in the Mystical Body of the church at the end of times.

The First Community of Asia — Ephesus

Image of the Lord:

> "...He Who holds the seven stars in his right hand, who walks in the midst of the seven golden lamp-stands."

This community must correspond to the image: The Lord among His angels, to represent the light and the love of God. He, first of all must be seen as the light which pierces our darkness and brings us over to the "other side." "light," with St. John is synonymous with love. (cf. Jn): Who does not see God is unable to love.

Praise and Reprimand:

> "...works and thy labor and thy patience, and that thou can'st not bear evil men; but hast tried them who say they are apostles and are not, and hast found them false. And thou hast patience and hast endured for my name, and hast not grown weary,"

"...hast left thy first love ... repent and do the former works; or else I will come to thee, and will move thy lamp-stand out of its place."

The Gift of Understanding will help to bring us back to our "first love." If we've lost that attraction, then we must repent, pray for the gift and return to Him Who has first loved us. What we "good Christians" easily forget in our "devotional practices" is that we are called to become new creatures in Christ. If we would live up to this challenge, every day would be a new day of creation. In relation to the first day, we should become "children of light." Looking up to Our Lady of Guadalupe enables the intuition of what this means: radiate the presence of the triune God in our heart.

Promise: "...I will permit to eat of the tree of life.."[9]

If we were to consider the deeper sense of "Ephesus": the chosen place for the deepest contemplation of Mary and St. John of the passion, death and Resurrection of Our Lord, we would find that the promise to this first community is really the fruit of contemplation, contemplation of the cross.

---

[9] Rv 2:7 In the first three communities the admonition: "He who has ears should hear what the spirit" tells the communities, is right before the promise. With the four last communities, the promise comes at the end. This difference helps to divide the seven communities into three and four. The three corresponding more to Most Holy Trinity, the four, more to the four principle qualities of God. This way the seven communities should be a complete mirror of the perfection of Most Holy Trinity.

The seven words of Our Lord Jesus Christ on the cross are His most precious legacy of His love to all those who look up to Him in adoration and gratitude. They are the "crystallizing point" for the Gospels, and so must also be for our life in the imitation of Christ. The sending of the Virgin Mary to the heathen country of Mexico enabled her to incarnate His....

First word from the Cross directed to the Father

"Father, forgive them, for they do not know what they do!" (Lk 23:34)

Again and again in the Gospels, the Lord is surprised and sometimes even angry over the lack of understanding of His disciples, especially when He speaks to them in parables, that is "in a veiled way," about the mysteries of the reign of God which cannot be understood in any other way.[10]

The clouds that envelop the image of Our Lady not only veil the mysterious presence of the Lord in her womb, but protect and wrap it in the living waters of grace which flow from the heart of the Father. God's mysteries are always life-giving mysteries. They can only be understood if we have a living and burning heart, one open to their beauty. Only God can take from us the blindness caused by sin, biblically referred by St. Paul as a "veil"(II Cor) causing us to fall into the ways of sin without knowing what we really do, and thus the need for the Lord's merciful intercession, *"'Father, forgive them, for they do not know what they do!'"* (Lk 23:34) We should never forget to pray the Rosary as a powerful instrument for the conversion of sinners. Certainly, this is why Our Lady insists so much on this prayer and even joined another intercession to it: "Oh My Jesus, forgive us our sins. Save us from the fires of hell. Lead all souls to heaven, especially those most in need of your mercy." It perfectly corresponds with the first word of Our Lord on the cross.

---

[10] Parables are like "images by way of words" referring to created things in this world or to situations which we can see or represent before our interior eyes.

First Day of Creation (Gen. 1:3-5)

The light of the first day can be understood in a triple way:

- as the creation of the angels as creatures of light
- as the creation of energy as the beginning of the material world
- in relation to man who will come to this world only on the last day light signifies the Gift of Understanding.

The "first day" in the Gospels always speaks about the light of Christ entering into the world of man, challenging his response.

Our prayers going up in the rosary, and the graces coming down from heaven, are part of making this world new, and at the same time bringing it back to the light it came from in the beginning.

The sacraments are living signs of the presence of Our Lord Jesus Christ in His church. The one common sign in them is the cross, which in the four-petalled flower is also the sign of His presence in the Image of Our Lady of Guadalupe. We can carry the Lord only in our hearts if we become "cruciform."

Baptism

In repeating the mysteries of the life, passion and Resurrection of Our Lord, we make an effort to enter deeper into them and so realize more fully the grace of Baptism received at the beginning of our Christian life. Although the grace of Baptism is an initial grace, it has to be consummated in a life according to the commandments of God, the word of God and obedience to the voice of our Guardian Angel. Only following the Lord on the way of the cross we also participate in the grace of His Resurrection.

This Sacrament is the fundament, the "rock" for our unique vocation in Christ, the Son of God. It is by Baptism that we enter into His Mystical Body, the church. The measure of our obedience

to the call of sanctity should reflect the importance of the mission God's Mercy will confer on us for the benefit of the whole church. The unique grace of Baptism for Juan Diego starts to unfold in its plenitude when he first meets Our Lady and accepts the mission she confers upon him. This is his unique vocation of serving the Lord, to form a new family of Christ in the New World which reflects the beauty and grace of Mary.

Part One of Holy Mass: The Introit[11]

We can come to consummation only if we continually keep in mind were we come from, and this is what Holy Mass continually reminds us of in its beginning: we have to confess ourselves as poor sinners before God, Whose first loving call resounds in our ears by the words of the Introitus. Even though there are many forms of Introitus, they can be reduced to one denominator: the outstretched arms of the Father Who is waiting on the hill for the return of his prodigal son. This is why also, when we pray the rosary, we should humbly accept the pious tradition to pray first our act of contrition, because we are not even worthy as poor sinners to take in our heart the most holy mysteries of the life of Christ.

---

[11] cf. Book VI or Rv 1:1-20

The Seven-Fold Candelabra of Book Two

1. Gift of the Holy Spirit: prayer for wisdom
2. Veil: rays
3. Community: Smyrna
4. Second word from the cross: "This day, you will be with me in para-dise."
5. Day two of creation
6. Sacrament: Holy Orders/ Matri-mony/Baptism
7. The Holy Mass: the readings

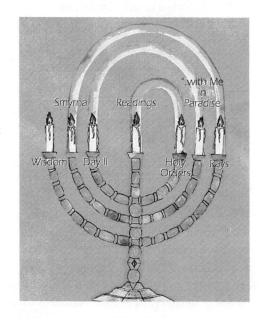

Prayer for Wisdom

"Oh God of wisdom, although we meet your wisdom wher-ever we turn our eyes, we are blind in recognizing it. It is a hidden wisdom, even in the image of Our Lady of Guadalupe, open only to the eyes of the pure, to the eyes of the angels. Give them power to turn our eyes away from the many things of this world and concentrate them on the one thing necessary: You, Oh God — and then let us look with Your eyes at the hidden wisdom of Your works so they will open for us as do the flowers to the rays of the sun. Amen"

Second Veil — The Rays

Passing from the veil of clouds, we encounter Our Lady's mantle of rays. They seem to radiate from her interior, proceeding from the glorious presence of God within her. There are 144 rays, counting those hidden by the angel (138 are visible, indicating that she is the image of the new Jerusalem coming down from heaven 1 + 3 + 8 = 12) representing the plenitude (12 x 12) of those who will be saved from among the twelve tribes of Israel (Apoc 7:4, 21:3).

The rays are a symbol of God's wisdom, because His wisdom penetrates the deepest of darkness. wisdom is always related to the "folly of the cross," first apparent in the second day of creation. (cf. Gen 1) wisdom is like the firmament between the waters of above and below: putting things in their right place in the sign of the cross.

Rays, in themselves, are fire, light, energy and radiation, and in the image, they seemingly emanate from the Most Holy Virgin, demonstrating that she bears the fountain and source of all life. The sun, for the Aztecs, was one of the most important symbols of God as the source and origin of all that is, "The God from Whom we have our existence," *in Ipalnemohuani*.[12]

When we speak of the love of God, we speak of a reality that all purified souls experience. It is the divine love which consumes. We see, in Mary, as did the Aztecs, a "woman transformed in the sun." The sun-fire represents the soul of her being, of her Immaculate Heart. It manifests the mystical union between Her, the "Immaculate Conception" and her Spouse: God. *"With you is wisdom who knows your works, who was with you when you made the world, who knows what is favorable in your sight...."* (Wisdom 9:9).

Second Community of Asia - Smyrna

Image of the Lord:

> *"...the first and the last, who was dead and is alive:"*

It is according to this image that the community will be judged.

---

[12] Term used by the Blessed Virgin indicating the True God in Whose name she came, cf. Nican Mopohua, vs. 26.

Praise (no reprimand):

> *"I know thy tribulation and thy poverty, but thou art rich;*
>> *"Fear none of those things that thou art about to suffer."*

The second community, a community recognized as being "poor," is blessed as being "rich." It is a community which must reflect the "One Who was dead and is alive." This One Who was dead is the very "One" Who entered salvation history, manifesting something of the infinite wisdom of God in the poverty of the Godman. (cf. Phil 2:7-8)

Remember: Jesus, He Who was born in Bethlehem, fled to Egypt, raised in humility, tempted by the devil, had nowhere to lay His head, was slandered, rejected, captured and condemned by the learned, persecuted, whipped, beaten, mocked, stripped and crucified by pagans, is the same One that must penetrate our life. We too will be judged by "Him Who was dead and is alive"!

Promise:

> *"...I will give thee the crown of life ... shall not be hurt by the second death."*

In Book II we see how the cross is extended from the Old World to the New World, to reform it according to the image of Christ Who came into this world as the poor and despised and the unknown. The history of the conquest of the New World, really reflects something of this poverty of Christ, because it was only a handful of men who started this adventure. Besides, we should remember that among this handful of men there were only very few who entered in the plan of God in total abandonment. Whatever critiques have been made in relation to Cortés, we have to confess that this great man really did his utmost to fulfill his mission.

It takes a lifetime to discover the plan of the wisdom of God on our life, but the sooner we look up to Our Lord Jesus Christ, as the missionary of the Father, we will discover more about this plan of mercy God has on our life. This is precisely what the angel of Portugal told the three shepherd children in his second spoken apparition. Though they are insignificant before the world, God has a plan on them which will change the face of the world, as He did by way of Cortés.

Second word from the Cross

> *"Amen I say to you, this day you will be with me in paradise."* (Lk 23:43)

Dismas, the "good thief," crucified beside Our Lord, merely looking upon Him, receives a ray of grace which enables him to recognize the Lord's innocence and to confess it publicly. The ray of the wisdom of God which penetrated his heart will become the fire of purification which will clean him from the darkness of sin.

In this context, "paradise" must be understood as purgatory, the place of purification now open for those who look up to the Lord in contrition of their sins. Paradise, for Adam and Eve, was the place of trial, where their fidelity to God's mandate was put to the test. Christ, by a life of perfect obedience to the Father, passed the trial of obedience which our first parents failed, and it is thus that He has become the "salvation for all those who look up to Him" (cf. Heb 5:9, 9:28)[13]

Juan Diego, chosen from amongst a people deeply enrooted in idolatry, is found by heaven to be the most beautiful flower on the stem of the tlamantini.[14] In blind faith and obedience he is ready to

---

[13] Remember: Even if man had not sinned he would have had to pass through many trials to become "cruciform" as His greater brother, as Mary, the Immaculate! Purgatory is the place where we will have the chance to be transformed into the image God had of us from all eternity in view of His Beloved Son. The more we are allowed to imitate Christ here on earth, collaborating with His Grace, the more we will pass our purgatory already here. Do not forget that purification, transformation and union is an organic process which takes time. The good thief by the blood of Christ was pardoned, but necessarily had still to be cleaned of the consequences of his sins in an organic process of purification. God is not a magician!

[14] tlamatine — Aztec or Toltecan wiseman.

fulfill what Our Lady asks of him, although we can see that it is absolutely contrary to human reason, i.e. picking flowers on an arid mountain top in the dead of winter.

Wisdom is learned in the school of life, not at a school, from books or conferences. It is usually found more abundantly with the simple than with the learned. This is clearly seen in the case of Dismas in opposition to the learned scribes and Pharisees, those guilty of Christ's condemnation because of human blindness and a lack of true wisdom.

Wisdom and poverty are inseparable, especially poverty of Spirit, that Beatitude which is first praised by Jesus in His Sermon on the Mount. (cf. Mt 5:3) The world has become lost in its hunger for earthly pleasure, and so those who are truly "poor" for the sake of Christ and the Gospel will be persecuted, but holding on to it in persecution or martyrdom will enable our entering into the fountain of life.

Even though man seldom consciously recognizes the plan of God on his life, if his heart is not as pure as that of Mary and Joseph and all the saints who followed up, as long as he does not resist God's call, he can become an instrument of His mercy. We should remember that there is like a current of the "thirst of Christ" going through the history of Christianity. It can be interpreted in many ways. One of this, in the beginning was that of the "crusade": we Christians must thirst with the Lord, that His cross will be lifted up in and over the entire world. The Spaniards and the Portuguese were the only nations in the beginning of the modern age which still listened to this call of the Lord "I thirst." We explained in Book II that they did it in the warrior perspective which has been their interpretation in their battle against the Moslems.

Precisely at the time when Christendom in Europe received its deepest wound from Protestantism (which today proved to be a mortal wound) the twelve Franciscans went out to discover the New World as "paradise lost" where Christian life should be realized again in plenitude according to the primary idea of the Jews that the reign of God should also be a political reign, because the whole man is called to live his faith and really by way of Our Lady, appearing to Juan Diego on the hill of Tepeyac, something of "paradise" was revealed precisely in the center of this New World. There is a hidden promise in this revelation that also the Old World will lose its faith and destroy itself and the Christian faith will come to its consummation in this New World, where Columbus first raised up the cross.

In a symbolical way, the discovery of the New World tells us that we necessarily have to cross over "the ocean" to arrive at the shore of the new Jerusalem. The "ocean" here is image of the trial we have go through in blind faith. Remember that even though Columbus had some basic instruments to orient his voyage to the New World, the stimulus to leave the shore of the Old World was his desire to serve God's greater plan. As Christians, we will never make this "voyage" if all our tendency, as it is in these times, is to establish our faith in this world. Time and again we have to break out of the comfort of the world to head out for a new destination which is not of this world.

Day Two of Creation

On the second day, God created the two elements: one visible, water, and the other more invisible, air. The firmament, between the waters, is not only a simple representation of the "physical heaven" above us,[15] but in the Spiritual and symbolic sense it represents the life, created by God which stays below and the one which is orientated towards heaven. This is, first of all, a reference to the angels after their separation on the first day. It also corresponds to man, who has lost the desire of heaven. This is why the Son of man has to be lifted on the cross. He will draw all those who look up to Him to His heart. (cf. Jn 3:14)

In the "second day of creation of the Gospels" the "firmament of separation" between those who

---

[15] This is what the ancients thought: the heaven as firmament with holes to let the rain come through." We should not laugh at this ingenuity — they had a better understanding of the transparency of things than we modern men.

follow Christ and those who stand up against Him is first becoming visible.

In the image of Our Lady of Guadalupe we recognize the "firmament of separation" in the vertical seam on her robe, separating the darker from the lighter side of her gown.[16]

Sacrament

Holy Orders: The corresponding Sacrament here is that of priestly Ordination. A sacrament of leadership, as St. Ignatius of Loyola saw it: of being captain under the banner of Christ in the fight against the fallen angels who have their banner with Lucifer on the other side. It is a challenge to be a confessor and if necessary to be a martyr in Christ, to reveal to the world that we are not living on our own, that we are not pure functionaries of some kind of a earthly institution but are representatives of the living God, who has revealed Himself to Abraham, Isaac and Jacob ... to all the saints who called out for Him. This is why the priest, more than the laity, needs the help of the an-gels, so as to be reminded every moment that his mission is not from this earth. The priests must be "angels of God," as St. Stephen appeared as an "angel" when his face irradiated the glory of his vision of the triune God.[17] This glory reflected by him was able to convert St. Paul from a staunch Pharisee to a fervent apostle, perhaps the most fervent of them all.

---

[16] In the reflection on the presence of the "golden rectangle" in the image of Our Lady of Guadalupe we note that the vertical seam also becomes the basis of finding nine perfect divisions of the sacred tilma, something which reflects the beautiful structure of the hierarchy of the holy angels, a structure which is also held together by the structure of the cross. C = cf. Appendix at the end of Book VII.

[17] cf. Acts 6:15 ff

Looking forward to the parts of the Holy Mass, we are reminded that it is the priest who is called to lead us from the Introitus to a deeper understanding of the word of God exposed in the readings. Juan Diego, participating in the general priesthood, even though not officially interested to pass on the message of Our Lady, became the most powerful help for the Franciscans to spread the faith in the New World. His way of announcing the good news was not so much by the word and the Sacraments (more reserved to the priest), but by the humble submission of his entire life to Our Lady, disappearing behind the image of Our Lady he was called to die to himself, day by day, but this way he helped to make living this image and so conserve it in its primeval splendor as it was handed on to him. This way, he really was, before being a missionary, a true contemplative of the glories of Our Lady. This we sometimes forget in a shallow understanding of Christian missionary activity: the deeper we contemplate the truths of faith the more we are able to confer the whole beauty of the good news.

Part Two of the Holy Mass: The Readings[18]

The more we confound the word of God with the word of this world the more it will become pure paper or "nice word." But the word of God is meant, first of all to bring fruit in our hearts, and the first fruit is that we recognize ourselves as poor sinners not worthy of the grace of Almighty God, the second fruit is that we try to reform our life according to this word of God and so really become "children of Light." This is what the manifold apparitions of Our Lady in our day want to bring to heart, that the word of God has to incarnate in our life as it did with her.

The adventure of the New World was a genuine attempt to bring the word of God to a world very different from ours, and so reform it according to the image we had in this Old World of Christ. This was necessarily also its limitation we come to see better today. But even though respecting our human limitation, it was not a pure "announcing of the word," but it was really "a reform of life" testifies up to our days in the Christian culture of this continent.

---

[18] cf. Book VI: The seven letters to the seven communities of Asia

Whoever enters one of its older churches will find moving representations of the Crucified Lord and His passion and always at His side, Our Lady of Sorrows. There are yet many places in the world, where the passion of Our Lord, during Holy Week, is made present even in its details.

The Seven-Fold Candelabra of Book Three

1. Gift of the Holy Spirit: Counsel
  2. Veil: Mantle
    3. Community: Pergamum
      4. Third last word
        5. Day III
          6. Sacrament: Confirmation
          7. The Offertory

Prayer for the Gift of Counsel

"Oh Lord, we are lost in the darkness and confusion of this world. Continually we need the grace of Your counsel so as not to go astray, but we recognize that the concrete counseling we need stems forth from the one counsel: Our unique vocation. It is the one necessary thing we must seek, because this vocation is You Oh Lord, by Your mystical Presence in our heart. Help us Oh Holy Spirit to find out ever deeper about this unspeakable grace and to correspond to it to the greater glory of the Father."

The Third Veil — The Mantle

The "turquoise mantle" of stars represents the constellations such as they were on the day the Virgin of Guadalupe appeared on December 12, 1531. These stars, representing the universe, are a symbol of the order and the beauty of all of God's works.[19] The light of the stars is symbolic of the invisible light of the hierarchy

---

[19] This veil is explained in greater detail in Book IV.

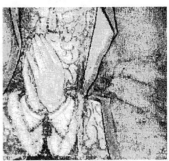

of the angels which was constituted in view of the mission of the Son of God on this earth, to help constitute the unshakable fundament of the church, symbolized in the earth separated from the chaotic waters. Her mantle is a symbol for water, the sea, of vegetation, of all of life, of the blue sky over us, of the life above us: the angels, the saints who have entered heaven. It is also a symbol of protection — we are so much under the mantle of Mary — of the waters of graces coming down continually from the Heart of God. For the Aztecs, the mantle is "xihuitl," all that is precious in the heavens and on earth. An image of the flowing down of the "waters of graces" is seen in the upper left side of Our Lady's mantle, especially where her arm bends. There also are noted three crosses, silently radiating the grace. Mary conceives for the second time under the cross in her heart opened by the seven swords of suffering. The Annunciation of the Archangel Gabriel comes to its fullness in the death of Our Lord on the cross. Salvation is confirmed for all eternity. Silently, Mary repeats her *"Fiat Mihi, secundum Verbum Tuum."*

The Third Community of Asia - Pergamum

Image of the Lord:

> *"…He who has the sharp two-edged sword:"*

Praise and reprimand:

> *"…you held fast my name and did not disown my faith, even in the days of Antipas, my faithful witness, who was slain among you where Satan dwells."*
>
> *"But I have a few things against you, because you have there some who hold the teaching of Balaam, who taught Balak to cast a stumbling-block before the chil-*

*dren of Israel, that they might eat and commit fornica-
tion. So you also have some who hold the teaching of
the Nicolaites. In like manner repent, or else I will come
to you quickly, and will fight against them with the sword
of my mouth."*

Promise:

*"...I will give the hidden manna, and I will give him a
white pebble, and upon the pebble a new name written,
which no one knows except him who receives it."*

The firmness of this earth is a manifold symbol: not only for
the "rock of the church" amidst the chaotic waters of destruction,
but also of the immutable truth of faith and of the doctrine of the
church. Glorifying Mary we dare to say: "You have overcome all
heresies. In you the word dwells in Its fullness, leaving no place
for doubt!" The "hidden manna" is a symbol for the mystical presence of Our Lord in our soul. In and through Him, it represents our
unique vocation which must grow in us day by day. In the end, our
individual judgment will be whether or not the Son of God recognizes Himself in us. "The white pebble" is another symbol for our
vocation. It is an allusion to the pebble of David which killed the
giant Goliath. It is a promise for the Christian, that in faithfully
living one's unique vocation, no power of hell will overcome.

The message of Our Lady by word and light goes deeper into
the heart than only a message by word. The union of word and
light is a promise given to the apostles of the last times who will
carry once more the Gospel over the whole world before the end
comes. All those who in their heart crave to be "children of light"
will receive this last message and so be saved. Even though the
apparition of Our Lady of Guadalupe is a message of love, understanding and mercy, it is nevertheless a "two-edged sword," this is
to say, a sword which clearly points to heaven, to the God of all
light, but at the same time reveals the darkness of the works of sin.
At the end of the last day, the separation of light and darkness,
which began on the first day, will be consummated.

Third word from the Cross

"Woman, behold, your son. Behold your Mother"
(Jn 19:26-27)

Mary and Juan Diego meet under the cross of the misery of
Mexico after the victory of the Spaniards. There is peace in the
country, as we hear in the beginning of the Nican Mopohua, but it
is more a peace of death than of life. The mother of the Lord appears with her wide mantle so as to mercifully take up all their
misery and heal it in the blood of her Son, shed for all men on the
cross. Like St. John, representing the "holy remnant of Israel" at
the foot of the cross, Juan Diego is the first called to share in the
graces of her mantle.

As Our Lady takes up "this son," recommended to her by her
Son, so too does Juan Diego, receiving her "into his house." First
he thought the "house" was the church of the Franciscans, dedicated to St. James the Elder, where he is inscribed, but later she
lets him know that he himself has to look for her house. Finally he
will be her sacristan at the newly built poor chapel until the end of
his life. Only under her starry mantle, sign that everything has its
place in the reign of God, can man discover his unique vocation
and so become a reflection of the Lord, as "a sharp two-edged
sword" (community of Pergamum). Only these vocations will break
the walls of indifference and lukewarmness which makes the Christian faith a form of "communism," a mass movement guided by a
common "ideal" which is nothing more than an ideology.

We need a mother so as to mature in our Christian vocation. By
her loving care, little by little, we are made to stand on our own feet
and to execute the responsibility and the privilege of being a baptized Christian. The more we lose Mary as our loving Mother in the
church, the more we construct our own maturity, which unfortunately is one of pride and pharisism. Whoever has found his unique
vocation in Christ, subordinated and in service to the whole of the
church, is immune to heresy, simplifications of the greater truth we
can only find in God. He does not have to fear the reign of satan,
which is a reign of suppression and violence, because the sharp
two-edged sword of his unique vocation will help him to be a confessor, and if necessary, as Antipas, a martyr of faith.

Day Three of Creation

In the order of material things, the "third day" represents the creation of this "smallest of all stars" on which Our Lord Jesus Christ took His residence. In relation to all the other stars, it is like Bethlehem in comparison to all the great cities of the world.

We should see the seven days of creation in a trinitarian sequence:

Day one and day four are correlated to the Father, day two and day five to the Son and day three and day six to the Holy Spirit.

Day I	Day II	Day III	Day IV	Day V	Day VI	Day VII
Father	Son	Holy Spirit	Father	Son	Holy Spirit	Creation returns to God

Why two times three? The days should be the reflection (two times) of the most Holy Trinity. In another perspective they represent the "spaces" of creation (first three days) and their inhabitants (second three days), in still another perspective divine and human life — *"in Him we live, move, and have our being"*[20] God is not only the deepest of our being, He comprises everything. In relation to the holy angels, day three represents the place of each angel in the heavenly hierarchy. After the trial (day one), the division between good and bad angels (day two); the third day confirms the special vocation of each angel in the plan of the wisdom of God.

In relation to man, the third day not only signifies the grace of a unique vocation for us Christians, it is also a symbol for the heavenly house God has already given us here on earth in the church. In

---

[20] Acts 17:28

the order of salvation, the "third day" is reflected in the Gospels when Our Lord Jesus Christ begins to form His "family," first with the election of the twelve apostles and the women who follow him on the way to Jerusalem and then, in a circle around them the disciples and all those who in some way look up to Him.

Again, we are reminded that the counsel most needed on our earthly pilgrimage is our vocation in imitation of Christ, and this in a unique way, responding to the call of love of God, destined personally to us. Only in this way can the church be built up by "living stones" and not bricks, each identical to the other. This is confirmed in the message of Guadalupe by this very personal and loving meeting between Juan Diego and Our Lady. To be truly a Christian is to correspond with one's whole being to the loving call of God, which in this case is transmitted by Our Lady in the most loving way. No where in literature can a purer relation between man and woman be found, as in the meeting of these two pure creatures who have one common aim: the service of God for His greater glory.

Sacrament - Confirmation

Confirmation is the Sacrament in which we promise to live a Christian life. As it is the Sacrament of the Holy Spirit. We pray for an outpouring of all His Gifts, but especially for the gift of counsel. Our Lady, as mediatrix of all graces, wants to help us to really become mature Christians, worthy of our vocation. This another maturity than that proclaimed in the church today, where man, in an attitude very much  alike to that of the fallen angels, proclaims the right to determine his own life.

A true child of the mother is never ashamed of her, but to the contrary, will always proclaim her glory. This mature humility is symbolically shown by the attitude of the seer, represented in the child at the feet of the Virgin, tightly holding onto the mantle of His Mother. With him we are called to enter into this mission under her mantle, guided by our Guardian Angel. Here again it is apparent that the last gospel to be proclaimed on earth is one by, through and with Mary, but as Mary's vocation is the most personal one among all Christians this requires on our part that also the way that we proclaim the good news must be as personal as possible.

This is quite a contradiction to the way the Gospel is many times proclaimed today, not only in an abstract and theological way, but also without the fire of the love of God which will give it life. Good news by Mary is one that comes from the heart and aims at the heart of those who hear it. As Mary gave her "yes," together with all her heart, when God called upon her, so also must our personal vocation become more and more, by way of her, an offering pleasing to God.

Part Three of the Holy Mass: Offertory[21]

The Offertory in Holy Mass is not as one might think, sitting comfortably on a church pew, some kind of preparatory work only the priest has to do. It is always a first act of an abandonment into the loving hands of the Father and this is why formerly the faithful used to kneel down, testifying their submission to the incomprehensible will of God. Juan Diego, already in the beginning, has to make a first painful experience of this truth.

His enthusiasm, taking on the mission of Our Lady, is cool to zero when the good bishop does not show the least sign of interest in what is being conferred to him. Mission is not only conferring an abstract truth to someone who is equally abstract from me, but it requires on our part, that together with the message, we give our hearts. This is best expressed with St. Paul in his letter to the I Thessalonians 2:8: "As if a nurse were cherishing her own children, so we in our love for you would have gladly imparted, not only the gospel of God, but also our own souls: because you had become most dear to us."

Louis M. DeMonfort, speaks in a beautiful parable about this simple truth, that any offering is increased in value if we hand it

---

[21] cf. Book VI: Offertory

over by someone more important than us. He speaks about a peasant who wants to give his fruit to the king, but on the way remembers that it would be much more profitable if to this purpose he would use the mediation of the queen. So also, our offertory, in this case, our personal vocation, is much more valuable to God if it is an offering by way of Our Lady.

The Seven-Fold Candelabra of Book Four

*"Oh Lord, cry out your thirst, that it will break all
the walls that man's sin, ignorance and self-sufficiency
have built up. Let your cry "I thirst" come over us
like a flood, that we will be torn along by it,
drowned in it — drowned in your thirst for the
salvation of souls, for the coming of the reign of God
in order, harmony and love — cry it out Oh Lord,
such that we forget ourselves and hear only You, feel
only Your thirst ... and thist with You. Amen"*

Prayer for Knowledge of the Gospel

1. Gift of the Holy Spirit: Prayer for knowledge
2. Veil: Earth-toned gown
3. Community: Thyatira
4. Fourth last word
5. Day IV
6. Sacrament: Holy Eucharist/Penance/Holy Eucharist
7. Holy Mass: Sanctus

Knowledge (of the cross): this gift isn't learned from books or from studying. It is the science taught by God Himself in the sacrifice of His Only Son. The more we enter with all our life into His sacrifice the more we are like Mary, able to participate in the redemptive work of Her Son. St. Francis certainly is one of the saints who had the best understanding of this gift. This is why also he didn't want his disciple to go back to the ecclesiastical status, but rather learn only by living the word of God in all tribulations of life. Unfortunately, his craving for this deeper science of Christ soon got lost, but it has to be resurrected in these last times when the whole church is called to enter in the way of the cross of Golgotha.

Fourth Veil - Earth-toned Gown

The *fourth* veil is Our Lady's earth-toned *gown*. Shown in all its various hues, it represents all mankind throughout the history of salvation. As co-redemptrix, Mary participates in the Redemption wrought by her Son. She takes upon herself the sins of men so that they might be washed in the blood of Christ her Son and through her tears.[22] There are various degrees of light and darkness in her dress, representing the battle between light and the darkness. We need the gift of the *science* of the cross in order to orient us towards the definite order of all things in the reign of God symbolically represented by the sun, the moon and the stars in heaven.

The earthly-toned color of the tunic symbolically reflects salvation history in its entirety and the mystery of iniquity. We note that a lace of golden flowers is superimposed on Her tunic. This speaks to us of the heavenly assistance of the holy angels in all battles. The more the angels are called to enter into the final battle for the reign of God, the more they will mysteriously have part also in the passion of Our Lord Jesus Christ, but we should remember that they have a different entry into the suffering of Our Lord. We men, first of all, see almost exclusively the dolorous part of His suffering; the angels, on the contrary, see the glorious part of it. Each moment of suffering has its glorious perspective, because it is only by greater glory of God, visible in the power of resurrection, that the power of sin was overcome. This is why we

---

[22] Recall Simeon's prophecy to Our Lady, Lk 2:35. It is here, for the first time, that Our Lady is being told about her coredemptive mission, certainly already before she knew about it, being singled out from all mankind in the mission of Incarnation. It is only by suffering that we come to know more deeply the immense love of God for us poor sinners, but suffering should be out of a pure heart which most of us have lost by sin. This is why only Mary Immaculate was dignified to participate in the sufferings of her Son. We can have part in them only according to the degree we are in Mary.

have to learn from the angels that suffering is "the noblest work" in which man is called to participate, and this is also why it requires the greatest purity of heart.[23]

Fourth Community of Asia - Thyatira

Image of the Lord:

> "...Son of God, who has eyes like to a flame of fire, and whose feet are like fine brass:"

Praise and reprimand:

> "...works, your faith, your love, your ministry, your patience and your last works....
> ...But I have against you that you suffer the woman Jezebel, who calls herself a prophetess, to teach, and to seduce my servants, to commit fornication, and to eat of things sacrificed to idols."

Promise:

> "...I will give authority over the nations. And he shall rule them with a rod of iron, and like the potter's vessel they shall be dashed to pieces, as I also have received from my Father and I will give him the morning star."

The Lord here represents the jealous love of God to bring man back to the order of the reign of God, out of which he fell with his first sin and continues to fall till the end of time when the chaos of the end will join up with the chaos of the beginning. The "feet of brass" represent the power of the Holy Spirit to realize this order

---

[23] Because in our times we have lost this purity of heart, in the flood of immorality which has come over us since the last World War, we are more and more unable to appreciate the value of suffering. This is why, even in the church, concepts like "sacrifice, expiation, reparation, etc." are part of the last vocabulary, and have been substituted by humanistic concepts, first of all a false concept of the love of one's neighbor. We have to recall soberly that there is no way to love one's neighbor if one has not first learned to love God.

against any opposition on the side of the fallen angels and man. Especially in our times in which man takes over his destiny, he makes himself his own redeemer. As many philosophies and ideologies, so many trials of man to save himself, but in the light of Christ this is the most futile attempt of man. He cannot draw himself out of the swamp waters of sin. Only by way of the cross is there salvation, and this is why we will find our way back to the order of God only if we take up our cross with the Lord.

This community should live the order symbolized in the order of the stars on the fourth day of creation. It is reprimanded because it suffers disorder, and sin enter, into its ranks. The sin of the Christians, as Pope Pious XII pointed out, is that they are lukewarm — this opens the entry for the demon and is cause of the loss of many souls, for which we are responsible. There is a perilous attraction to the "depths of Satan," especially for those who have no depth in their faith anymore and look out for compensation.[24]

The promise for this community is that if we live the order of the cross we will be a sign (a morning star!) for the pagans living in the disorder of sin. The "morning star" points to Mary who is the beauty of the order of God, as we learn to appreciate in the image of Guadalupe. The order of God is not the perfect order of computers but the living, mysterious and holy order of the living God!

Fourth Last word

"I thirst!" (Jn 19:28)

It is the outcry of the Lord: For bringing back the creation to the Father (repatriation).

It is the cry for saving the souls of men from eternal dam-

---

[24] More and more the sobriety of the truths of faith is substituted by fantastic and unreal speculations — products of the brilliant intellect of the fallen angels, who, revolting against God, have lost their fundament in reality.

nation. It is the challenge for the final union of all creation in God best expressed in the prayer of the great high priest written down by St. John in the farewell sermon (ch. 14-17) before entering his passion. The cry of the Lord will finally bring about this union of the three parts of creation as one: because this is our destiny, to praise the Holy God in union with the material and angelical creation for all eternity.

Day Four of Creation

The fourth day is the day of the creation of the lights in the heavens: the sun, moon and the stars. We recognize the order and harmony of the reign of God, first represented in the invisible hierarchy of the holy angels. The space of light opening up in the first day is filled and irradiates its wonderful order and harmony.

In relation to the angels it shows us the perfect order of their hierarchy, with its infinite correlations, in harmony of collaboration, in order to accomplish the plan of wisdom God has for this world.

In relation to man it is the order of the Mystical Body of the church which finally will be visible before the eyes of the world when the visible church will have adapted herself to the invisible order of the angels.

In the Gospels the "fourth day" is that of the multiplication of the bread — presymbol of the Holy Eucharist as "Bread of Life." It is by His Humble Presence in the Holy Eucharist that the Lord in the Holy Spirit will "reform the face of the earth." In relation to the Sacrament of Penance: it will bring fruit only if we receive it with a contrite and humble heart, recognizing that we have offended the Holy God.

Sacrament — The Holy Eucharist

The Greek fathers called the Sacrament of the Holy Eucharist "the Sacrament of Enlightenment" (photismos). It is by this Most Holy Sacrament that mankind, after purification, will learn more about the infinite holiness of God Who has humbled Himself so

much to be trodden upon in our days.[25] We have to learn "by God," this is to say that all our knowledge must be orientated to God and to His greater glory and not, as it is today, to the greater and vain glory of man, behind which is all the vanity of the fallen angels.

The Fourth Part of the Holy Mass: The Sanctus[26]

Holiness has to do with "whole," ever since man lost, by sin, the contact with God; he has gradually lost himself. In our times, he doesn't even know who he is, and this is why he tries to reproduce himself artificially and so he replaces life more and more by artifice. Man is split up in so many parts that he approaches the disaster of the first fallen angel, who is sometimes represented by millions of pieces of shattered glass. Only God is "whole," and therefore *holy*. Man will discover his identity only if he converts again to the living God.

In the liturgies of the eastern rite, after the offering, the priest disappears behind the icons and returns again for the "Our Father" and Holy Communion. This tells us symbolically that we will never find out about the depth of the Holy Mass beginning with the "Sanctus." The "Sanctus" is first of all, as we see in the vocation of the Prophet Isaiah the unending outcry of the angels before the greater majesty of God. It is the "Sanctus" which is the deepest veil over the next step in holy Mass: the consecration of bread and wine into the Body and Blood of Christ. Modern man is incapable of understanding that there was a discipline of Arcanum with the first Christians: nobody was admitted to assist holy Mass after the Liturgy of the

---

[25] Recall the angel's word in Fátima in his third apparition: "Receive the body and blood of Our Lord Jesus Christ terribly outraged by ungrateful men."

[26] cf. Book VI: Sanctus

word if he had not passed the examination not only about knowing the mystery of Incarnation, but also living it.[27]

The Seven-Fold Candelabra of Book Five

1. Gift of the Holy Spirit: Prayer for fortitude
   2. Veil: Inner white Tunic
      3. Community: Sardis
         4. Fifth word of Our Lord from the Cross
            5. Day five of creation
               6. Sacrament: Matrimony/Holy Orders/Confirmation
               7. Holy Mass (Transubstantiation)

Prayer for fortitude

> *"Lord God, grant us the fortitude of St. Stephen,*
> *stoned by the Jews for confessing his faith without*
> *fear. May we receive this gift by "looking up to You,*
> *seated at the right hand of the Father*
> *in Your glory. Amen."*

Fortitude is the most necessary gift in these times of battle against the more and more apparent dominion of satanic forces in the world. We must beseech this gift of the Holy Spirit through the purity of Mary. She lived the total surrender of the "Spouse of God." May our surrender, fortified in the purity of Mary, be a strength for the entire church … that we may be a worthy response to the will of Our Lord Jesus Christ in his command, *"love one another as I have loved you."* (Jn 13:34)

---

[27] The charismatic catechetical movement tries to reproduce this organic and gradual introduction of us Christians into this mystery of Incarnation. Learning in a purely rationalistic way we have completely lost the concept of a deeperm, that is, a mystical science which always implies the participation of the whole man. Catechism is not to know only about the truths of faith by letter; catechism implies that little by little we realize the mysteries of faith in our own life.

The Fifth Veil — Inner White Gown

The *fifth* of the seven veils is found in Our Lady's white cuffs and collar, a symbol of her angelic purity. She surpasses all the saints in angelic beauty. Even more than the angels, and in union with them, she is by her purity, *mediatrix* of all graces. If Christ Jesus is the head of His Mystical Body, then Mary is the neck, and it is for this reason the church calls upon her as the "gate of heaven," *porta coeli*. A sign of this mediation is the small golden brooch with the cross. It is specifically upon the white of the inner garment, but also as if closing the opening at the neck of the earth-toned gown (symbol of salvation history).

The white cuffs form the letters alpha and omega. The alpha seems to be more like the point of an arrow. The significance of the arrow can be found by means of the seven seals beneath her hands: our way to God, who is the alpha, is a sealed mystery. Mary is the alpha (small letter), God's first thought about creation, untouched by sin — the Immaculate One. She is also the omega (again small letter), that is, the consummation of creation according to this thought, through her Immaculate Heart.[28] Here her Immaculate Heart signifies that she has corresponded in all to the plans of the love of God. Her heart is not only the reflection of the Sacred Heart of Her Son, it is also that of the Heart (invisible and "white") of the Father.

This "white" veil also is a sign of the help of the holy angels in the final Spiritual battle for the kingdom of God. This is why the fifth community of Asia is in special need of their help. The angels will mediate to us the graces coming from God through Mary (neck), and at the same time they will be our strength (cuff) in combat. Therefore, it is also through them that we will be able to grow in the gift of fortitude, so necessary in this final battle for the kingdom of God. In relation to Genesis 1, the upward movement of the birds in the air is a symbol for a life in the Holy Spirit, a life which Mary lived to the fullness.

---

[28] Within the left hand of Our Lady can be seen a shadow in the form of a heart. Note that the small alpha and omega are in opposition to the capital ones, symbols of Our Lord!

The white color reflecting her angelic purity is also a symbol of the peaks of the volcanoes Popocatépetl and Iztaccihuatl (close to the capital). Covered by snow year round, they are a symbol of the nation and a challenge for a life according to the commandments of God. If Mexico continues on the way of the cross of the Lord, in the fight against the enemy, it will continued to be called "always faithful to the church."[29]

Fifth Asian Community - Sardis

Image of the Lord:

> *"...He who has the seven spirits of God and the seven stars...."*

Reprimand:

> *"...I know your works; you have the name of being alive, and you are dead.*
>
> *"Be watchful and strengthen the things that remain, but which were ready to die. For I do not find thy works complete before my God.*
>
> *"Remember therefore what you have received and heard, and observe it and repent. Therefore, if you will not watch, I will come upon you as a thief, and you shall not know at what hour I shall come upon you."*

Praise:

> *"But you have a few persons at Sardis who have not defiled their garments,*[30] *and they shall walk with me in white; for they are worthy."*[31]

---

[29] It is a statement of the Freemasons that as long as Mexico will continue in faith to the church, their dominion over Latin America will not be complete. The enemy knows better about the strategical importance of this country for the whole continent of America.

[30] The white garment is a symbol of baptismal innocence.

[31] Note the beautiful correlation with the fifth veil of the inner white garment of Our Lady of Guadalupe and that which Our Lord emphasizes to this fifth community of Sardis.

Promise:

> *"He who overcomes shall be arrayed thus in white garments, and I will not blot his name out of the book of life, but I will confess his name before my Father, and before his angels."*

The Lord revealing Himself as the "One who has the seven Spirits of God and the seven stars" is the Lord and King of the angels, at His service. Man, in his pride of doing everything himself, even in church, has forgotten that he is not only the last created, at the end of the sixth day, but that he is only a "third part" of this creation, together with mute (material) creation and the creation of the angels. We will not find our way in the growing confusion of these times if we do not avail the help of the heavenly Spirits and their light which pierces all darkness.

The Lord's blame for this community is one of the severest: *"you have the name of being alive, but you are dead."* How many so-called Christians rely on exterior "pious" works and prayers as a way to bargain with God? Through them, the name of God is shamed. Their faith is likened to that of the Pharisees, of self-justification. Besides the "pious," there are those who know everything better, who by their own effort want to create a church more adapted to the world, active only in social works. Both of them forget that faith must be fertile in good works, done in collaboration with the grace of God. Only these works will enter into heaven. The angel at our side is our best help to keep our eyes always lifted up to God.

The promise of the Lord for those who are "alive in faith" are the "white garments (as we see them in this veil with Our Lady of Guadalupe) to confess them before His Father and His angels. Those who really suffer for the situation of the church and the world in our days share with Our Lord His agony in the garden of Gethsemane. In these hours, Our Lord had to contemplate the exterior futility of all His efforts to bring man back to God. He was conscious, more than ever before, of the powers of the enemy.

In His humanity, He was almost crushed by this burden of sin, both of angel and man. It is in this hour that an angel from heaven came to comfort Him, that is to say, to give Him force to offer His last drop of blood for the salvation of mankind. If the Lord Himself, being at the same time God, needed to be comforted by an angel, how much more we poor Christians, so much lost in the desert of this world, must cry out for the help of the angels to assist us in this desperate situation.

It is a pious custom, especially in the holy hour of Thursday to offer the drops of the precious blood of Our Lord, that He sweated in the garden of Gethsemane, for all those who are recommended to our prayers and desperately need our help, in the first place, the priests, so much attacked by the enemy. Juan Diego's abandonment, in his common priesthood, to the will of God is a challenge for all priests to do the same and sacrifice their whole life to be like him, missionaries of the greater God as he was by way of Our Lady.

Fifth word of Our Lord from the Cross

> *"Eloi, Eloi, lama sabacthani?" "My God, my God, why hast thou forsaken me?"* (Mk 15:34, Mt 27:46)

It is to the greater God that we are called to "climb up," to the "mountain of sanctity," to share in the company of the angels and all the saints in heaven — this is a "*dark*" way, many times without any visible indications, without anybody to help us, the way of the "dark night of senses and of the Spirit." Any soul ambitious enough to draw closer to God necessarily has to pass through the abandonment Our Lord has suffered for all of us on the cross. That "God is" was never lost in the human consciousness of Our Lord Jesus Christ, but in His passion, taking upon Himself the sins of all mankind before and after Him, before the Father, He experienced the rejection of the Father as if He Himself was the greatest of all sinners. Adrienne of Speyer beautifully explains the deeper sense of sacramental confession: we confess our sins in and with Jesus on the cross to the Father, He Who takes upon Himself the just chastisement: the condemnation of death, which we have merited by our sins. But God the Father resurrects Him from the dead. This grace we receive by sacramental absolution; it is our part in the Resurrection of Christ.

Juan Diego, in his first visit with the bishop, met nothing but distrust and rejection, not only for his person, but also because as a messenger of Our Lady he must experience utter abandonment. He is tempted to give in, to put his mission back into the hands of Our Lady; if she hadn't reassured him, he would have given up. This also was the biggest trial for the shepherd children in Fátima: they were disbelieved by their parents, the pastor and the civil authorities. Because of this Lucia did not want to return to the Cova on the 13th of June as was requested by Our Lady. If it had not been for the intercession of prayers of Jacinta and Francisco she would have given up. This is to remind us that in the times of Spiritual combat we can not rely on ourselves. The trials will be too hard for us. Only by relying on the merciful help of Our Lady and in the grace of God will we be able to pass them. The fortitude we see in St. Stephen and other martyrs is not the fortitude of man, it is truly a gift of the Holy Spirit.

Day Five of Creation

The Population of the Waters and the Air

Life is called to rise over the force of gravitation of this world. We see this effort even in the plants, in the animals, especially the birds who serve here as symbol for a life turned to God. The angels living already in the presence of God are given to us as our good companions on the pilgrimage of this earth and not to drown in the dust of a purely pagan existence, as if there were no eternal life waiting for us. They have gone through the first trial at the beginning of times and they will help us to go through the last, which is to come over the whole world.

The "fifth day" in the Gospel is the approaching of Our Lord, with his apostles, to Jerusalem, most clearly seen with St. Luke (chapter 9-18). With St. Luke it is a journey of "nine steps," reminding us that we have to be born anew so as to enter heaven by the narrow door. It is on this "day" that Our Lord will teach them the science of the cross, as the key which will open the heavenly door.

Sacrament — Marriage

The Sacrament of Marriage unites again that which has been separated by original sin: man and women who together should be an image of the triune God. Infidelity and the breaking up of marriages, which are so prevalent today, is a very clear sign that even among Christians this sacrament is no longer understood as an inviolable "bond of God," a "bond" which necessarily infers: cross. Through the cross, Our Lord reunited heaven and earth. Through His passion He returned to man and woman the original orientation and destiny of their union: God. St. Paul speaks of marriage as the image of the union of Christ with His church. (cf. EPH 5:21-32) The mission of "union" is not only emphasized in the words of Our Lady of Guadalupe, but first of all in the pictorial message, in the "amoxtli"[32] to the Aztecs: she is standing on the moon, image of this earth, but enveloped by the rays of the sun, image of a life coming out of God. Why is marriage, in such a special way, under the shadow of the cross? The reason is certainly that the union of man and woman, fertile in a child, is meant to be an image of the triune God. The fallen angels, knowing about this plan of God, attacked at the most sensitive point: Adam and Eve fell, breaking the command of God, and so lost the guidance of the Holy Spirit that would have helped them to grow deeper and deeper into their destiny.[33]

---

[32] cf. Book I, virginity and motherhood
[33] The guidance of God was not completely taken away. A sign of this is that God Himself clothed man with animal skins. The warmth of the skin, being an image of the help of the Holy Spirit by way of the angels. By way of this guidance, man, in millions of years managed to climb up again to the point where God was able to send His Son to bring mankind back to Him.

By way of the Sacrament of Marriage a special grace was given to man to overcome the consequences of original sin, concupiscence, illness and death, but this only by way of entering into the way of the cross of Our Lord. Symbolically speaking, the consequences of the first sin of man are among men and women like an abysm which they can overcome only with the greater grace of God. This is why, necessarily, marriage is, and will remain a way of the cross which only those will enter who have the courage to ascend with the Lord to the hill of Golgotha.

In the image of Our Lady of Guadalupe the white interior gown reminds us of a wedding gown. Being so close to the holy body of Our Lady, it becomes a symbol that only in the purity of Mary will matrimony come to its consummation. Matrimony, as much as priesthood, is first of all, serving God, consecrating our life entirely to Him. It is by way of this consecration that we will become more and more instruments of the mercy of God, be it in Matrimony, be it in the priesthood. Only if we live these two sacraments in their holiness will the crisis in which they are found today be overcome.

The Fifth Part of the Holy Mass:

The Consecration[34]
The Lamb,
The Angels of Harvest and of Judgment

The only way of probing the depths of understanding with respect to the mystery of the Holy Eucharist is to see its relation to the sacrifice of Christ on the cross. Wherever this relation is obliterated, it becomes a "hieroglyph" which the fallen angels use to lead man into confusion. It is not by chance that Our Lord instituted the most holy Sacrament before he entered His passion: He wants to continue His presence and so also His passion in His faithful up to the end of times. The Lord wills to make present, in everyone of us, in a personal and unique way, His holy suffering on

---

[34] cf. Book VI; Consecration/Apocalyptic Mass.

the cross. If ever we were to understand this call more deeply, then we would also understand much better that the entire church, in these last times, is called in and through Mary Immaculate to collaboration in the fulfillment of Redemption. This is why the dogma of Mary co-redeptrix will be ripe for proclamation by the Holy Father only when the entire church will follow the Lord's call to share in His passion. To respond to the call of repentance of the first angel[35] is the condition for our having part in the final transormation of all things. Conversion in this final hour will ask for the complete denial of our own will, to die to the old Adam, so as to be able to resurrect in Christ as new men.

Juan Diego, in his way of the cross, has assimilated himself so much to Our Lady and by way of her to HER Son, that she in turn wants to reveal that he himself is his mission. The same thing we can observe with the children of Fátima — they completely identify themselves with their mission, forgetting about themselves, so they would be able to say with St. Paul, *"it is no longer I who live, it is Christ Who lives in me."*[36] In this last call for conversion there is only the choice between transformation into the new man in Christ or eternal condemnation, apparent in the two following angels of judgment. The sickle in the hand of the first angel of harvest is the beginning of the final harvest on earth, which is already prophesied by Our Lady of Guadalupe by her apparition at the beginning of the modern times, not by words but through the pictorial language of her image, the three "fishing instruments" and the constellation of Boötes.

---

[35] cf. Rv 2:4-5
[36] Gal 2:20

The Seven-Fold Candelabra of Book Six

1. Prayer for fear of the Lord
　2. Sixth veil: Mary's body
　　3. Sixth community of Asia: Philadelphia
　　　4. Sixth last word
　　　　5. Day six of creation
　　　　　6. Sacrament: Penance/Confirmation/
　　　　　　Extreme Unction
　　　　　　7. the holy Mass: Holy Communion

Prayer for the fear of the Lord
*"The closer you want to draw us to Your heart, oh God,
the more we need to know about the distance
of us poor creatures and sinners to you, O Holy God,
in order to better appreciate your Infinite love to us in
Christ Your Son!
May the fear of God, the angels experienced
in the first trial at the beginning of time
ever more penetrate our hearts;
then no temptation of the devil can tear us
away from you, oh God of love and Mercy. Amen"*

The fear of the Lord is the beginning of wisdom. It is the just distance between the Creator and the creature. This gift of the Holy Spirit is reflected in both the hands and face of the Virgin of Guadalupe. Her praying hands and inclined head both portray a profound reverence of God, her Creator. It is precisely this fear of God which is the main theme also of the Apocalypse: by way of the intervention of the angels, in the Spiritual battle of these last times, man will come again to know better about the greater God.

Sixth Veil — The Body of Mary Immaculate

The sixth veil enwrapping the mysterious presence of God in Mary is her most pure body; in the image we see only her hands and face. At the Annunciation, Mary had her eyes and her whole face turned to God. She was, "hanging on the face of God," and this is why her face, different from that of Moses, continues to radiate in a mysterious way, the presence of God in her heart. At the Annunciation, she opened her hands wide, in the form of a cross, to conceive with her whole being, body and soul, the Son of God. This is why these two parts of her body[37] represent in a special way the gift of the fear of God. As the most docile instrument among all creation, she submitted herself to the plans of the mercy of God. It is for this reason that Holy Mother the church calls her the "Ark of the Covenant," "House of Gold" and the "temple of God."[38] By way of Mary we can better understand the participation of material creation in Redemption and glorification. This is the most beautiful argument against all Gnostic heresies which try to do away with the material world.

Sixth Community of Asia — Philadelphia

Image of the Lord:

> *"...the Holy One, the True One, He Who has the key of David, he who opens and no one shuts and who shuts and no one opens:"*

Praise:

> *"I know your works. Behold, I have caused a door to be opened before you which no one can shut, for you have scanty strength, and you have kept my word and have not disowned my name.*

---

[37] A third part, seen in a veiled way, is her right foot. So also here we have a trinitarian relation: her face turns to God the Father, her hands, in similitude to her crucified Son, stretched out to receive the will of God in her heart and her foot, ready to carry the "good message" over the entire earth.

[38] Mary is the great mediatrix of graces. She veils the divine Mediator Jesus Christ like a crystal with a hundred facets and each facet is a reflection of her beauty, and of the greater beauty of God. Each facet is an avocation of Mary, like a precious image, like a precious stone, a crown around the triune God. This way we have to understand also the Laurentine Litany.

> *"Behold, I will bring some of the synagogue of Satan who say they are Jews, and are not, but are lying — behold, I will make them come and worship before your feet. And they shall know that I have loved you."*

Promise:

> *"...I too will keep you from the hour of trial, which is about to come upon the whole world to try those who dwell upon the earth.*
>
> *"I come quickly; hold fast what you have, that no one receive your crown. (The crown is symbolic of our vocation.) He who overcomes, I will make him a pillar in the temple of my God, and never more shall he go outside.*
>
> *"And I will write upon him the name of my God, and the name of the city of my God — the new Jerusalem, which comes down out of heaven from my God — and my new name."*

- For this community, the Lord is *"the holy, the true, the One Who has the key of David."* Where He opens, *nobody can close, where he closes, no one can open."*[39] It is He Who also opens the door to this community. In a fundamental way, Christ is for us the key to heaven when He died for us on the cross. This is why we can see the cross also as "a key," the only key which will open for us the doors of heaven. The power of the key of the church: to bind and to loosen is no other power than that of the cross. If we look deeper into the Apocalypse we will recognize that the cross is also the key for a deeper understanding of this mysterious book.
- *"You have little force, but you have kept My word faithfully, and didst not betray my name."* More and more whatever is pious tradition has been put aside, as the rosary, so much recommended by Our Lady, as the "prayer widows and old maids." The attack

---

[39] Rv 3:7-13

against the value of this sacramental is really a contamination by the "pride of the fallen prince," but the wisdom of God lifts up the lowly. The Lord will be victorious not by the strong but by the feeble, as with David in his fight against Goliath.

- The Lord gives the community of Philadelphia the promise of the conversion of some of those of the "synagogue of satan": "they will come and fall to your feet and will know that I love you." We must consider it a priority to be found in the favor of God, to be a "beloved son." We are to be "children of light" in a world of darkness. This is the best form of evangelization.

- *"As you have guarded My word of patience so I will guard you from the trial which has to come over the whole word to put them to test."* The test of the angels, at the beginning of time, was with respect to their submission to the incomprehensible plan of God for His Son. To serve or not to serve brought about the separation between good and bad angels. Mankind "come to maturity" is now faced with the same decision: humble submission to the indestructible will of God or revolt against God.

- *"I am coming soon, conserve what you have, so that you will not lose your crown."* We have to fight to be worthy of our "royal vocation in Christ." Whoever will not esteem it will lose it. Recall the parable of the "treasure hidden in the field" and of the "pearl of great price." The rosary helps us to appreciate the great "price" paid for our Redemption.

- *"He who overcomes, I will make him a column in the temple of My God."* We need to be in Christ all the time. We need to "carry Him from one communion to the next" in order to be a column in Him alone. We have to stand up in a time when the earth will be shaken as never before. Only He can help us not to move, when all things will be moved.

- *"And I will write the name of My God on him and the name of the new Jerusalem coming down from heaven and my new name."*

As the letter starts in a Trinitarian way: Holy God, True God, Omnipotent God, so it ends with a trinitarian promise to those who are faithful. In the name of God, we will become a "new man." In the new Jerusalem we will have our part in the glory of the Son, in the new name of the Son, revealed by the Holy Spirit (to those who adore God in Spirit and truth) we will receive our "new name" containing the mission we had on this earth in His name.

> *Admonition: "He who has ears, let him hear what the Spirit says to the church." Only in the Holy Spirit will we understand this outstanding promise for those who are faithful.*

Sixth Last Word

> *"Father, into Your hands I commend my Spirit."* (Lk 23:46)

Our way over this earth is a pilgrimage, many times on perilous roads, through many dangers and desperations, but we are never lost if we recommend ourselves in the hands of the Father Whose providence will never falter. In Complines, we pray this prayer of trust with the church everyday; we have to pray it most ardently in our last hour of transition from this world to the "other side," to the eternal light of God. The Apocalypse is also like the Complines on the world. All three parts of creation will be melted in the fire of the love of God to become one in His eternal praise.

Day Six of Creation

The "sixth day" in creation is the creation of animal life on the earth, and at its end, the creation of man, the "crown of creation." As  on the third day the earth became firm, so man has to become firm in God through Jesus Christ the Son of God Who became man, and not angel. In man, through Christ the triple creation is called to return to the Father, entering into the new Jerusalem, where God will dwell in their midst for all eternity.

Man appears on the "scene of this world" as the "Benjamin" in the "last hour" of the last day. God's infinite love has prepared for him, in the smallest of all stars, the most beautiful place he could think of. Everything is foreseen, even unto the smallest details. So already creation, in its beauty and perfection, is a challenge to man to become beautiful as Mary the most beautiful flower in the garden of God. Among all creatures he is the frailest of all. If not cared for in love from the very beginning of his life, he will suffer or even die. So among the two other creatures who surround him: material creation and the Spiritual creation of the angels he is in a special way a creature of hope. This hope can only be fulfilled if he attains the "fullness of his age and wisdom" in and by Jesus Christ, the Son of God. Recognizing his humble situation he should more and more avail himself of the help of his "elder brothers" and of the never failing love of God, which wants to transform him into "a son in the Son," giving him part in the eternal life of God. If he will follow the steps of the Lord which inevitably lead up to Golgotha, he will be admitted to enter into the rest of God on the seventh day!

Here again we have to remember the rosary as the prayer of harvest:

- Only with the Gift of the fear of God will we come to know about the greater God; this is why we have not only to go through the mysteries again and again, but they have to become life in us, the life of Christ.
- Looking to the community of Philadelphia we should not be afraid of our frailties amidst a world of power — we only need to be faithful, and the Lord will help us to go through the trial which necessarily has to come.[40] The rosary is the umbilical chord which ties us to our Lady, it is the climbing rope, with which we will reach God the holy.
- Every time we pray the Rosary we should commend our entireties into the hands of the Father in and through the Mys-

---

[40] the community of Philadelphia is the most outstanding among the communities of Asia. It is closest to the holy will of God concerning it. So it is also closest to Mary and to all her faithful servants, the saints. We can especially remember Juan Diego.

teries of Christ His Son. By praying the rosary we entrust ourselves, and this with each mystery, in the hands of the merciful God. It is by meditating the mysteries that we become more and more confirmed in our faith, and so acquire the gift of the fear of the Lord.

In the Gospels, the sixth day is that of the judgment of the Lord over Jerusalem, the unfaithful city. In the Apocalypse, the unfaithful city is exemplified by Babylon to show us that unfaithfulness is a universal sign of those who fall away from God. Jerusalem, even though elected to be the "holy city," had to give way later on to Rome, and at the end, also Rome, becoming unfaithful, will have to give place to this sixth community, which by its faithfulness is a living promise of all things in the new Jerusalem.

Sacrament — Penance

According to the "order of the Son,"[41] the Sacrament of Penance is the axle of the wheel of growth of the Spiritual life. The Sacraments have to help us to adapt our life ever more to the order of the reign of God, overcoming all egoism, arbitrariness and violence. Everything has to fit into the pattern of God's infinite love. The more we are conscious of our being poor sinners, nothing before God, the more we will be apt as instruments for God's infinite mercy. As the last phase of the history of salvation will be that of the justice of God, there is only, in the beginning, a last offer of con-

---

[41] The "order of the Son" is the order treated in the chaplet of the seven veils, the same order which corresponds with the seven Liturgical Hours: 1) Holy Eucharist, 2) Marriage, 3) Baptism, 4) Penance, 5) Holy Orders, 6) Confirmation and 7) Extreme Unction. In this order, Penance is the center, and therefore like the axis.

version to those who have not yet hardened their heart in the pleasures of an earthly life. The Apocalypse is mainly the accomplishment of the holy justice of God, which will reform the whole creation according to the face of the only "man" Who is just: Jesus Christ.

The Sixth Part of the Holy Mass: Communion

In the Apocalypse, "communion" is with the angels of the cups of the wrath of God. Here, we are reminded that "he who does not discern this bread from common bread" will "eat his own judgment"[42] The angels are sent by God to prepare us for a deeper comprehension of this Sacrament of the love of God which today, even in the Catholic Church, many times is only a "social sign," as with the Protestants and other sects. Only the angels can help us not to fall into this pit into which this sacred mystery has fallen in our days. Together with the shepherd children of Fátima we have the mission to help the Lord, the "horribly outraged Lord," out of this pit of depreciation, ignorance, coldness of heart and even hate. As this is a direct counter-attack against the enemies' strategy to make the Lord completely disappear from the church, we cannot enter into this fight without the powerful help of the angels. The loving cry of Our Lord to be consoled, as it was passed to little Therese Martin and to Francisco Marto should help crystallize the "little flock" of the faithful in this time of defection in the church.

Here again, we are reminded that the four-petalled flower on the womb of Our Lady is also a mysterious sign for the Holy Eucharist, which is, in this flower, symbolized by a circle, enveloped by the four petals of the Nahui Ollin. Curiously, the four petals are not connected with  each other. How do we understand this symbolism? If the four petals first of all signify the mystery of the cross, meditated in the heart of Mary, then the lack of connection should be a sign that

---

[42]   cf. I Cor 11:27

this meditation of the mystery of the cross has not yet come to its fullness. This is also why we do not yet understand more deeply the interior relation between those three entities: the Holy Eucharist, the word of God and the cross, which necessarily, even though different, must be one.

As the sixth community, by its number, is related to Our Lady,[43] it is this community which is called in a special way to realize this consummation: the consummation of unity. Unity is not, as in the world, a matter of agreement between different parts, but first of all unity in orientation to the One God. This One God is represented in the sign of the Holy Eucharist in such a hidden way that those who are of the world will never know about it. In God's infinite and incomprehensible wisdom the veiled presence of His Son necessarily at the end has to become not only the center of the heart of the faithful, of any Christian family or community, of the church, but also of the whole universe: this was the intuition of Teilhard de Chardin in his "Mass on the World."[44]

Seven-Fold Candelabra of Book Seven

1. Prayer for piety
   2. Veil: Mary's soul
      3. Community: Laodicea
         4. Seventh last word: "It is consummated."
            5. Day seven of creation
               6. Sacrament: Extreme Unction/Extreme Unction
                  Holy Orders
               7. The Holy Mass: The final blessing

---

[43] Remember that Our Lady's number is six: 2 x 3 (perfect reflection of Most Holy Trinity)

[44] There is no doubt that the intuition of Teilhard fundamentally is right, and this especially in an apocalyptic perspective (which he probably didn't note himself): the world can become one only in the One God Who in this Sacrament of love is present among us unto the end of times. The misinterpretation and misunderstanding of Teilhard is mostly due to the fact that he was not yet able to put into the corresponding language his Eucharistic vision.

Prayer for Piety

Lord, grant us Your gift of piety;
that we may recognize You:
the only living and true God,
Whom we ought to love with the
entirety of our faculties,
with our whole being.
We must die in You
so as to resurrect,
a "new man" in Christ,
Our Lord. Amen

God wills to encounter the heart and Soul of Mary Immaculate in every member of the mystical body of His Son so as to fully live His incarnate mystery of love in all. We must ask for the grace to be a child of Mary, living the "Who is like unto God" of St. Michael such that we live and give a worship worthy of God's majesty.

Seventh Veil — Mary's Soul

The *seventh* veil of the Virgin of Guadalupe is her angelic soul which guards and protects all the secrets of the life of God. Piety and beatitude reside within the most interior recesses, no longer visible for the world, because what God prepares for those whom He loves is beyond all word and comprehension. Mary's soul is the eternal magnificat. We should entone with her because God has done great things with us! He has opened our eyes to the unspeakable beauty of Mary Immaculate.

The veil of Mary's soul cannot be seen, but as a veil of the mystery of God Whom She bears, we can intuit it in her merciful glance and in the "movement of ransom" which comes forth from the same, participating in the "thirst" of her Son. By way of her eyes, we recognize Her to be the great fisher-maid. With the holy angels, she prepares the great harvest for the heavenly banquet in new Jerusalem.

Seventh Community of Asia — Laodicea

Image of the Lord:

> *"Thus says the amen, the faithful and true witness, who is the beginning of the creation of God:"*

Praise and reprimand:

> *"I know your works; you are neither cold nor hot.*
> *"I would that you were cold or hot. But because you are lukewarm, and neither cold nor hot, I am about to vomit you out of my mouth;*
> *"...because you say, 'I am rich and have grown wealthy and have need of nothing,' and do not know that you are the wretched and miserable and poor and blind and naked one.*
> *"I counsel you to buy of me gold (symbol of the fire of the love of God) refined by fire, that you might become rich, and might be clothed in white garments and that the shame of your nakedness may not appear, and to anoint your eyes with eye salve that you might see."*

Promise:

> *"As for me, those whom I love I rebuke and chastise. Be earnest therefore and repent, Behold, I stand at the door and knock. If any man listens to my voice and opens the door to me, I will come in to him and will sup with him, and he with me."*

> *"He who overcomes, I will permit him to sit with me upon my throne; as I also have overcome and have sat with my Father on his throne."*

This community is far from being what it should be. As the last amongst the seven, it represents the situation of the church of our day. It is not yet really aware of the grace it lacks so as to better correspond to the plans of love of God. As we see so clearly today, man has lost "looking up to eternity" (gold). Today's "better standard of living" has blinded our eyes to true values. The fire of divine love is dwindling, barely flickering, recalling the Lord's words: "will the Son of man when He comes back find faith on earth?"[45] Human effort alone will not suffice. The secular struggle of trying to improve our earthly conditions is enough to show us the true state of affairs. Perfection and consummation will only come when we stretch out for God's greater grace, in and through Mary, as her true children ("true devotees," as Louise Marie DeMontfort would say!) — only then will we be worthy to be clothed in white garments and join in the heavenly supper with the Lord to which we are invited at the end.

"Overcome!" Daily, this is the word we should hear our Guardian Angel call out to us. We must leave the old Adam aside and enter into the new life with Christ the Lord. There is no way of escaping the fire of purification, be it here on earth or in purgatory. Only when we are purified will we shine as fine gold, as the gold trimming of the mantle and the gown of Our Lady, of eternal life with God. The golden trimming at the bottom of her gown (like the lower part of the small omega) is a sign that mankind has entered into its final transformation by the victory of Christ on the cross; one day the whole earth-toned mantle will be gold. The golden trim at the bottom of her gown reminds us that God starts with the humble ones like Juan Diego, with those who cling with both hands to the golden trimming of the gown and the mantle, in ardent desire of this transformation. In the Holy Spirit, we must sigh in our hearts, that it be completed; this is our collaboration!

For centuries, the image of Our Lady of Guadalupe was a matter of devotion for the pious souls who always look up to their heavenly Mother. This has changed in our days when science tries to enter into the discussion of the authenticity of this image. The same thing happened with the only true image of Our Lord, the Shroud of Turin. Both images are still in the discussion which is getting progressively more negative than positive. This also is a clear sign that these true images of Jesus and Mary are a stum-

---

[45] cf. Lk 18

bling block God's providence has thrown into the confusion of these times.

Whoever will look at them with only human eyes, with the investigating eyes of a scientist, will find only "curiosities" or as Benitez, "enigmas," but those who look at them with the eyes of their heart will have the same experience as the simple pious people in Russia and other orthodox countries when they look up praying to an icon, because the icons are "windows to eternity." It is by them that we have a first glimpse of the other world and all receive by them graces which can only flow forth from this other world. This way these icons become a hidden presence of the triune God and so assemble all those who look up to God in true worship. They will become even more important in the time of persecution, when the churches are closed and public worship is no longer possible. Certainly there is no other image of Our Lady so prevalent, especially in America, than that of Our Lady of Guadalupe.

Last word from the Cross

"It is consummated!" (Jn 19:30)

This "last word" of the Lord will have to be repeated by every man as requisite for his participation in the eternal banquet. It is the powerful word which will comprise the totality of our earthly existence, having been purified in the blood of the Lamb, in the precious blood of Him Who was slaughtered for us on Golgotha. This word will be different for each of us, and thus will it become our eternal word of praise sung together with all the angels and saints in heaven. This word will be our new name, because the old will have passed away: the Father has renewed all things in His Son!

The Image of Our Lady of Guadalupe, as we have seen before, is the last message of God's mercy to the world.[46] It's not a message of the word, first of all, but a message in silence, and only those whose ears penetrate deeper into this silence will hear it. In it, they will hear the unspoken words of the love of God, which are always

---

[46] It comprises all the other revelations of Our Lady up to our times.

words of a personal love for each individual. The only intention of the noise of this world is to destroy our faculty of hearing, so as to make silence insupportable. At the end, corresponding to the seventh trumpet, God has to put an end to all these noises so as to put in His own word. Only those who have conserved a space of adoration and silence of and for the Greater God in their hearts, contrary and against the current of noise, will be able to hear this word.

Day Seven of Creation

On the seventh day, we will be allowed to repeat with God: "Everything is good, very good." Man lives in time, but God is in eternity. Future perfection and that which is still in the process of unfolding for us is already present for Him. Every Sunday, as the Lord's day, is a day of rest after a week of labor. It is a new promise for us that one day also, after the "six days of our life," we will be permitted to enter into the "eternal rest." The corresponding "day" of the Gospels is the day of the passion and the Resurrection of Our Lord. With the sixth day, the day of His judgment over Jerusalem, His active work is at an end. His passion in the mystical body of the church, at the end of time, will bring creation, as booty, home to the Father. On the "seventh day of salvation," the Son speaks the word of consummation in the Holy Spirit, for all of us.

Because the passion of Lord, in the Gospel of St. John, is the consummation of all things, it is another "creation of seven days;"[47] we have not been saved by the hidden life of Christ, nor by His apostolic life, but by His suffering on the cross. The fact that the passion is related to the seventh day underlines that by virtue of the passion, eternity already breaks into time, enabling "time" to

---

[47] There are "seven days" including the passion of Our Lord; the passion itself can be divided again into another "seven days" (divisions).

refind its course into eternity. The passion of Our Lord Jesus Christ comprises the entire history of mankind, and not only of mankind, but of all creation. Human understanding, as the "liberation" theologians would try to explain, cannot measure the suffering of Christ. His suffering touches the eternity of God; only thus it becomes a redemptive and saving suffering. This truth is symbolized by the seventh veil of the soul of Our Lady; the soul in man being closest to eternity.

It reminds us also that the suffering of the soul is of far greater value, just as the soul is of greater eternal value than the body.[48] Here we might recognize that the mystery of reparation is an apocalyptic mystery. It is for this reason that a church established on this earth, as if part of this earth, cannot understand it. The closer our approximation to the "consummation of all things," the more necessary does this mystery become, not only individually, but on the level of mankind.[49] As the Lord has taken upon Himself the death sentence so as liberate us from sin, so also is the "faithful remnant," in, through and with Mary, allowed to take upon themselves the sins of the "many" who otherwise would be lost.

Sacraments — Anointing of the Sick/Extreme Unction

This Sacrament is a preparation for our last decisive battle as well as our encounter and judgment with and by God. It is here, that we beseech the intercession of the Prince of the heavenly hosts, St. Michael the Archangel. He will assist us in the tremendous fight in our final hour  against the fallen Spirits: *"for you do not know the day of your Master's return."* (Mt 24:42) St. Michael is the great patron of the Holy Mother, the church, and it is his mission to help us in our daily battles and in our last journey, it is he who has to carry our soul to the other shore!

---

[48] The bodies of the faithful departed will only come to eternal life after the last judgment.

[49] Recall the seventh community of Asia.

In our days this Sacrament has been extended to become the Sacrament of the Anointing of the Sick. This is to remind us that sickness, concupiscence, and death are the three irremediable consequences of original sin. The only way to fight them is to rely on the greater force of the grace of God. The apparition of Our Lady of Guadalupe at the beginning of modern times is like another "sacrament of extreme unction" and therefore also of "unction for the sick," because it is by way of her that in these last times mankind, which is getting sicker and sicker, will find help and healing. She is the promise of God's love, that at the end God will "dry all tears." (cf. Rv 21:4)

The Seventh Part of the Holy Mass: "Ite Missa est."

Whenever we meet Our Lady, by way of her image, heart to heart, and take the time to rest in her Immaculate Heart, we will receive the command to go out, to bring the good news of this "last gospel" to the world. It is not only a command, but she herself will go with us to carry the good news to all those who still look out for the light of God. The more we take her in our house, as St. John did, the more it will be she who will pass on this word of apocalyptic consolation, which we so much need to find our way through the confusion of these last times.

But always, this "Ite Missa est" should remind us that we should cry out in our hearts "Maranatha, Lord Jesus come! Come deeper into our hearts, because only Your Light will penetrate the darkness of our days." The more Mary is in our heart the more the Lord will be in ours, and so we bring to the world a word about good news, but this good news itself, which is Jesus the Lord Himself. This is the mission entrusted to anyone who meditatively reads this book. We should do like the fathers recommended: "contemplata tradere," this is to say we should give on only what we have moved with Mary and in Mary in our hearts. Only this word, coming out of the heart, will reach other hearts, opening them to the beauty of God.

Appendix I

The Nican Mopohua

Plans of the Wisdom of God

God's wisdom manifests itself in the smallest of details. With respect to the unfolding of His will in the New World, we recognize this wisdom as a perfect reflection of, *"With you is wisdom who knows your works, who was with you when you made the world, who knows what is favorable in your sight, ... "*[1] As a written document, the Nican Mopohua is truly a divinely inspired work. God always uses the material world to bring about His greater glory, and so also here does He use the person of Antonio Valeriano to ascribe that which He Himself has already accomplished in His "Masterpiece of the Virgin of Guadalupe."

Antonio Valeriano was born very close to Tepeyac in 1520, very shortly after the arrival of the Spaniards to Mexico. His Aunt Papantzin, sister to Moctezuma II, was amongst the first Aztecs baptized, 1525. This may very well be the reason for his coming to live in Mexico in 1526. It is important to note that as "nephew" of Moctezuma II[2] he became recipient of his uncle's inheritance, good or bad.[3] At the age of thirteen, he began his studies at the first American University founded by Bishop Juan de Zumárraga. With hon-

---

[1] Wis 9:9
[2] P. Cuevas, historian
[3] cf. *Mi Niña, Duena de Mi Corazon*, page 47; the importance of the role of uncle amongst the Aztecs

honors, he was the first graduate in both Latin and Greek, and was only in his early twenties when he wrote the Nican Mopohua.

This autobiographical background helps us appreciate better the written masterpiece of the marvel of Guadalupe, as a spiritual testimony on behalf of the wisdom of God, preparing the soil such that His word and Work would not return to Him void.[4] Valeriano lived both in the "time" and the "space" of the apparition, and together, along with his educational preparation, he was the one chosen by God to relate in the "beauty of his culture" the beauty of God made manifest in the person of the Virgin of Guadalupe.

The "Nican Mopohua ..." was written in Nahuatl, in Valeriano's own hand, during the lifetime of both Bishop Juan de Zumárraga and Juan Diego. It is very possible that he was commissioned to write the account, but it is most probable that having repetitively heard from the mouth of Juan Diego he himself responded to the call of the Virgin to "build my sacred little house." He wrote the account on paper made of the maguey plant, the very same fiber of the ayate of Juan Diego. At the death of Valeriano, the Nican Mopohua was given to Don Fernando de Alva Ixlixochitl. While the original was in his care, it was sent to be printed by Luis de la Vega in 1649. From that initial printing there have been many translations. The son of Don Fernando de Alva Ixlixochitl inherited the original at the death of his father; he in turn willed it to the Jesuit Carlos de Sigüenza y Gongora. It was later transferred to the College of St. Peter and Paul and from there to the Royal University of Mexico. Some think that during the war with the United States of America it was taken along with other documents of Singüenza and so came to be found in the U.S.A. State Department in Washington, D.C. It has only been in the recent decades that the Nican Mopohua has really been made available to the majority of the Mexican populace,[5] and Christendom as a whole for that matter. The most integral translation of the document has been afforded us

---

[4] cf. Isaiah 55:11

[5] The message of Fátima has suffered a similar experience. Thousands of people come for every thirteenth of the month, but most of them, especially the humble on foot, have absolutely no idea of what the message of Our Lady of Fátima really is. They are simply attracted by the "remaining presence of Our Lady" in this place as in Mexico where she remains present in her image in the sanctuary.

by Fr. Mario Rojas Sanchez. It is on his translation from the Nahuatl, along with its division of 218 verses, that our following English translation is based.

The Nican Mopohua[6]

Here is told and set down in an orderly manner how a short time ago the Perfect Virgin Holy Mary Mother of God, our Queen, miraculously appeared there on Tepeyac, commonly known as Guadalupe.

She first caused herself to be seen by a humble Indian, named Juan Diego, and afterward her precious image appeared before the newly appointed Bishop Don Fray Juan de Zumárraga.

1   Ten years after the conquest of Mexico City, when the arrows and spears had been laid aside, when everywhere there was peace among the peoples,

2   Just as faith now sprouts, now grows green, now opens its corolla, so too, the knowledge of Him by whom we live: the True God.

3   At that time, the year 1531, a few days into the month of December, it happened that there was a humble Indian, a poor man of the people,

4   by name of Juan Diego; according to what is said, a resident of Cuauhtitlan,

5   and in religious matters, he belonged entirely to Tlatilolco.

6   It was very early Saturday morning, he was coming in pursuit of God and of his commandments.

7   And as he drew near to the little hill called Tepeyac it was beginning to dawn.

8   He heard singing on the little hill, like the song of many precious birds; when their voices would stop, it was as if the hill were answering them; their songs, extremely soft and delightful, surpassed that of the coyoltotl and the tzinitzcan and of other precious birds.

---

[6]   This translation of the Nican Mopohua is made by Davina Baca; it is based on Fr. Mario Rojas' translation from the Nahuatl to the Spanish.

9 Juan Diego stopped to look. He said to himself: "By any chance am I worthy, have I deserved what I am hearing? Perhaps I am only dreaming it? Perhaps I am dozing?

10 Where am I? Where do I find myself? Is it possible that I am in the place that our ancient ancestors, our grandparents spoke about, in the land of the flowers, in the land of the corn, of our flesh, of our sustenance, possibly in the land of heaven?"

11 He was looking toward the top of the hill, toward the direction from which the sun rises, from whence precious heavenly singing was coming.

12 And then when the singing suddenly stopped, when it was no longer heard, then he heard someone calling to him, from the top of the hill; the voice called: "Juan, dearest Juan Diego."

13 He then ventured in the direction of the voice; his heart was not troubled and he felt no anxiety, rather he felt extremely happy and contented; he began to climb the little hill to see from where he was being called.

14 And when he had reached the top of the little hill, when a young Maiden who was standing there saw him,

15 She bade him to approach her.

16 And when he reached the spot where she was, he was filled with wonder at the way her perfect grandeur surpassed all imagination:

17 her clothing shone like the sun, as if it vibrated,

18 and the stone, the promontory on which She stood, emitted something like rays of light.

19 Her resplendence was like precious stones, it seemed like an exquisite bracelet (it seemed beautiful beyond anything else);

20 the earth gleamed as with the splendor of the rainbow in the mist.

21 And the mesquites and cacti and all the other little plants that usually grow there seemed like emeralds. Their foliage appeared like turquoise. And their trunks, their thorns, their spines shone like gold.

22 He prostrated himself in her presence. He listened to her breath, her speech, which was full of esteem, extremely

kind, as coming from someone who attracted him to Herself and who greatly esteemed him.

23 She said: "Listen, my youngest Son, Juanito,[7] where are you going?"

24 And he answered her: "My Lady, my Queen, child, I am going to your little house in Mexico-Tlatilolco, to pursue the things of God that are given to us, that are taught to us by the ones who are the images of Our Lord: our Priests."

25 Then, and with this dialogue with him, she reveals to him her precious will;

26 She tells him, "Know for sure, my youngest son, that I am the perfect ever-Virgin, Holy Mary, Mother of the true God, through whom all being has existence, the creator of mankind, the Lord of all that surrounds and touches your lives, the Lord of heaven and earth. I ardently desire that my sacred temple, My "Teocalli"[8] should be built here,[9]

27 Where I shall introduce Him, I shall praise Him, as I make Him known,

28 (Where) I shall give Him to the people in all My personal love, in My compassionate gaze, in My help, and in My salvation:

29 Because I am truly your compassionate Mother.

30 Yours and of all the people who live as one in this land,

31 and of all the other people of different lineages, who love Me, those who cry to Me, those who seek Me, and those who confide in Me.

32 Because there I will listen to their weeping, to their sorrows, in order to remedy, to cure all their various afflictions, their necessities, their sufferings.

---

[7] The Blessed Virgin uses here the diminutive of Juan's name. This form is used in the language to indicate not only size, but also affection, endearment, fondness or love. It is almost impossible for a valid translation to convey the exquisite courtesy, almost reverence, inherent in the Nahuatl suffix "tzin."

[8] Literally "Teocalli," a term meaning "house of God (teotl = God and calli = house), was the name give to the shrines the Aztec built on top of their pyramid temples.

[9] Critical to our understanding of God's choice of this specific hill for his Mother's apparition is the fact that this very hill was the former site of the Aztecs' worship of "Tonantzin," mother of the gods.

33 And to achieve what My compassionate and merciful gaze is trying to realize, go to the residence of the bishop of Mexico, and tell him that I am sending you in order that you may reveal to him how I ardently desire for him to provide Me with a house here, that he should build My temple in the plain; you shall tell him everything, all that you have seen and marveled at, and what you have heard.

34 And know for sure that I shall be most grateful, and I shall repay you,

35 Because of it I shall enrich you, I will glorify you;

36 And because of it you will greatly merit the manner in which I will reward your efforts, the service you will render in going to request the matter for which I am sending you.

37 Now My dearest son, you have heard My breath, My word; go do your part."

38 And immediately he prostrated himself in her presence; and said to her: "My Lady, my Child, I am going right away to do your venerable breath, your word; I take my leave of you, for the moment, I, your poor Indian."

39 Then he descended the hill to put into action the errand entrusted to him; he came to the causeway, he came directly to Mexico.

40 When he arrived at the center of the city, he went straight away to the palace of the bishop, who had just recently arrived, the governing priest; his name was Fray Juan de Zumárraga, of the Order of St. Francis.

41 And as soon as he got there, he tried to see him, he begged his servants, his aides, to go and tell him so.

42 After a long time had passed, they came to call him, when the reverend bishop ordered that he should enter.

43 And as soon as he entered, he knelt before him, he prostrated himself, then he revealed to him, he told him the precious breath, the precious word of the Queen of Heaven, her message, and also all that he had marveled at, seen and heard.

44 And after hearing his whole story, his message, it appeared as if he really did not believe it to be true.

45 He answered him, saying, "Come again, my son, and then I will hear you out calmly, and will look into the matter from

the very beginning, I will consider the reason that you have come, your will, your wish."

46   He went out; he was downcast, because the mission that had been entrusted to him had not been realized immediately.

47   At the end of the day, he returned, he came straight from there to the little hilltop,

48   and he had the good fortune of meeting the Queen of Heaven: She was waiting for him there at the very spot where She had appeared the first time.

49   And as soon as he saw Her, he prostrated himself before her, he cast himself to the ground, saying to her:

50   "My dearest little Mistress, my Lady, my Queen, my dearest daughter, my Child, I already went to the place where you sent me to carry out your kind breath, your kind word; and although I gained entry to the place of the governing priest with a great deal of difficulty, I did see him, and made known to him your breath, your word, as you asked me to.

51   He received me kindly and he listened to it perfectly well, but, by the way he answered me, it seemed that he had not understood it, that he does not believe it.

52   He told me: "Come again, my son, and then I will hear you out calmly, and will look into the matter from the very beginning, I will consider the reason that you have come, your will, your wish."

53   By the way that he answered me, I could clearly see that he thinks that your house that you want built here, that maybe I am just making it up, or that maybe it does not come from your lips.

54   I beg you, my Lady, my Queen, my little One, to entrust one of the nobles, to bear your kind breath, you kind word, someone who is held in esteem, someone who is known, respected, and honored in order that he might be believed.

55   Because I am really just a man of the field, I am a mecapalli (a burden bearer)[10] a cacaxtli (a back frame), I am a tail, I am a wing, a man of no importance; I myself

---

[10] literally "mecapalli" a rope or hemp ladder type frame used to carry a load.

need to be led, to be carried on someone's back, the place to which you send me is a place where I am unaccustomed to going nor in which am I accustomed to spending any time, my Virgin, my youngest Daughter, my Lady, my Little One;

56 please forgive me; for I shall afflict your countenance with grief, your heart; I may fall into your anger, into your displeasure, my Lady, my Mistress."

57 The Perfect Virgin, worthy of honor and veneration, answered him,

58 "Listen, My youngest and dearest son, know for sure that I have no lack of servants, of messengers, to whom I can give the task of carrying My breath, My word, that they might carry out My will;

59 But it is very necessary that you, personally, go and plead, that My wish, My will, become a reality, that it be carried out through your intercession.

60 And I beg you, My youngest and dearest son, and I order you strictly, to go again tomorrow to see the bishop.

61 And in My name let him know, let him hear My wish, My will, so that he might fulfill it, might build My temple (My teocalli) which I ask of him.

62 And tell him again that it is I, personally, the ever-Virgin Mary, I, who am the Mother of God, who sends you."

63 Juan Diego, for his part, answered her saying, "My Lady, my Queen, my Little One, let me not afflict your face, your heart, with grief, I shall most gladly go to carry out your breath, your word. In no way shall I fail to do it, nor do I consider the means [of doing it] a bother.

64 I shall go and put your will into action, but perhaps I shall not be heard, and even if I am heard, I may not be believed.

65 Tomorrow afternoon, when the sun goes down, I shall come to return to your word, to your breath, with the response of the governing priest.

66 And now I shall respectfully take my leave of you, my Daughter, smallest of them all, Young Lady, my Mistress, my Little One, rest just a little more."

67 And then he went to his home to rest.

68 On the following day, Sunday, while it was still pre-dawn, everything was still dark, he set out from there, from his home, he came straight to Tlatilolco, he came to learn about God and to be included in the roll call; then to see the reverend bishop.

69 And about ten o'clock everything had been taken care of: Mass had been celebrated, roll taken and the crowd had dispersed.

70 And Juan Diego then went to the reverend bishop's residence.

71 And as soon as he arrived, he went through the whole struggle to see him, and after a great deal of effort, he saw him again;

72 he knelt at his feet, he wept, he became sad as he spoke to him, as he made known to him the word, the breath of the Queen of Heaven,

73 that hopefully the message, the will of the Perfect Virgin, might be believed, that of making her, that of building her little sacred house, where She had said, where She wanted it.

74 And the governing bishop asked him a great many things, he cross-examined him, in order to ascertain where he had seen Her, what She was like; he told the lord bishop absolutely everything.

75 And although he recounted everything with great exactitude and in each detail he saw, he was amazed that it appeared with obvious clarity that She was the perfect Virgin, the kind, wonderful Mother of Our Savior, Our Lord Jesus Christ.

76 Nevertheless, it was not realized right away.

77 He said that his petition could not be carried out, could not be realized based on his word alone,

78 that some other sign was very necessary if he was to believe that in fact the Queen of Heaven in person was sending him.

79 As soon as Juan Diego heard this, he said to the bishop:

80 "Lord Governor, think about what the sign you will ask for should be, because then I shall go ask the Queen of Heaven who sent me for it."

81 And when the bishop saw that he was in agreement, that he did not hesitate or doubt in the slightest, he dismissed him.

82 And as soon as he was on his way, he ordered some of his house-hold staff in whom he had absolute confidence to go along following him, that they should observe him carefully regarding where he went, whom he saw, to whom he spoke.

83 And that's what they did. And Juan Diego came directly. He took the causeway.

84 And those who were following him lost him on the wooden bridge where the brook comes out near Tepeyac. And even though they searched all over for him, they couldn't find him anywhere.

85 And so they turned back. Not only because they were greatly annoyed about this, but because he had also frustrated their intentions, he made them angry.

86 So they went to tell the lord bishop, they put it into his head that he should not believe him, they told him that he was only telling him lies, that he was only making up what he came to tell him, or that he was only dreaming or imagining what he was telling him, what he was asking of him.

87 Therefore they decided that if he came again, if he returned, they would seize him right there and would punish him severely, so that he would never again tell lies or agitate the people.

88 Meanwhile, Juan Diego was with the Most Holy Virgin, telling her the lord bishop's response,

89 which when She had heard it, She said to him:

90 "That's fine, My dear son, you will come back here tomorrow so that you can take to the bishop the sign that he has asked you for;

91 with this he will believe you, and he will no longer have any doubts about all this and he will no longer suspect you;

92 and know, My dear son, that I will reward your attention and the effort and fatigue that you have undertaken on My behalf.

93 So, go now; I will be waiting here for you tomorrow."

94 And on the following day, Monday, when Juan Diego was to take some sign in order to be believed, he did not return.

95   Because when he arrived at his house, the sickness had struck an uncle of his, named Juan Bernardino, and he was seriously ill.

96   He went to call the doctor, who even treated him, but it was too late; he was already very ill.

97   And when night came, his uncle begged him that he should go at daybreak setting out while it was still dark, to come call for a priest from Tlatilolco to go to him to hear his confession and to prepare him,

98   because he was sure that the time and place had now come for him to die, because he would never rise again, he would no longer get well.

99   And on Tuesday, while it was still quite night, Juan Diego left his house to come to Tlatilolco to get the priest,

100 and when he finally reached the little hill which ended the mountain range, at its foot, where the road comes out, on the side that the sun set on, which was his usual route, he said:

101 "If I continue ahead on the road, it is possible that this Lady will see me, and surely, She shall detain me, as before, in order that I might take the sign to the governing ecclesiastic as She has requested;

102 first let this trial leave us; first I must quickly call the religious priest; for my uncle is waiting anxiously for him."

103 Immediately he then went around the hill, ascending over the middle of it and crossing from there and emerging on the eastern side, so that he could go to Mexico quickly, so that the Queen of Heaven would not detain him.

104 He thinks that where he made the turn, She who sees everywhere perfectly, will not see him.

105 He saw how She was coming down from on top of the hill, and that She had been watching him from there, from that place where She had seen him before.

106 She came down to meet him on the side of the hill, She came to intercept him; She said to him:

107 "What's the matter, youngest and dearest of My sons? Where are you going, where are you headed?"

108 And he, perhaps he was somewhat distressed, perhaps a bit embarrassed? or perhaps he became afraid of the situation, he became fearful.

109 He prostrated himself before her, he greeted her, he said to her:

110 "My Young Lady, youngest of my children, my Child, I hope you are happy; how are you this morning? Are you in good humor and health this morning, my Lady, my little One?

111 Although it grieves me, I will cause your face and your heart anguish: I must tell you, my little Child, that one of your servants, my uncle, is very ill.

112 A terrible sickness has taken hold of him; he will surely die of it soon.

113 And now I shall go quickly to your little house of Mexico, to call one of our priests, the beloved ones of Our Lord, so that he will go to hear his confession and prepare him,

114 that is what we were really born for, we who came to await the affliction of our death.

115 But, if I am going to do it, then I will come back to go carry your breath, your word, Lady, my Young One.

116 I beg you to forgive me, be patient with me a little longer, because I am not deceiving you with this, my youngest Daughter, my Little One, tomorrow without fail I will come as soon as possible."

117 As soon as She had heard Juan Diego's explanation, the Merciful Perfect Virgin answered him:

118 "Listen, put it into your heart, My youngest and dearest son, that the thing that frightened you, the thing that afflicted you, is nothing: do not let your face be troubled; do not fear this sickness nor any other sickness, nor any sharp and hurtful thing.

119 Am I not here, I who am your Mother? Are you not under My shadow and protection? Am I not the source of your joy? Are you not in the hollow of My mantle? In the crossing of My arms? Do you need anything more?

120 Let nothing else worry you, disturb you; do not let your uncle's illness distress you, for he will not die of it now. You may be certain that he is already well."

121 (And at that very moment his uncle recovered, as they later found out.)

122 And when Juan Diego heard the lovely word, the lovely breath of the Queen of Heaven, he was greatly comforted by it, his heart became peaceful,

123 and he begged her to send him immediately to see the governing bishop, in order to take him something for a sign, for proof, so that he might believe.

124 And the Queen of Heaven then ordered him to go to the top of the little hill, where he had seen her before;

125 She said to him: "Go up My dearest son, the youngest one, to the top of the hill, to where you saw Me and where I told you what to do;

126 there you will see that there are a variety of flowers; cut them, gather them, put them all together; than come down here; bring them here, into My presence."

127 And Juan Diego climbed to the top of the hill right away.

128 And when he had reached the top, he was awed by how many there were, blooming, their corollas open, the greatest variety of flowers, lovely and beautiful, when it was not yet their season:

129 because, in truth, that season the frost was very harsh;

130 they gave forth an extremely soft fragrance, like precious pearls, as if filled with the dew of the night.

131 He then began to cut them, gathered them all up, he placed them into the hollow of his tilma.

132 The top of the little hill was certainly not the place in which any flowers might grow; there are only lots of rocks, thorns, stickers, prickly pears, and mesquite bushes,

133 and even if some small plants might grow, it was then the month of December, in which frost eats everything up and destroys it.

134 And he came down immediately, he came to bring the different kinds of flowers which he had gone up to cut to the heavenly Maiden,

135 and when She saw them, She took them with her precious hands;

136 then again putting them all together into the hollow of his ayate She said:

137 "My youngest and dearest son, these varied flowers are the proof, the sign that you are to take to the bishop;

138 you will tell him, on My behalf, that he is to see in them My desire, and that as a result he should fulfill my request, My will.

139 And you, you who are My messenger, in you I place absolute confidence;

140 and I strictly insist you that you should only open your ayate and show what you are carrying when alone, in the presence of the bishop.

141 And you shall tell him everything in detail, you shall tell him that I ordered you to climb to the top of the little hill to cut the flowers, and everything that you saw and admired,

142 so that you can convince the governing priest, so that he will in his turn do what lies within his responsibility so that My temple which I have requested should be built, should be erected."

143 And as soon as the heavenly Queen gave him her orders, he took the causeway, he came straight to Mexico City, he came happily now.

144 His heart was tranquil now, because his mission will turn out okay, he would fulfill it perfectly.

145 He came taking great care of the contents of the hollow of his clothing, lest something should fall;

146 he came delighting in the fragrance of the various exquisite flowers.

147 When he arrived at the Bishop's palace, the porter and other servants of the governing Priest went out to meet him,

148 And he begged them to tell him (Bishop Zumárraga) how much he wanted to see him, but no one was willing to do so; they pretended that they did not understand him, or that perhaps it was still too dark,

149 or perhaps because they felt by now that all he did was to bother them, to annoy them,

150 and their companions had already told them, those who had gone and had lost sight of him when they had followed him.

151 For a long, long time he waited for his request to be granted.

152 And when the noticed that he had been standing there a very long time, with his head downcast, not doing anything, lest he be called, and that he seemed to be carrying something, carrying it in the hollow of his tilma; then, they drew near to see what it was he was carrying and to satisfy their curiosity.

153 And when Juan Diego saw that he was no longer going to be able to keep what he was carrying a secret, and that therefore they might harass him, or push him around or even rough him up, he finally gave them a glimpse that they were flowers.

154 And when they saw that all of them were exquisite, myriad flowers, and that they were out of season, they were very much astonished by how fresh they were, how open their corollas were, how lovely their fragrance was, and how beautiful they seemed.

155 And they tried to grab and take a few of them;

156 they dared to try to take them three times, but in no way were they able to do so,

157 because when they would try, they could no longer see the flowers, rather they saw them as if they were painted, or embroidered, or stitched onto the tilma.

158 They went immediately to tell the governing bishop what they had seen,

159 and how much the lowly Indian who had come at other times wanted to see him, and that he had been waiting a very long time there for permission, because he wanted to see him.

160 And as soon as the governing bishop heard it, he realized that this was the proof which was to convince him, to put into action what the humble man was asking of him.

161 He immediately ordered that he should be shown in to see him.

162 And when he had come in, he prostrated himself in his presence, as he had previously done.

163 And he told him again what he had seen and admired, and his message.

164 He said to him, "Your Excellency, Sir, I have done as you ordered;

165 that is, I went to tell the lady, my Mistress, the heavenly Maiden, Holy Mary, the Beloved Mother of God, that you asked for proof in order to believe me, so that you might build her little sacred house, in that place where She has been asking that you build it;

166 and I also told her that I had given you my word to return [to you] and to bring you some sign, some proof of her wish, as you requested.

167 And she listened carefully to your breath, your word, and was pleased to receive your request for the sign, the proof, so that her beloved will should be done, should be a reality.

168 And today, while it was still night, She again sent me to come see you,

169 and I asked her for the proof so that I might be believed, as She had said that She would give it to me, and She complied immediately.

170 And She sent me to the top of the hill where I had seen Her before, to cut a variety of Castillian Roses.

171 And when I had cut them, I took them down to Her at the base [of the hill].

172 and She took them with her holy hands,

173 and She arranged them again in the hollow of my Ayate,

174 that I might bring them to you, that I might give them to you personally.

175 Even though I knew well that the hilltop was not a place where flowers grow, because there are only a lot of stones, thistles, thorny shrubs, cacti, and mesquite bushes, still I did not doubt because of that, nor did I hesitate on account of it.

176 When I reached the top of the hill, I saw that it was now paradise.

177 There was a variety of precious flowers there, each one perfect, the finest that there are, full of dew, splendid, so that I immediately cut them;

178 and She told me to give them to you on her behalf, and in this way I would prove to you; you would see the sign that you asked her for in order to accomplish her beloved will,

180 here they are; please accept them."

181 He then held out his white tilma, in whose hollow She had placed the flowers.

182 And as the various precious flowers cascaded to the floor,

183 at that instant it became the sign, the beloved image of the Perfect Virgin, Holy Mary, Mother of God suddenly it appeared exactly as we see it today,

184 where it is kept in her beloved little house, in her holy little house on Tepeyac, that is called Guadalupe.

185 And as soon as the governing bishop, and all those who were there saw it, they fell to their knees full of awe,

186 they stood up to examine it, they became saddened, they wept, their hearts and minds were ecstatic....

187 And the governing bishop weeping and sorrowful, beseeched her, begged her forgiveness for not having complied with her wishes, her holy will, her breath, her venerable word.

188 And when he rose to his feet, he released from around his neck where it had been tied, Juan Diego's garment, his tilma

189 on which the Queen of Heaven had appeared, on which She had become the sign.

190 And he took it and he placed it in his private chapel.

191 And Juan Diego remained another day in the house of the bishop who still detained him.

192 And on the next day, he said to him: "Come, let us go so you can show us where it is that the Queen of Heaven wants her chapel built."

193 People were immediately invited to do it, to raise it up.

194 And Juan Diego, as soon as he had shown them where the Queen of Heaven had ordered that her sacred house be built, asked permission:

195 he wanted to go home to go see his uncle, Juan Bernardino, who had been seriously ill when he had left him to go call a Priest from Tlatilolco to hear his confession and prepare him [for death], and whom the Queen of Heaven had told him had already been healed.

196 But he was not allowed to go home alone, but he was accompanied to his home.

197 And when they arrived, they saw that his uncle was already well, he suffered absolutely no pain of any kind.

198 And he, for his part, was very much surprised by the manner in which his nephew was accompanied and very honored;

199 He asked his nephew why they were honoring him so much;

200 and he told him how when he had left him to go call a priest to hear his Confession, to prepare him, how on the Tepeyac the Lady of Heaven had appeared to him;

201 and how She had sent him to Mexico to see the governing bishop, so that he might build a house for her there on Tepeyac.

202 And how She had told him not to worry, that his uncle was already happy, and how he had been very much consoled with the news.

203 His uncle told him that this was true, that he had been healed at that precise moment,

204 and that he had seen her in exactly the same manner that She had appeared to his nephew,

205 And She had told him that She was also sending him to Mexico to see the bishop;

206 and also that when he went to see him, he should reveal, should tell absolutely everything that he had seen

207 and the wonderful way in which She had effected his cure,

208 and that he should refer to her using the appropriate name, which would also be the proper name for her beloved image: the perfect Virgin, holy Mary of Guadalupe.

209 They then brought Juan Bernardino into the presence of the governing bishop, to speak with him, to give witness,

210 and together with his nephew, Juan Diego, the bishop lodged them in his home for a few days,

211 until the sacred teocalli of the Young Queen was built there on the Tepeyac, where She had appeared to Juan Diego.

212 And the lord bishop moved the revered image of the beloved heavenly Maiden to the main church

213 He took her cherished image from his palace, from his chapel where it had been, so that all the people might see it and admire it.

214 And absolutely this entire city, without exception, was

deeply moved as everyone came to see and to admire her precious image.

215 They came to acknowledge its divine character.

216 They came to present their petitions.

217 They greatly marveled at the miraculous manner in which it had appeared,

218 granted that no man on earth had painted her beloved image.

Epilogue

The ayate is made of ichtli, which comes from the maguey plant. This beautiful ayate, on which the ever-Virgin, our Queen, stamped her image, is in two pieces, joined together and sewn with soft thread. The blessed image is so tall, that from the sole of her foot to the top of her head, she is six and a half hands high. Her beautiful face is serious and noble, and somewhat dark in complexion. The lovely upper section shows her in an attitude of humility: the palms of her hands placed together in front of her bosom, at about her waist. Her sash is purple. Her right foot reveals only the slightly protruding tip of her ash-colored[11] slipper. Her clothing, as much as can be seen, is rose-colored, which looks like vermilion in the shadows of her folds; it is embroidered with various flowers, all buds, and gilt borders. At her neck is a golden circlet, with black lines around the edges, and in the center a cross. There is a slightly showing soft white inner garment, closely fitted at the wrist, with edges adorned with cutwork. Her veil, or mantle, on the outer surface, is a celestial blue: it sets well on her head, but fully reveals her face; reaching down to her feet, it fits a little more closely midway; the wide border is of gold; and gold stars are everywhere, forty-six visible in all.

Her head is inclined to the right; and above the veil is a gold crown whose spindle-shaped points have wide bases. At her feet is the moon, whose horns turn upward. She is placed exactly in the middle of them and likewise appears at the center of the sun,

---

[11] Actually this is the only area of the image that has no pigment whatsoever.

whose rays extend from her figure in every direction. There are one hundred golden rays, some very long and others small and flame shaped; twelve surround her face and head; in all there are fifty which radiate from each side. In configuration, there is a white cloud following the general outline of her garments. The beautiful image, and all the rest, is supported by an angel, who apparently terminates at the waist; none of its lower portion can be seen, being lost in the clouds. The extreme lower part of the tunic and mantle of the Lady of Heaven extend well below her feet and are held by the hands of the angel, whose robe is reddish vermilion in color, with a golden collar, and his extended wings display rich long-feathered plumage of green and other colors. She is borne aloft by the hands of the angel, who seems quite content to bear the Queen of Heaven in this manner.

"Call" in the Name of Holy God

The text of the Nican Mopohua is like a "mission document,"[12] in union with Juan Diego. We must remember that it is a challenge to follow up in his footsteps so as to realize our vocation for Mary. Together with all the other narrations of vocation in the Old and New Testament, the document of the Nican Mopohua is another precious example of a genuine Christian vocation. It beautifully corresponds with the call of all those who, in a humble way, are called to be "shepherds" in and through Christ, by mediation of Mary. It is a call by the Holy God; Who through the mediation of Mary, we must become another Christ by dying evermore completely to our own ego. The more we are "in Maria" the more we are to carry Christ Our Lord. This truth is depicted in a pictorial way in the image: the boy is with outstretched arms, his head is inclined in humility, his ears are wide open for the message and his eyes reflect interiorization.

---

[12] Document normally given by the ecclesiastical authority to those who are called to be catechists.

Beauty and Order

A Structural Analysis of the Nican Mopohua

I) Keywords in the Vocabulary and their interpretation

Revelation is not found in the narrative or the image alone, but is more profoundly witnessed in the deeper correlation of numbers. Something of the beauty and order of God will be revealed in the following vocabulary "statistics" of the Nican Mopohua. Only as a trinitarian revelation, revelation in Christ, will it come to its consummation.

"God"

"God" (prologue, vs. 2, 6, 24, 26, 62, 68, 165, 183) 9xs

One of the most important things we come to know in the evangelization of Our Lady of Guadalupe is a truth Our Lord exposes in the beginning of His apostolate in the parable of the sower and the seed and in other "organic" parables: faith has its growth along with the dangers that surround it.[13] The concept of God, during our earthly pilgrimage, has to grow in us as does the child, for "nine months," in the womb of its mother. Certainly this "birth" is best provided for, guided and protected by the nine choirs of the angels. They not only accompanied Our Lord in His initial descent from heaven, in His apostolate in Judea and Galilee and in His ascent to heaven, but they have the same mission with us who are called to be "sons in the Son of God." Necessarily, this growth is under the special care of Our Lady. This is eloquently found in the narration of the Nican Mopohua just as in her image. Faith is like a flower, slowly opening to the light of God.[14]

---

[13] cf. Mt 13:3-8, 19-23, Mk 4:3-8, 15-20, Lk 8:5-8, 11-18
[14] cf. Nican Mopohua, vs. 2

"Guadalupe"

"Guadalupe" (prologue, vs. 184, 208) 3xs

This is another confirmation that we must see the message of Guadalupe in a trinitarian way:
- as a message of the Father, in the image
- of the Son by the words she spoke
- of the Holy Spirit in the multiple correlation we try to discover in our meditations.

"Holy"

"Holy" Mary or Virgin (prologue, vs. 26, 88,
    165, 183, 208) 6xs
her "holy" hands (vs. 172) 1x
her "holy" little house (vs. 184) 1x
her "holy" will" (vs. 187) 1x
total 9xs

The mission of Our Lady of Guadalupe in Mexico is a holy mission in union with all the angels (9), to bring down the new Jerusalem. The holiness of God is best expressed in Mary, the ever-perfect Virgin. God, the triune, as in a mirror is most perfectly reflected in her. (6 = 2 x 3) Her hands are a symbol for what she does. Through them we most clearly see that her mission is, to bring her sons and daughters to holiness. The house she asks for is a "little" house, but as it is there where she wants to reveal the true God, it has to be a holy house, filled with the light of His holiness.

"Queen"

"Queen" 21xs
"Queen of Heaven" or "Heavenly Queen" (vs. 43, 48,
    72, 78, 80, 103, 122, 124, 143, 189, 192, 194, 195,
    200 and Epilogue) 15xs
"Lady of Heaven" or "Heavenly Maiden"(vs. 134,
    165, 200, 212 and Epilogue) 5xs

The fact that "Queen" occurs 21 times (3 x 7) is another sign that she is sent by God to represent God, the most Holy Trinity, in the Holy Spirit. At the same time she is a reflection of her Son, the king to come at the end of times, to be the king of all kings, to submit everything at his feet and at last surrender Himself to the Father. In 5x "Lady of Heaven" we have a silent allusion that the dignity of man is restored through the five wounds of Our Lord Jesus Christ.

"Mother"

"Mother" of God (prologue, vs. 26, 62, 165, 183) 5xs
"Mother" of the Savior (vs. 75) 1x
"Mother" (vs. 29, 119) 8xs

Total: 14 = 1 + 4 = 5

Remark: The Virgin of Tepeyac is first Mother of God. Then she is "Mother" of the Savior and only thus is she "Mother of Juan Diego" and of all men who on this earth want to be in one — in the One, who is her Son. In a mystical way, Mary has to represent the invisible Father on this earth, an idea not so foreign to the Aztecs, comprehension of the dual gender of Ometeotl. Her presence among them as Mother is that which helped them to break with the God of war and violence and slowly opened their heart for the mystery of Christian marriage, a concept even strange to them to this day. Motherhood is always in the sign of the cross (four), in the total self sacrifice of a wounded and opened heart (one), therefore five. Necessarily, it has both a natural and a supernatural dimension.

"Virgin"

"Perfect Virgin"(prologue, vs. 26, 57, 62, 73, 75, 117, 183, 208, and Epilogue) 10xs

Total : 12xs

Really, perfect virginity is not something "given" as our property, but is entrusted to us, as is our whole life: to bring fruit in this time and for eternity. The purer, the closer it will be to God, and the more it will bring fruit, because it will have part in God's infinite "productivity," fertility — most visible in the Son, engendered from all eternity, who is the life of all creation and of each living being. This fertility will be best seen in the end, in the most precious fruit of Redemption: the new Jerusalem with its twelve doors through which all redeemed mankind will enter.

"Breath" and "word"

"breath". . . . . (12xs before "word," *3xs after)
1st App. & with the bishop (vs. 22, 37,
      38 & 43) . . . . 3 + 1 = 4xs
2nd App. & with the bishop (vs 50-2xs, 54, 58,
      63, *65 and *72) . . . . 6 + 1 = 7xs
3rd App. 0
4th App. & with the bishop (115, *122 &
      167, 187) . . . . 2 + 2 = 4xs
5th 0

Total: 15xs

With respect to the first interview, "breath" appears as a word of the cross and therefore is found four times. Because it takes part in the "folly of the cross," it is not understood by the bishop. In the second apparition it is filled with the power of the Holy Spirit (7xs), thus helping the seer and the bishop to understand better. With respect to the fourth apparition, both participate in and accept the "folly of the cross."

"word" (15xs with "breath," 2xs other
      context, vs. 77 & 166) 17

Within the narrative of the Nican Mopohua, "breath" is always used in the same context with "word." It reminds us that our word becomes a living, and productive word only when it is accompa-

---

* When "word" appears before "breath" it is when Juan is animated by Our Lady *vs.65, 72, & 122: he is giving on the word in the "breath" of the Holy Spirit, the same way he has received it.

nied by the breath of the Holy Spirit who engenders life from the Father in the Son. To see that the words of Our Lady of Guadalupe are really life-giving words, we need only recall the eight million natives converted within the first seven years following Our Lady's apparition. Fifteen (15), in horizontal addition (1+5=6), makes six — recalling that all productivity and fertility should be a mirror, a reflection (2) of the triune God (3).

"Juan"

Juan Diego (prologue, vs. 4, 9, 12 (2xs), 23, 63, 70, 79,
    83, 88, 94, 99, 117, 122, 127, 153, 188, 191, 194,
    210, 211) 22xs
Juan Bernardino (vs. 95, 195, 209).................... 3xs
Juan de Zumárraga (prologue, vs. 40) 2xs
total — "Juan" 27xs

In the bible, the proper name of "John" reflects not only a most important personage, but those very personages become synthesized and links for and between Old Testament (St. John the Baptist), New Testament (St. John the Evangelist) and the Apocalypse. The translation of the name "John" from the Hebrew is "pure gift of God." (Lk 1) The "messengers of God," with this name, were representatives of all their predecessors of different names. Indeed, the message of Our Lady of Guadalupe has been a "pure gift" for Mexico, for all America and in an apocalyptic perspective for the whole world.

"Son"/"Daughter"

"Son" (vs. 23, 26, 37, 45, 52, 58, 60, 90, 92, 107,
    118, 125, 137) 13xs
"Daughter" (vs. 50, 55, 66, 116)...................... 4xs

Nothing is more humiliating for the fallen angel, who arrogates himself the number thirteen, than to see man, taken from the dust of the earth and accepted by God as "son in His Son." The fact that Our Lady, together with the bishop, uses the term thirteen times with Juan Diego is not only a sign of a special maternal love for the seer, but in this perspective also a sign of special protection against the snares of the devil which will become more and more perilous for all mankind the more we are nearing the last times. "Four" tells us that we become sons/daughters only when we enter through the narrow door of the cross.

"Child"

"Child" (always directed to the Virgin — vs. 24, 38, 50,
111, 110-2xs) 6xs

Juan Diego beautifully reflects the Beloved Apostle. St. John the Evangelist, at the foot of the cross was commissioned by Christ to "take the Mother of God into his home," likewise do we find with Juan Diego. In this sense, she really is "his child" (not only because he is older, and she is still "a girl"); it is also an expression of his tender and respectful love for the Virgin — he cares for her as would the best of all fathers (reminding her that she "should rest," asking her if she has "slept well" (vs. 66, 110), etc.

"Uncle"

"Uncle" (vs. 95, 97, 102, 111, 120, 121, 195,
197, 202, 203) 10xs

The use of "uncle" ten times emphasizes the authority of the uncle over the whole family — maternal line. He is in the natural order of things, the representative of the One God and his authority on man.

"Morning"

"Morning" (vs. 6; 2xs in vs. 110) 3xs

"Morning," used three times, and at crucial points in the narrative, is a clear sign, that something new is going to happen. It is a sign of a new creation and recalls the morning of Resurrection.

The first apparition takes place, not on Sunday morning as with Our Lord, but on Saturday morning, the day of Our Lady. She, hidden by the brightness of the Light of her Son in the New Testament, in these "modern times," "will come forth as the sun…" and precede the second coming of Her Son as judge of the living and the dead. The triple occurrence of "morning" reflects the Most Holy Trinity. The "new day" will be a time in which the deepest mystery, that of the most Holy Trinity, will be revealed to those who love God like Juan Diego.

"Dawn"

"Dawn" (vs. 7, 68) 2xs

The use of this "morning" word also gives us the notion of the emergence of something new coming out of the Mystery (night) of the greater God. In this case though, it is the relation to the sun which is emphasized. The light of God pierces the dark night of paganism; not only that of the poor Aztecs but also the night of the neo-paganism of our times, a night much denser than that of the pagans.

"Hill"

"Hill" (vs. 7, 8; 2xs, 11, 12, 13, 14, 39, 47,
    100, 103, 105, 106, 124, 125, 127, 132,
    141, 170, 171, 175, 176 . . . . 22xs

The hill of Tepeyac where Our Lady meets Juan Diego should always be seen in correlation with the hill of Golgotha (22 = 2+2 = 4 = the cross), where Our Lord Jesus Christ was crucified and thus merited the Redemption of us poor sinners. Mary Immaculate was exempt from original sin by the merits of the passion of her Son. When she appears on the hill of Tepeyac She makes present the sacrifice of Her Son. At the foot of the cross she received the precious blood of Christ, the expiatory price of our Redemption. Now, she is pouring this grace not only upon Mexico, but more and more on the whole world. Only the precious blood of Her Son will bring the final victory over the serpent. The simple terms used in the Nican Mopohua help us to penetrate ever deeper into the apocalyptic and universal meaning of the apparition of Our Lady of Guadalupe.

"Hilltop" or "top of the hill" (vs. 11, 12, 14, 28, 47, 105, 124, 125, 127, 132, 141, 170, 175, 176) 14xs

Mountains and hills as places for theophanies, of revelations of God. Remember what we suggest the three "covenants," the "third" and last one in Mary Immaculate on the hill of Tepeyac.[15] The allusion to the Holy Spirit is apparent: two times seven — a revelation in view of the Son who wants to make Himself known in these last times first of all by his Mother and by way of the cross (one and four make five — the wounds of Christ)

"Sun"

"Sun" (vs. 11, 17, 65, 100 and Epilogue) 5xs

Again, we have a correlation to the five wounds of Christ. Only the passion of the Lord can bring about the final liberation of man, held bound in his captivity to sin. Although this is still veiled, this is the greatest promise of the apparition of Our Lady of Guadalupe. The closer our union with the holy angels the clearer will be our vision of the glorious aspect of the sacrifice of Christ: literally, light is breaking out of the wounds of Our Lord. We must remember that this reality is expressed in a veiled way, not by words, but through the simple "parable of five."

"Tepeyac"

"Tepeyac" (prologue, vs. 7, 84, 184, 200, 201, 211) 7xs

We must see the hill of Tepeyac in the light of the Holy Spirit so as to better understand the universality of Redemption promised to all mankind in this apparition. Tepeyac is like a "new

---

[15]   The one covenant is in the Son of God; this is a trinitarian interpretation.

Golgotha," but this time in the glory of the Holy Spirit Who will bring Redemption to its fullness.

"Voice"

"Voice" (vs. 8, 12, 13) 3xs

Again it is formally confirmed: the revelation of Our Lady is a trinitarian mystery.

"Hear"

"Hear," "heard," "hearing" (vs. 8, 9, 12-2xs, 33,
    37, 43, 44, 45, 52, 61, 64; 2xs, 79, 89, 97, 113,
    117, 122, 160, 195, 200) ..... (cross = 4 = 2+2 = 22) 22xs

All our hearing is orientated to the second Divine Person, the word of God. This word is only heard if we are looking up to the cross, the climax of our salvation. Only if we are crucified can we hear. Before Juan Diego sees something in the first apparition, he first hears the heavenly singing of the birds. Hearing goes deeper into the soul of man. Seeing only confirms that which we've first heard. This is emphasized in the apparition of Our Lord with St. Thomas.

"See"

See, seen 40xs
saw 16xs

The verb "to see" appears 56xs. The horizontal addition (5+6) gives us (11), which again when added in the horizontal (1+1) gives us (2). Whatever we look for should be sought in the Son of God (2), in view of Him everything has been created.(cf. Col 1:16) Through Him we will enter into beatific vision for all eternity.

"Sing"

"Sing" or "singing" (vs. 8, 11, 12) 3xs

All singing is for the praise of the triune God.

"Smell"

"Disfrutando del aroma" — "delighting
in the aroma" (vs. 146) 1x

All our senses must open before God. Man has five spiritual senses which correspond to the outward.[16]

"Bird"

"Bird" (2xs in vs. 8) 2xs

We recall that *"flor y canto"* — "flower and song" for the Aztec were the only means of coming close to God. The singing of the birds is part of the revelation of the Son of God, of Him Who for us has reopened the doors of heaven.

"Flowers"

"Flower"(s) (vs. 10, 126, 128, 132, 134, 137,
141, 146, 153, 154, 157, 175, 177, 181, 182, Epilogue)   16xs

In matters of revelation, "flowers" are messengers of the Holy Spirit," $16 = 1 + 6 = 7$

"Heart"

"Heart" (vs. 13, 56, 63, 111, 118, 122, 144, 186) 8xs

Eight, as two times four ($8 = 2 \times 4$), is a symbol for the plenitude of the graces which come from the cross. It is also a symbol for creation (in the four directions of the wind) coming to its fullness. Our heart, noblest symbol of man's destiny, will come to this fullness only crucified in Christ, or in view of Mary, pierced by the swords of suffering.

---

[16]   cf. I Jn 1:1 ff.

"Appear"

"Appear"(ed) (prologue, vs. 2xs, 21, 44, 48, 75, 183,
189, 200, 204, 211, 217, Epilogue) 13xs

Already in Mexico, this number is closely related to her apparitions in Fátima. Our Lady of the Rosary deliberately chose the 13th of the month for her apparition to counteract the malicious influence the evil one has placed on this number for his purposes.

"Mary"

"Mary" (prologue, vs. 26, 62, 165) 4xs
"Mary" in the image 2xs

Although for the Aztec, the Virgin of Tepeyac appears as the "glorious woman," we must remember that she is only "glorious" because she has passed through the "narrow door" of the cross. The presence of the cross in her image is not something "added or even superimposed," it is an integral part of her and is easily recognized by the vertical line formed by the central folds in her gown, entering the horizontal one formed by her arms and praying hands. Both the formal and material expressions are one.[17] "Six" is really a symbol of Mary, as she is the perfect mirror of the most Holy Trinity (two times three).

"Sign"

"Sign" (vs. 78, 80, 90, 94, 101, 123, 126,
137, 167, 178, *183, 189) 12xs

Again we have the unison of a formal and material identity. Our Lady of Guadalupe really is the great apocalyptic sign of Apoca-

---

[17]   By formal expression we mean the "form" used to express something. In this case the unique repetition of words in the Nican Mopohua are part of the "form" used by Valeriano and they are found in perfect unison with the "material" reality of the image. They both reflect the same truth.

lypse 12. She is the unrefutable promise of the consummation of all things in the new Jerusalem with its twelve doors.

"Proof"

"Proof" (vs. 123, 137, 160, 165, 166, 167, 169) 7xs

Only the Holy Spirit can convince us in matters of supernatural things, material proof is vain.

Resumé

Anyone having a true insight into the deeper significance of numbers in holy Scriptures,[18] will be awed at just how much the Nican Mopohua testifies the unspeakable mystery of God's harmony in revelation. This humble analysis alone should be a sufficient "proof" that indeed, this document really is a document of the Holy Spirit. We may rely on its authenticity with as much confidence as placed in her God-painted image. The two testimonies of the word and the image of the revelation need only the third testimony of the Holy Spirit Himself to reveal the authenticity of the revelation of Our Lady of Guadalupe on Tepeyac.

---

[18] Unfortunately the fallen angels have a great insight to the importance of numbers and they use it to confuse man in anything which is "gnosis."

Appendix II

Analysis of the Structure of the First Apparition as Recorded in the Nican Mopohua

(Prologue to Verse 39)

This first scheme is only to orient the reader. Looking close, one will note a beautiful and harmonic order within this first apparition. We first note seven divisions or steps in the encounter and then a harmonic balance between the steps. Consider this "seven" in light of a seven-fold candelabra.* The following extended analysis will employ the use of the Spanish translation of the Nican Mopohua so as to capture something of the "flor y canto" of the marvel of Guadalupe. The purely English reader need only refer to the document beginning on page 11.

---

* There is not a little similarity to the "historical prologue" of the Gospel of St. Luke. The apparition is circumscribed in its three dimensions: time, place and mode — another trinitarian relation; everything here should be seen and understood in relation to the most Holy Trinity. It is a trinitarian revelation from the very beginning.

Prologue

"Aqui se cuenta, se ordena, como hace poco, milagrosamente se apareciola perfecta Virgin Santa Maria Madre de Dios, nuestra reina, alla en el Tepeyac de renombre Guadalupe.

"Primero se hizo ver de un indito, su nombre Juan Diego; y después se apareció su Preciosa Imagen delante del reciente Obispo Don Fray Juan de Zumárraga."

1. The Day, Time and Pursuit of Juan Diego (Vs. 6)	2. Arrival to the nose of the Hill – Tepeyac at Dawn (Vs. 7-10)	3. Call and Response (Vs. 12-13)	4. The Encounter (Vs. 14-22)	5. The Dialogue Begins (Vs. 23-24)	6. The Request (Vs. 25-37)	7. Adsum (Vs. 38-39)
The foundation of the First Apparition – Mary, New Birth and loging for God.	A. He **hears.** B. He **sees.** C. He **wonders.** 1. worthy? 2. meriting? 3. dreaming? a. land of the flowers? b. land of the corn? c. land of one's flesh? d. land of sustenance? e. earthly paradise?	A. The **song** of the birds **stops** B. He **hears** 2xs his named called by the Queen of Heaven. C. He **ventures to go** to where he is being called to. 1. nothing worries his heart. 2. nothing changes his mind. 3. above all he is happy. 4. he is extremely content. 5. he ascends the hill (responds).	A. He is **seen** by the Doncella. B. She **beckons** him. C. Description of the Virgin and of nature transformed new Jerusalem. D. He prostrates in her presence. E. He **listens** to her breath / her word.	A. She Initiates the dialog. B. He responds.	A. Who – She is and in Who's Name she comes B. What – She wants, Her Mission (a home) C. How — She will give God to the people. D. Revealing her Heart. E. Mother 7xs. F. Reason – to hear, to heal and to cure. G. Mission and recompense.	A. Prostrates self. B. On his way. C. Courteously excuses himself from her presence. D. Descends. E. Finds the road again. F. Straight ahead to Mexico

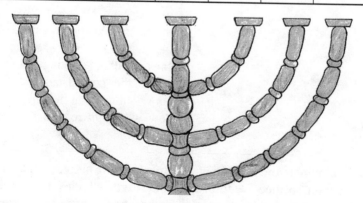

1. Diez años después de conquistada la ciudad de México, cuando ya estaban depuestas las flechas, los escudos, cuando por todas partes había paz en los pueblos,	* This peace recalls the peace of the times of Our Lord's first coming. It is only an outward peace, under the control of an exterior and armed power, that of the Spaniards. Nevertheless it is the condition for the "deeper peace" to come.
2. así como brotó, ya verdece, ya abre su corola la fe, el conocimiento de Aquel por quien se vive: el verdadero Dios.	As there is only the way of "flowers and song" to speak about God, so also faith, directed to the true God, can only grow organically, in similitude to nature. After all the destruction, brought on by war, the burnt soil irresistibly brings forth new growth.
3. En aquella sazón, el año 1531, a los pocos días del mes de diciembre, sucedió que había un indito, un pobre hombre del pueblo,	The month of the apparition, December, normally the coldest in Mexico, is emphasised. No growth whatsoever is to be expected during this time; nature is as if "dead." The same holds true for man. He was yet living in the terrible consequences of the "winter of war." The Mexicans were as "nothing" in the eyes of the "conquistadores": "a poor nothing of an Indian" — is how we ought to understand: "indito."
4. su nombre era Juan Diego, según se dice, vecino de Cuauhtitlan,	But already in his name, there is some light which pierces the darkness of winter: He carries the name of the predilected

		Apostle St. John. This light is not coming from below, but from heaven.
5.	y en las cosas de Dios, en todo pertenecía a Tlatilolco ... * The end of the introduction to this narration.	The effort of the hagiograph is to lay out the fact of this apparition: Juan Diego is a newborn son of the Holy church, he is registered in Tlatiloco, where the Spanish Franciscans had their headquarters.
6.	Era sabado, *muy de madrugada*, venía en pos de Dios y de sus mandatos.	Saturday as day of Our Lady symbolically: the beginning of Her reign preceding the second coming of Her Son. 1. Day and number of Our Lady, day six of creation (creation of man), — the sixth day is not at an end — man is not yet what he should be: Image of the triune God, this is the unspoken promise of the apparition of Our Lady On his way for the things of God: the only thing we can offer in return to the gratuity of salvation is a holy nostalgia for God; here testified by this early going for the "things of God."

7. Y al llegar cerca del cerrito llamado Tepeyac ya amanecía.	2. As he arrives to the "nose of the hill" it dawns. There is an invisible and inaudible breeze coming from the hill; promise of the proximate encounter in the Holy Spirit.
8. Oyó cantar sobre el cerrito, como el canto de muchos pájaros finos; al cesar sus voces, como que les respondía el cerro, sobremanera suaves, deleitosos, sus cantos sobrepujaban al del coyoltototl y del tzinitzcan y al de otros pájaros finos.	A. He hears on the hill - The songs of precious birds - they represent the angels surrounding this revelation of Our Lady - again nature helps us to better understand the invisible things of God. - The echo of their voices is like a first invitation to enter into dialogue with God.
9. Se detuvo a ver Juan Diego. Se dijo: ¿Por ventura soy digno, soy merecedor de lo que oigo? ¿Quiza nomás lo estoy soñando? ¿Quizá solamente lo veo como entre sueños?	B. He sees – Hearing the wonderful voices has opened more deeply the sense of seeing. C. He wonders – Wondering with the pre-Socratic philosophers was the beginning of philosophy. 1. worthy? Juan Diego does not refer anything to himself — he continues in perfect poverty = openness to the things to come. 2. Meriting? Only the humble will "see."

	3. Dreaming? Those who are not expecting anything "extraordinary."
10. ¿Dónde estoy? ¿Dónde me veo? ¿Acaso allá donde dejaron dicho los antiguos nuestros antepasados, nuestros abuelos: en la tierra de las flores, en la tierra del maíz, de nuestra carne, de nuestro sustento; acaso en la tierra celestial?	a. Land of the flowers? b. The land of corn? c. Land of one's flesh? d. Land of sustenance? e. Earthly paradise? This is why he looks out for a "natural" explanation of what is happening. In five steps (five is symbol of plenitude) he approaches truth. Only when we enter heaven through the wound of the heart of Our Lord we will see the fullness of Truth.
11. Hacia allá estaba viendo, arriba del cerrillo, del lado de donde sale el sol, de donde prodecía el precioso canto celestial.	He looks in the direction from where the beautiful sounds are coming from, intuiting already something of their celestial proveniance.
12. Y cuando cesó de pronto el canto, cuando dejó de oírse, entonces oyó que lo llamaban, de arriba del cerrillo, le decían: "Juanito, Juan Dieguito."	3. Call and Response A. The song of the birds stops B. He hears his name being called (2xs) by the Queen of Heaven.
13. Luego se atrevió a ir a donde lo llamaban; ninguna turbación pasaba en su corazón ni ninguna cosa lo alteraba, antes bien se sentía	C. He ventures to go to where he is being called to. This is his state of mind: he is in perfect interior peace and harmony

alegre y contento por todo extremo; fué a subir al cerrillo para ir a ver de dónde lo llamaban.	1. Nothing worries his heart 2. Nothing changes his mind 3. Above all he is happy 4. He is extremely content 5. He ascends the hill (responds)
14. Y cuando iba a llegar a la cumbre del cerrillo, cuando lo vió una Doncella que allí estaba de pie,	4. The encounter at the top of the hill. A. Standing there, she **sees** him. We are in her glance before we look up to her. It is as if he is entering deeper into her eyes.
15. lo llamó para que fuera cerca de Ella.	B. She calls him closer. First he is attracted by her eyes, then called by her.
16. Y cuando llegó frente a Ella mucho admiró en qué manera sobre toda ponderación aventajaba su perfecta grandeza:	C. The description / nature transformed 1. He obeys and is found before her. 2. He admires her perfect countenance. Again his first reaction: the admiration of a child, which equals adoration of the angels. (She represents the Holy God).
17. su vestido relucia como el sol, como que reverberaba,	3. Her dress shone like the sun, as if reverberating

18. y la piedra, el risco en el que estaba de pie, como que lanzaba rayos;	4. The rock beneath her also irradiated — Nature around her is like another dress.
19. el resplandor de Ella como preciosas piedras, como ajorca (todo lo más bello) parecía	5. Her splendor was as precious stones — she represents the new Jerusalem
20. la tierra como que relumbraba con los resplandores del arcoiris en la niebla.	- The earth glistened with the resplendence of the rainbow (sign of eternal peace: consummation of the new covenant.)
21. Y los mezquites y nopales y las demás hierbecillas que allí se suelen dar, parecían como esmeraldas. Como turquesa aparecia su follaje. Y su tronco, sus espinas, sus aguates, relucían como el oro.	- The desert plants seemed as emeralds (turquoise) and gold. There is no "desert" any more, everything reflects the glory of God, first in O.L.G.

22. En su presencia se postró. Escuchó su aliento, su palabra, que era extremadamente glorificadora; sumamente afable, como de quien lo atraía y estimaba mucho.	D. In her presence he prostrates himself.
	
	E. He listens to her breath, her word; four qualities:
	
	   1. extremely glorifying,
	
	   2. infinitely amiable
	
	   3. as someone who attracted
	
	   4. and esteemed him.

23. Le dijo: "Escucha hijo mio el menor, Juanito. ¿A donde te diriges?"	5. She initiates the dialogue, he responds A. She is attentive to his mission before she reveals hers.
24. Y él le contestó: "Mi Señora, Reina, Muchachita mía, allá llegaré, a tu casita de México Tlatilolco, a seguir las cosas de Dios que nos dan, que nos enseñan quienes son las imágenes de Nuestro Señor: nuestros Sacerdotes."	B. He responds 1. "My Lady" (My Queen) 2. "My young girl" 3. "to your house…" 4. "to follow the things of God that the images of Our Lord, the Priests, give us." Remark the triple address — he recognizes her even before she will tell who she is (by her "breath").
25. En seguida, con esto dialoga con él, le descubre su preciosa voluntad;	6. The request (there is mutual respect from the beginning)
26. le dice: "Sabelo, ten por cierto. hijo mio el mas pequeno, que yo soy la perfecta siempre Virgen Santa Maria, Madre del Veraderisimo Dios por quien se vive, el creador de las personas, el deuno de la cercania y de la inmediacion, el dueño del cielo, el dueño de la tierra. Mucho quiero, mucho deseo que aqui me levanten mi casita sagrada	A. Who she is — "The ever-perfect Virgin Mary" and In Who's Name She comes: 1. Mother of the True God 2. For Whom we live 3. The Creator of persons 4. Lord of Salvation History 5. The Lord of heaven and earth (five=plenitude)

27. En donde lo mostrare, lo ensalzare al ponerlo de manifiesto:	B. What she wants — a sacred home Her mission: 1. Manifest Him, 2. Give birth to Him, 3. Making Him known.
28. Lo darea las gentes en todo mi amor personal, en mi mirada compasiva, en mi auxilio, en mi salvacion:	C. How she wills (mode) — to give Him (God) to the people 1. in all her personal love, 2. in her compassionate glance, 3. in her help, 4. in her salvation:
29. Por que yo en verdad soy vuestra madre compasiva,	D. Revealing her heart Because I am a compassionate Mother,
30. tuya y de todos los hombres que en esta tierra estais en uno.	E. Universal Motherhood 1. to him (Juan) 2. and of all those in this land who will to be one
31. y de las demas variadas estirpes de hombres, mis amadores, los que a mi clamen, las que me busquen, los que confien en mi ,	3. of the various races 4. of her lovers 5. of those who implore her 6. of those who seek her 7. and of those who confide in her.

32. por que alli les encuchare su llanto, su tristeza, para remediar, para curar todas sus diferentes penas, sus miserias, sus dolores.	F. The reason for her "sacred house..." is: there she will hear: l. their grief 2. their sadness so as to heal, to cure 3. all their different hurts 4. their miseries 5. their sorrows

33. Y para realizar lo que pretende mi compasiva mirada misericordiosa, anda al palacio del obispo de mexico, y le diras como yo te envio, para que le descubras como mucho deseo que aqui me provea de una casa, me erija en el llano mi templo; todo le contaras, cuanto has visto y admirado, y lo que has oido.	G. The mission for Juan Diego, apparent already in her compassionate and merciful glance, to go to the bishop and reveal it:
	
	1. A house on the hill, a temple below.
	
	2. Everything he should tell what he saw, admired, heard.
	
	3. "I will gratefully
	   a. be indebted for it,
	   b. I will repay you for doing it,

35. Que por ello te en-riquecere, te glorificare;	c. I will enrich you d. I will glorify you;

36. Y mucho de alli mereceras con que yo retribuya tu cansancio, tu servicio con que vas a solicitar el asunto al que te envio.	e. ...your fatigue will merit retribution, f. your service for soliciting that for which I send you."
37. Ya has oido, hijo mio el menor, mi aliento mi palabra; anda, haz lo que este de tu parte."	4. "You have heard, the smallest of my sons, my breath, my word; go, do your part."
38. E inmediatamente en su presencia se postró; le dijo: "Señora mía, Niña, ya voy a realizar tu venerable palabra; por ahora de Ti me aparto yo, tu pobre indito."	7. The "Adsum" A. Immediately he prostrated himself in her presence B. He responds with "My Lady, little one, I'm already on my way to bring about your venerable word (request); C. He politely excuses himself from her presence as her "poor Indian"
39. Luego vino a bajar para poner en obra su encomienda: vino a encontrar la calzada, viene derecho a México.	D. He descends so as to bring to effect her mandate: E. He left to find the highway F. He goes straight to Mexico.

General Review of the First Encounter According to its Seven Main Parts

The sevenfold structure of the first apparition, is another sign of the presence of the Holy Spirit in the "Nican Mopohua..." of Our Lady of Guadalupe. Looking more closely, we will not only see the harmonious construction of this first part of the narration, but also the multiple relations with the other "rows of seven." Here, we will specifically highlight a correspondence with the "seven days of creation" in Genesis and the Gospels.

The *first* step: like a prologue, putting down the most important historical details and presenting the "hero" Juan Diego. Our Lady has already looked down on him, she is attracting him by her light which is no other than the light of God Himself. She comes in the name of her Son and as her Son called his first apostles on the "first day" so does she with Juan Diego: he is called to be "her messenger" as she is of the Lord.

The *second* step: his arrival on the hill breaks the frontier of the material visible world and opens the sight to the world of wonders of God: to His glorious presence in Our Lady. This "second step" is in relation to the "second day" of Genesis. Tepeyac becomes the firmament upon which he will have to stand in the completion of his mission. He wonders where he has come, thinking over several possible solutions which come to his mind. Finally he comes close to reality: it is like "paradise."

He is called to announce this "glorious world of God," the shadow of which, even in the church is hardly intuited. It is within this "glorious" world" that we are called to settle down, more than on the firm ground of this earth. Necessarily, the message will be a challenge to our faith, for it cannot be put into our categories, not even the religious ones.

The *third* step: the call of Our Lady directed to him personally. First it is coming from afar, indirectly, through the singing of the birds; they are not birds of this world, even though they have a certain similarity with them. We can only meet them on a different and higher level. We cannot reach them by our own effort. Are they symbols for the angels preparing this decisive hour of the history of salvation for the New World?

That he is called by his name makes him a new man in Christ — again a beautiful parallelism to the call of the twelve apostles before they were sent out. As the apostles were the first called to constitute the family of Christ on the "third day" in the Gospels,[1] so also is he admitted to a new, celestial family. They were allowed to share in the "family of the most Holy Trinity" and at the same time they were sent to spread it. Along with his compatriots, this will also be Juan Diego's mission. All that is entrusted to him has to be passed on by way of the corresponding authority, the bishop.

The "new being" he shares with Our Lady finds its expression in his new state of mind: "nothing worries him, nothing changes his mind, above all he is happy and extremely content." These four attributes naturally correspond to the cross with its four directions. In some way he has part in the "before-Redemption" of Mary through the blood of Christ. Only as a "new man" is he able to ascend the hill and to approach Our Lady more closely.

The *fourth* step: He enters deeper into the loving glance of Our Lady of Guadalupe. This "fourth step" is the middle one amongst the other six: it is a trinitarian encounter. Only by entering deeper into her glance is he afforded the grace of seeing her as well as the nature surrounding her. It is like a continuation of her glorious dress; as Our Lady of the Assumption, she represents nature as it will be one day in the heavenly Jerusalem. She is it! It is thus that she stands before him in the name of the Father. Prostrating in her presence he responds to the humiliation of the Son of God who became man to save us of our sins.

Before listening to her words, he is attained by her breath, the very breath of the Holy Spirit Who inspires her words. This same "breath of the spirit" will be the inspiration of Juan Diego's words as he presents himself before the bishop. Again four attributes characterize her way of speaking and consequently relate it to the glorious cross: "extremely glorified, infinitely amiable, as someone who attracted and esteemed." These attributes circumscribe their mutual relation as a relation established in and by the cross, therefore everything is in its place. The disequilibrium man inherited through original sin, throwing him out of balance, so much so that

---

[1] cf. Book Five, Way of the Cross of Blessed Juan Diego

even human relations become difficult and at times impossible, is not found here. There is just measure — temperance. In Genesis, day four consists in the creation of the lights of heaven as well as the two greater lights of the "sun and the moon," the beautiful expression of the order of the reign of God. In the Gospels we find "day four" centered on the multiplication of the bread, a foreshadowing of the Holy Eucharist, the sun of our supernatural life.

The *fifth* step marks the initiation of "the dialogue." In relation to the seven days of creation of Genesis it corresponds to day five: the population of the "spaces" of day two — water and air — with fish and birds. Day five should bring to our attention the "ascending" movement of the birds and of that overcoming the attraction to this earth. The birds are symbols of man's nostalgia for and coming closer to God. Our Lady, in the name of God, initiates the dialogue, lost by the first sin. This is more than a historical moment of utter importance. In the person of Juan Diego, the Aztecs, lost in the confusion of a blood-thirsty cult, are called to approach the only true God.

In all purity of heart, Juan Diego is able to respond on behalf of all his countrymen; he is already on the way to "her house, to follow the things of God that the images of Our Lord, the priests give us,"[2] meeting her, he is already "at home." Our Lady, primitive image of the church, is by far much more than any stone-built house, more shadow than image of the true God. We should soberly remark that Our Lady does not answer his cordial invitation to come "to her house," she wants her own house, not in a sense of competition, but as to be closer to the real God.

The *sixth* step is her request. She explains who she is, what she wants, how she wills, why and being Mother to all. Again four attributes to be related to the cross in its four directions, pointing to the four main qualities of God. Her motherhood is sevenfold, in the Holy Spirit, beyond any natural motherhood. Being the Mother of God she is truly able to *help*: She will "hear" their grief, their sadness and will "cure" all their different hurts, miseries and sorrows — in the five wounds of Her Son. Only now does he receive his mission. Our Lady emphasizes that he must to tell all that he

---

[2]   Mary cf. I Kings 19:12b , Ex 13:21, Nm. 9:15, I Rom 8:10

has seen, admired and heard. (Note the inverted order: starting from outside (seeing) orientated to the heart: admire, hear.) Already here we want to recall a beautiful parallelism to the first letter of St. John — where he speaks about the "experience of the word"; first he speaks of hearing and seeing, at the end, in view of announcing the good news he inverts this order: to see first and then to hear. Hearing goes deeper into the soul of man if one is truly able to hear with his whole being.[3]

In this "sixth step" of the encounter with Our Lady, we have another seven steps.[4] Materially and formally it is a mission in, through and with the Holy Spirit Who will bring creation and salvation to its ultimate perfection in Jesus Christ, the Son of God. The "sixth day" in the Gospels is the Lord's last preaching in Jerusalem, before He is judged by the Jews, He judges the infidelity of the "City of Peace." There is another parallelism with St. John. In his Gospel, there are also "seven steps" in the Lord's arrival to the third Pascal feast in Jerusalem. There are another "seven steps" with respect to His passion in Jerusalem, coming forth from the previous "seventh step" (the resurrection of Lazarus). In day six and seven of St. John's Gospel we have "fourteen steps" just as we will find fourteen stations in the "way of cross of Juan Diego" in Book Five.

Mexico has received an abundance of graces. Is she corresponding to the dignity of her vocation? will she bring forth fruit for the Great Harvest? The same questions have to be posed in relation to the church, so many times addressed by Our Lady, in our own day.

The *seventh* step is Juan Diego's acceptance of the Mission in a true spirit of "piety."[5] We have six steps relating to Our Lady. He can only fulfill his mission in, with and through Mary. Only now, if already he is "Her true image" will he be able to touch the heart of the bishop and so fulfill his mission, his vocation.

That his mission will necessarily be a way of cross he cannot yet foresee. The apostles did not foresee that their way up to Jerusa-

---

[3] *Flor y Canto*, pg. 270.

[4] Wisdom 9:9

[5] cf. Nican Mopohua vs. 26

lem would end in Golgotha. This will be the trial for Juan Diego and of any true apostle of Mary. Only in and through the cross will the doors of heaven open. This also is what the Gospels tell us on this "seventh day": only through death will we come to resurrection.

Similitude of the Nican Mopohua with the Gospel of St. John

1 — We can best see this similitude by way of the symbolism of the numbers: In the Nican Mopohua, as in the Gospel of St. John, the main theme is: *"The Light shines into the darkness ... to those who accept it is given the power of becoming children of God."* (Jn 1:2) The light here comes through the Mother of God and her seer. It breaks its way into this pagan country and into the situation of destruction: it is a healing and consoling light, in the same way as the "healing miracles" of St. John: healing the servant of the centurion, chapt. 4, causing the lame to walk, chapt. 5, giving both interior and exterior sight to the blind, chapt. 9, and resurrecting Lazarus from the dead, chapter 11.

It is a light of apocalyptic dimensions, a victorious light, breaking exterior and interior obstacles and transforming man who is far away from God, to a proximity with Him, and this not only with the Aztecs, but also in view of the Spaniards whose faith is too much a faith of domination. It is a light of reconciliation coming out of the heart of Our Lady by way of her merciful eyes which will even heal the deepest opposition in this growing church in Mexico: the opposition between charisma and hierarchy.[6] Here Mary reveals herself as the Bride of the Holy Spirit.

2 — The Lamb of God, invisibly present in the four petalled flower, is a symbol of the Holy Eucharist irradiating from the womb of Our Lady of Guadalupe. It is in the center of the cross, made out of the vertical beam of opposition between heaven and earth, and the

---

[6] Jn 13:34

horizontal beam between Juan Diego and Our Lord present in the womb of Our Lady. From this center reconciliation starts and, little by little, will conquer the entire reign of Moctezuma and irradiate over the whole continent.

Let us here recall the parallelism to the Adoration of the Wise Men coming from the Orient. The apparition of Our Lady is really another Epiphany, but now in the perspective of the second coming of Our Lord in glory. Another similitude lies in the simplicity and profoundness of expression close to the Hebrew language, not only in the syntactical form of parataxis, repetitions and other stylistic forms. Here we would need a deeper study of the Nahuatl language.

3 — It is a trinitarian light

- The light coming down through Our Lady and her servant Juan Diego is a "light" of the Father which will create the New Man in Christ.
- It is the glorious light of the Son Who frees man from the captivity of sin and makes him a "son of light."
- It is a gospel of reconciliation in the light of the Holy Spirit overcoming and resolving all oppositions in the heart of the triune God.

4 — The structure of four is already known to the Aztecs as symbol of plenitude, revealed by Christ to be the saving structure of the cross. It is as the crystallization point of the entire narration, the same way as the four-petalled flower is the center of the person of Our Lady in the image. But as in the image, it is a rounded cross, so also in the narration of the Nican Mopohua. In the womb of Mary, by her continual meditation, it has lost all the rough edges and become a sign of God's merciful love for us poor sinners.

5 — The number five, also typical for the Gospel of St. John, best seen in the miracle of the lame one at the pool of five porticos (ch. 5), and even more in the wounded heart of Our Lord (ch. 19), is known by the Aztecs as a sign of consummation. It is not only found in the five apparitions of Our Lady, but also in several de-

tails of the narrative:[7] everything is orientated towards the pierced heart of Our Lord.

7 — The number seven, as a way of development in the Holy Spirit has been mentioned at the end of the analysis of the first encounter of Juan Diego with Our Lady of Guadalupe.

12 — The twelve and the two stations of the way of the cross of Juan Diego (cf. Book V) are really an interior structure of this narration, the same as the mantle of rays of Our Lady in the image, they point out to the new Jerusalem as the goal of all salvation. Here the glory of the transformed nature in the beginning has found its formal expression.

---

[7]   cf. Lk 1:35

Appendix III

One Way of Praying the Seven Veils

A. Begin with the sign of the cross. We adore God's eternal wisdom in choosing it as the instrument of our salvation, we confess the holy cross as the symbol of our faith and we beseech to be sealed by and in it. We remember that to be sealed with the holy cross is a unique privilege which not only brings special graces, but great responsibilities.

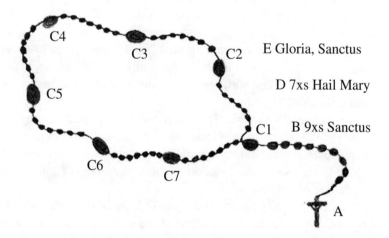

C4

C3

C2 E Gloria, Sanctus

D 7xs Hail Mary

C5

C1 B 9xs Sanctus

C6

C7

A

B. Nine times we pray the Sanctus; one time for and with each of the heavenly choirs. We begin with our own Guardian Angel and pray with all the angels of the Ninth Choir. We continue by invoking the 2) the Archangels, 3) the Virtues, 4) the Principalities, 5) the Powers, 6) the Dominations, 7) the Thrones, 8) the Cherubim and the 9) the Seraphim. Praying in union with the entire heavenly court has great value and significance. The holy angels are always before God, adoring and glorifying Him. It is they who carry our prayers to the heart of the Holy, Mighty and Immortal God.

A   The Sign of the cross
B   9xs Holy, Holy, Holy
C   Our Father (the particular veil)
D   7xs Hail Mary (meditating the correlations)
E   After each veil, pray the Gloria and the Holy, Holy (continue with each corresponding veil, C.2, C.3, etc.)
F   St. Michael Prayer 9xs

C1   The first veil: the clouds; already, the first veil will take us in to the contemplation of the mystery of God, symbolized in the cloud, i.e.[1] another attribute of the "One and Only True God," Ometéotl, "He that covers the earth with cotton."[2] The first veil, representing the mystery of God, is the foundation of the participation in the life of God.

Liturgical Hour: Matins; the first "hour" given to us by God. We unite ourselves with the light of the new day and we begin the day with hearts filled with praise and adoration of God, the Author and Origin of "The Light."

Sacrament: The Most Holy Eucharist; we recognize in the first lights of the day, as in the clouds, the first opportunity for making a spiritual Communion and for receiving "the Mysterious One." It also gives us our sacramental orientation: The Bread of Life at the beginning of the new day.

Gift of the Holy Spirit: Understanding; the light of understanding which we are lacking is received from Our Lord Jesus Christ truly present in the Most Holy Eucharist. Adoration of Our Lord in

---

[1]   Mary cf. I Kings 19:12b, Ex 13:21, Nm 9:15, I Rom 8:10.
[2]   Flor y Canto, pg. 270.

this Sacrament of love and light is the goal of the holy angels with respect to mankind. It is their only desire to bring all creation to the heart of God.

C2 The second veil: The rays; fire, light, energy and it is radiating from the Most Holy Virgin, demonstrating that She Herself bears the fountain and source of all life. The sun, for the Aztecs, was one of the most important symbols of God as the source and origin of all that is, "The God from Whom we have our existence," *in ipalnemohuani.* When we speak of the love of God, we speak of a reality that all purified souls experience. It is the divine love which consumes. We see, in Mary, a fire which is now the soul of her being, of her Immaculate Heart. It is a mystical marriage between Her, the "Immaculate Conception" and her Spouse: God. *"With you is wisdom who knows your works, who was with you when you made the world, who knows what is favorable in your sight ..."*[3]

Liturgical Hour: Lauds; the morning prayer the hour of the holy sacrifice of the Mass, living expression of the saving love of God. There is no greater praise of God than that of the Holy Mass. Through the light of God which has already reached us, we are able to recognize not only the beauties of nature, but the wonders of the redemptive work of Our Lord Jesus Christ: the first light of the sun awakens the singing of the birds and the praise of colors.

Sacrament: Matrimony; the Sacrament of life of the propagation of the family of God. The 138 visible rays (1+3+8=12) in the image of Our Lady of Guadalupe teach us of the finality of the family: the consummation of the love of God in the new Jerusalem.

Gift of the Holy Spirit: wisdom; teaching us that God is Author, Origin, Creator and Omega. All the names and attributes given by the Blessed Virgin in the first apparition (Dec. 9, 1531) demonstrate this holy wisdom of God;[4] In Huelnelli Téotl Dios: God of Great Truth; In Ipalnemohuani: He from Whom all being has ex-

---

[3] Wisdom 9:9.
[4] cf. Nican Mopohua vs. 26.

istence; in Teoyocoyani: Creator of mankind (of Self and of others), in Tloque Nahuaque: The Lord of all that surrounds and touches our lives. It is also translated to "He Who supersedes us," this is the name of the God of history. In Ilhuicahua in Tlaltipaque: The Lord of the heaven and earth, Teimattini: The Provider.) Another sign of the union of God and the Holy Virgin is found in the Book of Wisdom 9:9, "With you is wisdom who knows your works, who was with you when you made the world, who knows what is favorable in your sight …"

C3 The third veil: Her mantle; symbol of protection, of water, of life, of the heavens, of the angels and of "xihuitl" (all that is precious in the heavens and on earth). The gospel of the stars found with the constellations represented on her mantle announce in and through the light. Here, we can make a beautiful tie with the Annunciation of the Archangel Gabriel. He, as the guardian of the earth, proclaims the good news to Mary. He brings the word of God to Her and She responds to His voice with her *"Fiat Mihi, secundum Verbum Tuum."* This reminds us also of the third day of creation; by her fiat, this earth became firm.

Liturgical Hour: Terce; the hour which is our entrance into the work of the day. We go forth from Holy Mass, carrying the word of God to the world; this is Mission. As the seer, Juan Diego, represented in the child at the feet of the Virgin holds tightly onto the mantle of His Mother, let us enter into this hour under the mantle of her protection.

Sacrament: Baptism; the Sacrament of New life which incorporates us into the family of God, giving us dignity and an eternal mission.

Gift of the Holy Spirit: Counsel; the gift that orients us to God. The holy angels, symbolized in the stars of the mantle of the Virgin of Tepeyac, are light and orientation on our way and journey to God. The counsel and advise to all Christians is to live one's baptism so that with, through and in Mary we are enabled to be "servants and handmaids of the Lord."

C4 The fourth veil: Her tunic; is of an earthly-toned color reflecting salvation history in its entirety. We recognize in the play of lights and darkness a teaching on the cross as symbol of the spiritual battle in which we must participate if we wish to live united with the Master. We note that a lace of golden flowers is superimposed on Her tunic. This speaks to us of the heavenly assistance of the holy angels in our daily battles. It also tells us of their desire to participate in the passion of Our Lord Jesus Christ. The four-petalled flower, the "nahui ollín," is cruciform and speaks to us of sacrificial life in God, also the other nine small eight-petalled flowers: we need to be crucified with Christ in order to live our common priesthood.

Liturgical Hour: Sext; midday, being the hour in which Our Lord was raised up on the cross, it should be for us the hour of transformation. Let us unite ourselves with this liturgical hour that we also may benefit from the graces of His Sacred passion. It is an hour in which we can reflect, examining and seeing our lives in the light of the holy cross, participating in the redemptive work of Christ.

Sacrament: Penance; the Sacrament of purification. By the grace of the sacred passion and the most precious blood of Our Lord Jesus Christ we can experience the healing and transforming waters of this Sacrament. We ask for the grace of preparing ourselves well so as to benefit from the fullness of the Sacrament of penance.

Gift of the Holy Spirit: Knowledge (of the cross); This gift isn't learned from books or studying. It is the science taught by God Himself in the sacrifice of His Only Son. Like Mary, we should participate in the redemptive work of Her Son.

C5 The fifth veil: Her interior white tunic; the white color reflects her angelic purity, symbol of the peaks of the volcanoes Popocatépetl and Iztaccihuatl, covered by snow year round.

Liturgical Hour: None; the hour of the death of Our Lord Jesus Christ. His total surrender to the will of His Father is the surrender that fortifies us in this vale of tears. It is a time of thanksgiving, of repentance and of resolution. It is a time for the saving graces of the Son of God.

Sacrament: Holy Orders; We pray for all priests, especially those in most need of the mercy of God. We beseech the grace of Mary's angelic purity for all priests such that they may be fortified in her purity.

Gift of the Holy Spirit: Fortitude; the most necessary gift in these times of battle against the impurities of the world. Let us ask for the Fortitude of the Holy Spirit through the purity of Mary. Mary's purity is really a total surrender as "Spouse of God." We pray that our surrender, fortified in the purity of Mary, be a strength for the entire church ... that we may be a worthy response to the will of Our Lord Jesus Christ in his command, *"love one another as I have loved you."*[5]

C6 Sixth veil: Her body; only her hands and her face are seen. In her left hand we see the shadow of Her Immaculate Heart, and in her glance we encounter but a shadow of the infinite and merciful love of God.

Liturgical Hour: Vespers; it is the hour when we come to the end of the day's work and once again we present it to the Lord. It is also the hour in which we unite ourselves with the Archangel of the love of God, St. Raphael, and ask for his powerful and special assistance. Vespers brings to mind the mercy and compassion exercised by the holy women after the lifeless body of Our Lord was taken down from the cross. If we pray this hour with St. Raphael, we can beseech him to wound us with his arrow of love, that we are never healed from this wound ... and that all is conquered through love.

Sacrament: Confirmation; it is the Sacrament in which we promise to live a Christian life. As it is the Sacrament of the Holy Spirit, let us ask for all His Gifts, but most especially for the Fear of the Lord. The virginal body and soul of Our Blessed Mother received the Holy Spirit and the power of the Most High overshad-

---

[5] Jn 13:34.

owed her[6] making of Her "the promised woman" of Genesis 3:15. It is She who will "crush the head of the serpent." It is through Her that we are enabled to live our confirmation and we announce Her, with all the heavenly court, "conqueror of hell"!

Gift of the Holy Spirit: Fear of the Lord; this gift teaches us the just distance between the Creator and the creature. The gift is recognized in both the Virgin's hands and face, namely that part of her virginal body that shows: her hands, in the praying position, and her inclined head, are both gestures of profound reverence of God, her Creator.

C7 Seventh veil: Her soul; Our Lady's soul cannot be seen, but as a veil of the mystery of God Whom She bears, it is present in her glance and in the "movement of ransom" which comes forth from the same. through her merciful eyes, we recognize Her to be the great fisher-maid. With the holy angels, She prepares the great harvest.

Liturgical Hour: Complines; it is the hour when we commend our spirits unto the Lord. Night prayer offers us the grace to remember that one day the hour of our own death will approach, so we ask the preparatory grace of final repentance.

Sacrament: Anointing of the sick; the Sacrament which prepares us for our encounter and judgment with and by God. It is here, at this hour that we beseech the particular intercession of the prince of the heavenly hosts, St. Michael the Archangel, in the preparation of our final hour, but we should not limit our prayer for his assistance at this final hour; for his help is a continual aid ... *"for you do not know the day of your Master's return."* (Mt 24:42) St. Michael is the great patron of the Holy Mother, the church, and it is his mission to help us in our daily battles and in our last journey, it is he who is to carry us to the other shore!

The gift of the Holy Spirit: Piety; the seventh gift of the Holy Spirit. God wills to encounter the heart and Soul of Mary Immaculate in every member of the Mystical Body of His Son so as to fully live His incarnate mystery of love in all. We must ask for the

---

[6] cf. Lk 1:35.

grace to be a child of Mary, living the "Who is Like unto God" of St. Michael such that we live and give a worship worthy of God's majesty. The praying of the seven veils is not meant to be presented in a restricted form. Neither is it necessary to be prayed in the same style . One should find in it a means of praying any of the groupings of seven. It can be prayed all at once at any time of the day. One can make a small meditation with one of the veils and the particular corresponding liturgical hour at the corresponding hour. We recommend the meditation of one veil in a special way for each day of the week, starting on Monday with the first veil. In this way, we are under the "mantle" of Our Lady throughout the week, but every day in a special way. It can be prayed alone or with others. As Book One will present in the seven-fold candelabra, it is an excellent preparation for a deeper penetration of any of the Seven Books. The following scheme will also be of assistance in the keeping of the groupings.

The following table will serve as a help in your meditation of the seven veils. Note that one can begin to integrate former contemplations: of the days of creation, the last words of Our Lord and the seven apocalyptic communities with the veils of Our Lady of Guadalupe. Now, having the visual of the image of Our Lady before us, it becomes much easier to pray in union with the Liturgical Hours, asking for the anointing of the Holy Spirit and His Gifts, as well as begin to contemplate the seven major divisions of the holy sacrifice of the Mass. Do not try to pray several relationships at once. Pray one at a time, and little by little take in others. Soon a beautiful harmony of correlations will present themselves.

Clouds	Rays	Mantle	Gown	Inner Gown	Body	Soul
Under-st-anding	Wisdom	Counsel	Know-ledge	Fortitude	Fear of the Lord	Piety
Father forgive them for they know not what they do	This day you will be with me in paradise	Behold your Mother	I thirst	My God, My God, why have You forsaken me?	Father, into Your hands I com-mend my spirits	It is finished
Ephesus	Smyrna	Perga-mum	Thyatira	Sardis	Phila-delphia	Laodicea
Day I	Day II	Day III	Day IV	Day V	Day VI	Day VII
H. Eucharist - Matins	Marriage - Lauds	Baptism - Terce	Penance - Sext	Holy Orders - None	Confir-mation - Vespers	Extreme Unction - Comp-lines
Introit	Readings	Offertory	Sanctus	Conse-cration	Com-munion	Ite Missa est

About the Author

Anonymous writings were the rule in Middle Ages, because what matters is the contents of books and not the person of the author. For the most part, works which bear the name of no man imply the source of inspiration as being divine, that is, crediting the work as having a sole author, namely, God, the Creator and Author of all that is: material and immaterial, including our very thoughts. Even before we begin to contemplate the image of Our Lady of Guadalupe, we need to fundament ourselves in the reality that God alone is Author, Center and Finality.

More than a name, Miguel Guadalupe should be a concrete symbol of God's authorship. By way of the pseudonym, the book of seven is characterized as a member of the family of Our Lady, specifically of Our Lady of Guadalupe; a title given to Our Lady, as well as her miraculous image, by Holy Mother the church shortly after her appearances to Juan Diego in Mexico, in 1531. As *"the woman clothed with the sun and the moon beneath her feet,"* she is the *"Great Sign"* who not only marks the brink of modern times, but who also by way of St. Michael wages war against the *"dragon."*(cf. Rv.12:1, 12:7)

Miguel is the Spanish name for Michael, the Archangel and "Prince of the heavenly hosts," for he also has his part in *The Seven Veils of Our Lady of Guadalupe*. It is in San Miguel del Milagro, Mexico, the only church-approbated apparition site of St. Michael in North America (apparitions of St. Michael 1631), and then in missions throughout Mexico, the U.S.A. and several European countries, that this topic was first treated. The book was written in team-work and aims at creating "family" with the One Necessary Center, symbolized by the "nahui ollin," the four-petalled flower on the womb of Our Lady of Guadalupe. It is a hidden promise that she will bring Our Lord to this world again, veiled by the same seven veils which surround His Eucharistic Presence among us.

The second coming of Our Lord, even though at the end it will be like a lightning bolt, is necessarily linked to His Eucharistic Presence. For this we have to give testimony as the martyr St. Jeanne D'Arc, who daily received Holy Communion and listened to the voice of St. Michael the Archangel. Nobody knew about this element of her mission, but she was still burned at the stake as a heretic in 1431, exactly 100 years before the apparitions of Our Lady in 1531. Something similar might happen to the remnant of faithful souls who are ready to "wash their garments in the blood of the Lamb." They are already being gathered by the "Hidden Lord" from the "four winds."

The image of Our Lady of Guadalupe, with the assistance of St. Michael the Archangel, should be like unto the banner of St. Jeanne, leading to the victory and triumph of the Immaculate Heart of Mary by way of St. Michael's cry "Who like unto God." The image should penetrate the deepest of our souls so that not only exteriorly we are assured of her living presence with us, but by way of her, become that "new man" we are called to be in Christ Jesus. It is thus that the threefold creation: material, angel and man, come together to sing the eternal praises of the triune God.

May 13, 1995.